John A. Straayer / Robert D. Wrinkle / J. L. Polinard

Colorado State University · University of Texas-Pan American · University of Texas-Pan American

STATE AND LOCAL POLITICS

Second Edition

St. Martin's Press
New York

Sponsoring editor: Beth A. Gillett
Development editor: Susan Cottenden
Manager, Publishing services: Emily Berleth
Senior editor, Publishing services: Douglas Bell
Project management: York Production Services, Inc.
Senior production supervisor: Joe Ford
Photo research: Rose Corbett Gordon
Cover design: Evelyn Horovicz
Cover photo: Ken Tannenbaum/Image Bank

Library of Congress Catalog Card Number: 97-65186

Manufactured in the United States of America.

3 2 1 0 9 8
f e d c b a

For information, write:

St. Martin's Press, Inc.
175 Fifth Avenue
New York, NY 10010

ISBN: 0-312-14989-1

We'd like to dedicate this book to ten special students—*to Keith and Sean, to Elizabeth, Tracie, Lisa, J. T., and Christy, and to Kathy, David, and Jeffrey*. We urge them to read it, even though it's not assigned.

Contents in Brief

• • •

Preface xv
About the Authors xvii

Chapter 1 A State and Local World 1
Chapter 2 Federalism 27
Chapter 3 State Constitutions 67
Chapter 4 The State Legislature 95
Chapter 5 The State Executive 145
Chapter 6 State Judicial Systems 185
Chapter 7 Political Parties 227
Chapter 8 Special Interest Groups 253
Chapter 9 Elections 285
Chapter 10 The American Metropolis 313
Chapter 11 Local Governments 341
Chapter 12 Community Power and Politics 377
Chapter 13 State and Local Fiscal Policy 405
Chapter 14 Commencement 447
Glossary 453
Index 465

Contents

• • •

Preface xv

About the Authors xvii

Chapter 1 A State and Local World 1

What State and Local Governments Do 4

The Politics of State and Local Government 9

An Expansive and Complicated System 17

Common Features and Variety 21

Summary 24

Chapter 2 Federalism 27

Organizing Government 28

Alternative Organizational Formats 31

The American Organizational Framework 33

Focus 2.1: *Full Faith and Credit: Maybe* *41*

Intergovernmental Relations 45

Consequences of Institutional Design 59

Focus 2.2: *Support Your Local Sheriff* *60*

Summary 62

Policy Perspective 62

Chapter 3 State Constitutions 67

State Constitutions Are Important Political Documents 68

Multiple Levels of Law 71

The Contents of State Constitutions 73

• • •

The Length and Detail of State Constitutions 75
State Constitutional Amendments 77
Criticisms of State Constitutions 78
Constitutional Politics 83
The Functions of State Constitutions 88
Summary 89
Policy Perspective 89

Chapter 4 The State Legislature 95
Institutional Design 96
Institutional Transition 97
Focus 4.1: *Alcohol and Legislators* *99*
Legislative Functions 101
The Legislative Process 102
Informal Rules and Strategies 107
Legislative Organization 108
Focus 4.2: *The Unsinkable Willie Brown* *113*
Legislative Committees and Their Assignments 115
Focus 4.3: *Mr. Speaker versus the NRA* *117*
Legislative Support 119
Representation 120
Representational Roles 130
The Demographics of Legislators 131
Tenure and Turnover 133
Summary 136
Policy Perspective 137

Chapter 5 The State Executive 145
The Modern State Governor 146
Focus 5.1: *Mudslinging in Minnesota* *150*
Focus 5.2: *Running for Governor* *151*
Roles of the Governor 152

Focus 5.3: Pottys and Priorities 155

SOURCES OF GUBERNATORIAL POWER 156

LIMITS ON EXECUTIVE POWER 161

GOVERNORS' POWERS: A COMPARISON 171

EXECUTIVE STRENGTH AND LEADERSHIP 173

OTHER STATE EXECUTIVES 174

THE GOVERNOR AND SEPARATION OF POWERS 177

SUMMARY 178

POLICY PERSPECTIVE 179

CHAPTER 6 STATE JUDICIAL SYSTEMS 185

MOST JUSTICE IS ADMINISTERED BY STATE AND LOCAL SYSTEMS 187

JUDGES ARE HUMAN BEINGS 187

THE COURTS ARE POLITICAL ENTITIES 188

THE STRUCTURE OF STATE JUDICIAL SYSTEMS 189

JUDICIAL REFORM 195

SELECTING JUDGES 196

DEMOCRACY AND THE COURTS 203

Focus 6.1: *Judicial Selection and the Voting Rights Act* 204

Focus 6.2: *Religion, Sexual Orientation, and Parades* 206

CONTEMPORARY PROBLEMS IN THE COURTS 206

Focus 6.3: *Crowded Dockets and Their Consequences* 210

STATE COURTS AND CIVIL LIBERTIES 213

RECENT DEVELOPMENTS IN THE STATE COURTS 215

SUMMARY 218

POLICY PERSPECTIVE 219

CHAPTER 7 POLITICAL PARTIES 227

THE FUNCTIONS OF POLITICAL PARTIES 228

POLITICAL PARTY ORGANIZATION 234

A RESURGENCE IN PARTY VITALITY 239

PARTY COMPETITION 239

Focus 7.1: Selected Third Parties in the United States 246

CRITICISMS OF THE POLITICAL PARTIES 246

SUMMARY 248

POLICY PERSPECTIVE 248

CHAPTER 8 SPECIAL INTEREST GROUPS 253

PARTICIPANTS IN SPECIAL INTEREST GROUPS 256

THE LOBBYISTS 259

Focus 8.1: Lobbying: An Insider's Game? 260

TECHNIQUES OF INFLUENCE 262

Focus 8.2: The Lobbying Industry 263

WHAT MAKES A SPECIAL INTEREST GROUP EFFECTIVE? 267

LOBBYISTS IN STATE POLITICS 272

Focus 8.3: Do—Do Not 273

SPECIAL INTEREST GROUPS IN A DEMOCRACY 276

SUMMARY 278

POLICY PERSPECTIVE: WHAT'S OUR POLICY ON SPECIAL INTERESTS? 279

CHAPTER 9 ELECTIONS 285

ELECTION LAWS 286

Focus 9.1: From Classroom to Boardrooms 290

ELECTORAL PARTICIPATION 292

Focus 9.2: Women in the Legislature 297

THE IMPACT OF INSTITUTIONS ON ELECTORAL PARTICIPATION 299

MODERN CAMPAIGNS 301

DIRECT DEMOCRACY 305

IS DIRECT DEMOCRACY GOOD GOVERNMENT? 307

SUMMARY 308

POLICY PERSPECTIVE: THE VOTING RIGHTS ACT AND THE STATES 308

Chapter 10 The American Metropolis 313

Population Shifts in the United States 314

Some Consequences of the Population Shifts 319

Problems Associated with Fragmentation and Suburbanization 322

Focus 10.1: *Avoiding Annexation in Portage Township* *323*

Benefits of Suburbanization 325

Extreme Proposals for Reform 325

Focus 10.2: *Abolish the Suburbs?* *326*

Modest Proposals for Reform 327

The Politics of Metropolitan Reform 330

The Downside of the Metropolitan Scheme 332

Future Trends 334

Summary 336

Policy Perspective 336

Chapter 11 Local Governments 341

Characteristics of City Government 342

The Organization of City Government 345

Focus 11.1: *A Conservative Big City Mayor?* *347*

The Distribution of Structural Forms of City Government 352

Political Influence and City Government Structure 353

City Governments Differ in Many Ways 356

Counties, Schools, and Special Districts 358

Focus 11.2: *County Reform* *363*

Focus 11.3: *Politics in the New York City Schools* *365*

Focus 11.4: *Education and Taxes: The Michigan Model* *367*

Summary 370

Policy Perspective: Educational Reform 371

Chapter 12 Community Power and Politics 377

Power in the Local Community 378

WHO CARES WHO GOVERNS? 379

DO POWER ELITES GOVERN THE COMMUNITY? 380

IS COMMUNITY POWER PLURALISTIC? 383

Focus 12.1: *Students and Community Power* *386*

DO EXPERTS GOVERN THE COMMUNITY? 386

DO LOCAL ELECTION SYSTEMS BENEFIT THE ELITE? 388

Focus 12.2: *Term Limits—No Problem at the Local Level* *389*

DO THE FEDERAL AND STATE GOVERNMENTS RULE THE COMMUNITY? 395

Focus 12.3: *The Impact of a Federal Mandate on a Small Town* *397*

SUMMARY 398

POLICY PERSPECTIVE: ECONOMIC DEVELOPMENT AND OUTSIDE CAPITAL 399

CHAPTER 13 STATE AND LOCAL FISCAL POLICY 405

THE PUBLIC DEMAND: MORE SERVICES, NO MORE TAXES 407

FISCAL POLICY: A COMPLEX SYSTEM OF INSTITUTIONS AND BUDGETS 407

TRENDS IN FISCAL POLICY 416

THE POLITICS OF MONEY 418

Focus 13.1: *The Return of the Toll Road?* *427*

Focus 13.2: *Would You Like Higher Tuition and Pay Toilets?* *434*

THE PROBLEMS AND POLITICS OF BUDGET MAKING 438

SUMMARY 442

CHAPTER 14 COMMENCEMENT 447

PLURALISM 448

DECENTRALIZATION 449

POWER 450

IS THE SYSTEM IN CRISIS? 450

FUTURE TRENDS 452

GLOSSARY 453

INDEX 465

Preface

• • •

In so many ways our world is a state and local world. The water we drink, the streets we drive, the schools we attend, and the ballots we cast are provided by our cities, counties, schools, special districts, and states. If the students in the college classrooms of the late 1990s come to hold public office, it will in all likelihood be in a state or local government; there are, after all, 85,000 state and local governments compared to just a single national government. It is with this in mind that we embarked on a second edition of this text.

The fundamental purpose of this second edition of *State and Local Politics* is the same as it was in the first edition, namely, to help undergraduate students understand and appreciate those governments that affect their lives on a daily basis, and within which many of today's students will assume positions of responsibility in the not-too-distant future.

New to This Edition . . . .

New Chapter One

A wholly new first chapter attempts to convince students that state and local governments are important, are very relevant to their daily lives, and that what goes on within them is inevitably and properly political. By emphasizing this relevance here and throughout the text, we hope to encourage students to think about their communities with a new interest and vigor.

Policy Perspectives

Instead of separate policy chapters, we have woven policy issues throughout the book. Eleven of the fourteen chapters conclude with a "policy perspective" where we link some aspect of substantive policy to the treatment of institutions and process contained in that chapter. The one exception to this altered treatment of policy is the updated chapter on fiscal policy. In our view, the politics of taxing and spending are so intertwined with the basic features of government structure and process as to require fairly expansive independent treatment.

Expanded Focus Boxes

In response to reviewer comments, we have increased the number of focus boxes. This feature is useful in providing contemporary illustrations of the general observations

• • •

and principles contained in the text. In addition, they represent opportunities to capture the students' attention with real-life examples of state and local politics.

Attention to County Government

Many readers told us that they liked the attention to local governments—the counties especially—in the first edition. We have expanded this coverage and included new information provided in recent academic literature and updated the book's statistical materials.

Highlights and Acknowledgments

While we believe the changes discussed above will make this second edition more attractive and useful to students, there are some very important ways in which this book has not changed. First, our focus upon institutions, beginning with an updated treatment of federalism in Chapter 2, is intact. Our experience indicates that students more readily grasp the complexities and subtleties of political behavior if they have first come to understand the way the system is constructed. Second, we have kept the book comprehensive, with coverage of institutions and processes at both the state and local level. In addition, we have tried to maintain the conversational writing style of the first edition. We strive to make the students interested, not sleepy.

Finally, we continue to draw upon both mainline academic literature and materials from the popular press. Newspapers and magazines such as *Governing* and *State Legislatures* contain contemporary descriptions and analyses of local and state politics, and are useful in conjunction with what is reported by our professional journals and presses.

With the first edition, we worked to keep the language clear, straightforward, and short on academic jargon. We made a point of covering all the critical aspects of institutions and processes. The book was published in paperback. We have repeated that approach in this second edition so that, once again, professors need not make a choice between comprehensiveness and cost.

The editorial staff at St. Martin's Press was cooperative, encouraging, and truly professional. We would like to thank Beth Gillett, our sponsoring editor; Susan Cottenden, our development editor; Doug Bell, senior editor; assistant editor, Jayme Heffler; and John Britch, marketing manager. We are also grateful to several academic colleagues who reviewed drafts of the manuscript and contributed valuable comments and suggestions for the second edition: Nasir Ahmed, Grambling State University; William K. Hall, Bradley University; William E. Kelly, Auburn University; June Lang, Suffolk Community College; Joseph R. Marbach, Seton Hall University; James L. McDowell, Indiana State University; John D. Redifer, Mesa State College; Thomas F. Richards, Brookdale Community College; and Homer E. Williamson, St. Cloud State.

John A. Straayer
Robert D. Wrinkle
J. L. Polinard

About the Authors

• • •

John A. Straayer is professor of political science and past department chair at Colorado State University. He is director of the department's legislative internship program and has served as a lobbyist for the university. He has published *The Colorado General Assembly*; *American State and Local Government*; *The Study and Teaching of Political Science*; *Introduction to American Government*, with Robert D. Wrinkle; *American Government: Policy and Non-Decisions*, with Robert D. Wrinkle; and *The Politics of Neglect: The Environmental Crisis*, with R. L. Meek.

Robert D. Wrinkle is professor of political science at the University of Texas–Pan American, where he teaches in the Master of Public Administration program. He has published articles in journals such as *American Politics Quarterly*, *Criminal Justice and Behavior*, *Hispanic Journal of Behavioral Science*, *State and Local Government Review*, *Western Political Quarterly*, *Social Science Journal*, and *Social Science Quarterly*. He is a coauthor of *Electoral Structure and Urban Policy: Impact on Mexican American Communities*. He is coauthor, with John A. Straayer, of *American Government: Policy and Non-Decisions*.

J. L. Polinard is professor of political science and chair of the Department of Political Science at the University of Texas–Pan American. His primary teaching interests are in minority politics and public law. He is past chair of the Pre-Law Advisors National Council and has served on a panel of the State Bar of Texas. He has published articles in such journals as *American Politics Quarterly*, *Hispanic Journal of Behavioral Science*, *Publius*, *State and Local Government Review*, *Western Political Quarterly*, *Social Science Journal*, and *Social Science Quarterly*. He is coauthor of *Electoral Structure and Urban Policy: Impact on Mexican American Communities*.

CHAPTER
I

• • •

A State and Local World

• • •

The Arizona state capitol building *(foreground)* surrounded by a more recent extension. Phoenix, Arizona. *(Miro Vintoniv/Stock, Boston)*

• • • **What State and Local Governments Do**

Public Health and Safety
Public Utilities
Crime and Corrections
Education
Social Services
Land Use Control
Jobs and Economic Development
Public Fun
Citizenship and Civil Life

• • • **The Politics of State and Local Government**

Public Health and Safety
Public Utilities
Crime and Corrections
Education
Social Services
Land Use Control
Jobs and Economic Development
Public Fun
Citizenship and Civic Life

• • • **An Expensive and Complicated System**

Federalism
Separation of Powers
Boards and Commissions
Urban Sprawl
Bureaucracy
Decentralization

• • • **Common Features and Variety**

Commonalities
Differences

• • • **Summary**

There are several reasons why you should read this book and master the materials presented in your class. All the reasons are tied in some way to the quality of your life. At this point in time state and local governments may not seem all that relevant but, trust us, they are, and they will be all the more so as the years pass. What are the reasons that these governments are relevant?

First, you live in a state and local world. Your schools, streets, police protection, water, and parks come from state and local government. Second, if you marry or divorce, buy a house or run a restaurant, teach English or practice law, drive a car or steal one, you'll have to deal with your state and local governments. It's clearly an advantage to know something about governments, when you have to deal with them. Third, state and local governments provide the services and climate that make your world civilized.

There are times and places where citizens are not safe and life is lousy—no protection from political thugs, no clean water, sewage in the streets, threats to life and limb for those who speak out or seek change. But in the United States, at least most often, police and fire protection are available, public health is adequate, and political speech and participation are protected, indeed, even encouraged. Who does all this? It is your cities, counties, school districts, and state agencies.

Whether you simply want to be on the receiving end of the services provided by government, or you want to participate in the processes of deciding when and how to provide them, you need to know something about how governments are organized, how they function, and what they do. One quick way to gain a sense of the relevance of state and local government is to ask yourself what you're doing, how you got here, and what your plans are.

Consider the experience that you may have had during your first few days as a college student. You pack up your belongings and leave home, driving first on a city street and obeying city traffic policies. You then travel on a county road, built with state and county funds, before moving onto a state highway, built largely with federal money but patrolled and maintained by state employees. You might, in your haste to get to school, be the sad recipient of a citation for a violation of the state speed laws and have to go to a state court. The court would be housed in a county building. You might park in a city parking lot while in court. In the county building you could "wash up," using water and sewerage pipes attached to city facilities. The attorney you might hire would have had to pass a state bar examination. Like other professionals, including funeral directors, hairdressers, architects, nurses, social workers, and teachers, lawyers are regulated by the state.

Assuming that you avoided jail and made it to school, you would need to find housing at or near the university. When initially constructed, the housing had to be in conformance with city building codes. Such codes regulate the size and placement of the structure on the lot, the electrical and plumbing systems, and, perhaps, the size and condition of the rental unit. If you have a pet, you may have to deal with a leash law, purchase a pet tag, and secure required immunization shots for the animal. If your pet runs away or get lost, it might end up in a city or county pound.

On weekends, you may spend time in a state or local park. When you stop for a meal, the restaurant will have been inspected by a local government health agency. If you become sick or have an accident, you will likely end up in a state or local hospital.

Some day you will leave school and in all likelihood you'll be looking for a job. You may seek public employment since, often, governments are among the largest employers. There are over 86,000 governments in the United States and all except one is state or local. They employ millions of people, from teachers to cops, to computer analysists, to social workers, to engineers, to park employees. If you're a teacher, you'll probably work in a public school. You may work in a university as a professor or member of the large supportive staff. You might seek employment in law enforcement as a city cop, a state trooper, or with the FBI. You might want to join the staff in your state legislature, or work in planning or budgeting in the city or county.

You'll need a home some day. Whether you build or have someone build for you, you'll need to know about zoning, about required lot sizes and setbacks from the street. You'll have to pay a development fee of some sort and you will want to know how much it is, just as you'll be concerned about the levels of city, county, school district, and special district property taxes. The city, or county if you build outside the city limits, will have requirements for your plumbing, electrical system, and window sizes. You'll need upstairs windows large enough to permit escape in case of fire.

Whether you buy or build, you'll have to complete a ton of title work. Your lender will want to be assured that the title to the property is clear of any secondary liens, and that it is properly filed with the county clerk and recorder. If you screw up, you could find yourself unable to sell your property at a later date, or discover that someone else owns a part of it.

You'll have kids someday. Then the schools will begin to matter. Are they close? Is there busing? What are the class sizes? Are there good special education opportunities? Is the local school board squabbling over sex education and prayers in school, or are local school politics tranquil? Eventually you may be drawn into local school district governance.

Chances are that after a few years in your community you'll become warned about the economic health of the area, or about the impact of growth on the surrounding environment, or both. Maybe your business or job is in jeopardy because of an economic slow down, or maybe you're concerned that there are ample employment opportunities for your kids. Alternatively you may become increasingly irritated by the clogged streets and slowing traffic and by the dirty air, and you blame that on all the newcomers who are wrecking your nice town.

As you sit in a city or county and in a public classroom you are right now intertwined with state and local government. When you get a job, start a business, get married, register to vote, license a car, exceed the speed limit, buy or build a house, send kids to school, turn on the water or flush the toilet, you are interacting with your state and local governments.

By now we trust that we've established the fact that state and local governments are ever present and relevant parts of our life and yours. Now let's look a little more systematically at what it is that they do.

What State and Local Governments Do

State and local governments are involved in almost everything that relates to your daily life. They provide public safety and most of our public utilities such as sewers and water; they build, maintain, and patrol our roads; they educate us and our kids; they operate our social service systems; they set up the framework for much of our entertainment; and they maintain the basic infrastructure for our civics — that is, they conduct our elections.

Public Health and Safety

There are over a million police officers and firefighters in the United States and nearly all of them are employees of our state and local governments. In fact, most are local employees — city police officers and county sheriff department officers. The national government employs around 90,000 officers of the law in its various offices, a number roughly equal to the total of state patrol officers and other state police officers. While there are about a third of a million local firefighters, there are virtually none at the state or federal level. Clearly public safety is in state and local hands, the occasional presence of the feds in such places as Waco, Idaho, and Montana, notwithstanding.

Similarly, public health is largely a state and local concern. Most hospitals are private and nonprofit, but the twenty percent or so that are public, are local, not federal. Most of these are city facilities.

In addition to hospitals, public health is protected through such measures as building codes, restaurant licensing and inspecting, and the maintenance of sanitary land fills. These are state and local functions. Cities and counties maintain dumps. Counties check on restaurants to be sure that customers don't become ill or die from contaminated food or drink. City building inspectors seek to minimize the presence of rat infested slum rental properties. In recent years, states and localities have made and enforced a variety of regulations designed to reduce air pollution.

Imagine yourself in a world without state and locally provided health and safety services. Traffic would be helter-skelter, your food could be toxic, there'd be no 911 lines, your house could burn to the ground, crooks could steal you blind, trash would pile up, and there might be no local hospital. That might be fun if you were the only one speeding, drinking illegally, and spending other people's money. But clearly such would not be the case. Your local environment would look much like Thomas Hobbes' world of all against all.

Public Utilities

We take for granted that drinkable water will run from our taps and that the contents of the toilet will disappear when we pull the handle. We expect streets and road and traffic signals to be there each day, and we want our gutters to carry away water in rainstorms. When it snows, we want the streets plowed.

These are public utilities, and they are provided by our states and particularly our localities. Some localities provide utility services beyond sewer, water, and streets, in the form of public electricity systems and trash pickup. Cities build and maintain city streets, and the counties do the same with rural roads and bridges. States build some highways and help cities and counties by financially assisting with state thoroughfares that pass through them. The interstate system is funded largely with federal money derived from fuel taxes, but it is constructed, maintained and patrolled by the states. So when you travel you're dependent fully on your states and localities.

Crime and Corrections

Often on hears, "don't make a federal case of it," as if big deals are federal and little ones are state or local. As it turns out, most cases big and small are state or local, not federal. Most of our criminal laws, most of our courts, most of our prisons and prisoners are state and local.

There are about 225,000 employees in our judicial systems; just over 200,000 of these are state and local. In 1993 our corrections systems employed roughly 245,000 people; all but 22,000 of them were state or local. There were just under 75,000 federal prisoners, but 836,000 inmates in state or local confines. Most crimes violate state and local laws, most of our judges wear state or local robes, and most of our correctional employees work in state prisons or county jails.

Education

Presidents, would-be presidents and scores of other national politicians like to talk about our schools, citing their shortcomings and spinning out recipes to fix them. The federal government does spend money on the schools, but it is a tiny fraction of the total costs.

For all the national level rhetoric and regulation, the schools in America are not federal. With the exception of some private institutions, they are state and local. Our elementary and secondary schools employ over six million people, or more than twice the total number of federal employees. In addition, public colleges and universities have over a half a million professors.

Most of our elementary and secondary schools are run by locally elected boards in school districts. They are funded by a combination of locally levied property taxes and money appropriated by the state legislature. The states impose some controls on the local schools, such as minimum curricular and reporting requirements, but most policy decisions are made locally. One exception to this would be requirements mandated by Congress but unaccompanied by money to pay for them, such as special education requirements and gender parity in athletics.

Social Services

All the debate over welfare in recent years makes it seem as though provision of social services is a completely federal operation. So far as funding and eligibility for benefits are concerned, that has been the case. But the administration of welfare programs is anything but federal. Most of the hard work, the "on the street" confrontation of poverty and its associated maladies, is done by employees of county government.

For several decades, and until the sweeping 1996 revisions of federal welfare policy, the foundation of the social services system was AFDC (Aid for Families of Dependent Children). AFDC was actually an amendment to the Social Security Act of 1935. The federal government established guidelines for eligibility to receive AFDC payments and the states set the particulars of eligibility within those guidelines. The federal government picked up the tab. It paid the money to the states and counties, and armies of county social workers administered the program, working with the poor to determine eligibility and making the payments to them.

Another mainstay of the social services system was, and remains, Medicaid. Like AFDC, Medicaid was enacted in 1965 by Congress as an amendment to the foundational 1935 Social Security Act. Medicaid is a program, jointly funded by the states and national government, that provides medical care for some of the poor. Other poor people are classified as "medically indigent" and are too rich to qualify for Medicaid, but too poor to afford private health insurance. States foot the bill to help these people.

Other social services programs have included SSI (Supplemental Security Income), which helps the blind, aged and disabled. Virtually all the funds for these programs have been fully or partially supplied by the national government.

It remains to be seen exactly what shape the welfare system will take. What is clear is that Congress's 1996 law limits recipients to five years of benefits in a lifetime. Family heads have two years to find employment, and teen moms receive no help unless they live at home and stay in school. Eligibility for legal immigrants will be restricted and food stamp funds reduced. Some argue that these changes will toss millions of people onto the streets and hurt the kids of the poor. Others contend that welfare careerists will be stimulated to become self-sufficient. Clearly even more changes will be made in Congress and state legislatures as the impacts of the new system become felt.

Social services programs differ from education, public safety, and public utilities in that much of the money is federal. But since the national government has no local level administrative structure, it has fallen to the states and their localities, mostly the county governments, to administer the programs. Following the 1996 welfare changes, the responsibilities of the states and localities will increase even further.

Land Use Control

We are a nation in which "private property," as the institutionalized, government-backed option to individually claim exclusive ownership of some segment of God's creation, has taken hold with a vengeance. Yet such claims are not without qualification. One cannot, for example, erect rock concert or rodeo areas in the center of a middle class residential area, even if one holds title to the property. Nor can one willy-nilly open a bar between an elementary school and a church.

There are all sorts of controls on how we may use land and the structures we place upon them, and most of these controls are state and local. Most cities adopt zoning plans to specify which areas of the municipality may be the site of single family residences, or apartments, or retail outlets, or heavy industry, and so forth. Indeed, much of local politics revolves around fights about how to zone or rezone property. Land use controls outside cities, out in the county, exist as well, although they tend to be less restrictive.

As with all that local governments do, their legal prerogative to place strictures on the use of land comes from their parent unit, the state. State legislatures, in statute, tell cities and counties what they may do with respect to land use control. All of this is good to know, because anyone who plans to build a home or start a business will have to know what is on the books with respect to permissible uses of the property, and will have to deal with the city, the county, or both.

Jobs and Economic Development

As noted earlier, governments in the United States employ a large slice of the work force. Indeed, state and local government employ nearly sixteen million people, or more than five times the number of federal civilian employees.

But beyond the direct employment of their own workers, state and local governments struggle constantly to expand private sector job opportunities. This effort takes several forms. One common approach is to offer to adjust the tax bills of businesses that are willing to move in. Tax breaks may include waiver of initial development fees for facility construction, forgiveness of property taxes due as a result of improvements (tax increment financing), or even elimination of taxes on machinery or inventory.

Other tactics include active recruitment programs designed to sell the attractiveness of a community to the executives who make business location decisions, and establishment of "industrial parks," which are sections of the community equipped with the streets and utilities needed by a business or industry.

Public Fun

A state and local activity easily confused with economic development is the provision of opportunities for entertainment. This comes in the form of museums, zoos, parks concerts halls, tennis and softball facilities. It also comes in the form of millions of dollars of tax-paid construction of sports arenas for million dollar ball-players. The recent construction of stadiums in Baltimore and Nashville are examples.

These activities are easily confused with economic development because their partisans generally promote them as, among other things, job creating. Cultural facilities, it is argued, make a community attractive to tourists who spend money, and to corporate executives who may be contemplating a move. Stadiums, like the pyramids of old, are said to employ workers during the construction stages thus giving the locality an economic boost. The conclusions of some studies dispute this later claim, arguing that without the stadiums the money would be spent on other projects and activities and these then would add to economic activity.

Citizenship and Civil Life

The United States isn't simply a representative democracy. It is 86,743 democracies, almost all of them the representative type. This means that elections are held and records are kept. It also means the creation of campaign and election laws, and their enforcement.

This is a big and important job, and if we want our democracy to survive, it must be done well. It is our state and local governments that do it. State laws define political parties and govern their structure, finances, and many aspects of their operation. State laws also control election practices and lobbying. They limit campaign contributions and spending. They require financial reports of the parties, candidates, independent political committees, corporations, unions, political action committees, and lobbyists. They require financial disclosure by candidates. And state laws provide penalties for noncompliance. It is state agencies, including secretaries of state and attorneys general, who enforce the rules and provide public data drawn from the reports.

The workhorses in our civic life are the counties. It is the county clerks who register voters, arrange the elections, count and report the ballots, and keep the records. Cities and school districts do some of this too, albeit only for their own elections. The county does it not only for county contests, but for all state and national elections as well. Without the work of the states and their "children," the counties, we would have no elections, no records, no democratic decision-making system.

State and local governments, the local ones especially, are the foundation of civil life in America in another all-important way; this is where most participation in civic life occurs. There is just one United States president and only 535 members of the U.S. Congress. But there are over seven thousand state legislators and hundreds of thousands of city council and school board members. Knowledge and participation lead to understanding and support of institutions. This system of extensive participation, thus, helps to create a base of knowledgeable, experienced civic activists in the political system.

The Politics of State and Local Government

It's not impossible to conclude that what goes on in state and local governments, in the local units especially, is somehow nonpolitical. Candidates for office frequently claim to eschew politics in favor of a "pursuit of the common good." Voters like to say that they don't vote for a party or for politicians, but instead just "vote for the best person." In the some 14,500 school districts, about two-thirds of our cities and all the 33,000 special districts, elections are "non-partisan"; that is, candidates do not run as members of a political party. Indeed, it is in only about 10,000 of our 86,743 American governments (the counties, 49 states, and some cities) that candidates for office run on political party tickets. Beyond this, citizens, public officials, and editorialists alike are fond of claiming that the provision of such public services as water, politic protection, and schooling for our kids should be "done on a businesslike basis," and "politics" should be kept out.

All of this nonpolitical and antipolitics rhetoric may sound good but, in truth, it is nonsense. Public decisions, collective choices, are inherently political for they involve the making of choices among competing options. They involve conflict, compromise, and coercion. If everyone agreed on everything, there'd be no politics. But that's not our world. Consider, as examples, these policy areas and the choices that must be made.

Public Health and Safety

Public health and safety, as we saw earlier, involves police protection. Is it political? City council members and mayors must make a host of tough choices. Should the cops get a raise, or should funds be spent to hire more of them? Which areas of the community should be most heavily patrolled. In some areas, a heavy police presence triggers complaints about harassment, but with thin coverage city officials are accused of neglect.

Should there be a police review board composed of citizens to hear complaints about police behavior? If so, who should be on it and who should decide who its members will be. Will such a board become a cop-harassment body, damage police morale, and cause cops to avoid aggressive law enforcement?

If the cops get a raise, how about the firefighters and how about the "invisible bureaucrats" who process tax bills and building permit applications? To give them all a healthy raise might break the bank or require a tax increase.

In tight budget times, which seem to be all the time, choices must be made. Should a branch library be opened in a new upscale part of town, or should the inner-city parks and basketball courts be improved and expanded? Folks who live in the newer areas are generally better organized and politically skilled. Should they get their way?

When choices such as these and others, like choosing levels of traffic law enforcement, must be made, there are multiple options, multiple opinions, and organized pressure groups on the multiple sides of the issue questions. Is this political?

Public Utilities

Some cities own electrical power plants and distribution systems, and some do not. Opponents of public electric systems argue that they rob the private sector providers of market share. Some say that public systems are inefficient, although this claim is by no means anchored in fact. Still others say that public systems are inherently bad because they are socialistic, and things socialistic are bad — "just because." The battle over public ownership has gone on for most of this century and will surely continue beyond the year 2000.

Public utilities, like city-provided electricity, give money to the city general fund. These are called "in lieu of taxes" payments. They compensate for the tax revenues lost to cities by the absence of private (and thus tax-paying) utility systems. The money for these "in lieu" payments comes from the customers; it is an extra charge built into the fee structure.

Is this right? How high should the charge be for such payments. In a sense, this practice amounts to a tax system based upon one's consumption of electrical power. Does this make sense? Whether it does or not, it constitutes a policy choice, just like the choice of relying upon a sales tax rather than a property tax. Different taxes have different impacts on taxpayers in various income categories. So decisions to have or not have a city-owned utility system and to impose or not impose an "in lieu of taxes" charge are conflict causing policy choices; they are political decisions.

The same is true of decisions about whether, and to what extent, to impose a "development fee" on new construction. If the city, county, or school district does not, then existing taxpayers, whose money has built the schools, parks, roads, bridges, and jails, are subsidizing the newcomers.

Both the newcomers to the community and the builders would like to duck such a fee to reduce the cost of new housing and business properties. But the longtime locals want new development to "pay its own way."

So the battles go on and on. Public electrical systems or private ones? High development fees, low ones, or none? Elected public officials have the job of making the calls and for that they take the political heat.

Crime and Corrections

What in the world could be political about crime? Wouldn't anyone with sense apprehend, convict, and lock up thieves and rapists? The answer, of course, is yes, but the deeper one probes into questions of crime, the murkier they become.

For example, what are the answers to these questions? A twelve year old girl tries to slip out of a Banana Republic clothing store with a sweater hidden in a shopping bag from Sears. She has been expelled from school for disruptive behavior twice, but has no criminal record. Should she go to jail? A stockbroker knowingly gives bad advice to his clients, and while he makes money buying and selling securities for them, he loses most of the clients' money. Should he go to jail? A teenager loses his temper, slams his pickup truck into a row of bicycles in the school parking lot, and in the process badly injures a fellow student. Is this an accident or vehicular assault?

The prisons in your state are full; there is a backload of those convicted, still housed in the county jails, which are themselves overcrowded. A growing proportion of the inmates are there for drug-related offenses, including sales of small quantities and personal usage. Should we increase taxes to construct and staff more prisons, or change the laws in order to de-criminalize personal usage of certain drugs? Should we let 75-year-old cancer patients smoke a little weed, or should we put them and their suppliers in prison at the cost of $25,000 per year in taxpayers' money?

These are all political questions, of course, and their resolution will come in the form of political answers. Matters of crime and corrections no longer look to be so simple. Indeed, our elected state legislators find that their plate is full of such questions.

What is or is not a crime is determined by legislative bodies, and usually reflects the current societal values. A minimum drinking age, a speed limit, the line between a misdemeanor and a felony charge are all political questions because they call for the exercise of judgment where opinions differ. The same is true of penalties for those actions defined in law as crimes.

We might decide to put the little girl with the stolen sweater on probation, or we might just release her to the custody of her parents (if she lives with them) and make her clean the floor in the store. We might put the stockbroker in jail, or we might not. It depends on how the legislature has chosen to define the crime and what penalties it has prescribed. It also depends on the inclinations of the prosecutors and the judges. And we will surely do what we've done before, namely adjust penalties for crimes up and down, depending upon the mood of the public and its tolerance for taxes.

Now, crime and corrections policy doesn't look so simple. Rather, the policies on the books at any one point in time represent our tentative answers to a host of complicated questions, made in the context of competing opinions and pressures, shifting public opinion, and limited resources. It is political.

Education

School board elections are "nonpartisan" in the sense that candidates do not run on party tickets. We all agree that schools should do what is "best for kids," and their activities should not be politicized. So it's easy to believe that politics should be kept out of education policy.

But that belief turns out to be absurd, for today, whether in the state legislature or at the local level, nothing is more politicized than the schools and education policy.

Let's begin with the legislature. In virtually all the states, one half or more of the funds for elementary and secondary schools comes from the state. So how should that money be distributed? Should it be an across-the-board equal dollar allocation per student, with a district of, say 100,000 students receiving four times as much as one with an enrollment of 25,000? Should a distribution formula take into account special circumstances?

For example, even a district with one student needs a building and a teacher. The per-pupil costs in such very small districts will be higher than those larger districts. Per pupil costs will also be higher in cities with a higher cost of living, and in districts where counsellors and health care professionals are needed to provide special services for kids from troubled homes.

Now we've got a political fight. Every legislator will be out to protect the schools in his or her legislative district, and will advocate whatever formula that produces the most dollars. Rural lawmakers will be pitted against urban ones, and those from suburbs may well constitute yet a third coalition. Those same legislators will also fight over bills designed to funnel public money into charter schools, and to support or thwart "back-to-basics" curricula requirements.

Matters are testy locally too. Should kids in neighborhood schools be bussed to a charter school so a building and a fancy curriculum is provided for the bright and college-bound youngsters from elsewhere? Should we set aside time for private devotions? Is evolution a fact or a theory, and how should it be presented in the classroom?

As with crime and corrections, these are matters over which people differ, and over which they organize and fight. The political parties may be absent at school board election time, and we may agree that it is "what's best for kids" and not petty politics that should be our preoccupation, but guess what? Education and schools are political.

Social Services

Are welfare recipients just lazy bums and leaches, or are they people just like the rest of us who took one wrong turn or who are disadvantaged through absolutely no fault of their own? Either way, what is the most promising strategy to get them to self-sufficiency?

We can't even agree on what constitutes "welfare," much less agree on how to eliminate its need. Most folks who do not receive AFDC help, food stamps, or SSI payments agree that these programs are welfare. They may not, however, view their child's Pell grant, their corporations forgiven local property tax, or farm subsidies in that way. All of these expenditures constitute targeted payments from the collective treasury to exclusive populations. Since we don't agree on which programs are aptly called "welfare," fights about welfare reform target some programs and people, but not others.

Should a promiscuous teenage high school dropout and her child be supported with taxpayer dollars? If so, for how much and for how long? What about the corporation that exports its products to foreign markets. Should taxpayers foot part of the bill for overseas advertising? Should taxpayers guarantee American farmers income and profits in exchange for their agreement to create artificial commodity shortages so they do not glut the market, drive prices down, and bankrupt themselves?

Politicians decide who is and who is not called a welfare recipient, and politics decide how much these recipients, and others not so designated, receive from the public treasury. People have differing views on who is deserving of public help, and for how long. They disagree about whether public assistance to teen moms and farmers alike helps or makes matters worse. Research has yet to uncover the correct formula to produce universal self-sufficiency, so in the meantime we vote on popular experiments to write into law.

Land Use Control

How political is land use control? Just ask any city council member who has just watched a state legislature fight over "takings" legislation. Takings is the term used to describe what occurs when an action by government diminishes, or is seen to diminish, the market value of a piece of property. If a city requires, as a condition of rezoning or issuance of a building permit, that a portion of the land in question be deeded to the city for some public purpose, that action is viewed as a taking. If public policy restricts the use of land by prohibiting disturbance of wetlands used by wildlife, that action may be viewed as a taking. In these instances, the government is alleged to be taking from an owner some portion of the value of the private property.

Takings bills in legislatures are typically designed to make state and local governments responsible for compensating landowners when their land use decisions reduce property values. Cities and counties obviously oppose such legislation, arguing that erodes the ability of the community, through its elected government officials, to control the quality of life. Advocates of takings bills argue that government should not take away one's private property, or some value thereof, without fair market value compensation. Interestingly, they do not argue that landowners should share with government (and as such, their neighbors) windfall profits that accrue to them when a public improvement increases their property value.

More frequently, cities and counties referee fights among community members over issues of zoning, rezoning, and traffic. Property owners routinely seek rezoning for land in or near residential areas in order to permit construction of grocery stores, gas stations, or apartment houses. Megabusinesses like WalMart and Safeway seek to place giant discount stores close to population centers. Neighbors complain and resist, citing the problems of noise, parking and traffic congestion.

It's a never-ending process. As citizens seek to profit by use of their land or protect the tranquility of their neighborhoods and towns, or both, land use control spells a continuous succession of political battles.

Jobs and Economic Development

The political fights here are akin to those associated with the control of land usage. Everyone wants a job, one that pays well. Merchants like growth because it means more business and more profits. So do developers and realtors. Longtime locals are skeptical because growth also means more traffic, pollution, and crime.

Cities and counties are in the middle. Tax break give-a-ways to entice new businesses generally mean a transference of government costs to others. Often too, they trigger demands by existing local businesses for their own brand of special treatment. At the same time, any sign of softness in the local economy will stimulate calls for action to shore it up. Therefore, local officials are forced to make all sorts of choices. Some political forces will press for growth-promoting policies and others will fight back.

Public Fun

One variety of economic development policy has to do with public fun. In many communities a social elite will support spending for museums, zoos, and cultural structures, and as long as expenditures are modest they face little or no opposition. But a modern variation of spending for fun is different and is highly contentious—the use of public money to build the amphitheaters demanded by professional sports franchises.

This issue has become increasingly prominent as franchise owners have elevated their demands for the taxpayers' money. Al Davis, owner of the Oakland-then L.A.-then Oakland Raiders may have started the ball rolling. More recently owner Art Modell moved the Browns football team out of Cleveland when he didn't get what he wanted when he wanted it. Jerry Jones of the Dallas Cowboys wants the workers in his local world to pay for a dome to keep his millionaire gladiators out of the rain. Denver Bronco owner Pat Bowlen insists that taxpayers buy him a new stadium to increase the value of his team and his cash flow. He did this following a taxpayer gift of a baseball facility for the Rockies; now, on the heals of the Bronco plea, the owners of the Colorado Avalanche and Nuggets want the fans to chip in for them, too. So far, none of the owners plan to include the fans and the non-fan tax-payers in on the increased profits.

One strain of argument in favor of such public subsidies (seldom referred to as welfare) is that it is the community which is the winner. Large scale construction provides jobs and, with the multiplier effect, it provides an economic stimulus to the entire community. In addition, sports teams give citizens a sense of community pride. Apparently it costs to get proud.

These are hot political issues. Community leaders often feel blackmailed by the team's threat to leave town if it doesn't get it's way. Most teams have an intense following of loyalists, and they are poised to blame the politicians if the team leaves. Others ask why, if there are tens of millions of dollars in public money available for the already rich, can't the schools be more generously supported. The elected officials are in the middle, and they must make the tough political choices unless, of course, they toss the ball to the voters via a referendum—as has been done in Denver, Dallas, and Tampa.

Citizenship and Civic Life

One might believe that civic life is removed from politics. But not so. Indeed some of our most intense political battles are fought over questions of how to run a democracy.

What do these battles involve? They involve when to schedule primary elections, whether to force local governments to conduct elections in November in conjunction with state and national elections or let them be conducted at various times throughout the year, what kinds of reports lobbyists must make, whether to impose campaign contribution limits, and whether to allow lawmakers to move directly from elective office into the lobbying business or require a "cooling off" period first.

These can be intense political battles. For example, groups and lobbyists who support public schools fight to retain the option for school districts to schedule elections in the spring. Local government spring elections have much lower voter turnout and thus the clout of the pro-public school forces, composed of teachers, administrators, parents of kids and school volunteers, is much greater. In November elections the power of their numbers is diluted by the extra voters who are drawn to the polls by presidential or statewide contests, and these folks are, taken as a whole, less likely to back teacher-supported school board candidates or mill levy increases.

Obviously, matters of campaign financing are highly contentious as well. Habitual political activists and high rollers resist limits on campaign contributions, and so do corporations and unions. Some incumbent office holders also resist limits since they traditionally are able to raise more money than their challengers. But some challengers also oppose limits because they need all the money they can raise to neutralize the name identification advantage held by incumbents.

As a result, even questions of how to conduct elections and associated matters of politics in a democracy become highly political. Everyone, from the parties to their candidates to the money people and lobbyists, are angling for an advantage.

An Expansive and Complicated System

As suggested, ours is an expansive and complex political system. Indeed, it needs to be in order to do everything from issuing driver's and marriage licenses to running hazardous waste dumps and kindergartens. Ours is also a highly decentralized system. Some of the decentralization is a product of the sheer size of the enterprise, and some of it comes from purposeful fragmentation of political power, done for a variety of reasons. Most of the rest of the book is devoted to descriptions and analysis of our state and local governments, but the balance of this chapter will overview the structure of the system.

Federalism

The single most prominent and consequential feature of our political system is federalism. In fact, all of Chapter Two is devoted to federalism. Federalism is the term for a political system in which public authority is divided and shared by two governments or sets of governments. The United States Constitution provides the structure for our federal system. The Constitution creates both a central government and a series of states. Certain powers and limits are assigned to each.

Federalism has the effect of decentralizing political power, and purposefully so. Our framers, James Madison most prominently, were worried about the dangers of concentrated political power. Indeed, their experience under the British Crown gave them good cause for such concern. As a result, they created a much needed central government, but one with strictly limited authority and functions. The range of national government activity has expanded greatly since 1789, of course, but our system retains the division of labor between a central unit and regional ones, namely, the states.

This decentralization has had a number of consequences, some good and some not so good, although what's good and what's not is largely in the eyes of the beholder. Clearly, federalism has dispersed power and kept any one person or group from fully dominating American politics. With fifty states now, it provides for a variety of settings to experiment with public programs — "laboratories of democracy," they've been called. Decentralization also allows states to tailor policies, from highways to taxation, to their peculiar needs and circumstances.

Federalism can also produce confusion and discrimination. Our sad "separate-but-equal" legacy was possible because of federalism. With fifty different consumer protection laws, businesses and customers alike can be confused about what laws pertain to what products in what jurisdiction. Citizens, ranging from taxpayers to children on welfare, can be treated quite differently. California has a rather steep state income tax; Wyoming has none and neither does New Hampshire. Wisconsin's public assistance programs are quite generous, but those in Mississippi are not at all. For a child whose family is poor, then, it's the luck of the draw. The child's food and future may well be determined by where the child's mom happens to live.

When first adopted, the U.S. Constitution created fourteen governments — the national government and thirteen state governments. Beyond that, of course, each state set up its own system of local units. Now we have fifty-one governmental systems, plus their tens of thousands of local subunits. Governmental authority and functions are widely decentralized.

Separation of Powers

Federalism wasn't enough for those who feared political centralization. As a result authority was, and is, further dispersed by the separation of the policy making, policy executing, and judgment functions. Judges, presidents, and state governors are not to make our public policy. That's the job of the elected legislators. Governors and presidents are to implement the legislators' policy. Judges are charged with resolving disputes. Although it doesn't always work that way, each is supposed to stay out of the realm of the others.

So now the system is further decentralized. From federalism's fifty-one governments, the system splits into one hundred and fifty-three branches, plus all the localities.

Even the separation of powers on top of federalism wasn't enough. The lawmaking function is divided by the creation of two-chamber legislatures in every state except Nebraska. Counting the national government, the system now has one hundred and one legislative chambers, all of them participating in the creation of America's public policies.

Boards and Commissions

Our governmental landscape is covered with boards and commissions. These are multimember bodies that make policies of various sorts or govern different parts of the executive branches in the states. Some boards govern colleges or universities. Some are entrusted with state highway departments. Still others manage state game, fish, and park departments. Members of some boards and commissions are elected at the polls, usually in November elections. Others are appointed to their posts by governors, subject often to state senate confirmation.

Why do we have these boards? Two major factors prompted their creation. First, there was, and remains, a desire by recipients of public services and those subject to government regulation to control the agency itself. People who enjoy hunting and fishing, for example, want to be able to control the use of the funds derived from license fees. They want streams kept natural and perhaps stocked, and they want to dictate hunting season dates when they can. The best way to do this is to have a state fish and game department run by a board or commission, the membership of which is dominated by hunting and fishing partisans.

The same is true with highway departments. Trucking and auto interests would rather have the highway department under the thumb of their own people than that of the governor. This phenomenon helps explain why it is politically difficult to push through state executive branch reorganizations designed to centralize gubernatorial authority. A strong governor spells weaker boards and commissions; indeed, it may even mean their elimination.

Some boards and commissions are the product of Populist and Progressive era reforms back around the turn of the twentieth century. During the latter years of the nineteenth century, big money commercial and industrial interests, such as lumber, mining, and railroads, bribed legislators and governors in successful quests for authority to grab land and rape the earth.

Eventually, outraged public response to such chicanery took the form of creating multimember boards and commissions, composed of "nonpolitical" laypeople, and placing them, rather than governors or legislators, in charge of state agencies. The notion was that a state's land, water, and minerals would be better protected by such governing bodies than by elected politicians, who could be tempted by the cash of the robber barons.

Whatever the reasons for creating boards and commissions, the result is further decentralization of our state and local political systems. So now we've divided authority between governments, branches, chambers, and executive branch units as well. It's not always easy to remember "who governs."

Urban Sprawl

Detroit is not just Detroit; its literally hundreds of cities, counties, school districts, and special districts in the south-eastern corner of Michigan. Likewise, Los Angeles is not just one city with a mayor and city council; it's a huge chunk of southern California, north of Mexico and San Diego.

In truth, Detroit is just a single city, with defined boundaries and a city government, and the same is true of Los Angeles. But these two cities, and scores of others, are also the hubs of urban regions which are replete with governments of all sorts — other cities, counties, school districts, and a bewildering array of special single-function units such as mosquito abatement, recreation, and baseball stadium districts. Indeed, there are over 86,000 such local governments.

How this pattern developed is a lengthy and interesting story, which we will look at later in this book. For now it is sufficient to note that such a fragmented pattern of local governments adds greatly to the dispersion of public authority. The pattern surely works against the emergence of dictatorships, and for that James Madison would give thanks. The pattern also provides hundreds of thousands of opportunities for citizens to play roles of elected decision maker, and Andrew Jackson would surely like that. But it also makes it quite difficult to plan sensible land usages and traffic patterns, and it surely complicates law enforcement and a host of other public functions.

Bureaucracy

No matter how you structure them, organizations become difficult to administer when they grow large. And large is surely what many of our state and local governments have become. In large organizations, communications often move slowly and messages get murky and misread. There are all sorts of ways that people scattered throughout a large organization can ignore or thwart the wishes of those who are supposed to be in charge, for example the agency head or governor.

In addition, bureaucracies are labor-divided, and the persons and offices within them are specialized. Some may deal with engineering, some with accounting, others with planning or the budget. Some are computer experts. You don't have to have read all the Dilbert comics to know that no one can know everything. Thus, organizational specialization leads in some measure to independence on the part of the specialists. Top-down control becomes more and more difficult as specialization advances, especially if it occurs in organizations that are large.

Decentralization

We're now back to where we began in this section of the chapter. For a host of reasons, our political system is an expansive and complicated governmental system. We've purposefully dispersed power in order to thwart tyranny. We've decentralized further to check the illicit impact of big money upon our environment. Urbanization and suburbanization have led to the multiplication of governmental units. Simple growth has made bureaucracies, public as well as private ones, hard to control from the top or the center.

This is the political system, the state and local system, which is of such enormous consequence to us all. Those of us who participate in civic life will, in all likelihood, do so in a state or local governmental unit. What we need and do daily traces to state and local units, whether it is a drink of water or a license to practice law or cut hair. Washington, D.C., may monopolize the news on TV, but cities, counties, and other state and local units are most dominant in our lives.

Common Features and Variety

As our study of state and local government and politics proceeds, it will become clear that the fifty states and their localities are alike in some ways but very different in others. Indeed, with fifty systems and 86,000 local units within them, it could hardly be otherwise. In closing this chapter, we will illustrate briefly these commonalities and differences.

Commonalities

American state and local governments share many historical, cultural, linguistic, and legal characteristics. All states are part of the constitutionally established federal system. They relate to the national government in the same legal fashion and are subject to the same constitutional restrictions (for example, restrictions on ex post facto laws and bills of attainder). Article IV of the Constitution requires each state to afford full faith and credit to the "public acts, records, and judicial proceedings of every other state."

The states also share many features related to their common northern European and British background. Of course, English is the dominant language for both written and spoken communications. British common law provides part of the basis for judicial decisions in all states except Louisiana, where French legal custom prevails. In addition, the state and local systems are structurally similar. Each state has a constitution with a bill of rights and separates the functions of government into three branches — legislative, executive, and judicial. All states have an elaborate network of local governments and, except for Nebraska, a bicameral legislature. The states are similar in still other respects. Each state has two representatives in the Senate, spends more on education than any other activity, and encounters challenges related to employment, schooling, poverty, and race relations.

The various similarities among American state and local governments make them politically alike in many ways. In these respects, it is possible to generalize about their functions.

Differences

Obvious differences exist among the states. In particular, differences in population size, concentration, and ethnic distribution affect the politics of states and localities. In terms of population, the states differ considerably: California has 28 million inhabitants, New York has 17 million, and Wyoming has less than one-half million. As a result, public assistance programs such as welfare are more expensive in California than in Wyoming. In some states, including Illinois, Arizona, and Colorado, a large proportion of the population is concentrated in one or two major urban centers, but in other states, such as Montana and Vermont, the population is more scattered. In the former case, politicians need to be more concerned about urban transit, smog, housing, and the urban vote. Ethnic composition also varies among the states. For example, Hispanics are concentrated in the Southwest, while African Americans are more likely to inhabit northern, eastern, and southern states. Some states and localities contain very small percentages of ethnic minorities.

In addition, industry, personal income, and taxes vary greatly among states and localities. In Michigan, particularly in the Detroit area, the automobile industry is critical, both politically and financially. In Montana the copper industry plays a similar role. In 1994, per-capita personal income was $29,402 in Connecticut and over $25,000 in three other states (Massachusetts, New Jersey, and New York), whereas it was less than $17,000 in Mississippi and Arkansas and under $18,000 in eight other states (South Carolina, Kentucky, Louisiana, Montana, New Mexico, Oklahoma, Utah, and West Virginia). The per-capita taxes collected Alaska and Hawaii in 1993 amounted to nearly $3,725 and over $2,357, respectively, while South Dakota collected just $823 and New Hampshire a mere $884. The variations in income and taxes mean that some states can provide more services of higher quality, such as education and health care, than other states. Moreover, the states often differ in terms of election laws, in the structure of local governments, and in the nature of the tax system.

Just as the states vary in terms of their geography, industries, and wealth, so too do they differ in their political cultures, public attitudes, and public policies. According to politics professor Daniel Elazar, three political subcultures exist. The **individualistic political subculture** is comprised of groups that immigrated to America in search of self-advancement without government influence. They initially settled in New England and later migrated to the Midwest. The **moralistic political subculture** is made up of people who came to America with a more collective concern for their well-being and who demonstrated that concern by their community-oriented focus. They settled in the Great Lakes region and in the upper Midwest. Finally, settlers in the South brought with them a political subculture that Elazar refers to as traditionalistic. In a **traditionalistic political culture**, the status quo is the norm, while change is not. Those at the top of the social hierarchy are also dominant in government and politics.

As the nation was settled, the three political subcultures became somewhat mixed. However, recent studies by political scientists indicate that the subcultures tend to reflect regional variations in public attitudes about government and politics that translate into policy differences.

The tradition, structure, and political style of state governments vary as well. In Louisiana, for example, certain instances of corruption were tolerated that would not have been permitted in North Dakota. In the South and West, most cities have adopted the city manager system and nonpartisan elections, both products of the early-twentieth-century reform movement. In eastern cities these reforms are much less prevalent. In some states, including Georgia and California, the governor derives considerable political clout from a major role in the budgeting process. In Texas and Colorado, however, the governor's role is much less central. In New Jersey, local governments and politicians strongly guard their independence from state encroachment. The funding of local government in Hawaii is largely centralized at the state level, as is political power.

In some respects American state and local governments are much as they were decades ago, whereas in other ways they have changed dramatically. All states still have three branches of government, and 49 states have had bicameral legislatures since statehood. In addition, local governments continue to be subordinate to the state government, and the states' constitutional relationship with the federal government has not changed. Finally, two major political parties still dominate U.S. politics.

However, state and local governments have undergone several major changes, many of which have had lasting and significant consequences. Following a period of economic growth, change, and corrupt politics as practiced by some wealthy industrialists in the late 1800s, Populist and Progressive reformers successfully fought back with a host of political reforms, including the adoption by many state and local governments of the initiative and the referendum. These devices give the individual citizen a direct role in lawmaking. Civil service replaced the spoils system, in which government jobs were dispensed on the basis of political considerations. Locally, reforms brought the city manager system and nonpartisan, at-large elections, which replaced the political machine, the elected mayor, and the ward.

More recent changes of major consequence have involved state-nation relations and the vitality of state governments. Following several decades of increasing amounts of federal money being transferred to states and localities to support a variety of programs, the tide turned in 1980 when the Reagan administration required states to rely more on their own tax resources. The modernization of state institutions, particularly the legislature, began in the 1960s and has made state governments more active and more responsive to contemporary problems and needs. In these major ways, then, state and local government units operate differently than they did in the past.

Summary

Most services are provided by state and local governments, and Americans are most likely to have contact with government at the state and local levels. These government units provide for such services as education, water, sewers, streets, fire protection, parks, and prisons. They regulate businesses, utilities, and the professions, maintain vital statistics, and conduct elections.

The United States has more than 86,000 governing bodies, including state, city, and county governments as well as school districts and special districts. The American political system is highly decentralized.

The highly decentralized nature of the U.S. government system has advantages and disadvantages. Dispersed power helps guard against tyranny and provides extensive citizen access to government as well as opportunities for participation. However, decentralization makes planning and problem solving difficult, can confuse citizens' understanding of the government system, and can cause inequalities in the quality and quantity of services available to Americans.

The state and local governments are necessarily political in nature. People want different things from their government, and disagreements must be worked out by government through political processes — debate, compromise, and voting.

The shape of the American institutional apparatus structures American politics. At the same time, politics help to determine government structures. Institutions determine areas of authority and the processes by which decisions can be made. Power struggles over the shape of governments occur, and the particular configuration helps to determine who wins and who loses. The areas of power and the rules of the game, in turn, dictate appropriate political strategies and behavior. The structure of national-state-local relations, the division of authority through the separation of powers, bicameralism, the plural executive, boards and commissions, legislative committee systems, the proliferation of local governments, and still other structural characteristics of American institutions determine in large measure what governments do and how they behave politically.

This book pays special attention to U.S. institutions for two reasons. First, we cannot hope to understand the American political system without first knowing something about the governments that make up that system — their functions, their organization, and their structural relationship to one another. Second, an appreciation of the patterns of political behavior requires an understanding of why politicians and the public act in certain ways. Their behaviors are in large part determined by the organization of authority in government institutions.

KEY TERMS

individualistic political subculture
moralistic political subculture
traditionalistic political subculture

CHAPTER
2

. . .

Federalism

. . .

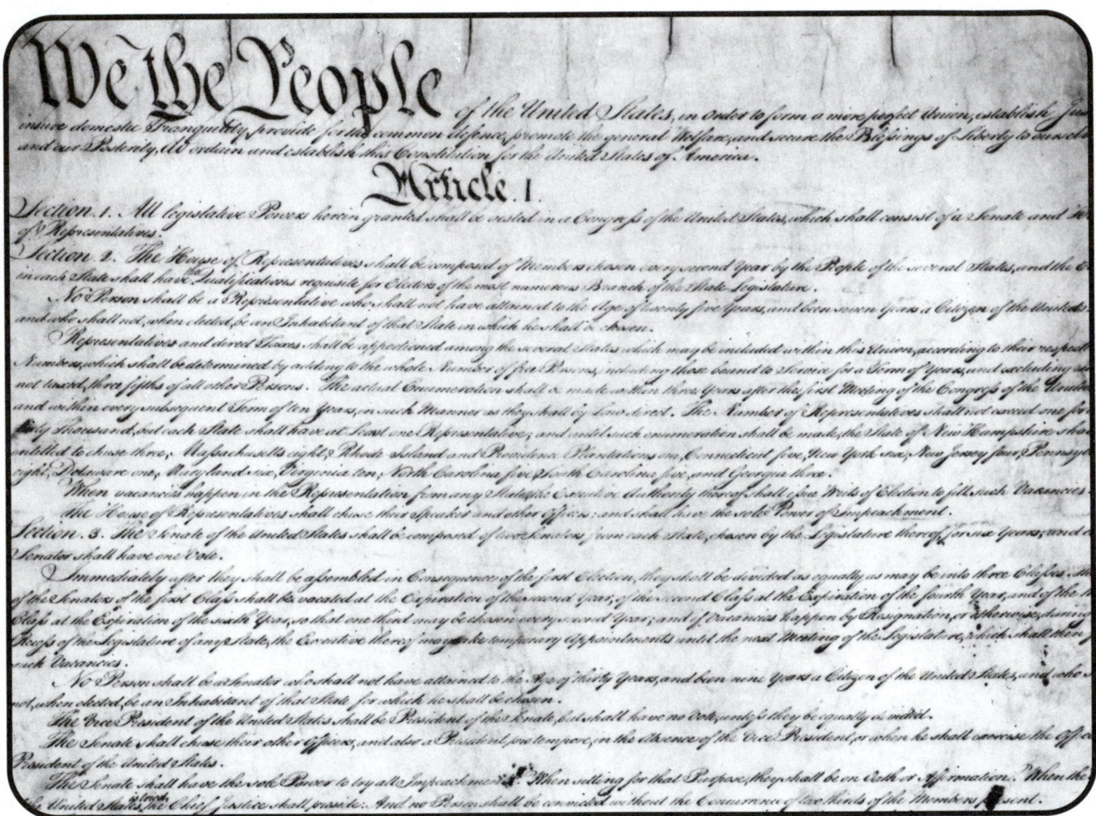

We the People of the United States, in Order to form a more perfect Union, establish Jus
insure domestic Tranquility, provide for the common defence, promote the general Welfare, and secure the Blessings of Liberty to ourselv
and our Posterity, do ordain and establish this Constitution for the United States of America.

Article. I

Section. 1. All legislative Powers herein granted shall be vested in a Congress of the United States, which shall consist of a Senate and Ho
of Representatives.

Section. 2. The House of Representatives shall be composed of Members chosen every second Year by the People of the several States, and the E
in each State shall have the Qualifications requisite for Electors of the most numerous Branch of the State Legislature.

No Person shall be a Representative who shall not have attained to the Age of twenty five Years, and been seven Years a Citizen of the United
and who shall not, when elected, be an Inhabitant of that State in which he shall be chosen.

Representatives and direct Taxes shall be apportioned among the several States which may be included within this Union, according to their respect
Numbers, which shall be determined by adding to the whole Number of free Persons, including those bound to Service for a Term of Years, and excluding
not taxed, three fifths of all other Persons. The actual Enumeration shall be made within three Years after the first Meeting of the Congress of the Unite
and within every subsequent Term of ten Years, in such Manner as they shall by Law direct. The Number of Representatives shall not exceed one for
Thousand, but each State shall have at Least one Representative; and until such enumeration shall be made, the State of New Hampshire sha
entitled to chuse three, Massachusetts eight, Rhode Island and Providence Plantations one, Connecticut five, New York six, New Jersey four, Pennsylv
eight, Delaware one, Maryland six, Virginia ten, North Carolina five, South Carolina five, and Georgia three.

When vacancies happen in the Representation from any State, the Executive Authority thereof shall issue Writs of Election to fill such Vacancies.

The House of Representatives shall chuse their Speaker and other Officers; and shall have the sole Power of Impeachment.

Section. 3. The Senate of the United States shall be composed of two Senators from each State, chosen by the Legislature thereof for six Years; and e
Senator shall have one Vote.

Immediately after they shall be assembled in Consequence of the first Election, they shall be divided as equally as may be into three Classes. Th
of the Senators of the first Class shall be vacated at the Expiration of the second Year, of the second Class at the Expiration of the fourth Year, and of the t
Class at the Expiration of the sixth Year, so that one third may be chosen every second Year; and if Vacancies happen by Resignation, or otherwise, during
Recess of the Legislature of any State, the Executive thereof may make temporary Appointments until the next Meeting of the Legislature, which shall then
such Vacancies.

No Person shall be a Senator who shall not have attained to the Age of thirty Years, and been nine Years a Citizen of the United States, and who
not, when elected, be an Inhabitant of that State for which he shall be chosen.

The Vice President of the United States shall be President of the Senate, but shall have no Vote, unless they be equally divided.

The Senate shall chuse their other Officers, and also a President pro tempore, in the Absence of the Vice President, or when he shall exercise the Off
President of the United States.

The Senate shall have the sole Power to try all Impeachments. When sitting for that Purpose, they shall be on Oath or Affirmation. When the
United States is tried, the Chief Justice shall preside: And no Person shall be convicted without the Concurrence of two thirds of the Members present.

The Preamble to the Constitution of the United States of America. The basic principles of federalism are set forth in the Constitution.

• • • **ORGANIZING GOVERNMENT**

• • • **ALTERNATIVE ORGANIZATIONAL FORMATS**

Centralization
Decentralization
Federalism—A Compromise

• • • **THE AMERICAN ORGANIZATIONAL FRAMEWORK**

Background
Federalism: National and State Relations
Expressed Powers of the National Government
Implied Powers of the National Government
National Supremacy and Guarantees

Focus 2.1: FULL FAITH AND CREDIT: MAYBE

A Unitary System: State and Local Relations

• • • **INTERGOVERNMENTAL RELATIONS**

Overview
The 1960s and 1970s
The 1980s: Reaganomics
The 1990s
The Design Affects Political Tactics

• • • **CONSEQUENCES OF INSTITUTIONAL DESIGN**

The Design Provides Variety

Focus 2.2: SUPPORT YOUR LOCAL SHERIFF

The Design Configures Elections
The Design Has Changed over Time

• • • **SUMMARY**

• • • **POLICY PERSPECTIVE**

In the early 1990s, a Utah resident was wanted by the police for a robbery allegedly committed in Lawrence, Kansas. The fugitive was stopped by a Wyoming state patrol officer, who shot the suspect in the head as he emerged from his car carrying an AK-47 assault rifle. He was hospitalized in Laramie, Wyoming, but was later brought by a Wyoming county sheriff to a hospital with better facilities, in Fort Collins, Colorado, just a few miles from the Wyoming border. The hospital was operated by a special hospital district. The Wyoming authorities then left the fugitive and returned to Wyoming. The Fort Collins police and the sheriff of Larimer County, Colorado, had to guard him, and the local hospital had to pay for expensive medical treatment. Wyoming authorities washed their hands of responsibility. The Kansas authorities said they wanted the fugitive extradited to them, but not until his medical condition improved.

Every year in April, Kathy and Steve of Canyon Country, California, file their income taxes with the federal government. At the same time, they file their California state income tax returns. Each spring their mortgage company sends the Los Angeles County treasurer money to cover Kathy and Steve's property taxes (see Figure 2.1). They have paid a little of this money to the company each month as part of their total mortgage payment. The treasurer disperses portions of the property tax funds to the local governments within whose jurisdictions Kathy and Steve reside. These include Los Angeles County, the schools, the city, a flood control district, a water district, and a sanitation district. In addition, Kathy and Steve pay special additional levies (voted for by the citizens) to the city for lighting, flood control, sewer maintenance, and sanitation.

Organizing Government

When Americans talk about government, it is often in the singular: "The government did this or that"; "Government is necessary"; "The less government the better"; "A government investigation is needed"; "The government should mind its own business"; "Government is the problem, not the solution." However, the United States has not one government but more than 86,000 governing bodies (see Chapter 1). As the examples that open this chapter demonstrate, the American system of government is highly decentralized, not in the sense that all authority is at the local level, but rather in the sense that authority and responsibility for public affairs are widely dispersed. The case of the fugitive involved four states, two counties, a city, a special district, and the question of who would pay the hospital bill. When Kathy and Steve pay taxes, they are interacting with a national government, a state government, a county

1992

JOINT CONSOLIDATED ANNUAL TAX BILL

1992

CITIES, COUNTY, SCHOOLS AND ALL OTHER TAXING AGENCIES IN LOS ANGELES COUNTY
SECURED PROPERTY TAX FOR FISCAL YEAR JULY 1, 1992 TO JUNE 30, 1993
SANDRA M. DAVIS, TREASURER AND TAX COLLECTOR

COUNTY OF LOS ANGELES

OWNER OF RECORD AS OF MARCH 1, 1992
SAME AS BELOW

ACCOUNT NO.	PRINT NO.	REG.	DIVISION INDEX BATCH NO.	Year	Seq. No.	Map Book	Page	Parcel	TRA
				92	000				

PROPERTY LOCATION AND / OR PROPERTY DESCRIPTION

ROLL YEAR 92-93	CURRENT ASSESSED VALUE		TAXABLE VALUE
LAND	101769		101769
IMPROVEMENTS	106545		106545
FIXTURES			
		TOTAL	208314
		LESS EXEMPTION HOME	7000
		NET TAXABLE VALUE	201314

DETAIL OF TAXES DUE	RATE	AMOUNT
GENERAL TAX LEVY		
ALL AGENCIES	1 000000	2013 14
VOTED INDEBTEDNESS		
COUNTY	001409	2 84
SPECIAL WATER	037437	75 36
SANITATION DIST	001363	2 84
FLOOD CONTROL	003397	7 07
COMMNTY COLLEGE	002654	5 34
HIGH SCHOOLS	002627	5 29
DIRECT ASSESSMENTS		
CONS SEWER MAINT		14 50
SAN DISTRICT 26		59 40
MOSQUITO ABATE		2 10
STA CLARITA LTG		5 00
FLOOD CONTROL		30 18
CFPD-BENEFIT ASM		43 09
FIRST INSTALLMENT TAXES DUE		1133 08
SECOND INSTALLMENT TAXES DUE		1133 07
TOTAL TAXES DUE		2266 15

BEFORE CALLING A COUNTY OFFICE SEE REVERSE SIDE FOR IMPORTANT TAXPAYER INFORMATION

THERE WILL BE A $49.85 SERVICE CHARGE FOR ANY CHECK RETURNED BY THE BANK.
KEEP THIS UPPER PORTION FOR YOUR RECORDS ; YOUR CANCELLED CHECK IS YOUR RECEIPT

Figure 2.1 Sample Property Tax Bill—Los Angeles County, California

government, a city government, and a host of other governments. Table 2.1 outlines the number and types of U.S. governments.

Particularly in the making of public policy, the decentralized institutional arrangement employed in the United States has far-reaching consequences. Levels of taxes and of public service vary widely among states and among jurisdictions within states. The presence of thousands of governments means there are tens of thousands of opportunities for citizens to hold public office. However, it also makes coordinated problem solving difficult, and the large numbers of elections and offices can confuse voters. The division of authority between (1) a central (national) government and (2) the state governments and their tens of thousands of political subdivisions makes intergovernmental struggles for power an ongoing part of the U.S. political environment.

Chapter 2 examines the institutional (structural) framework of the American political system. The relationship between the national government and the states has changed considerably over the years, and especially during the last six decades. The appropriate distribution of powers within this relationship has moved to the top of the national agenda as a result of the policy debates from the 1994 and 1996 elections. Following the 1994 congressional elections, President Clinton declared that the era of big government was over, and by 1996 such policy areas as welfare, health care, and immigration were relocated as state and local issues. Also, in the early 1990s, the U.S. Supreme Court, for the first time in sixty years, restricted congressional use of the commerce clause to expand national power, ensuring that this debate likely will continue through the rest of this decade.

TABLE 2.1 AMERICAN GOVERNMENTS

Type of Government	Number *1977*	*1987*	*1992*
Federal Government	1	1	1
State Governments	50	50	50
Local Governments	79,862	83,186	84,955
Counties	3,042	3,042	3,043
Municipalities	18,862	19,200	19,279
Townships	16,822	16,691	16,656
School Districts	15,174	14,721	14,422
Special Districts	25,962	29,532	31,555
Total	79,913	83,237	85,006

Source: U.S. Statistical Abstract, 1996 (Washington, D.C.: GPO), p. 295.

Alternative Organizational Formats

The governments of other nations are structured in a variety of ways. In some nations, decisions are made by a central government and carried out by a network of regional or local administrative departments; this high degree of centralized power is called a **unitary system**. In other nations, decisions are both made and carried out by regional or local units; often this decentralization of power is described as a **confederacy**. In still others, decisions are made centrally and administered locally, made and carried out locally, or made and administered centrally; this is a **federal system**. There are advantages and disadvantages to each of the three organizational patterns.

Centralization

In a **centralized (unitary) system**, decision-making authority, or sovereignty, is located in the central government. Most important decisions are made by the central government and are administered by its administrative arms—regional units (called states, prefects, or districts) or regional suboffices of an agency or department of the central government. The critical point is that decision-making authority resides in a central decision-making unit and the subunits exercise only those powers authorized by the main unit. Great Britain and France, for example, are unitary systems. Although both countries have regional and local units of government, these subunits are not sovereign; that is, they do not have the authority to make independent decisions. Their organizational structure, functions, duties, operating procedures, and personnel are controlled by the central decision-making unit.[1]

Advantages of Centralization

There are both advantages and disadvantages associated with the centralized or unitary system of government. On the positive side, centralization can be effective in solving problems that affect people in large geographic areas and in coordinating public programs. Air pollution and poor water quality are examples of problems that can affect many people in diverse areas; it is difficult to remedy such problems on a local or piecemeal basis. Thus, in these cases, an organizational scheme that permits decisions to be made by a central authority makes it easier for the government to develop and coordinate programs addressing these problems and providing needed services. Centralization may also keep various independent regional government units from pursuing contradictory policies on the same issue.

Disadvantages of Centralization

Centralization can cause problems as well. Large centralized governments have the potential for becoming highly bureaucratic, impersonal, and unresponsive to local concerns. Those who value small, proximate, and highly sensitive government sometimes find that the vast size of the centralized government represents a definite disadvantage. When considerable discretion is not given to regional or local administrative units, local problems (with sewer or water service, roads, parks, or public assistance, for example) may have to be communicated through numerous layers of bureaucracy before responses are received. This can be a time-consuming process; the time involved and the distant relationship can cause the main decision makers to see a distorted picture of the actual local problems and to give inappropriate responses. Some administrators may even deliberately use the complexity of the unitary system as an excuse to delay or avoid responding. As a result, local citizens become frustrated and lose confidence in their government.

The centralized system is easier to establish and operate in some countries than in others. In countries with a common heritage, culture, and language, where racial, ethnic, and religious variations do not divide the population, and where people are not isolated geographically from others, centralization may be established and function with little or no difficulty. However, in countries where there are many segments of society and where people differ significantly in terms of language, race, religion, culture, and history, or where they are separated geographically, it is more difficult to unite the people under a centralized system of government.

In other words, centralization at the expense of local autonomy is not a problem in homogeneous societies. But in many nations, where regional or tribal ties are very strong, it is difficult to fabricate a new nation out of previously isolated or independent units. Recent struggles for regional independence within the former Soviet Union and what was once Yugoslavia illustrate the difficulty of politically centralizing diverse peoples. Still, the governments of all fifty American states today are unitary systems, as are the vast majority of the more than 150 nation-states currently in existence.

Decentralization

The **decentralized system** of government organization differs in many respects from the centralized scheme. Here, the sovereign authority to decide most policy matters resides with the regional or local units. Like the Continental Congress during the formative years of the American Union, the central government in a decentralized system may represent the unity and purpose of member units and thereby have symbolic significance. It may also serve to enhance communication and program coordination among the member units. However, the local or regional units remain sovereign, and the centralized government lacks sovereignty. Under a decentralized plan, the member units and the central unit relate to one another in a loose, leaguelike arrangement in which the central unit has no legally binding powers over the local or regional units.

The United States as it existed under the Articles of Confederation provides an excellent example of a decentralized nation. Following the American War of Independence, neither public opinion nor the political alignment allowed government authority to be centralized. The best that could be achieved politically was a loose, decentralized organization of the states. Today, the United Nations provides an example of a decentralized, or confederal, structure. Although its formation cannot be considered an attempt at global governmental unity, the use of the Security Council veto and the United Nations' limited success in its peacekeeping efforts illustrate the difficulties involved in combining peoples with different social, ethnic, and religious characteristics into a single system of government.

Federalism—A Compromise

Federalism represents a compromise between centralization and decentralization. It divides sovereignty between a central government and its subunits, such as states. A situation may arise, as it did under the Articles of Confederation, in which decentralization leads to unacceptable chaos but the formation of a strong central government remains politically infeasible. A workable compromise may be found by assigning to a central government those functions that cannot be conveniently performed on a local or regional basis (for example, national defense) and leaving certain other functions in the hands of the localities (for example, police and fire protection). Federalism may thus provide enough centralization and coordination to avoid conflict or chaos in domestic or international relations, as well as help to avoid political problems resulting from attempts to compromise the integrity of local or regional units. Although the compromise arrangement of federalism can blend degrees of centralization and decentralization, it can also make it difficult to resolve jurisdictional conflicts between the central government and the regions. In many cases, the central government gradually preempts the prerogatives of the regional units, and the system becomes centralized in a *de facto* sense.

The American Organizational Framework

Federalism is an important part of American political history. Today we have what is sometimes called **coercive federalism**, in which the central unit employs its fiscal and constitutional powers to subordinate the state and local units. However, this was not always the case.

For 150 years the states and the national government functioned in parallel fashion. Beginning in the 1930s and accelerating in subsequent decades, the central government has wielded power over the states, while at the same time curtailing what had been a growing flow of federal dollars to help support state and local programs, many of which were begun with federal money as the stimulus (see Table 2.2). In the 1990s, however, this trend to national power has slowed.

In order to understand the American organizational framework, we need first to examine the background and structure of that system as it was initially framed. We also need to trace the changes that have occurred over the years.

Background

In the United States, the relationship that exists between the national government and the states is federal in nature; that is, it represents a compromise between centralization and decentralization. In contrast, the relationship that exists between the fifty states and their local governments is unitary in nature; in other words, it is centralized.

The Articles of Confederation

The first official organization of the American states was accomplished through the **Articles of Confederation**, which brought the thirteen American colonies together in a loosely knit confederation. Written in 1776 and legally ratified in 1781, the confederation plan remained in effect until it was replaced in 1789 by the current U.S. Constitution. However, the loose union created by the Articles of Confederation led to a host of organizational and operating problems for the thirteen states, and the perceived need to remedy many of those problems had a profound impact on the nature, formation, and adoption of the Constitution.

The Articles of Confederation established a unicameral Congress as the legislative or policymaking body for the loose union of the thirteen states. Each state had only one vote in Congress, though it could send a multiple-member delegation if it so desired. The unicameral body constituted the only branch of the central government—there were no separate executive and judicial branches. From time to time the Congress set up *ad hoc* executive committees to administer programs, but there was no permanent executive branch to implement congressional decisions. Likewise, there was no judicial branch to re-

Table 2.2 Three Brands of Federalism

	Basic Responsibilities		
	National	*State/Local*	*Characteristics*
Dual Federalism (1789–1930s)	National defense Regulation of commerce Post offices and roads Immigration Currency Foreign policy	Safety Health Utilities Education	National and state/local in largely separate, independent fashion
Cooperative Federalism (1930s–1960s)	National defense Regulation of commerce Post offices and roads Immigration Currency Foreign policy	Safety Health Education Utilities	More and more national programs are developed provide financial support for state and local actions, with a few conditions imposed by the national government
Coercive Federalism (1970s–1990s)	National defense Regulation of commerce Post offices and roads Immigration Currency Foreign policy	Safety Health Education Utilities	Flow of national aid to states slows; use of spending power to impose national policy goals on state and local governments accelerates
Cooperative Federalism II (1990s–?)	National defense Regulation of commerce Post offices and and roads Immigration Currency Foreign Policy	Safety Health Education Utilities Welfare	National aid to states continues to slow; use of commerce and taxing power to impose national policy goals slows

Source: U.S. Statistical Abstract, 1996 (Washington, D.C.).

solve disputes between the states or jurisdictional quarrels between the Congress and the various states. Finally, the Congress did not have the authority to act directly on individual citizens but instead found it necessary to go through the states; this was known as the doctrine of interposition. Thus, to enforce laws or collect taxes, Congress had to gain the cooperation of the individual states—a situation that, in effect, gave each state the power to veto actions proposed by the Congress.

As in all confederations, the central organ of government was weak; and, in the case of the thirteen states, this weakness led to several problems. First, the Union was financially weak. Debts remained from the Revolutionary War, and the Continental Congress found it hard to collect the taxes to pay the debts. In addition, its inability to regulate commercial relations among the states resulted in chaotic interstate commerce. States often refused to cooperate with other states and, in some cases, even erected interstate trade barriers. The lack of unity among the states and the weakness of the center made international dealings with such nations as England, France, and Spain difficult and placed the fledgling Union at a comparative political disadvantage—the Congress simply could not speak with authority for the consortium of states. On the western frontier there was dissatisfaction as a result of a perceived failure by the Congress to provide protection against the Native American population. The inability of the Congress to act directly upon citizens made tax collection and program implementation difficult. Finally, the operations of the Congress were hampered by certain requirements of the Articles of Confederation—that laws be passed by an abnormal majority of at least nine of the thirteen states and that amendments to the articles be made by unanimous vote.

The U.S. Constitution

The **U.S. Constitution**, written in 1787 and ratified in 1789, was in large part intended to remedy the problems confronting the Union. It contained provisions for the establishment of the executive and judicial branches of government, for more central and forceful conduct of international relations, for more orderly interstate trade relations, and for the direct enforcement of laws and implementation of programs by the central government vis-à-vis the citizen.

In many respects, however, the new Constitution was a compromise. The most important long-term compromise was the blending of centralized and decentralized government styles. The Constitution established a central government to perform one set of functions and left to the state governments the performance of other functions. Federalism thus emerged, characterized by dual, or divided, sovereignty.

The federal scheme was a workable compromise between two contending forces. On the one hand, there existed a clear need to centralize the power to conduct foreign relations, regulate interstate commerce, and collect taxes. On the other hand, the experience with British control, the prior existence of operating units of state government, and the desire for independence created by revolutionary war rhetoric made the abolition of the states in favor of a centralized scheme impossible. The states already existed, they had a structure, they carried on programs, and each had a battery of public officials and government employees—people who were very unlikely to agree to the abolition of their government. Likewise, propaganda designed to whip up the revolutionary drive for independence and to support the war against England was not easily forgotten, and the colonists were highly suspicious of a strong central government. Thus, the federal arrangement provided a workable compromise. The states were retained, but certain critical functions, such as the regulation of interstate commerce and the conduct of foreign affairs, were transferred to a strengthened central government.

Upon ratification, the Constitution became the supreme law of the land. It provided in general terms for the establishment of a central or national government, and it recognized the existence of the state governments. It established in skeleton form the structure of the national government. It specified in general terms the powers of the national and state governments, and it identified the activities in which neither the national nor the state governments could engage. As the supreme law of the land, the Constitution took precedence over any national government statute, any administrative edict, any action by public officials of the national and state governments, and any state constitutional provision, statute, or administrative edict.

Federalism: National and State Relations

The federal system that the Constitution established may be defined as follows: Two levels of government—national and state—exist side by side, neither being a creature of the other but both being subordinate to the legal authority of the Constitution. Each level of government is sovereign; that is, each exercises authority that the other does not.

Figure 2.2 depicts the national government–state government relationship of the federal system. As the figure shows, the sovereign people acted to establish a basic law (or contract) known as the Constitution; the Constitution, in turn, legally established a dual system of government; and each level of government was designed to relate directly to each individual citizen. However, it should be noted that the Americans living today do not constitute the "sovereign people" who initially agreed to the federal arrangement. Figure 2.2 de-

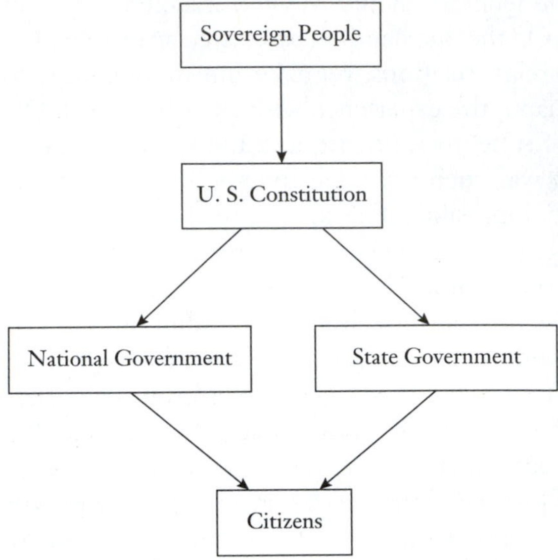

Figure 2.2 The Federal System

picts, in theoretical terms, the relationships among the people, the Constitution, and the two levels of government.

Expressed Powers of the National Government

The Constitution explicitly details the legal or **expressed powers** of the national government and a number of activities in which the national government and the state governments may not engage. It is not as explicit, however, in detailing the legal powers of the states. The various powers and limitations outlined by the Constitution are shown in Table 2.3.

The Constitution established the three branches of the national government. Article I established the **legislative branch**—a bicameral (two-house) legislature with representation in one house (the lower house) based on a state's population, and with each state, regardless of its geographic size or population, holding two seats in the upper house, or Senate. Article I also stipulated that representatives in the lower house be elected by the people and serve two-year terms, and that those in the upper house be selected by the legislatures of the various states and serve six-year terms. As a result of the Seventeenth Amendment, however, senators in all states now are popularly elected.

Article II of the Constitution established the **executive branch** of the national government. It also vested the power of the executive branch in the president and conferred upon the president various powers and duties. Finally, the Constitution created a court system known as the **judicial branch**. Article III

TABLE 2.3 THE U.S. CONSTITUTION: LEGAL POWERS OF NATIONAL AND STATE GOVERNMENTS

National Government	State Governments	Intergovernmental Relations
Expressed powers Inherent powers Implied powers Powers denied	Reserved powers Powers denied	National supremacy Full faith and credit

established the Supreme Court and empowered Congress to create lower courts as it deems necessary.

In most other respects, however, the Constitution does not provide much detail about the structure of the national government. As a result, congressional statutes and administrative orders have formed most of the vast national government apparatus.

The Constitution conferred on the national government, in explicit terms, the authority to perform certain functions. For example, in Article I, Section 8, Congress is given the authority to lay and collect taxes, to borrow money, to regulate commerce with foreign nations and between the states, to constitute courts inferior to the Supreme Court, and to raise and support the armed forces, among a series of other expressly delegated powers. Also in Article I, the Constitution gave Congress the authority to "make all Laws which shall be necessary and proper for carrying into Execution the foregoing Powers, and all other Powers vested by this Constitution in the Government of the United States, or in any Department or Officer thereof."

Implied Powers of the National Government

The activities of the national government have expanded over time, in part because of technological advances and changing socioeconomic conditions, and in part because the Supreme Court has supported increased national government activity in its interpretations of the Constitution. Historically, the Supreme Court has defined the constitutional authority of the national government broadly, thus giving rise to what are called the **implied powers** of the national government.

In the landmark case of ***McCulloch v. Maryland*** (1819), Chief Justice John Marshall, citing the "necessary and proper" clause of Article I, Section 8 of the Constitution, held that the national government could legally establish a national bank system because such action would be implied from the government's explicit authority to "coin money and regulate the value thereof."

Marshall, a Federalist and an advocate of a strong central government, contended that the expressed powers found in the Constitution be viewed as the ends or goals of the national government, and that any means necessary to reach those goals and not prohibited by the Constitution were considered constitutional. In addition to the *McCulloch* case, changing conditions and a host of subsequent Supreme Court decisions that broadly interpreted the authority of the national government also contributed to the vast expansion of national activity.

Inherent Powers of the National Government

In addition to its expressed and implied powers, the national government exercises what are called **inherent powers**. The national government and the president in particular possess full constitutional authority to conduct foreign relations and enter into treaties. In the case of *United States v. Curtiss-Wright Export Corporation* (1936), the Supreme Court affirmed the inherent powers of the national government in foreign affairs, noting that such powers are inherent because of the United States' membership in the family of nations.

Interstate and State–National Relations

As noted earlier in the chapter, the Constitution does not include explicit provisions for the structure of state governments or state authority. It does, however, deny certain powers to the states, address the subject of interstate and state–national relations, and provide a series of guarantees to the states. The one constitutional provision that deals affirmatively with the authority of the states is in the Tenth Amendment: "The powers not delegated to the United States by the Constitution, nor prohibited by it to the States, are reserved to the States respectively, or to the people." Because of the wording of this amendment, the states are generally said to possess **reserved powers**. Article I, Sections 9 and 10 of the Constitution, list a series of **powers denied** both the states and the national government, including the power to enter into a treaty, to coin money, and to pass bills of attainder or *ex post facto* laws (criminal laws that are applied retroactively).

On the subject of interstate relations, Article IV of the Constitution is fairly elaborate. Section 1 of this article orders the states to grant **"full faith and credit"** to the public acts, records, and judicial proceedings of every other state. Section 2 commands each state to grant its "privileges and immunities" to the citizens of all other states and charges each state with the duty of rendering up to other states fugitives from the law (a provision with which states do not always comply).

Article IV is of considerable importance because it requires that states enforce their laws impartially, treating their own citizens and citizens of other states as equals in most areas. Deeds, contracts, wills, and other legal documents from one state must be honored in all other states. Although states can have their own legal provisions in such areas as residence requirements for voting, driver's licenses, out-of-state tuition rates for colleges and universities, and marriage laws, they nearly always administer them in a reasonable fashion. States allow, for example, drivers from other states to pass through with a driver's license and registration plates from their home state, and they recognize marriage and birth certificates from other states. From time to time problems may arise, however; for example, there was a time when North Carolina refused to recognize a Nevada divorce decree. In most cases, though, the states adhere to the requirements of "full faith and credit" (see Focus 2.1 "Full Faith and Credit: Maybe") and "privileges and immunities" stipulated in Article IV.

National Supremacy and Guarantees

Whereas Article IV of the Constitution addresses the relationships among the states, Article VI specifies the relationship between the states and the national government. It reads, in part:

> This Constitution, and the Laws of the United States which shall be made in Pursuance thereof; and all Treaties made, or which shall be made, under the Authority of the United States, shall be the supreme Law of the Land; and the Judges of every State shall be bound thereby, any Thing in the Constitution or Laws of the State to the Contrary notwithstanding.

Focus 2.1
FULL FAITH AND CREDIT: MAYBE

• • •

In 1996, when it appeared that Hawaii would recognize the legality of same sex marriages, Congress passed a bill, and President Clinton signed it into law, that permitted states to withhold recognition of such marriages. As the "full faith and credit clause" is a part of the Constitution, a question arises about whether the Congressional action is constitutional; that is, is a constitutional amendment required to establish an exception to the full faith and credit clause?

This provision, often referred to as the **national supremacy** clause, specifies that no state laws may conflict in any way with national government laws that are constitutional, with provisions of the Constitution, or with the provisions of treaties. For example, in *Missouri v. Holland* (1920), the Supreme Court held that the national government could write legislation based on the provisions of a treaty (in this case, a treaty related to the international protection of migratory birds), and that a state may not ignore or contradict such a law. Treaty-based legislation is, thus, constitutional even if the same legislation would be unconstitutional in the absence of the treaty.

Although the states have sovereign authority through their reserved powers, in a head-on clash of the laws of the national government and the laws of a state, Article VI of the Constitution provides for national supremacy if the Supreme Court deems the national law constitutional.

Finally, the Constitution provides a series of guarantees to the states in Article IV, which specifies that no state may be split to form another state without the consent of Congress and of both states involved. The article also commands the national government to protect the states from invasion and requires the national government to guarantee every state a republican form of government—that is, one based on the consent and representation of the people.

The Constitution as Compromise

As suggested, the Constitution represents a compromise by its authors as they sought to cope with the pressing problems of their era. The states already existed, so their elimination was not politically feasible. At the same time, a lack of strong central direction caused the consortium of new states a host of irritating problems. The solution was to retain the states and let them continue to perform most of their traditional functions (such as the maintenance of local law and order), but at the same time create a central government to handle problems and services that demanded centralized decision making (such as the regulation of interstate commercial relations). Federalism, therefore, provided a mixture of centralization and decentralization and maintained the political integrity of both central and regional governments.

The process for amending the Constitution illustrates the legal relationship between the national government and the states. The amending process most often used involves the initiation of a proposed constitutional change by the national government—by a two-thirds vote in both houses of Congress and subsequent ratification by the legislatures of three-fourths of the states. Constitutional amendments may also be proposed by a national convention, called by Congress at the request of two-thirds of the states; again, ratification must be by legislative action or special conventions in three-fourths of the states. Whatever process is employed, both the national government and the state governments must be parties to the constitutional change. Neither unit of government can unilaterally amend the Constitution or increase or decrease the powers, duties, or limitations of the other. Rather, they are partners in the sense that they are equally bound to the legal authority of the Constitution.

A Unitary System: State and Local Relations

The legal relationship between state and local governments is very different from that of the national government and the states. Whereas the national government and the states are partners, both bound by the Constitution and both sovereign, all units of local government are part of and subordinate to the states. State governments create local governments; assign powers, duties, and limits to local governments; and, if they wish, may legally abolish local governments. In other words, local governments (counties, cities, townships) are subdivisions or administrative arms of the state; local governments have no sovereignty.

State constitutions and statutes demonstrate this superior–inferior legal relationship. All state constitutions provide for the existence of local units. In some cases local governments are given some of their legal authority in constitutional home-rule provisions, but in most cases local governments are assigned their powers and duties and have limits imposed on them by state statutes—acts of the state legislature.

Legal Relations

A generalized model of the legal relations between the state and local governments is as follows: First, the constitution of the state provides for the existence of county governments, school district governments, special district governments (for example, water, sewer, and recreation districts), and city and town governments. It may specify the structure of county government, the number of members in and the terms of office for the county board of supervisors, and county duties (such as maintaining vital statistics and records). In addition, the state constitution may empower the legislature to grant home rule to cities and counties; that is, to allow them, by statute, to tailor their own government structure and range of functions. In reference to schools, the constitution may call for the establishment, by legislative statute, of a system of free and compulsory schools to be managed by local school districts and supervised by a state board of education. Regarding towns and cities, the constitution may instruct the legislature to classify towns and cities according to size, and to prescribe for each size its structure, powers, duties, and limitations. It may order the legislature to do likewise for special districts.

Furthermore, the state constitution may contain a variety of other provisions that affect the operations of local governments. It may, for example, restrict state and local governments by establishing in a bill of rights such basic freedoms as those of speech, press, assembly, and religion. In the area of taxation, the constitution may limit the kinds of taxes that local governments can collect and the rates they can impose. For example, the constitution may forbid local governments to impose an income tax or may limit the use of the property tax to a specified rate.

Other than providing for the creation and operation of local governments and the occasional prescription of structural features, state constitutions generally leave the detailed specifications of local government structure, powers, duties, and limits to the state legislatures. Thus, one must look to the statutes of a state for detailed descriptions of its local governments. Whether found in state constitutions or statutes, the laws regarding local governments tend to be restrictive.

Local Governments and Dillon's Rule

As noted earlier in the chapter, the federal courts tend to accord a broad interpretation of the constitutional powers of the national government. For local governments, however, the tendency is in the opposite direction. The propensity for narrow court interpretations of local government powers is termed **Dillon's rule** after an Iowa judge, named John F. Dillon, who stated:

> It is a general and undisputed proposition of law that a municipal corporation possesses and can exercise the following powers, and no others: First, those granted in express words; second, those necessarily or fairly implied in or incident to the powers expressly granted; third, those essential to the accomplishment of the declared objects and purposes of the corporation,—not simply convenient, but indispensable. Any fair, reasonable, substantial doubt concerning the existence of power is resolved by the courts against the corporation, and the power is denied. [2]

Although there seems to be a recent trend of the courts to be less strict in their interpretations of local government powers, there is no evidence of dramatic change. Local governments remain the legal wards of the state. They were created by the state, they receive their instructions from the state, and they may do only what the state permits through its statutes and constitution. Occasionally, state courts interpret municipal home-rule laws, which grant cities greater discretion over governance, in ways that give cities some independence from their state. But even home-rule laws are state laws. State-local relations are still much as Judge Dillon described them.

Finally, whereas an amendment to the Constitution must be approved by both partners of the federal union—the national government and the states—local governments do not play a similar role in their relationship with the states. The constitutional powers, duties, limits, and geographic boundaries of the states cannot be altered without their consent. In contrast, local governments have no opportunity to alter proposed state constitutional changes. The state legislature plays a role, as do the voters of a state, but local governments do not.

Intergovernmental Relations

Overview

The relationships that exist among the various levels of American government provide a legal picture of intergovernmental relations, but there are also many important modern-day realities to consider. From an examination of the legal nature of the federal system and the unitary relationship that exists between state and local governments, it may seem that each of the three levels of government operates independently of the other units. However, this is not how American government operates.

Intergovernmental relations in the latter half of the twentieth century have been characterized by the existence of an elaborate and complicated maze of legal and financial ties among national, state, and local units of government. By the 1970s this maze had become so complex that a succession of presidents—Nixon, Carter, Reagan, Bush, and Clinton—sought to simplify it and restore some independence to the states. This process accelerated following the 1994 congressional elections as the Republican-controlled Congress focused on shifting power from the national government to the states.

The Impact of Federal Grants

The instrument most responsible for the development of complex legal and financial ties is the national government's **grants-in-aid** program. Grants-in-aid are funds that the federal government makes available to state and local governments for support of state and local programs. Some grants are **categorical grants** and are used for narrowly defined purposes. Others are **block grants**, meaning that state and local governments have some discretion in the use of the funds. Today, almost every sphere of governmental activity—from the construction of sewer systems and golf courses to the training of police officers—involves cooperative programs among the different levels of government.

Intergovernmental relations have undergone dramatic changes over time, including increased interaction between the national government and the state and local units. The financial scope of national government grants-in-aid to state and local governments has increased over the past several decades, and cooperative programs now involve the national government in a wide array of activities and services (see Table 2.4).

Several observations may be made concerning grant-in-aid programs and their growth. Clearly the dollar volume of the programs is large. Growth was especially dramatic between the 1930s and the 1970s, but has since slowed. Moreover, not all national government money finds its way into state and local coffers in large blocks of cash. Instead, hundreds of categorical grant programs exist, each created by some act of Congress and each designed to help state or local government solve a particular problem or set of problems. Some programs help local schools purchase student lunches, some help colleges and universities conduct research, and some help cities improve older neighborhoods. Other programs are designed to help the states and localities attack various problems.

A More Complex System

Not surprisingly, the federal grant system is confusing and unwieldy. The programs are so numerous and complicated that many colleges, universities, state

TABLE 2.4 FEDERAL AID TO STATE AND LOCAL GOVERNMENTS, 1970–1996

	Dollars Spent (millions of dollars)			
				(estimated)
Type of Federal Aid	*1970*	*1980*	*1990*	*1996*
Total grants and revenues	$24,065	$91,451	$135,377	$236,730
National defense	37	93	241	25
Natural resources/environment	411	5,363	3,745	4,009
Energy	25	499	461	482
Agriculture	664	569	1,285	676
Transportation	4,599	13,087	19,225	26,617
Community/regional development	1,780	6,486	4,965	9,690
Education, employment, training, social services	6,417	21,862	23,359	35,561
Health	3,849	15,758	43,980	99,173
Income security	5,795	18,495	35,189	54,909

Source: U.S. Statistical Abstract, 1996 (Washington, D.C.: GPO), p. 300.

agencies, and local governments employ people just to keep track of the programs that might be of benefit.

Most importantly, however, grant programs have brought the various levels of government together into a complicated set of legal and financial relationships. Unlike in the past, when the various units and levels of government could go about their business relatively unaffected by other governments, today's city, county, special district, state, and national bureaucracies must interact constantly with their counterparts in agencies of other governments. Moreover, federal money, or incentives, have the effect of speeding up states' adoption of new and innovative policies.[3]

Why the Change?

A number of factors contributed to the development of the massive network of intergovernmental relationships that exists today. The historical propensity of the Supreme Court to interpret broadly the authority of the national government made it legally possible for Congress to create various kinds of grant programs. As noted earlier in the chapter, Chief Justice John Marshall began this trend with his ruling in *McCulloch v. Maryland* (1819). The grant programs are based on the Constitutional authority of Congress to spend money, including money earmarked to support state and local activities.

In addition, the grant programs emerged as the national government sought to deal with problems related to the failure of the states to come to grips with urban issues during the Great Depression of the 1930s and the later period of rapid urbanization (from about 1950 to 1970). In 1790 only 5 percent of the U.S. population was classified as urban, but in 1890, for the first time in American history, more people lived in cities than on farms. By 1970 that figure had soared to over 70 percent. The increasing U.S. population combined with greater numbers of urban dwellers meant that American society was becoming more crowded, more complicated, and less agricultural as millions of people moved into relatively small cities. All sorts of urban problems emerged, including air and water pollution, poor and insufficient housing, mass-transit difficulties, and increased crime.

Until the Supreme Court reapportionment decisions of the mid-1960s, political power remained in the hands of the rurally oriented and tight-fisted state legislatures. The legislatures were thus unwilling to raise taxes or to address the growing needs of the urban areas.[4] In addition, cities were perceived negatively during the heyday of the urban political machines, so that state decision makers tended to ignore the problems of the burgeoning cities. Thus, with the woes of the urban areas increasing and the states somewhat indifferent to urban problems, the cities turned to Washington, D.C., for help. They received it in the form of grant programs approved by Congress.

Another factor contributing to the expansion of national government activity has been the changing nature of many important public issues. Unlike the local problems that dominated the agendas of government in the past—such as wheat blight and potholes in county roads—today's decision makers must wrestle with more difficult issues—such as a polluted environment and rising unemployment, that are regional or national in scope.

Many contemporary problems, such as mass transit and clean air, plague entire metropolitan areas. As a result, they cannot be handled locally but require the help of the state and national governments. Their causes and consequences extend far beyond the jurisdictions of local governments. This pervasive quality of modern-day issues keeps the national government on the scene. In addition, problems are increasingly national in character in that they tend to affect large areas of the country. They are thus perceived as national problems and are put on the agenda of the national government. For example, air pollution is a problem in Denver, Detroit, New York, Phoenix, and Los Angeles, to name only a few cities.

Finally, the technologically advanced and complicated nature of the U.S. economy and communication and transportation systems has contributed to national government involvement, particularly in urban areas. Modern communication technology makes it possible for the events and problems of one city or region to become known across the nation within minutes. The transportation system permits millions of people to move about throughout the country, making Americans more familiar with the conditions, events, and problems in other areas. Mass production and distribution systems have made various areas of the country dependent on one another.

Reasons exist for placing many modern problems on the agenda of the national government. In a sense, technology has made the nation smaller, identifying problems common to many regions. Politicians promise voters that national programs will be established to attack the problems, including urban slums, run-down schools, and air and water pollution.

A Layer Cake Becomes Marble Cake

Over thirty years ago Morton Grodzins first used what is now known as the **marble-cake federalism** analogy to describe the nature of intergovernmental relations, or cooperative federalism as it is often called.[5] According to Grodzins, the U.S. government system can no longer be viewed as a three-tiered layer cake of national, state, and local governments with each layer performing its own functions independently of the others. Through the grants-in-aid programs and cooperative federalism, intergovernmental relations now look more like a marble cake, with a maze of vertical financial and legal ties integrating the activities of the three sets of governments.

More recently, in an analysis of the expansion of national government programs and spending, Thomas Anton has characterized the contemporary federal system as composed of "coalitions of beneficiaries."[6] Private beneficiaries of congressional programs—such as farmers, water barge operators, students, the elderly, and public assistance recipients—are in league with the federal and state bureaucrats who administer the benefits programs. They are tied to the reelection-oriented members of Congress who sit on the committees that consider and review the programs and who seek to please their voting constituencies. These parties work together to advance their various personal and professional desires by protecting and expanding the programs from which they all benefit. Some call these mutually supportive networks **iron triangles**; others refer to them simply as **subgovernments**. In either case, these coalitions make it politically difficult to cut spending by reversing what has already been established.

The 1960s and 1970s

From the founding of the Union through the nineteenth century, fiscal federalism—the financial interdependence of the national and state governments—developed at a leisurely pace. Congress authorized financial aid to assist states with the construction of postal roads. The federal government also made funds available to assist with vocational education, aid the blind, and help universities conduct research. However, even as late as 1930, less than 3 percent of all state and local revenues came from the federal coffers.

The situation began to change significantly at the turn of the century, and accelerated in the mid-1960s and later. The adoption of the Sixteenth Amendment in 1913 legitimized the federal income tax, which greatly increased the amount of revenue available to the federal government. The Great Depression stimulated Congress to enact programs in states and localities designed to spur economic recovery and growth. In the decade or so following World War II, Congress authorized federal financial support of urban planning and renewal efforts in America's cities.

The Great Society

From the mid-1960s to the 1970s, the expansion of federal programs was enormous. Federal legislation made federal dollars available to states and localities through a wide variety of programs. Included were new or expanded funding programs in elementary and secondary education, higher education, the arts, mental health, drug and alcohol treatment, maternal and child health, family planning, legal services, highways, airports, job training, and wastewater treatment plants. Lyndon B. Johnson, a master of congressional politics, was president. Earlier, John Kennedy, elected president in 1960 and assassinated in 1963, had called on the nation's people to recognize their obligations to their fellow citizens. Johnson continued that theme and, with the help of Congress, expanded Kennedy's dream into the **Great Society**—countless domestic programs designed to fix our broken cities, educate our children, and train our unemployed. The period of the Great Society affected fiscal federalism dramatically.

But Congress wasn't finished. Just as the Great Society was in full swing, the nation developed a new consciousness about both the environment and consumer protection. On the heels of domestic legislation—in areas such as education, jobs, and health—the administration in Washington began passing consumer and environmental protection laws, making even more money available to state and local governments.

The period of 1965 to 1975 transformed intergovernmental relations. But it was also significant for another related reason. When Congress passed legislation making financial support available to state and local governments, it also accelerated the establishment of highly complicated and costly conditions that state and local governments had to meet in order to qualify for financial help. In other words, the programs came with strings attached. But this was not new to state and local governments. Congress had long imposed construction and accounting standards in such grant areas as highways, welfare, and education. For the most part, the guidelines were designed to ensure the responsible use of the funding.

Crossover Sanctions

The strings attached to federal funds took on a new dimension in the 1960s and 1970s. By this time many state and local units were dependent on federal dollars. Decision makers, both in Congress and in bureaucratic federal agencies, began to realize the extent to which they could impose national government policy objectives on state and local units by threatening to withhold federal funds. Washington decision makers thus imposed on state and local units, by means of congressional acts and agency guidelines, a wide variety of requirements, some of which were not directly related to the purposes for which the state and local units received funding. These became known as **crossover sanctions**. State and local governments, now "hooked" on Washington's financing, found themselves subject to requirements ranging from equal opportunity in women's athletics to the development of drug-free workplace programs. An example of the former occurred at Colorado State University when a federal judge ruled that CSU's 1992 decision to save money by eliminating its women's softball program violated Title IX of the Educational Amendments Act of 1972. The judicial order was quite specific, directing CSU to hire a permanent coach for the team, begin active recruiting, and offer an exhibition schedule by the fall of 1993. The judge left undisturbed a companion decision that eliminated the men's baseball program.

At stake is states' continued receipt of funding in such areas as sewerage, transportation, student aid, and research. Debates over national policy objectives raged in areas ranging from affirmative action and removal of barriers for the handicapped to consumer protection and clean waters. The costs, in time and dollars, to state and local governments accepting the aid grew. Intergovernmental relations became ever more complicated. Among the results were intergovernmental conflicts, a paperwork blizzard, and significant state and local dependence on federal money. Moreover, the stage was set for such political events as the passage of Proposition 13 in California in 1978, the election of Ronald Reagan to the presidency in 1980, and his "new federalism" of the 1980s.

Proposition 13 and the Taxpayer Revolt

The much-heralded **Proposition 13**, an initiative measure passed by California voters, reduced the levels of assessment on property (such as residential homes) and limited the permissible levels of property taxation. Most commentators viewed its passage as part of a national property tax revolt. In addition, voter support of Proposition 13 was interpreted as a statement by voters that they had enough government and enough regulation and wanted relief. A vote on federal regulation was not available; a vote on state and local taxes was. Voters in other states responded to ballot initiatives in a similar antigovernment fashion.

Another factor, one fundamentally associated with the nature of the U.S. political system, also lay behind these events. People were fed up with increased government intervention in their lives. The proportion of state and local revenues derived from the federal treasury had grown from less than 3 percent in 1930 to over 25 percent by 1978. This growth was accompanied (especially from 1965 forward) by a wide array of new mandates to state and local governments from Washington—some from Congress but most the product of bureaucratic interpretation. Private-sector federal contractors had similar experiences. The result, right or wrong, was a growing sense of being bullied by Washington, of being caught in a paper tangle, of being helpless before the enormous federal establishment. Small businesspeople were angry, state lawmakers felt pushed around, state and local employees and public officials were pressured.

The 1980s: Reaganomics

Following his election, President Ronald Reagan assembled a program designed to translate his campaign pledges into policy.[7] For Reagan, it was imperative that federal spending be brought under control, that state and local governments return to a financially more self-reliant status, that fiscal intergovernmental relations be simplified and made more efficient, and that the extensive network of federal regulations designed to push state and local governments into compliance with federal policy objectives be reduced. His program is referred to as **Reaganomics**.

Block Grants

Early in 1981 President Reagan presented Congress with proposals to consolidate eighty-five categorical grant programs into seven block grant programs, including education, health, social services, urban development, and community development. He further proposed to reduce funding levels for the programs by one-quarter, with the programs to be "enriched" by the presumed savings of administrative efficiency. Fewer strings were to be attached to the blocked programs, allowing states and localities increased flexibility to reduce administrative costs. Reagan wanted the national government to assume full responsibility for Medicaid, while placing the cost of Aid for Dependent Children (AFDC) and food stamps on the states.

President Reagan did not get all he wanted from Congress, but he got some of it. In the Omnibus Budget Reconciliation Act of 1981, Congress consolidated seventy-seven categorical programs and two existing block grants into nine block grant programs. The newly created block grant programs were in the areas of community development; elementary and secondary education; preventive health and health services; alcohol, drug abuse, and mental health; maternal and child health services; primary care; social services; community services; and low-income home energy assistance. Funding was reduced in most areas, with the greatest reductions in employment and training assistance, child nutrition, public assistance, and low-income energy help.

The changes had a significant impact on state and local governments. They changed the nature of intergovernmental relations, with the role of the states strengthened and the role of local governments weakened. Many of the programs—in areas such as job training, community development, education, health, primary care, and community services—had been characterized by direct federal–local financial ties. With the blocking of formerly categorical programs, funds were targeted to the states and state officials had to play a larger role in distributing federal funds to local governments.

Less Federal Money

The changes in the grant system also reduced the amount of federal money available to support state and local programs. In 1982 there was a reduction in the size of the grants-in-aid system for the first time in the history of the programs. In 1978 federal money constituted 9 percent of local government revenues and 22.3 percent of the revenues for the states; by 1987 these numbers had fallen to 4.2 percent and 18.5 percent, respectively (see Figure 2.3). The cutbacks, combined with other troublesome features of the economy and of state and local finances, created severe budgetary pressures for many states and localities.

The trends set into motion by Reaganomics in 1980 continued throughout that decade and into the next (see Figure 2.4). Presidents Reagan and Bush restricted continued growth in the flow of federal money to the states and localities. Indeed, their goal was to shrink it. In addition, Reagan and the Congress cooperated in running up enormous annual budget deficits in the 1980s, leading to constant pressure to control spending. That pressure continues to plague President Bill Clinton's administration. One result has been growing congressional resistance to spend more in support of state and local programs. This has caused more of the financial responsibility for many domestic programs to be placed on state and local units, as Reagan wanted. One consequence of the 1994 congressional elections was to increase pressure to reduce the number of unfunded mandates imposed on the states by federal entities; the GOP Contract with America captured much of the spirit of the Reagan goals. By the 1996 presidential election, the issue was no longer whether there should be a reduction of the influence of the national government, but rather to what degree. President Clinton declared that the era of big

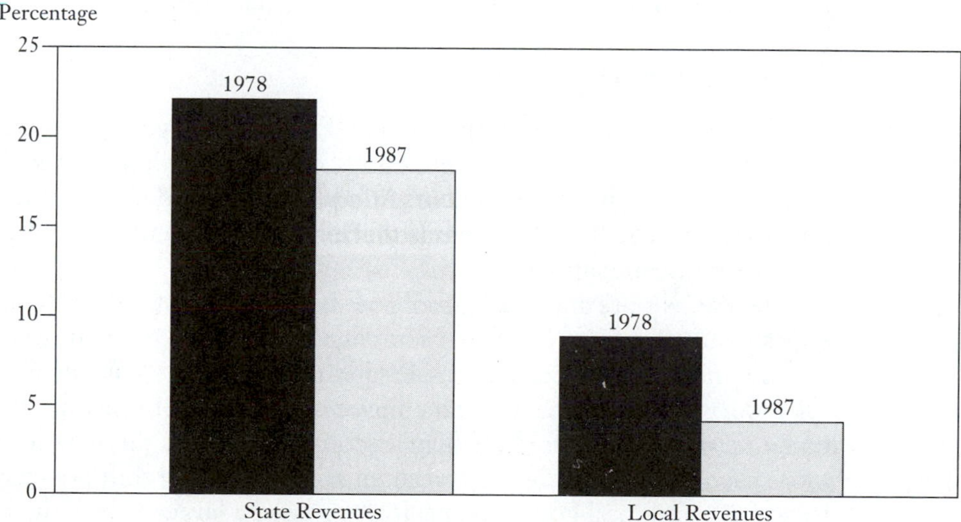

Figure 2.3 Federal Funds as a Percentage of State and Local Revenues, 1978 and 1987
Source: Robert Gleason, "Federalism's Fiscal Shifts," *ACIR Intergovernmental Perspective* (Fall 1988): 26.

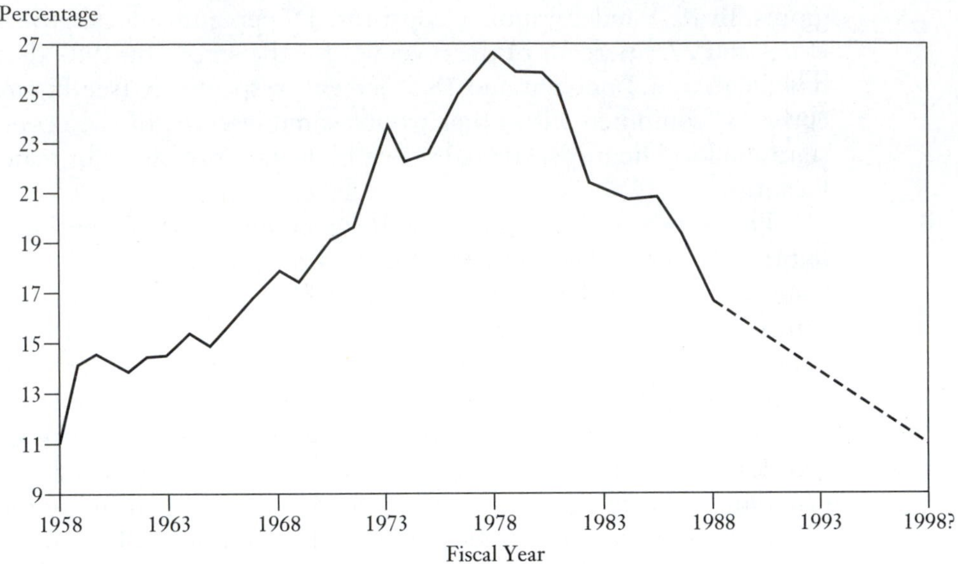

Figure 2.4 The Rise and Decline of Federal Aid, 1958–1988, and 1998? (as a percentage of state and local outlays)
Source: ACIR Intergovernmental Perspective (Winter 1988): 13.

government was over, and, while that may have been more rhetoric than reality, it spoke to the change in philosophy that had occurred in a generation.

Redistributing the Tax Burden

Reaganomics had redistributive effects. Programs targeting low-income people were hit quite hard, with reductions in education, job training, and community and regional development. At the same time, defense spending, Social Security, and Medicare, programs that primarily benefit the middle class, received significant support.

Insofar as state and local governments replaced lost federal funds with revenues generated from their own sources, the overall tax structures of the states became more regressive. Today sales and property taxes, on which state and local governments rely heavily, take higher proportions of income from low-income people than does the federal income tax. Thus, the new federalism did more than simply alter intergovernmental relations and shift policy responsibility to state and local governments; it also passed a larger part of the bill for government services to those in lower-income categories by shifting the cost of many programs to the states and localities.

The 1990s

The relationships among the national, state, and local governments today are significantly different than a decade ago. Due to the changed fiscal relations triggered by Reagan, state and local governments have had to rely on their own sources of revenue. As a result, the states emerged from the 1980s more self-reliant than they had been in the two preceding decades. State and local governments had to raise taxes to pay their own way. From 1982 to 1988, general fund spending increased by 51 percent for the states and by 62 percent for the localities.[8] This trend is likely to continue at an accelerated pace as the GOP Congress first elected in 1994 and reelected in 1996 continues to press for shifting federal programs to the states. In 1996, President Clinton signed a bill from Congress that would shift the funding of welfare from the national government to the states (see the Policy Perspective in Chapter 4). State governors and legislatures now must search for sources of money to support these shifts.

Local governments now rely more heavily on their political parents—the states. In 1988, for example, state aid to local governments totaled $143 billion, in contrast to only $17 billion in local aid from the national government.[9] Just as aid from the national government comes with strings attached, so does aid from the states. The flow of state money has grown together with state controls. For example, nine states recently enacted legislation empowering the states to take over failing local school systems, and twenty others provide for some form of state intervention in troubled local schools.

Money Shrinks but Mandates Don't

Although one might expect national government influence to moderate or decline with the stabilization or reduction in federal financial help, this has not happened. Instead, government controls have increased to the point that in 1989 the governors called on Congress to stop placing mandates on the states. Congress has made continued state receipt of highway money contingent on compliance with congressional preferences about the speed limit and legal drinking age, and continues to impose clean air and water standards as well as wage and hour laws on state and local governments.

State and local officials do not like many of these mandates because they find them costly and unresponsive to regional and local conditions. But in numerous policy areas, Congress, through federal agencies, continues to tell state and local governments what to do. One observer put it this way:

> State governments are required to develop programs, expend resources and participate in federal programs based on federal priorities instead of, or to the detriment of, state defined goals and missions.[10]

In the mid-1990s, Congress began to respond to these complaints; it is likely that there will be fewer unfunded mandates during the latter part of the decade.

Federal Courts Send Mixed Signals

However, Congress has not acted alone in altering intergovernmental relations. The courts, which played a significant role in strengthening the hand of the national government over the states, have also responded to and participated in the more conservative changes of the 1990s. In the 1976 case of *National League of Cities v. Usery*, the Supreme Court concluded that the commerce clause of the Constitution does not give the national government the authority to enforce the provisions of the Fair Labor Standards Act on the states and localities. In a 5–4 decision, the Court held that Congress may not "operate to directly displace the states' freedom to structure integral operations in areas of traditional governmental functions." The definition of a "traditional" function was difficult to define, however, and by 1985, in *Garcia v. San Antonio Metropolitan Transit Authority*, the Court reversed its ruling in Usery by allowing the imposition of the Fair Labor Standards Act on the states. Critics argue that this represents a damaging blow to the principle of federalism in that it strips away the semiautonomy of the states in the formerly dual system of federalism. The position of the Court is that if the states want to be shielded from the policy desires of Congress, they must seek their remedy through the political process (that is, they must lobby Congress).

Other cases have reinforced the *Garcia* ruling. In *South Carolina v. Baker* (1988), for example, the Court concluded that it is permissible for Congress to levy federal taxes on interest earnings on state and local bonds (previously, these bonds had been immune from such taxation). The 1987 case of *South Dakota v. Dole* is another example of the Supreme Court's approval of the congressional propensity to tell the states what to do. Shortly after it began providing financial help in 1921 to the states for the construction and maintenance of highways, Congress imposed conditions on the states for continued receipt of the money. These included creation of state highway departments, imposition of weight limits, highway maintenance to suit federal desires, imposition of heavy vehicle use taxes, billboard control, the visual screening of junkyards, speed limits, air-quality programs, and a minimum drinking age of 21 years.[11] Most recently, Congress required the states to revoke the driver's licenses of persons convicted of drug offenses, even if no driving was involved.

South Dakota and several other states challenged Congress's authority to impose the minimum drinking age, but the Court sided with Congress. One critic of the decision notes that "in *Dole* the Court effectively abrogated the notion that Congress is a government of delegated powers. . . ."[12]

Some federal requirements on the states and localities include forced uniformity in the keeping and reporting of information. It is argued that the requirements are necessary to provide Congress and federal agencies with comparable and reliable data for use in distributing funding and assessing program results.[13] However, they also add to the federal government's list of Supreme Court–sanctioned implied constitutional powers to influence state and local governments. Table 2.5 lists the regulatory statutes and amendments passed by

TABLE 2.5 MAJOR ENACTMENTS AND STATUTORY AMENDMENTS REGULATING STATE AND LOCAL GOVERNMENTS, 1982–1990
Age Discrimination in Employment Act Amendments of 1986
Americans with Disabilities Act of 1990
Asbestos Hazard Emergency Response Act of 1986
Cash Management Improvement Act of 1990
Child Abuse Amendments of 1984
Civil Rights Restoration Act of 1987
Clean Air Act Amendments of 1990
Commercial Motor Vehicle Safety Act of 1986
Consolidated Omnibus Budget Reconciliation Act of 1985
Drug-Free Workplace Act of 1988
Education of the Handicapped Act Amendments of 1986
Emergency Planning and Community Right-to-Know Act of 1986
Fair Housing Act Amendments of 1988
Handicapped Children's Protection Act of 1986
Hazardous and Solid Waste Amendments of 1984
Highway Safety Amendments of 1984
Lead Contamination Control Act of 1988
Ocean Dumping Ban Act of 1988
Older Workers Benefit Protection Act of 1990
Safe Drinking Water Act Amendments of 1986
Social Security Amendments of 1983
Social Security: Fiscal 1991 Budget Reconciliation Act
Surface Transportation Assistance Act of 1982
Voting Accessibility for the Elderly and Handicapped Act of 1984
Voting Rights Act Amendments of 1982
Water Quality Act of 1987

Source: Timothy J. Conlan and David R. Beam, "Federal Mandates: The Record of Reform and Future Prospects," *ACIR Intergovernmental Perspective* (Fall 1992): 8.

Congress between 1982 and 1990 that significantly affected intergovernmental relations. As you can see, the legislation covers a diverse array of topics.

Recently, however, the Supreme Court has handed the states some important victories. In 1995, the Court signaled that it may no longer simply rubber-stamp Congress's use of the Commerce Clause to expand national power at the expense of the states. In 1990, Congress, relying on the Commerce Clause, enacted the Gun-Free School Zones Act, making it a federal offense for any individual knowingly to possess a firearm within a school zone. Lopez, a senior at a San Antonio high school was arrested and charged under the law with carrying a .38 caliber handgun at school. He subsequently was convicted. On appeal, Lopez' lawyers argued that the law exceeded Congress's legislative power. In *Lopez v. U.S.* (1995) the Supreme Court agreed, stating in a 5–4 decision that possession of a gun in a local school zone is in no sense an activity that affects interstate commerce. For the first time in over sixty years the Court had restricted Congress's use of the Commerce Clause as part of the "federal police power." The ruling raised the question of a possible return to the notion of dual federalism.

In the 1995–96 term, the Court further reined in the powers of the national government by ruling in *Seminole Tribe of Florida v. Florida* that a federal statute giving private parties the right to sue states violated the Eleventh Amendment's grant of state sovereign immunity. This trend continued during the 1996–97 term of the Court. In June 1997, by a 5–4 decision, the Court ruled that the section of the Brady Bill requiring county sheriffs to conduct background checks on potential handgun buyers exceeded congressional authority (*Printz v. US*, 95-1478).

What's next? Most scholars agree that these recent decisions are simply "corrections" to the 60-year trend of expanding national power and do not portend dramatic change in national–state relations. Still, there may be future "corrections." For example, the federal motor-voter law requires state officials to oversee federal voter registration; certainly, the *Printz* decision invites a challenge to this practice. Then, there is the Violence Against Women Act (VAWA). In this act, Congress, relying on its commerce authority, created a federal cause of action for rape victims by asserting that gender-motivated violence affects the ability of women to engage in commerce. In July 1996, a federal district court in Virginia dismissed a VAWA suit, concluding that the connection between gender-based violence and interstate commerce was too tenuous. This decision was appealed to the 4th Circuit U.S. Court of Appeals in the spring of 1997.

The state–local relationship is unitary, not federal. Since local governments are creatures of the state, they do what their state dictates; within any single state, local policies are similar. Policies in all cities, counties, or special districts may not be identical because the states typically allow for local variation. But since state law establishes systems of local government, standardization is extensive. All cities in a given size classification, for example, employ the same form of government, and all counties are subject to state-specified powers, duties, and limitations.

The states must ratify proposed amendments to the Constitution, as they are partners in a federal relationship. No such role is provided within the states for their political subdivisions with reference to changes in state constitutions.

The Design Affects Political Tactics

Both the behavior of special interest groups and lobbyists and the organizational characteristics of political parties are heavily influenced by the shape of American institutions. For example, just a few decades ago, civil rights proponents, unable to persuade state and local officials to eliminate racial segregation, shifted their focus to national decision makers. In *Brown v. Board of Education* (1954), the Supreme Court did what state officials would not do—outlaw the separate treatment of the races in public education. Congress enacted a number of significant civil rights laws in the 1960s.

Recently, interest groups have been readjusting their focus on the states. This is the result of the devolution of program responsibilities to the states, of the states' undertaking some regulatory activities where national law is silent, and of a more conservative federal judiciary following the Reagan/Bush years of GOP presidential appointments. The design of our institutions thus provides the road map that guides and directs the activities of political interests.

Consequences of Institutional Design

Does it matter how a polity designs its government institutions? Yes, for institutions are the foundation of the political system. According to the principle of federalism, both the setting and implementation of policy are left to the states and their local units. Public safety, for example, is a state and local matter (see Focus 2.2 "Support Your Local Sheriff"). Police officers and firefighters are local government employees. Public utilities—sewers, water, streets—are state and local matters, as are most parks and landfills. Public health programs and hospitals are state and local concerns. Most criminal laws, courts, and prisons are as well. If the founders had institutionalized a unitary relationship between the national government and the states, all of this would be different. Policies would be made centrally, and local options and state variations would not exist.

The Design Provides Variety

Variety does exist, for state and local governments differ widely (and sometimes wildly) in their priorities. Revenue systems vary among states and among

Focus 2.2
SUPPORT YOUR LOCAL SHERIFF

• • •

In 1993, Congress passed the Brady Act. The Brady Bill imposes a five-day waiting period on handgun purchases, and also requires local law enforcement officials during that time to check prospective buyers' backgrounds to determine if they meet any of the conditions established by the bill for denial of the permits. These conditions include being a convicted felon or being mentally ill.

In June 1996, the U.S. Supreme Court agreed to hear the cases of two county sheriffs from Arizona and Montana, who had sued the federal government over the constitutionality of the provision ordering local law enforcement officials to perform federal background checks. The sheriffs argued that this federal requirement violates the Tenth Amendment.

Since the passage of the Brady Act, six federal judges heard similar cases in various jurisdictions. Five of the federal courts ruled in favor of the local law enforcement officials. Subsequent appeals resulted in one appellate court finding the background-check provision constitutional and one striking the provision down.

In June 1997, the U.S. Supreme Court ruled that this section of the Brady Bill exceeded the authority of Congress (*Printz v. U.S.*).

cities. Some states and localities spend heavily on police and fire protection, whereas others do not. The tax burden is heavier in some states than others, as are levels of public assistance and health care benefits. Some states foot most of the bill for elementary and secondary education; others leave the tax collecting to local school districts.

The Design Configures Elections

The consequences of our institutional arrangements are evident in the electoral system as well. When we go to the polls, we are confronted with a formidable ballot featuring elections for national, state, and local offices. We may be able to vote on the same ballot for a president, a U.S. senator, a congressional representative, a state governor, an attorney general, a secretary of state, a state senator and house representative, state judges, members of a state university governing board, and a host of local offices. Why? Because of the way our government is structured.

In a many ways, then, the shape of American political institutions affects the nature of our politics and policies. Election systems, policy and program variations, and political strategies and behavior are products of those institutions.

The Design Has Changed over Time

Over two hundred years ago America's political activists faced a serious problem. After difficult years under the thumb of the English crown and following the Revolutionary War, not many favored installing governmental institutions that centralized authority. Yet in the face of such pressing problems as interstate commercial squabbling and war debts, the existing decentralized scheme, in which the states were autonomous, was not working. The political resolution was found in a federation. Some functions were handed over to a newly created national government, while most others remained with the states (and remain with the states today).

But times change, and over the years Congress, basing its decisions on the Constitution's commerce and tax clauses, the spending power, and the necessary and proper national supremacy provisions, has greatly expanded the scope of national government activities. Today, state and local governments find themselves forced to help implement a wide variety of national policy objectives and to comply with a host of national rules and regulations.

And, yet, Dylanlike, the times they are a-changing. Federalism is a dynamic concept, and, as this chapter has indicated, the relationship between the national government and the states rarely is static. The political debates of the mid-1990s plus the Supreme Court decisions restricting congressional authority give promise of yet another period of change between the national government and the states.

Still, the system seems to work. In one of the most perceptive and fresh analyses of federalism in several years, Professor Paul Peterson suggests two theories of federalism—functional and legislative.[14] The functional theory of federalism posits the two main economic purposes of domestic government to be developmental (e.g., physical and social infrastructure) and redistributive (e.g., the reallocation of resources from the "haves" to the "have-nots"). The former is the appropriate province of the state governments, the latter that of the national government. When these boundaries generally are acknowledged, as Peterson suggests has happened over recent decades, the "price" of federalism is bearable. The second theory, however, recognizes that it is in the interests of legislators at the national level to claim credit for actions that weaken federalism (e.g., shifting redistributive functions to the states) and that political pressures may cause the "price" of federalism to rise. As we approach the end of the 1990s, Peterson is cautiously optimistic, while recognizing that the compromises that form the dynamic of the interplay between the functional and legislative theories may not produce the desirable outcomes.

Summary

In an attempt to resolve the differences between those in favor of a highly centralized government and those supporting a decentralized system, the framers of the Constitution developed a federal system. Federalism is a system of dual or divided sovereignty: The central government is sovereign in those policy areas with national impact, and the individual states are sovereign in those policy areas with more limited impact.

For the first 150 years of the Republic, there was some cooperation between the national and state governments; however, they were largely independent of each other. For the past half-century, there has been increasing interaction among the different levels of government. Most noticeably, the national government has used financial incentives to expand its influence over and to impose its policy preferences on the states. Now, during the latter part of the 1990s, national influence over the states appears to be lessening.

As is evident throughout the book, the federal principle is pervasive in American politics. Almost every political institution is affected by this notion of divided sovereignty. Our system of justice, our political parties, and our elections of public officials all function the way they do because of the influence of federalism.

As this chapter has indicated, federalism is not a fixed principle. Rather, it evolves in response to changing political demands and values. There is no reason to believe this evolution will cease. James Madison might have trouble recognizing federalism in its current form, but if he could see it ten years from now, who knows what he might think? Almost certainly, the federalism that characterizes American politics in the year 2008 will be different from that of today.

Policy Perspective

On the face of it, policy development in a federal system is simplicity itself. Problems that affect the nation will be the province of the national government, and problems of more limited impact will be addressed by the individual states. Even identifying specific national and state powers is not very difficult. Obviously, foreign policy should be the concern of the national government; no one wants Arizona engaging in unilateral foreign policy negotiations with Mexico, or Michigan declaring war on Canada. It's clear that the problems of education in Oregon may be (indeed, are likely to be) quite different from those in South Carolina. Each of these states should be free to establish their responses to these problems. Commerce, too, is an easy call: Let the national government regulate commerce between the states, interstate commerce, and each state will be responsible for governing the commerce that occurs within the state, intrastate commerce.

The devil, of course, is in the details. When does interstate commerce end and intrastate commerce begin? When does a problem begin to have sufficient national impact as to justify national intervention? Who decides? How?

Historically, the U.S. Supreme Court ultimately has defined the boundaries of the federal arrangement; there is a reason this text is full of Supreme Court citations. But this, at best, begs the question. After all, the Court is a branch of the national government. This doesn't mean that the Court always will rule in favor of the national government, and it has not, but, certainly over the two hundred years of the Republic, it has done so more often than not. Why should the views of these particular nine men and women be the final authority about the conflicts between the states and the national government?

Of course, there is no precise answer to this question. Nor can there be. Reasonable people will disagree about what constitutes national versus state problems. Most of us are comfortable today with the notion that the national commerce power can be used to regulate racial discrimination; certainly, in 1964 racial discrimination was a problem of national scope. But should that power be used to protect the safety of local schools by prohibiting firearms within certain distances of the schoolgrounds? Many would agree that schoolground safety is a laudable goal, but is it an appropriate task for the national government? This is not a rhetorical question.

Similarly, there is probably widespread agreement that the need for clean air and clean water cross state boundaries and merit national attention. But what if a state decides that, in the interests of the state's health concerns, landfills within the state should not accept waste products from outside the state? Is this an appropriate exercise of control over intrastate commerce or is it an interference with interstate commerce? (The Court ruled the latter.) Is it within a state's intrastate commerce power to establish a limitation on the weight and length of trucks traveling over the state highways (yes to the issue of weight, no to the issue of length), and to establish a requirement that trucks traveling over its highways use a specific shape of mudflap (again, no according to the U.S. Supreme Court)?

Thus, as indicated in this chapter, making public policy within a federal arrangement is a constant exercise of determining which level of government has the appropriate jurisdiction to act. In other words, there is a constant drawing of lines, and, consequently, a constant movement of those lines. In the early part of the century, child labor was labeled the province of the states; by the 1940s the interpretation of the federal principle in this policy area changed and the national government assumed authority over child labor (again, on the basis of the commerce clause).

The federal grants-in-aid programs offer perhaps the best examples of this shifting of lines. The grants often come with strings attached, allowing the national government to condition its aid on state acquiescence to national goals. In the late 1980s, Congress offered aid to the states for the maintenance of their state highways. Part of the funds, however, were conditioned on the state's willingness to raise their drinking age to twenty-one. Again, few of us would argue that the states and national government should be able to cooperate in the maintenance of public highways, but the linkage between maintaining the highways, the drinking age of teenagers, and interstate commerce may be less clear. Although, in theory, no state sovereignty was violated as any state could decline such aid; in reality, most states are dependent on such aid if they are to maintain their roads.

Poverty, crime, welfare, education, transportation, environmental protection, and housing are all examples of policy areas that have at one time been considered issues properly addressed by state policies, and at other times, properly addressed by the national government. Many of these policies are addressed in depth throughout this book, but all continue to be influenced by the most important principle in our system—the federal principle.

KEY TERMS

unitary system
confederacy
federal system
centralized system
decentralized system
federalism
coercive federalism
Articles of Confederation
U.S. Constitution
expressed powers
legislative branch
executive branch
judicial branch
implied powers
McCulloch v. Maryland
inherent powers
reserved powers
powers denied
full faith and credit
national supremacy
Dillon's rule
grants-in-aid
categorical grant
block grant
marble-cake federalism
iron triangle
subgovernment
Great Society
crossover sanction
Proposition 13
Reaganomics

ADDITIONAL READING

Advisory Commission on Intergovernmental Relations. *Regulatory Federalism: Policy, Process, Impact and Reform* (Washington, D.C.: GPO, 1984).

Anton, Thomas J. *American Federalism and Public Policy* (Philadelphia: Temple University Press, 1989).

Beam, David R., and Timothy J. Conlan. "The Growth of Intergovernmental Mandates in an Era of Deregulation and Decentralization." In *American Intergovernmental Relations*, ed. Laurence J. O'Toole, 2d ed. (Washington, D.C.: Congressional Quarterly Press, 1993).

Conlan, Timothy. *New Federalism: Intergovernmental Reform from Nixon to Reagan* (Washington, D.C.: Brookings Institution, 1980).

Derthick, Martha. "American Federalism: Madison's Middle Ground." *Public Administration Review* 47 (Jan.–Feb. 1987): 66–74.

———"The Enduring Features of American Federalism." *Brookings Review* (Summer 1989): 34–38.

O'Toole, Laurence J., ed. *American Intergovernmental Relations* (Washington, D.C.: Congressional Quarterly Press, 1985).

Peterson, Paul E. *The Price of Federalism* (Washington, D.C.: Brookings, 1995).

Walker, David. "Intergovernmental Relations and Dysfunctional Federalism." *National Civic Review* (Feb. 1981): 68–76.

Wrightson, Margaret T. "The Road to South Carolina: Intergovernmental Tax Immunity and the Constitutional Status of Federalism." *Publius* 19 (Summer 1989): 39–55.

NOTES

1. Alex N. Dragnich, "The Government of Great Britain," in *An Introduction to Political Science*, ed. Alex N. Dragnich and John C. Wahlke (New York: Random House, 1966), p. 71.
2. Quoted in Clyde F. Snyder, *American State and Local Government* (New York: Appleton-Century-Crofts, 1965), p. 353.
3. Susan Welsh and Kay Thompson, "The Impact of Federal Incentives on State Policy Adoption," *American Journal of Political Science* (Nov. 1980): 715–29.
4. Some observers challenge the notion that malapportionment was a major factor in the failure of states to tackle urban problems; see, for example, Thomas R. Dye, "Malapportionment and Public Policy in the States," *Journal of Politics* (Aug. 1965): 586–601.
5. Morton Grodzins, "The Federal System," in *Goals for Americans*, ed. the American Assembly (Englewood Cliffs, N.J.: Prentice-Hall, 1960), pp. 265–82.
6. Thomas Anton, *American Federalism and Public Policy* (Philadelphia: Temple University Press, 1989), p. 32.
7. Much of the material in this section is drawn from *ACIR Intergovernmental Perspective* (Winter 1982).
8. John Herbert, "The Growing Role of the States Is Greater Than We Knew," *Governing* (March 1990): 11.
9. Ibid.
10. Ali F. Seven, "Highway Sanctions: Circumventing the Constitution," *State Legislatures* (Feb. 1989): 28.
11. Ibid.
12. Thomas R. McCoy and Barry Friedman, "Conditional Spending: Federalism's Trojan Horse," *Supreme Court Review* (Chicago: University of Chicago Press, 1988), pp. 85–127.
13. Cheryl Arvidson, "As the Reagan Era Fades, It's Discretion versus Earmarking in the Struggle over Funds," *Governing* (March 1990): 22.
14. Paul E. Peterson, *The Price of Federalism* (Washington, D.C.: Brookings, 1995).

CHAPTER 3

• • •

State Constitutions

• • •

Preamble.

We, the People of Colorado, with profound reverence for the Supreme Ruler of the Universe, in order to form a more independent and perfect government; establish justice; insure tranquility; provide for the common defense; promote the general welfare, and secur the blessings of liberty to ourselves and our posterity, do ordain and establish this Constitution for

"The State of Colorado."

Article I.

Boundaries.

The boundaries of the State of Colorado, shall be as follows: Commencing on the thirty-seventh parallel of north latitude, where the twenty-fifth meridian of longitude west from Washington crosses the same; thence north, on said meridian, to the forty-first parallel o north latitude; thence along said parallel, west, to the thirty-second meridian of longitude west from Washington; thence south, on said meridian, to the thirty-seventh parallel of north latitud thence along said thirty-seventh parallel of north latitude to the place of beginning.

Article II.

Bill of Rights.

In order to assert our rights, acknowledge our duties, and proclaim the principles upon whi our government is founded, we declare:

Section 1. That all political power is vested in and derived from the people; that all govern-ment, of right, originates from the people, is founded upon their will only, and is instituted solely fo

The opening page of the Colorado state constitution. Every state has a written constitution that establishes the basic framework and procedures for collective decision making. In this case, the constitution also establishes the location and boundaries of the state. *(Colorado State Archives)*

• • • **STATE CONSTITUTIONS ARE IMPORTANT POLITICAL DOCUMENTS**

Constitutions Structure State Governments
Constitutions Impose Limits on States

• • • **MULTIPLE LEVELS OF LAW**

• • • **THE CONTENTS OF STATE CONSTITUTIONS**

Bills of Rights
The Framework of State Government
Local Governments
Control of State and Local Finances

• • • **THE LENGTH AND DETAIL OF STATE CONSTITUTIONS**

• • • **STATE CONSTITUTIONAL AMENDMENTS**

• • • **CRITICISMS OF STATE CONSTITUTIONS**

Too Much Detail
Poor Design
Outdated
The Reformers' Preferred Model
State Responses

• • • **CONSTITUTIONAL POLITICS**

High-Stakes Politics
Special Interests
Vested Interests versus Reformers' Interests
The Difficulty of Introducing Changes
Enduring Issues
Arkansas: An Example of Constitutional Politics

• • • **THE FUNCTIONS OF STATE CONSTITUTIONS**

Constitutions Distribute Power
Constitutions Govern Finances

• • • **SUMMARY**

• • • **POLICY PERSPECTIVE**

The U.S. Constitution written in Philadelphia in 1787 is not the only American constitution. Every U.S. state also has its own written **state constitution**. Many states have had several constitutions. Indeed, over the course of U.S. history, Louisiana has had eleven constitutions, Georgia has had ten, South Carolina seven, and Alabama, Florida, and Virginia six each. Nineteen states have had just one constitution. State constitutions also differ in certain ways. The state constitutions of Connecticut, Indiana, Minnesota, New Hampshire, and Vermont are, like the U.S. Constitution, each less than 10,000 words in length. However, Alabama's constitution is about 174,000 words, New York's is 80,000 words, and Oklahoma's and Texas's each exceed 60,000 words. Furthermore, whereas the constitutions of Alaska, Illinois, Michigan, Montana, Pennsylvania, and Virginia have been amended fewer than twenty-five times, Alabama's constitution has more than 500 amendments and California's and South Carolina's constitutions have over 400 amendments each.[1] (See Table 3.1.)

Historically, many state constitutions have been long and full of detail, some of it outdated (prohibitions against dueling, for example). Constitutional reforms have been emphasized throughout the country over the past decades; when they have been successful, some of the length and detail of state constitutions have been eliminated. Although state constitutions contain common elements, they also display rich and interesting variety.

State Constitutions Are Important Political Documents . . . .

From the lack of public attention that state constitutions receive, one might misjudge them as unimportant. However, in the U.S. federal system, these documents establish the institutions of government within each state. State constitutions prescribe the structure, powers, duties, and limits of each branch of government. They lay the foundations for tax policies and systems of local government. Each state constitution contains a bill of rights; increasingly, the states' bills of rights provide the foundation for legal decisions that affect American civil liberties. Under what is called the "new judicial federalism," the courts have recognized individual rights granted by state constitutions that are not guaranteed by the national constitution. The answers to a wide array of modern political questions lie in the constitutions of the American states. You and I may pay property taxes on our homes, but must the elderly and war veterans pay them too? Must churches that operate stores or day-care centers on their premises pay taxes? Can cities enact an income tax? Who dominates the state budget process—the governor or the legislature? How are state judges selected? Do citizens have the right to privacy and to a quality education? In the

TABLE 3.1 GENERAL INFORMATION ON STATE CONSTITUTIONS (AS OF JANUARY 1, 1996)

State or Other Jurisdiction	Number of Constitutions*	Dates of Adoption	Effective Date of Present Constitution	Estimated Length (number of words)	Number of Amendments: Submitted to Voters	Number of Amendments: Adopted
Alabama	6	1819, 1861, 1865, 1868, 1875, 1901	Nov. 28, 1901	220,000 (a)	818 (a)	582 (a)
Alaska	1	1956	Jan. 3, 1959	15,988 (b)	34	25
Arizona	1	1911	Feb. 14, 1912	28,876	218 (c)	119 (c)
Arkansas	5	1836, 1861, 1864, 1868, 1874	Oct. 30, 1874	40,720	171	81 (d)
California	2	1849, 1879	July 4, 1879	54,645	823	491
Colorado	1	1876	Aug. 1, 1876	45,679	265	128
Connecticut	4	1818 (e), 1965	Dec. 30, 1965	9,564	29	28
Delaware	4	1776, 1792, 1831, 1897	June 10, 1897	19,000	(f)	127
Florida	6	1839, 1861, 1865, 1868, 1886, 1968	Jan. 7, 1969	25,100	97	69
Georgia	10	1777, 1789, 1798, 1861, 1865, 1868, 1877, 1945, 1976, 1982	July 1, 1983	25,000	58 (g)	44 (g)
Hawaii	1 (h)	1950	Aug. 21, 1959	20,744 (b)	110	86 (i)
Idaho	1	1889	July 3, 1890	23,239 (b)	194	114
Illinois	4	1818, 1848, 1870, 1970	July 1, 1971	13,700	16	10
Indiana	2	1816, 1851	Nov. 1, 1851	10,230 (b)	70	38
Iowa	2	1846, 1857	Sept. 3, 1857	13,430 (b)	52	49 (j)
Kansas	1	1859	Jan. 29, 1861	11,900	119	91 (j)
Kentucky	4	1792, 1799, 1850, 1891	Sept. 28, 1891	27,234 (b)	66	33
Louisiana	11	1812, 1845, 1852, 1861, 1864, 1868, 1879, 1898, 1913, 1921, 1974	Jan. 1, 1975	54,112 (b)	112	72
Maine	1	1819	March 15, 1820	13,500	194	164 (k)
Maryland	4	1776, 1851, 1864, 1867	Oct. 5, 1867	41,349	241	207 (l)
Massachusetts	1	1780	Oct. 25, 1780	36,700 (m)	145	117
Michigan	4	1835, 1850, 1908, 1963	Jan. 1, 1964	25,246 (b)	54	20
Minnesota	1	1857	May 11, 1858	23,700	208	113
Mississippi	4	1817, 1832, 1869, 1890	Nov. 1, 1890	23,508	152	119
Missouri	4	1820, 1865, 1875, 1945	March 30, 1945	42,000	139	86
Montana	2	1889, 1972	July 1, 1973	11,866	38	21
Nebraska	2	1866, 1875	Oct. 12, 1875	20,048	294	198
Nevada	1	1864	Oct. 31, 1864	20,770	189	115 (j)
New Hampshire	2	1776, 1784	June 2, 1784	9,200	280 (n)	143 (n)
New Jersey	3	1776, 1844, 1947	Jan. 1, 1948	17,800	60	47
New Mexico	1	1911	Jan. 6, 1912	27,200	252	127
New York	4	1777, 1822, 1846, 1894	Jan. 1, 1895	51,700	284	215
North Carolina	3	1776, 1868, 1970	July 1, 1971	11,000	35	27
North Dakota	1	1889	Nov. 2, 1889	20,564	238 (o)	132 (o)
Ohio	2	1802, 1851	Sept. 1, 1851	36,900	259	157
Oklahoma	1	1907	Nov. 16, 1907	68,800	300 (p)	151 (p)
Oregon	1	1857	Feb. 14, 1859	26,090	397	201
Pennsylvania	5	1776, 1790, 1838, 1873, 1968 (n)	1968 (n)	21,675	27 (q)	21 (q)
Rhode Island	2	1842 (e)	May 2, 1843	19,026 (m)	105	59
South Carolina	7	1776, 1778, 1790, 1861, 1865, 1868, 1895	Jan. 1, 1896	22,500	650 (n)	465 (r)
South Dakota	1	1889	Nov. 2, 1889	25,000	196	101
Tennessee	3	1796, 1835, 1870	Feb. 23, 1870	15,300	55	32
Texas	5 (s)	1845, 1861, 1866, 1869, 1876	Feb. 15, 1876	80,806 (b)	532 (t)	364
Utah	1	1895	Jan. 4, 1896	11,000	134	84
Vermont	3	1777, 1786, 1793	July 9, 1793	6,880	210	52
Virginia	6	1776, 1830, 1851, 1869, 1902, 1970	July 1, 1971	18,500	31	26
Washington	1	1889	Nov. 11, 1889	29,400	159	89
West Virginia	2	1863, 1872	April 9, 1872	26,000	113	66
Wisconsin	1	1848	May 29, 1848	15,531 (b)	177	129 (j)

(continued)

State or Other Jurisdiction	Number of Constitutions*	Dates of Adoption	Effective Date of Present Constitution	Estimated Length (number of words)	Number of Amendments: Submitted to Voters	Number of Amendments: Adopted
Wyoming	1	1889	July 10, 1890	31,800	104	62
American Samoa	2	1960, 1967	July 1, 1967	6,000	14	7
No. Mariana Islands	1	1977	Jan. 9, 1978	11,000	50	47 (u,v)
Puerto Rico	1	1952	July 25, 1952	9,281	6	6

*The constitutions referred to in this table include those Civil War documents customarily listed by the individual states.

(a) The Alabama constitution includes numerous local amendments that apply to only one county. An estimated 70 percent of all amendments are local. A 1982 amendment provides that after proposal by the legislature to which special procedures apply, only a local vote (with exceptions) is necessary to add amendments to the constitution.

(b) Computer word count.

(c) One of four proposals was adopted in 1994–95. The total number of proposals and adoption has been reduced by one each to conform to authoritative counts of all amendments proposed and adopted since statehood.

(d) Eight of the approved amendments have been superseded and are not printed in the current edition of the constitution. The total adopted does not include five amendments that were proposed and adopted since statehood.

(e) Colonial charters with some alterations served as the first constitutions in Connecticut (1638, 1662) and in Rhode Island (1663).

(f)Proposed amendments are not submitted to the voters in Delaware.

(g) The Georgia constitution requires amendments to be of "general and uniform application throughout the state," thus eliminating local amendments that accounted for most of the amendments before 1982.

(h) As a kingdom and a republic, Hawaii had five constitutions.

(i) Seven amendments approved by voters in 1994 are not counted because final certification has been delayed by litigation.

(j) The figure given includes amendments approved by the voters and later nullified by the state supreme court in Iowa (three), Kansas (one), Nevada (six) and Wisconsin (two).

(k) The figure does not include one amendment approved by the voters in 1967 that is inoperative until implemented by legislation.

(l) Two sets of identical amendments were on the ballot and adopted in the Maryland 1992 election. The four amendments are counted as two in the table.

(m) The printed constitution includes many provisions that have been annulled. The length of effective provisions is an estimated 24,122 words (12,400 annulled) in Massachusetts. In Rhode Island before the "rewrite" of the constitution in 1986, it was 11,399 words long (7,627 annulled).

(n) The constitution of 1784 was extensively revised in 1792. Figures show proposals and adoptions since the constitution was adopted in 1784.

(o) The figures do not include submission and approval of the constitution of 1889 itself and of Article XX; these are constitutional questions included in some counts of constitutional amendments and would add two to the figure in each column.

(p) The figures include five amendments submitted to and approved by the voters which were, by decisions of the Oklahoma or U.S. Supreme Courts, rendered inoperative or ruled invalid, unconstitutional, or illegally submitted.

(q) Certain sections of the constitution were revised by the limited constitutional convention of 1967–68. Amendments proposed and adopted are since 1968.

(r) In 1981 approximately two-thirds of the 626 proposed and four-fifths of the adopted amendments were local. Since then the 24 proposed and 12 adopted amendments have been statewide propositions.

(s) The Constitution of the Republic of Texas preceded five state constitutions.

(t) The number of proposed amendments to the Texas constitution excludes three proposed by the legislature but not placed on the ballot.

(u) The 47 amendments were adopted in 1985. One amendment was proposed in 1994, but was rejected.

(v) The total excludes one amendment ruled void by a federal district court.

Source: The Book of the States, 1996–97 (Lexington, Ky.: Council of State Governments), pp. 5 and 6.

past, state constitutions also addressed important political questions, such as voting rights for women and former Confederate soldiers.

State constitutions are inherently political in nature, and their execution often involves high-stakes politics. Power relationships between legislators and governors and between state and local governments are formed by state constitutions. Taxation policies are affected by state constitutional provisions. The institutional designs for state and local governments, as established in state constitutions, structure state–local political power relationships, provide the parameters for much political behavior, and in large part determine the content of public policy.

It is useful to think of the fundamental nature of state constitutions by considering the word *constitution*. Constitutions "constitute"; that is, they form, create, or establish something. In the case of state constitutions, they establish the basic anatomy and procedures of government.

Constitutions Structure State Governments

A basic function of the state constitution is to establish the framework and procedures for collective decision making. Individuals and groups in any society find it necessary to accommodate their differences. One way to settle differences is to fight; another is to agree on a set of processes and establish an organizational arrangement through which disagreements may be resolved. Constitutions help perform this function. Generally, they spell out the fundamental organization of the governmental apparatus and specify procedures for proposing policy (the introduction of bills), implementing policy (the administration of bills that have passed), and settling disputes and interpreting laws (roles typically played by the courts). As noted in Chapter 2, the U.S. Constitution establishes organizational and decision-making procedures for the national government. The state constitutions do the same for state and local governments. Many features of governmental structure and procedure are, of course, spelled out in detail by legislative acts and administrative agency decisions, but the basic framework is established in state constitutions.

Constitutions Impose Limits on States

Both the U.S. Constitution and state constitutions identify certain activities in which government may not engage. This feature is important because it identifies, for citizens, for the legislative and executive branches of government, and for the courts, those freedoms that are viewed as especially valuable and deserving of special protection from government interference. State constitutions, like the U.S. Constitution, contain bills of rights, though the states' tend to be longer and more detailed.

Multiple Levels of Law

Americans are frequently exposed to many different types of law—the Constitution, bills that have passed through legislatures, county zoning ordinances, parade permit rulings issued by city managers, and so on. But how these various types of law relate to one another, and especially when they come into conflict, may not be readily apparent. Before examining modern state constitutions in detail, let us consider briefly the relationship of the various levels of law in the American system.

The U.S. Constitution is the supreme law of the nation. Congress, in implementing the powers given to the national government by the Constitution, passes laws called **statutes**. But Congress may not pass just any law. It may only pass laws and establish programs that are authorized by the Constitution. When questions arise about whether Congress has exceeded the authority given it by the Constitution, a Supreme Court interpretation, or **judicial review**, may take place. In judicial reviews, the Court decides whether Congress has created a lower order of law that is beyond the range of activity authorized by the higher law—the Constitution.

Similarly, other lower levels of law cannot conflict with or involve the government in activities beyond the range authorized by the higher levels of law. Thus, state constitutions cannot in any way conflict with provisions of the U.S. Constitution or with congressional actions that are deemed constitutional. Furthermore, a state's legislative statutes cannot conflict with its constitution. State administrative agencies, such as the highway and fish and game departments, can engage only in those activities authorized by state statutes. Public officials may engage only in activities authorized by formal administrative procedures or guidelines, state statutes, state constitutions, congressional actions, and the U.S. Constitution. Figure 3.1 diagrams the relationships among the various levels of law.

These relationships are highlighted by Elder Witt in his characterization of Oregon's State Supreme Court Justice Hans A. Linde, a leader in what is called the new judicial federalism (see Chapter 6):

> The first question [Linde] asks when a state action is challenged in his court—whether it's a police request for a driver's license or a regulatory board's revocation of a dentist's license—is whether the action is authorized by law. If it is not, the government loses. If it is, he asks whether it is in line with the state constitution. If it is not, the government loses. If it is, only then does Linde look to a challenge based on the federal constitution.[2]

It is important to recognize that laws do not define themselves or interpret their own legitimacy. People do so in courts of law. The legislature may pass laws that the Court may later declare unconstitutional. Moreover, state and local statutes likely contain numerous provisions that might be deemed unconstitutional if they were ever challenged in the courts. However, such provisions are treated as legal since they have not been challenged or found to be otherwise.

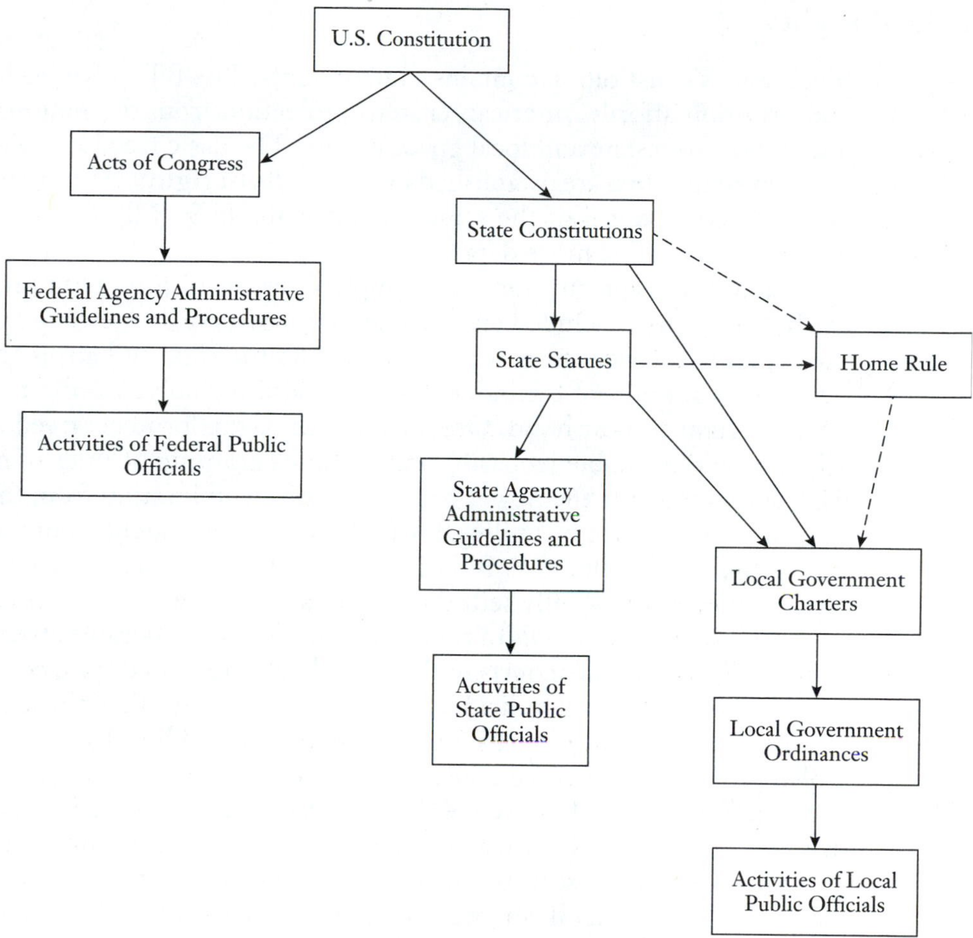

Figure 3.1 Levels of Law and Their Relationships

The Contents of State Constitutions

State constitutions establish the basic structure of state and local government systems. They allocate authority to various units and branches of government and prohibit state and local governments from engaging in certain activities. Although they vary along a number of dimensions, state constitutions are also similar in many respects. Most are long and detailed. They also tend to be restrictive, affording little flexibility to state and local governments.

Bills of Rights

Each state's constitution contains a bill of rights. The Bill of Rights in the U.S. Constitution affords American citizens protection from the national government, not from state and local governments. The basic freedoms afforded citizens in state courts are established by **state bills of rights**. Although state bills of rights cover much of the same ground as the U.S. Bill of Rights, they are typically longer and more detailed.

California's constitution, for example, contains twenty-eight provisions in its Bill of Rights. Included are the common provisions regarding the right of free speech, the right to petition government, the right of habeas corpus, and freedom from bills of attainder. However, also included are the right to fish and the right to post bond. Oregon's Bill of Rights protects freedom of religion, prohibits double jeopardy, and prohibits granting of titles of nobility. It also denies the state the power to prevent citizen emigration from the state. In Florida, the freedom from illegal search and seizure is spelled out more elaborately than it is in the U.S. Bill of Rights, and there is an explicit prohibition against the use of illegally seized materials as evidence against a defendant.

Provisions in state bills of rights have received considerable attention in recent years, as supreme courts in the states have often cited state constitutional provisions as providing individual rights more expansive than those established by the U.S. Supreme Court's interpretations of the Bill of Rights. In cases involving the rights to equal educational opportunity and privacy, for instance, state supreme courts have rendered significant decisions based on state constitutional provisions. This trend has received increased attention as the U.S. Supreme Court's conservative members have become less receptive to civil libertarian claims. Federalism, the operation of dual systems, appears to be working well with respect to judicial politics. One commentator notes that "since 1980, dozens of state courts, in more than 350 cases, have declared their constitutions more protective of individual rights than the federal Constitution."[3]

The Framework of State Government

State constitutions also provide the basic framework for state governments. All fifty state constitutions create three branches of government—legislative, executive, and judicial. The legislature is divided into two houses in all states except Nebraska. In the executive branch, state constitutions typically establish the office of governor, specify the length of term, and describe the powers and duties of the office. These usually include the powers to call the legislature into special session, to veto legislation, and to require written reports of executive agencies. Likewise, state constitutions specify legislative terms of office, some legislator privileges, and the lawmaking powers of the legislature itself. In judicial articles, state constitutions generally call for the establishment of a state supreme court and a system of lower courts, indicate the procedure by which judges are selected, and, together with state statutes, specify the powers and jurisdictions of the courts at each level of the judicial system.

In addition, state constitutions provide for the establishment of a variety of state boards, agencies, and institutions. These include such bodies as state boards of education, which oversee the operation of the elementary and secondary school systems in the state; public utility or "corporation" commissions, which license public utilities and other kinds of business corporations operating in the state; and boards of regents, which govern state colleges and universities. In some cases state constitutions establish elective governing boards for these agencies; in others, board members are appointed by the governor.

Local Governments

State constitutions also establish elaborate systems of local government. These include cities, towns, counties, school districts, special districts, and in some cases township or parish governments.

Some state constitutions go into great detail about the structure, powers, duties, and limitations of local governments. Others are brief and leave the details of these matters to legislative bodies.

Control of State and Local Finances

Many state constitutions have highly restrictive fiscal provisions that earmark certain revenues for specified uses and place low ceilings on the permissible levels for state and local sales and property taxes. Some state constitutions allow, while others prohibit, income taxes.

State constitutions contain sections relating to numerous other matters as well, such as water and mineral rights, the conduct of elections, the allowable debt level for the state, and others. Table 3.2 outlines the Illinois and Texas constitutions, and illustrates the sorts of matters with which state constitutions deal.

The Length and Detail of State Constitutions

As noted earlier in this chapter, many state constitutions are quite long. The constitution in effect in Louisiana until 1975 contained over 250,000 words, or

TABLE 3.2 ORGANIZATION OF TWO STATE CONSTITUTIONS

Illinois Constitution		Texas Constitution	
Article I	Bill of Rights	Article I	Bill of Rights
II	The Power of the State	II	The Powers of Government
III	Suffrage and Election	III	Legislative Department
IV	The Legislature	IV	Executive Department
V	The Executive	V	Judicial Department
VI	The Judiciary	VI	Suffrage
VII	Local Government	VII	Education—The Free Public Schools
VIII	Finance	VIII	Taxation and Revenue
IX	Revenue	IX	Counties
X	Education	X	Railroads
XI	Environment	XI	Municipal Corporations
XII	Militia	XII	Private Corporations
XIII	General Provisions	XIII	Spanish and Mexican Land Titles (repealed)
XIV	Constitutional Revisions	XIV	Public Land and Land Office
		XV	Impeachment
		XVI	General Provisions
		XVII	Mode of Amending the Constitution of This State

more than four hundred book pages, with its amendments. It was said that the old Louisiana constitution weighed thirty-six pounds. In contrast, the U.S. Constitution, including its amendments, contains fewer than 10,000 words.

Not surprisingly, these long and detailed constitutions often lack clarity. Some are much more detailed than others, but most contain detailed provisions for taxing and spending; for the powers, duties, and limitations of local governments; and for bills of rights. The Texas Constitution, for example, contains detailed provisions on several issues: the teachers' retirement fund; rural fire protection districts; limits on state appropriation of anticipated revenue; the issuance and sale of bonds by the state to create the Texas Water Development Fund and Texas Water Development Board; a tax levy authorized for Confederate soldiers and sailors and their widows; compensation to persons fined or imprisoned for offenses of which they are not guilty; and land for psychiatric hospitals, among other provisions.

Numerous examples of highly detailed state constitutional provisions exist. Some are even humorous, such as the old Louisiana constitution that declared Huey P. Long's birthday a holiday forever. The Oklahoma Constitution requires all public schools to teach agriculture, horticulture, stock feeding, and domestic science. In Alabama, the constitution provides for the continuity of the state legislature in the event of an enemy attack.

State Constitutional Amendments

Long and detailed state constitutions become long and detailed through the amending process. **Amendments** are modifications made to existing laws or bills. The **amendment process**—that is, the procedures used to make changes—varies among the states. However, it is typically a slow process that involves initiative through legislative action and popular ratification at the polls. Some state constitutions have been amended hundreds of times, whereas those drafted or redrafted recently have only a few amendments.[4]

Most proposals for state constitutional amendments begin in the state legislatures, and most proposed amendments pass. As of 1995, legislative proposal of an amendment required a simple majority in both houses in nineteen states. Nine states require a three-fifths majority, and nineteen others require a two-thirds majority. Three states have procedures requiring either an abnormal (two-thirds, three-fifths, or three-fourths) majority in one legislative session or a simple majority in two sessions. Eighteen states permit constitutional amendments to be proposed by way of a citizen initiative, a method requiring the signatures of a specified number of voters on a petition. For the most part, these states are located in the midwestern or western United States (Arkansas, Florida, and Mississippi are exceptions). The inclusion of this **direct democracy** method of constitutional change in some states is a product of nineteenth- and early-twentieth-century Progressive and Populist movements.

Table 3.3 lists the states with the most and fewest constitutional amendments. As one might expect, states that have recently adopted entirely new constitutions have the fewest amendments. Modifications to older constitutions that have been made through amendments are often incorporated into the revised documents.

In the 1980s alone, approximately 1,500 state constitutional amendments were proposed and nine out of ten were placed on the ballot by legislatures. Roughly three-fourths of the proposed changes met with voter approval. The 1990s show no sign of this pace decreasing significantly. In the early 1990s almost seven out of ten proposed amendments were adopted.

Although only a small number of proposed constitutional amendments reach the ballots by way of citizen initiative in the 18 states that authorize the process, the initiative is gaining popularity. Whereas in 1982 and 1983 there

TABLE 3.3 CONSTITUTIONAL AMENDMENTS IN SELECTED STATES

State	Year of Most Recent Constitution	Number of Amendments
States with the Most Amendments:		
Alabama	1901	582
California	1879	491
South Carolina	1895	465
Texas	1876	364
New York	1894	215
States with the Fewest Amendments:		
Illinois	1970	10
Michigan	1963	20
Montana	1973	21
Pennsylvania	1968	21
Alaska	1959	25

Source: Data from *The Book of the States, 1996–97* (Lexington, Ky.: Council of State Governments, 1996), p. 20.

were sixteen such proposals involving nine states, in 1990 and 1991 there were twenty-nine citizen-initiated proposals in ten states. Citizen-initiated amendments fare more poorly with the voters than do those submitted by the state legislatures, with less than a 50 percent success rate.[5] Table 3.4 identifies the various procedures used by those states that permit the initiative.

Criticisms of State Constitutions

Over the past several decades, state constitutions have been attacked for their excessive length, detail, and restrictiveness. They also have been blamed for much of the inability of states and localities to cope with many contemporary problems.

Too Much Detail

For the sake of flexibility in changing times, it is argued that state constitutions, like all basic documents, should be brief and indicate succinctly general government principles. Although they should sketch the basic government struc-

TABLE 3.4 CONSTITUTIONAL AMENDMENT PROCEDURE: BY INITIATIVE

Constitutional Provisions			
State	*Number of Signatures Required on Initiative Petition*	*Distribution of Signatures*	*Referendum Vote*
Arizona	15 percent of total votes cast for all candidates for governor at last election.	None specified.	Majority vote on amendment.
Arkansas	10 percent of voters for governor at last election.	Must include 5 percent of voters for governor in each of 15 counties.	Majority vote on amendment.
California	8 percent of total voters for all candidates for at governor last election.	None specified.	Majority vote on amendment.
Colorado	5 percent of total legal votes for all candidates for secretary of state at last general election.	None specified.	Majority vote on amendment.
Florida	8 percent of total votes cast in the state in the last election for presidential electors.	8 percent of total votes cast in each of one-half of the congressional districts.	Majority vote on amendment.
Illinois	8 percent of total votes cast for candidates for governor at last election.	None specified.	Majority voting in election or three- fifths voting on amendment.
Massachusetts(b)	3 percent of total votes cast for governor at preceding biennial state election (not less than 25,000 qualified voters).	No more than one-quarter from any one county.	Majority vote on amendment which must be 30 percent of total ballots cast at election.
Michigan	10 percent of total voters for governor at last gubernatorial election.	None specified.	Majority vote on amendment.
Missouri	8 percent of legal voters for all candidates for governor at last election.	The 8 percent must be in each of two-thirds of the congressional districts in the state.	Majority vote on amendment.
Montana	10 percent of qualified electors, the number of qualified electors to be determined by number of votes cast for governor in preceding general election.	The 10 percent to include at least 10 percent of qualified electors in each of two-fifths of the legislative districts.	Majority vote on amendment.
Nebraska	10 percent of total votes for governor at last election.	The 10 percent must include 5 percent in each of two-fifths of the counties.	Majority vote on amendment, which must be at least 35 percent of total vote at the election.
Nevada	10 percent of voters who voted in entire state in last general election.	10 percent of total voters who voted in each of 75 percent of the counties.	Majority vote on amendment in two consecutive general elections.
North Dakota	4 percent of population of the state.	None specified.	Majority vote on amendment.

(continued)

State	*Number of Signatures Required on Initiative Petition*	*Distribution of Signatures*	*Referendum Vote*
Ohio	10 percent of total number of electors who voted for governor in last election.	At least 5 percent of qualified electors in each of one-half of counties in the state.	Majority vote on amendment.
Oklahoma	15 percent of legal voters for state office receiving highest number of voters at last general state election.	None specified.	Majority vote on amendment.
Oregon	8 percent of total votes for all candidates for governor at last election at which governor was elected for four-year term.	None specified.	Majority vote on amendment.
South Dakota	10 percent of total votes for governor in last election.	None specified.	Majority vote on amendment.

(a) Only Article IV, The Legislature, may be amended by initiative petition.
(b) Before being submitted to the electorate for ratification, initiative measures must be approved at two sessions of a successively elected legislature by not less than one-fourth of all members elected, sitting in joint session.

Source: The Book of the States, 1996–97 (Lexington, Ky.: Council of State Governments, 1996).

ture and allocate authority in very general terms, the more detailed aspects of the law should be left to legislative statute. The excessive length and detail of state constitutions make change difficult. The hands of the governor, legislature, state agencies, and local governments are often tied, for enacting new laws or modifying old ones often requires constitutional amendment—a much more cumbersome and time-consuming process than the simpler enactment of a state statute or local ordinance.

Furthermore, much of the detail in state constitutions focuses on the limits and restrictions placed on state and local government, particularly in the area of finance. For example, the typical state constitution earmarks large proportions of the state's revenues for specified uses, severely limiting the ability of the legislature to allocate funds flexibly. Regarding local governments, state constitutions often place ceilings on the property tax and prohibit the use of an income tax, which restricts the ability of local governments to provide expensive services and attack costly problems.

Poor Design

State constitutions also have been criticized for the manner in which they organize the legislative and executive branches of state government. Until the Supreme Court reapportionment decisions of the early 1960s, some state constitutions provided for representation in one house of the legislature on a basis other than straight population—that is, not in terms of a "one person, one vote" formula. Many observers believed that this practice kept political control in the hands of rural interests, who were not likely to raise taxes and expenditures to fight growing urban and metropolitan problems.

In the executive branch, many state constitutions disperse authority to such a degree that firm executive leadership is difficult to achieve. For example, many permit the direct election of a series of executive branch officials (for example, attorney general, secretary of state, and tax commissioner), giving the officials an independent constituent base and allowing them to operate without control by the governor's office. Further, many state agencies are headed by multimember boards or commissions that maintain their autonomy from the governor.

Outdated

The perceived shortcomings of state constitutions are widely publicized. Almost thirty years ago, James N. Miller began an article for the *National Civic Review* with this comment:

> In the next few years, Americans in as many as half the states will have a chance to vote on one of the most important government reforms facing the country: modernization of our ancient and ludicrous state constitutions.[7]

Miller added that if voters did not choose to modernize their state constitutions, "they [would] be missing one of their last good chances to pull our state and local governments out of their present rapid decline into senility and ineffectuality."[8]

Many state constitutions were written in the latter decades of the nineteenth century, when state and local governments were plagued by corruption. Attempts to thwart the chicanery led to the inclusion of many lengthy and restrictive constitutional provisions. For example, West Virginia's constitution, written in 1872 after a series of scandals involving the railroads, bars railroad officials from legislative office and devotes 6,300 words to functions in which the legislature *may not* engage. Miller argued that the excessive detail in constitutions encourages lawmakers to ignore or subvert the documents. Irrelevant passages designed to cope with problems of an earlier time are simply ignored. Provisions that are highly restrictive invite subversion. Very low debt ceilings, for example, have tempted states such as Pennsylvania to set up "public corporations," which borrow money for the state.

The Reformers' Preferred Model

As Miller anticipated, there have been demands in recent decades for constitutional revision in almost every U.S. state. In most cases the proposed changes followed a set pattern.

Proponents of constitutional revision typically seek shorter and less restrictive documents, a streamlined executive branch, a shortened ballot, a longer term in office for the governor, increased executive powers, and elimination of the mass of antiquated irrelevancies. These proposed revisions generally follow those of the model state constitution, first proposed by the National Municipal League in 1921. (The league proposed shorter and less restrictive state constitutions with increased powers for local governments.)

State Responses

Montana's constitution, adopted in 1972, provides for an apportionment commission, the election of the lieutenant governor and governor on the same ticket, and a maximum limit of twenty major executive branch departments. In addition, it lowers the age at which one is legally recognized as an adult to eighteen, provides for open legislative sessions, contains an environmental protection provision, and relaxes restrictions on state and local taxing and borrowing.

Many other states also have revised their constitutions. Illinois, North Carolina, and Virginia adopted new documents in 1970, Louisiana adopted a new constitution in 1974, and Georgia did so in 1976 and again in 1982. Other states failed to revise their constitutions. In 1967 New York voters rejected a new document, as did voters in Arkansas, Idaho, Oregon, North Dakota, and Texas in the 1970s. During the 1980s and early 1990s, the move to reform state constitutions subsided somewhat, as shown in Figure 3.2. The number of **constitutional conventions**, which are held to revise constitutions, declined, the number of new adoptions fell to just one, in Georgia, and voters' interest in conventions decreased. In fourteen states the law requires that voters be asked periodically whether they want a constitutional convention to be called. In Hawaii this must occur every nine years; in Alaska, Iowa, and Rhode Island it is done at ten-year intervals; and in the other ten states it occurs less frequently.

State constitutional change is still difficult to implement despite reformers' efforts. Even those who seek change soon realize the difficulty of achieving it and tend to turn to the more successful tool of piecemeal constitutional amendment.

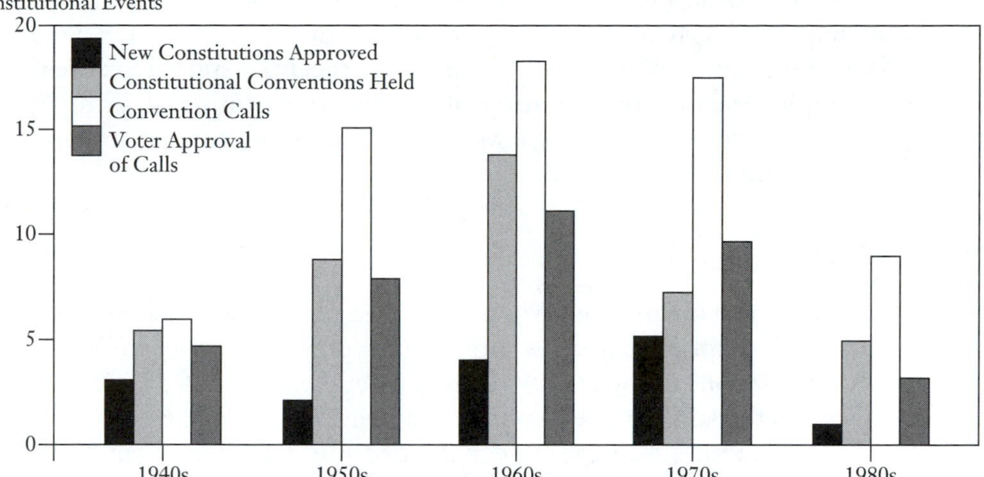

Figure 3.2 Trends in Constitutional Change, 1940s–1980s
Source: Adapted from data in Albert L. Strum and Janice C. May, "State Constitutions and Constitutional Revisions: 1988–89," in *The Book of the States* (Lexington, Ky.: Council of State Governments, 1988), pp. 2–13.

Constitutional Politics

Although it is tempting to view constitutions as higher laws that are somehow nonpolitical, they are the products of the same political processes from which other laws emerge. Many people associate the U.S. Constitution with the founding fathers and the founding of the nation. As a result, the document is often viewed as a statement of "truths," rather than as a politically spawned set of laws. The propensity to hold constitutional documents in high esteem affects perceptions of state constitutions as well.

High-Stakes Politics

Constitutions are as political as any other law. They allocate authority, structure decision-making processes, specify rights and duties, and, as a result, help to determine who gets what, when and how. Examples of how state constitutions help to allocate scarce resources abound. To varying degrees, all state constitutions earmark tax revenues for specific uses: gasoline taxes for highway construction; hunting license fees for game, fish, and park programs; sales tax money for schools; and, in the case of Wisconsin, a portion of the property tax for the support of a statewide forestation program. Likewise, state constitutions provide a variety of tax exemptions for various special interests: veterans and the elderly may be exempt from part of the property tax; homesteads and certain classes of agricultural lands may receive a special tax break. Other examples include the granting of special water, mineral, and timber rights. Constitutions, like other laws, are not neutral—they favor some individuals and groups over others.

Special Interests

That state constitutions play a role in the allocation of scarce societal resources helps to explain why constitutional conventions are the site of hot debate and competition, and why newly drafted documents are often rejected at the polls. When the subject of a new state constitution is raised, vested interests that receive special advantages under the existing document fight for its retention, whereas new interests fight for the inclusion of provisions that would benefit them. For example, veterans' groups support preference points on civil service examinations and property tax exemptions. Taxpayer groups push for the retention or imposition of very low ceilings on the property tax. The education lobby, made up of teachers and administrators, fights to earmark funds for the schools and to increase the level of state support for local school districts. Sporting groups insist that hunting and fishing license fees be constitutionally tagged for fish and wildlife programs. Churches lobby for property tax exemptions. These and other vested interests seek to establish or protect, in their states' most basic law, special advantages for themselves.

Special private interests are especially vigorous in their efforts to influence the content of state constitutions because constitutions are more difficult to alter than are statutes or administrative rules and procedures. Administrative rules and procedures can be changed by administrative fiat, and statutes can be altered or repealed by a majority action in the legislature and the concurrence of the governor. It is much more difficult to change a constitution. In a majority of the states, the proposal of a constitutional amendment requires abnormal majorities (two-thirds or three-fourths votes) of the members of both houses of the legislature, or the securing of a very large number of signatures of registered voters on a petition and ratification by a majority vote at the polls. It is, quite obviously, a long and difficult process; and, as a result, it is of great advantage to a special interest group to have its particular provision included in a document that is so difficult to change.

Vested Interests versus Reformers' Interests

An earlier study of constitutional conventions in three states suggested that success or failure to revise state constitutions reflected the relative strengths of vested interests versus those of the reformists. Elmer Cornwell, Jay Goodman, and Wayne Swanson suggested several trends regarding vested and reformers' interests. First, voting divisions in conventions tend to involve "good government" reformers versus groups that may be affected by changes in the constitution and thus have a stake in the status quo. Second, the methods by which constitutional convention representatives are chosen have an impact on the character of the document that is produced.

Finally, new documents that are either highly innovative or not at all innovative are not likely to receive public acceptance. A highly innovative document draws the wrath of "standpatters," whereas a less innovative one is likely to be rejected by proponents of reform. A document promising incremental change, therefore, has the best chance of popular adoption at the polls.[9]

The Difficulty of Introducing Changes

Given that state constitutions are hard to change and tend to be long and detailed, it is no surprise that they are also conservative in nature. Provisions that favor special interests are hard to remove. New approaches that would allow government to move in new directions or attack new problems are difficult to secure. The hands of governors, legislatures, and state agencies are tied by constitutional restrictions on the earmarking of funds, the imposition of debt ceilings, and the exemption of properties from the tax rolls. In a period of rapid social, economic, and political flux, constitutional change is extremely difficult.

Enduring Issues

Some issues in state constitutional politics are universal and enduring, whereas others are more episodic in nature or the products of a particular state or region. Writing about the Virginia experience, for example, state constitutional expert A. E. Dick Howard points to several issues that he views as fundamental and common: To what extent should there be restrictions on popular preferences? How should legislative, executive, and judicial relationships be structured? What roles will state and local governments play? How much detail is appropriate in a foundational document? As Howard notes, questions such as these may never be fully answered.[10]

Other issues are less enduring or universal in nature. For example, in 1889 the Wyoming constitutional convention debated the issue of whether people need to be able to read in order to vote; the Wyoming convention resolved in the affirmative. The delegates also considered a tax on mined coal and the need for a civil service system. They decided not to tax coal and concluded that patronage "is one of the rewards of politics."[11] In a debate on the ownership of water, it was decided that all water belonged to the state of Wyoming. And, since there was no universal suffrage in 1889, the delegates discussed the wisdom of permitting only men to vote on ratification of the state constitution. They chose to have qualified electors of both sexes vote.[12]

During the late nineteenth and late twentieth centuries, certain issues became matters of constitutional politics. The last two decades of the nineteenth century witnessed widespread public and private sector corruption and abuse of power. These conditions spawned interest in the initiative, the referendum, and the recall as tools to control government and curb corrupt practices. The **initiative** is a process in which citizens sign petitions to place policy questions directly before the voters. The **referendum** is similar in that citizens vote directly on proposals that have been referred to them by the legislature. The **recall** is a process in which citizens vote on a proposal to remove (recall) a public official before the end of the normal term. More recently, in many of the eighteen states that allow citizen initiative, it has been employed in efforts to enact constitutional limitations on taxes and spending. California, Massachusetts, Michigan, and Colorado are among the many states where such measures have appeared on recent ballots. In addition, many original state constitutions provided for weak executives. Consequently, one additional area of proposed constitutional reform has featured debates over such issues as centralizing executive branch authority and expanding the influence of governors in the budget-making process.

Arkansas: An Example of Constitutional Politics

The political nature of state constitutional politics is illustrated vividly in Diane Blair's description and analysis of constitutional history and politics in Arkansas.[13] That state has had five constitutions. The first, ratified in 1836, was modeled after the U.S. Constitution. The second was adopted in 1861, when Arkansas joined the Confederacy at the start of the Civil War. References to the Union became instead references to the Confederacy, but not much else was changed. After the war between the states, the constitution was changed in 1864 as Arkansas was reassociated with the Union. In this third version, slavery was outlawed.

In 1868 Arkansas adopted what became known as the "carpetbag constitution"—its fourth. African Americans could vote but former Confederates could not. State government power, including gubernatorial power, was centralized. Six years later, in 1874, a fifth constitution was ratified in Arkansas, this one in reaction to the 1868 document and the excesses and corruption of the postwar Reconstruction period. The 1874 document reflected widespread fear and distrust of the state government. It was long and went into detail to prescribe authority carefully and to limit the state. Many terms of office were shortened to two years and a number of appointed executive branch offices were made elective. In addition, many public office salaries were constitutionally set and the state's taxing and spending powers were limited. Clearly, each of the five constitutions reflects the politics of the day.

Arkansas continues to operate under the 1874 constitution, though there have been efforts to replace it. Between 1968 and 1980, when reformers nationwide were seeking to modernize state constitutions, reform efforts were launched in Arkansas. In one instance, the reform attempt was terminated when the Arkansas Supreme Court ruled that the directive given to the constitutional convention unlawfully tried to limit the scope of the delegates' agenda. Other attempts at reform failed to receive voter ratification at the polls, despite the apparent support of public officials, many interest groups, and the public.

In Arkansas, as in many other states, why do voters reject modern documents designed to streamline state government? Blair cites as reasons general voter indifference to constitutional reform, coupled with the opposition of many special interests. Voters for whom state constitutional reform is not a major concern may well decline to vote at all, or they may be easily persuaded by opponents. A few small special interest groups may favor much of the new arrangement but oppose one or two changes that would take away some special benefit. The opposition of small groups can add up to a negative majority. Blair describes the process by which many small objections to constitutional reform add up to the rejection of the entire proposal:

> In 1970, for example, county judges feared loss of power to a newly strengthened county legislature, chancery judges resisted their potential consolidation with courts of law, realtors feared potential increases in property taxes, and various professional associations opposed the rumored consolidation of their separate licensing boards with one administrative authority. In 1980 organized labor opposed removal of the 10 percent usury limit, the Arkansas Educational Association feared the loss of the Education Department's independent status to greater gubernatorial direction, some legislators resented the redistricting that mandated single-member districts would necessitate, and fundamentalists suspected an attempted backdoor to get an equal rights amendment into the constitution through reference to "sex" in the revised equal protection clause.[14]

It is no wonder that attempts at wholesale constitutional revision so often fail and that most constitutional change comes about through a piecemeal amendment process. When a host of special constitutionally anchored advantages are threatened with change, there is inevitably much opposition. However, when only one or two interests are threatened (as is usually the case with proposed amendments), the opposition is not as strong and the chances for passage are greater.

The Functions of State Constitutions

Does it matter what the people of a state include in their constitution? Does it matter how constitutions "constitute" the institutional apparatus of state and local government? Judging from the interest that political groups have in defeating reforms, in Arkansas and elsewhere, the answer to both questions clearly must be yes.

Constitutions Distribute Power

Consider again the functions and content of state constitutions; the features of these documents are often the targets of reform. The relationships between the legislative and executive branches are set forth. In the critical process of budget making, it is determined whether the governor or the legislature will play the dominant role, and whether the governor will have veto authority over legislative actions. In Wisconsin, for example, the governor's role in the budget and the governor's authority are strong. Recently, and to the consternation of the legislature, Wisconsin Governor Tommy Thompson rearranged some numbers and words in the budget, thus altering legislative intent. Until 1997, in North Carolina the governor had no veto power.

The state constitution structures state executive branches. It determines whether the attorney general, secretary of state, treasurer, highway department director, and others will work for the governor or be directly elected by the voters and thereby possess an independent constitutional base and freedom from gubernatorial control.

Constitutions Govern Finances

Unlike the federal government, which struggles with huge budget deficits, especially in recent years, all states except Vermont are required by law to balance budgets annually (Vermont does so as a matter of practice). In most states this is a constitutional requirement, though in a few it is a statutory one.

The balanced budget requirement is of no small consequence—it keeps the states out of the type of deficit trouble that plagues Washington. However, it also makes budgeting difficult for states. Matching expenditures with revenues during twelve-month fiscal-year cycles is not an easy task. Revenues must be forecast well over a year in advance, often in the context of an unsettled economy. The potential for agency spending overruns in program areas that are not easily controlled, such as social services and health, is always a danger. As a result, states maintain reserve accounts. But there is constant political pressure to reduce or raid reserve accounts to meet one spending demand or another. Overall, though, state constitutional barriers to deficit spending provide effective parameters to the budget process.

Summary

Each of the fifty states has its own state constitution. Some states have had many different constitutions over the years. State constitutions are important because they organize the branches of state government, distribute powers and privileges among agencies and officeholders, and impose limits and restrictions on government activities. Although most state constitutions are excessively long and detailed, modern reformers are emphasizing a shift to briefer, more basic documents. Most attempts at sweeping reform have failed; the groups that benefit from the existing provisions often work together to defeat the changes or the new documents. State constitutions embody high-stakes politics; like all laws, they help to determine the distribution of power and material resources.

When reformers seek to reorder or modify institutional arrangements, groups whose current interests are best served by the status quo resist the changes. Legislators, judges, governors, agency heads, universities, cities, and counties all seek maximum constitutional authority and flexibility. Similarly, teachers, realtors, morticians, lawyers, and taxpayers want support of their endeavors addressed by the state constitution, with the cost or a good portion of it paid by the government. The most basic rules of the political game—including the structure of the playing field and the tools needed to work the system successfully—are thus set forth in the constitutions of the fifty American states.

Policy Perspective

At first blush, citizen initiatives would seem to be very desirable mechanisms for translating public preference into public policy. The initiative process is one form of "direct democracy"; that is, the citizens can directly initiate and develop public policy by popular vote. The initiative, along with the referendum and recall, were measures that emerged at the beginning of this century as part of the Populist movement. They were reforms designed to take power away from the big bosses in the political machines and transfer it directly to the people. Progressives believed that both political parties were controlled by the economic monopolies, and that the elected representatives of the people—legislators and governors—were in the pocket of the moneyed interests. Therefore, they sought means by which to bypass the elected officials and give the "little people" a chance to address their needs by direct action. Progressives viewed politics as corrupt and distasteful; the solution was to avoid working within the political institutions and provide the people mechanisms by which to directly make their wishes known. The initiative, referendum, and recall are the best known of these reforms.

The Progressive Movement had a definite geographical cast to it, rooted largely in the agrarian midwest and the new western states (even today there are only three southern states that permit the initiative). The Progressive Movement enjoyed its peak popularity at the turn of the century, with most of the reforms being adopted before World War I.

The initiative permits the public to initiate public policy; the referendum provides the electorate a means by which it approves legislative action before the latter can become law, and the recall allows voters to "recall" an elected official before the completion of his or her formal term of office.

So, what's the problem? Direct democracy seems to speak to the most attractive aspects of a democratic society. Proponents contend that not only does it allow the citizenry to directly address their needs, the threat of the direct democracy tools influences the elected representatives to be more sensitive to public opinion. And, especially in the policy areas that create great controversy (e.g., abortion, gambling, gay rights), a device such as the initiative permits the voters to bring to public debate issues that might otherwise be avoided by the elected representatives.

Opponents argue that it is just such actions that make initiatives (and other forms of direct democracy) unwise. That is, initiatives enable voting majorities to threaten the rights of unpopular sociological minorities, implement hastily and ill-advised public policy without the extended debate and deliberation that characterizes the legislative process, and enables well-financed special interests to use their monetary superiority to conduct expensive media campaigns that overcome the responses of opposing groups with fewer resources.

The issue might be cast in terms of this chapter: if a state's constitution is the fundamental legal document governing the state's political processes, is it desirable to permit a mechanism by which these processes may be bypassed by popular vote? Of course, there is no correct answer to that question. What we do know is that after a period in which direct democracy seemed relatively dormant, there has been a resurgence in the past twenty-five years of the use of the initiative, and that, as we turn toward the end of the decade, the use of the initiative is increasing.

Citizen-initiated propositions have begun to attract considerable attention, not just within the state where the proposition has been placed on the ballot, but also from national media in certain cases. California's propositions in 1994 limiting immigration and in 1996 banning affirmative action became the focus of national as well as statewide debate. The subjects targeted for change in initiative propositions vary widely. Term limits have been a favorite topic. Georgia voters recently rejected a proposal to lengthen the term of state representatives from two to four years. Voters in California, Colorado, and Oklahoma voted to limit the term for legislators in 1990, and a host of other limits followed in 1992.

Texas voters defeated two proposals to raise legislator salaries. In Utah voters approved a change in the maximum allowable size of their state senate, and in South Dakota a proposal to allow gambling in the city of Deadwood was approved. Colorado voters approved a similar limited gambling amendment in 1990, but defeated four others in 1992. California voters recently voted to increase the cigarette tax. In seven states—California, Colorado, Florida, New Jersey, New Mexico, Texas, and Washington—proposals to exempt veterans, widows, and the elderly from some taxes were endorsed. Colorado voters in 1992 approved a constitutional amendment prohibiting the state and local governments from protecting gays, lesbians, and bisexuals from discrimination in housing or employment (overturned by the U.S. Supreme Court in *Romer v. Evans* in 1996).

As can be seen, citizen initiatives address some of the most controversial, and colorful, issues facing the nation, and, therefore, attract attention. In addition to fiscal issues, such as voter approval of tax raises or the prohibition of a state income tax, various social issues also have been placed on the ballots of several states. Between 1984 and 1994, seven states proposed initiatives that would either place or ease restrictions on the right of women to obtain abortions. Eight states offered voters the opportunities to permit or prohibit some form of gambling. Three states passed initiatives making English the official language of the state. In 1994 Oregon voted to allow terminally ill individuals to obtain lethal drugs, and in 1996, Arizona and California voted to allow marijuana to be used for medicinal purposes (President Clinton promptly announced the national government's opposition to these actions). Also in 1996 Florida's voters approved a proposition amending their constitution to establish an Everglades Trust Fund to help with the costs of environmental restoration of the Everglades, and, then, at the same election, rejected the proposition that imposed a tax to provide the funds for the Trust Fund.

A look at the initiative battles in Colorado in the early 1990s perhaps best identifies the strengths and weaknesses of the initiative as a policy device.

On November 3, 1992, Colorado voters approved two highly controversial constitutional amendments, both of which were placed on the ballot through the citizen-initiative procedure. Amendment I limited both state and local taxing and state and local spending. Within months the impact was felt in the state's schools, which were hit with a 4 percent reduction in per-pupil spending for the next fiscal year.

Amendment II made it unconstitutional for the state and local governments to enforce prohibition of discrimination against persons because of their sexual orientation. Existing antidiscrimination policies in Aspen, Boulder, and Denver were thus rendered unenforceable. The intended effect of the measure was to provide a shield under which private discrimination against persons because of their sexual orientation cannot, by law, be stopped. Both amendments created controversy following their adoption. Amendment I triggered an immediate fiscal crisis in the school districts, many of which instantly prepared to lay off personnel, reduce or eliminate funds for busing and sports programs, and freeze salaries. Similar prospects were forecast for other Colorado cities and counties, as well as for the state government itself. Amendment II ignited nationwide efforts to convince tourists to boycott Colorado. A war of words continued between Colorado for Family Values, which promoted the measure, and its opponents, who viewed the amendment as a license to discriminate. In 1996, the U.S. Supreme Court ruled that Amendment II violated the U.S. Constitution *(Romer v. Evans)*.

Where does this leave us? Should the citizens have a direct method of amending their constitution and making public policy? Or is a representative government, restricted by the state constitution, preferable?

KEY TERMS

state constitution	amendment	initiative
statute	amendment process	referendum
judicial review	direct democracy	recall
state bill of rights	constitutional convention	

ADDITIONAL READING

The Book of the States. Each issue contains information updates on state constitutions as well as a wealth of statistical data. (Lexington, Ky.: Council of State Governments), published biennially.

Cronin, Thomas E. *Direct Democracy: The Politics of Initiative, Referendum and Recall* (Cambridge, Mass.: Harvard University Press, 1989).

Finkelman, Paul and Stephen E. Gottlieb. *Toward a Usable Past: Liberty under State Constitutions* (Athens, Ga.: U. of Georgia Press, 1991).

National Municipal League. *Model State Constitutions*, 6th ed. (New York: NML, 1968).

Tarr, Alan G. *State Constitutions of the United States* (Greenwood Press, 1995).

Witt, Elder. "Hans A. Linde: The Unassuming Architect of an Emerging Role for State Constitutions." *Governing* (July 1989): 58.

NOTES

1. Up-to-date information, statistical and otherwise, may be found in the biennial issues of *The Book of the States* (Lexington, Ky.: Council of State Governments).

2. Elder Witt, "Hans A. Linde: The Unassuming Architect of an Emerging Role for State Constitutions," *Governing* (July 1989): 58.

3. Ibid.: 56.

4. See *The Book of the States, 1992–93* (Lexington, Ky.: Council of State Governments, 1993), p. 20.

5. Janice C. May, "State Constitutions and Constitutional Revision: 1990–91," in *The Book of the States, 1992–93* (Lexington, Ky.: Council of State Governments, 1993), p. 2.

6. See ibid., pp. 8–9; and Janice C. May, "State Constitutions and Constitutional Revision, 1988–89 and the 1980s," in *The Book of the States, 1990–91* (Lexington, Ky.: Council of State Governments, 1991), p. 21.

7. James N. Miller, "The Dead Hand of the Past," *National Civic Review* (April 1968): 183.

8. Ibid.

9. Elmer E. Cornwell, Jr., Jay S. Goodman, and Wayne R. Swanson, "State Constitutional Conventions: Delegates, Roll Calls and Issues," *Midwest Journal of Political Science* (Feb. 1970): 105–30.

10. A. E. Dick Howard, "Constitutional Government," in *Virginia Government and Politics*, ed. Thomas R. Morris and Larry Sabato (Charlottesville, Va.: Institute of Government Research, University of Virginia, 1984), p. 11.

11. Tim R. Miller, *State Government: Politics and Wyoming*, 2d ed. (Dubuque, Iowa: Kendall/Hunt, 1985), p. 13.

12. Ibid.

13. Diane D. Blair, *Arkansas Politics and Government* (Lincoln: University of Nebraska Press, 1988), p. 130.

14. Ibid.

CHAPTER 4

...

The State Legislature

...

The house of representatives of the Texas state legislature in session. Texas has a bicameral legislature, modeled on the U.S. Congress, as do all states except Nebraska. Austin, Texas. *(Bob Daemmrich/The Image Works)*

• • • **INSTITUTIONAL DESIGN**

• • • **INSTITUTIONAL TRANSITION**

Legislative Supremacy
Trouble in the Legislature
The Reformers Triumph

Focus 4.1: ALCOHOL AND LEGISLATORS

Did Reform Backfire?

• • • **LEGISLATIVE FUNCTIONS**

• • • **THE LEGISLATIVE PROCESS**

Death Traps for Bills
Is the Process Effective?
Recent Improvements

• • • **INFORMAL RULES AND STRATEGIES**

• • • **LEGISLATIVE ORGANIZATION**

Division of Labor
Party Caucuses
Leadership Positions
Powers of Leadership
Trends in Leadership

Focus 4.2: THE UNSINKABLE WILLIE BROWN

• • • **LEGISLATIVE COMMITTEES AND THEIR ASSIGNMENTS**

Focus 4.3: MR. SPEAKER VERSUS THE NRA

• • • **LEGISLATIVE SUPPORT**

• • • **REPRESENTATION**

Apportionment
Malapportionment Develops
Gerrymandering

• • • **REPRESENTATIONAL ROLES**
Representatives as Mirrors
Representatives as Oracles
Representatives as Brokers

• • • **THE DEMOGRAPHICS OF LEGISLATORS**

• • • **TENURE AND TURNOVER**

• • • **SUMMARY**

• • • **POLICY PERSPECTIVE**
Origin of the Current System
Welfare from 1935–1996
Pressure for Change
The New Welfare System

Institutional Design

entral characteristics of the institutional design of state government include the separation of powers in all fifty states and bicameralism in all states except Nebraska. Voters in Indiana provided a striking illustration of the effects of such institutional arrangements in November 1988. They elected Democrats as governor and lieutenant governor, and a senate with a Republican majority of twenty-six to twenty-four over which the Democratic lieutenant governor would preside. For the house of representatives the voters selected fifty Democrats and fifty Republicans. In 1996 they managed to do it again; the Republicans controlled the senate, the governor a Democrat, and the house is again tied.[1]

The stage is thus set for conflict—within each house, between the house and the senate, and between the legislative and executive branches. Yet Indiana was not alone in this regard. In recent years, well over half of the American states have had split party control either between the house and the senate or between the legislative and executive branches. Going into the 1997 legislative sessions, thirty-one of the fifty states were split. Eleven states featured Republican party control of both legislative chambers and the governorship, and seven others were dominated by the Democrats. Nine of the eleven

Republican states were west of the Mississippi, and five of the seven Democratic states were east of the river. Divided government and its attendant conflict are no longer the exception but the norm.

To those who cherish neatness, order, and speed in decision making, this combination of institutionally dispersed authority and political competitiveness must be a nightmare. For others who fear concentrated power and cherish representation above all, the carnival that such divided government is certain to produce is a small price to pay. But no one should fail to see the impact of a state's institutions on its politics.

Institutional Transition

Legislatures are the centerpieces of the institutional arrangements in the American states. The legislature is where U.S. policies are made. Elected legislators decide how much to spend on schools, how much zoning power cities may exercise, which professions will be regulated, what acts will constitute crimes, and who will pay for it all. The legislature is the institution that produces most of the nation's laws.

American state legislatures have had a varied and interesting history. During the early decades of the Republic, they were the dominant branch. Later they fell into disrepute and became, quite often, subservient and sometimes corruptible rubber stamps for state governors and lobbyists. More recently, the state legislatures have been reformed and have reasserted themselves as the central institution of state government, although they are still not free of problems and criticism.

Legislative Supremacy

Following the Revolutionary War, public fear and dislike for executive authority was high, and thus representative bodies—legislatures—were fashioned as the dominant institutions of government. The Virginia constitution of 1776, for example, provided for a strong legislature and a weak executive. The governor was elected by the legislature itself for a term of just one year and could serve no more than three years in a row. There were few limits on the power of the legislature. Indeed, Thomas Jefferson, who served as Virginia's second governor, commented on the extent of legislative power by observing that "173 despots would surely be as oppressive as one."[2]

Trouble in the Legislature

The later years of the nineteenth century witnessed widespread political corruption and a decline in trust of government. State legislators, like many governors and both local and national officials, joined hands with big-money interests to enrich themselves at public expense. Such behavior fueled the Progressive and Populist movements and led to efforts to restrict government. For example, in 1901 the state of Alabama adopted a constitution that allowed the legislature to meet for just fifty days once every four years. Other states instituted similarly limiting reforms. Public confidence in the legislative institutions of the time was not high.

Throughout much of the period from World War II to the reapportionment revolution of the mid-1960s, however, state legislatures remained under the dominance of special interests and rural-oriented lawmakers. They teamed up with their lobbyists (see Chapter 8) to work out public policy in "capitol hill" pubs like the Bull Ring in Santa Fe, the Broken Spoke in Austin, Clyde's in Tallahassee, and the Galleria Tavern in Columbus, Ohio.[3] (See Focus 4.1 "Alcohol and Legislators.")

The Reformers Triumph

In the 1960s the U.S. Supreme Court kicked off a revolution of sorts with its decision in the case of *Baker v. Carr* (1962). In *Baker* and subsequent related decisions, the Court declared that state legislative districts must contain approximately equal numbers of people. These decisions broke many old patterns of power and many old habits. The **reformed legislatures** have not been the same ever since.

America's state legislatures have continued to change in many ways over the past three decades. Years ago they were roundly criticized for being malapportioned and exhibiting a rural bias in an urban age; for not offering members decent staffing, space, equipment, and pay; and for being internally undemocratic and rife with cronyism. Pundits said that the legislatures should modernize and become more like the U.S. Congress, with good salaries and ample staff and space, that they should meet every year in long sessions, that they should open up and clean up internally, and that they should be reapportioned to be more representative of the population. Much of that has happened, and now the state legislatures are sometimes criticized for being too well endowed with pay, staff, and space. The members are becoming careerist just like—some say unfortunately like—members of Congress.

Prior to *Baker v. Carr*, state legislatures were heavily dominated by rural interests. Legislative leaders and majorities had little interest in expanding tax bases to raise money to deal with growing urban problems. **Legislative**

Focus 4.1
ALCOHOL AND LEGISLATORS

• • •

The political "watering hole" is as old as American politics and American legislatures themselves. Over two hundred years ago, Thomas Jefferson and Patrick Henry met at the Raleigh Tavern in Williamsburg, Virginia, to complain about the actions of King George III. For years, legislators and lobbyists in Denver bought each other hamburgers and beer at the Congress lounge—called Nick's—or French dip and martinis nearby at the Quorum as they exchanged information and lobbied each other. Stories have it that at Santa Fe's Bull Ring, a state senator named "Diamond Tooth" Miller wore a button advertising himself as "the Best Goddamn Senator Money Can Buy" as he filled himself with drinks bought by lobbyists. In Texas, tax bills were written over lunch and drinks in the Deck Club. Florida's lobbyists used to supply food and drinks to legislators in rooms near the capitol, compliments of the "booze fairy."

The situation has changed in recent years. Modern post-reapportionment, career-oriented state legislators drink less. The media are more apt to report their off-the-floor behavior. The public is impatient with lawmakers. So today it's less booze, more soft drinks and coffee. Some say that the modern legislature is cleaner and better. Others lament the trend, arguing that better policy emerges from an environment in which elected officials can cut deals away from the glare of the press, and without constant concern for the impact of their frank discussions and their compromises on their reelection fortunes. We may have fewer barroom and backroom deals than before, but do we have better public policy?

Sources: Jonathan Walters, "A Night on the Town Isn't What It Used to Be in Jefferson City," *Governing* (July 1989): 26–31; and Alan Ehrenhalt, "An Embattled Institution," *Governing* (Jan. 1992): 28–33.

turnover, the election of new freshman lawmakers, was quite high, running near and often over 50 percent following some elections. As a result, novice lawmakers could be tightly led by old-hand leaders and effectively coached by special interest lobbyists. Sessions were short, often running just thirty, sixty, or ninety days, and in many states legislators met just every other year. Session-end **logjams** or deadlocks were frequent, and some legislation was sloppy and hastily adopted. Alan Ehrenhalt describes these old-time legislators as "racist, sexist, secretive, boss-ruled, malapportioned, and uninformed."[4]

The 1960s and 1970s were periods of major change. In the wake of Watergate and Vietnam, and in the context of the civil rights, consumer protection, and environmental movements, the nation was ripe for reform, and the reformist sentiment touched state legislatures. Following the *Baker* case, the legislatures were reapportioned and thus came to represent urban and suburban interests more fully. Sessions in many states were lengthened and more of them began to meet annually. Pay was increased, expense allowances expanded, new offices built, and staffs enlarged. (In many states now, staff help is available for committees, party caucuses, leadership members, and even members' home offices.) State after state passed laws requiring members to report their finances, and lobbyists to report their income, expenses, and clients. The media began to watch legislators more closely.

The modernization of state legislatures proceeded unevenly across the country. The states of California, Florida, Pennsylvania, Michigan, New York, and Wisconsin led the way. Others, such as Wyoming and Kansas, moved more slowly. A number of states remain unreformed today, preferring to stay with the **citizen legislature model**, in which lawmakers do not make a career out of politics; New Hampshire is a prime example.

As many state legislatures became more like Congress, legislators became more like the representatives in Congress, viewing their position in careerist terms and gearing more of their behavior toward reelection. Over half of the members in Pennsylvania, New York, Wisconsin, and Massachusetts define themselves as full-time legislators. Campaigns became increasingly expensive, political consultants were hired more often, and running for reelection became a full-time enterprise for many. Legislative leaders took on the role of fundraisers to help members' campaigns.[5]

Did Reform Backfire?

Today, state legislatures are again the subject of criticism and, ironically, it is often because they did exactly what the pre-1960s critics asked of them. The opening of all legislative decisions to public scrutiny has made it more difficult for members to sit down and work out compromises. Like Congress, some state legislatures are faulted because they are heavily staffed and the staffers devote energy to the reelection of their bosses. High pay has made the job so attractive that some members want to stay in office forever. The preoccupation with reelection, critics say, drives members to endless pandering to district interests, often to the neglect of statewide problems and needs. All the while the costs of running a campaign have escalated; contests commonly cost $25,000 to $100,000 per candidate, and in some instances have increased to over $1 million. Members now must devote far too much of their time to fund-raising and pander to special interest groups' **political action committees (PACs)**, which are the political arms of professional associations, unions, corporations, and other groups. (See Chapter 8 for a more detailed discussion of PACs.)

Perhaps, some say, the states would be well served by a return to the citizen legislature. And, indeed, this may come as a result of term limits that are now in place in nearly half of the states. Others suggest that the answer lies in an intermediate position, with fair representation and reasonable but limited staffing, pay, and so forth. In any case, the state legislatures have undergone significant change in recent years (see Table 4.1). For better or worse, they have been modernized, or professionalized, as early critics wanted.

Legislative Functions

All fifty states follow the national pattern of instituting a formal separation of the lawmaking, the law-implementing, and the law adjudication functions through the establishment of three branches of government. Separation of powers does not, of course, completely compartmentalize these three govern-

TABLE 4.1 STATE LEGISLATURES BEFORE AND AFTER MODERNIZATION

Before Modernization	After Modernization
Malapportioned	One person, one vote
Rural dominance	Improved pay
Internally undemocratic	Expanded staff help
Strong leaders	Better facilities
High turnover of members	Longer sessions
Short sessions	More independent of governor
Limited staff	Conflict of interest laws
Low pay or no pay	Sunshine laws
Many conflicts of interest	More costly elections
Strong influence by governor	More PAC money
Strong interest group influence	Careerist legislators
Sometimes corrupt	More independent legislators
	Weakened leadership

mental functions, but it does place most of the responsibility for each function with a specified branch of the government. One of the major tasks of state legislatures, then, is the enactment of statutes, or state laws. In the process of fulfilling their formal responsibilities of lawmaking and budget review, state legislatures interact closely with the other two branches of government—the executive and the judiciary—and perform the critical function of legitimizing public policy.

Thus, laws are passed—an almost endless string of national, state, and local measures that place limits on behavior and establish public programs. State constitutions allocate to legislatures the authority to pass laws. In some cases, constitutions contain detailed measures that specifically restrict behavior and establish public programs. But it is in the statutes—the laws enacted by the legislature—that most of the provisions that authoritatively restrict behavior and establish public programs are found.

The range of subject matter contained in the flood of legislative proposals considered by state legislatures is considerable. Bills have to deal with such weighty matters as agriculture, health, roads, education, local governments, state agencies, water rights, the environment, taxation, motor vehicles, insurance companies, children's codes, and others. Some are of much less consequence than others, and a few are, in fact, patently silly. But by and large the business of legislatures is serious.

Another important function of state legislatures is controlling the budget. This is the oldest legislative function and predates the enactment of laws. In a sense, the budgetary powers of legislatures are part of their overall policy formation role and, again, this is a role that legislatures share in a *de facto* sense with the executive branch. But legislative control of the public purse is important for both real and symbolic reasons. Most state legislatures must approve state budgets annually: They have the authority to review, revise, or eliminate any or all items, and they may add new items if they wish. In reality, of course, modern state budgets are so voluminous and complicated that the legislatures' role is often one of reviewing and making minor alterations in the budget as it is proposed by the governor. But the legislature does retain the final legal budgetary sanction, and this fact alone conditions the contents of the budget that the governor submits.

The Legislative Process

The **legislative process** is the pathway by which a bill becomes a law. In most states, the process is similar both to that of other states, and to that of Congress. (The legislative process in Nevada is shown in Figure 4.1.) Although

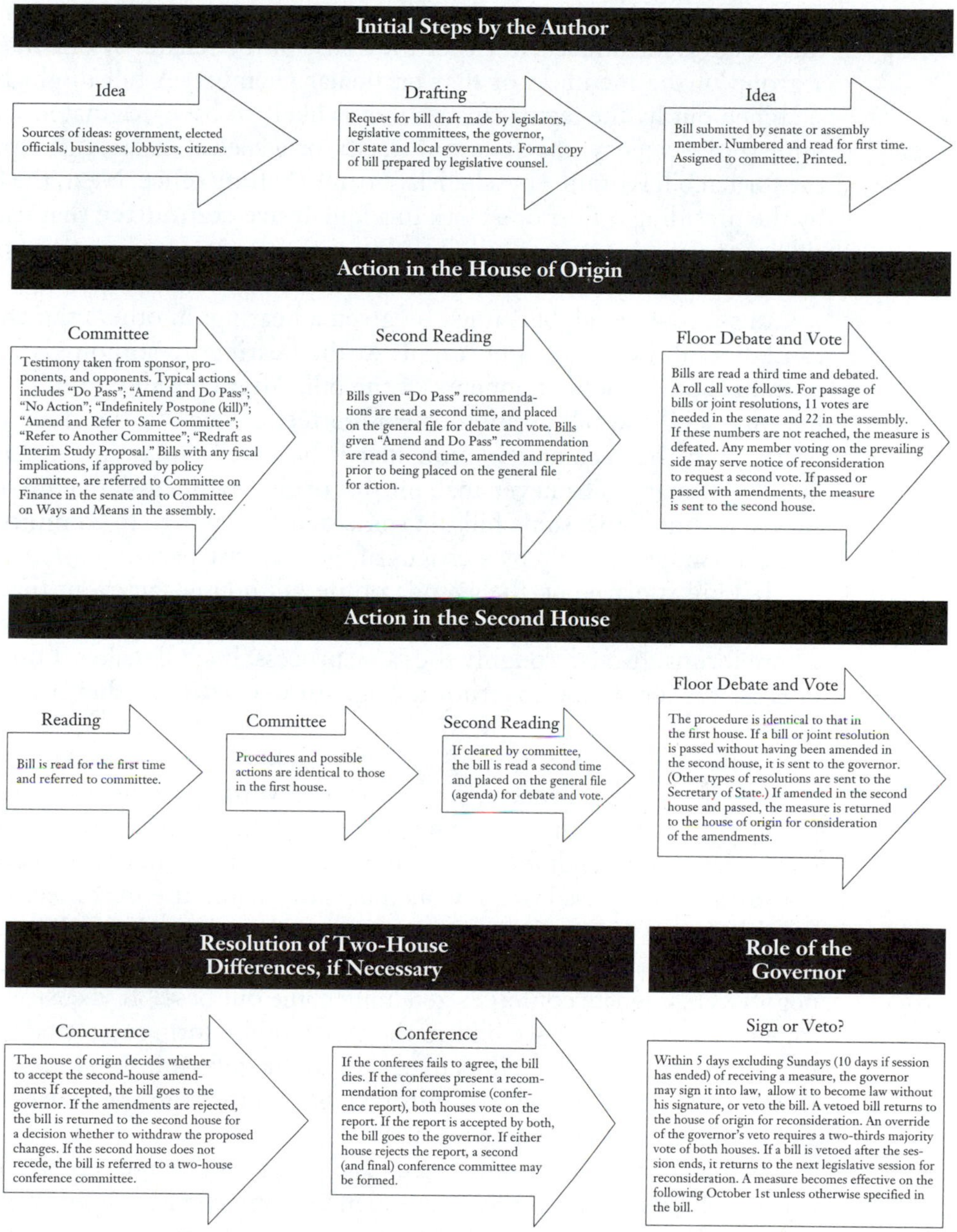

Initial Steps by the Author

Idea

Sources of ideas: government, elected officials, businesses, lobbyists, citizens.

Drafting

Request for bill draft made by legislators, legislative committees, the governor, or state and local governments. Formal copy of bill prepared by legislative counsel.

Idea

Bill submitted by senate or assembly member. Numbered and read for first time. Assigned to committee. Printed.

Action in the House of Origin

Committee

Testimony taken from sponsor, proponents, and opponents. Typical actions includes "Do Pass"; "Amend and Do Pass"; "No Action"; "Indefinitely Postpone (kill)"; "Amend and Refer to Same Committee"; "Refer to Another Committee"; "Redraft as Interim Study Proposal." Bills with any fiscal implications, if approved by policy committee, are referred to Committee on Finance in the senate and to Committee on Ways and Means in the assembly.

Second Reading

Bills given "Do Pass" recommendations are read a second time, and placed on the general file for debate and vote. Bills given "Amend and Do Pass" recommendation are read a second time, amended and reprinted prior to being placed on the general file for action.

Floor Debate and Vote

Bills are read a third time and debated. A roll call vote follows. For passage of bills or joint resolutions, 11 votes are needed in the senate and 22 in the assembly. If these numbers are not reached, the measure is defeated. Any member voting on the prevailing side may serve notice of reconsideration to request a second vote. If passed or passed with amendments, the measure is sent to the second house.

Action in the Second House

Reading

Bill is read for the first time and referred to committee.

Committee

Procedures and possible actions are identical to those in the first house.

Second Reading

If cleared by committee, the bill is read a second time and placed on the general file (agenda) for debate and vote.

Floor Debate and Vote

The procedure is identical to that in the first house. If a bill or joint resolution is passed without having been amended in the second house, it is sent to the governor. (Other types of resolutions are sent to the Secretary of State.) If amended in the second house and passed, the measure is returned to the house of origin for consideration of the amendments.

Resolution of Two-House Differences, if Necessary

Concurrence

The house of origin decides whether to accept the second-house amendments If accepted, the bill goes to the governor. If the amendments are rejected, the bill is returned to the second house for a decision whether to withdraw the proposed changes. If the second house does not recede, the bill is referred to a two-house conference committee.

Conference

If the conferees fails to agree, the bill dies. If the conferees present a recommendation for compromise (conference report), both houses vote on the report. If the report is accepted by both, the bill goes to the governor. If either house rejects the report, a second (and final) conference committee may be formed.

Role of the Governor

Sign or Veto?

Within 5 days excluding Sundays (10 days if session has ended) of receiving a measure, the governor may sign it into law, allow it to become law without his signature, or veto the bill. A vetoed bill returns to the house of origin for reconsideration. An override of the governor's veto requires a two-thirds majority vote of both houses. If a bill is vetoed after the session ends, it returns to the next legislative session for reconsideration. A measure becomes effective on the following October 1st unless otherwise specified in the bill.

Figure 4.1 The Legislative Process in Nevada
Source: State of Nevada, *Legislative Manual*, Bulletin no. 92–23, 1993.

there are variations among the states, in general terms the process goes like this: A bill is introduced, in either the house or the senate, by one individual or a group of the members of that particular chamber. A bill might have been sketched out by the legislator, but it is as likely to have originated with an administrative agency, the governor's staff, or a special interest group. Usually, the formal bill is drafted by a legislative bill-drafting office. Next, the bill is sent by the presiding officer or a clerk to a **legislative committee** that usually considers a particular type of bill. The bill is then considered by that committee, and hearings may be held.

In some states all bills must be given a hearing; in others the chairperson can kill a bill by simply ignoring it. At the hearings, testimony is heard from both proponents and opponents of the bill. After consideration, the committee may send the bill to another committee, or back to the floor of the full house with the recommendation that it be voted either up or down. As in Congress, many bills never make it out of the state legislative committee. It should be noted that some bills, in some states, do not go to committee but are instead handled directly by a caucus of the majority party.

If a bill is placed on the agenda of the full house—an event that is not always automatic—and if the bill is passed, it is then sent to the other house, where it runs through roughly the same process. If a bill makes it through both houses, it is sent to the governor for signature or veto, whichever the governor chooses.

In many cases, bills passing both houses have some amendments attached at some point in the process. Therefore, the wording of the house version of a bill may differ from that of the senate version. In such cases, the first chamber may accept the amendments of the other chamber. If it does not, a **conference committee** comprised of a few members of each house may meet to iron out the differences between the two versions and send a uniform bill back to the two houses. Researcher Donald Gross suggests that in conference committee negotiations, senate conferees generally come out best.[6] It is customary, then, for each house to approve bills in the compromise form suggested by the conference committee. The bill is then sent to the governor for signature or veto. In some instances, whole new bills may be run through the process, bills that embody house-senate compromises.

While conference committees are often vital stages in the legislative process, stages where highly consequential compromises or even changes are made in legislation, most bills never go to conference. The most common method of resolving differences in the house and senate versions of a bill is for one of the houses to recede from its position and accept the version of the other. Compromises are usually worked out informally among the bills sponsors and other interested parties, legislators and lobbyists alike. A study of over a thousand bills introduced over two years in Colorado, for example, found that:

> Only about 1 bill in 11 that are introduced, or 1 bill in 6 that pass both houses, or roughly a quarter of those that emerge in different form, go to conference.
>
> The preferred method of accommodation is concurrence by the first chamber with the amendments of the other.[7]

Death Traps for Bills

The state legislative lawmaking process is, of course, more complicated than the preceding brief sketch suggests. As many commentators correctly suggest, the legislative process, as it currently operates in American national, state, and local governments, has a strong conservative bias. As a result, it is much easier to use the procedures to stop a bill from becoming a law than it is to secure its passage. The legislative process thus lends itself to obstructionism. As in Congress and many city councils, there are several critical points in the legislative process, called **power pockets**, whereby a strategically placed individual or minority coalition in a state legislature can kill or radically alter a bill.

The speaker of the house of representatives and the president of the senate are sometimes able to affect the fate of a bill through their power to refer bills to committees. As we will see later in the chapter, all state legislative bodies are broken down into subject-matter-oriented committees. Some bills, however, may properly be sent to more than one committee. An education bill, for example, might legitimately be sent to either a committee on local government or a committee on education or to both. The chair and members of one of these committees might be inclined to look favorably on the proposed law, whereas the chair and members of the other committee might be hostile to the bill or to some of its provisions. In Colorado, for example, former House Speaker Carl "Bev" Bledsoe, a cigarette smoker and a rancher, opposed no-smoking laws and daylight savings time. A fellow Republican introduced bills to curb smoking and institute year-round daylight savings time in the state. Bledsoe sent the bills to Colorado's House Committee on Agriculture. His friends on that committee "smoked" both bills, and neither one saw the "light of day."

Legislative committees themselves exercise extensive control over bills. Committees always have more work than they have time for; as a result, some bills are considered and others are left to die. If a committee chairperson is opposed to a certain bill, that committee chair can, within limits, refuse to schedule hearings, or delay them. In some states the committee chair can send the bill to a subcommittee that the chair knows will ignore it, amend it to the point where it loses its original intent, or recommend that it not be passed upon favorably by the full committee and the full house.

Full committees can do likewise: In some states they can ignore bills, amend them to death, postpone indefinitely or table them, or report them out to the full house knowing that the bills will be defeated. As one would expect, the degree of influence that such committees have over proposed legislation varies greatly among the states. For example, according to Malcolm Jewell, committee influence is weak in Illinois, due in part to the strength of political parties, but strong in Minnesota. As a general rule, though, committees, their members, and their chairpersons are in a position to critically affect the fate of bills.[8]

The governor is obviously in a critical position. Governors in every state except North Carolina possess some sort of **legislative veto** power, and many have a **line-item veto** over specific items in the budget.[9] Since a two-thirds or three-fifths vote in both houses of the legislature is typically needed to override an executive veto, the governor is in a position to thwart the enactment of laws that are found displeasing. In most states the veto power is strengthened further by the tendency of legislators to rush the most important and most controversial bills (for example, education, welfare, taxation, budget) through the legislature in the final few days of the session, for legislatures in most states cannot call themselves back into special session. Therefore, critical legislation sometimes appears on the governor's desk toward the end of a session; should the governor decide to veto or pocket veto a measure, the legislature is left without enough time to reconsider the bill or attempt to override the veto.

Some legislative houses have powerful agenda-setting committees of some sort, often called **rules committees** or **calendar committees**. They become powerful, in many cases, because of the voluminous flow of bills sent to the floor, especially during the final few days of a session. The extensive flow of proposed legislation means that if bills are considered on the floor in the order in which they emerge from various committees, the most important legislative proposals may never be considered. Thus rules committees often have the authority to restructure the legislative calendar, giving priority to certain bills and ensuring their consideration. Clearly, this makes the rules or calendar committee a powerful body, for it can, in many instances, determine the fate of a bill. In Utah, the leadership performs this function through a process called "sifting." As the session end nears, the leaders gather informally and "sift" through the remaining bills, placing those deemed most important on the calendar. Others die.

In short, there are many stages in the lawmaking process at which an individual or group may sabotage policy proposals. To become law, a bill must successfully make its way through a process rife with pitfalls. It is no wonder, then, that in most states fewer than half of the bills introduced ever make it all the way through the legislative process; in some states the rate is below 20 percent.

Is the Process Effective?

It may be implied from what has been said that the slow, cumbersome, and hazardous state legislative process is not effective. Given the ability of individuals and small groups to use the procedures to thwart majority rule, it is difficult for some to come to a different conclusion. Others argue, however, that the process works to serve the public interest in that it mitigates potentially rash and hasty action. Supporters of the slow legislative process suggest that there are times, especially during crises or perceived political pressure, when the temptation is great to rush a host of new bills through the process. Its slow-moving nature forces legislators to take the time to reconsider, dispassionately, the proposed laws that at first may seem wise and necessary. Bicameralism, the committee system, the gubernatorial veto, and other factors that slow down the legislative process are, therefore, considered effective.

Recent Improvements

During the recent era of state legislative modernization, many states instituted a variety of procedures to streamline the process. In most states today legislators may pre-file bills; that is, they may have bills prepared, and submit them, before the legislative session actually begins. In about half the states, a bill that has not passed in the first year of a two-year session may be carried over into the second year.

Most state legislatures also now operate with a calendar that sets deadlines for the introduction of bills, for the completion of committee work on bills, and for action on bills in the two chambers on second and third readings. All of these innovations in procedure are designed to expedite the work of committees and to relieve some of the pressure of the old end-of-session logjam.[10]

Informal Rules and Strategies

In addition to the formal rules and procedures that govern the lawmaking activities of state legislatures, there are a number of informal yet powerful rules that guide behavior. Informal rules tend to exist, of course, in almost all types of organizations.

In a classic study of four state legislatures, John C. Wahlke and his associates identified several informal rules that expedite the operations of state legislatures and make the legislative process reasonably coordinated and predictable for the lawmakers:

> Keep your word; abide by commitments; support another member's local bill if it doesn't affect you or your district; don't make personal attacks on other members; oppose the bill, not the [person]; observe common courtesies; be friendly and courteous even if you disagree; take a stand, don't be wishy-washy; notify in advance if you are going to change your stand or can't keep a commitment; be willing to compromise; don't fight unnecessarily; follow caucus or conference decisions; keep your temper; don't introduce too many bills or amendments; don't divulge confidential information; defend legislature and members against outsiders; be fair, show good judgment, maturity, responsibility.[11]

Sanctions can be applied against individuals who violate these and other informal rules of the game. The most commonly applied sanctions include obstructing the violator's own bills, applying the "silent treatment," indicating mistrust by cross-examination, and stripping away political tools such as patronage, good committee assignments, and the support of local organizations and constituencies.

Similarly, lawmakers have access to a wide variety of tactics that they can use to political advantage. One way to help ensure passage of one's bills is to seek well-placed cosponsors. It doesn't hurt a bill's chances, for example, to have as a cosponsor the chairperson of the committee that hears the bill or a legislative leader in either or both houses. It also doesn't hurt to have multiple cosponsors, for any lawmaker willing to add his or her name to a bill is unlikely to oppose the measure.

All sorts of other informal strategies are employed in state legislatures. Lawmakers sometimes lean on lobbyists to help sell a bill or an idea to other legislators—a sort of reversal of the lobbying role. Presiding officers selectively send bills to certain committees, depending on whether they want a bill supported or killed. Legislators and lobbyists collaborate to generate home-district pressure on committee chairs to bring bills up for hearings. The tactics are endless, spurred at times by purely partisan or personal motives and at other times by a genuine desire to get the votes needed to convert good ideas into public policy.

Legislative Organization

Forty-nine of the fifty states have a **bicameral legislature**—one composed of two houses. The lone exception is the state of Nebraska; it shifted to a **uni-**

cameral legislature—the single-house system—in 1937 because of a desire to save money on lawmakers' salaries and the conviction that this is a more efficient system than the two-house body. As Table 4.2 shows, the ninety-nine state legislative houses vary greatly in size, ranging from a senate of twenty members in Alaska to a house of representatives of four hundred in New Hampshire. Senators in all except twelve states serve four-year terms, and house members in every state except Alabama, Louisiana, Maryland, and Mississippi serve two-year terms.

Division of Labor

Like sizable organizations of almost any kind, state legislatures find it both convenient and necessary to organize and divide the labor in order to get the work done. Although the nature of the organizational scheme varies among the states and legislative houses make their own operating rules, three common features include party or factional caucus formation, a leadership structure, and a committee system.

TABLE 4.2 MEMBERSHIP IN THE FIVE LARGEST AND FIVE SMALLEST STATE LEGISLATURES

State	Number of Members		
	House	*Senate*	*Total*
Largest			
New Hampshire	400	24	424
Pennsylvania	203	50	253
Georgia	180	56	236
New York	150	61	211
Minnesota	134	67	201
Smallest			
Hawaii	51	25	76
Delaware	42	21	63
Nevada	41	21	62
Alaska	40	20	60
Nebraska (unicameral)	—	—	49

Source: The Book of the States, 1996–97 (Lexington, Ky.: Council of State Governments, 1996), p. 68.

Party Caucuses

Organization in state legislative houses usually begins with the formation of majority and minority **party caucuses.** In most two-party states, caucus formation follows party lines; thus, in each house at the start of the session, a Democratic caucus and a Republican caucus form and meet.

In some states, however, such as the one-party Democratic states in the South and the nominally nonpartisan state of Nebraska, caucus formation, if it exists, is based on factions rather than party. The Mexican-American caucus in Texas is an example. So is the cross-party conservative "cowboy coalition" in New Mexico's senate. On occasion, caucuses cross party lines, particularly when there is a move to dump party leadership. This occurred fairly recently in a number of states, including California, Connecticut, Florida, New Mexico, and Oklahoma.

Leadership Positions

Majority and minority party caucuses make decisions regarding the organization of the house or senate and, in some cases, membership on committees. Where they are operative, majority caucuses decide whom they will support for the offices of speaker of the house and presiding officer of the senate (the "pro tem") where there is no presiding lieutenant governor. Since, in most cases, voting on matters of organization is according to strict majority–minority lines, the nominees of the majority caucus prevail. The selection of presiding officers is critical, especially in the house of representatives, because the speaker in most states has the power to appoint committee members and to refer bills to the various committees.

In addition to the selection of presiding officers, majority and minority caucuses usually select their own informal leadership. This may consist of a floor leader, who guides the activities of the majority in its attempt to control procedure and to secure or thwart the passage of legislation on the floor, and perhaps one or more assistants or "whips" to assist the floor leader in communicating with members and counting votes. In some states, the majority or minority caucus meets periodically to identify its position and strategy on particular pieces of legislation.

The number of leadership positions and their degrees of authority vary from house to senate and from state to state. Typically, the presiding officer in the house, the speaker, has greater power than does the senate counterpart, the president or president *pro tempore*. State senates are smaller and more informal than state houses; senate members usually serve four-year terms, whereas a two-year term is the norm for state houses of representatives; and many senators have had previous experience in the house. In general, then, individual senate members tend to be less inclined than their house colleagues to take orders from leadership. In some state legislatures, New York being an extreme case, a large number of leadership slots exist. They carry extra pay and prestige for those who hold them, and can be parceled out in exchange for the political support of top leaders.

Table 4.3 outlines the most common state leadership structure. However, it is important to remember that state-to-state variation is extensive and the relationships among leaders are not necessarily hierarchical or authoritarian.

Powers of Leadership

Legislative leadership positions are prized, and for good reason—they generally bring with them considerable power and sometimes serve as launching pads for higher office. For example, house speakers and senate presidents in many states appoint committee members and committee chairs. Since committee positions are highly valued, members may be willing to support a leader in exchange for a desired committee assignment. Furthermore, the power to direct bills to the various committees provides presiding officers with opportunities to affect the fate of bills. Some state legislative leaders are empowered by the rules to waive certain other rules, such as bill introduction deadlines and bill limits. This, too, gives them influence over members. Following an election, minority party leaders may become majority party leaders; therefore, members generally want to remain in their good graces. The floor leaders, whips, and caucus chairs are close to the presiding officers and may at some time succeed them. Members are aware of this and as a result often pay them deference as well.

Table 4.3 State Legislative Leadership Positions

House of Representatives		Senate	
Majority Party	*Minority Party*	*Majority Party*	*Minority Party*
Speaker (presiding officer)		President (presiding officer)	
Majority floor leader	Minority floor leader	Majority floor leader	Minority floor leader
Asst. Majority leader (whip)	Asst. Minority leader (whip)	Asst. Majority leader (whip)	Asst. Minority leader (whip)
Caucus chair	Caucus chair	Caucus chair	Caucus chair

For a variety of reasons, then, including their ability to win leadership contests in the first place, legislative leaders wield considerable **leadership powers**. Yet the powers, roles, and perils of legislative leadership have changed significantly in recent decades. Improved pay, staff help, and facilities as well as longer, annual legislative sessions have attracted more career-oriented politicians who want a share in the power and the action. Many of today's state legislators have no other job. They use questionnaires, newsletters, constituent service, and often their own state-paid staffers to campaign year-round. They look to their legislative leaders to help them raise money to secure reelection. (See Focus 4.2 "The Unsinkable Willie Brown.")

Trends in Leadership

Contemporary legislative leaders in the states are weaker than their historical counterparts. The new members want to share power. In exchange for their support of the leadership, they expect to receive help with their fund-raising efforts and legislative agendas. Legislative committees are stronger now, and they too sometimes become little centers of power able to rival that of the leadership.

When modern legislative leaders seek to exert their influence, they often do so at some risk. In 1989 in Connecticut, for example, Speaker of the House Irving Stolberg was deposed after serving two terms in that position and shortly after having been selected to serve a third. Stolberg met his demise at the hands of a **bipartisan coalition** in which many of his former Democratic supporters joined Republicans in a cross-party alliance. One of Stolberg's younger colleagues described the context of the situation this way:

> We were a new generation of professional legislators. . . . We had our own staff, our own offices. And there was a sense among the younger generation that Irving was just not allowing any upward mobility.[12]

Commenting on the trend toward weaker leaders, legislative scholar Alan Rosenthal notes that a more professionalized legislature leads to more careerists in office, which leads to more ambition on the part of more members, which leads to challenges of strong leadership.[13] Legislative leaders in California, New Mexico, Florida, Oregon, Vermont, New York, and elsewhere also have been deposed in recent years, often by bipartisan coalitions. In 1992, in the context of a general anti-incumbent and antigovernment mood, the American voters joined in: Some eighty-five state legislative leaders chose not to seek reelection and another eight were defeated.[14]

As the ability of strong-armed leaders to survive declines, traditions of short-tenure rotation in leadership slots are dissolving in some states, too. As

Focus 4.2
The Unsinkable Willie Brown

• • •

State houses of representatives have seen many legendary speakers come and go, including Ohio's Vern Rife, Georgia's Thomas Murphy, and Maine's John Martin. But there's never been one quite like California's Willie Brown.

Willie Brown is a Democrat. He sought the California assembly speakership in 1974, 1976, and 1978 and lost. He finally made it in 1980 by assembling a coalition of fellow Democrats and minority party Republicans to win over the opposition of a majority in his own party.

The Democratic caucus was in disarray at the time, obviously. After taking over the speaker's slot, Brown overhauled the Democratic caucus and solidified his leadership position, in part by collecting and spending campaign funds to ensure the election of Democrats who would be loyal to him. The Republicans, who had helped him ascend to the speaker's position and received a share of the committee chairmanships for their efforts, were soon dealt out of the power loop and back into their minority party posture.

Willie Brown ruled California legislative politics from 1980 on, through his skillful use of the prerogatives of his position, brokering the distribution of interest group campaign money, his unrivaled knowledge of the rules and process, and his interpersonal skills. He was buoyed, of course, by a Democratic house majority.

That is, until 1994. In 1994 a Democratic majority of 47–33 was transformed into a 39–41 minority. Republicans had been in the minority for twenty-five years and were salivating over the prospects of electing one of their own as speaker, and controlling all committees.

But Brown didn't sink. He convinced a disgruntled Republican to switch to Independent and support Willie for speaker. Now there was a 40–40 tie. After weeks of stalemates and negotiation, including a quorum-blocking boycott by Republicans, Brown maneuvered himself into the chair, triggered a vote to oust another Republican who, by a quirk of election timing, held both a House and Senate seat. This produced a 40–39 advantage for Democrats.

By a 40–39 vote, Willie became speaker once again. What did he do? He treated Republicans well, giving them one-half of the assembly's twenty-six committee chairmanships. Then he quit and ran for mayor of San Francisco. But in his departure he left one final reminder of his

Focus 4.2 *(continued)*

political skill by maneuvering the election as speaker of Republican Doris Allen, with just her vote and that of all the Democrats. He won his race for mayor in a runoff. Why is that not a surprise?

Sources: Daniel M. Weintraub, "Power Play in California," *State Legislatures*, February, 1995, pp. 16–19; Richard A. Clucas, "The Political Skills of California Assembly Speaker Willie Brown," *Comparative State Politics*, August, 1995, pp. 1–4.

Malcolm Jewell notes, strong one-term traditions are practiced in Arkansas, Florida, Wyoming, Alaska, North Dakota, and South Dakota, but two-term stints are in place in Connecticut, New Jersey, Kansas, Montana, Nevada, and Utah.[15]

There seem to be changes, then, in two directions. Rotation is giving way to some continuity in many states, and long-term, strong leaders are increasingly at risk in others. It appears that in the modern state legislature, a successful leadership strategy increasingly must include the provision of political opportunities and assistance for members as well as broad consultation and inclusion in decision making.

Legislative leaders are playing a larger role as fund-raisers to support the election and reelection of members of their party. Leaders require the support of their members, and they cannot be influential speakers, senate presidents, or majority leaders if their party is in the minority. Therefore, more legislative leaders are hosting fund-raisers and leaning on the lobby corps to build election war chests for their legislative candidates.[16]

In the 1960s California's house speaker, Jesse Unruh, pioneered the practice of building leadership campaign funds. One of his modern-day successors, House Speaker Willie Brown, raised and spent between $2 million and $4 million per election. This helped to keep Brown's Democratic party in the majority in California's house and also kept house Democrats beholden to Brown. In the same vein, writer Rob Gurwitt describes the fund-raising process in Ohio:

> House Speaker Vern Riffe will throw a birthday party for himself. . . . There will be a small combo playing jazz off in the corner as guests spread through the huge hall, stopping to fill up at the bar or graze the buffet tables of fried chicken legs, egg rolls, pasta, vegetables, broad trays of cheeses. . . . As many as two thousand politicians, union officials and corporate executives will have come by to pay their respects to the Democratic speaker at a cost of $300 each.[17]

How can we characterize such practices and events? Lobbyists with interests in policy decisions are squeezed for money by legislative leaders who make the decisions and also have an interest in remaining as the leaders. These leaders in turn help members who have an interest in reelection. The money that changes hands is used, legally, to purchase mostly issueless propaganda designed not to inform the public but to persuade it to vote in a particular way.

Almost half of the states now have term limits for state legislators, and these limits will undoubtedly affect leadership patterns. Politically ambitious lawmakers may well feel compelled to attempt upward movements into positions of leadership very soon after election since they can no longer watch and wait through an apprentice learning period. California law limits legislators to six years in the house and eight in the senate. In Oklahoma, Nevada, and Utah the limits are twelve years and, with a few exceptions, they are eight years in other term-limited states.

Among the probable consequences of the limits are that turnover in leadership will be higher, fights over leadership slots will be more frequent, and leaders will increasingly be legislative novices. Exactly how this will impact the operations of our state legislatures remains to be seen.

Legislative Committees and Their Assignments

At the heart of state legislative organization is the committee system. As noted earlier in the chapter, division of labor is necessary because legislatures consider hundreds of bills covering a wide range of subject matter. Further, the chambers can range in size from twenty to four hundred members. Thus, the work of American state legislatures is divided among a number of committees organized by subject matter. The typical state legislative chamber includes committees on education, highways, health and welfare, state institutions, local government, judiciary, finance, interstate relations, and others. Table 4.4 lists the twenty-four senate committees in operation in California.

As Table 4.5 (page 117) shows, the number of committees varies among the state legislatures. Whereas Missouri has seventy-one legislative committees, Maryland has only fifteen. The states also vary in terms of their use of **joint committees**—that is, committees made up of members from both the senate and the house of representatives. Connecticut, for example, has twenty-two committees, all with joint membership. The typical state legislator serves on two or three committees, though this also varies, as some lawmakers in certain states serve on more than a half-dozen committees. Like many other aspects of state government structure and procedure, the committee system is in a constant state of flux.

The method by which committee assignments are made in state houses of representatives is fairly standard, but in state senates the committee assignment

Table 4.4 Standing Committees in the California Senate

Committee
Agriculture and Water Resources
Appropriations
Banking and International Trade
Budget and Fiscal Review
Business and Professions
Constitutional Amendments
Education
Elections and Reapportionment
Energy and Public Utilities
Government Organization
Health and Human Services
Housing and Urban Affairs
Industrial Relations
Insurance, Claims, and Corporations
Judiciary
Local Government
Natural Resources and Wildlife
Public Employment and Retirement
Revenue and Taxation
Rules
Toxics and Public Safety Management
Transportation
Veterans Affairs

Source: State Legislative Leadership, Committees and Staff, 1993–94 (Lexington, Ky.: Council of State Governments, 1993), pp. 10–11.

process varies considerably. In thirty-nine states the speaker makes the committee assignments for both parties in the house of representatives. In four states the speaker appoints majority party members and the minority leader appoints minority party members. Three other state houses use a committee called a **committee on committees**. In Hawaii a party caucus appoints members to committees.

In the senates of most states, committee assignments are made by a committee on committees, by the president of the senate, or by the president *pro tempore*, who presides in the absence of the senate president or lieutenant governor. There are certain variations in procedure, of course. In California, committee assignments in the senate are made by the committee on rules, whereas in Virginia they are determined by election.[18]

In an old study of the U.S. House of Representatives, Nelson Polsby concluded that the House has become increasingly "institutionalized" over time—that is, legislative turnover had declined, committees had become more im-

TABLE 4.5 LEGISLATIVE COMMITTEES IN SELECTED STATES

State	Number of Committees			
	House	*Senate*	*Joint*	*Total*
Missouri	42	23	6	71
Illinois	28	16	0	44
California	26	24	10	60
Connecticut	0	0	24	24
Alaska	9	9	4	22
Maryland	7	6	11	24

Source: The Book of the States, 1996–97 (Lexington, Ky.: Council of State Governments, 1996), p. 113.

portant and more autonomous, and their operations had become more routine.[19] Using these measures, it appears that state legislatures are relatively uninstitutionalized, for personnel turnover is high, the committees are sometimes weak, and the seniority principle is not followed rigidly. In a study of selected committees in six state legislatures, Keith Hamm found that committee members tend to have a special interest in the type of legislation considered by their particular committee. This special interest, in turn, often translates into an advantage for interest groups, which have a special stake in the bills handled by those committees. The same phenomenon is, of course, very pronounced in the committees and subcommittees of the U.S. Congress.[20]

The organizational and procedural features of state legislatures thus affect the distribution of power and influence among legislators. The speaker of the house is usually quite powerful, given the speaker's power of recognition in floor debate, power to refer bills to committee, and power to appoint committee members and, in some cases, committee chairs. (See Focus 4.3 "Mr. Speaker versus the NRA.") Given their role in the appraisal of bills, state leg-

Focus 4.3

MR. SPEAKER VERSUS THE NRA

• • •

Mr. Speaker is Tom Loftus, former speaker of the Wisconsin house of representatives. The NRA is the National Rifle Association, Wisconsin Chapter. The NRA wanted state legislation prohibiting local governments from enacting any controls whatsoever on the possession of firearms. The speaker did not. He characterized his political battle

Focus 4.3 *(continued)*

with the gun lobby this way: "A fight with the NRA was baseball bats at close range, and I learned to swing first."

An Illinois community called Morton Grove had enacted an ordinance that banned all handgun possession. The NRA said it feared such laws could spread to Wisconsin, so it pushed for a state law denying local governments such authority. The gun lobby's real goal was much broader, namely, to strip local gun controls altogether. Speaker Loftus opposed such legislation even though he was, in his words, " . . . a former military policeman, medal winner with the Colt 45, and an owner of two handguns."

For his efforts Loftus became the NRA's chief villain. It ran radio spots characterizing him as an enemy of the sportsman. It sent its 80,000 Wisconsin members Loftus' home phone number and urged them to call him. It similarly triggered a storm of "grass roots" calls to other legislators.

But the NRA's attacks and political threats failed to beat the power of the speaker. Loftus used the speaker's access to the air waves and printed press to paint the NRA leadership as extreme, as misrepresenting the issues, as misleading its own members. As Loftus put it, "In order to expose this powerful group to the sunlight of public debate, where it could be made to blink, like rats emerging from the sewer, the fight had to be made personal: them versus me, the NRA versus the Speaker."

While he was personally polite to NRA callers, Loftus' wife chastised them for waking the baby with late night calls. In the legislature Loftus employed the speaker's power to refer bills to committees so as to stall NRA supported measures. He helped the NRA pass the anti-Morton Grove bill it said it wanted, but really did not want, and engineered the death of the more sweeping anti-gun control measures that were at the core of the NRA strategy.

In Wisconsin, as elsewhere, the NRA has money, members and zeal; it's a tough political player. At the same time, Wisconsin's house speaker, like those in other states, wields extensive power over legislative operations. In this case, Mr. Speaker prevailed.

Source: Tom Loftus, *The Art of Legislative Politics*, Washington: C.Q. Press, 1994, Chapter 7.

islative committees are influential, though not always as strong as their congressional counterparts.

Legislative Support

Legislators cannot function without help. They need clerical assistance, researchers, some type of income, financing for their housing and transportation expenses, and a place to work. Before the modernization of many state legislatures in the 1960s and 1970s, both staff and financial help was minimal in most legislatures. In some states there was no staff assistance at all, and many legislators received no salary. Some had no place to work, except for their desk on the floor of the chamber itself. In addition, many legislatures met in very short sessions, some only every other year.

There have been significant changes in state legislative support in recent years. As in the case of Congress, staffing in the more professionalized state legislatures is becoming increasingly decentralized. Some legislatures, including those in California, Illinois, Michigan, and New York, now provide staffing for individual members, leaders, committees, party caucuses, and, in a few instances, home district offices. Legislator salaries are still low in some states but substantial in others, exceeding $20,000 a year in most cases and reaching $50,000 in some others. New Hampshire pays its legislators just $100 a year, whereas New York lawmakers receive almost $60,000 annually. (See Table 4.6.) Allowances for housing, per diem, and travel expenses are much more generous than they were formerly. Space and equipment have also improved in many states.

Expanded staffing can affect state legislatures in many ways. It can make legislators much more self-reliant and less dependent on lobbyists for infor-

TABLE 4.6 LEGISLATORS' SALARIES IN SELECTED STATES, 1994

Highest (yearly)		Lowest (daily)	
California	$ 72,000	New Mexico	$ 0
New York	57,500	Rhode Island	5
Pennsylvania	47,000	Alabama	10
Michigan	45,450	Kansas	63

Source: The Book of the States, 1996–97 (Lexington, Ky.: Council of State Governments, 1996), pp. 80–81.

mation. Lawmakers must cast votes on hundreds of complicated measures every year and must turn somewhere for information and advice. To the extent that they have their own staff members, they are able to discount, or at least supplement, the information fed to them constantly by representatives of interest groups. Better staffing can also give the state legislature a measure of strength and independence in its relationship with the governor, particularly in the area of budgeting. If the legislature and its committees (which bear the responsibilities of budget preparation and review) lack their own cadre of analysts, they will be largely captive to the numbers, projections, and estimates of consequences given them by the governor's staff. In recent years many reformed and resurgent state legislatures have become increasingly free of gubernatorial influence, in part as a result of improved staffing.

Staffing levels also have implications for legislative careers. Even though staffers on state payrolls technically should not perform partisan work to advance the political careers of their superiors, much of what they do has that effect. Staff members handle constituent inquiries and help solve constituent problems. They send out questionnaires and newsletters, all of which bear the name and picture of the lawmaker and thereby advance his or her name recognition and chances for electoral success. As in Congress, a few states now provide staff help for district offices, which functions to maintain the incumbent's presence in the home district. Some critics argue that expanded staffing reinforces the trend toward career-oriented politicians, whose major objective then becomes repeated reelection, and who eventually lose touch with their workaday-world constituents.[21]

Representation

In large and complex communities such as the American states, it is not possible to pursue the democratic dictum of "government of, by, and for the people" through direct democracy. There are simply too many people and complicated issues to make collective decisions in that fashion. Thus, out of necessity, the states resort to some form of representative government, and state legislatures are among the nation's most representative institutions.

Apportionment

To establish and operate any representative system, an important normative question must be resolved regarding **apportionment:** On what basis shall representatives be selected? Should the seats in state houses and senates be apportioned on the basis of local government units, just as those in the U.S. Senate are doled out on the basis of two per state? Should they be apportioned on the basis of land area, with each legislative district containing the same number of square miles or acres? Or should districts be drawn so as to include roughly the same number of people within each district? Selecting the criterion by which to apportion legislative seats is a normative issue because there is no absolutely right or wrong way to do it. It is a question of values.

A search for historical precedent in the United States on the matter of apportionment is of relatively little help. The Constitution provides for representation on the basis of population in one house of Congress and for equal representation for political units (the states) in the other. The situation is different in the states, however, because local units of government (for example, counties and townships) are not legally related to the states in the same way that the states are to the national government.

Likewise, a search for precedent in the states themselves is of no help. Some states entered the Union with representation in both houses based on population. Others based representation in one house on population and employed other criteria, such as local governmental unit, in the other house. Before the "one person, one vote" decisions of the 1960s, many state constitutions provided for representation in at least one house on a basis other than straight population. In Vermont, for example, each organized town received at least one seat in the lower house; in seven other states, each county was given at least one seat in the state senate.

Although there are no clear-cut clues to proper apportionment criteria in the history of apportionment schemes in the United States, a fairly obvious suggestion is implicit in democratic theory. Democratic decision making at its best provides for political equality. Influence is not, of course, equally distributed throughout society, but democratic theory still insists that this be the case—or at least that no overt attempts be made to enforce political inequality.

Malapportionment Develops

In the past many states deliberately employed apportionment schemes in which the one person, one vote criterion was violated. However, the drive for **reapportionment** did not become a salient political issue in America until the massive population shifts of the twentieth century, which created dramatic imbalances in the number of individuals in the legislative districts of many states. Then, throughout the early decades of the twentieth century and into the 1960s, malapportionment was increasingly criticized as inherently undemocratic and the cause of many of the social, economic, and political ills of the cities. Thus, **malapportionment**—gross imbalances in the number of individuals residing in state legislative districts—emerged as a by-product of twentieth-century population shifts. As Figure 4.2 demonstrates, astounding rural and urban population shifts have occurred in the United States since 1910.

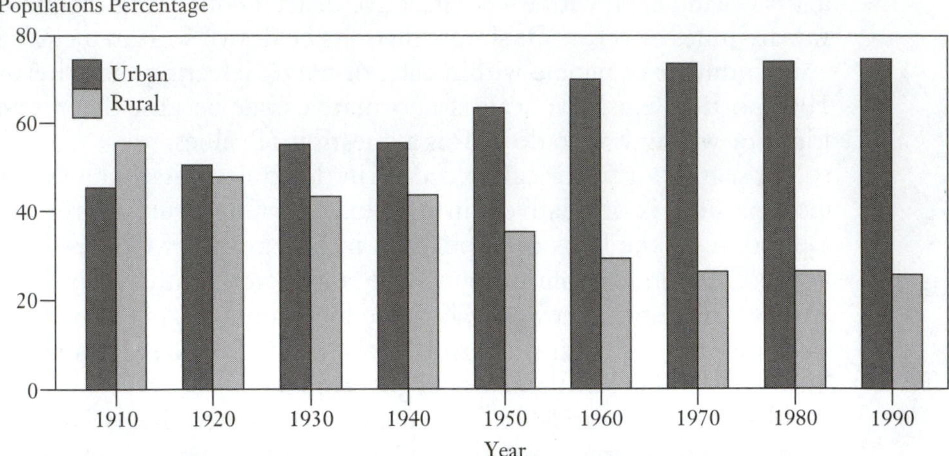

Figure 4.2 Urban and Rural Populations in the United States, 1910–1990
Source: U.S. Bureau of the Census, *Statistical Abstract of the United States* (Washington, D.C.: GPO, 1981 and 1992).

In the nineteenth century, state legislative houses whose membership was based on population, were regularly reapportioned to match population shifts, in accordance with state constitutional requirements. Throughout the first half of the twentieth century, however, when much of the U.S. population moved from farms to cities, state legislatures became increasingly reluctant to redraw their district lines in accordance with the movements of the people.

Yet state legislatures' reluctance to obey the provisions of state law regarding the redrawing of district lines was understandable. Typically, the task of reapportioning state legislatures has been that of the legislatures themselves. Therefore, if representatives and senators had supported reapportionment, many would have been voting to eliminate their own seats, to combine their own districts with other districts, or to create additional districts in the urban and suburban areas, thus diminishing their own relative political power. Like most people and nearly all politicians, state legislators sought self-preservation, which almost invariably meant refusal to reapportion, despite the demands of state law.

The existing political power arrangements and the American grassroots ethic supported the persistent refusal of state legislatures to reapportion themselves. Malapportionment itself meant that legislative control remained in the hands of the rural representatives. They could, and did, thwart most attempts to redraw district lines. Their refusal to act received substantial support from a deeply rooted American notion about the romantic character of the hinterland. Rural people themselves opposed reapportionment. Many claimed a need for an inflated rural vote in order to protect the farming and cattle economy against the antirural onslaughts of urban politicians, which, it was feared, would result in a trampling of rural interests.

Many urban people, too, supported malapportionment. In Colorado in 1962, for example, a "federal plan" for apportionment that did not comply with the one person, one vote principle carried by better than three to two in a statewide election. In addition, the plan received a majority of votes in every county in the state, including the highly populous counties in and around Denver. The U.S. Supreme Court later voided the Colorado federal plan, even though thousands of urban and suburban voters seemed willing to help their rural neighbors diminish the value of the urban vote.[22]

The Extent of Malapportionment

While the extent of malapportionment varied among the states, at least one house in nearly every state was seriously out of balance by the 1960s. The Arizona senate, for example, was composed of twenty-eight members—two from each of its fourteen counties—even though 75 percent of the people in that state lived in just two counties (Maricopa County, which contains Phoenix and its surrounding suburbs, and Pima County, where Tucson is located). Similarly, in California in the 1960s, one senate district contained over six million people whereas the population in another barely exceeded 14,000. In Vermont the largest house district had a population of 33,155 and the smallest a scant thirty-eight. It was not unusual for states to have at least one chamber in which fewer than 20 percent of the state's voters could elect enough representatives to constitute a voting majority in that house. Table 4.7 displays the extent of malapportionment in selected states in the 1960s.

Complaints about malapportionment and its ill effects grew in number and intensity throughout the 1950s and into the early 1960s. Some of the criticism was ideological in nature, asserting that it was unfair and undemocratic to minimize the value of the urban and suburban votes. Other observers blamed malapportionment for the growing ills of the cities.

Yet there was no universal agreement about the impact of malapportionment on state politics, and some observers were skeptical about its supposed ill effects. In 1964, for example, Herbert Jacob warned that reapportionment would not have a dramatic impact on the behavior of state legislatures.[23] Similarly, in a study of the public policies of states with varying degrees of malapportionment, Thomas Dye concluded in 1965 that:

> On the whole, the policy choices of malapportioned legislatures are not noticeably different from the policy choices of well-apportioned legislatures. Most of the policy differences which do occur turn out to be a product of socio-economic differences among the states rather than a direct product of apportionment practices.[24]

TABLE 4.7 SELECTED STATES' LEGISLATIVE APPORTIONMENT IN THE 1960S

State	District Population		Minimum Popular Vote for Majority
	Largest	*Smallest*	
California senate	6,038,771	14,294	10.7
Connecticut house	81,089	191	12.0
Florida senate	935,047	9,543	12.3
Kansas house	68,646	2,069	18.5
Montana senate	79,016	894	16.1
New Jersey senate	923,545	48,555	19.0
Rhode Island senate	47,080	486	18.1
Vermont house	33,155	38	11.6

Source: National Municipal League, *Compendium on Legislative Apportionment*, 2d ed. (New York: National Municipal League, Jan. 1962).

However, Allan Pulsipher and James Weatherby argued in 1968 that malapportionment depressed spending in some service categories in the states, whereas party competition elevated it.[25] Thus, while we cannot lay a major portion of the blame for urban woes on state legislative behavior resulting from malapportionment, it may have had some impact on state policy.

A Remedy for Malapportionment

The remedy for malapportionment came in the early 1960s by way of Supreme Court decisions. Until 1962 the federal courts had steadfastly refused to involve themselves in the apportionment question, arguing that the selection of a criterion for the drawing of representative boundaries was essentially a policy or "political" question, not a legal issue. The subject of apportionment criteria was not considered a judicial matter based on the constitutionally established separation of powers doctrine, which gives the legislative branches of government the chief responsibility for matters of public policy and specifies that the courts concern themselves only with legal questions.

The pre-1962 position of the Supreme Court is often illustrated by its decision in the 1946 case of *Colegrove v. Green*, in which the malapportionment of congressional seats in the state of Illinois was challenged as constituting a denial of the Fourteenth Amendment guarantee of equal protection of the law to everyone. In Colegrove, the Supreme Court ruled that the federal courts did not have jurisdiction over apportionment cases and that the remedy for malapportionment should be sought in the legislatures. But the Court was minus two members when the Colegrove decision was rendered, and one of the majority judges wrote an independent decision. Thus, the four-to-three decision was rather "soft." Nevertheless, the federal courts refused jurisdiction in apportionment cases until 1962.

The Supreme Court's decision in *Baker v. Carr* in 1962 overturned the Colegrove ruling. In the *Baker* case, which involved a Tennessee apportionment controversy, the Supreme Court decided that the federal courts did have jurisdiction in apportionment cases, since malapportionment violated the Fourteenth Amendment guarantee of equal protection of the laws. The *Baker* decision quickly led to many other suits in nearly every state challenging the apportionment schemes of state houses, state senates, and congressional districts. For example, in *Wesberry v. Sanders* (1964) the Supreme Court ruled that all congressional districts must contain substantially the same number of people, and in *Reynolds v. Sims* (1964) the Court applied the same principle to both houses of state legislatures. Several decisions rendered by the Court in the early 1970s indicated that, while the one person, one vote principle need not be realized with absolute precision, districting must be fair and deviations may not be extreme.

One Person, One Vote

Through reapportionment cases the Supreme Court firmly established the principle that one person's vote must count substantively as much as another's. Before the end of the 1960s, reapportionment had been accomplished in all states, either by the legislatures themselves or, when the legislature was unable or unwilling to do so, by the federal courts. Chief Justice Earl Warren, speaking for the Supreme Court majority in *Reynolds v. Sims* (1964), indicated clearly the position of the Court on districting:

> Legislators represent people, not trees or acres.
>
> Legislators are elected by voters, not farms or cities or economic interests.
>
> Weighting the votes of citizens differently, by any method or means, merely because of where they happen to reside, hardly seems justifiable. . . .
>
> Our constitutional system amply provides for the protection of minorities by means other than giving them majority control of state legislatures. . . .[26]

In some instances, however, the one person, one vote dictum has not translated into equal apportionment. The Court has insisted on strict equality when states are districted for the U.S. House of Representatives. But in terms of the states themselves, the Court has said that when a substantial state interest in some small deviation from perfect apportionment exists, such deviation is allowed.

Room for Flexibility

Through a series of decisions in the 1970s, the Supreme Court arrived at what some have called a "*de facto* plus or minus 10 percent" rule. That is, when the deviation in population between a state's most populous and least populus house or senate districts is less than 10 percent, any plaintiff challenging the plan carries the burden of proof as to why it should be disallowed. When a plan exceeds the 10 percent variance and is challenged, the state must show a clear state interest to justify the departure from strict equality.

The Court has allowed several states, including Wyoming, Virginia, Connecticut, and Texas, to operate with plans containing some departure from precise population equality. In a truly unique instance the Court allowed Wyoming in 1983 to employ a districting plan in which one district contained such a small population that there was a difference of 89 percent. The extreme deviation occurred because of a longstanding state constitutional rule that provided for at least one house member from each county. The Court found a state interest in preserving that historical condition (*Brown v. Thompson*, 1983). By and large, however, the Court has held the states to substantially equal population in legislative districts.

Many early critics had hoped that the end of rural domination of state politics would mark the start of a period of revitalization in state government and the allocation of increased public resources to urban problems. There is little evidence that this has happened, however. While rural influence has diminished in state legislative politics, it has not disappeared. Perhaps more important, there is often considerable friction between the urban and suburban blocs. Although the twentieth century has been marked by tremendous urban population growth, it was the suburbs, not the cities, that experienced the greatest growth between 1950 and 1970.

Gerrymandering

The phenomenon of gerrymandering is related to the apportionment issue. Although the Supreme Court now demands that all districts in a given state legislative or congressional chamber contain roughly the same number of people, it also indicates a willingness to invalidate apportionment schemes when districts are formed with the clear purpose of assigning certain people to one or another district on the basis of their party identification or race (*Davis v. Bandemer*, 1984; *Gomillion v. Lightfoot*, 1961). The opportunity still exists, however, for subtle manipulation of district lines to favor one group or party over another.

A **gerrymander** is an attempt to draw district lines in such a way as to maximize the voting power of one faction and minimize that of another. It often results in the creation of odd-shaped districts. A district may be perfectly apportioned and even have a rather normal shape, yet be horribly gerrymandered. While the term *gerrymander* often suggests very odd-shaped districts, it is also used to refer to attempts by political parties to draw district lines so as to maximize the electoral impact of their voters and minimize those of the opposition party.

A Hypothetical Case

Suppose that Congress and the Census Bureau entitle our hypothetical state to four seats in the House of Representatives. It is the task of the legislature of our state to come up with a plan to divide the state into four districts. Given the ruling of the Supreme Court, each of the districts must contain substantially the same number of people. Our state has 800,000 registered voters—485,000 registered Democrats and 315,000 registered Republicans. (Let us suppose, unrealistically, that these 800,000 registered voters are the only people in the state and that they all vote for their registered party.)

It is possible for the legislature of our hypothetical state to draw the four districts in any number of shapes, including plans A–F as suggested in Figure 4.3. Just as the shape of congressional districts can vary, so too can the distribution of registered Democrats and Republicans within the various districts, with a highly significant impact on the electoral outcome. Table 4.8 shows the electoral outcomes of districting plans A, B, and C in the figure. Note how partisan distribution can vary and change the outcome of elections without violating the Court's one person, one vote dictum. Although each district in the three hypothetical plans contains the same number of persons—200,000—the electoral outcomes would clearly differ. Under districting plan A in Table 4.8, the Democrats would have a significant edge in statewide voter registration and would likely win all four congressional seats. However, if we shuffled the voters around according to plan B, the Republicans would capture two of the four seats even though they are the minority party. Under plan C (which is admittedly absurd), the minority party would capture three of the four congressional seats, and the Democrats would have a 200,000 to 0 landslide victory in district 1.

The hypothetical districting options suggested here and in Figure 4.3 and Table 4.8 are, of course, grossly oversimplified. Even so, they point to the

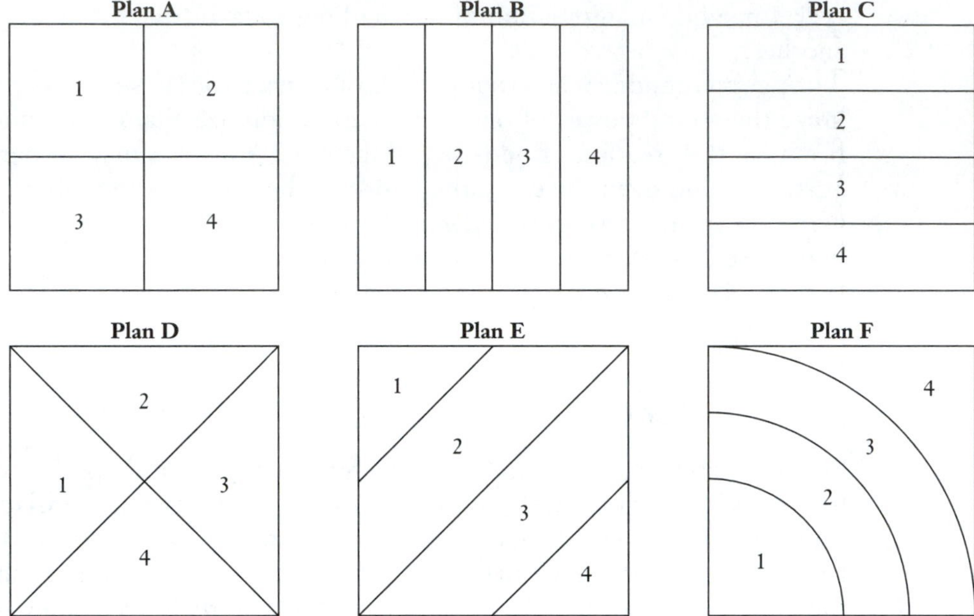

Figure 4.3 Six Hypothetical State Districting Plans

kinds of advantages a party can gain through manipulation of district boundaries. The courts have long held that gross and obvious tinkering with district boundaries and the creation of contorted district shapes will not be tolerated when it can be shown that such districting results in the denial of equal protection of the law to someone. But the door is still open to all sorts of subtle maneuvering to gain partisan advantage. It obviously matters very much, then, which political party is in the majority in a state legislature at reapportionment time.

Table 4.8 Hypothetical Districting Plans and Electoral Outcomes

	Plan A		Plan B		Plan C	
District	*Democrats*	*Republicans*	*Democrats*	*Republicans*	*Democrats*	*Republicans*
1	120,000	80,000	150,000	50,000	200,000	0
2	120,000	80,000	150,000	50,000	95,000	105,000
3	120,000	80,000	90,000	110,000	95,000	105,000
4	125,000	75,000	95,000	105,000	95,000	105,000
Total	485,000	315,000	485,000	315,000	485,000	315,000

The Position of the Courts

The voting rights legislation of 1982 requires that any jurisdiction with a history of denying electoral political equality to racial minorities secure clearance from the U.S. Department of Justice or the U.S. District Court in Washington, D.C., before altering district boundaries or making any other election system changes. The legislation also prohibits states from using voting systems that result in discriminatory practices or that reduce the political role of racial minorities.

In addition, recent Supreme Court decisions may affect the ability of parties to gerrymander for political purposes. In *Davis v. Bandemer* (1984), for example, the Court ruled that gerrymandering is within the Court's jurisdiction when it functions to harm the other party. In this Indiana case, Democrats accused controlling Republican legislators of unconstitutionally depriving them of equal protection of the law. The Court consented to hear the case but found insufficient evidence to justify the claim. More recently, in the California case of *Badham v. Eu* (1988), Republicans accused Democrats of districting California's U.S. House seats to reduce their fair share of members. Here the Court found that the Republicans' claim of being shut out of the political process could not be sustained.

Today the Court has yet to disallow a districting plan just because it has the effect of advantaging one or the other party. But the Court is quick to void plans that, by either intent or results, diminish the voting and representative power of minorities.[27]

Control of state houses, state senates, and the governorship is always important to political parties, but especially so at the start of each decade, when state legislatures and U.S. House district lines are redrawn. Both houses of a state's legislature and the state's contingent of congressional seats must be reapportioned after each census. As is the case with legislative bills generally, new congressional districting plans are developed and passed by the legislature and signed by the governor—unless, for some legal reason, the courts must step in. In many states, the reapportionment of state legislative seats is handled in the same fashion.

Once district lines are set, they remain for ten years. In the 1990 elections, for instance, the biggest prize to be won was generally considered that of the governor's chair, especially in such large and growing states as California, Florida, and Texas. Because of the 1990 census, those three states gained thirteen new U.S. House seats and, for the final decade of the twentieth century, would be sending 105 members to the 435-member U.S. House. In all three states Democrats controlled the legislatures. Democratic governors, thus, could work with Democratic legislators to devise districting schemes that would help their party. Republican governors, possessing the veto, could bargain with the Democrats and press for districting plans that helped Republicans or were somewhat neutral in their impact. As it turned out, Democratic governors won in Texas and Florida, while a Republican prevailed in a close contest in California.

Representational Roles

The selection of a criterion for legislative districting involves in part a normative judgment and, because of recent Supreme Court decisions, a primary focus on population. However, other matters related to the question of representation also merit attention. What should the role of the representative be? How does the representative actually view that role? What might the role of the representative encompass? Here are three different views on the role of the representative in a democracy.

Representatives as Mirrors

Some observers argue that a representative should only strive to function as a link between constituents and public policy decisions. In the **mirror role**, the representative "mirrors" the preferences of the people. The representative is a device for simplifying the problem of achieving government by the people.

For those who support this view, direct democracy is preferable to representative government because the individual is the best judge of his or her own values and does not need others in the legislative chambers or in the courtroom to make decisions. But since direct democracy is an impractical way to arrive at collective judgments in a crowded and complex world, people must resort to representative government and try to make it reflect voters' wishes.

Representatives as Oracles

Others argue that representatives should use their superior insight and access to information to benefit the people. This is called the **oracle role** because lawmakers predict rather than attempt to figure out constituents' needs.

Supporters of the oracle role prefer it over the mirror role because they believe that the electoral processes seek out the best people to serve in communities. Others support the oracle role for a more practical reason: Given legislators' access to information and their proximity to the seats of power, they are privy to facts and problems unknown to the average voter and, therefore, can make informed judgments.

Representatives as Brokers

Another view of the legislator's role is termed the **broker role**. Here lawmakers neither try to transfer constituents' preferences into law nor follow their own wisdom. Rather, legislators' major task is to play the game and make the trades that will benefit constituents' interests. The broker role is actually a combination of the mirror role, the oracle role, and a little crass self-interest.

Knowing that public policy results in the allocation of scarce societal goods and services, legislators as brokers make the trades and deals necessary to ensure that their district is the beneficiary of a fair share of what is available. Of course, legislators must make judgments about what their district wants and needs, and they may be assisted in making these judgments by consulting constituents. In general, though, these legislators do what is necessary to bring into their district public benefits for schools, roads, parks, and so on. Supporters of the oracle role might call a broker an immoral dealer. The broker might reply that the real world is composed of conflicting interests and many diverse images of the public good, and that as such it requires compromise. It also requires that members stick with their party and party leaders much of the time if they wish to be successful.

The Demographics of Legislators

If being a representative means possessing the characteristics of one's constituents, then American state legislators are unrepresentative in many ways. Compared to the larger population, state lawmaking bodies are overly populated with men, whites, older people, people with higher-than-average incomes, better-educated Americans, and professionals and businesspeople.

Not everyone has the desire or resources to run for public office, and not everyone can afford to take time away from other pursuits to sit in a legislature from sixty to two hundred days a year. Young people often lack the money, experience, and occupational flexibility to serve. Poor people are too busy trying to support themselves. Working people seldom have the occupational flexibility needed to run a campaign and trot off to the state capitol. Therefore, many Americans cannot serve in public office, for a variety of reasons.

Over the years, legislatures have had relatively few women and minority members. Until recently there were few women and minorities who possessed all or most of the resources needed for successful pursuit of a state legislative seat—interest, education, money, and flexibility. They may have had the interest but lacked the money or occupational flexibility. Or they may have had the ability, money, and time, but no interest. In addition, deeply rooted attitudes among voters often discouraged either the candidacy or the electoral success of women and minorities. For years the laws and political practices in some southern states made it difficult for African Americans to vote, much less run successfully for public office.

Many of these patterns have been changing. The heavy representation of lawyers in state legislatures is receding, though the number of businesspeople and other professionals (educators, for example) is growing. In 1990 there were 422 African American state legislators, or 5.7 percent of the total of 7461. Hispanics totalled 119, or just 1.6 percent. The 1992 election produced an increase to 514 African Americans and 161 Hispanics. The increases in African Americans were concentrated in the South, Georgia, Louisiana, Mississippi, and Florida especially. Hispanic gains were most pronounced in California, New Mexico, Texas, and New York.[28]

The number of women legislators is increasing as well. Whereas in 1969 only 4 percent of the states' lawmakers were women, by 1990 that figure had grown to over 17 percent and by 1995 to over 20 percent (see Figure 4.4). The states with the highest percentages of women legislators are Washington (39.5 percent), Nevada (34.9 percent), Colorado (32 percent), Arizona (30 percent), and New Hampshire (30 percent). States with the most modernized legislatures rank well in this area.[29] Southern states rank low.

Women are making their presence known in positions of leadership, too. In 1989, fifteen women held the position of either presiding officer of a

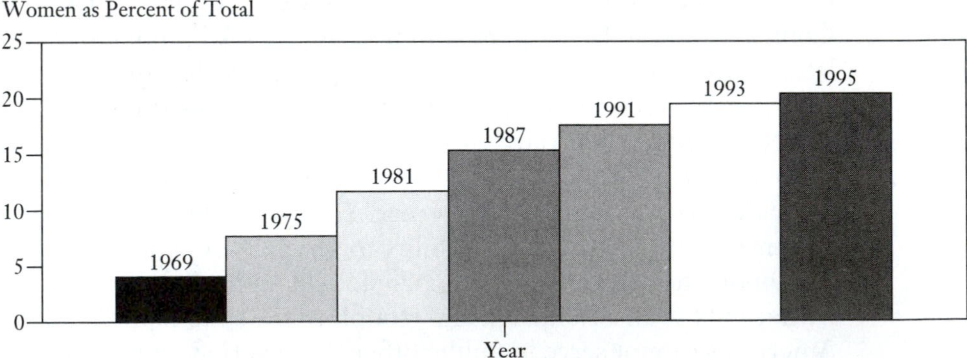

Figure 4.4 Women in State Legislatures, 1969–1997
Sources: Rutgers University Center for the American Woman and Politics, "Women in State Legislatures, 1997" and *Statistical Abstract*, various years.

chamber or majority or minority floor leader. One such leader, Vera Katz, a speaker of the Oregon house of representatives and a Democrat, was first elected to the Oregon house in 1972. Over the years she joined forces with other women in the chamber, members of both parties, to press issues of concern to women.[30] Vera Katz is not alone as a female legislative leader. In the early 1990s women have held the senate presidency in Connecticut, Vermont, Delaware, and North Dakota. Ramona Barnes served as Alaska's house speaker. Women were minority party leaders in a dozen senates and a half dozen houses. In 1995 and 1996 the entire Colorado minority party leadership contingent was female, and in 1997 both the majority and minority leaders are women. Female legislative leadership is no longer an anomaly in states.

There is some evidence that changing legislative demographics can lead to changing public policy. A study conducted by the Center for American Women and Politics at Rutgers University indicates that women legislators are more apt than their male counterparts to resist state laws banning abortion. For example, 38 percent of the men polled and 26 percent of the women polled strongly supported laws banning abortion. The study also suggests that Republicans of both sexes are more favorably disposed than Democrats to such legal prohibitions.[31]

Various factors thus influence the voting behavior of state lawmakers—political party, constituents' desires, advice from other legislators or the leadership, and personal values.[32] Gender and race, like schooling, age, and economic and occupational circumstances, also shape attitudes and behavior. As the demographics of state legislatures continue to change, albeit slowly, public policy will shift as well.

Tenure and Turnover

Legislative turnover is both a problem in and of itself and a reflection of conditions within state legislatures. Before modernization, the chambers were internally undemocratic and often under the thumb of one or a few heavy-handed veterans. With little chance of playing a meaningful role in the process, the newly elected soon left. Of course, the poor or nonexistent pay and the absence of staff assistance and adequate office space contributed to high turnover as well.

With high turnover, most premodernized legislatures were composed primarily of novices—lawmakers unfamiliar with many issues, with the arguments on two sides of an issue, and with the probable consequences of proposed legislation. Their lack of background knowledge, coupled with the absence or shortage of staff, tended to force lawmakers to rely on the lobby corps for information and voting cues. Although lobbyists had to be honest and reliable to be effective in the long run, they were also in the employ of special interests with self-serving stakes in legislative outcomes.

The remedy, critics argued, was longer tenure. Indeed, with the improved pay, staff help, and facilities that came with the reforms of the 1960s and 1970s legislative turnover declined significantly (see Table 4.9). For example, whereas in 1978 at least 30 percent of the membership in state legislatures was new in thirty-four of the ninety-nine chambers, by 1988 the number had dropped to just nine. The decline in legislative turnover was especially high in the most modernized states. In California, for example, new membership fell from 25 percent in the senate and 31 percent in the house in 1978 to just 8 percent and 10 percent, respectively, in 1988. The decline in Ohio in the same period went from 15 percent to 6 percent in the senate and from 18 percent to 7 percent in the house.

Scholars who study state legislative turnover link the increasing stability of legislative membership to modernization. In a 1988 study of twenty-five states, Squire Perverill indicates that improved salaries and opportunities for advancement lead to membership stability.[33] In a related finding, legislative experts Malcolm Jewell and David Breaux document the growth in the winning electoral margins of state legislative incumbents—an indication that legislators are finding careers in state houses and senates more to their liking and are replicating the political strategy of members of Congress when they attempt to maintain their positions.[34] In a 1986 study on why state legislators voluntarily leave office, Wayne Francis and John Baker note that one common reason given is the pursuit of other political ambitions.[35] It appears, then, that the re-

TABLE 4.9 LEGISLATIVE TURNOVER RATES, 1978, 1988, AND 1994

		New Membership (as a percentage of total membership)					
	Year	−10%	10–19%	20–29%	30–39%	40–49%	+50%
Number of	1978	1	19	41	22	9	3
Legislative	1988	13	40	28	7	2	0
Chambers*	1994	8	29	28	11	4	0

*Number of chambers does not total 99 because not all states held elections shortly before 1978 and 1988, and in 1994.
Source: Calculated from data in *The Book of the States, 1980–81, 1990–91, and 1996–97* (Lexington, Ky.: Council of State Governments, 1981, 1991, and 1996), pp. 103, 124, and 70 respectively.

cent era of modernization has produced meaningful changes in legislative membership.

In an ironic turn of events, the extension of legislative tenure called for by early critics is now producing complaints of a different sort. Many contemporary critics argue that a growing number of state legislators are behaving like their counterparts in Congress. With better pay and working conditions, it is claimed, many legislators are looking to make elective office a career and thus spend an increasing portion of their time solidifying their electoral base. Newsletters, questionnaires, and constituent service—anything that keeps the incumbent's name in the forefront—become the agenda, it is argued. At the same time, the costs of election campaigns are soaring and the role of political action committees in financing them is growing. It is argued that career advancement is displacing effective governing as the legislator's main objective.

Disillusionment with some of the consequences of a modernized, or "congressionalized," legislature was recently expressed in citizen-initiated efforts to limit the legal tenure of lawmakers. In 1990 voters in three states—California, Colorado, and Oklahoma—had the opportunity to approve constitutional amendment proposals to impose tenure limits. All three proposals passed. In California, house members may serve six years and senate members eight years. Service in the affected legislative and executive public offices is limited to twelve years in Oklahoma and to eight years in Colorado. In 1992 voters in fourteen other states followed suit and adopted term limits. By 1997, nearly half of the states had term limits for their state legislatures.

Opponents argue that tenure limitations deprive the voter of a full range of choices, saddle legislators with a constant flow of inexperienced lawmakers, and spell a return to the troublesome days when lobbyists were informed and experienced but elected officials were not. Whatever the pros and cons of tenure restrictions, it appears that voters do not fully support all of the results of the modernized, professionalized legislatures. The virtues of the citizen legislature are thus receiving renewed attention.

Evidence suggests that term limits are having an early impact on legislative turnover and are pushing us back to the higher rates of decades past. Referring once again to Table 4.9, we see that the number of legislative chambers experiencing turnover of 30 percent or more jumped to eleven in 1994, up from just seven in 1988. Even though term limits do not yet impact many sitting lawmakers, some incumbents are leaving early to seek other offices or move from the house to the senate in anticipation of being ousted by the limits. Ironically, if this trend continues, we may expect to hear critics complain about the shortcomings of legislatures populated by inexperienced amateurs, just as we did before the reforms of the 1960s and 1970s.

Summary

Today's state legislatures are arguably the centerpieces of the institutional arrangement of American state government. The state legislature writes the laws and controls the purse strings. The shape of much of the executive and judicial branches is determined by legislatively drawn statutes. The size of the budget and the configuration of tax laws are set by the legislature. The shape, roles, and powers of local governments are products of legislative action.

Early in U.S. history, the legislature was indeed the supreme branch. The founders feared concentrated executive authority. Over the years state legislatures fell into some disrepute and were often manipulated by governors and special interests. The public good suffered. More recently state legislatures reformed themselves to varying degrees, and they are now more effective and reputable institutions.

The manner in which state government in general and state legislatures in particular are organized has significant political consequences. The deliberate separation of the legislative and executive functions builds into the system the potential for conflict. So does the division of the legislature into two chambers. In recent years well over half of the states experienced divided government, in which one political party controlled one or both legislative chambers while the other party held the other chamber, the governorship, or both. This combination of institutional design and split party control leads to conflict.

The states have modernized their legislative institutions, and this too has had consequences. Better pay, enhanced staffing, longer sessions—these and other changes have freed legislatures from some gubernatorial and special interest group influence, thus addressing some of the criticisms of decades past. But modernization has also created more career politicians. Many citizen legislators still serve, but there are fewer of them. Institutional modernization, contemporary observers argue, has led to increased power of incumbency and lower electoral competition, more costly elections, greater reliance on special interest group money, weakened legislative leadership, and greater internal decentralization and fragmentation. In their heightened concern for reelection, legislators may tend to worry more about their district and less about the larger statewide good.

The powers of legislatures, governors, courts, and local governments, the levels of conflict and cooperation among the branches of government and chambers of a legislature, the behavior of politicians and the strategies they employ—these are all determined in large measure by the shape of the institutions within which they operate.

Policy Perspective

In the most fundamental sense, legislatures are the fount of virtually all public policy. Our most basic policies, those housed in constitutions, are often proposed by citizens through initiative processes or constitutional conventions and then ratified by the full electorate, but aside from this, policy is legislatively created. Executive branch agencies too may be said to create policy as they write rules and regulations. But rules and regulations themselves are rooted in the policies adopted by legislatures. This is the way the system is designed; legislatures are supposed to be the policy bodies.

As we close out the twentieth century, our state legislatures find themselves grappling with one of the more complicated and difficult policy areas of all, namely welfare. For decades now, welfare policy as well as all social services policies have been intergovernmental. The national government has formulated the basic structure of the system and paid for a good share of it; the states have provided the details about eligibility and benefit levels and paid much of the welfare bill; and local governments and counties have administered the programs. But in 1996 the Congress wrote into law a radically changed welfare system, and President Clinton signed the bill. Since then, state legislatures have struggled to rewrite their laws to conform to the new model.

Origin of the Current System

The roots of America's welfare system go all the way back to the "poor laws" of Elizabethan England. The poor were viewed as slothful or improvident or both, and their care was viewed as the concern of local governments, or as private matters. This perspective carried on into early America where churches and private charities cared for the poor, and county governments maintained "poor farms," "poor houses," and county hospitals.

This all changed in the 1930s. The Great Depression hit, and it did so with such force to render unemployed, and poor, an enormously enlarged portion of the American public. In the depths of the Depression one could no longer argue that bad luck, God's will, or sheer laziness fully explained a person's need for help. The economy was in the dumps and millions of hardworking middle-class moms and dads were on the street and unable to care adequately for their families.

In this environment in 1935, Congress, with President Franklin Roosevelt leading the way, enacted the Social Security Act that laid the foundation for a new social services system, which has endured, with some periodic modifications, until 1997.

Welfare from 1935–1996

The 1935 Social Security Act is best known for its establishment of a system of old age payments, but it also contained a provision for Aid to Families with Dependent Children. AFDC, as it is known, has been the core program in our social services system from 1935 to 1997, and it established the national government as a central figure in the system. Under AFDC, states established eligibility for receipt of welfare payments, and also set the payment levels, albeit within guidelines established by Congress. The national and state governments shared the cost.

There were other programs too. The Social Security Act also created programs for the poor, the blind, the elderly, and the disabled; in 1972, these were combined into "supplemental security income," or SSI. The national government ran the SSI Program, although states were authorized to supplement federal payments and many did so.

In 1940 the national government established the Food Stamps Program, and in 1965 it created Medicaid. Food stamps are designed to help poor people buy food, of course, and Medicaid, not to be confused with the Medicare program for the elderly of all income levels, is a program of medical care for poor people. The Food Stamp Program is funded by the national government, while Medicaid has been jointly paid for by the national and state governments. In addition to these, the states have established a variety of smaller targeted programs for various categories of needy persons.

The programs cited above, from AFDC and SSI to Food Stamps and Medicaid and individual state programs collectively constitute "welfare" or social services. This bundle of programs have been both increasingly costly to the states, and the object of extensive criticism and controversy.

Pressure for Change

During the 1980s and into the 1990s, the costs of social services, Medicaid especially, placed growing pressure on state budgets, and thus state legislatures. Along with the rapidly rising costs associated with crime, corrections and prisons, social service budgets began to eat away at the funds available for schools, roads, and other state programs. In the 1980s, for example, Medicaid costs grew three times faster than that of state budgets generally. This was caused in part by the expanded and increasingly costly array of medical treatments, and expanded eligibility for Medicaid as dictated by Congress. State legislatures responded by experimenting with managed care systems in which primary care doctors serve as gatekeepers to specialized treatments.

But the welfare system was also controversial for its failure to eliminate, or at least reduce, the need for its own existence. Rather than helping the poor climb out of poverty and into gainful employment and self-sufficiency, the system seemed to trap people into lives of poverty and dependence. Notwithstanding the fact that the vast majority of the poor were and are young, occupationally unskilled mothers with young children, the image of welfare recipients as lazy freeloaders who preferred welfare to work became widespread.

Pressure to change the welfare system mounted, and in 1996 Congress and President Clinton agreed to scrap much of the old system that had been in place for over sixty years. The president and members of Congress used language like "ending welfare as we know it," and "moving Americans from welfare to work."

These 1996 changes took place in an environment characterized by broad opinion held by both citizens and political leaders that much of what the national government does should be decentralized. The term "devolution" enjoyed widespread use in the early 1990s, as governors and mayors, joined by national politicians and many citizens, called for a reduction, if not an end, to congressional mandates imposed on the states in one policy area after another. The push moved governmental functions to the state and local level, and let the states and localities figure out how to run them.

The 1996 changes in America's welfare policies, thus, were responses to several political pressures. There was pressure to control the costs of social services that were squeezing state budgets. There was pressure to scrap what was widely viewed as a failed welfare system. And there were political demands to rid states of what were viewed as rigid and excessive rules and regulations—mandates—emanating from Washington, D.C.

The New Welfare System

What does the new welfare system look like? How does it compare to the old one? Is it better? Under the old system, which allowed for individual state waivers of certain federal requirements, there was some state experimentation, in Wisconsin most notably. Now, in the late 1990s, experimentation is the name of the game in all fifty states, and thus the shape of the system will be evolving for some time to come. Quite simply, it will be years before we know the results of the new approach with any degree of certainty.

As with the old system, the general parameters are set forth by Congress in national statutes. Congress has said that there will now be a lifetime eligibility limit of five years on welfare. States may make legal and illegal immigrants ineligible. Teen moms must live at home and go to school to be eligible. Recipients must work or be in a job-training program, and by 2002 half of all recipients in each state must be working, although 20 percent of the recipients may be exempted from this requirement. States are now given block grants from the national government and, within such guidelines as those just noted, the states may design their own system.

Now, more than in the last sixty years, welfare decisions are in the hands of state legislators, and as we approach the end of the century, they are making tough choices. State legislators are having to decide how much benefits will be. They will have to decide what to do about day care for young parents, who now must leave home to work. They will decide if grandparents who end up mothering their grandkids are eligible for benefits and if so, whether they must work. Lawmakers will have to decide which state pays for a child from one state cared for by a parent or grandparent in another. They will be deciding which, if any, poor legal aliens may receive medical care under Medicaid. They will have to figure out what to do with grandparents with grandkids who used up their five years of eligibility raising their own children. Will teen parents be pressured to live in group homes? Will divorced parents be allowed to keep whatever child support they can get out of a deadbeat parent?

The list of questions goes on and on, and will be answered by different sets of lawmakers in the fifty states. There will be variety among the states, and there will be modifications from year to year when some approaches seem to work while others do not. The states may well discover that moving people "from welfare to work" is costly and that new approaches cost more, not less. The federal block grants may prove to be inadequate, putting even more pressure on state budgets. In addition, the Congress is sure to tinker with the law; it always does.

Welfare policy will continue to be an intergovernmental affair. With less congressional micromanagement, the role of the states has increased, but so too have the hard choices and the headaches. Special interest group pressure at the state level is greater than ever, as advocates for seniors, children, and the disabled all fight for broad eligibility and generous benefits within the context of limited resources.

The states have long lobbied for a greater voice in social services policy. Now they have it.

KEY TERMS

reformed legislature
legislative turnover
logjam
citizen legislature model
political action committees (PACs)
legislative process
legislative committee
conference committee
power pocket

legislative veto
line-item veto
rules committee
calendar committee
bicameral legislature
unicameral legislature
party caucus
leadership powers
bipartisan coalition
joint committee
committee on committees
apportionment
reapportionment
malapportionment
gerrymander
mirror role
oracle role
broker role

ADDITIONAL READING

Chasen, Daniel J. *Speaker of the House: The Political Career and Life of John L. O'Brien* (Seattle: University of Washington Press, 1990).

Ehrenhalt, Alan. "An Embattled Institution." *Governing* (Jan. 1992): 30.

Hanson, Royce. *Tribune of the People: The Minnesota Legislature and Its Leadership* (Minneapolis: University of Minnesota Press, 1989).

Jewell, Malcolm E., and Penny Miller. *The Kentucky Legislature: Two Decades of Change* (Lexington, Ky.: University of Kentucky Press, 1988).

Rosenthal, Alan. *Governors and Legislatures: Contending Powers* (Washington, D.C.: Congressional Quarterly Press, 1990).

———. *Legislative Life: People, Process, Performance* (New York: Harper & Row, 1981).

Straayer, John A. *The Colorado General Assembly* (Niwot, Colo.: University Press of Colorado, 1990).

NOTES

1. Robert X. Browning, "Indiana Elects Democratic Governor and Equally Divided House," *Comparative State Politics* (April 1989): 1–2, and *State Legislatures* (December 1996): 14.
2. Quoted in Thomas R. Morris and Larry Sabato, eds., *Virginia Government and Politics* (Charlottesville: Institute of Governments, University of Virginia, 1984), p. 79.
3. Jonathan Waters, "A Night on the Town Isn't What It Used to Be in Jefferson City," *Governing* (July 1989): 26–31.
4. Alan Ehrenhalt, "An Embattled Institution," *Governing* (Jan. 1992): 30.
5. For an excellent discussion of the modernization of state legislatures since the mid-1960s and its consequences, see Alan Rosenthal, "The Legislature: Unraveling of Institutional Fabric," in *The State of the States*, ed. Carl E. Van Horn (Washington, D.C.: Congressional Quarterly Press, 1996), pp. 77–107.
6. Donald A. Gross, "House-Senate Conference Committees: A Comparative State Perspective," *American Journal of Political Science* (Nov. 1980): 769–78.
7. John A. Straayer, "How Prevalent Are State Legislative Conference Committees?" *Comparative State Politics* (April 1996), p. 6.
8. See Malcolm E. Jewell, *The State Legislature* (New York: Random House, 1969), ch. 3.
9. *The Book of the States, 1996–97* (Lexington, Ky.: Council of State Governments, 1996), pp. 98–99.
10. See *The Book of the States, 1996–97* (Lexington, Ky.: Council of State Governments, 1996), pp. 93–97.

11. John C. Wahlke, Heinz Eulau, William Buchanan, and L. C. Ferguson, *The Legislative System* (New York: Wiley, 1962), pp. 146, 147, 154.
12. Quoted in Alan Ehrenhalt, "A Coup in Connecticut: The Unmaking of a Leader—and Its Consequences," *Governing* (Aug. 1990): 74–79.
13. Alan Rosenthal, "A Vanishing Breed," *State Legislatures* (Nov.–Dec. 1989): 30–34.
14. Karen Hansen, "Elections 1992: The Message Is Mixed," *State Legislatures* (Dec. 1992): 13.
15. Malcolm Jewell, "The Durability of Leadership," *State Legislatures* (Nov.–Dec. 1989): 10–11, 21.
16. Alan Rosenthal, "There's Power in Campaign Bucks," *State Legislatures* (Nov.–Dec. 1989): 34.
17. Rob Gurwitt, "How to Succeed at Running a Legislature: Pack a Mighty Wallet," *Governing* (May 1990): 26–31.
18. *The Book of the States, 1996–97* (Lexington, Ky.: Council of State Governments, 1996), p. 113.
19. Nelson Polsby, "The Institutionalization of the U.S. House of Representatives," *American Political Science Review* (March 1968): 144–68.
20. Keith Hamm, "The Role of Subgovernments in U.S. State Policy-Making: An Exploratory Analysis," *Legislative Studies Quarterly* (Aug. 1986): 321–52.
21. For discussions of consequences of well-staffed professional legislatures, see William T. Pound, "Legislatures: Our Dynamic Institutions," *State Legislatures* (Jan. 1993): 22–25; and Rich Jones, "The Legislature 2010: Which Direction?" *State Legislatures* (July 1990): 22–25.
22. Susan W. Furniss, "Reapportionment in Colorado" (M.A. thesis, Colorado State University, 1967).
23. Herbert Jacob, "The Consequences of Malapportionment: A Note of Caution," *Social Forces* (Dec. 1964): 256–61.
24. Thomas R. Dye, "Malapportionment and Public Policy in the States," *Journal of Politics* (Aug. 1965): 599. See also Richard I. Hofferbert, "The Relationship between Public Policy and Some Structural and Environmental Variables in the American States," *American Political Science Review* (March 1966): 82; and John C. Grumm, "The Effects of Legislative Structure on Legislative Performance," in *State and Urban Politics*, ed. Richard I. Hofferbert and Ira Sharkansky (Boston: Little, Brown, 1971), pp. 298–322.
25. Allan G. Pulsipher and James L. Weatherby, Jr., "Malapportionment Party Competition and the Functional Distribution of Governmental Expenditures," *American Political Science Review* (Dec. 1968): 1207–19.
26. *Reynolds v. Sims*, 377 U.S. 533 (1964).
27. Task Force, "Reapportionment Law: The 1990s" (National Conference of State Legislatures, Denver, Colorado, Oct. 1989).
28. Rich Jones, "The State Legislatures," in *The Book of the States, 1990–91* (Lexington, Ky.: Council of State Governments, 1991), p. 111.
29. Ibid. See also *Women in Elective Office*, fact sheet (Rutgers University, Center for American Women and Politics, Eagleton Institute of Politics, 11 July 1988), p. 2.
30. Foster Church, "Just Like a Woman," *Governing* (Sept. 1990): 26–30.
31. "Lawmakers' Abortion Votes Are Influenced by Gender," *Governing* (Aug. 1989): 17.
32. See Cole Blease Graham, Jr., and Kenny J. Whitby, "Party-Based Voting in a Southern State Legislature," *American Politics Quarterly* (April 1989): 181–93; Gregory A. Calderia and Samuel C. Patterson, "Political Friendship in the Legislature," *Journal of Politics* (Nov. 1987): 953–75; Warren E. Miller and Donald E. Stokes, "Constituency Influence in Congress," *American Political Science Review* (March 1963): 45–56; Herbert McCloskey, Paul J. Hoffman, and

Rosemary O'Hara, "Issue Conflict and Consensus among Party Leaders and Followers," *American Political Science Review* (June 1960): 406–27; and Herbert McCloskey, "Consensus and Ideology in American Politics," *American Political Science Review* (June 1984): 361–79.

33. Perverill Squire, "Career Opportunities and Membership Stability in Legislatures," *Legislative Studies Quarterly* (Feb. 1988): 65–82.

34. Malcolm E. Jewell and David Breaux, "The Effects of Incumbency on State Legislative Elections," *Legislative Studies Quarterly* (Nov. 1988): 495–514.

35. Wayne L. Francis and John R. Baker, "Why Do U.S. State Legislators Vacate Their Seats?" *Legislative Studies Quarterly* (Feb. 1986): 119–26.

CHAPTER 5

The State Executive

Governor Christine Todd Whitman waves to supporters as she departs for a reelection campaign bus tour of New Jersey. *(Charles Rex Arbogast/AP/Wide World Photos)*

The Modern State Governor

Increased Responsibility
Greater Visibility
Tough Competition for the Job

Focus 5.1: Mudslinging in Minnesota

Focus 5.2: Running for Governor

Roles of the Governor

Chief Administrator
Party Leader
State Symbol
Policy Leader

Focus 5.3: Pottys and Priorities

Policy Coordinator

Sources of Gubernatorial Power

Visibility
Executive Authority
The Political Party
The Veto
Appointment Power
Budget Power
Tenure
Lobbying

Limits on Executive Power

The Plural Executive
Reform Proposal: The Integrated Executive
The Bureaucratic Organization
Bureaucratic Reform
Bureaucratic Control
Agency–Clientele Ties
Sunk Costs

Governors' Powers: A Comparison

Executive Strength and Leadership

• • • **OTHER STATE EXECUTIVES**
The Lieutenant Governor
The Attorney General
The Secretary of State
The State Treasurer

• • • **THE GOVERNOR AND SEPARATION OF POWERS**

• • • **SUMMARY**

• • • **POLICY PERSPECTIVE**

The Modern State Governor

wo days before the November 1990 elections, a *New York Times* article reported that:

> From New England to California, the fiercest battles of the 1990 election are being fought for governor, as voters pick the men, and perhaps women, who will shape everything from taxes to the political districts that [U.S.] House members will serve for the next decade. The political stakes are so high that when all the accounts are tallied, more than a quarter of a billion dollars will have been spent.[1]

In recent years the post of governor has been an increasingly attractive political position. Just as modernization has changed the state legislative institution, so too has it affected the state executive branch. A number of states have lengthened their chief executive's term of office from two years to four years; today only the governors of New Hampshire, Rhode Island, and Vermont serve for two years.[2] Several states that previously had not permitted a governor to serve two consecutive terms have now relaxed that restriction. In addition, there has been some reduction in the number of other directly elective executive branch slots, positions from which the incumbents could operate independently of the governor.

Governors have been given broader powers to reorganize their bureaucracies without having to await legislative action. In many states the governor's staff has been expanded, which has enhanced the chief executive's capabilities with respect to budgeting and planning.[3] Together, these recent changes have strengthened state governors and enhanced their political roles and visibility.

Increased Responsibility

The devolution of responsibility from the national government to the states for funding many domestic programs over the past decade or so has contributed to the expanded, more visible role of the state governor. Increasingly, the states have had to fend for themselves in the underwriting of environmental, health, and educational programs. While the national government has imposed more and more requirements on the states as conditions for continued federal funding, governors have had to become involved in complying with the requirements and paying the bills.

Enhanced executive authority and the states' expanded policy responsibilities have combined and have dramatically transformed the position of state governor from one of mild importance to one at center stage in American politics. Several widely respected scholars of the American governorship recognize the modern role of the state chief executive. According to Thad Beyle and Lynn Muchmore: "During the mid-twentieth century, the American governorship has grown in importance not only within the states themselves, but also within the context of our federal system of government."[4] Similarly, Coleman Ransone observes that "During the last thirty years the American governor has emerged as a policy leader of no mean proportions."[5]

This increased importance of the position of governor is evident both in the credentials of individuals who seek the post and in the fact that former governors have recently been presidents or presidential candidates. In 1990, for instance, former U.S. Senator Lawton Chiles of Florida and sitting U.S. Senator Pete Wilson of California ran for governor of their respective states. Both won. Cecil Andrus of Idaho served as governor, left to become U.S. Secretary of the Interior, and then returned to run successfully for his old slot as governor. Others have served once as a state's chief executive, left that office, but then sought it again, including Orval Faubus of Arkansas, George Wallace of Alabama, Michael Dukakis of Massachusetts, John Y. Brown of Kentucky, and Richard Snelling of Vermont. Jimmy Carter and Ronald Reagan both served as state governors before winning the presidency. Dukakis, California's Jerry Brown, Michigan's George Romney, Lamar Alexander from Tennessee and Wallace of Alabama have all sought the presidency. In 1992 and again in 1996 Bill Clinton won the presidency having previously served as governor of Arkansas.

Not all governors have been former U.S. Senators or are destined to become presidents or presidential candidates. Many have had political careers as state legislators, state treasurers, state attorney generals, or in some other elected position. One recent study shows that most state governors have served in their state legislature, in another statewide office, or both.[6]

Greater Visibility

The growing importance of state governors is also evident in the changing public roles they are playing. The National Governors Association (NGA) has emerged in recent years as an increasingly visible and respected voice for states and governors alike. In late 1990, the NGA joined other groups in publicly criticizing a new federal policy that would have withheld highway funds from states refusing to revoke the driver's licenses of drug offenders. Following the 1994 Republican takeover of Congress, Republican governors including Michigan's John Engler, Wisconsin's Tommy Thompson, and New Jersey's Christine Todd Whitman became significant voices in national policy debates. The governors were important participants in the 1995 and 1996 discussions leading to changes in the welfare system. Governors do not always get their way, but they do constitute a meaningful and respected collective voice in American politics.

Modern governors are also increasingly visible policy leaders within their own states. Wisconsin's Governor Tommy G. Thompson describes the expanded role of the modern American governor in this way:

> American governors consider two of their most vital tasks to be broadening their state's economic base and providing opportunities for their citizens. Thus, governors have led efforts to guide and stimulate economic development and job creation for more than twenty years. As the world has become smaller, so governors' economic development strategies have become more far-reaching. Now that economic opportunities are more international in scope, governors' efforts must extend beyond state and national borders.[7]

Not all governors employ the same strategies in their public life, and for some the highly public role can compensate for shortcomings in other areas of gubernatorial responsibility. Marc Landy describes the style of two Kentucky governors, Happy Chandler and John Y. Brown:

> Chandler was widely considered to be the best storyteller in Kentucky political history. He campaigned for office by tirelessly traversing the state, regaling and beguiling audiences, in every little crossroad and rural hamlet with his songs, jokes and tales.
>
> Brown's skills have proven themselves to be more appropriate to the onset of the television age. He skillfully exploited the same marketing flair that he had used to develop his Kentucky Fried Chicken empire.[8]

Today's more public gubernatorial role can often be a major political resource, for the accompanying visibility allows governors to keep their faces and names continuously before the voters. But the center stage position can sometimes be damaging as well. Following the U.S. Supreme Court's decision in the 1989 Webster abortion case, Florida's Governor Bob Martinez led a charge to press the legislature to enact antiabortion policies. The failed attempt contributed to Martinez's November 1990 defeat. Similarly, Kansas Governor Mike Hayden and Nebraska Governor Kay Orr were associated with unpopular tax increases, and both lost in 1990.

In 1990 Texas's Clayton Williams lost his first and only bid to become governor, and his defeat is widely attributed to the extensive publicity he received. Williams assumed a "good old boy" posture and took a host of "six-shooter tough-guy" positions on such issues as drugs. Polls showed that the voters loved it at first, but became increasingly uneasy the more they saw of it. In a $17 million campaign, Williams spent $8 million of his own money—too much, it appears, for in his case familiarity bred the contempt of voters. During 1996 and 1997 Arizona's Fife Symington was the target of federal fraud charges and demands mounted for his impeachment or resignation. He was convicted and resigned in October 1997. The fame that governors and would-be governors so often enjoy as a political advantage became hard on Martinez, Hayden, Orr, Symington, and Williams.

Tough Competition for the Job

It is not surprising that as the post of governor has become more important and more desirable, the contests too have become increasingly expensive and, in some instances, contentious or downright nasty. In 1956 the average cost of a gubernatorial election was $100,000 (or $418,410 in 1987 dollars) and the costliest races in the largest states averaged $300,000 (or $1.3 million in 1987 dollars). For the 1986 elections, however, the average cost had soared to $7.4 million (in 1987 dollars). The Texas campaign alone ran over $55 million in 1990. In California, it was almost $60 million. In 1992 dollars, the average cost per vote from 1977 to 1993 ranged from $28.82 in Alaska and $10.98 in Louisiana, to just under $1.12 in Wisconsin and $1.70 in North Carolina.[9] The enormous amount of money spent on gubernatorial elections parallels the escalating costs of all types of elections, particularly statewide races. The objectives of the modern campaign—building an image and gaining media coverage—involve the use of consultants, polling, mass mailings, and especially television, all extremely expensive.

Negative campaigning also seems to be a popular modern strategy in gubernatorial races, as it is in American elections generally. (See Focus 5.1 "Mudslinging in Minnesota.") Incumbents who have been in office during any form of tax increase are sure to be blamed. In the 1990 California Democratic

Focus 5.1

MUDSLINGING IN MINNESOTA

• • •

In Minnesota a particularly nasty gubernatorial campaign developed during the 1990 elections. Republican candidate Jon Grunseth called incumbent Governor Rudy Perpich "the supreme liar." Stories about Grunseth also circulated—it was rumored that he had had extramarital affairs and had invited teenage girls to swim naked in his pool. Grunseth eventually withdrew from the race, and Perpich lost to an eleventh-hour Republican replacement candidate.

Sources: "Road to Governor's Mansion in California Is Paved with Mud," *Rocky Mountain News*, 4 June 1990; "Mud Gets Thick in Minnesota Race," *Denver Post*, 21 October 1990; and "Minnesota Governor Candidate Quits," *Rocky Mountain News*, 29 October 1990.

primary, for example, the advertisements of John Van de Kamp blasted Dianne Feinstein as "a Republican in Democratic clothing." In Texas, candidate Clayton Williams refused to let voters forget about his opponent's earlier personal problems with alcohol, while the opponent and eventual winner, State Treasurer Ann Richards, blasted Williams for spending $8 million of his own money on the campaign and for failing to pay 1986 income taxes.

Incumbents enjoy a large advantage in gubernatorial elections, just as they do in virtually all American elections. Beyle reports that incumbents win more than 70 percent of the time.[10] Voters are crossing party lines increasingly and generally lack detailed information about candidates and their positions on the issues. Name identification and image are important cues for most voters. Therefore, the public stage that governors enjoy during their term in office later provides them with a significant edge in election years.

Modern governors are usually very deliberate and purposeful in their use of the public spotlight. (See Focus 5.2 "Running for Governor.") Writer Paul West captures the essence of their electoral life in a 1990 article entitled "They're Everywhere! For Today's Governors, Life Is a Never-Ending Campaign," in which he describes former New Jersey Governor Thomas Kean's early days in office as "such a disaster that his pollster, Robert Teeter, said privately that Kean's career might already be over."[11] In response, Kean's handlers set about to change his image. They manufactured televised town meetings that aired on cable television in all New Jersey counties. Kean appeared with actors Bill Cosby

Focus 5.2
RUNNING FOR GOVERNOR

• • •

Kenneth Gorman ran for Governor in 1994. His literature was a card that read "Ken Gorman for Governor of Colorado in '98. Keep on smoking them joints."

Gorman, 50 years old and a former air traffic controller, has a simple platform: legalize marijuana. He says he smokes it three or four times a day for his migraine headaches. His current job, he reports, is "marijuana salesman," and he only sells it for medicinal purposes. His father died a painful death from emphysema, he says, and the drug gave his father some relief.

In 1995, Gorman was arrested in Lakewood, Colorado for selling a 17-year-old three pounds of pot for $2,100. He claims he is not a dealer, though, citing his lack of wealth, his old car, and the modest apartment that is his home.

When arrested Gorman said of the sale, "of course I did it. That's my job." One purpose of his business, Gorman says, is to fund his campaign for governor. Lakewood police officer Mike Rose says he probably won't vote for Gorman. In a letter to the editor, Chuck Seevers suggested that Gorman be hung at the state capitol during one of the smoke-ins that Gorman promotes.

In 1996 Ken Gorman was in jail on drug charges and his bail was set at $45,000. He seems not to be worried, claiming that he's never been convicted. Still, pending charges could land him in the slammer for twenty-four years and that could well crimp his political ambitions.

In 1998, Governor Roy Romer will conclude twelve years in that post and term limits prevent him from serving further. So it's an open seat, so to speak, and that's when challengers have their best shot. Maybe Mr. Gorman knows something we don't know.

Source: Rocky Mountain News, 20 September 1995 and 1 August 1996; *Denver Post*, 20 August 1996.

and Brooke Shields in advertisements geared toward promoting tourism in the state. The governor hosted a televised talk show. In short, Kean's image changed, and at least for a while he became an enormously popular governor.

Colorado's Governor Roy Romer employed a different but equally successful approach to image building. Romer worked constantly to project an image of energy and identification with the common folks. During an election in which the construction of Denver's new airport was a central issue, the governor had breakfast in small cafes with early risers on their way to work—his so-called oatmeal circuit. His image carried constantly in the media became one of a hardworking, shirtsleeves governor who associates with the average working person. When the eastern Colorado town of Limon was devastated by a tornado, Romer was there on local streets and on televised news shows, dressed in his worn and ever-present leather bomber jacket, and promising state help.

However, even with the media focus, the contemporary state governor is not unbeatable. The more than 70 percent success rate that gubernatorial incumbents enjoy is not as strong as the 97 percent or 98 percent success rate enjoyed by incumbent members of the U.S. House of Representatives. Governors and senators run statewide. During campaigns, as during their service in office, they receive considerable media exposure. Although this is usually an advantage that sitting governors can exploit, media exposure can be a liability at certain times, such as when a scandal breaks out or when unpopular policies, tax increases in particular, must be adopted.

The intense media attention given gubernatorial contests can in some cases help the challengers. As in U.S. Senate contests, which are also statewide, challengers enter the race without the advantage of extensive name recognition enjoyed by the incumbent. Media coverage can narrow that gap and thereby diminish the incumbent's initial advantage. For the governor who remains visible, stays out of trouble, and either ducks or shares the blame for unpopular actions or policies, though, the political future remains reasonably secure.

Roles of the Governor

The range of formal authority that a governor possesses varies among the fifty states. In some states, such as Kentucky and Wisconsin, the governor has extensive power to appoint top-level state administrators, to veto legislation, and to influence the size and shape of the budget. In other states, including Texas, the governor's formal powers are more limited. Indeed, governors in most states share some executive branch authority with other directly elected officials and may be politically constrained by the legislature or by special interest group power. At the same time, they are often able to augment their institutional authority with political clout, derived variously from exploitation of the media, hard work, force of personality, intelligence, and, perhaps, a central position in the political party.

One factor common to all states is the public's expectation that the chief executive officer will play a host of roles. Some gubernatorial roles are formal and institutional, whereas others are symbolic and ceremonial. In virtually all cases the responsibilities that fall on the shoulders of the state governor are not matched by a parallel allocation of formal authority. Thus, successful governors often combine their formal authority with personal political skills and effective exploitation of public opinion.

Chief Administrator

Perhaps the most important, best-known role played by governors is that of chief administrator. Although not the only high-level position in the executive branch of state government, the office of governor is generally considered the top job because it carries the most authority, responsibility, and visibility. At the same time, the legal authority and political power of governors vary among the states and are in some cases fairly limited. Still, the public image is that the governor "runs" the state. If things go well the governor takes the credit, and if things fail the opposition party or faction sees to it that the governor takes the blame. When the legislature passes a law, it is the governor's duty to enforce it. If an agency is not doing its job, the governor is expected to investigate. In the event of a scandal in state government, the governor has to explain and rectify it. The media demands it and so does the opposition party.

Although the authority and power of the governor vary among the states, and although in some states the governor's powers are few and relatively weak, the public's image of the chief administrator remains constant. The governor is widely viewed as a state's chief administrative officer and as ultimately responsible for conducting the state's affairs.

Party Leader

The governor is frequently looked upon as a party leader, though here there are also great variations among the states. In one-party states, such as some of those in the South, the governor may be the leader of just one faction of the majority party. Or, with the Republican party enjoying growing success in other southern states, the governor may be someone who has bucked traditional partisan trends and built political success via party organization and extensive media play. In other states the governor may be a maverick personality, having obtained a party's nomination for office by challenging the choice of the party regulars in the statewide gubernatorial primary. Party mavericks and governors in one-party states may still be viewed as the most significant and most visible members of their party, but they may not be considered the true leaders of their party.

The governor's role as party leader may also depend on the composition of the legislature. When the governor's party has a majority in both houses, the governor may well be the acknowledged rallying point for party maneuvers. When the opposition party controls the legislature, which is increasingly the case, the governor may be the opponent of the legislature rather than a source of direction and strategy.

Regardless of the chief administrator's status in the political party or the composition of the legislature, the governor remains the most visible elected official in the state and is almost always an asset to the party. Governors command vast amounts of television, radio, and newspaper attention. They speak at hundreds of social and political gatherings. They are asked to campaign for and support members of their party, who are candidates in legislative contests. And they are the key attraction at their party's fund-raising affairs.

State Symbol

Chief executives (including mayors, governors, and U.S. presidents) are visible symbols of their community and its government, and as such they perform a wide range of ceremonial functions. In effect, then, the governor is a state symbol.

Governors welcome dignitaries from other states and nations. They dedicate new bridges, highways, and public buildings. They make speeches on holidays, march at the head of parades, and warn children not to experiment with drugs or eat the apples they collect on Halloween until the fruit has been checked by their parents. They express alarm at the growing number of highway deaths and appeal to motorists for caution on holiday weekends. And often governors, like the president, are, in the minds of children, the personification of government itself.

The symbolic role that governors play can be both a liability and a political asset. It can be a liability because of the tremendous demands it places on the people who serve as governors. However, the widespread visibility of the role translates into a significant advantage at the polls.[12]

Policy Leader

Another role of the governor, one of growing significance and importance, is that of policy leader. Like other chief executives, governors are involved increasingly in policy-related activities—anticipating and identifying problems and issues, proposing goals and programs for the states, as well as fabricating and implementing legislative policy.

Three critical factors have combined to increase the salience of the policy role of the governor. First, the need to attack such problems as air and water pollution, crime, and illegal drugs through public policies has increasingly involved state government programs and spending. Second, twentieth-century developments in mass communications have increased the visibility of such politicos as state chief executives. Third, the number and complexity of the problems with which state governments wrestle and the web of ties with local units of government and the national government have made it increasingly necessary to coordinate public policies and programs; this has been done increasingly through the office of the governor.

As a result, party leaders, legislators, bureaucrats, and the public expect governors and gubernatorial candidates to act like policy leaders. They are expected to identify issues and anticipate public problems. When they run for office, they are expected to do so on platforms that call for specific policy options. Once in office, governors are expected to help determine the legislative agenda, to bring to the legislature a program (a set of specific policy recommendations as well as some written legislation), and to play the political game to secure passage of that program. This is the case even if legislative leaders of the other party fully intend to scrap or sabotage the governor's recommendations.

Governors can work with and cajole their own party and legislative leaders. They can appeal to the public for support. Through patronage and other devices, they can pressure various special interest groups and individual legislators to gain their support of a program. Their ability to push certain policies also gives governors great power. Therefore, the role of policy leader is a source of power for most governors. (See Focus 5.3 "Pottys and Priorities.")

Focus 5.3
POTTYS AND PRIORITIES

• • •

In the very early days of the Republic, governors were both feared and disliked. Stemming from our experience with the English Crown and the King's use of colonial governors as hammers in the royal tool box, our founders lodged public power in the hands of legislators and kept governors weak. Among other things, this meant that early state executives played no significant role in establishing government priorities.

That state of affairs has long since changed, and now we expect, even demand, that our governors take the lead in articulating an agenda and priorities for the state. This expectation is both symbolized and institutionalized in the universal "state of the state" address given to state legislatures. But as both Vermont's governor and its legislature discovered recently, the annual address is not the only occasion when state priorities are hatched.

Focus 5.3 *(continued)*

Vermont planned to close seven highway rest stops. They were either "under-utilized, outdated, environmentally unsound or inaccessible to the handicapped." The plan, it was thought, would entice motorists to stop instead at small tourist towns.

The planned action got the goat of Vermont Representative Bob Walker. He dramatized his opposition by getting 25,000 signatures on a pro-potty petition, locating a port-a-potty at the state capitol next to the governor's car and distributing bumper stickers that read, "No rest area fix, No governor Dean in '96."

Representative Walker commented, "The 25,000 people who signed are saying they'd like to go to the bathroom." Governor Dean said, "I figured it was just a cost-cutting measure." His advice to others contemplating such closures is, "don't."

Vermont's leaders then set about looking for other ways to keep those who stopped, rested and comfortable. Priorities had changed.

Source: Charles Mahtesian, "The Outhouse Rebellion," *Governing* (May 1996): 16.

Policy Coordinator

Closely related to the governor's role as policy leader is that of **policy coordinator**. Governors are in a position to coordinate and integrate public policy—in preparing party platforms and legislative program proposals, in preparing and reviewing state budgets, and in acting as the state's chief administrative official. Bills are introduced in the legislature on a variety of subjects and from a variety of sources; they are considered in a variety of committees; and, if passed, they are administered by a variety of disparate departments and agencies of the state government.

All the ingredients are present, then, for an incremental and totally undirected and uncoordinated implementation of public policy. Some duplication, waste, and lack of coordination are inevitable, but the governor, like other executives in U.S. government, is in a position to maintain a degree of perspective on state government activities.

Sources of Gubernatorial Power

Like the roles of a governor, **gubernatorial power** can be both formal and informal. **Formal powers** are institutional; that is, they come with the position.

Informal powers, such as the ability to influence public opinion, are derived in part from a governor's personality and in part from the visibility of the position itself.

Visibility

Governors' policy roles and symbolic positions provide them with an almost continuous public platform. They can command front-page newspaper coverage and radio and television time almost at will. Many of the little things they do find their way into print and rebound to their political benefit. Montana's Governor Marc Racicot garnered headlines when he traveled a hundred miles by car, on roads that were often muddy and remote, to give a junior high graduation address to a class of one. The address was given to an eighth-grader, who said of the governor, "He was pretty much my only choice."[13]

If governors want to generate an issue, argue on behalf of pending legislation, indicate their displeasure with someone's actions, or focus public attention and put pressure on some legislator or committee, they can call on their publicity resources and gain visibility faster and more effectively than perhaps any other state official. Of course, this does not always guarantee governors success, but it is one of many tools in their collection of political resources.

Executive Authority

Although some degree of power accrues to all state governors by virtue of their formal authority, many governors are restricted by constitutional and statutory limitations on budgetary, appointive, and veto powers, as well as by the establishment of several other elected executive posts. Nevertheless, all governors retain some power to appoint executive personnel, influence the content of the budget, demand written performance and progress reports from executive departments, and issue administrative orders. Formal executive authority, though it varies among the states, adds significantly to the governor's political powers.

The Political Party

The political party of a governor is usually a source of political power, though to varying degrees. It is a strong source of power for governors who have been active within their party, who have built a network of political alliances, and whose party controls both houses of the legislature. In this case, the legislature is likely to look to the governor for policy direction, to consult the governor throughout the legislative session, and to be supportive of the governor's policy preferences.

However, divided government is more prevalent than ever before. As a result, governors often do not enjoy a united and supportive legislative party. Following the 1990 election, only nineteen states had governments in which the party of the governor also controlled both legislative houses. An identical number remained divided after the 1996 elections. Partisan division can reduce governors' powers, whereas unity can mean significant legislative support of their major policy objectives.

The political party can also help gubernatorial candidates at the polls. In most states, the two major parties are organized at the precinct, county, and state levels; this organization helps candidates raise funds, get potential voters registered, and disseminate political propaganda. Party identification is the single most reliable predictor of an individual's vote, and a candidate's firm identification as a Democrat or a Republican automatically guarantees the candidate an electoral base. Of course, some states are dominated by one party; as a result, political contests can be based on factional fights rather than party competition.

The Veto

The governors in all states except North Carolina possess some sort of veto power over legislative action. In over 90 percent of the states governors are empowered to use the line-item veto (usually in regard to appropriations, or budget, bills). The veto is a significant political tool for the chief executive. Given the nature of the legislative process, important, controversial bills tend to be reported out of committee and placed before the full house late in the session. Therefore, governors can appraise and veto critical bills when the legislature is about to adjourn and after it has disbanded. A few states allow governors to **pocket veto** legislation; that is, the governor may neglect to sign bills after the legislature has adjourned. In addition, it takes an abnormal majority of two-thirds or three-fourths to override an executive veto in most states (two-thirds is most common). Some states do not allow the legislature to call itself back into session. As a result, it is difficult for the legislature to override a gubernatorial veto.[14]

The potential for executive veto can affect the governor's powers in two very different ways. First, the fact that the governor has the opportunity to void legislation means that the legislature is apt to keep controversial provisions out of bills. The governor thus can have an impact on legislation even without acting. Second, there are ways of structuring legislation to minimize the risk of a veto. Provisions that a governor is known to favor may be tied to other unfavorable ones, making it difficult for the governor to eliminate a provision without voiding the entire legislative package. For example, a legislature might effectively avoid a budget item veto by lumping endangered items with other appropriations. As in all areas of politics, the outcome tends to be one of compromise.

The veto powers of governors vary among the states. Although in a few states a veto can be overridden by a simple majority vote in the legislature, a two-thirds majority is the norm in most states. Some governors have only a limited period in which to sign or veto legislation; others are granted extended periods. For example, Indiana has no line-item veto, and the governor's veto can be reversed by a simple majority. North Carolina's governor has no veto power. In contrast, the governor in Wisconsin may veto parts of bills. Governor Tommy Thompson has employed that authority to alter legislative intent. Despite legislative protest, Wisconsin's supreme court has upheld his actions, stating that the governor can apply his or her veto authority to individual words, letters, and punctuation marks in bills.[15]

Appointment Power

The power of governors to appoint administrative personnel varies considerably among the states. For governors with a significant degree of appointment power, it is an important executive tool. When an official in the executive branch is popularly elected or appointed by a board, has civil service protection, or is appointed by the governor with the confirmation of the senate, that official is in a position to exercise considerable independence from the governor. In contrast, when an official is appointed by the governor and may be dismissed by the governor, that official is likely to remain closely attuned to and comply with the chief executive's preferences. Similarly, the agency head who can be fired by the governor and whose paycheck depends on courting the governor's wishes is more apt to cooperate with the governor than the agency head who is appointed by a multimember board and has a degree of independence from the chief executive. In short, appointment power is of immense value to governors in their efforts to get members of the state executive branch to comply with their directives.

As with veto powers, the degree of executive appointment power varies. The governors of Oklahoma, Mississippi, Georgia, and Texas have only weak appointment power; the heads of many agencies in those states are elected or appointed by a board, a commission, or another state official. In contrast, the appointment power of the governors of Alaska, Colorado, Delaware, Indiana, Kentucky, Massachusetts, and Tennessee is strong.

Budget Power

Playing a major role in the development of the state budget and in the dispersal of appropriated funds can give governors power in relations with the legislature and administration. Governors in all fifty states play some role in the budget-making process, but the degree of their power varies considerably. In some states the governor and staff members solicit requests for funds from various state agencies, review the funding requests (in terms of their reasonableness and the degree to which they reflect the governor's goals and legislative program), and make upward or downward monetary adjustments on the basis of their compatibility with the governor's program and the anticipated state revenues.

In other states the governor's role in the budget-making process is more limited. The governor may participate in budget formation along with a state budget director, a state comptroller, or a state finance director. Such a situation exists in Texas, where the lieutenant governor and the speaker of the house share most budget-making powers. The individual with whom the governor shares the budget preparation role may also be an elected state officer, a civil service employee, or an officer chosen by the legislature; in these cases the individual is less influenced by gubernatorial control. In all states, however, governors' budget powers, like those of the legislature, are restricted by state constitutional or statutory earmarking of certain tax revenues.

Budget preparation is an extremely critical function of state politics. The greater the governor's role in budget making, the more likely it is that the legislature and the administration will respond positively to the governor's proposals. Legislators know that modern-day state budgets are large and complex and that legislative time is limited; as a result, the legislature often reviews the governor's budget and makes some incremental adjustments. Similarly, the heads of administrative agencies know that if they cross the governor they may be shortchanged in the next budget. The legislature's role tends to be one of budget review rather than of budget formation, which gives the governor the power to make budget cuts.

Tenure

In decades past many governors served only two-year terms and were prohibited by law from serving consecutive terms. This has changed in recent years. Today the governors of forty-seven states serve four-year terms; in eighteen of these states the governors may serve an unlimited number of consecutive terms as long as they win the elections. Four states prohibit consecutive terms, and in some other states the governor may serve only two consecutive terms, a restriction similar to that imposed on the U.S. presidency.

In some ways appointment power of governors is restricted. Often governors find that a majority of the members of executive boards and commissions serve longer terms than the governor. Obviously, the longer a governor stays in office, the more appointments he or she can make. Longer tenure may also give the governor greater political freedom and a stronger hand in exercising other gubernatorial powers.

Lobbying

Straightforward lobbying is an important political tool for state governors both within their own states and in their collective interactions with the national government. At home, governors must deal with their own state legislature in getting bills passed, appropriations made, and measures vetoed. It is thus critical for governors to maintain ongoing contact with the legislature. In order to do so, governors have on staff a **legislative liaison**—a person who lobbies the legislature on a daily basis and keeps legislators informed of the governor's preferences (including unacceptable provisions of bills that will be vetoed). As noted earlier in the chapter, the threat of a veto can influence the content of bills and the behavior of lawmakers.

Governors and other elected state officials have now become important lobbyists in their own right. Much of a governor's time is spent in lobbying within the intergovernmental system. Former Governor Ann Richards of Texas spent a considerable amount of time lobbying President Clinton and Congress on a host of issues, including NAFTA (the North American Free Trade Agreement) and the Supercollider, both important issues to the Texas economy.

Limits on Executive Power

Although the governors of the American states derive political power from a variety of legal and political sources, their executive power is limited by a host of legal and practical restrictions. Governors bear the responsibility for, but often lack the power to control, large and unwieldy state bureaucracies. They frequently lack strong veto, appointment, and budget powers. Since many of their counterparts in the executive branch are independently elected, governors must often bargain for what they want for their states. Some of the severest limitations on executive power have been the target of recent reform proposals geared toward strengthening the governor's power.

The Plural Executive

In many states the governor is a member of a **plural executive**—in other words, one of a number of directly elected members of the executive branch. It is not uncommon for states to elect the lieutenant governor, the secretary of state, the attorney general, the treasurer, the auditor, and other top state officials, as well as the governor. The governors of all fifty states are popularly elected. Forty-three states directly elect the attorney general, thirty-eight elect the treasurer, thirty-seven elect the secretary of state, and forty-two elect the lieutenant governor. Voters in some states also elect an assortment of other executive branch officials, including the comptroller, the insurance commissioner, the land commissioner, and the mining commissioner. In addition, most states have a host of boards and commissions whose members are sometimes elected at the polls. In Arizona, the three members of the state's corporation commission are directly elected; in Michigan, the governing boards of three state universities (University of Michigan, Michigan State University, and Wayne State University) are directly elected in statewide elections.

Some elective executive posts are established by constitutional provision; others are provided for in legislative statutes. However they are created, elective posts exist in every state and, as a general rule, executive authority is widely dispersed. The plural executive model diagrammed in Figure 5.1 is similar to that of most states. A number of implications of the plural executive approach to administrative organization are immediately apparent. Since several major executive officials are directly elected and possess independent constituent bases, they may not have much incentive to follow the governor's directives or preferences. Because the governor does not hire and cannot dismiss the secretary of state, the attorney general, the treasurer, or many other executive branch officials, they are free to choose whether or not to cooperate with the governor. However, such executive branch officials are required by constitutional and statutory provisions and encouraged by public opinion to cooperate with other public officials and to assist in the smooth, effective conduct of public affairs. Still, they owe their jobs to the voters who elected them. As a result, elected officials tend to be much less indebted to the governor than those who are appointed by the chief executive.

Many gubernatorial candidates campaign while holding another state office, such as that of state treasurer, attorney general, or secretary of state. It is not unusual for one of these statewide officeholders to see political advantage in embarrassing the incumbent governor while keeping his or her own name

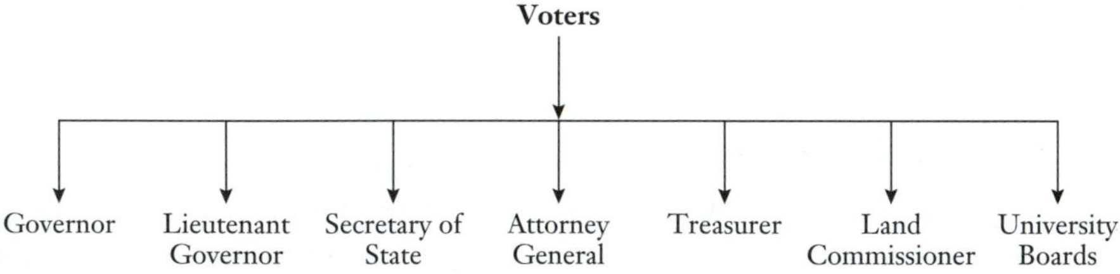

Figure 5.1 The Plural Executive Model*

*This figure shows a hypothetical sampling of offices; the actual selection varies from state to state.

in the headlines. When Governor Jerry Brown of California was out of the state, his lieutenant governor, as acting governor, often countermanded the executive orders Brown had issued.

The diffusion of executive authority and responsibility in the American states not only weakens the political power of governors but also adds to voter confusion. As every voter knows, American ballots are extremely long. It is difficult for even the most conscientious voters to make informed choices from wide and diverse lists of candidates and offices. Voters dissatisfied with their state government, and with the executive branch especially, must attempt to choose from among dozens of individuals running for election and reelection to executive branch posts.

In addition, the plural executive model in state government complicates the process of maintaining administrative coordination of responsibilities. Most of the functions performed by state government departments and agencies are related in some way to the functions of other departments and agencies. Under the plural executive model, many functions and duties are performed semi-independently with no overall coordination. The governor can create some degree of coordination through persuasion, and the legislative budget committees, unwieldy as they often are, through budgetary threat and intimidation. But no comprehensive approach to the coordination of responsibilities exists.

Reform Proposal: The Integrated Executive

The elimination of the plural executive is among the countless administrative reforms that have been proposed over the course of American history. Most reformers propose replacing the plural executive with a strong integrated executive model. An organizational arrangement borrowed from the business world, the **integrated executive** model would eliminate several elective posts and increase the governor's appointive and administrative powers. Heads of cabinet-type departments, such as the secretary of state, the attorney general, and the treasurer, would no longer be elected in statewide elections but would be appointed by the governor. They would also be responsible to the governor and subject to removal by the governor.

The governor in the integrated executive approach would serve as chief executive in both fact and theory. Like the U.S. president, governors would have the power to select department heads and, together with cabinet members, would be responsible for the administration of their departments. Governors would also be able to remove department heads whose performance was lacking. Lines of authority and responsibility would be more clearly established than in the plural executive model. Figure 5.2 diagrams a hypothetical integrated executive model of state government.

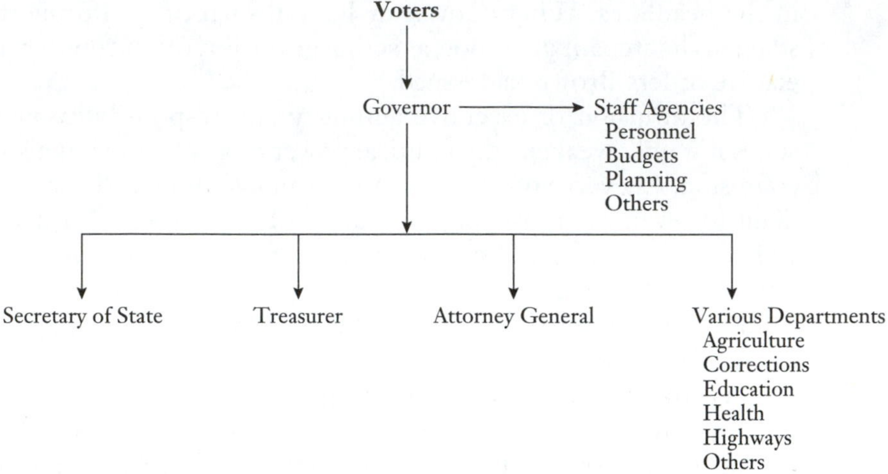

Figure 5.2 The Integrated Executive Model

Progress in securing adoption of the integrated executive model has been slow but steady. *The Book of the States* reports that in the last decade, nearly half of the states underwent some form of reorganization.[16] However, reorganization does not necessarily reduce the number of bureaucratic units or strengthen the power of the chief executive. In some cases reorganization may be little more than a rearranging of existing units, with no reduction in the proliferation of those units.

In none of the fifty states does the actual organization of the executive branch perfectly match the model of either the plural or the integrated executive. Some tend toward one side or the other. Each state's organizational scheme is the product of the political history of the state and the success or failure of reform movements. Figures 5.3 and 5.4 show the contemporary organizational schemes in Oklahoma and Alaska, respectively. Oklahoma's institutions were created initially when it entered the Union in 1907, a time of Progressive reforms designed to disperse power and thus weaken corrupt institutions. Today formal authority is still widely dispersed in Oklahoma. In contrast, Alaska became a state in 1959, in the midst of the executive reform movement. Not surprisingly, the Alaska executive branch resembles the integrated executive model.

The Bureaucratic Organization

The structure and operation of most state bureaucracies further reduce the political strength of many governors. Most states have well over a hundred agencies, many headed by multimember boards or commissions, existing in dis-

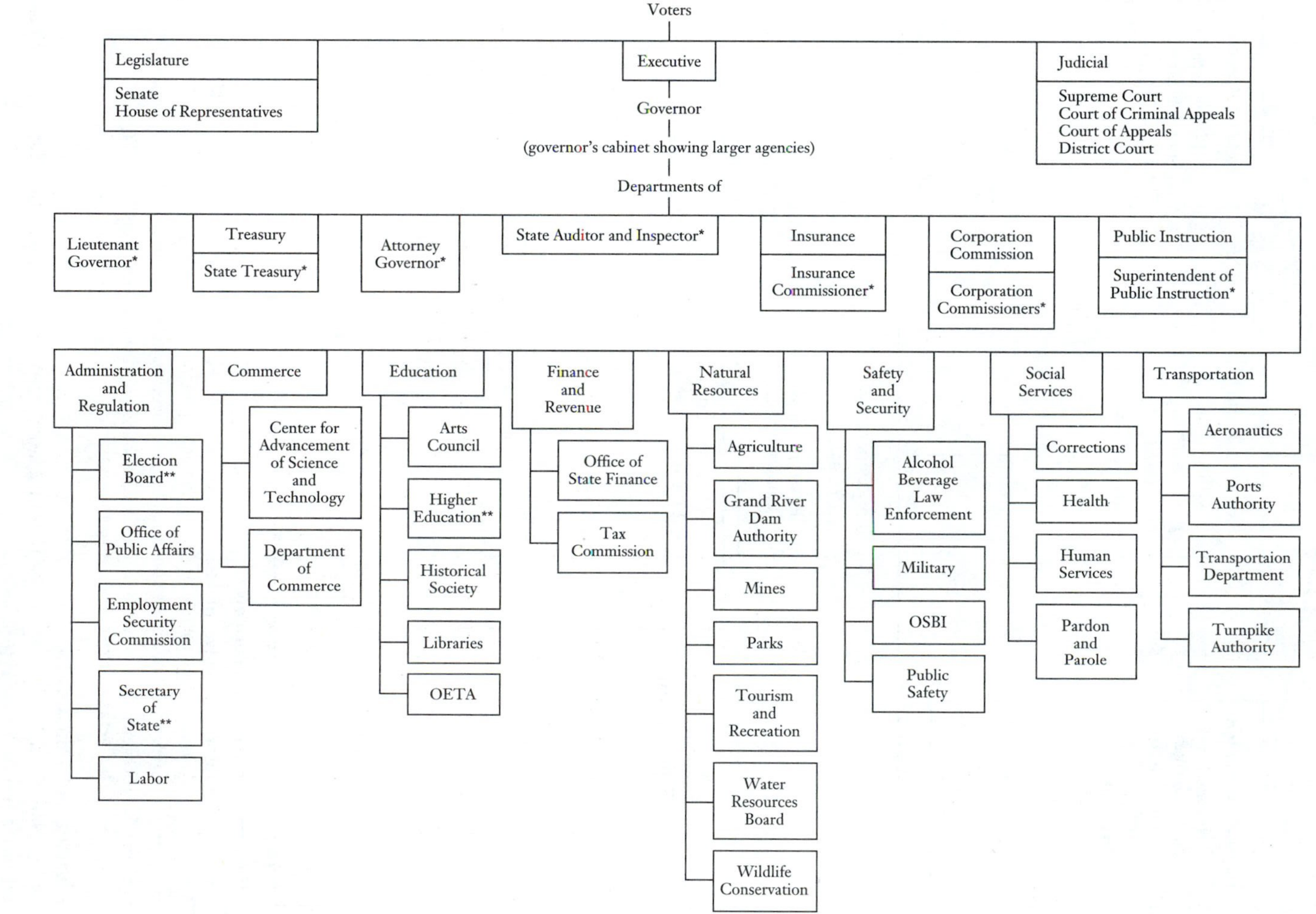

Figure 5.3 Oklahoma's Executive Branch
*Elective office established by constitution.
**Appointive office established by constitution.
Source: Oklahoma 1989–1990 (Oklahoma City: Oklahoma Department of Libraries, 1990).

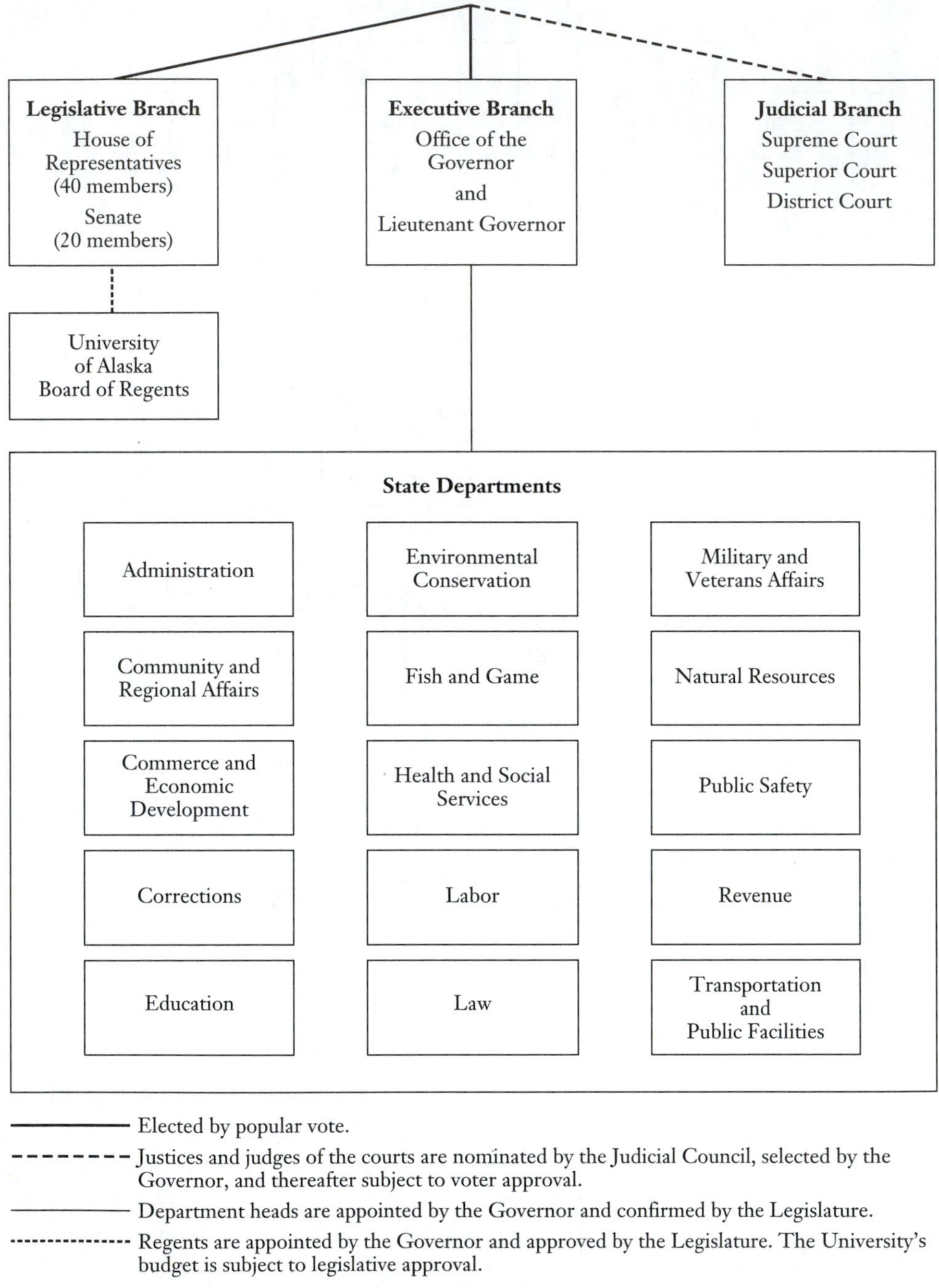

Figure 5.4 Alaska's Executive Branch
Source: Alaska Blue Book, 1989–1990 (Juneau: Alaska Department of Education, Division of State Libraries and Archives, 1990).

persed fashion in sprawling bureaucracies. Much of the activity of the agencies is uncoordinated or overlaps with that of other agencies. The result of this lack of coordination is clear. The governor or other state officials have difficulty exercising meaningful coordination and control over the state's activities. When administrative units are headed by multimember boards or commissions, the governor may be able to exert only little influence because the members' terms are longer than the governor's. Moreover, the governor can neither appoint nor dismiss many members of boards and commissions.

In addition, governors may find it impossible to keep track of the numerous individuals and functions for which they are responsible. Further, the various administrative units, especially those headed by boards and commissions, may respond to a variety of different "publics."

American state governments attained their present bureaucratic structure through the combination of several circumstantial factors over a long period of time. The nineteenth-century Jacksonian penchants for representativeness and maximum public participation in decision making provided the initial impetus for multiple membership on governing boards of state and local administrative agencies. Boards and commissions became even more popular in the late nineteenth and early twentieth centuries, when there was rampant corruption in state government. State legislatures were viewed, often correctly, as the tools of such special interests as the railroads and big corporations; and governors, it was thought, could be persuaded by the rich and powerful.

The remedy offered by reformers involved the insulation of government in general and of public administration in particular from corrupt public officials in the legislative and executive branches. Thus emerged the widespread use of multimember boards and commissions with representation from a variety of economic sectors, terms that exceeded those of the governors, and nonpartisan or bipartisan membership. Of course, in the process of insulating state agencies from corruption, the reformers also may have insulated them from control by the public.

Another factor contributing to the bureaucratic state of administrative affairs in state government was the constant need for government to respond incrementally to an increasing number of emerging problems associated with the new programs and new agencies. In no state did the present administrative structure take shape overnight. Rather, like all public and private bureaucracies, state bureaucracies are the product of numerous decisions—made incrementally at various points in time—to take on new public programs and to create new departments for implementing those programs and policies.

Bureaucratic Reform

There have been attempts in almost every state to reform the bureaucratic organization in order to facilitate assignment of authority, accountability, and responsibility as well as to increase the economy and efficiency of state government. Figure 5.2 diagrams the integrated executive model, the envisioned shape of the reformed administrative structure. No state bureaucracy, whether reformed or unreformed, is exactly like the model depicted in the figure, and no two state bureaucracies are exactly alike. But the reform proposals that have been adopted in many states call for administration restructuring along the lines shown in Figure 5.2.

The numerous existing agencies are grouped according to function into a few departments. Internally, these departments are organized along hierarchical lines, with authority flowing downward and responsibility upward. Each department is run by a department head who is appointed by and responsible to the governor. Because the number of departments is reduced, the governor's span of control—the number of individuals the governor supervises directly—is reduced to a more manageable level. The governor is better able to perform in an informed manner, and the voter knows that the governor is responsible for poor government. In turn, the governor can easily identify the responsible department head, and so on. The lines of authority and responsibility are simplified and clearly fixed.

In addition, the governor is given the needed staff to manage the tasks of budget making, personnel hiring, and planning. The governor's powers are strengthened and the bureaucracy is more logically arranged. The governor can administer the affairs of the state with more order and dispatch, and the people can better evaluate their government in action.

Do not overestimate the effect of reorganization on human behavior. All organizations tend to develop elaborate informal authority and communication systems, quite apart from the formal channels. Employees become acquainted with their counterparts in other agencies and departments; the work of the organization is then expedited as communication is conducted laterally throughout the organization by phone, E-mail, note, or in person. When the law changes the formal structure of the organization, it does not immediately or necessarily eliminate personal acquaintances or change behavior and communication patterns.

Researchers disagree about the impact of government structure on behavior and performance. Some studies suggest that government structure may be of secondary or no importance in determining output and performance.[17] The efficiency objective is questioned as well. Kenneth Meier reports that:

> The conventional wisdom that executive reorganization along the principles of classical organization theory introduces economies into bureaucracy is not supported by major American state government reorganizations from 1965 to 1975.[18]

Scholar James Conant, in a review of the arguments and evidence supporting the push for a streamlined, more efficient executive branch structure, concludes that the ultimate effects of reorganization remain largely unknown.[19]

At the same time, however, it is clear that the current complicated government apparatus makes it difficult for the average voter to remain informed. There is also some debate over the assumption that economy, efficiency, and simplicity in government are good. Some critics argue that, in light of democratic theory, it is more important for government to be responsive to the people than efficient and economical. Questions about the impact of government structure on policy output are subject to some degree of empirical measurement, but questions that focus on values in decision making are normative and thus subject to debate rather than empirical proof.

Any successful reorganization is required to (1) reduce internal and external resistance to and develop support for the proposed changes. An example of the skillful achievement of these ends is described by Phillip Foss's case study of the reorganization of the California highway patrol.[20] Foss points out that the proponents of the plan to reorganize took great pains to "reduce the costs of change." Employees who were to be affected by the changes were consulted before the plan was announced. Great efforts were made to avoid demotions or cuts in pay and to avoid moving employees against their will. The reorganization did not necessitate a change in state statute, which could have precipitated trouble with or in the legislature. The reorganization, in short, was successful because the political groundwork was carefully planned.

Bureaucratic Control

Modern bureaucracies, whether state, local, federal, or private, provide their administrative subunits with multiple opportunities to develop autonomy within the larger organization and some degree of immunity from executive and public control. As organizations become larger and more complex, as communication systems become more elaborate and impersonal, and as employees master increasingly specialized skills, administrative departments and agencies and the offices within them become harder to control. As a result, the problems of executive leadership also increase.

State bureaucracies and other large organizations share a number of characteristics. Perhaps among the most important features are specialization, division of labor, and elaborate systems of communication and authority. Recent massive technological advances have created ever-increasing specialization. The jack-of-all-trades who could adequately perform a number of functions has been replaced by the expert who is skilled in a narrow range of activities. Modern bureaucracies are full of them—accountants, attorneys, computer programmers, mechanics, typists, engineers, and a variety of other technicians. These individuals are usually adept at their trade but may be unable to understand or perform other organizational tasks. Likewise, their functions may be beyond the comprehension of their coworkers.

The same sort of specialization characterizes entire administrative units, such as libraries, research services, budget offices, data-processing centers, and motor pools. The organization is dependent on its specialist employees and departments; indeed, they may increase its productivity considerably, providing they function properly. It makes sense, of course, to staff public administration with the best experts available—to employ skilled typists, computer programmers, biologists, and mechanics instead of people with relatively low skill levels. However, the widespread use of expertise can also create problems of coordination and control.

Experts and specialized administrative units can derive considerable autonomy from their expertise. Motor pools can structure their regulations, procedures, requirements, and schedules and demand compliance from any state employee who wants the use of a vehicle. Libraries on university campuses can make their own rules. Data-processing personnel can insist on compliance with the information-collecting and -reporting procedures that they prefer. It should not be implied that large organizations or state government bureaucracies are typically in a state of chaos and rebellion, for this is clearly not the case. But the possession by an individual or department of an expert skill on which the organization depends and that cannot be easily replaced gives that individual or department a base of independence. In this case, it is no easy task for an administrator or chief executive to obtain the performance desired of subordinates just because he or she has formal authority over them.

Agency–Clientele Ties

Another factor that can reduce the ability of the governor to control an administration is the tendency for government agencies to forge links with private interests, often called **clientele groups**. Such ties can prove advantageous to both the agency and the clientele group. The latter may be given opportunities to appraise agency programs and plans before they are implemented. The agencies and groups may even swap personnel. For example, it is common for the relevant clientele groups to be contacted before administrative appointments are made to the boards that govern the agencies with which they interact, or before a department head is selected. As a result, an individual who is not acceptable to a special interest group rarely wins appointment to the state agency with which that group deals.

The collective result of agency–clientele ties is that government agencies tend to be staffed with personnel who share the values and goals of the private interests with which they interact. Indeed, the agencies are often staffed with persons who formerly worked for those interests and who may work for them again in the future. Private interests, in short, are formally plugged into the official decision-making apparatus.

Sunk Costs

The money, staffing, and physical facilities that a government, an industry, or another type of organization has already invested in ongoing programs may be referred to as **sunk costs**. The widespread existence of sunk costs—in terms of money, staffing, buildings, institutions, programs, behavior patterns, and expectations—restricts the political power and decision-making options of both the governor and the legislature. As a result of decisions made in the past, of policies already adopted, of programs presently in existence, and of staff already employed, a widespread network of public expectations exists and policy options are thus restricted.

The drastic reduction of ongoing programs in such areas as education, public health, parks, or highways is not a politically feasible option for a governor or a legislature. In the area of education, for example, millions of dollars' worth of buildings and materials exist; thousands of people have been trained, licensed, and employed; millions of children are involved in the school programs; and millions of parents expect educational programs. The most a governor can hope to accomplish under such circumstances is to seek small, incremental adjustments in the programs and the budget.

Similar conditions exist in other policy and program areas. Budgets for highways, mental health care, and other social services can often be adjusted upward or downward by up to 10 percent. The political climate is sometimes ripe for the institution of new programs or the reduction of others, but wholesale reversals are almost never feasible policy alternatives. Consideration of new mass-transit programs must recognize the existence of billions of dollars of investment and thousands of miles of expressway systems; new building plans must include strategies to deal with existing structures; plans to close or relocate recreational facilities must anticipate citizen expectations and behavior; and plans to expand or move an airport must accommodate existing physical facilities, citizen resistance to expansion or relocation, and the networks of communication and transportation that service existing facilities. Clearly public programs and annual budgets are not drastically transformed by governors or legislatures. Decisions made earlier restrict the powers of governors and legislators.[21]

Governors' Powers: A Comparison

Scholars who study state governors have developed numerical indices used to evaluate levels of formal gubernatorial authority. One recent study conducted by the National Governors Association (NGA) examined six areas of gubernatorial power: (1) the governor's ability to run for repeated reelection, (2) the extent of the governor's authority to appoint and remove the heads of executive branch departments, (3) the governor's role in the budget-making process, (4) the legislature's prerogatives to change what the governor proposes, (5) the nature of the governor's veto power, and (6) the extent of legislative control exercised by the governor's political party.[22] Each state was assigned a score in each category, and from that a combined point total was computed (see Table 5.1).

Although the NGA study cannot account for the political clout enjoyed by a governor as a result of political savvy, hard work, intelligence, a powerful personality, or skill in the use of image and the media, its measures do display the range of authority that exists among state governors. As shown in the table, most states received a score in the 19 to 24 range, although some were at the high or low end. The two extremes—Rhode Island and Maryland—show that not all governorships are created equal in terms of authority. Some governors

TABLE 5.1 DEGREES OF FORMAL GUBERNATORIAL AUTHORITY AMONG THE STATES

Degree of Authority (on a scale of 15–29)	States
29	Maryland
27	Massachusetts, West Virginia
26	New York
25	Minnesota
24	Arizona, Connecticut, Hawaii, Kansas, Nebraska, New Jersey, Oregon, Tennessee, Utah
23	Arkansas, Delaware, Illinois, Iowa, Louisiana, Michigan, North Dakota, Ohio, Pennsylvania, South Dakota, Virginia
22	California, Colorado, Georgia, Mississippi, Montana, Washington, Wisconsin, Wyoming
21	Arizona, Florida, Idaho, Kentucky, Missouri
20	Indiana
19	Alabama, Maine, Nevada, New Mexico, Oklahoma
18	New Hampshire, South Carolina, Vermont
17	North Carolina
16	Texas
15	Rhode Island

Source: National Governors' Association data from Thad L. Beyle, "Governors," in *Politics in the American States*, 5th ed., ed. Virginia Gray, Herbert Jacob, and Robert B. Albritton (Glenview, Ill.: Scott, Foresman/Little, Brown Higher Education, 1990), p. 228.

enjoy extensive formal authority, whereas others have only weak authority and may need to compensate for it through informal sources of power.

Executive Strength and Leadership

Clearly our discussion of gubernatorial roles, powers, and limitations show that executive strength and leadership are enormously complicated and can vary widely. Institutional structure, formal authority, executive and legislative branch partisan lineups, the governor's personality and political savvy, and other factors all contribute to executive strength and leadership.

Kentucky's governors have historically been leaders in their political party and have enjoyed extensive appointment powers as well as a political environment conducive to a strong leadership role. Government has not been divided, since the Democrats have controlled both legislative chambers and the executive. The Kentucky governorship has been quite strong with respect to both formal institutional authority and informal political powers.[23]

In Georgia governors have also been quite strong, but not because of their formal authority. The governor's appointment powers are only moderate, due to the direct election of many department heads, including the lieutenant governor, the secretary of state, the attorney general, the commissioners of insurance, agriculture, and labor, and the superintendent of schools. The governor in Georgia does play a major role in the budget process and has strong veto powers. Both tradition and one-party Democratic domination of state legislative and executive elections provide the governor with a strong political base from which to operate. Until the 1960s Georgia's governor could select legislative leaders, and there is still a tradition of gubernatorial appointment of people to judicial and other elective offices. For example, the incumbent resigns voluntarily before the end of the term, the governor fills the vacancy, and the appointee can then seek reelection running as an incumbent. Clearly, this strengthens the governor's hand by helping to ensure that the governor's appointee stays on the job.[24]

Texas's governor enjoys neither strong appointment powers nor a central role in budget making. Texas has a host of boards and commissions, including the Railroad Commission, which regulates state oil and gas leases. The lieutenant governor presides over the senate and, together with the house speaker, plays a large role in the budget process.[25] Former Republican governor Bill Clements faced a Democratic house and a Democratic senate headed by long-term and powerful Democratic lieutenant governor Bill Hobby. Limitations such as these restrict the ability of the governor to forge a strong electoral base.

California's governor enjoys extensive institutional authority but may encounter political problems. The governor's budget, appointment, and veto powers are extensive, and there are no limits on reelection. However, during much of the recent past, the state government has been politically divided, with a Republican governor and a Democratic majority in the legislature.[26]

Other State Executives

As noted earlier in the chapter, the governor is not the only elected administrative official in state government. In most states voters also elect a lieutenant governor, an attorney general, a secretary of state, and a treasurer; some also elect a state auditor, a comptroller, and commissioners of education, agriculture, labor, and insurance (see Table 5.2). Although reformist efforts to streamline state government and centralize authority have included proposals to make some of these positions appointive by the governor, the array of directly elected posts has remained substantially unchanged in recent decades.

The Lieutenant Governor

All executive offices are of some administrative and political importance. The lieutenant governor may preside over the state senate (twenty-six states), cast a vote in cases of ties (twenty-five states), assign bills to senate committees (thirteen states), or appoint members to senate committees and committee chairs (seven states). The lieutenant governor functions as the governor when the latter is disabled (in forty-two states) and when the governor is out of state (twenty-seven states).[27]

TABLE 5.2 DIRECTLY ELECTED STATE EXECUTIVE OFFICERS

Position	Number of States
Governor	50
Attorney general	43
Lieutenant governor	42
Treasurer	38
Secretary of state	36
Auditor	25
Comptroller	9

Source: Calculated from data in *The Book of the States, 1996–97* (Lexington, Ky.: Council of State Governments, 1996), p. 33.

Typically, the lieutenant governor has no direct administrative duties other than special tasks assigned by the governor. Further, lieutenant governors whose duties include presiding over the state senate often decline to do so much of the time. There are exceptions, however; in Texas, the lieutenant governor's role in the senate is of major political importance. Some critics argue that the lieutenant governor position is not needed, and there has been a movement in several states to eliminate the position.

The position of lieutenant governor can be a launching pad for mischief, for a run at the position of governor, or both. In states where the governor and the lieutenant governor are not elected on a single ticket, they may be from different political parties. For example, a Massachusetts lieutenant governor, an announced candidate for the governorship, proposed a new state budget during the governor's absence from the country.

In addition, some governors have given the lieutenant governor significant duties. Florida's Lawton Childes is an example. He assigned Buddy Mackay the task of coordinating policy within his cabinet, and sent him to the senate from time to time to lobby members on the governor's policy preferences.

The Attorney General

We've noted that authority in the executive branches of the states is widely distributed, and that the power of the governor can be weakened because of the direct election of major executive branch department heads. Attorneys general,[28] who exist and run the departments of law in all fifty states, constitute one such position. In five states the attorney general is appointed by the governor and is subject to the governor's direct influence. But in forty-three states the attorney general answers only to the people at election time, and is rather independent as a result. It is small wonder that attorneys general are often members of the opposite party as the governor, or that the position is frequently used as a springboard for the governorship itself.

The position of attorney general is an important one and, indeed, increasingly so. The attorney general is the chief legal office of the state. Responsibilities of the position include representing public officials in civil suits related to their official duties; offering advisory opinions on the constitutionality of laws, regulations, or actions to the legislature or others in the executive branch; helping local prosecutors when asked or sometimes intervening; defending the laws of the state in court actions; and routinely reviewing new legislation.

Increasingly, state attorneys general have played the role of public watchdog and advocate in matters of environmental pollution and consumer protection. In recent years, they have initiated legal action against Mitsubishi Electronics and

Nintendo for price-fixing on television sets, they've sued VISA and Mastercard for monopolistic credit card practices, and they've challenged the veracity of the advertising of Nabisco, Kellogg, Quaker Oats, and Campbell Soup with respect to the health aspects of their products, as well as "environmental friendly" advertisements of Mobil Oil and Proctor and Gambel. In a number of states, Florida being one prime example, they have sought damages against tobacco companies on behalf of the state, seeking to recover state-paid health costs.

Clearly, the office of attorney general is important to others within state and local government as well as ordinary citizens. State officials look to the attorney general for legal defense and legal advice. The interest of citizens on matters ranging from a clean environment to consumer fraud and price-fixing are often advanced by that office.

Given both the wide sweep of responsibilities and the elective nature of the position it is little wonder that the job can become highly political. Many a governor has served first as attorney general and used the position to generate visibility and political support. An aggressive and well-publicized campaign against polluters, recapture of fraudulently obtained welfare benefits, or pursuit of organized crime can do good things for a politically ambitious attorney general. So can a drumbeat of attack on a sitting governor who is of the other political party.

The Secretary of State

In thirty-six states voters elect their secretary of state[29] directly, making the position one of the many in the plural executive model. Three states have no secretary of state, and the duties usually performed by that office are done by the lieutenant governor. In three other states the legislature elects the secretary of state and in the remaining eight the governor makes the appointment.

The duties of the secretary of state are of vital importance even if they're not flashy or the focus of headlines. Perhaps the most important function is to serve as the state's chief elections officer. The election tasks performed by this office generally include determining the eligibility of political parties and candidate eligibility, overseeing voter registration, publishing election results, certifying nominations and elections, receiving initiative and referendum petitions, receiving financial disclosure and campaign funding reports from candidates and, often, receiving legally mandated registration forms and financial reports from lobbyists. Anyone seeking information on elections or lobbying is well served by visiting the office of secretary of state first.

In addition, the secretary of state's office is typically the place where corporations and trademarks are registered and public notaries are commissioned. These are important records for both businesses and government as they provide a tracking of the formation and dissolution of business enterprises as well as their names and some financial records.

Secretary of state offices are heavy with citizen traffic. Streams of people come in daily seeking information, inquiring about legal requirements for political candidacy, lobbying, or registering a business. Therefore, office personnel must be "client friendly," and accurate and up-to-date records must be maintained.

The State Treasurer

One other executive branch position that is elective in most states is that of state treasurer.[30] Voters in thirty-eight states elect their state treasurer. In seven others the governor makes the appointment and in four the treasurer is elected by the legislature. In Georgia, the State Depository Board makes the appointment.

Basically, the treasurer is the custodian of the state's money. Just as with a family's finances, the flow of tax revenues into state coffers does not match the ebb and flow of expenditures, the result is that there is often "money in the bank" for short periods of time. For a state, the amount can be a lot of money, with significant interest-raising potential. The treasurer's job is to invest the funds for short periods of time, maximizing the return but avoiding risk. In addition, treasurers manage a state's debt on capital matters, issuing bonds and seeing to proper payoffs of the state's capital borrowing.

The Governor and Separation of Powers

The governor and the legislature are rivals for control of the budget process. Governors can and do employ the veto, and they threaten its use to coax from the legislature policies they prefer. Governors also use their visibility in the media to press on the legislature those parts of their agendas that are supported by public opinion. But the legislature ultimately controls the lawmaking process; it can exert control over the authority, the resources, and the shape of both the executive branch and the courts.

The internal structure of a state's executive branch can have a pronounced impact on state politics. When executive authority is dispersed among a variety of directly elected officials, the governor's power is weakened somewhat. The governor may even face public political opposition from other executives, especially if they belong to the other party. But U.S. institutions do divide authority. When the various parts of the institutional apparatus are controlled by different parties—which is the case in the vast majority of states—implementing a particular political philosophy is difficult. A Democratic legislature may thwart a Republican governor and vice versa. A Republican attorney general may give a Democratic governor a rough time with unwanted advisory opinions, investigations, or prosecutions. Boards and commissions that govern regulatory bodies or large educational institutions may pursue policies and priorities—with respect to environmental pollution or tuition rates, for example—that both the governor and the legislature dislike.

Clearly, the hallmark of executive branch organization in the American states is decentralization. Like federalism and legislative bicameralism, executive branch decentralization disperses power and, when combined with partisan division, creates a political system characterized by extensive conflict. Of course, there are some centralizing features in the system as well. With a mixture of available budgetary, appointment, and veto powers, as well as skillful use of the media and political party connections, some governors can overcome the effects of institutional decentralization and push their preferred policies into public law.

Such successes are the result of the triumph of informal gubernatorial power over formal fragmentation. The place of the states in the federal system has changed over the years, most recently with an increase in their role and importance. Within that context, the nature of the governorship has changed as well. Today's governorship is a prized position. Some past governors want the job back. Many already successful politicians are willing to surrender their U.S. House and Senate seats to seek the position of state governor. Many attorney's general, state treasurers, legislative leaders, and individuals with successful records in the private sector want to be governor. As formally instituted, the governorship is not all that powerful a position, and the increasingly prevalent party-divided government makes the job more difficult than ever before. But the states are major actors in the contemporary federal system, and, with skillful supplementation of formal authority with public relations and political savvy, an energetic politician can indeed make a difference.

Summary

The modern state executive system is one in which the governor occupies a primary place, often among a host of other elected executive officials. Governors play a variety of formal and informal roles, many of which contribute to the expansion of executive power. However, today's governors also face limitations. The plural executive system was designed to limit executive authority and continues to do so. An established bureaucracy with strong agency–clientele ties also limits the power of the governor. While most modern governors are not formally endowed with extensive powers, there are ways to create a stronger gubernatorial office. Some states continue to amend the executive structure by placing additional formal powers in the hands of the governor. Informal powers and bureaucratic expertise can increase the power of the governor who possesses the political expertise and public support to make effective use of them.

Policy Perspective

The most literal interpretation of the separation of powers doctrine would tell us that governors have no role in the creation of public policy. Legislatures are properly the policy bodies, and the governor's job is to take the policy as presented by lawmakers and implement it.

Of course, it is not quite that simple. At the very best governors have an affect on public policy by the manner in which they and those who work for them implement policy. Implementation can be vigorous or lax. Regulations can be enforced rigorously, or ignored. Governors can appoint highly qualified administrators to head important departments, or they can use such posts as payoffs for the marginally competent.

The role that governors play in policy formation has varied considerably in time, by state, and by the personality and skills of the individual. In the pre-Constitutional colonial days governors were, in effect, the government. They were most often Royal appointees, agents of the British Crown and, while roundly unliked, they were in charge. In response to this executive hegemony, the early post-Constitutional states limited the tenure and powers of governors and generally reduced them to mere figureheads. Legislatures reigned supreme.

Following the Civil War and on into the twentieth century, legislative–executive relationships reversed themselves until part-time, unrepresentative, and often incompetent legislatures were led by the nose by dominating governors. This *de facto* executive dominance was reinforced by a private sector business ideology that championed centralized and top-down authority in the organizational world.

Over the past decade or two the picture has been mixed. Governors generally play important roles in policy making, but they are not always dominant. Chief executives are singular; they are easily and heavily covered by the media. The public knows who the governor is and tends to equate the person with the state government itself. Legislatures, on the other hand, are complicated and multimember bodies, much less well covered in the media and less well known and understood by the public. As a result, governors are expected to talk about major public problems and they are expected to have ideas about how to deal with them. In short, we have come to expect modern governors to have policy agendas and to push them.

The ability of state governors to influence the content of public policy has also been bolstered by the growth in size and competence of executive budget and planning staffs. No longer must governors rely upon a mere handful of aides, or the legislatures staff, to assemble budgets and policy proposals. Most governors today have dozens, even scores, of professionals to aid them.

But there have been some countertendencies that act to restrict the modern governor's impact upon policy. Perhaps most importantly, legislatures too have become modernized. Conditions vary widely among the states but, generally, and as compared to the situation several decades back, legislatures are populated with well-educated members, they have capable staff assistance, their facilities and equipment are modern, and they meet in session or interim committees much of the year. Most modern state legislatures have reasserted themselves as the states' central policy bodies.

Changes in the political landscape have also served to affect the policy role of governors. Over the course of the past two decades divided government has become so prevalent that today it is the norm. Indeed, by 1997 thirty-one states were divided, with no single political party in control of both legislative chambers and the governorship as well. This means that whatever policy package a governor chooses to push will be countered by that of the other party. The other party may not prevail, but neither will the governor alone rule the policy agenda.

Still other factors constrain a governors policy role; some of these were discussed earlier in the chapter. In some states the plural executives model hampers a governor's ability to control policy implementation. In some instances, staffing is short. In still other states, the law or custom leads to total legislative control of the budget process.

While such institutional and political factors clearly play a role in shaping gubernatorial impacts upon policy, so do the personalities and skills of the governors themselves. The behavior of such recent governors as Wisconsin's Thompson, Michigan's Engler, Wilson of California, Whitman of New Jersey, and even Joan Finney of Kansas and Gary Johnson of New Mexico are cases in point.

Tommy Thompson is a Republican in a state with a strong progressive tradition and a legislature that has been controlled by Democrats more often than not over the past few decades. Thompson exercised the veto in a way never before seen in his state, striking out words and letters in the budget bill to actually alter the meaning of policy. He also led an effort to restructure the state's welfare system well before the Congressional changes to 1996, and in a way that garnered national attention and made Thompson a visible and important figure in both the national Republican party and the National Governors Association. In Michigan Thompson's Republican colleague John Engler similarly landed in the national spotlight by successfully pushing for major state tax cuts, and an overhaul of the state's system of financing public schools.

In California Pete Wilson took a firm, controversial, and highly visible stance in opposition to affirmative action and public assistance for illegal immigrants, and he had partial victories on both counts. New Jersey's Christy Whitman ran on a platform of major tax cuts. She won and followed through on her promises, although the cuts have led to other problems, such as school finance, that may come back to haunt her politically.

These are examples of recent governors, who with a combination of personal assertiveness and political risk, and effective use of the public platform and media attention enjoyed by chief executives, were able to impact policy in major ways and, thus far, survive.

Not all governors are so successful. Joan Finney served just one term in Kansas and was generally considered to have done poorly. Many of her administrative appointments were poorly received, as were her policy stances.

The jury is still out on New Mexico's Gary Johnson. A political novice Republican businessman in a Democratic state, Johnson won in a three-way race in which some sour-grape primary losers splintered the Democratic vote and let Johnson slip in with less than 50 percent of the vote. Following the first legislative session, Johnson proceeded to veto almost half of the legislature's bills, shocking and angering majority party Democrats and Republicans alike. Going into the 1997 session he suggested that the legislature write a budget giving him the nonfederal and nonearmarked general fund portion in a single lump sum; then he'd just go ahead and run things. One of his cabinet secretaries told an interim legislative committee that the governor would be assembling a policy group, presumably his cabinet, and they'd vote thumbs up or thumbs down on 1997 legislative measures. While Governor Johnson claims to dislike politics and argues that he is not a politician, he is clearly intent on making an impact on policy. Indeed, his comments and budget actions suggest an interest in displacing the legislature itself as the fount of New Mexico's public policy.

The policy role that governors play is a function of institutional, political, and personal factors all rolled together. Without the institutional veto power neither Thompson nor Johnson could have done what they did to the legislatures' budgets and bills. With the public relations and media skills of Pete Wilson and Christie Whitman, Joan Finney might well have had a more pleasant and consequential experience as governor of Kansas. Except for widespread divided government, more governors might well do better pushing their policy preferences.

Professor Thad Beyle, a foremost scholar on the subject of American governors, developed an analysis that combines both the personal and formal powers of governors. Interestingly, some governors with rather weak formal powers do well on the personal power scale, and vice versa. Professor Beyle's rating of personal power is based upon a combination of opinion poll data, ratings by observers of the governors, and information on election results and gubernatorial careers. For the formal power he looked at appointment, budget, and veto authority, as well as political party control and tenure potential. In Missouri, the formal powers of the governor rank about in the middle of the fifty states; for Colorado it is toward the weakest end. Yet the governors of those two states are the highest of the fifty on the personal power scale.[31]

What does this all mean? It means that modern state governors do indeed play major roles in the establishment, as well as the implementation, of public policy. But the roles and the impact of the governors vary. They vary from great (in Wisconsin) to slight (in Kansas). The impact comes in politically smooth fashion in California and New Jersey, but like a loose bull in New Mexico. And the policy impacts are significant, not trivial, affecting matters ranging from welfare and tax policy to public school finance.

KEY TERMS

policy coordinator
gubernatorial power
formal powers
informal powers
pocket veto
legislative liaison
plural executive
integrated executive
clientele group
sunk costs

ADDITIONAL READING

Beyle, Thad, and J. Oliver Williams, eds. *The Governor in Behavioral Perspective*. New York: Harper & Row, 1972.

Beyle, Thad L., and Lynn R. Muchmore, eds. *Being Governor: The View from the Office*. Durham, N.C.: Duke Press Policy Studies, 1983.

Rosenthal, Alan. *Governors and Legislatures: Contending Powers*. Washington, D.C.: Congressional Quarterly Press, 1990.

Sabato, Larry. *Goodbye to Goodtime Charlie*. 2d ed. Washington, D.C.: Congressional Quarterly Press, 1983.

NOTES

1. Michael Oreskes, "Governors' Races, Close and Costly, Are Richest Prize," *New York Times*, 4 Nov. 1990.
2. *The Book of the States, 1990–91* (Lexington, Ky.: Council of State Governments, 1991), pp. 85–86.
3. See Thad L. Beyle, "Being Governor," in *The State of the States*, 3rd ed., ed. Carl E. Van Horn (Washington, D.C.: CQ Press, 1996), pp. 78–82.
4. Thad L. Beyle and Lynn R. Muchmore, eds., *Being Governor: The View from the Office* (Durham, N.C.: Duke Press Policy Studies, 1983), p. 3.
5. Coleman B. Ransone, Jr., *The American Governorship* (Westport, Conn.: Greenwood Press, 1982), p. 3.

6. Thad L. Beyle, "Governors," in *Politics in the American States*, 6th ed., ed. Virginia Gray and Herbert Jacob (Washington, D.C.: C.Q. Press, 1996), pp. 207–52.
7. Tommy G. Thompson, "Going Global: A Governor's Perspective," *Intergovernmental Perspective* (Spring 1990): 15.
8. Marc Landy, "Kentucky," in *The Political Life of the American States*, ed. Alan Rosenthal and Maureen Moakley (New York: Praeger, 1984), p. 206.
9. Beyle, "Governors," pp. 208–9.
10. Beyle, "Governors," p. 214.
11. Paul West, "They're Everywhere! For Today's Governors, Life Is a Never-Ending Campaign," *Governing* (March 1990): 51–52.
12. The symbolic role of the U.S. chief executive develops in Americans' minds at a very early age. See David Easton and Jack Dennis, "The Child's Image of Government," *Annals of the American Academy of Political and Social Science* (Sept. 1965): 40–57.
13. *Denver Post*, 19 May 1994.
14. *The Book of the States, 1996–97*, p. 98.
15. Tony Hutchinson, "Legislating via Veto," *State Legislatures* (20 Jan. 1989): 20–22.
16. Thad L. Beyle, "The Executive Branch: Organization and Issues, 1988–89," in *The Book of the States, 1988–89* (Lexington, Ky.: Council of State Governments), p. 75.
17. Thad L. Beyle, "The Powers of Governors," in *State Government*, ed. Thad L. Beyle (Washington, D.C.: Congressional Quarterly Press, 1990), pp. 124–25.
18. Kenneth J. Meier, "Executive Reorganization of Government: Impact on Employment and Expenditures," *American Journal of Political Science* (Aug. 1980): 396–412.
19. James K. Conant, "In the Shadow of Wilson and Brownlow: Executive Branch Reorganization in the States, 1965–1987," *Public Administration Review* (Sept.–Oct. 1988): 892–902.
20. Phillip O. Foss, *Reorganization and Reassignment in the California Highway Patrol* (Indianapolis: Bobbs-Merrill, Inter-University Case Program, 1962), case no. 75.
21. Ira Sharkansky suggests that the best predictor of the content of a new budget is the content of past budgets. See his "Agency Requests, Gubernatorial Support and Budget Success in State Legislatures," *American Political Science Review* (Dec. 1968): 1,220–31.
22. Reported in Beyle, "Governors," pp. 201–51, esp. pp. 217–30.
23. Landy, "Kentucky," pp. 208–13.
24. Lawrence R. Hepburn, "Georgia," in *The Political Life of the American States*, ed. Alan Rosenthal and Maureen Moakley (New York: Praeger, 1984), pp. 191–93.
25. Anthony Champagne and Rick Collis, "Texas," in *The Political Life of the American States*, ed. Alan Rosenthal and Maureen Moakley (New York: Praeger, 1984), pp. 144–47.
26. Charles G. Bell, "California," in *The Political Life of the American States*, ed. Alan Rosenthal and Maureen Moakley (New York: Praeger, 1984), pp. 53–54.
27. *Book of the States, 1990–91*, p. 56, and *1996–97*, p. 46.
28. See Jeffrey L. Amastey, "The Attorney General," in *The Book of the States, 1992–1993*, pp. 102–13.
29. See James H. Douglas, "The Secretary of State," in *The Book of the States, 1992–1993*, pp. 95–101.
30. See Mary Ellen Withrew, "The State Treasurer," in *The Book of the States, 1992–1993*, pp. 115–121.
31. Beyle, in "Governors," pp. 228–38.

CHAPTER
6

• • •

State Judicial Systems

• • •

Most judicial activity in this country occurs in the state and local courts, not at the federal level. Minnesota's supreme court, the highest court in that state, has seven justices: *(seated, from left)* Justice Ester M. Tomljanovich, Chief Justice A.M. (Sandy) Keith, Justice Sandra S. Gardebring; *(standing, from left)* Justice Edward C. Stringer, Justice Alan C. Page, Justice Paul H. Anderson, Justice Kathleen A. Blatz. *(Courtesy of the Supreme Court of Minnesota)*

• • • Most Justice Is Administered by State and Local Systems

• • • Judges Are Human Beings

• • • The Courts Are Political Entities

• • • The Structure of State Judicial Systems

State Courts and Federal Courts
Federal versus State Cases
State Supreme Courts
Intermediate Appellate Courts
Trial Courts
Lower Courts
Special Courts
Legislative Control of the Courts

• • • Judicial Reform

• • • Selecting Judges

Judge Selection Varies among States
Should Judges Be Elected or Appointed?
Choosing the Best Judge Selection Method
The Methods Are Political

• • • Democracy and the Courts

Focus 6.1: Judicial Selection and the Voting Rights Act

Political Equality
Legal Precedent

Focus 6.2: Religion, Sexual Orientation, and Parades

• • • Contemporary Problems in the Courts

Attitudes and Values
Judicial Delay

Focus 6.3: Crowded Dockets and Their Consequences

Bargain Justice
Unequal Resources

Lack of Diversity
Searches for Remedies

• • • **STATE COURTS AND CIVIL LIBERTIES**
State Bills of Rights
The Fourteenth Amendment
Rights by Case Law

• • • **RECENT DEVELOPMENTS IN THE STATE COURTS**
New Judicial Federalism
Alternative Dispute Resolution
Other Approaches to Expediting the Courts' Business
Gender and Ethnic Fairness

• • • **SUMMARY**

• • • **POLICY PERSPECTIVE**

Like the legislative and executive branches, the judicial branch makes authoritative decisions and allocates scarce goods and values in the states. That is, the judiciary is a political as well as a legal institution. This may be the single most difficult characteristic of the judiciary for most of us to understand. The conventional view is that the courts, and the judges who preside over them, are somehow removed from politics. We like to believe that justice is indeed blind, and so we embrace a **cult of the robe**—the notion that when an individual puts on the robe of a judge, he or she sheds all biases and prejudices and becomes an impartial dispenser of justice. In reality, the cult of the robe is based on a myth—but a functional myth, because it helps us to accept judicial decisions with which we disagree.

In order to maintain respect and support for the judicial system it may be important that the image of judicial impartiality be preserved. Still, the courts, like the legislative and executive branches of government, are highly politicized. As in most other areas of government and politics, opinion and prejudice help to determine who wins and who loses in the courts. This is not to suggest that the judicial environment is the same as the legislative and executive environments; it is not. But it is a political environment nonetheless.

The principle of **judicial review**—the determination by the judiciary of the constitutionality of the actions of public officials—operates at the state as well as the federal level. Through this principle, state courts hear thousands of cases every year, and in the process they settle disputes, interpret the law, and help to shape public policy. Many cases that come before the courts involve minor events (for example, the prosecution of individuals for disorderly conduct or traffic violations); others are more serious (murder trials or million-dollar lawsuits). Some cases may have implications for just one individual, while others may involve an interpretation of a statute or of the powers and duties of a local government or state agency and may affect many people for years to come. Albeit rarely, a state case can sometimes transcend the confines of the case itself to serve as a window to the nation's values, such as in the O.J. Simpson case and the Timothy McVeigh/Oklahoma City bombing case. Whatever the nature of the case—whether it involves an intergovernmental dispute over the powers of local governments, a contest for the custody of children, a suit for land or money, or a prosecution of an individual accused of a crime—the courts are involved in the creation and application of law and in the authoritative resolution of conflict.

Most Justice Is Administered by State and Local Systems

Most of the courts, judges, and criminal and civil cases in the United States are in the state and local systems, not in the federal courts. The reason is simple: most of our laws are state-made laws. Virtually all property, contract, domestic relations, and criminal law is embodied in state-made common law, state statutes, or local ordinances. The federal laws and federal courts deal with matters of federal taxation, bankruptcy, racketeering, and civil rights and liberties, as well as a host of other matters. The bulk of the action involving crime, property, families, children, and the general health, peace, and safety of the public, however, is in the state and local domain.

Most legal matters, criminal and civil, are not settled as a result of lengthy and full-blown judicial proceedings. Rather, criminal cases are often settled before they ever go to trial, through plea bargains struck between defendants and prosecutors, deals that are then accepted by a judge.

Judges Are Human Beings

Judges, like the rest of us, have sets of attitudes and policy preferences—and these creep into their decisions. Prosecutors in most states possess broad discretionary powers, with the result that some people are prosecuted and others are not. As we will see later in the chapter, decisions are made and political equality is violated through a system of bargain justice. Prosecutors are actually a part of the executive branch of government, but their roles have obvious implications for the court system. Some judges have reputations as being "hanging judges" (meaning that they are tough on crime). Other judges are more sympathetic than some of their colleagues to the defense or the prosecution, to citizens or corporations, to women or men. In some courts, students, African Americans, or poor people may be at a definite disadvantage. After all, the courts are called "courts of law," not courts of justice.

Some judges also enjoy reputations for being hard-working, knowledgeable, and fair. Unfortunately, the process of selecting judges in many states (discussed more fully later in this chapter) sometimes produces judges whose abilities are widely disparaged by the local members of the bar. One Texas district judge had the nickname "Reversible Error" by fellow practicing lawyers; the attorneys knew that this judge was likely to make an error during a trial that would lead a higher court to reverse the decision on appeal. Unfortunately, this type of judge is hardly unique.

This chapter describes the structure and operation of the judicial systems in the American states. It also outlines the structure of the state courts, including their relationship to the federal judiciary, a few of the more salient characteristics of the judicial process, the various methods employed to select judges, a number of problems that continue to plague state courts, and the role of the courts in the maintenance of political equality and civil rights.

The Courts Are Political Entities

As noted earlier, we often think of courts as nonpolitical institutions. Formulating public policy is normally perceived as a function of the legislative and executive branches, not of the courts. Judges often take great pains to maintain judicial restraint and to avoid the appearance of judicial activism by claiming to look to statutes and legislative intent rather than their own preferences when making decisions. The terms **judicial restraint** and **judicial activism** describe the relationship between the courts and the elected branches of government. Advocates of judicial restraint believe that the courts should defer to the elected branches on questions of public policy. Proponents of judicial activism view the courts as equals of the elected branches and believe that the courts should be directly involved in the policy-making process. Our definition of democracy calls for equality for all before the bench. In many ways, then, our understanding of the judiciary role in the separation of powers, our assumptions about democracy, and judges' stated intention to exercise restraint all seem to create a picture of a court system that is not political.

But, of course, the judiciary is political. If the term politics refers to the determination of public policy, then the courts are very much political institutions. No matter how detailed and specific our constitutions and statutes are, judgments about their meanings in specific situations must be rendered. What does prohibition of "cruel and unusual punishment" mean when it comes to living conditions in some state prisons? What does it mean to provide equal educational opportunity in elementary and secondary education? How much money should a person recover as "damages" in a case of personal injury? How far does "due process" go in preventing a city or state agency from firing an employee? The courts end up making many of these decisions, and their choices often have enormous policy consequences. When a court disallows "double-bunking" or requires a certain number of square feet in living space per inmate in a state prison, it can set off a capital construction program with major fiscal consequences for a financially beleaguered state. A court decision that finds a state's educational funding system to be an impediment to equal educational opportunity among school districts can do the same. Texas grappled with the latter problem for several years, with increasing costs to the taxpayers, before resolving the problem to the satisfaction of the state courts.

Courts also have a political character as a result of the backgrounds and attitudes that judges bring to their jobs. Judges, like governors, legislators, and lobbyists, come to their job with a set of values and preconceptions, and, try as they may (and some do not try), they are never able to shed their prejudices and apply the law objectively. Although the courts may try to be fair, although they may attempt to minimize partisan considerations in their judgments, and although they may be the least political of the three branches of government, they remain political institutions.

No one can deny that the choices made by judges have major impacts on public policies or that the preferences of judges find their way into decisions, just as attitudes and values affect the way legislators vote. At the same time, although the avowed responsibility of legislators is to translate voter preferences into public policy, the duty of judges is to minimize the impact of personal political preferences in general and try instead to "discover" what the people want, as evidenced in the words and intent of constitutions and statutes. This task may not be feasible, or even desirable according to some, but the very perception on the part of the public that this is the proper role of the judiciary is a constraint on judicial behavior.

The Structure of State Judicial Systems

While the judicial systems of all states share many characteristics, there is also extensive diversity. By and large the courts are, like much of the U.S. government system, highly decentralized. Some courts handle minor cases, while others deal with more serious ones. Courts may have original jurisdiction, appellate jurisdiction, or both. In general, all states have a three-tiered judiciary made up of trial courts, appellate courts, and a supreme court (although not all states call their top court a "supreme" court). In most states various parts of the court system operate independently of one another. Sometimes more than one set of courts has jurisdiction over similar cases. Often the administration of the courts is decentralized, too. As we will see later in the chapter, methods of selecting judges vary among the states and even among the courts within individual states.[1]

State Courts and Federal Courts

The judicial systems in the American states are structurally separate from the national court system. Here again we see the influence of the federal principle. As in American government generally, decision making in the judiciary is widely diffused—both between and within the national and state court systems. The output of the judicial system is the cumulative result of thousands of decisions made in literally thousands of courtrooms.

Our use of the federal system results in the parallel existence of two sets of government—the national government and the fifty state governments. As a result, there are actually fifty-one sovereign governments and, consequently, fifty-one court systems. The national courts (or federal courts, as they are usually called) have **jurisdiction** over matters involving national laws and personnel, and the state courts deal with state matters. When the national government, an employee of the national government acting in an official capacity, or a national law is involved, the case is heard in national court. If the state government, a state employee acting in an official capacity, or a state law is involved, the state courts have jurisdiction. Because local governments are legally a part of the state governmental system, matters involving local governments, their official representatives, or their ordinances are usually heard in the state courts as well. The major exception involves U.S. constitutional issues; that is, under some circumstances when there is a question about the constitutionality of a law or act of a state or local government, the U.S. Supreme Court may hear the case.

There are a few other exceptions to the various jurisdictional rules. For example, if a state employee breaks a federal law by violating someone's civil rights, he or she may be tried in a federal court. Some criminal actions run afoul of both federal and state laws (for example, bank robbery); a person accused of such crimes may be tried in both federal and state courts (there is no double jeopardy violation, as the accused is not being tried twice under the same law). The highly publicized Rodney King case in Los Angeles is such an example. The police officers accused of beating King were first tried in a local court under California law; they were acquitted. Then, they were tried in a federal court, on the charge of violating King's federal civil rights; two of the officers were found guilty.

Federal versus State Cases

At one time or another we all have heard the quip, "Don't make a federal case out of it." The intended implication is that somebody is making a "big deal" out of a minor matter. But the unintended implication is that the issues before the national courts are always more significant than those addressed by the states. Not so. Jurisdiction between the national and state courts is determined by the government, the public official, or the law that is involved, not by the seriousness of the case. Murder, rape, assault, and reckless or drunk driving are all serious matters, but they are state cases because they involve violations of state law. Likewise, disorderly conduct and illegal parking or drinking after hours are state cases because they involve violation of local ordinances, and local governments are legally a part of the state government. However, the theft or purposeful destruction of a mailbox is a federal offense; it involves obstruction of the U.S. mail, a violation of a federal (national) law, and a person accused of such an act would be tried in a federal court.

In some cases, both state and federal courts have jurisdiction in a particular civil matter. If an individual chooses to sue a firm engaged in interstate commerce, he or she may bring the case in federal court. If the firm is engaged in intrastate commerce only, the suit will be heard in a state court (unless the matter involves a U.S. constitutional issue, such as alleged civil rights violations or a breach of federal law). Sometimes the case can be brought in either court, if there is concurrent jurisdiction. For example, some years ago a serious automobile accident resulted in a case in which the injured party brought suit for personal injury against a consortium of a railroad and two construction companies. In this particular case, the suit could have been brought in either a state or federal court. The incident was a crash involving an automobile and a train at a construction location where highway work was being done by two construction companies, each of which maintained its central office in a different county of the state. The individual injured in the accident actually had a choice of five courts in which to bring an injury suit. Since the railroad was involved in interstate commerce, suit could have been brought in federal district court—the lowest major court in the federal judicial hierarchy. But a suit could also have been brought in any one of four trial courts in the state in which the accident occurred. It could have been brought in the state court in the county where the accident happened, or it could have been brought in state court in the county where the plaintiff (the person filing the suit) resided. Finally, the suit could have been brought in state court in either of the two counties where the construction companies maintained their home offices.

The national judiciary is structurally uncomplicated, consisting of three levels of courts plus a group of special courts. State court systems are often not so simple. All states have a supreme court, an intermediate appellate structure, and a group of trial courts. Some states have a number of other courts as well. No two states have identical court systems. In some states, such as Wyoming, the judiciary consists of just three tiers. In other states, such as New York, the judiciary contains a host of special purpose courts in addition to the major trial courts and the supreme court.

State Supreme Courts

At the top of every state court system is a court of last resort, usually called the **supreme court**. Two unusual deviations are found in Oklahoma and Texas, where there are two courts of last resort—one for civil cases and another for criminal matters. State supreme courts typically are composed of five or seven justices, although Alabama, Iowa, Mississippi, Oklahoma, Texas, and Washington each have nine. In some states the justices are appointed by the governor or legislature; in others they are elected on either partisan or nonpartisan ballots. In a few states the judges serve life terms on the top court, while in others they are elected to two-, six-, eight-, or ten-year terms. (The methods of judicial selection are examined more fully later in the chapter.)

Most of the business of state supreme courts involves hearing appeals from lower court decisions; in a few states the supreme court has original jurisdiction (that is, it can be the court in which the case originates). Decisions by these courts are made by majority rule and usually are recorded in written opinions. In considering appeals from lower court decisions, state supreme courts play an important role in the political process. Often cases that reach the appellate court are controversial and hinge on disagreement about the interpretation of a law. When the court renders a decision, therefore, it sets a precedent that the lower courts are expected to follow. As a result, state supreme courts play a critical role in the actual establishment of the law, and, since their decisions bind the lower courts, the decisions of the supreme courts may affect large numbers of people.

Intermediate Appellate Courts

State supreme court dockets have become extremely overloaded in recent decades. As a result of the serious and growing problem of delayed justice, nearly two-thirds of the states now have some form of **intermediate appellate court.** These appeals courts are higher on the judicial totem pole than the major trial courts, but lower than the supreme court. Their task is to relieve the supreme court of some of its burden and to reduce the long delays that have become a serious problem in cases under appeal. With few exceptions, such as death penalty cases in some states, cases that eventually reach the supreme court must be heard by the intermediate appeals court first. The number of judges on intermediate appellate courts varies from three in Alaska, Hawaii, and Idaho to eight in Texas. In most states appellate judges are selected for terms ranging from five to twelve years.

Trial Courts

Below the supreme court and the intermediate appellate courts (in states where they exist) are the **trial courts**, or the courts of general jurisdiction. The names and numbers of courts of general jurisdiction vary considerably, but they handle the bulk of the most serious cases in every state. These trial courts go by several names, the most common of which are district, superior, circuit, county, and common court. In some states there are just a few such courts, and in others there are dozens of them. In some states each county has one or more major trial court, whereas in other states one court may serve several counties. In the most complex systems there are trial courts of record (that is, courts whose proceedings are recorded) as well as trial courts, usually addressing minor issues, that do not keep a written record.

Courts of general jurisdiction possess both original and appellate jurisdiction. They may hear appeals from such lower courts of limited jurisdiction as probate, municipal, or magistrate courts, and, while they possess original jurisdiction in both serious and petty matters, most of their work entails civil cases involving large sums of money and criminal cases involving large fines or lengthy jail sentences. Felony cases, for example, are heard for the first time in the major trial courts. When these major trial courts hear appeals from the lower courts of limited jurisdiction, the case is heard *de novo* (literally, "anew"); that is, since many lower courts are not courts of record, the cases that are appealed are heard all over again, from the beginning.

Unlike appellate courts, where there are no juries, major trial courts may use juries in both criminal and civil cases. As is the case with state supreme courts and intermediate appellate courts, trial court judges are appointed in some states and elected in others for terms ranging from four to fifteen years.

Lower Courts

At the bottom of the judicial hierarchy are the **lower courts**, or courts of limited jurisdiction. These may be county, municipal, or justice of the peace courts, depending on the exact structure of a state's system. These lower courts process the thousands of minor cases involving traffic violations, misdemeanors (such as disturbing the peace), and suits involving small amounts of money. Compared to the courts of general jurisdiction and state supreme courts, the lower courts are less significant politically because the cases they handle affect only the individuals involved. Unlike supreme court decisions, the actions of the trial courts do not set precedents that are followed by other courts.

Special Courts

Finally, many states include certain types of **special courts** in their judicial systems. States with heavy urban concentrations, such as Michigan and New York, may make constitutional or statutory provision for special municipal courts in the large cities. Other states have established special purpose probate, juvenile, small claims, tax, or domestic relations courts.

As noted earlier in the chapter, no two states have identical judicial systems. The names of the courts, the methods of selecting judges, the length of judges' terms, and other features of the judicial system vary among the states. Most states employ one or more courts that handle specialized cases of one sort or another. Table 6.1 outlines the relatively simple court structure of Hawaii, the moderately complex system of Iowa, and the highly complicated arrangement of New York.

Legislative Control of the Courts

Although some basic features of state court systems are established in state constitutions, the state legislatures make most of the decisions that shape the structure, jurisdiction, and operation of the courts. What constitutes a felony or a misdemeanor, and what should the penalties be for conviction? How much sentencing latitude should judges have? What should be the salaries of judges? Will there be a public defender system and, if so, what will it look like? How many courts and how many judges will there be in the state? These are the types of questions answered by state legislatures.

Each year state legislative agendas contain many bills related to the judiciary. Often the bills are pushed to change or clarify laws in direct response to a court decision with which the legislature may have disagreed. Sometimes legislators, angry with a court decision, may seek to remove jurisdiction from a court. Of course, it is the legislature that writes the statutes that the courts apply and interpret. It is also the legislature that creates most of the court system. While to some degree the courts are supported by fees, it is the legislature that appropriates much of the money needed to run the judicial system.

TABLE 6.1 JUDICIARY STRUCTURE IN THREE STATES

Hawaii	Iowa	New York
Supreme court	Supreme court	Courts of appeals
Intermediate courts of appeals	Court of appeals	Appellate divisions of supreme court
Circuit courts	District courts	Supreme court
District courts	Superior courts	Court of claims
	Municipal courts	Surrogates' courts
	Judicial courts	Family courts
	Magistrate courts	County courts
	Police courts	Civil court (New York City)
		Criminal court (New York City)
		District courts
		Justice courts
		City courts
		Town and village courts

Sources: Adapted from data in *State Court Systems* (Chicago: Council of State Governments, 1962); and *The Book of the States, 1988–89* (Lexington, Ky.: Council of State Governments, 1989).

Judicial Reform

Reformers have been busy in recent decades pressing for structural changes in the courts. Criticisms of and recommendations for the courts follow the same line as those targeted at other parts of the government. State judicial systems are faulted for instances of overlapping jurisdiction and for their generally decentralized character. Critics accuse the court systems of being inefficient and confusing. They should be restructured and centralized, it is argued.

Reformers often advocate what is called a **unified court system**. In theory, a unified system would be hierarchical, with the supreme court at the top, serving both as a court of last resort and as the body that possesses final administrative power over the entire court system. The rest of the courts would be subordinate to the supreme court. The jurisdiction of each set of courts would be clearly defined, with no overlapping or conflict. Procedures would be the same in all courts that share similar responsibilities and jurisdiction. Personnel and pay systems would be standardized and centrally administered.

The benefits of such an orderly system, reformers argue, would include greater public understanding of the courts, increased speed in the processing of cases, and financial savings.

However, like reformist campaigns in government generally, court reforms are acknowledged more in word than deed. As is the case with any existing organizational arrangement, many people have a stake in the existing system. Judges and lawyers develop useful routines that they do not want disturbed. Many of the people most closely associated with the court system oppose any type of radical change. In addition, proposals for unified court systems often require that the state assume more of the costs of running the courts, with perhaps less reliance on support from local governments or from fees. This could create problems for legislators, especially in times of tight budgets. The legislature must modify state statutes to reorganize the judicial system, and legislatures are reluctant to do so if there is a significant price tag associated with the changes. Although there has been some modernization of the structure and operation of state courts in recent years, it has not been as sweeping or as extensive as reform advocates would like it to be.[2]

Selecting Judges

Although all federal judges are appointed by the U.S. president, considerable variation exists among the states in the procedures of judicial selection. Indeed, some states employ one system of selecting judges for some courts and a different system for other courts. Still, there are five general patterns of judge selection:

1. Appointment
2. Election in nonpartisan elections
3. Election in partisan elections
4. A combined appointment–election plan
5. Legislative selection

The appointment–election plan, often called the **Missouri plan** or the **merit plan**, has enjoyed some popularity recently. Although the details vary among states, basically the Missouri plan involves the appointment of judges by the governor from a list of nominees submitted by a judicial nominating panel. The nominating panel is supposedly made up of experts—knowledgeable attorneys and laypersons who are assumed capable of identifying candidates who will make good judges. After appointment by the governor, the judge serves a brief term in office and then runs for election against his or her record (that is, the judge faces no opposition). These elections are called retention elections. The voters determine whether to retain the judge for another specified term or to reject the judge and have the governor appoint a replacement.

Judge Selection Varies among States

Although changes in judge selection procedures are constantly being made, the state variations are as follows: nineteen states elect all or some of their judges in partisan elections; in three states all or some judges are elected by the legislature; twenty states elect judges in nonpartisan elections; nine states permit the governor to appoint all or most judges; and twenty-three states employ the Missouri plan. Where changes are being made in the selection processes, the process of choice usually is some form of the merit plan.

The judge selection scheme of each state can be classified as one of the five general types, but there are many variations among the states in terms of the details of the selection plans. For example, Ohio has partisan primaries but nonpartisan general elections. In Rhode Island the legislature elects the members of the state supreme court but the governor makes the appointments to the trial courts. In Arizona the selection process varies by the population of the county in which the court is located, with still other variations for certain local jurisdictions.[3] Maryland's judge selection process varies not only with the level of the court but also with the county involved. New Mexico employs a hybrid system in which a nominating convention provides the governor with a list of judicial nominees, the governor makes the appointment, the appointee runs in a partisan election in a first retention attempt after a period on the bench, and thereafter runs unopposed in a typical Missouri plan fashion.[4]

Most judges in Alabama, Arkansas, Texas, Illinois, Mississippi, New Mexico, North Carolina, and West Virginia are elected on partisan ballots, and all judges in Kentucky, Michigan, Minnesota, Montana, Nevada, North Dakota, Ohio, Oregon, Washington, and Wisconsin are elected in nonpartisan elections. A number of other states elect most, but not all, of their judges in either partisan or nonpartisan elections. Table 6.2 indicates the various methods by which states select their Supreme Court justices.

The method of judge selection utilized by any given state is usually the result of decisions made at the time the state entered the Union. It is often conditioned by the precedents set in and around that state in pre-statehood days as well as the reform movement that was in vogue at the time of statehood. This explains the widespread use of the elective procedure in the western states, for example. In a few states, though, later reform movements brought about the adoption of new judge selection methods. The complex mixture of procedures that exists in some states today may well be the result of incremen-

Table 6.2 State Supreme Court Selection Methods

Partisan Election	Nonpartisan Election	Legislative Appointment
Alabama	Georgia	Connecticut
Arkansas	Idaho	Rhode Island
Illinois	Kentucky	South Carolina
Mississippi	Louisiana	Virginia
New Mexico	Michigan	
New York	Minnesota	
North Carolina	Montana	
Pennsylvania	Nevada	
Tennessee	North Dakota	
Texas	Ohio	
West Virginia	Oregon	
	Washington	
	Wisconsin	

Governor Appointment	Missouri (Merit) Plan
Delaware	Alaska
Hawaii	Arizona
Maine	California
Maryland	Colorado
Massachusetts	Florida
New Hampshire	Indiana
New Jersey	Iowa
Vermont	Kansas
	Missouri
	Nebraska
	Oklahoma
	South Dakota
	Utah
	Wyoming

tal modification of the basic system brought on by such changes as rapid urbanization, which led to the addition of municipal courts in some cities.

Should Judges Be Elected or Appointed?

Arguments have been made both in support of and in opposition to the various methods of selecting judges. An old saying has it that the appointment process makes judges out of politicians and the electoral process makes politicians out of judges.

Elections

It is argued that direct election, the most widely used method, is effective because it makes judges, who clearly play policy-related roles in the governmental process, accountable to the sovereign public. Governors, legislators, mayors, and other public officials are held accountable for their behavior in public office and, the argument continues, the same level of accountability should be required of judges, since their actions, like those of other public officials, affect large numbers of people.

A counterargument contends that, although it makes sense in a democracy to maintain a popular check on all public officials, elections can tempt judges to "bend the law" in order to muster political support at the polls. The goals of the courts are to apply the law and to administer justice in an impartial and nonpolitical fashion. However, this counterargument continues, elections may subject judges to a host of political pressures and make it difficult for them to remain impartial on the bench. The contention is that the judiciary should be kept out of electoral politics; that the courts and judges are, or at least should be, "above the law."

As noted earlier in the chapter, the courts are very much a part of the political process. Still, in the name of judicial impartiality, opponents of the popular election of judges would rather minimize the political pressure to which judges may be subjected. The use of nonpartisan elections in many states represents an effort to avoid the "taint" of partisan politics. While the removal of party designations from the ballot may reduce the overt role of the political party in the judicial selection process, it does not purge the process of its partisan nature. Elections, by their very nature, are political affairs because they involve contestants for designated positions.

In addition, judicial elections are usually down-ballot races; that is, the candidates' names appear near the bottom of the election ballot and as a result attract a relatively low voter response because most voters are not likely to be familiar with them. A few years ago Texas voters elected a candidate whose last name was identical to that of a well-known candidate from the recent past. There is little doubt that most Texas voters mistakenly assumed the current and past candidates were the same person. They were not, and the public was dismayed to learn that they had elected an individual whose personal legal problems led eventually to his fleeing the state to avoid imprisonment.

Then there is the issue of financing judicial campaigns; money can taint the process. It is not uncommon for successful judicial candidates at the district court level to hold receptions for the purpose of paying off their campaign debt shortly after winning an election. Obviously, local law firms feel strong pressure to contribute to a judicial campaign or risk alienating a judge before whom they may appear in court. This is hardly "blind" justice.

Appointments

Some argue that the gubernatorial or legislative appointment of state judges removes the worst of partisan politics from the courtroom. The judicial system needs both qualified people and the highest possible degree of objectivity; therefore, it is important to insulate judges from the political combat of elections. Opponents of the appointment method reverse this argument. They contend that judges are public officials and an integral part of the government apparatus. Because their decisions affect the public, judges, like all other public officials, should be subject to public oversight and public control. Of course, there is nothing about the appointment process that is any more likely than the electoral process to filter out political hacks, individuals who might receive judicial appointments as rewards for longtime party service.

There is widespread agreement about the goal that should be pursued: Judges should avoid partisanship and favoritism in their official decision-making capacity, and as public servants they should be responsible to the people. The disagreement hinges on the methods that best achieve that goal. Are judges best made impartial and accountable when they are periodically forced to encounter the judgment of the people at the polls? Or is justice best served by appointing judges and thus insulating them from the pressures of elective politics?

The Missouri Plan

The solution to this problem, many contend, is the adoption of the Missouri or merit plan. As noted earlier in the chapter, the Missouri plan is a "merit" system that combines aspects of the elective and appointment methods of judge selection. In theory, it is intended to eliminate the worst and preserve the best of both the appointment and elective systems. Various forms of the method are employed in almost two dozen states. Advocates of the Missouri plan argue that it ensures the selection of competent judges, reduces the political nature of judge selection, and still sees to it that judges remain accountable to the people.

Critics of the Missouri plan, however, respond that it combines the worst, not the best, of the appointive and elective methods. First, they argue, it eliminates much of the public accountability that is supposedly inherent in the elective system. The popularly elected governor is restricted to the choices proposed by the nominating commission, so that the public cannot justifiably hold the governor responsible for the appointment of an incompetent judge.

Second, once a judge has served a short initial term, reelection is almost guaranteed for two reasons: (1) the judge is not likely to face serious opposition and (2) the public's knowledge of the affairs of the court is all but nonexistent. One way in which voters become informed about the record of incumbents seeking reelection, and one way in which incumbents are replaced by new officeholders, is through the debate and publicity that accompany most contests for public office. The contention is that when judges are allowed to run without opposition, they face no opponent whose campaign rhetoric might inform voters about the incumbent judge's past record. As a result, Missouri plan judges are almost never voted out of office.

It is important here to qualify the word *never* with *almost*, for occasionally voters do decline to return certain Missouri plan judges to the bench. Usually reelection fails when a judge runs afoul of the law or otherwise does something extreme and widely publicized. Perhaps the best-known example of an ouster of a judge in a retention election occurred in California in 1986, when Chief Justice Rose Bird and two of her associates failed to be retained. Bird had voted repeatedly against imposition of the death penalty, and she and her colleagues were painted as liberal and soft on crime in a sophisticated $4 million television campaign.

Another criticism of the Missouri plan is that the informal role of state bar associations is enlarged and strengthened by its use. Attorneys are given an official role in the selection of the short list of nominees from which the governor must appoint judges, since they are given a number of slots on the judicial nomination commissions. Critics of the Missouri plan argue that the courts should belong to the people and not to a privileged set of lawyers.

In addition, critics note that the jockeying for appointment to the recommending panel is very political, because attorneys campaign for these positions. The result is that the formal process of the merit system may mask a highly politicized informal process of selection.

Choosing the Best Judge Selection Method

The debate over which judge selection method is best hinges in part on the assumption that it makes a difference which plan is used—that better judges or better decisions can be achieved by using one plan instead of another. Research addressing this issue is inconclusive. While the various plans may result in the selection of different kinds of judges, it is not certain whether better decisions are also a result. One reason for this is the difficulty of determining what "better" decisions are. In addition, other factors tend to standardize the selection processes and minimize the potential differences.

In a study of twelve states, Herbert Jacob found that the various systems lead to the selection of judges with different social and political backgrounds (though his evidence is not considered conclusive).[5] Jacob compared judges selected through partisan, nonpartisan, and legislative election as well as by gubernatorial and Missouri plan appointment, according to their localism (roots in the state), education, and previous political experience. While he found slight variations, no clear patterns emerged. The larger question remains unanswered—do any of the plans produce better judicial decisions?

The Methods Are Political

At the same time, differences among the various judge selection methods are lessened somewhat because the methods are all political and because gubernatorial appointment plays a major role in all of them. Both partisan and nonpartisan elections are obviously political. Partisan elections more overtly bring the political parties into the selection process, but even in nonpartisan elections many candidates have had previous political experience. In fact, Jacob's study indicated that over half of all judges elected on nonpartisan ballots had held previous political office.[6] In addition, contestants in any election, whether labeled partisan or nonpartisan, are involved in a struggle for funds, visibility, popularity, and, most importantly, votes.

Judge selection by way of legislative election, gubernatorial appointment, or the Missouri plan is a political process as well. Nearly 60 percent of the judges selected by gubernatorial appointment, over 90 percent of those selected by state legislatures, and almost one-third of the Missouri plan judges studied by Jacob had held previous political office.[7] Appointments to the bench have always been a popular way for governors and legislatures to reward staunch party supporters, and so it is unlikely that an individual with little or no earlier participation in partisan activities would attract the attention of a governor, a legislature, or even a Missouri plan nominating commission. In other words, it is difficult to demonstrate that some judge selection methods are political whereas others are not.

The differences among the plans are also minimized by the fact that the gubernatorial appointment of judges plays a major role in judge selection even when elective systems are employed. Judges may die or retire from the bench in the middle of their terms, giving governors numerous opportunities to appoint replacement judges. Since incumbent judges are defeated in bids for reelection less than 10 percent of the time, gubernatorial appointments turn out to be extremely significant, even in elective states. It is likely that as many as one-half of the judges in elective states come to the bench by way of executive appointment.

Craig Emmert and Henry Glick also pursued the question of the differential impact of judicial selection methods. Like Jacob, they found that the method used makes little difference. Their work focused on state supreme court justices, and, while they found background differences among the judges, they concluded that the variations were best explained by region of the country, not by the selection method.[8]

In general, we can say that variations in judge selection plans can have some impact on the kind of person who ends up on the bench. However, we cannot say with certainty that any one selection plan removes politics from the courtroom or that it leads to better judicial decisions.

Judicial elections might become even more political as voters become more aware of the political impact of judicial decisions. In 1980, a candidate for the bench in Texas campaigned on an avowedly political platform, calling for prayer in the schools, elimination of pornography, and lower taxes. Lately Texas supreme court races have been major battlegrounds concerning tort reform, with one slate of candidates (usually Republicans) receiving strong support from insurance companies and the medical profession, and another slate of candidates (usually Democrats) drawing a major portion of support from trial lawyers associations. In short, judicial selection involves issue politics, ethnic politics, party politics, and personal politics just as do all other contests for positions of authority. (See Focus 6.1 "Judicial Selection and the Voting Rights Act.")

Democracy and the Courts

The relationship between democratic theory and the courts has long been a focus of scholars. This is especially true at the federal level, where judges are appointed and therefore are not directly accountable to those affected by their decisions. It is also true with respect to state and local courts. Historically, the courts have been viewed as the defenders of basic American values, especially those associated with civil liberties. A realistic appraisal of this role must acknowledge an "accordion" effect; that is, the protection of civil liberties expands when the courts are staffed with liberal judges and contracts when the courts are staffed with conservative judges. This is yet another indication of the political role of the judiciary.

There are several important aspects of the courts' role in protecting civil liberties. First, one of the most basic assumptions underlying democratic thought is that people should be politically equal, and judicial precedents have been a critical device for the maintenance of political equality. Second, the courts currently are plagued with a host of serious problems that make the maintenance of political equality all but impossible. Third such civil liberties

Focus 6.1

JUDICIAL SELECTION AND THE VOTING RIGHTS ACT

• • •

The courts themselves have been used to attack judicial election systems in certain jurisdictions. For some years now, courts have employed the 1965 Voting Rights Act to declare that at-large city council elections have discriminatory impacts on ethnic minorities. Recently, judicial elections have been attacked on the same basis in Alabama, Florida, Georgia, Louisiana, Mississippi, Ohio, and Texas.

The position of the courts on this matter remains unsettled. In 1987 one U.S. District Court found that the at-large system did indeed have a discriminatory impact, and in 1989 a U.S. Court of Appeals agreed. In addition, the U.S. Department of Justice, which has some direct enforcement powers for the Voting Rights Act, found in 1990 that the Georgia at-large system of choosing state judges disadvantaged African-American voters. However, also in 1990, a U.S. District Court held that because judges are not "representatives," the Texas system of electing judges was not subject to challenge under the provisions of the 1965 act. Next, a divided three-judge panel on the Fifth Circuit Court of Appeals reversed this decision in 1992, and the Texas attorney general recommended that the state adopt a plan for judicial districts in selected urban areas. In August 1993, the full Fifth Circuit Court of Appeals reversed the three-judge panel and ruled that the Voting Rights Act should not be applied to judicial selection in Texas.

as free speech, free press, and **due process** of law (which includes such procedural rights as the right to counsel and the right to a jury trial) are considered necessary for democracy, and historically the courts have played a major role in the protection of these rights.

Political Equality

In some totalitarian states elitist theories of government advance the notion that some people should rule others because they are inherently superior in terms of race, religion, wealth, gender, family, knowledge, or some other ascriptive characteristic. Political equality does not and cannot exist, it is contended. Rulers in some totalitarian states purposely undermine political equality by programming a sort of randomness into public decision making. The prospect of an unpredictable midnight "knock on the door" is used to terrorize the population. Due process of law and equal protection of the law are nonexistent. One person, one vote at the polls is a joke, although the myth may be maintained.

Things are supposed to be different in a democracy. Here special claims to rule are rejected, and, supposedly, all people are politically equal. Nobody gets two votes at the polls; traffic tickets are not supposed to be fixed just because one has a friend or relative in city hall; contracts for the construction of public buildings are supposed to be let on the basis of competitive bidding, not on the basis of "who you know"; and every person is supposed to be treated equally before the law.

We all know that this is not really how things work all of the time, but most of us agree that this is what a democracy should strive for. The use of legal precedent and the rule of law—both matters deeply involving the courts—are critical in the effort to achieve the goal of political equality. The **rule of law** means that public decisions affecting such activities as the establishment and enforcement of traffic regulations, the issuance of parade permits, and courtroom trials for everything from disorderly conduct to rape are to be made and conducted according to known legal provisions, and not on the basis of the preferences of some individual or group. (See Focus 6.2 "Religion, Sexual Orientation, and Parades.") In short, a democracy is supposed to be a government of laws, and no one person is supposed to be "above" those laws.

Legal Precedent

Legal precedent means that the procedures used and the decisions rendered in one situation should match those in other situations involving similar circumstances. In other words, it is assumed that there is value in maintaining some degree of predictability in the application of law.

The decisions of the higher courts, usually the federal and state supreme courts, establish legal precedents that bind the lower courts. Such precedents are intended to standardize the decisions and procedures followed throughout the federal and state judiciaries and thereby increase the probability that individuals will receive equal treatment before the law regardless of the courtroom they find themselves in. However, the standardizing effect of higher court precedents is reduced somewhat by judges' different perceptions of the meaning of decisions as well as by the intrusion of judges' individual values. Any judge who systematically deviates from the decisions and interpretations of the higher courts will be overruled with considerable frequency. Thus, the use of

Focus 6.2

Religion, Sexual Orientation, and Parades

• • •

In the early 1990s, the annual St. Patrick's Day parades in Boston and New York spawned lawsuits aimed at forcing the events' sponsors to allow a gay Irish group to join the parades. Each year the city of Boston has granted the South Boston Allied War Veterans Council, an association of various veterans groups, authority to organize and conduct the annual parade, an event that drew as many as 20,000 marchers. In 1992, the council denied the request of the Irish-American Gay, Lesbian and Bisexual Group of Boston (GLIB) for permission to march in the parade. The council contended that GLIB represented a lifestyle incompatible with the traditional religious and social values the parade was intended to represent. GLIB contended that this refusal constituted discrimination on the basis of sexual preference under Massachusetts public accommodations law. The state trial court agreed with GLIB and was upheld on appeal by the Massachusetts Supreme Judicial Court. In a similar case emanating from New York, however, a U.S. District Court judge refused to order the sponsors of that city's parade to allow a similarly identifiable gay liberation group to march under its banner.

In 1995, the U.S. Supreme Court reversed the Massachusetts courts, holding that requiring private citizens who organize a parade to include among the marchers a group imparting a message the organizers do not want to convey violated the organizers' First Amendment rights.

(Hurley v. Irish-American Gay, Lesbian, and Bisexual Group of Boston).

legal precedent—the similar interpretation and application of the law in similar circumstances—is critical for the maintenance of political equality.

Contemporary Problems in the Courts

It is important to acknowledge that numerous real-life conditions lead to something less than total political equality in the courts. Ideally, for example, courts in a democracy would provide citizens with speedy and impartial justice.

Individuals arrested for a crime would be swiftly charged, arraigned, and brought to trial. Persons who suffer injury as a result of an accident or breach of contract would be able to file suit and have the courts reach a quick and just decision. This ideal comports with the familiar saying that "justice delayed is justice denied." Unfortunately, however, this is not the way our courts work today. Rather, clogged dockets and large backlogs of cases are the norm, and swift justice is the exception.

Attitudes and Values

The values of judges and juries reduce objectivity and equal treatment before the law. The combination of delayed trials and the availability of plea bargaining may have unfortunate consequences. For example, an innocent person may be advised to cut a deal with the district attorney by pleading guilty to a lesser offense in order to expedite the process and avoid the vagaries of a jury trial. This is not to say that most judicial decisions make a mockery out of equal protection of the law, or that there is no attempt to run the judicial process according to democratic norms. Rather, the conditions in the courts are such that there is a gap between the reality of the courtroom and the goal of equal and impartial justice.

Judges, like everyone else, are in part products of their past. Their attitudes, values, and ways of looking at the world are partly the result of their life experiences. Different judges, having had different sets of experiences, will vary in terms of their attitudes and values. These variations will lead to different patterns of judicial decisions. Such variables as party affiliation, sex, and race may influence judicial behavior.

Early studies of state supreme court justices conducted by Stuart Nagel found differences in the behavior patterns of Democratic and Republican judges, Catholic and non-Catholic judges, liberal and conservative judges, and white and nonwhite judges.[9] For example, Nagel found that, compared to Republican judges, Democrats more frequently decided in favor of the defense in criminal cases, of the tenant in landlord-tenant cases, of the consumer in sale-of-goods cases, of the injured in motor vehicle accident cases, and of the employee in employee injury cases. They were also more likely to find a constitutional violation in criminal cases. Judges of color, compared to white judges, more often found in favor of the defense in criminal cases and of the wife in divorce cases, and they more often found a violation of procedure in criminal-constitutional cases. Catholic judges were more likely to find in favor of the defense in criminal cases, of the wife in divorce settlement cases, of the debtor in creditor-debtor cases, and of the employee in employee injury cases than were non-Catholic judges. Finally, liberal judges were more apt than conservatives to side with the defense in criminal cases, with the injured party in motor vehicle accident cases, and with the employee in employee injury cases.

More recent studies show that a judge's political party affiliation and local political culture will have the greatest effect on decisions. Race and sex are less influential. Not surprisingly, Democrat judges tend to be more liberal than Republican judges. In terms of race some studies indicate African-American judges are slightly more lenient than white judges toward African-American defendants, but the differences are not very great and vary from city to city. Studies also show that female and male judges are more alike than different. One study found female judges more likely to convict defendants charged with rape, but also more likely than male judges to sentence female defendants to longer terms.[10]

Although not usually systematically gathered and reported, additional evidence of the intrusion of personal attitudes and values into judicial decision making is available in almost any city or county courthouse. For example, following an extensive "drug bust" in Colorado that culminated in scores of arrests, large numbers of young people appeared for arraignment in a state district court. Some were released on personal recognizance bonds, pending trial. Others, appearing before a different judge in the same court, were required to post cash bonds of up to $2,500—an event that led the district attorney to complain that the propensity of the more lenient judge to release the accused without a cash bond was extremely discouraging to the local police. The district attorney was probably correct; the behavior of the more lenient judge regarding the bonds was probably discouraging to the police. The obvious dual standard created by the two judges' behavior was doubtless discouraging to those who did not have the $2,500 for bail and who may have spent time in the county jail awaiting trial. The behavior of two sincere judges, trying to do their best, led to inequality before the law.

Jurors' Prejudices

Jurors come to the jury box with their own preconceptions. This unfortunate fact is illustrated at its extreme by the comments of a male juror who had been dismissed on a peremptory challenge by the defense attorney in a Colorado courtroom in 1975. In reference to the case, which involved a convicted felon then being tried for rape, the juror commented to a fellow juror, "If they hadn't kicked me off that jury, I'd have saved the taxpayers some money by getting a short trial. I could have told you that son-of-a-bitch was guilty by just looking at him."[11] The use of dismissals from the jury both for cause and by peremptory challenge (the prerogative of both the defense and the prosecution to remove a specified number of potential jurors for no stated cause) is designed to minimize the intrusion of this sort of overt prejudice into judicial decisions. Although attorneys are allowed considerable discretion in exercising peremptory strikes during the *voir dire* ("to speak the truth") phase of jury selection, recent court decisions have held that peremptory challenges may not be used to exclude jurors because of their race. Still, many believe race plays an important role in jury decisions. Many analyses of the 1995 O. J. Simpson verdict conclude that the predominant African-American membership of the jury was a key element in the decision to acquit.

Juries are one of the most important links between democracy and the judicial process. Although they are instructed by judges to consider only the law and the facts entered into evidence, virtually all studies of jury behavior reveal that jurors view their role as that of dispensers of justice rather than interpreters of law and facts. For example, juries often refuse to convict, regardless of the evidence, when they view the law being applied as silly or unjust. Again, African Americans tended to view the O. J. Simpson trial in dramatically different terms than white Americans. African Americans were more willing to accept evidence pointing to police tampering while white Americans were more likely to focus on evidence pointing to Simpson's guilt.

As might be expected, jury practices vary from state to state. Several states permit nonunanimous verdicts, especially in civil trials. The trend among the states now is toward six-person rather than twelve-person juries.

There are two types of juries: **grand juries** and **petit juries**. A grand jury does not determine guilt or innocence; rather, it decides whether sufficient evidence exists to warrant an indictment (that is, to bring the accused to trial). The determination of guilt or innocence is left to the petit jury, or trial jury.

Judicial Delay

Another serious problem that makes the administration of impartial justice difficult is the tremendous case backlog of many state courts. Tens of thousands of cases are handled by the courts each year and, as a result, delays of up to five years between filing a case and final resolution are not uncommon in civil cases. In contrast, criminal cases must be brought to trial within three months in most states. Although there are many reasons for the growing case backlog, appeals of lower court judgments and the growing interdependence and general complexity of our society are among the most basic reasons. Delays of this sort are serious in both civil and criminal matters. Some civil suits, for example, involve the attempts of individual citizens to recover damages from insurance companies for injuries or losses suffered in accidents. When such a case drags on for months or years, evidence gets old, witnesses forget what they saw, and injured parties must get along without payment for the injury or loss.

Focus 6.3
Crowded Dockets and Their Consequences

• • •

Attempts to address the crowded dockets of state courts sometimes have less than desirable consequences. In 1992 the chief justice of the Texas Supreme Court acknowledged that almost one out of every eight state district court cases was being heard by an ex-judge through a state-based visiting judge program. The chief justice conceded that some infirm or controversial ex-judges, despite having been rejected by the voters, were still adjudicating cases around the state. These ex-judges included individuals who had been reprimanded by the state's Commission on Judicial Conduct, one ex-judge whose family life was such a scandal that his own children endorsed his opponent during the latter's successful election campaign, and an ex-judge so feeble that he was cited for lacking the basic vision and hearing needed to make competent decisions.

Families who have lost their homes, widows and widowers who have lost their spouses, or breadwinners who have become disabled as a result of an accident may be seriously hurt by long delays. Cases involving insurance companies may be aided by the aging of evidence. Also, the plaintiff may tire of waiting and be willing to settle for less than stipulated in the original claim. Some research suggests that the failure of some judges to manage their dockets, and the dilatory habits and tactics of many lawyers also contribute to the delays.[12] (See Focus 6.3 "Crowded Dockets and Their Consequences.")

Bargain Justice

Crowded court dockets and uncertainty about the behavior of judges in many instances lead to what is called **bargain justice**, or the making of deals—**plea bargaining**—between the district attorney's office and a defendant. Indeed, most civil and criminal cases are settled without ever coming to trial. Every year defendants in literally thousands of criminal cases agree to plead guilty to a less serious crime than the one for which they were first indicted. District attorneys often promote such deals when they are not sure their case is strong enough to ensure a conviction on the first and more serious offense, or when they are simply too busy to follow through with full trials on every indictment. Bargains of this sort often benefit the defendant in that they expedite the processing of the case and ensure a much lighter sentence than if the defendant had been convicted on the original indictment. At the same time, plea bargaining may also influence the innocent defendant to plead guilty to a lesser charge in order to avoid the risk of conviction.

A study of New Orleans area courts illustrates the political nature of the prosecution process. Over a six-year period fewer than 40 percent of the defendants pled guilty to their original charge. Over 5 percent of the others pled guilty to a reduced charge, roughly 10 percent pled innocent and were tried, and nearly 45 percent had their case dismissed for a variety of reasons.[13]

One might logically ask why bargain justice is a problem, especially since it expedites the business of the courts. Even though plea bargaining only recently became a public topic, it dates back over a hundred years. Measured against the democratic demand for political equality, however, it can become a serious problem, for it places tremendous judicial power in the hands of the district attorney's office—an office the people did not establish to pass judgment on citizens. When district attorneys are in a position to make deals with defendants, inequality before the law is almost ensured. District attorneys make deals in some cases but not in others. They are most likely to deal when the case is weak, when their office is overly busy, when the court dockets are full, or when they are on familiar terms with the defendant's attorney. This means, then, that the fate of many accused persons rests not with the facts and merits of the case but with such circumstantial factors as the business load of the court and the mood and prejudices of the district attorney.

Sometimes district attorneys with future political ambitions press a case because it may bring them great publicity and the opportunity to create a favorable public image. At other times they may drop a case because a rash of new and serious crimes demands their attention. The result is inequality in the application of law. Some people are subjected to the full weight of a state's laws. Other people who should be prosecuted are not, and the public loses.

Recent emphasis on the public fear of crime and consequent political ramifications have led to "no plea" policies in some jurisdictions. A growing number of prosecutors have announced that their office will refuse to plea bargain. "No plea" policies have been adopted in jurisdictions in Alaska, California, Florida, Indiana, Louisiana, Michigan, Missouri, New Jersey, and New York. The results have been mixed, with the "no plea" policies already abandoned in some jurisdictions, but praised in others. The term is somewhat misleading since the prosecutor usually refuses to accept plea bargains following a grand jury's indictment, but will negotiate before taking the case to the grand jury.[14]

Unequal Resources

A problem that is not peculiar to the courts is the unequal distribution of benefits that results from gross inequities in wealth. Rich people are better equipped than poor and moderate-income people to influence politics—from the county and states to the federal government. They are also in a better position to employ skilled legal help, thereby increasing their chances of success in the courts. The services of a skilled attorney are essential to success in the courtroom. The legal process and the law itself are extremely complicated. Since the average citizen is understandably overwhelmed and confused by what goes on in a courtroom, the services of a lawyer or a public defender are necessary. The wealthy can avail themselves of the best legal services; the poor cannot. Although certain Supreme Court decisions have helped to eliminate some of the most serious disadvantages that formerly haunted the poor in terms of legal representation, inequities still exist. Generally, the rich continue to receive better-quality legal representation than the poor. In death penalty cases especially, a disproportionate number of poor defendants in capital cases find themselves represented by inexperienced and overworked public defenders or court-appointed counsel.

Lack of Diversity

Ethnic minorities and women are underrepresented in the state judicial system. The number of judges of color is low and is growing only slowly. The same is true of the number of minority lawyers and minority law school students. Although the number of women lawyers and judges is on the upswing, the judicial system is still dominated by men. These imbalances are an ongoing problem, for it is difficult to maintain the legitimacy of any government institution when one group disproportionately controls the seats of power.

Recently the lack of diversity in the judiciary became a source of concern in two states. In 1990 the U.S. Department of Justice found that Georgia's system of electing judges in large judicial districts by majority vote conflicted with the law. The Justice Department claimed jurisdiction over the matter based on the 1965 Voting Rights Act, which requires states to clear their electoral processes with the department under certain circumstances. It was argued that the election system in Georgia worked to discourage the election of African-American judges. Similarly, in Colorado in 1991, minority spokespersons addressed the issue of their underrepresentation when a judicial selection panel sent a list of six nominees—all white—to the governor. The critics further noted that only thirteen of the state's 248 trial court judges were Hispanic (even though Colorado has a significant Hispanic population) and nine of those thirteen had been appointed within the previous three years.

Searches for Remedies

Little can be done about the personal attitudes of judges; lawyers can only try to choose jurors whose personal attitudes make them sympathetic to the lawyer's position. There is a growing awareness of and concern about the crowded dockets, delayed justice, inequities in quality of legal representation, and minority underrepresentation of the American state judicial system. In efforts to deal with the volume of cases and the resulting backlog, many states, including California, Pennsylvania, New Jersey, and New York, are experimenting with alternative methods of dispute settlement.[15] These include arbitration and mediation, which are methods of settling disputes without a trial. Both involve a third party who serves as an "umpire" between the two opposing sides. The major difference between the two methods is that decisions reached through arbitration are legally binding, whereas decisions reached through mediation are not. Mediation services are sometimes called citizen dispute settlement programs and are sometimes provided in locations known as neighborhood justice centers.

The quality of justice is a matter of increasing concern in the states. Since it can be affected by the abilities and integrity of judges and attorneys, nearly a dozen states have established continuing legal education programs, or CLEs. Other states are exploring methods of monitoring the performance of judges.

Clearly the courts face many problems, but the judicial system does have many relatively unbiased and competent judges and district attorneys. While some judges may be biased and incompetent and some district attorneys may engage in questionable tactics, the sources of these problems lie in the system itself. Perhaps the primary purpose of the law and the judiciary in any society is to give people's lives and the application of law some degree of regularity and predictability—to eliminate unnecessary uncertainty and randomness in interpersonal, intergroup, and government relations. Hence, the system emphasizes the rule of law, the use of precedent, and the general attempt to make every person equal before the law in a democracy. At the same time, differences in interpretations of the law are inevitable, as is inequality before the law. Caseloads are such that delayed justice must often be taken for granted.

State Courts and Civil Liberties

The American state courts are deeply involved in protecting **civil liberties**—the freedoms of speech, press, and religion; due process of law; and apportionment. Citizen contact with government occurs most often at the state and local levels, and most serious cases addressing civil liberties arise in the localities and the states.

State Bills of Rights

Civil liberties are specified in the national Bill of Rights, in the states' bills of rights, and in U.S. Supreme Court interpretations of the Fourteenth Amendment to the U.S. Constitution. These documents typically guarantee the freedoms of religion, speech, and press, protection against capricious deprivation of property, and a variety of other civil liberties. In addition, there are procedural rights, generally categorized under the umbrella of due process, which include the Miranda warnings, the right to counsel, and the right to have evidence that is seized in violation of one's constitutional rights excluded from use in trials. The latter is called the **exclusionary doctrine**.

Perhaps the best-known statement of freedoms in the U.S. legal system is contained in the First Amendment to the Constitution:

> Congress shall make no law respecting an establishment of religion, or prohibiting the free exercise thereof; or abridging the freedom of speech, or of the press; or the right of the people peaceably to assemble and to petition the Government for a redress of grievances.

The legal application of civil rights to the states by the courts is complex. In 1833 in *Barron v. Baltimore*, the U.S. Supreme Court held that the Bill of Rights afforded citizens protection only from the national government, not from the states, and that state bills of rights restricted the states. The Court held to that interpretation until the twentieth century. This meant that systems of justice varied greatly among the states, as well as between states and the national government.

The Fourteenth Amendment

In the twentieth century, Supreme Court interpretations of the Fourteenth Amendment have had the effect of expanding and standardizing citizen rights in the states. The Fourteenth Amendment states that:

> No State shall make or enforce any law which shall abridge the privileges or immunities of citizens of the United States; nor shall any State deprive any person of life, liberty, or property, without due process of law; nor deny to any person within its jurisdiction the equal protection of the laws.

Note that the opening line of the First Amendment reads, "Congress shall make no law . . . ," but that the opening line of the Fourteenth Amendment refers specifically to the states. In 1925 the Supreme Court began what is known as **selective incorporation**—giving specific meaning to the

Fourteenth Amendment's concepts of liberty, due process of law, and equal protection of the laws by linking the protections found in the Bill of Rights to the Fourteenth Amendment's due process clause.

In *Gitlow v. New York* (1925), the Court held that the freedoms specified in the First Amendment (speech and press) were among the liberties that, according to the Fourteenth Amendment, could not be compromised by a state without due process of law. In *Palko v. Connecticut* (1937), Justice Benjamin Cardozo held that the Fourteenth Amendment required states to protect those rights "implicit in the concept of ordered liberty" and basic to an "enlightened system of justice." He went on to suggest that the freedoms of speech, press, assembly, and religion were among the rights selectively incorporated through the Fourteenth Amendment in order to ensure ordered liberty. In subsequent cases the Court has, through the Fourteenth Amendment, applied numerous other restrictions on the states, most of them similar to those of the national Bill of Rights. They include the use of the exclusionary principle (*Mapp v. Ohio*, 1961), the right to counsel (*Gideon v. Wainwright*, 1963), and several others. Indeed, most of the liberties of the Bill of Rights have been effectively incorporated. The application of many Bill of Rights freedoms to the states via the Fourteenth Amendment has helped to standardize justice among the states.

Rights by Case Law

In essence, the Supreme Court has built a body of case law that establishes the parameters for the states in a host of policy areas. Reading much of the meaning of the U.S. Bill of Rights into the words of the Fourteenth Amendment, the Court has circumscribed the ability of state and local governments to restrict speech, the press, and rights of assembly. It has given definition to the concept of freedom of religion, and it has told states and localities how to handle those accused of crimes. The Court has forced desegregation of schools. State courts, as well as all state and local governments, are obligated to obey the "supreme law of the land," and that law is what the Supreme Court says it is.

Recent Developments in the State Courts

New Judicial Federalism

There have been several interesting developments in the state courts in recent years. One is the emergence of the **new judicial federalism**—that is, the expanded use by state courts of provisions in state bills of rights as the legal bases for decisions. For example, the courts in California and Texas cited their own state constitutions in decisions requiring modification of school financing schemes to achieve more equity in educational opportunity. Some state courts have restricted the employer's right to fire employees "at will." The courts have also relied on their state bills of rights to anchor such civil liberties as free speech, sexual equality, and freedom from illegal search and seizure, often going beyond the protections outlined by Supreme Court decisions.

Most of these developments occurred in the 1980s and 1990s. It was during this period that the U.S. Supreme Court retreated from its earlier tendency to base decisions on interpretations of the Fourteenth Amendment. The shift toward new judicial federalism has led to some expansion of civil liberties and diversity among the states.[16]

Utah's Supreme Court Justice Christine Durham explains the trend toward new judicial federalism as a result of the emergence on the bench of a new generation of judges. Many of today's justices grew up and received their legal training during a period of general social activism in the late 1960s and the 1970s, when the courts, like other institutions, were used strategically to press political agendas in such areas as civil rights, consumer rights, and environmental protection. State judges today bring to their cases the perspectives and understandings that they learned and internalized during that era. They tend to be active and innovative in the search for and use of fresh sources of judicial guidance and precedent.[17]

In a related trend, the state courts have shifted the perspective of some laws through judicial decisions. State courts have long played a major role in the development of policy in areas not addressed by or not fully covered by state statute, including tort (legal wrongs), contract, and property law. Thus, the cumulative impact of the decisions of state judges has been the basis of law.

Historically, the judge-made law was conservative, protecting the holders of money and property and providing substantial protection to businesses from product liability. This has changed some in recent years, for state courts have begun to side more often with injured plaintiffs in cases involving such matters as medical malpractice and product liability. In some instances state legislatures have responded by legislating limits on liability; this process usually is called **tort reform**. Physicians and businesses push for such limitations, of course, whereas trial lawyers are opposed to them. Tort reform was a central campaign theme in the Texas judicial elections in the late 1980s and early 1990s. The willingness of some citizen interest groups throughout the nation to seek relief through the state courts has increased as the effects of conservative Reagan and Bush appointments to the federal court system have begun to assert themselves. Whereas during the 1960s and 1970s, the federal courts were viewed as relatively friendly to litigation involving civil rights or consumer protection, today the state courts are considered safe havens because of the more conservative federal bench.

Changes in Federal Court/State Court Relationships

In 1996, Congress passed the Anti-Terrorism and Effective Death Penalty Act of 1996. Included in the act were provisions that altered the ability of the federal courts to review state court criminal judgments that have raised potential constitutional objections. Before the passage of this act, state prisoners could petition the federal courts for *habeas corpus* relief, arguing that the state courts had ignored or violated their constitutional rights. If granted, their case would be reviewed by a federal court to see if constitutional infirmities existed. While federal courts were obligated to defer to a state court's determination of fact, the state courts were required to hold hearings on the merits of the petition and issue written findings and conclusions that could be challenged by the petitioner. Critics of this process argued that having an additional layer of post-conviction review was unnecessarily duplicative and was an undesirable intrusion of the federal government into state authority. The new act addressed that criticism and is expected to severely curtail federal involvement.

Those who opposed the new restrictions on *habeas corpus* relief note that 40 percent of the state death sentences imposed during the past twenty years have been overturned in federal courts, demonstrating a clear need for federal oversight. In addition, federal judges are appointed, while state trial judges frequently face the pressures of reelection campaigns, usually in the communities where the crime occurred, and, consequently, it is contended, they are less sensitive to the rights of the accused.

Alternative Dispute Resolution

In response to the continuous high volume of legal activity, many states have experimented with alternatives to full-blown courtroom litigation. Although the approaches vary, they are often referred to generally as **alternative dispute resolution (ADR)** and include mediation, binding and nonbinding arbitration, short "mini-trials," court-mandated arbitration, and summary jury trials. The abbreviated proceedings are binding only when both parties agree to them in advance. Roughly half of all ADR schemes were developed in the 1980s or later. They are employed in various forms and combinations by the states.[18]

Other Approaches to Expediting the Courts' Business

Approaches geared toward speedier and more effective processing of the legal business of the states also include automation of fines, jury selection, judge access to case law and child-support payment records; videotape recording of court proceedings; long-distance audio and video communication in certain court proceedings; the use of more specialized courts (for example, drug case courts); and a general tightening of procedures to reduce the number of postponements and delays.[19] The public, in turn, has been made more aware of the judicial process through the televising of state and local trials. Although not all states permit televised trials, and no federal trials are televised, the Supreme Court has held that there is no constitutional prohibition against televising courtroom proceedings. In 1995, much of the nation watched the O.J. Simpson trial, arguably the most-watched trial in history. Not only was the trial televised, but numerous other programs were spin-offs of the trial. In the typical fashion of American popular culture many cable systems now carry the Court Channel, which televises state and local trials of interest. Despite the circuslike nature that often characterized the Simpson trial, televised trials sometimes perform an educational function, offering a basis of comparison and contrast between the court system in reality and that portrayed in countless television shows and movies.

There is widespread opinion that many contemporary problems facing the courts are the result of a litigation explosion. But at least one study disputes that claim. An investigation conducted by the National Center for State Courts in 1986 found no evidence of such an explosion.[20] The need for ways to expedite the courts' business seems to be a long-standing problem caused by many factors.

Gender and Ethnic Fairness

More than half of the states have recently established commissions or task forces to investigate and seek remedies for gender bias in the courts. Their recommendations include changes in procedures, modified law school curricula, and the use of gender-neutral language.

Some states have also established bodies to look into the problem of racial and ethnic bias. For example, a New York group found that the domination of the legal system by whites leads to distrust of the system by nonwhites; the O. J. Simpson trial will be a textbook example of this for several years. The courts will continue to change, albeit incrementally, as a result of the findings of such study groups, as well as in response to political pressures (such as those now challenging judicial election systems).

Summary

The role of state courts in the American judicial system is complex. Because of federalism, both the national government and the state governments have courts. Because of the separation of powers, the judiciary is only one of three branches within each state.

Courts are often viewed by the public as removed from politics, handing down legal decisions that have little policy import. But this view of the courts, based on the cult of the robe, is a myth. In reality, courts make policy through decisions that are influenced by the attitudes and worldviews of the judges who make them. Thus, state and local judicial systems are actively involved in the political process because they render decisions that have an impact on public policy.

Perhaps the most striking characteristic of state judicial systems is their diversity; no two state court systems are alike. Unfortunately, they are also characterized by overloaded dockets, which often means that justice is not served swiftly. The states use various methods of selecting judges, although studies indicate that there is little substantive difference in the types of judges selected.

Finally, the diversity of state courts also results in inequities in the quality of justice that is dispensed. Nonetheless, contemporary state judicial systems have been willing to extend state rights beyond those guaranteed by the U.S. Constitution, in a trend called new judicial federalism.

Policy Perspective

What should happen to the woman who shoplifts a dress and shoes, to the boy who steals a car, to the distinguished looking gentleman who takes a million dollars per year in salary from a savings and loan that he helps to ruin, or to the prostitute who is caught both soliciting and using cocaine? Should they all go to jail?

Which government should worry about shoplifting, about theft, about sex and drugs? The Congress, the state legislature, the city council?

These are political questions with political answers. We've answered some of them in our foundational documents that structure our governments and allocate authority. The U.S. Constitution makes trade, defense, currency, and certain other matters the province of the national government. Most of the rest is left to the states and their local governments. Choices about what, if anything, to do about theft, sex, and drugs is then allocated to the national or state–local policy bodies—to their legislatures.

Sometimes the public and thus our lawmakers grow impatient with certain kinds of behavior and decide to become tough on crime. That often plays well at election time. But it also results in significant increases in the costs of government—more police, judges, prisons, and guards are then needed. The increased spending does not play so well. So the laws, the penalties, and the costs all become political questions, and they change from year to year.

American local and state governments pass laws by the thousands, hire people by the tens of thousands, and spend money by the millions and billions to try to keep the public safe. The "reserved powers" in the United States Constitution that are reserved to the states include what are commonly known as "police powers," and these refer to the authority of the states and their political subdivisions to provide for the public health, welfare, and safety of the citizenry.

In part due to political pressure there has been an increasing nationalizing of crime fighting. Virtually every Congress in recent memory has expanded the number of offenses that violate federal law. Although it was announced in early 1997 that the rate of violent crime had fallen for the fifth straight year, people still do not feel safe and, therefore, being "tough on crime" brings a big payoff for the elected representatives in Washington, D.C.

Still, crime is considered primarily a state and local problem. The largest slice of local and state government efforts to keep us safe, and even pure, involves crime and corrections. Over 95 percent of all crimes committed are violations of local or state laws, not transgressions of acts of Congress. Laws against murder, rape, assault, robbery, or littering are enacted by state legislators or city councils, not the Congress. The same is true of statutes that prohibit drug use or sale, fraudulent representation of mileage on used vehicles, prostitution, speeding, and disorderly conduct.

Most law enforcement officials in the United States are employees of state and local governments. State legislatures and city councils enact thousands of laws every year that declare various sorts of behavior to be against the law. Penalties are prescribed for those convicted of engaging in such activities. Courts are created and staffed to determine guilt. Prisons are built to house some of the guilty. All sorts of rehabilitation and probation programs are established to try to turn offenders into law-abiding citizens or, at the least, gain retribution for what they did to somebody else or to themselves. Most jails and prisons are local and state, too, and so are most of the guards and occupants.

Quite clearly, American public policies having to do with crime and corrections, both in the formation of policies and in their execution, reflect our employment of a federal system. All of this means that our entire criminal justice system is highly decentralized and that the laws and the structure of law enforcement varies considerably from one jurisdiction to another. Given our early history in which the states preceded the central unit in time and assumed initial responsibility for public health and safety, the business of crime and corrections is mostly state and local.

Crime and corrections are also intergovernmental matters, involving local, state, and national institutions. We've noted most criminal laws, most criminals, and most judges, courts, and jails are state and local, and not national. But the U.S. Constitution and the U.S. Supreme Court impact the state and local units in important ways. The high court has set the parameters with respect to the rights of the accused, and it plays an important role in determining the acceptability of prison conditions in the states.

Similarly, state criminal laws and corrections funding policies have dramatic impacts upon the local units. When states become "tough on crime," the state courts fill up. These courts are housed locally by the counties, and in the early stages of the process, prisoners are held in local jails, which are usually county facilities. When state criminal justice systems become jammed, it is the local units that feel the pressure initially. If the states are slow to expand the courts and the prisons, local facilities are overloaded. In our structurally complicated and interrelated system, what one institution does soon has an impact upon the others.

With increased emphasis on crime fighting, not surprisingly, the size of the prison population has increased also. In the 1970s there were roughly 200,000 persons in America state prisons. By 1990 that number was about 700,000. The states were adding to their prison population by 35,000 to 40,000 per year. In 1988 the states added an average of 800 prisoner beds per week. In the first six months of 1989 that figure was 1800 per week.[21] Between 1980 and 1989 the prison population grew by almost 90 percent. One in 420 Americans was in jail or prison, the highest rate in the world.[22] In California in 1980 there were fewer than 25,000 state prisoners; by the early 1990s that number will be 100,000.[23] Nationwide it was estimated that the total number of persons on probation, out on parole, or still in jail or prison exceeded four million, or more than the entire population of twenty-seven of our fifty states.

Why the change? What led to such an explosion in the prison population if the crime rate was rising slowly? The answers lie in a series of widespread policy changes in the states. Stimulated in part by growing discomfort with long-standing and vast case-to-case discrepancies between sentences for serious crimes and actual time served, in part by the impact on public and legislative opinion of a "tough on crime" stance taken by President Ronald Reagan, and by a growing concern with the spread of drugs, state legislatures joined in a collective stampede to "get tough on crime."

This was done in several ways. The simplest but most consequential action lengthened sentences for felony offenses such as murder, assault, rape, and robbery. "Three strikes and you're out" policies began to be popular, and some politicians, playing to the voters' fears, urged a "two strikes and you're out" policy. States doubled, even tripled the length of sentences and some states eliminated parole.

Many states also modified sentencing policies in which judges had wide sentencing latitude and could consider a variety of factors in each case in setting sentences. Such systems often led to wide sentencing discrepancies among judges with similar cases, and also left the time of prisoner release up to parole boards. Policy changes constricted judicial latitude by more specifically specifying sentences or by setting forth sentencing guidelines, and by curtailing the powers of parole boards.

These factors in combination, namely longer sentences and reduced judicial and parole board latitude, explain in large measure the explosion in prison population. The explosion in the size of the prison population was a function of policy changes, and not the result of dramatic changes in the crime rate. But while the states were getting "tough on crime," they were not calculating the inevitable, and surely predictable, impact on the prison population.

Nor were they calculating the increased costs of prison maintenance. It costs much less to build a prison, than to maintain it. The lengthening of sentences and reduction of judicial and parole board discretion, coupled with the increase in drug-related convictions has affected the size of the prison population, and the cost of corrections. With increases in the prison population came increasingly crowded conditions. Court orders led to massive prison construction efforts in several states.

Clearly the growing costs that recent developments have created cause some difficult financial problems for the states. One commentator remarked that "Getting tough on crime has come to mean getting tough on taxpayers."[24] Oregon's former Governor Neil Goldschmidt lamented that "Imprisonment rates are rolling toward numbers that will eat our budgets whole."[25] As a result, the states have been trying a variety of approaches to control corrections costs.

Cost control efforts have run the gamut from simply releasing prisoners early, to wholesale sentencing reform and expanded community-based correctional programs. A number of states have emergency release systems in place so that when the prison population reaches institutional capacity, the governor activates a provision to simply add to the time served by some selected set of prisoners so that a number of them are immediately ready for release. States that employ such systems include Arizona, Connecticut, Florida, Iowa, Michigan, New Jersey, Ohio, South Carolina, and Washington.

States are also relying heavily on community-based corrections to keep costs under control. Indeed, roughly three-quarters of those convicted of crimes are not in prison but are in the community, usually on parole or probation. While there are differences of opinion on the question about which offenders should be kept in prison and for how long, it is clear that not all those behind bars are violent or present a physical danger to others. The National Conference of State Legislatures notes that only 30 percent of those now in prison have been convicted of violent crimes.[26] Others are there for theft of property, use of drugs, or some other nonviolent offense.

One way of looking at public policy and crime is simple· find the lawbreakers, convict them, and put them away. But the more carefully one examines the matter, the more complicated and the more political it appears. What should be considered a criminal act? Why do people violate the law? What should we do with those who do break the law? How much of our collective resources should be spent to cage the convicted? What rights should we extend to the accused — who are, really, some of us? These are just some of the tough questions, and their resolutions are, of necessity, arrived at politically.

Clearly, then, there are trade-offs to be made in the formation of criminal laws, and clearly there will be differences of opinion. What should be outlawed in the mind of one person is acceptable to another. What appears worth paying for with respect to prison costs to one taxpayer may not be acceptable to others. What was legal in 1900 may well be illegal in 1950, or in the year 2000, and what draws a fine in Montana may send you to prison in Florida. The sentences set by one legislature may be altered by the next one. Determinations about what is criminal and what is not, rest upon a blend of facts—hard, cold facts about crime, about budgets, and about public opinion and the current values and beliefs held by both the public at large and the politically influential, and our lawmakers.

KEY TERMS

cult of the robe
judicial review
judicial restraint
judicial activism
jurisdiction
supreme court
intermediate appellate court
trial court
lower court
special court
unified court system
Missouri plan
merit plan
due process
rule of law
legal precedent
grand jury
petit jury
bargain justice
plea bargaining
civil liberties
exclusionary doctrine
selective incorporation
new judicial federalism
tort reform
alternative dispute resolution (ADR)

ADDITIONAL READING

Fino, Susan P. *The Role of State Supreme Courts in the New Judicial Federalism*. Greenwood Press, 1989.

Glick, Henry R. *Courts in American Politics: Readings and Introductory Essays*. New York: McGraw-Hill, 1990.

______. *Courts, Politics and Justice*. New York: McGraw-Hill, 1993.

Grilliot, Harold J., and Frank Schubert. *Introduction to Law and the Legal System*. 4th ed. Dallas: Houghton Mifflin, 1989.

Rosenberg, Gerald N. *The Hollow Hope: Can Courts Bring About Social Change?* Chicago: University of Chicago Press, 1991.

Stumpf, Harry P., and John H. Culver. *The Politics of State Courts*. Longman, 1992.

Wice, Paul. *Judges and Lawyers*. New York: Harper Collins, 1991.

NOTES

1. See *The Book of the States, 1990–91* (Lexington, Ky.: Council of State Governments, 1991), pp. 210–22; and Lawrence Baum, *American Courts: Process and Policy*, 2d ed. (Boston: Houghton Mifflin, 1990).

2. See, for example, U.S. Department of Justice, *Court Unification* (Washington, D.C.: GPO, April 1988).

3. Baum, *American Courts*, pp. 100–101; and *The Book of the States, 1992–93* (Lexington, Ky.: Council of State Governments, 1992), p. 233.

4. See Dixie K. Knobel, "The State of the Judiciary," in *The Book of the States, 1990–91* (Lexington, Ky.: Council of State Governments, 1991), p. 200.

5. Cited in Kenneth Vines, "Courts as Political and Governmental Agencies," in *Politics in the American States*, ed. Herbert Jacob and Kenneth Vines (Boston: Little, Brown, 1965), pp. 239–87.

6. Ibid.

7. Ibid.

8. Craig F. Emmert and Henry P. Glick, "The Selection of State Supreme Court Justices," *American Politics Quarterly* (Oct. 1988): 445–65.

9. See Stuart Nagel, "Political Party Affiliation and Judges' Decisions," *American Political Science Review* (Dec. 1961): 843–51; Stuart Nagel, "Ethnic Affiliation and Judicial Propensities," Journal of Politics 24 (1962): 92–100; and Stuart Nagel, "Off-the-Bench Judicial Attitudes," in Judicial Decision-Making, ed. Glendon Schubert (Glencoe, Ill.: Free Press, 1963), pp. 29–55.

10. See, for example, Cassie Spohn, "The Sentencing Decision of Black and White Judges: Expected and Unexpected Similarities," *Law and Society Review*, 24 (1990): 1197–1216; Susan Welch, Michael Combs, and John Gruhl, "Do Black Judges Make a Difference?" *American Journal of Political Science*, 32 (1988): 126–36; John Gruhl, Cassia Spohn, and Susan Welch, "Women as Policymakers: The Case of Trial Judges," *American Journal of Political Science*, 25 (1981): 308–22; and David W. Allen and Diane E. Wall, "The Behavior of Women State Supreme Court Justices: Are They Tokens or Outsiders?" *Justice System Journal*, 12 (1987): 232–45.

11. Witnessed by one of the authors.

12. James H. Bradner, Jr., ed., *Advancing Justice: May We Approach the Bench?* (Schaumburg, Ill.: Alliance of American Insurers, 1987).

13. Herbert Jacob, "Politics and Criminal Prosecution in New Orleans," in *Studies in Judicial Politics*, ed. Kenneth Vines and Herbert Jacob (New Orleans: Tulane University, Studies in Political Science, 1963).

14. See Andrew Blum, 'No Plea' Policies Sprout Across US." *The National Law Journal* (Sept. 9, 1996): 1.

15. *The Book of the States, 1988–89* (Lexington, Ky.: Council of State Governments, 1989), p. 148.

16. See Elder Witt, "Hans A. Linde: The Unassuming Architect of an Emerging Role for State Constitutions," *Governing* (July 1989): 56–60; and Stanley Mosk, "The Emerging Agenda in State Constitutional Rights Law," *Annals of the American Academy of Political and Social Sciences* (March 1988): 54–64.

17. Lawrence Baum and David Frohnmayor, eds., *The Courts: Sharing and Separating Power* (New Brunswick: Rutgers University, Eagleton Institute of Politics, 1989).

18. Bradner, *Advancing Justice*.

19. Knobel, "The State of the Judiciary," pp. 194–203.

20. National Center for State Courts, *Court Statistics and Information Management Project* (Williamsburg, Va.: NCS, April 1986).
21. "Record jump in prison population," *Rocky Mountain News*, 11 September 1989.
22. Julie Lays, "The Complex Case of Costly Corrections," *State Legislatures* (February 1989): 15–17.
23. The National Council on Crime and Delinquency, *Crime and Punishment in the Year 2000: What Kind of Future* (San Francisco, Calif., 1988): 22.
24. Sharon Randall, "Sensible Sentencing," *State Legislatures* (January 1989): 14–18.
25. The National Council on Crime and Delinquency, *Crime and Punishment in the Year 2000*, p. iii.
26. Donna Huzaker, "Can States Make Sentencing a Science?" *State Legislatures* (October 1992): 4.

CHAPTER 7

• • •

Political Parties

• • •

Partisan politics is everywhere. This booth and the political activity it stimulated were photographed at the Monterey County Fair in California. *(David Conklin/Monkmeyer)*

• • • **The Functions of Political Parties**
Educating the Public
Increasing Political Involvement
Recruiting Candidates
Organizing the Lawmaking Process
Fusing the Fragmented System
Forming Majorities
Resolving Conflict

• • • **Political Party Organization**
Three Levels of Party Organization
One-Party States
Variety among States
An Untidy Structure
Weakened Political Parties

• • • **A Resurgence in Party Vitality**

• • • **Party Competition**
Divided Government
Perspectives on Political Competition
Third Parties

Focus 7.1: Selected Third Parties in the United States

• • • **Criticisms of the Political Parties**
Do Elites Control the Parties?
Are the Parties Directionless?
Are the Parties Too Much Alike?

• • • **Summary**

• • • **Policy Perspective**

Chapters 7 through 9 focus on the organizations and activities within the political system that link citizens to the formal institutions discussed in the previous chapters. Chapter 7 addresses political parties; Chapters 8 and 9 cover interest groups and elections, respectively. In a democracy, public policies are intended to reflect the preferences of the people, and it is through political parties, interest groups, and elections that the people most often make their desires known. The links between institutions and citizens are not perfect, of course, but collectively parties, interest groups, and elections help to keep decision makers informed of voter preferences.

The Functions of Political Parties

Most political parties in most political systems have two primary goals: winning elections and making public policy. The first goal is the means to implementing the second goal. Political parties win elections in order to organize the government and make public policy. Indeed, parties must win elections with some degree of regularity or endless defeats will make it extremely difficult to recruit and maintain a cadre of party regulars and a viable party organization. In their search for success at the polls, political parties perform a number of additional functions considered essential to the successful operation of democratic political systems. These **latent functions** include contributing to the political education of the public, increasing citizen involvement in politics, recruiting people for political office, organizing the government, partially fusing a government fragmented by federalism and the separation of powers, forming the majorities necessary for the development of legitimate public policy in a democracy, and serving as vehicles that negotiate conflict into compromise.

Educating the Public

Without the participation of an informed citizenry, democratic government is meaningless. Scholars of democracy agree that informed citizen participation is an important check on political leadership. In this regard Americans have traditionally assigned a major educational role to the mass media, arguing that free press and free speech are necessary to the full and free flow of ideas and information. Without such a flow it would be impossible for the voter to participate intelligently in the decision-making processes.

The media must have something to report to the people, and it is here that the parties play a critical role. Much of our political news is party news—news of the controlling party in the legislature doing battle with the governor who is of a different party; news of a partisan minority in the state senate struggling to block the passage of a bill supported by the majority party; news of the entry of new candidates into an upcoming race for governor; or news of the leadership of the minority party blaming the majority party for bad roads, prison riots, or rising taxes.

It is the political struggle that the media reports, and it is the parties that have organized and are engaged in that struggle. The political parties create and publicize platforms. They search for and create issues. They criticize the opposition party's policies and offer alternative policies. They publicize all of this through the mass media as well as through other traditional campaign channels. During election campaigns, the parties consciously seek to inform the public through their influence with the media, giving rise to the use of **spin doctors**, whose job is to offer the media the party's interpretation of campaign events. Most of the activities in which parties engage in their search for electoral success have the effect of disseminating information throughout the system.

Increasing Political Involvement

When an individual becomes involved in politics, the chances are that the person is affiliated with one of the two major political parties—the Republican party or the Democratic party. Of course, there are other ways to be politically active and other parties to join. One can work with a special interest group or be politically active in nonpartisan city elections, or one could declare membership in the Libertarian Party or Ross Perot's Reform Party. But more likely an individual's involvement in politics is defined largely through contact with a major party.

Thus, it is the major parties, with their permanent and ongoing organizations, that more than any other single factor inform political activism. One may be active in a precinct or the county organization, or even be a candidate for local, state, or national office. Whatever the nature of an individual's involvement in the political process, political parties are useful vehicles in enhancing the political activism considered essential to a democratic decision-making process.

Recruiting Candidates

State constitutions and statutes establish and assign powers, duties, and limitations to public offices. But they have little to say about who will fill these offices. In part, this is deliberate; the legislatures are organized by the parties, and it is to the parties' advantage to retain discretion over the recruitment of candidates. As noted in more detail later in the chapter, the laws in most states govern the formation and operation of the parties, but the laws fail to provide the informal routines for the recruitment of candidates for public office. This role is filled by the parties.

Obviously, screening devices of some sort must operate to select from the vast general public those few who will contend for office in public elections. Some people will run for office but most will not; some procedures, either formal or informal, must operate to form the selection process. With rare exceptions, an individual with aspirations for public office must start by affiliating with and working for a political party. This alone does not ensure success, but it almost always is a prerequisite to political success. Again, it is the political party that recruits most of the people needed to fill elective public offices in the states.

Organizing the Lawmaking Process

Although much of the formal structure of American governments is prescribed by law, the law is largely silent concerning other organizations that are equally necessary to the smooth functioning of government. For example, the laws of a state may establish three branches of government, but may say nothing about how the three branches will relate to one another or how the hundreds of members of the legislature will conduct business. To expedite the operations of an otherwise unwieldy legislature, committees must be formed, leadership selected, and procedures established. Working relationships among the three branches of government, and between the legislative and executive branches especially, must be forged. Political parties generally perform these functions.

Most legislatures divide into majority and minority factions, usually along party lines. The majority faction controls the selection of formal leadership for each house, and both the majority and minority select their own floor leadership. Likewise, the parties usually play major roles in the selection of personnel for legislative committees and in the maintenance of communications with the governor—matters about which the law is generally silent. But this is not always so. In some states, ideology has been more important than partisanship in organizing the state legislature; conservatives battle liberals more than Republicans battle Democrats. The essential point here is that government bodies, like all organizations, do not run themselves—people run them. The political parties play a major role in organizing the government so that issues may be identified, alternatives proposed, bills introduced and processed, and public programs effectively administered.

Fusing the Fragmented System

One of the most salient features of American government is the extent to which it is structurally fragmented. Federalism divides authority between the national and state governments. The separation of powers employed at both the national and state levels further divides authority. So do bicameral legislatures, the plural executive model (employed to some degree in all of the states), and the vast systems of local government.

Most of the factors that divide decision-making authority were adopted purposefully to reduce the opportunities for individuals and groups to exert excessive influence on public decisions; federalism and the separation of powers are examples of such intentionally adopted institutional features. Other fragmenting structures, such as the proliferation of governments in many metropolitan areas and the expansion of bureaucracies at all levels, have been the result of changing social and technological circumstances and purposeful design. Whatever their cause, the fact remains that decision-making power is widely dispersed in the American government system.

To a degree the political parties glue the fragmented system back together. Sometimes the two houses of a bicameral state legislature are controlled by different political parties, or one party may control the legislature while the other party occupies the governor's chair. In the latter case, the effects of structural fragmentation may be further aggravated by interparty wrangling. For example, a Republican legislature may refuse to help a Democratic governor push a legislative program; or the governor may refuse to place items on the call (agenda) of a special legislative session that the majority leadership in the legislature wants to consider. In many other cases the same party controls both houses of a legislature, or even the entire legislative branch and the governorship as well. Under these circumstances the controlling party may fuse what the structure has fragmented. The governor and the legislative leadership may work closely as a team to propose, enact, sign, and implement a package of policy proposals.

The capacity of the political parties to transcend structural divisions can also link the states with the national government. Although communication may not be extensive, the congressional representation of a given state usually maintains contact with the party and its elected officials back home. Senators and members of Congress return for reelection campaigns as well as for a variety of other reasons, and their agenda almost always includes a round of meetings and speeches involving members of the party. Problems are discussed, information is exchanged, and promises are made. Since more and more programs at all levels of government involve cooperative efforts, discussions almost always include some consideration of how the Washington representatives can be of assistance to the home state. The existence of linkages of this sort can be seen in the frequent announcement by Senators and members of Congress of federal grants to such state institutions as universities and to local governments in the representative's home state.

Forming Majorities

In the United States, two seemingly contradictory truths operate simultaneously. On the one hand, we profess to adhere to the concept of majority rule, and in many cases actually live up to it (for example, majorities, not minorities, pass legislation in city councils, state legislative committees, and state supreme courts). On the other hand, we experience and often encourage considerable social, cultural, and political diversity. How, then, do we get anything done? How can effective public programs be designed to attack our numerous pressing problems if, in the face of a culturally, socially, and politically pluralistic system, we require majority approval of public actions?

Political parties help to answer these questions by creating voting majorities out of a maze of minorities—both at the polls and in legislative bodies. The parties assist their members who are running for political office, and in return they expect some loyalty from those who win (though their loyalty is not always forthcoming). In addition, the parties play a key role in the organization of legislative bodies, and those who occupy such critical posts as committee chairperson or house speaker owe some of their success to the party. Ideological commonalities provide another basis for party unity. This is not to say that American political parties are tightly knit and disciplined organizations, for they are not. But they do provide an organizing and rallying point for politicians.

When majorities form to pass laws, the parties more than any other single factor are responsible. Scholarly studies indicate that the single best predictor of legislative voting behavior is party affiliation. On most legislative proposals, those lawmakers who lack a vital interest in the particular issue up for a vote frequently rely on party direction to govern their vote. This is not to say that all votes are determined by the party line, that parties are the only institutions to which lawmakers are loyal, that all divisions fall along party lines, or even that a majority vote invariably indicates widespread agreement on the issue at hand. On many occasions different individuals favor an item for quite different reasons. Nevertheless, the democratic expectation of majority rather than minority rule demands that public measures be passed by majority votes. The political parties thus play a critical role in assembling majorities out of what is often a vast network of minorities.

Resolving Conflict

For a political party to select a nominee for public office, put together a platform, or reach a party position on a legislative proposal, it must successfully negotiate a number of compromises. There are few issues on which all the members of a party can agree. Differences of opinion between party members often are of a lesser magnitude than the differences between the party itself and the opposition; but differences are almost sure to exist within the party as well. Sometimes the parties, both national and state, can unite and pull together after ironing out their internal differences; at other times the differences run too deep and the party is weakened by internal division.

The capacity of political parties to make compromises has implications for the political styles found in legislative bodies and for the relationships between governmental branches and agencies. Some commentators argue persuasively that there exists a widespread consensus in the United States on such political fundamentals as the proper institutions and procedures for decision making, but few claim that a majority of the people, be they leaders or followers, can agree on such narrow and specific issues as the proper level for the property tax, the best expenditure levels for parks or roads, or the wisest approach to addressing the problem of crime. When we move from the general, such as the need for better schools, to the particular, such as the best way to achieve better schools, consensus rapidly gives way. Thus, if the parties did not effect compromises, if all the differences of opinion that exist on nearly every issue were fed into legislative deliberation, if all of the latent points of disagreement had to be fought out in the official decision-making arenas, it would be difficult to accomplish anything at all.

The preceding description of the functions performed by political parties is necessarily generalized because in no two states are the political systems exactly alike. Indeed, rarely does a given party have exactly the same political stance and agenda in one state as it does in another. Within the larger states, it is not uncommon for Democrats and Republicans in one region of the state to differ ideologically from their counterparts in another region. Whatever their shape or style, parties do have in common the fact that they perform a number of significant functions in the political system. It is important that some individual or organization inform the public, nominate candidates, publicize issues, organize the legislatures, facilitate communications among the branches of government, effect compromise, and put together the majorities needed to pass bills. For these reasons the political parties are vital components of the political system.

Political scientist John Bibby suggests that modern-day political parties may be "likened to public utilities in the sense that they perform essential public functions."[1] They nominate and run candidates for office and do much of the work to organize U.S. governments. And they perform these public functions within the confines of state law.

Political Party Organization

There are laws in every state that control various aspects of political parties and elections. In all except a few states, the statutes speak to the structure and organization of the parties. They control party finances. State laws specify the means by which parties can place candidates for office on the ballot, and they do so in ways that make it easy for the two major parties to run candidates, but difficult for third parties to enter the game (the two major parties control the legislatures that pass these laws, and they have no desire to facilitate the emergence of a third party). In some instances, the states establish in law the dates for such party functions as precinct caucuses. To varying degrees, then, the political parties operate within parameters established by state law.

Three Levels of Party Organization

There are basically three levels of party organization in most states—the precinct, the county, and the state—though the law in many states also provides for organization along such lines as congressional districts.

The **precinct** is the basic unit of party organization. There are hundreds of precincts in every state, and a total of over 100,000 in the entire country. A precinct typically takes in an area covering several blocks and contains hundreds of individuals. In competitive two-party areas, each party may have viable precinct organizations. Periodically—once a year in some cases—a meeting called a **caucus** is held in the precinct and is open to anyone who lives within that precinct and who wishes to affiliate with the party. Officers called precinct captains are chosen. In areas where one party is dominant, the weaker party may find it difficult to maintain an effective organization in many precincts; even in competitive states, one party may dominate an area with the result that the other party has no effective organization in that area. In addition, the activity of many precinct organizations tends to surge around election time and grow dormant between elections. The precinct level is where much of the hard and unrewarding work is done, but it is also the level at which elections often are won or lost. Precinct workers typically do much of the legwork in getting people registered, peddling campaign materials, and hustling the voters to the polls on election day.

The next unit of party organization is the county. The typical county has a Democratic party organization and a Republican party organization. Each party periodically holds a county convention, sometimes once a year or perhaps just in election years. Representatives to the county convention usually are selected by the precincts. The convention elects a set of permanent officers, including a county central committee, a county chair, a county vice-chair, and a secretary-treasurer. In some years the convention also nominates candidates for such offices as county board of supervisors and sheriff, as well as delegates to the state convention, if there is one that year. In some states there is a party organization in each congressional district, and the county conventions may elect delegates to that unit as well. Party organization at the county level tends to sustain more continuity and vigor than it does at the precinct level. This is true in large part because the county is larger, containing dozens or hundreds of precincts.

The third and top level of party organization in the states is the state party itself. Just as the parties hold countywide conventions, they also periodically hold statewide conventions, at which they may nominate or endorse candidates for statewide office and select officers for the state central committee. In most states candidates for statewide office are selected in direct statewide primaries, but in others the convention can endorse a candidate or give the candidate top-line designation on the ballot, thus providing the candidate with an advantage in the primary.

In addition to the party organizations at the precinct, county, and state levels, other organizations may exist to serve the purposes of individual candidates. Senators and members of Congress, for example, typically maintain some sort of home organization of their own.

One-Party States

In one-party states or regions, there may be organizations linked not to a particular office but to a particular agenda. For example, there is a county in south Texas that has never elected a Republican to a district or countywide office. The county is a key player in statewide politics because of its monolithic Democratic vote. There are two longstanding organizations that operate within the county as **vote brokers**. During the Democratic primaries, candidates seeking statewide nomination attempt to lock in the endorsement of these two organizations as a key to success in the primary. If one organization endorses one candidate, the other usually supports an alternative candidate. Whichever candidate wins the primary is expected to reward the appropriate organization with patronage. As Republicans rarely contest all offices on the ballot in this county, the conflict between the two "broker" organizations sometimes has been more pronounced than that between the two political parties.

Variety among States

There are tremendous variations within and among the states as to the shape and operating procedures of the parties. Some states have many more precincts and counties than others, and thus their party organizations are more expansive. Some states, and even regions within them, are two-party competitive, with the result that there is vigorous organization and competition within most of the precincts and counties. In one-party dominant areas, the party that chronically loses may be unable to sustain any organization at all in some precincts and counties.

The procedures for selecting delegates to national presidential nominating conventions and the ways in which members of county and state executive committees are selected also vary among the states. But again, in most states the parties are organized at three levels (see Table 7.1).

An Untidy Structure

One major characteristic, and perhaps the defining characteristic, of American political parties is that they are structurally untidy, from the precinct to the national level. This is a gentle way of saying that each level of party organization enjoys considerable autonomy. Charles O. Jones, commenting on the degree of cohesion and unity characteristic of American parties, aptly refers to them as "non-things."[2] Unlike the political parties in certain Western European nations, those in the United States are relatively undisciplined, for one level of organization is rarely able to control the activities of those below it. Precincts are free to operate independently of the county. County officials, when they do accede to the wishes of state or national party officials, do so because they want to, not because they have to; and state officials are similarly independent of the national party. Neither U.S. presidents nor state governors can instruct county organizations on how to conduct their campaign activities or how to spend their money. American parties tend to be loosely knit confederations of largely independent fiefdoms.

TABLE 7.1 POLITICAL PARTY ORGANIZATION

Nation	States	Counties	Precincts and Wards
National chairperson National committee	State chairperson Other officers State committee	County chairperson Other officers County central committee	Precinct and ward chairs Precinct committee members

The loosely organized nature of American political parties can be explained in part by the structure of the U.S. government. Here, again, the federal principle is at work. The government structure disperses decision-making authority. Federalism permits the existence of one national and fifty state governments. The separation of powers and bicameralism further divide authority within these and other local units. In most states there exist hundreds of local government units. Because many of the officials of these governments are elected on partisan ballots, especially at the county level and above, political parties compete for the offices. Thus, the structure of the parties follows the structure of the government. The government is decentralized and so are the parties.

The decentralization of government is also reflected in the great diversity of the American polity. For example, the Republican party in Alabama is very different from the Republican party in Oregon. A Democratic governor in Rhode Island is likely to pursue quite different policy goals from the counterpart governor in Massachusetts.

In addition, the loose and rather unstructured nature of American political parties is a product of reforms adopted during the twentieth century. Until the early twentieth century, the parties, at the local level especially, were tightly organized and exerted significant control over nominations, elections, and the behavior of elected officials. Nominations for political office were made in caucuses of the party "big cheeses." Government jobs were passed out by the winners to the party faithful; this process was known as patronage. As a result, there were powerful incentives for people to associate with one of the two major parties and to work to keep their party in power.

This was an era of great **political machines**, which were highly disciplined, hierarchical organizations controlling precinct, ward, city, and sometimes county politics. They maintained an iron hand and dictated electoral outcomes through their grip on the local vote. They were headed by such well-known individuals as Boss Crump in Tennessee, Tom Pendergast in Kansas City, and the late Richard Daley in Chicago, perhaps the last of the classic machine bosses. Probably the most famous political machine of the era, Tammany Hall in New York City, exercised virtually complete control over municipal patronage.

Local political organizations still exist, of course, but the reduction in immigration combined with the impact of World War II and various reform movements have made the old-style political machines a relic of the past. Immigration restrictions reduced the steady flow of people on whom the machines depended for votes and day-to-day political work in exchange for patronage appointments. Similarly, the end of World War II brought with it the G.I. Bill, which provided a college education to thousands of individuals who otherwise might have remained dependent on the machines for their livelihoods.

Weakened Political Parties

Civil Service

Most state government employees today are part of a civil service system in which employment is based in large measure on training and merit, rather than on patronage. It is one's education, training, and skills, not one's contributions to a political party, that lead to a job. There are some exceptions to this rule, most notably in policy-level positions, in which devotion to a victorious governor's or mayor's policies is required, and in many county and municipal governments, where long standing traditions of patronage have won out over reformist sentiment. Even here, personnel turnover often is a function of personalized, nonpartisan political organizations that are not identified with either of the two major political parties.

Therefore, control over most public employment is no longer in the hands of the political parties. As a result, the parties are weakened by their inability to distribute rewards to the party faithful.

Direct Primaries

Similarly, the introduction of the **direct primary** in the early twentieth century deprived the parties of control over a major set of political prizes. The direct primary provided voters the opportunity to choose a party's candidate for the general election. Before the 1920s, long-term service to one of the two major parties was the necessary route for anyone seeking a place on the ballot. In contrast, the direct primary allows politically ambitious persons to launch a drive for a party's nomination by appealing directly to the voters. The laws governing primaries and nominations vary somewhat among the states, but the direct primary has universally loosened party control over nominations.

Candidate-Centered Campaigning

Another development that has weakened the American political parties is the candidate-centered campaign. Before the 1960s, the parties were the major source of the money and staffing that candidates needed to run their campaigns. Today, however, without the patronage, jobs, and control over nominations needed to entice large numbers of people to stay involved and loyal, the modern parties can seldom provide such support. Rather, political action committees (PACs) provide much of the money needed to fuel campaigns, and political consultants increasingly run sophisticated campaigns featuring computer-supported polling and targeted mailing as well as fund-raising.

The candidate is at the center of the campaign and is supported by money and skills obtained outside of the political party. The party role has thus become one of assisting, not directing, political campaigns. Furthermore, at the municipal level, the trend toward nonpartisan elections has rendered the parties irrelevant to most local governments.

A Resurgence in Party Vitality

The various reforms—civil service, direct primaries, and candidate-centered campaigning—coupled with such sociological factors as immigration patterns, steadily reduced the influence of political parties over the course of the twentieth century. However, there are recent signs of renewed vitality, primarily as a result of changes in the financial relations between the national parties and the state parties.[3] In particular, the Republican and Democratic National Committees are increasingly resourceful in raising money, and both are pumping some of the funds into state party organizations and state-level elections.

At the state and local levels, the parties are using the additional resources to add more permanent staff. Previously, many state and local political units would fold their tents between elections or maintain a minimal presence, perhaps only in the town or the home of the party chair. Today, more money means more organizational permanency. In addition, increased resources allow the parties to be more vigorous and regular in their polling, in their get-out-the-vote efforts, and in developing mailing lists for fund-raising and targeted campaign mailings. The infusion of national money into state parties and to state candidates is drawing the different levels of party organization closer. It is also putting the national committees in a position to exert previously nonexistent leverage on the state parties.

Party Competition

Before the 1970s, political scientists often addressed such issues as voters' tendency to inherit their parents' political leanings, the tendency of Americans to identify with one of the two parties, and the frequency of voting straight party-line ballots. They also wrote about the "solid South," where after the Civil War the southern and border states remained solidly in the Democratic party camp for almost a century.

What a difference a generation can make! Contemporary political scientists focus on an array of very different issues because so much has changed. A growing number of voters are **ticket-splitting**—that is, not voting a straight party ticket, but rather choosing one party's candidates for some offices and the other party's candidates for other offices—as the bonds that once held them tightly to one of the two major parties continue to dissolve. The extensive use of television in statewide contests—for governor, for example—fueled with enormous sums of money gives today's candidates the opportunity to promote an attractive personality instead of party loyalty. The South is no longer solidly Democratic; indeed, it is increasingly Republican in national and statewide elections, and Democratic electoral successes in such traditional Republican strongholds as Vermont, Arizona, and Idaho are no longer shocking.

Divided Government

Table 7.2 demonstrates the extent to which solid party control of regions has dissolved throughout much of the nation. For example, in 1992 three states in the formerly solid Democratic South had Republican governors—Alabama, Mississippi, and South Carolina; Texas followed suit in 1994. The Republican-leaning states of Colorado, Idaho, Kansas, and Wyoming all elected Democratic governors in 1992. Indeed, in only twenty of the fifty states did voters that year elect a fully united government with both legislative chambers and the governorship in the hands of the same party. Conversely, 60 percent of the states were operating with divided government.

This trend continued in 1996. Following the 1996 elections, a record thirty-two states have divided control at the state capitol, with a governor of one party and at least one house of the state legislature controlled by the other party.

The traditional geographical alignments of the parties also continue to be in a state of flux. In the last two decades, eleven southern or border states have elected Republican governors. These included Alabama, Arkansas, Florida, Louisiana, Missouri, North Carolina, Oklahoma, South Carolina, Tennessee, Texas, and Virginia. As a result of the 1996 elections, Florida became the first southern state to elect Republican majorities to both houses of the state legislature.

It is interesting to observe the actual divisions of state governments in 1996 (see Table 7.2). While partisan control in thirty-two states (an all-time record) was split in some fashion, thirty-eight states had both houses of the legislature under one party's control. Of these legislatures, twenty were Democratic and eighteen Republican. The Republican upsurge is significant; in 1994 Democrats controlled twenty-four legislatures and Republicans only eight. Much of the divided control came in the form of united legislatures with governors from the opposite party, but eleven states have one chamber of the legislature controlled by the Republican Party and the other house controlled by the Democrats.

Divided party control has deep roots in American history. The results of the Civil War affected American elections for a hundred years after the conflict

Table 7.2 Divided Party Control: State Legislatures and Governors in 1996

Fully United (18 States)		
Democratic Legislature and Governor (6)	*Republican Legislature and Governor (12)*	
Georgia	Arizona	North Dakota
Hawaii	Idaho	Ohio
Kentucky	Iowa	Pennsylvania
Maryland	Kansas	South Dakota
Missouri	Montana	Utah
Vermont	New Jersey	Wyoming

Split Control (31 States)			
Alabama	Illinois	Nevada	Tennessee
Alaska	Indiana	New Hampshire	Texas
Arkansas	Louisiana	New Mexico	Virginia
California	Maine	North Carolina	Washington
Colorado	Massachusetts	Oklahoma	West Virginia
Connecticut	Michigan	Oregon	Wisconsin
Delaware	Minnesota	Rhode Island	New York
Florida	Mississippi	South Carolina	

Party Control of Legislatures		
Democratic Control (20)	*Republican Control (18)*	*Split (11)*
Alabama	Alaska	Delaware
Arkansas	Arizona	Illinois
California	Colorado	Indiana
Connecticut	Florida	Michigan
Georgia	Idaho	Nevada
Hawaii	Iowa	New York
Kentucky	Kansas	North Carolina
Louisiana	Montana	South Carolina
Maine	New Hampshire	Texas
Maryland	New Jersey	Virginia
Massachusetts	North Dakota	Wisconsin
Minnesota	Ohio	
Mississippi	Oregon	
Missouri	Pennsylvania	
New Mexico	South Dakota	
Oklahoma	Utah	
Rhode Island	Washington	
Tennessee	Wyoming	
Vermont		
West Virginia		

ended. In reaction to the activities of the postwar Republican president and Congress, the southern and border states embraced the Democratic party. Indeed, they did so with such tenacity that the Republican party was all but nonexistent in those states and all meaningful political competition took place within the Democratic party. Virtually all local and state officeholders were Democrats, the Democratic primaries constituted the only meaningful elections, and Democratic presidential candidates could count on the support of the solid South. The Great Depression of the 1930s began during the tenure of another Republican, Herbert Hoover, and reinforced the Democratic solidarity.

Beginning in the 1960s, however, the situation gradually changed. The civil rights movement of the 1960s and 1970s, supported by Democratic presidents and Congresses controlled by the Democratic Party, but opposed by many Democratic political leaders in the South, weakened the loyalty of many white southern voters to Democratic presidential candidates. From 1968 to 1988 Republican candidates (Richard Nixon, Ronald Reagan, and George Bush) enjoyed widespread southern support. At the same time, the considerable southward migration of many easterners and midwesterners with Republican party affiliation or leanings also helped to expand the Republican electoral base in the South. Since 1982 Republicans have gained state legislative seats in the South in every election. Until 1978, Democrats controlled over 80 percent of the state legislative seats in the South; in 1996 their share of those seats fell to 62 percent, the lowest since Reconstruction.

Aided by the presence of two southerners on the ticket, in 1992, the Democrats broke through the Republican southern stronghold at the presidential level with the election of Bill Clinton. The 1996 election, however, saw a return to the voting pattern of previous years. Although Arkansas, Florida, and Louisiana voted for President Clinton, the rest of the deep southern states supported the Republican ticket.

The style of campaigning, especially in statewide contests, also has changed in recent decades. As noted earlier in the chapter, elections are increasingly expensive candidate-centered media events, and money, television, and personality have diminished the importance of political party affiliation as a factor in voters' choices.

Electoral success and organizational strength go hand in hand. When one party dominates elections for a long time, it is difficult for the minority party to remain active. People simply are not motivated to contribute their time, money, and energy to losing causes. But a few victories can change that situation. Thus, when Republican presidential and gubernatorial candidates enjoyed some success in the solid South, new life was given to the Republican party organization. Democrats continue to win many local and state contests, but, increasingly, both parties are active, functioning organizations.

In the American states, then, there may be two-party competition but one-party dominance. Voters in most states provide some support for both major parties. Hence, divided government is common. At the same time, many state legislatures remain under the control of one party, most often the Democratic party, albeit by a narrow margin. In addition, within the states many local offices and state legislative seats belong to the same party after repeated elections.

Perspectives on Political Competition

In addressing the issue of whether competitive politics or one-party dominance is best, political scientists generally advocate two-party competition. It is argued that in states with one-party control, there is a tendency for factions to form within the dominant party. This was particularly true in the South when the Democrats long controlled elections.

In his classic study of politics in the South conducted in 1949, V. O. Key suggested that some characteristics of factional politics may be unhealthy for a democracy.[4] In representative democracies, the political parties provide the link between the mass of voters and the seats of power. They nominate candidates, publish policy platforms, organize and run the government, and, in periodic elections, take the credit or blame for what has gone on. In addition, organized political parties are like most other organizations in that they provide assistance to their members, command a degree of loyalty in return, and operate according to sets of rules and norms that help to control and direct the behavior of their members.

The Downside of Factional Politics

When political struggles among factions replace interparty competition, problems result. For example, without the parties there is no highly organized and visible "in-group" or "out-group" for voters to hold responsible for successes and failures. Voters cannot easily or accurately decide whether the party in power has done a bad job and on that basis proceed to vote for the other party; in fact, there may be no "other" party, and the voter may be unaware of the other faction. In addition, parties operate according to sets of rules and norms that factions do not employ. Without the parties it is possible for candidates and politically active types to behave in an irresponsible, freewheeling, and self-serving fashion. Furthermore, without viable political parties, candidates are much more "on their own" in their search for campaign funds and other forms of political support. As a result, they may be more susceptible to the influence of special interest groups. There are other problems as well. Without party support and the need to conform to party norms, candidates may be tempted to resort to demagogic tactics, focusing their attention on such factors as personalities or race.

Therefore, when political parties are weak, or when legislative competition revolves around a series of factions within a single dominant party so that policy leadership is not provided by the parties, influence will flow elsewhere. It will flow to dominant personalities, to committees and their chairpersons, and to the lobbies.

The Advantages of Competition

Political parties, of course, are not perfectly representative of the American public or even of the American voting public. The highly educated, financially well-off, occupationally prestigious, and politically involved "elite" tends to dominate the voting, candidate, and decision-maker ranks. Nevertheless, political parties are more reflective of popular preferences than the alternatives—individuals, small legislative committees, and narrowly focused lobbies. In its search for some person or institution to represent its values and views, the American public is better off casting its lot with the party than with any of the available alternatives. But the option of the party is available only so long as the political environment remains competitive.

In short, vigorous interparty competition is healthy in a representative democracy. The parties broaden the base of support for candidates, freeing them from the possible control of special interests. The out-party criticizes the in-party, thus helping to keep the public informed. The out-party also provides a ready, visible alternative for a dissatisfied public. Where effective two-party competition exists, party organization in the legislature tends to be more cohesive, with the healthy result that public policy is more heavily influenced by the parties than by strong committee chairs or special interest groups. With competition, the quality of candidates offered by the parties is higher, whereas the absence of competition allows the dominant party to nominate anyone it wants. (This absence of competition in the South led to the term **yellow-dog Democrat**, which was used to identify voters who would vote the Democratic ticket even if the candidates were yellow dogs.) The parties articulate and press for the interests of large numbers of people. Factions, in contrast, are not nearly as effective or responsible as links between the people and their government. Without healthy two-party competition, the preferences of the unorganized and the inarticulate often are ignored in public policy.

Competing Views

A number of studies question Key's suggestion that the level of party competition has an effect on the public policies of a state. Studies conducted by

Dawson and Robinson,[5] Hofferbert,[6] and Dye[7] conclude that differences in the taxing and spending patterns of the states are affected more by social and economic variations than by differences in political factors (such as party competition, apportionment, and government structure). Yet studies conducted by Cnudde and McCrone[8] and Sharkansky and Hofferbert[9] modify this suggestion that political variables and policy outcomes may be causally unrelated. They point out that political factors may have a greater effect on policy outcomes in some policy areas than in others. For instance, Cnudde and McCrone suggest that in the policy areas of greatest concern to society's less well-off, such as aid to dependent children and unemployment compensation, increased party competition works to their benefit, whereas in policy areas of less concern to this group, the level of party competition has little or no impact. One explanation for this tendency is that the less well-off often lack access to the decision makers, money, positions, and status needed for placing their concerns on the public agenda. Thus, in areas of concern to them, they take advantage of the potential of the political party to champion their needs.

Similarly, Sharkansky and Hofferbert contend that political factors such as party competition and governmental structure affect policy in the states but to varying degrees according to the particular policy:

> Welfare–education policies relate most closely with the competition-turnout dimension of state politics and with the affluence dimension of the economy. Highway–natural resources policies show their closest (inverse) relationships with the industrialization dimension of the state economy.[10]

It might also be argued that two-party competition, insofar as it leads to divided government, makes it difficult to assign responsibility for government actions. When a legislature is divided, or when a governor is from one party and the legislature is controlled by the other, each party tends to blame the other for problems (a pattern not uncommon at the national level as well) and both parties seek to take credit for accomplishments. Governors may argue that their state's legislature ignored their priorities or failed to fund their programs adequately. The legislature, in turn, may blame the governor for budget shortfalls or scandals in state agencies.

Third Parties

The preceding discussion of political parties has referred only to the Republicans and Democrats, for the American party system is typically described as a **two-party system**. However, there have been many more parties in the history of American politics, and even today there are several **third par-**

Focus 7.1

SELECTED THIRD PARTIES IN THE UNITED STATES

• • •

Farmer-Labor Party (Minnesota)
La Raza Unida Party (Texas)
Conservative Party of New York State
Libertarian Party
Socialist Labor Party
Socialist Workers Party
Theocratic Party
New Alliance Party
Consumer Party
Right-to-Life Party
Peace and Freedom Party
Populist Party
American Independent Party
Worker's League Party

ties offering choices to voters. (See Focus 7.1 "Selected Third Parties in the United States.") Still, usually only two parties—Democrats and Republicans—have a realistic chance of winning the vast majority of elections in the U.S. political system. Therefore, competition is defined in terms of the two-party system.

Criticisms of the Political Parties

Political parties have long been the topic of heated discussion regarding both their performance as conduits of public preferences and their proper role in the political system. The first question is an empirical one, for it simply asks whether political parties are effective links between the people and their government. The second question is normative, addressing the question of what parties should try to do.

Through the years American political parties have been criticized for being insensitive to the desires of the masses and insufficiently cohesive to allow the voters to make meaningful choices. These twin critiques may appear contradictory, and to some extent they are.

Do Elites Control the Parties?

It has been argued that the parties—from county organizations to presidential nominating conventions—are controlled by a few party leaders. In a classic study, scholar Robert Michels[11] called this an "iron law of oligarchy," a sentiment echoed by Phyllis Schlafly,[12] who asserts that both major American parties are controlled by a big-money eastern establishment.

Are the Parties Directionless?

The parties are also criticized for being so incohesive that the public is not given a clear-cut choice at the polls. From the county to the national level, it is argued that the parties lack tight organization. As a result, they cannot effectively articulate and institute a "party line" and the voters cannot effectively hold any party fully responsible for the public decisions that are made.

This criticism has some merit, for the fragmented nature of the political system works against party cohesion. Governors, state representatives, others elected to the executive branch, and the various boards and commissions all respond to slightly different constituencies. Thus, the parties are both controlled by an elite group and, at the same time, insufficiently cohesive to present the voters with as meaningful a set of choices as some would like. As Samuel Eldersveld suggests, the parties constitute a multiplicity of oligarchies.[13] On both counts, then, it is argued that the preferences of the masses are slightly obscured.

Are the Parties Too Much Alike?

In addition, the two major parties are criticized for being too much alike in that they both seek middle-of-the-road candidates and platform stands designed to alienate as few voters as possible. As a result, the voter ends up with a choice between Tweedledum and Tweedledee—a rather meaningless differentiation at best. In common terms, as many observe, "there's not a dime's worth of difference between the two major parties."

Although there is some merit in this observation, it should not be carried too far. It is true that the two major American parties lean toward the middle of the road on issues, but they must do so if they hope to win votes and elections. A radical stance, whether to the far left or far right of the political spectrum, would prove suicidal for the parties. Several political observers argue that the parties reflect, rather than create, the political leanings of the American people. Thus, both major parties are in the middle of the political spectrum because that is where most of the people are.

In a sense, American society is consensual; people tend not to want or need more extreme choices at the polls. While there is division on specifics, there is consensus on basics. Indeed, if Americans were presented with more radical choices, a host of changes could lead to the development of a potentially dangerous situation. For example, great ideological divisions would exist within society, which radical parties would exploit in search of votes. The lack of consensus would, in turn, create widespread disagreement on fundamental questions and make it difficult to arrive at compromise decisions. Decision making would likely be characterized by rigid factional adherence to ideological and policy positions, and thus by immobility. As a result, it would be relatively easy to form a majority to stop something from happening but impossible to generate majority support to get anything done. In other words, our political parties serve the central functions of creating consensus in our system, balancing the system between the extremes, and helping us, as a people, to "agree to disagree."

Summary

Political parties perform many important functions in the political system. These include nominating candidates for office, contributing to the political education of the public, maintaining a check on those in office, drawing people into political activities, organizing the government, and bridging some of the gaps created by federalism and the separation of powers.

The United States is characterized as having a two-party system, but there are great variations among the states, some of which are dominated by one party. In addition, some are predominantly Democratic, whereas others lean toward the Republican side. The parties vary in terms of their organization as well. Although they are governed by law in nearly all states, the exact pattern of party organization varies. So do the number of elective offices, the frequency of elections, and the time of year at which elections are held.

Finally, the two major parties have been the subject of much criticism. While some of the criticisms have a degree of merit, effective counterarguments can be made. Both parties tend toward the middle of the political spectrum and avoid radical positions on issues, which many contend is a reflection of the political leanings of the American people. Therefore, parties do not create political beliefs but mirror those of the masses.

Policy Perspective

It sounds so good: a responsible party system. Who could be against "responsibility"? There are political scientists who endorse a responsible party system as an ideal way of facilitating the development of public policy in the states. In reality, no such animal exists among the fifty states, and there are many who contend that a responsible party system actually would be undesirable. Desirable or not, it is very unlikely that a responsible party system will become a characteristic of any state's policy process.

In theory, a responsible party system makes sense. The basic idea is that a political party will be organized along the traditional model of a pyramid, with authority flowing from the top to the bottom. Come election time, so goes the theory, state parties in a responsible model will meet and agree upon a specific set of policy goals to offer voters meaningful and distinct choices. Then, the parties will recruit candidates at the state, county, and local levels who pledge to support the specific planks of the platforms. Democrat candidates will say to the voters, elect us and we'll do *X*; Republican candidates will promise to do *Y*. In other words, the voters will be presented with a clear choice as to a policy preference—none of this tweedledee-tweedledum business.

Then, if elected, under a responsible party model, the representatives of the majority party are expected to translate their platform into public policy. In other words, they're expected to do what they said they would do. This means the parties will be in charge of policy making in the legislature; the majority party will organize and direct the policy process. After all, in the campaign, the party told the voters that if they wanted, say *X*, then vote for our candidates. The voters did so, and now, since the party has a majority of the representatives, it's simply a matter of bringing *X* to a vote and passing it. What could be more democratic?

Such party systems actually exist, although not in United States. Most of the time, responsible party systems go hand in hand with parliamentary systems (e.g., England). In such systems there is no separation between the legislative and executive branches, and, consequently, it is very rare that the political leader (usually called the Prime Minister) will be of a different political party than the majority of the representatives. This, in part, enables political parties in a responsible system to exercise considerable control over its membership in the legislative chamber. In other words, there is a high degree of party discipline that often is missing in state party systems. Check Table 7.2 again; well over half of the fifty states have executives of one party and legislatures controlled by the other party.

As discussed briefly earlier in this chapter, there are a number of reasons why our parties are not organized along the lines of a responsible party system. Fundamental is the impact of the federal principle. Just as the nation is organized along federal lines, so are the parties. Each state has a party unit at the state, county, and local level, but there is no pyramid model here; rather each level operates more or less autonomously. Thus, a state party organization may have as a major goal the election of candidate *X*, who must take positions on statewide issues during the campaign. At the same time, the county organization may be involved in working for candidates for countywide offices whose positions on county issues may be very different from or even incompatible with those of the statewide candidates of the same party. Since the major goal of our political parties is to get candidates elected, each level seeks those positions that will attract votes, making it difficult to establish the explicit policy positions characteristic of the responsible party model.

Think of the difficulty in a state of crafting a specific platform that will attract voters from, say, minority populations in the urban centers, while at the same time pulling in the rural, predominately white vote as well. While there may be some coordination between the different levels of party organization, each level goes its own way. As a result, this diminishes the policy-making power of the parties as the majorities that are elected to the legislature may not be as cohesive as those found in responsible party systems.

In a sense a responsible party system is more democratic, while our system is more representative; that is, most state political parties respond to the demographic differences that are manifest in almost all fifty states. Democrats in Chicago differ in significant ways from Democrats down state; Republicans in San Diego may hold different policy views from those in San Francisco.

Sometimes, the existence of different levels of autonomy may work to the detriment of a state party. A few years ago, one of the western states was embroiled in redistricting litigation. Such litigation is hardly unique, since redistricting may well be the most bitterly fought political battle of each decade; a shift of just a precinct or two can literally change the outcomes of elections for the next several years. Both political parties were engaged in drawing maps of legislative districts to present to the court. Not surprisingly, the Democrats wanted to design a map that would elect more Democrats, and the Republicans were working hard to draw a map that would ensure the election of Republicans for the next decade.

The Democratic County Party in one of the major urban counties was responsible for drawing the Democratic map for the state legislative districts in their county. The state Democratic Party already had done some preliminary work on population and voting data and had a draft of a map ready. They offered it to the county party and were told, politely, to butt out. As the Democratic County organization completed its work, it became clear that their map would not enhance Democratic electoral chances as much as the state party map. Frantic pleas from the state party officials to the county party leadership were unavailing; in so many words, the county leadership said stay off our turf. As it turned out, the state party was correct (the county party had worked with inaccurate data). Unbelievably all belonged to the same party with the same goals. No pyramid organization here.

KEY TERMS

latent functions
spin doctor
precinct
caucus
vote broker
political machine
direct primary
ticket-splitting
yellow-dog Democrat
two-party system
third party

ADDITIONAL READING

Frendreis, John P., James L. Gibson, and Laura L. Vertz. "The Electoral Relevance of Local Party Organizations." *American Political Science Review* (March 1990): 225–35.

Hawley, Willis D. *Non-Partisan Elections and the Case for Party Politics*. New York: Wiley, 1973.

Jewell, Malcolm E., and David M. Olson. *Political Parties and Elections in American States*. Chicago: Dorsey, 1988.

Keefe, William. *Parties, Politics and Public Policy in America*. Washington, D.C.: Congressional Quarterly Press, 1987.

NOTES

1. John F. Bibby, "Party Organization at the State Level," in *The Parties Respond*, ed. L. Sandy Maisel (Boulder, Colo.: Westview Press, 1990), p. 22.
2. Classroom comment by Charles O. Jones, professor of political science.
3. See Bibby, "Party Organization," p. 22. See also Samuel C. Patterson, "The Persistence of State Parties," in *The State of the Party*, ed. Carl E. Van Horn (Washington, D.C.: Congressional Quarterly Press, 1989), pp. 153–74; and John F. Bibby, Cornelius P. Cather, James L. Gibson, and Robert J. Huckshorn, "Parties in State Politics," in *Politics in the American States*, 5th ed., ed. Virginia Gray, Herbert Jacob, and Robert B. Albritton (Glenview, Ill.: Scott, Foresman/Little, Brown Higher Education, 1990), pp. 85–122.
4. V. O. Key, Jr., *Southern Politics* (New York: Knopf, 1949).
5. Richard E. Dawson and James A. Robinson, "Interparty Competition, Economic Variables and Welfare Politics in American States," *Journal of Politics* (May 1963): 265–98.
6. Richard I. Hofferbert, "The Relation between Public Policy and Some Structural and Environmental Variables in the American States," *American Political Science Review* (March 1966): 73–82.
7. Thomas R. Dye, *Politics, Economics and the Public: Policy Outcomes in the American States* (Chicago: Rand McNally, 1966).
8. Charles F. Cnudde and Donald J. McCrone, "Party Competition and Welfare Policies in the American States," *American Political Science Review* (Sept. 1969): 858–66.
9. Ira Sharkansky and Richard I. Hofferbert, "Dimensions of State Politics, Economics, and Public Policy," *American Political Science Review* (Sept. 1969): 867–79.
10. Ibid.: 878.
11. Robert Michels, *Political Parties* (1915; reprint New York: Collier Books, 1962).
12. Phyllis Schlafly, public comment made during the 1964 election.
13. Samuel J. Eldersveld, *Political Parties* (Chicago: Rand McNally, 1964), esp. ch. 6.

CHAPTER 8

• • •

Special Interest Groups

• • •

Interest groups are various means to influence political outcomes. Here, a group of striking United Auto Workers participate in a rally in downtown Chicago, Illinois. *(Robert Kusel/Tony Stone Images, Inc.)*

• • • Participants in Special Interest Groups

Educators
Local Governments and Professionals
Business Interests and Volunteer Groups
Similarities and Differences among the States
Single-Issue Noncompromisers
Why Interest Groups Are Formed

• • • The Lobbyists

Focus 8.1: Lobbying: An Insider's Game?

Employee and Contract Lobbyists
Volunteer Lobbyists and Legislative Liaisons

• • • Techniques of Influence

Focus 8.2: The Lobbying Industry

Direct Communication
Image Building
Activating Grass Roots
Common Interests
Personnel Exchanges
Role Reversals
PAC Money

• • • What Makes a Special Interest Group Effective?

Size
Money
Cohesion
Leadership
Image
Political Efficacy

• • • Lobbyists in State Politics

The Defensive Advantage

Focus 8.3: Do—Do Not

Failure and Success
Strong Parties Weaken Special Interest Groups

• • • SPECIAL INTEREST GROUPS IN A DEMOCRACY

• • • SUMMARY

• • • POLICY PERSPECTIVE: WHAT'S OUR POLICY ON SPECIAL INTERESTS?
Watching the Lobbyists
Campaign Money
Factions: To Control or Not Control?

n any day in any state during any legislative session one can find the capitol crowded with **lobbyists**—the hired guns of powerful interests, some would say. The hallways, or lobbies, just outside a state's house and senate chambers and near the committee rooms buzz with the talk of lobbyists and lawmakers. Testimony on critical bills is given by lobbyists or by persons they have brought in. Lobbyists trek in and out of legislators' offices all day long. Lawmakers can, if they want, enjoy meals at the expense of the special interest groups that hire the lobbyists. Legislators summon lobbyists routinely to ask for data, or to ask how their group feels about a proposed bill, or even to ask the lobbyist if an amendment to a bill is acceptable to the special interest group. Many bills are written by lobbyists or their lawyers before final technical drafting by the legislative staff.

A large and growing proportion of the money that fuels electoral campaigns comes from **special interest groups**—corporations, professional associations, labor unions, educators' organizations, local governments, and other groups that spend some of their time and money trying to influence government. Legislators and legislative leaders solicit money from special interest groups directly. Sometimes large checks arrive by mail, unsolicited. Even incumbents with no electoral opposition receive special interest group money. Lobbyists maintain ongoing communication with legislators, agency personnel, and members of governors' staffs about their groups' policy preferences. Sometimes lobbyists initiate court action to support their position (as in seeking an order to void a statute or agency rule that they oppose). Often they run radio, television, newspaper, magazine, and billboard advertisements portraying themselves as good citizens whose desires reflect the public good.

What are the effects of special interest groups and lobbyists? Bill Schluter, a Republican member of the New Jersey House, cites the candid comments of the director of public relations for that state's Chamber of

Commerce: "I have not seen legislators who could be bought, but I met a lot who could be rented, who can be influenced by the need to finance their campaigns."[1] The efforts of special interest groups and lobbyists, and their money, have a tremendous impact on government activities. Legislators, governors, and other elected state and local officials obtain their positions by appealing successfully for public support. To continue in public life, they must continue to satisfy enough people to secure reelection. Thus, when a lobbyist who represents a slice of the electorate tells a politician how the people stand on some matter, the lobbyist's comments are influential. In addition, elections cost money, and lawmakers know that special interest groups support candidates who support them.

While political self-interest is a powerful motivation to listen to special interest groups and their lobbyists, it is not the only one. Lawmakers must make hundreds, even thousands, of choices every year. For legislators, votes must be cast both on the floor and in committee. Governors and other state executives must similarly make decisions constantly. Where can they obtain the information needed to guide their choices? Decision makers come to their jobs with a set of values and at least some information, but none can be fully informed on all matters. Legislative and executive staff personnel provide information to varying degrees, depending on the state or local government involved, but in no cases can staff members provide everything. In many smaller states, such as New Mexico, Wyoming, and Idaho, staff support is in very short supply, and thus the lobbyists are an important source of information and voting cues.

In an ideal world of perfect democracy, everyone would be politically equal, for political equality is an important value in democratic theory. In the real world, however, people are not equal politically. In general political inequality is not the result of forceful denial of access to the political process; rather, it is largely due to the fact that some people are active in politics and others are not. Many well-educated and well-to-do business and professional people understand how the political system works and how to exert influence. They organize and spend time and money to advance their own interests. Sometimes political organization and action is triggered by the actions of other groups. But many Americans do not get involved, whether due to a lack of interest or a shortage of time. As a result, they are largely irrelevant to the political process. Yet politicians listen to those who speak out, especially when the comments may be instrumental to their political fortunes. They do not listen to those who fail to speak out. E. E. Schattschneider once remarked that democracy's choir sings with an upper-class accent.[2] Special interest groups are in that choir, and the songs they sing express largely their own interests.

Participants in Special Interest Groups . . . .

Who are the groups in the state political systems and what do they seek to accomplish?[3] To gain a sense of the types of special interest groups that operate within any particular state, first one needs to consider what it is that the state does and then look at the state's economic foundation. What do states do? They establish and fund educational institutions at all levels, from kindergartens to graduate, medical, and law schools. Indeed, education consumes more than half, and often two-thirds, of annual state budgets. States also establish local governments—counties, cities, special districts—and control their structures, authority, and limitations. States license professions and businesses, ranging from hairdressers and morticians to taxi companies and boxers. Much of our tort law now exists in state statutes. So do provisions controlling the use of water, timber, and minerals. States tax both businesses and individuals. They promote economic development but discourage and penalize drug use, rape, and murder.

So who are the people who try to influence policy outcomes by lobbying lawmakers, executive branch officials, and even the courts? They are individuals and groups that have stakes in the laws and the budgets that legislatures adopt.

Educators

In every state, teachers' organizations are an important and usually effective lobby. The state controls teacher credentials, teacher tenure, and much school funding, so it is to be expected that educators would lobby. Associations of school districts, school board members, and school administrators also lobby the state, often joining forces with the teachers but sometimes opposing them.

Local Governments and Professionals

Associations of cities, counties, and special districts are highly visible and effective interest groups and lobbying forces in the states as well. The structures, duties, and resources of local governments are state controlled, so the fact that they lobby is not surprising.

Similarly, physicians, lawyers, planners, psychiatrists, social workers, and most other professionals lobby. They donate to campaigns, spend to gloss up their public images, and send lobbyists to the legislature and other decision points in state government. These professions are state-regulated. Why? Because regulation advances public health and safety, and also helps to limit access into the professions. These lobbyists thus have a stake in convincing lawmakers to maintain regulatory laws.

Business Interests and Volunteer Groups

Business interests are important and powerful lobbying groups in the states. Business people often oppose taxes and regulation but favor receipt of government contracts, government spending, and tax breaks. Public officials worry constantly about the economic health of the state, so they are usually receptive to the arguments of businesses. Farmers often lobby successfully for tax breaks on farm machinery. Mining operations receive depletion allowances. In recent years businesses have pressed for cost reductions of worker compensation taxes and for some freedom from labor unions.

Similarly, realtors lobby to stay free of state regulations establishing health and safety standards for rental properties. Doctors lobby for statutory caps on malpractice damage awards. Trial lawyers oppose damage caps; they make their living in the courts, often through shares of damage awards. And so it goes. Group after group works the political system in search of laws and appropriations that give it an edge, or money, or both.

Professional interest groups are often joined by volunteer groups seeking public policy that advances their ideological positions. The pro-life movement wants bans on abortions. Parents seek tougher drunk-driving penalties. Some want certain chemicals outlawed. Still others like the League of Women Voters are interested in reforming the political system.

Similarities and Differences among the States

Table 8.1 lists special interest groups that are viewed as especially influential in the politics of two states. It is interesting to note both the similarities and the differences between them. In both Arizona and Ohio, business interests and public employees are listed. This is to be expected, and it is common among all the states. Businesses are understandably concerned with state regulations and taxes. Every year the legislative agenda will be loaded with bills that can impact a business's success, as well as its costs and profits. Similarly, employees of state and local governments have much at stake, since their pay, benefits, working conditions, indeed their jobs, ride on state budgets and related state policies.

But notice, too, some differences between Arizona and Ohio. While cities and towns and teachers are listed as among the more influential interests, businesses and business associations dominate the listing. But in Arizona, traditional organized labor is absent altogether. In Ohio, by contrast, labor and

TABLE 8.1 INTEREST GROUPS IN TWO STATES

Arizona	Ohio
Manufacturers Association	Education Lobby
Chamber of Commerce	AFL-CIO
Business Council	Public employees unions
Mining Association	Council of Retail Merchants
League of Cities and Towns	State Medical Association
Education Association	Trial Lawyers
Utilities	AARP
Railroad Association	Manufacturers Association
	Insurance Federation
	Nurses Association

Source: These listings are drawn from data assembled by Professors Ronald Hrebener and Clive Thomas as a part of their ongoing study of interest groups in the states.

public employees are well represented in the listing of influentials. Businesses and trial lawyers are there too, but they do not dominate.

These differences, like the similarities, are to be expected, and can be found among other states as well. In Arizona, like other western and southern states, labor has not been well organized and powerful traditionally, and the values of the larger population tend to be conservative and sympathetic to money and management. In Ohio, the Midwest generally, and the East, labor's history and roots go much deeper, and community values reflect that fact as do the sympathies of many legislators.

Overall, the groups that show up on the Arizona and Ohio lists of influentials reflects the situation in the states generally. Teachers, businesses and their various associations, utility companies, lawyers, doctors, and other professionals along with labor and local governments are universally present and consequential in state politics even though their relative clout varies from state to state.[4]

Single-Issue Noncompromisers

There has been an increase in recent years in the number of **single-issue interest groups** that champion some policy stance on a single issue. These groups are often ideological in nature and press moral rather than economic values, though this is not always the case. Pro-life activists, parents against drunk driving, parents in favor of home schooling or school choice, and opponents of gun control are examples. The participants in recent tax-limitation campaigns include some who just don't want to pay taxes and others who are ideologically attracted to minimalist government.

Single-issue groups and their lobbyists are sometimes rigid and therefore difficult for lawmakers to deal with. In the long run this can work to the disadvantage of the groups. For example, those whose stance on abortion or pornography is deeply rooted in moral values often view compromise as an unacceptable breach of moral virtue. But collective choices in democracies are by their nature the product of compromise. It is one thing for an individual or group to live by a particular standard of behavior; it is quite another to insist that a particular standard be imposed through law on an entire society.

Public officials who, by definition, represent or work for entire polities find it hard to deal with single-issue noncompromisers. For example, legislators who refuse to embrace a group's rigid position risk losing the support of that group. But lawmakers who do support such a position must then forsake compromise with all the others. It is difficult for legislators to muster support for their own bills, and, indeed, even to stay in office, if they are unwilling to compromise with their colleagues. Linda Wagar cites the comment of an Alaska state senator: "Lawmakers who try to adjust their votes to the demands of every special interest group eventually lose the respect of their colleagues and constituency."[5]

Why Interest Groups Are Formed

One could easily gain the impression that politically active special interest groups exist solely for the purpose of pressing their positions and preferences on the government. More often than not, this is not the case. For most special interest groups, political action represents just one of their many activities, and generally not even the primary one.

Professional associations of physicians, counselors, lawyers, and teachers, for instance, are formed to share professional information, keep members abreast of professional developments, advance job security, and generate collective insurance or recreational opportunities. These pursuits often lead the groups into the political arena, but political objectives per se do not explain the groups' existence.

The Lobbyists

One needs only to wander through a state capitol when the legislature is in session to gain a sense of the role of special interest groups in the political process.

The lobbies just outside house and senate chambers are crowded with lobbyists milling around, often calling legislators off the floor and into the lobby for consultation as debate and voting proceed (hence the term lobbyist). The same activity can be seen in the hallways outside committee hearing rooms. Indeed, lobbyists often consult with legislators during hearings and are frequently called on to answer questions about bills that the sponsoring lawmakers themselves cannot answer. (See Focus 8.1 "Lobbying: An Insider's Game?")

Focus 8.1

LOBBYING: AN INSIDERS GAME?

• • •

One does not need to hang around a state legislature very long before noticing that it feels like a summer camp for adults, where everyone knows everyone else, and has for years. Lobbyists know each other, so do legislators, and so do members of the staff and press and high-level executive branch personnel. They stroll around the capitol like it's been home for years and, for many, it has. Many lobbyists are former legislators. So are some in the executive branch. Hanging around the capitol and exchanging ideas, information, and influence becomes a way of life for many politicos, even as they move from one job to another.

Karen Reinertson provides an example. Karen lobbied in the legislature for the Association of Counties in Colorado for a while, left, came back, and lobbied for it again twice more. She lobbied for Denver's mayor. Karen lobbied for an assortment of clients as a member of a contract lobbying firm. She worked for Colorado's governor, twice in his budget office, once heading the state's Local Affairs Department and once running the Office of Energy Conservation. Her most recent occupation is lobbying with the state's largest lobbying firm.

Governors come and go. So do legislative staffers. Members of the press are often transient. With term limits, there'll be more and more new faces in the legislature. But in some capacity the regulars, like Karen Reinertson, will always be there to help steer the ships of state. Is this good? Is this bad? Whatever it is, it's real, it is a phenomenon that is here to stay, and it involves people who are paid by special interests, and elected by no one.

Source: Peter Blake, "The 'should not' of state ethics policy," *Rocky Mountain News*, 24 December 1993; *Denver Post*, 16 December 1993.

The lobbying business is not easy. Lobbyists must hustle constantly, counting favorable and unfavorable votes by legislators both in committee decisions and on the floor. Sometimes they must combat the pressure from special interest groups on the other side of the issue. Lawmakers often request information, and lobbyists must round it up. Increasingly, lobbyists are pressured for campaign donations, or they help in pressuring one lawmaker on behalf of another. But through all of this, clearly the door is open for special interest groups and their lobbyists to be highly influential, particularly when they judiciously and skillfully use good information and campaign money.

Lobbying, like much of state government, is said to have become more professionalized in recent years. Governors are well educated and capable managers. State legislators enjoy improved staffing, office space, and pay. Similarly, the lobbying game has become less a matter of legislators and lobbyists deciding public policy in local watering holes. The mix of whiskey and political deals, it seems, has given way in some measure to a meld of information and larger campaign contributions. Backroom wheeling and dealing may be fading, but the same cannot be said for the impact of interest groups and their lobbyists on public policy.

Just as there are many different types of interest groups that seek to influence the course of public policy in the states, so too are there different types of lobbyists.

Employee and Contract Lobbyists

Some lobbyists are hired as employees of businesses or industries. Manufacturers, large retail outlets, utility companies, breweries, associations of local governments, and others often maintain their lobbying presence in the capitol through such **employee lobbyists**.

Other interests hire **contract lobbyists**, persons who, like attorneys and accountants, represent someone or some organization for a fee. Many contract lobbyists are former legislators who rely on their knowledge of the system as well as on the friendships and political networks they have developed over the years.

Contract lobbyists may represent anywhere from a few to two dozen or more clients. Their tasks are to watch carefully for bills that might affect their clients and to represent their clients' preferences to lawmakers. They do this through ongoing personal conversations, presentations of data, and the orchestration of expert or citizen testimony in committee hearings. Sometimes they testify themselves. They count votes constantly. Sometimes contract lobbyists attempt to secure the passage of legislation; at other times they seek to stop bills. The annual income of an effective contract lobbyist can run into hundreds of thousands of dollars.

Volunteer Lobbyists and Legislative Liaisons

Some interest groups' views are represented to lawmakers by **volunteer lobbyists**. Environmental, consumer, and good government groups, such as the Sierra Club, Common Cause, and the League of Women Voters, often fit this category.

In addition, many lobbyists work for the government itself. One study estimates that from 25 percent to 50 percent of all lobbyists represent some government or government agency.[6] These people are often called **legislative liaisons** because they are state agency employees whose job it is to communicate for their agency with the legislature or another agency or government. They are, nonetheless, lobbyists, for they advocate particular policy positions and do so in statehouse "lobbies."

In recent years statehouse lobbyists or legislative liaisons have become more numerous. The devolution of many responsibilities to the state level has made state policy a high-stakes matter for many interest groups. In addition, with federal deregulation of a number of activities, the states have stepped in with their own regulations, and this has brought out many more lobbyists for professions and businesses.

For example, with the states assuming vastly increased responsibility for public welfare, advocates for health care, children, social workers, counties, and others will swarm legislators as they construct the new state welfare programs.

The increased importance of state policy is illustrated by the emergence of Washington, D.C.–based firms whose business it is to maintain lists of recommended lobbyists, by state, for national organizations or groups seeking lobbying help in a particular state.[7] It should be noted, too, that a significant proportion of modern-day lobbyists are women, unlike the earlier male monopolization of such influence.[8]

Techniques of Influence

Interest groups use a variety of **techniques of influence**.[9] Sometimes their activities involve direct contact with lawmakers; at other times they try to affect the administration of laws that have already passed; and at still other times they attempt to pressure decision makers indirectly through public opinion. Periodically, they may try to determine the outcome of an election or a court decision. Their tactics, in short, are many and varied. Direct communication, building a public image, establishing links, exchanging personnel, role reversals when lobbyists pressure legislators on behalf of other legislators, and PAC money contributions are among the most popular techniques.

Focus 8.2

The Lobbying Industry

• • •

Some organizations and interest groups use their own employees to do their lobbying. These people are called employee lobbyists, public relations specialists, governmental relations specialists, or legislative liaisons. Other special interest groups communicate to lawmakers through contract lobbyists—people who, like other professionals, charge a fee for their services. Some organizations use both their own employees and contract lobbyists, and some lobbyists serve in both capacities.

For example, in Colorado U.S. West, a telecommunications company, has critical interests in such political issues as deregulation of telecommunications. It maintains a staff of employees who lobby the state legislature and employs the services of several prominent contract lobbyists, especially at critical times during legislative sessions. Danny Tomlinson, a one-time employee of U.S. West who lobbied the state legislature, is now a contract lobbyist who represents the interests of over a half-dozen organizations—from insurance companies and agricultural interests to a land title association and a major state university.

As this example indicates, there is no single pattern of interest group representation; rather, each group chooses one or more methods that it finds most effective. As a result, a veritable lobbying industry has emerged.

Direct Communication

A common special interest group tactic involves direct communication with decision makers about the concerns of the group. Sometimes it is accomplished through testimony by a special interest group spokesperson at committee hearings, such as when a bill of interest to the group is under consideration. More often, however, it involves personal contact between the group's lobbyist and the lawmaker. As is the case at the national level, professional lobbyists are common in state legislative halls.

The task of the professional lobbyist can be difficult, but it is not very complicated. Basically it involves vigilance in monitoring the flow of legislation, in keeping track of upcoming administrative appointments, policies, and emerging court cases that affect the group, and making certain that the relevant decision makers are fully aware of the preferences of the group. Lobbying is an informal process that involves extensive direct communication and personal contact.

The successful lobbyist maintains a close watch on bills introduced into the legislature. When a bill of concern to the special interest group is introduced, the lobbyist appraises it in terms of its potential impact on the group's interest. Next the lobbyist conveys the preferences of the group to the lawmakers, especially to those in strategic positions, such as the chairperson of the committee that will hear the bill and the leaders of the majority party. The lobbyist only rarely attempts to twist the arm of a legislator and almost never tries to "buy" a vote with money or gifts. The commodity that the lobbyist peddles is information, and the lobbyist's major sources of capital are friendship, trust, and access to decision makers.

Lobbying, then, is largely a matter of good public relations. Lobbyists want the decision makers to be aware of their groups' positions on the issues. They want access to the decision makers so they can freely communicate with them. They also want to be thought well of so their preferences and those of the groups they represent will be given serious consideration. Decision makers are more apt to give credence to a lobbyist who has a reputation for honesty, who provides consistently reliable information, and who represents reputable interests.

The success of lobbyists depends in part on the interests they represent and the backgrounds of the lawmakers with whom they deal. Lawmakers, like everyone else, are in part a product of their past, and so their values and preferences are conditioned by their experiences. Thus, a lobbyist representing agricultural interests may have a distinct advantage over counterparts representing organized labor in dealings with lawmakers with a farm background. The spokesperson for labor may have a similar advantage in gaining access to a governor who once served as a union official.

Image Building

In addition to the common tactic of direct communication through paid lobbyists, organized interests often seek to influence the content of public opinion, and thereby exert indirect pressure on decision makers by creating for themselves a positive public image. The behavior of both elected and appointed officials is conditioned by public opinion. Elected officials must concern themselves with public preferences, of course, since their political future is dependent on their ability to win votes. Appointed officials are less directly controlled by the voter, but they too must give some attention to public desires to avoid adverse public opinion or pressure for their removal. Thus, special interest groups frequently devote some of their attention and resources to the creation of a favorable public image of themselves and voter sympathy for their goals.

Public utilities use the mass media to try to convince the public of their critical role in providing valuable public services. Farmers, cattle raisers, and mining companies spend sizable sums to point out how their industry provides jobs, pays taxes, and thereby makes the state a nicer place in which to live. Insurance companies, chambers of commerce, teachers, truckers, and laborers do the same. Each group tries to gain favor with the public, hoping that lawmakers will be more receptive to the group's demands if they believe "the public" is on its side.

Special interest groups occasionally employ test court cases in their efforts to influence public policy. When a newly passed bill is ambiguous, or when some of its provisions are of questionable constitutionality, a group may file suit to clarify the meaning of the bill or to test its constitutionality.

Activating Grass Roots

Increasingly special interest groups have sought to organize and activate their memberships at the grassroots level. Lawmakers, whose political lives hinge on their ability to get elected and reelected, are usually hypersensitive to communications from voters back home in the district.

Special interest group leaders know this, and so they'll sometimes supplement direct lobbying efforts with orchestrated communications from voters. For example, state associations of police chiefs can lean on their members to call or make a quick trip to the capitol when a concealed weapons bill is up for a vote. Teacher associations can alert teachers all across the state to contact their legislators at budget time and, of course, there are teachers in every legislator's district.

One example of such grassroots effort is that done by Farmers Insurance Group. From its offices in Los Angeles, the company supplies its agents with monthly news bulletins called "Grass Roots Activism: Farmers Focus." The short publication briefs agents on the nature of the legislative process, the technique of coalition building and, of course, the importance of grassroots work.

In addition, the company briefs agents on its position on such issues as drunk driving, rate regulation, no-fault insurance, and product liability. Farmer's objectives, like that of other groups, is to prime its people for political action. If agents know a little something about policies and issues deemed important to the company, they can be asked to push a local legislator's button at some critical moment.

Common Interests

A common and quite effective interest group activity involves the formation and maintenance of linkages with the government agencies whose functions are of interest to the group. Wildlife enthusiasts, for example, commonly maintain close ties with state game, fish, and parks departments. Local governments maintain close contact with state departments of local government, and teachers' organizations and school districts tend to interact frequently with state departments of education.

Relationships of this sort are natural in some respects, since the interests and activities of the group and agency are similar. There is mutual advantage in forging and cultivating them. The special interest group benefits in that the agency may be charged with the administration of the policies and programs of most concern to the group. Thus, the group has an "inside track" in being able to communicate with the agency and to influence both agency personnel appointments and the vigor with which the policies and programs are implemented. The agency, in turn, benefits in that it can look to the special interest group for support in the legislature and with the governor at times of budget review.

Personnel Exchanges

Special interest groups and public agencies often exchange personnel, or have, in effect, a veto over administrative appointments in the agency. No group has an official veto over administrative appointments, of course. A governor or senate committee can often solicit informally the opinion of the most interested groups before making or confirming an administrative appointment. Only in the most unusual circumstances would someone vigorously opposed by the bar association be appointed and confirmed as a state judge or a person opposed by the wildlife interests be made head of state game, fish, and parks operations.

Much of what state governments do involves regulation. The states license or regulate the insurance industry, teachers, engineers, physicians, lawyers, realtors, and others. Thus, groups and their lobbyists often interact with executive branch officials as agencies develop rules and regulations, or in the instigation of proposals for new legislation. Agencies routinely circulate drafts of proposed rules and regulations to the affected groups. The representatives of these groups testify at hearings. In short, there is much routine interaction between the executive branch regulators and the regulated.

Role Reversals

There are what might be considered role reversals in state politics, particularly in the legislature. We generally think of lobbying as special interest group communication and pressure brought to bear on lawmakers. But often it is the other way around. Increasingly, individual legislators, legislative leaders, and the legislative parties lean heavily on groups and their lobbyists for campaign funds. Lawmakers routinely tell lobbyists to sell expensive tickets to fund-raising events, or just straightforwardly demand contributions. Often, legislators seek the help of lobbyists in counting the votes of other lawmakers or in stirring up grassroots support of or opposition to particular bills. The capitol environment is an enormous market in which all participants seek advantages through deals and bargains with each other.

PAC Money

Quite often, mutually supportive relationships develop between special interest groups and legislators. Many groups, such as professional associations, unions, businesses, and others, form **political action committees (PACs)**—the political arms of these organizations. PACs pool funds from individual donors and disperse them in small, medium, or large sums to candidates. Gifts of $100 to $5,000 are not unusual. Most PAC campaign contributions go to incumbents, lawmakers chairing critical committees, and legislative leaders. Like seasoned gamblers, special interest groups prefer to place their bets on winners.

What Makes a Special Interest Group Effective?

Some special interest groups are more successful than others, and the success of any particular group can vary with time, place, and the issue at hand. Not all groups make out equally well in the distribution of benefits allocated through public policy and that is not just a product of accident or chance. To win in the political arena a special interest group must do several things successfully. It must draw public attention and concern to what it perceives to be problems. It must be able to place the problem on the agenda of government. It must muster enough support among decision makers to ensure the introduction and passage of legislation favorable to its cause. It must command enough political power to secure both adequate funding and meaningful administration for its programs.

This sort of political success, in turn, requires that special interest groups accumulate and use several critical elements of political power. These include size, money, votes, leadership, group cohesion, shrewd strategy development and use, symbol manipulation, general public support, and others.[10]

Size

Size is clearly an important determinant of the political effectiveness of a special interest group. Except for civil servants and other appointed officials, public officials in the United States are in office because they won elections, and they remain in office only if they can continue to win elections. Since votes are all-important to governors, representatives, and city council members alike, a large special interest group with the potential for delivering large numbers of votes for or against a candidate can command that candidate's attention and can usually affect decisions more easily than can a small group.

In terms of sheer numbers, teachers and union members are typically more resourceful than physicians or farmers. Tom Loftus, a former Speaker of the House in Wisconsin, noted that there are kids in all legislative districts. There are also teachers who are both voters and opinion leaders in all districts, and representatives are well aware of this. Insofar as a large group can control and deliver the votes of its membership, it must be reckoned with by candidates for public office.

Money

Another critical political resource is money. Virtually every technique for influencing the political system requires the expenditure of funds, and without at least a minimal budget a special interest group is all but powerless. The very organization and maintenance of a group requires funds to rent offices or meeting halls, to pay phone, printing, and postage bills, and to do some traveling. If the organization itself is without funds, the leadership may have to meet the expenses "out of pocket." If the group is to be permanent in nature—which it must be to have any sustained impact on politics—it may be necessary to employ salaried leadership, staff, and lobbyists. It may want to support a periodic publication, such as a weekly newsletter or a monthly bulletin. It may be desirable to run expensive advertisements in newspapers and magazines to build sympathetic public opinion. The Sierra Club, public utilities, and major oil companies have done so in the past.

Special interest group money has become increasingly important and plentiful in state elections. In Florida, PAC contributions to legislative campaigns rose from $1.1 million in 1976 to $10 million in 1987—an increase of over 800 percent in only 11 years.[11] In California, state legislative campaigns sometimes cost $1 million or more, and in states both large and small, amounts of $50,000 to $250,000 are common. Races for governor can exceed $10 million.

Today, special interest groups are expected to contribute generously to candidates' campaigns. Not surprisingly, those that do are often among the most influential groups—including teachers, business people, lawyers, realtors, labor unions, and others.

Cohesion

Generally, a special interest group that is tightly knit internally is more effective politically than one that acts as an umbrella for several factions that share some goals but disagree on other matters. A group with diverse membership is not likely to reach agreement frequently or easily on such issues as specific candidates or programs to support. As a result, the behavior of members may be difficult to mobilize and control, and members' time, money, and other resources may be hard to obtain or coordinate. Furthermore, internal fragmentation can dissipate the potential power of a special interest group as well as confuse its goals. As the various factions of the group push for different issues and in different directions, decision makers may be unable to respond favorably to the group's preferences simply because those preferences cannot be identified. Moreover, decision makers, usually loath to resolve disagreements within interest groups, prefer to be presented with clear-cut preferences. Thus, any type of special interest group reduces its political effectiveness when it fails to articulate a united, coherent set of policy preferences.

Group cohesion, then, is critical, though it may be difficult to create and maintain. In the early days of organized labor's fight for legitimacy and better wages, hours, and working conditions (a period that covered roughly the first half of the twentieth century), unions were quite successful in commanding allegiance. Workers had much to gain and comparatively little to lose through collective action. Today, the social and economic status of labor has improved tremendously, and the individual worker is much less dependent on the union. Cohesion within the ranks is, as a result, more difficult to maintain.

Cohesion is a problem in other areas as well. Large and small banks may fight over the issue of branch banking. Manufacturers may split on the issue of returnable or nonreturnable beverage containers. Differences between colleges and research-oriented universities may divide the educational community, dissipating the impact of its lobbying efforts. Within state municipal or county associations, the needs of those in core metropolitan areas often diverge from those of the smaller rural cities and counties. In short, group cohesion is an important political resource but often a difficult one to achieve.

Leadership

The politically effective special interest group is able to formulate and articulate its goals clearly, identify the points at which it can gain access to decision makers, place its concerns on the agenda of government, and gain the political support necessary to see the programs it favors safely through the legislative and administrative processes. But such a group does not automatically organize itself in these ways; rather, the group does so through its leadership.

Energetic, imaginative, and articulate leadership is critical at every stage of special interest group activity. Leadership persuasion is necessary to hold the membership together, whereas lackluster direction or internal wrangling can easily weaken or destroy a group. Organizational skills are required of leaders to keep the group moving effectively over time. Skills in communication are essential to leaders for articulating group goals and ensuring they are known and understood by members and decision makers alike. An uninformed or confused membership can easily drift away, and uninformed or confused decision makers cannot be relied on to articulate the preferences of the group. Furthermore, leaders' knowledge of political personalities and of the political system is important in the selection and timely use of political tactics. The use of an untimely tactic or the application of pressure on the wrong person at the wrong time can easily backfire.

Finally, it is the task of leadership to identify and articulate the points of common interest among a group's membership. All groups, regardless of their size, will agree on certain issues but disagree on others. The successful leader stresses the points of agreement and thereby focuses the group's attention on those points, rather than on areas of contention and potential disruption.

Image

The public's image of an interest group can have a significant impact on the group's degree of political effectiveness. When voters and public officials perceive a group as productive, patriotic, and reasonable, as comprised of people of stature and goodwill, and as having roots in the state, the group's preferences are likely to be received and considered in a positive and sympathetic way. In contrast, a group perceived as lazy and unproductive or as unreasonable and destructive is likely to have its concerns viewed with skepticism. Indeed, the effectiveness of lobbyists hinges in large measure on the positive image of their client.

Examples of special interest groups with a good public image are numerous, although it is important to remember that a group's public image may change as the social and economic situation in the nation evolves. Physicians have historically been viewed as friends of the sick, exemplars of science and wisdom, pillars of the community, and esteemed persons generally, and for good reason. But their image may be changing somewhat, given the dramatic increases in the cost of medical care. Teachers have been viewed as poorly paid but dedicated people concerned with the mental and physical development of the nation's greatest resource—its youth. But they have also been portrayed as union members demanding concessions from governments ill equipped to grant them. Business entrepreneurs have been perceived as efficient and hard-working, as risk-takers, and as the backbone of the U.S. economic system; they have also been seen as exploiters of labor. Farmers and veterans have generally enjoyed a favorable public image. Farmers have been viewed as a part of the Jeffersonian tradition so vital to the nation's development, while veterans are given credit and praise for their sacrifices in defense of the country. These and other interest groups devote a lot of money, time, and effort to maintaining a positive public image.

Political Efficacy

Belief in one's **political efficacy**—the conviction that one can have an impact on political decisions—plays a critical role in the propensity of an interest group to seek to influence the political system. Groups that fail even to try to affect the system will have no political influence. Such politically inefficacious groups are subject to a vicious cycle of failure: (1) members fail to see the potential benefits of political action; (2) they remain politically inactive; (3) their political inactivity prohibits them from deriving any benefits from the system; and (4) their initial assumption about the nonresponsive nature of the system is confirmed.

A person's sense of political efficacy is largely a product of the socialization process. If throughout the early formative years both the spoken word and the behavior of friends and family communicate the notion that civic involvement is good and can produce results, an individual is apt to feel politically effective. This person has learned that attempts to influence decisions are proper—even a responsibility or duty—and that actions will lead to results. In addition, the politically efficacious person often has been taught enough about the structures and processes of government to enable effective action. He or she knows something about how and when political decisions are made and who makes them. The result is that people whose backgrounds have equipped them with both the will and the tools to be politically active tend to have the most impact on the system. In contrast, individuals who have by word and example been taught that political action is futile usually tend to be politically inactive and ineffective.

Similarly, special interest groups view the political system and respond to it in different ways. In a study involving five nations—the United States, Great Britain, Germany, Italy, and Mexico—Almond and Verba identify a variety of "political cultures."[12] They contend that people's expectations of their own ability to affect the decisions of and receive benefits from the government vary according to their nation's political history and their own wealth, education, occupation, and other factors. In rural Mexican towns, Almond and Verba found that some people had little hope of influencing decisions, were not motivated to attempt to do so, and did not expect to receive much in the way of government benefits. In contrast, the researchers found that well-to-do Britons generally considered themselves able to influence decisions and expected the government to pay attention to their concerns. The British, unlike the Mexicans, had what Almond and Verba call "input" expectations (to affect decisions) and "output" expectations (to receive benefits).

Studies of the American voter likewise display correlations between political efficacy and such factors as income, education, race, and occupational status.[13] Well-educated persons, the well-to-do, and those in high-status occupations tend to vote regularly, to be confident in their ability to influence political decisions, and to associate with politically relevant groups (for example, fraternal organizations, labor unions, and professional societies). Indeed, it is just these sorts of people, the local "elites," who often dominate local politics and local elections. In general, the poor, unemployed, and undereducated tend to be less confident in their ability to be politically effective and, therefore, tend to be relatively inactive in politics. There are numerous individual exceptions, of course, but as a group the upper class is highly politically active and, as a result, fares better in terms of the output of the political system. (See Focus 8.3 "Do—Do Not.")

Lobbyists in State Politics

The structure of the U.S. government system helps to determine the strategies employed by special interest groups. Because decision-making authority is widely dispersed, there are many so-called **veto points** at which special interest groups have the opportunity to affect government decisions. Federalism, the separation of powers, bicameralism, the plural executive, the existence of a host of boards and commissions, and other structural features of the political system create literally hundreds of points at which authoritative decisions are made. As a result, special interest groups can attempt to influence court decisions, legislative decisions, gubernatorial appointments, agency policies, the operations of boards and commissions, and other official behaviors or decisions.

The Defensive Advantage

Interest groups typically find it easier to stop unfavorable policies from being implemented than to precipitate action. The structure of government, with its host of veto points, makes this possible. Legislative committees can sometimes

Focus 8.3
DO—DO NOT

• • •

Lisa Kinney is a state senator in Wyoming. By profession she is both a librarian and a lawyer. Senator Kinney authored a short book in which she offers lobbying advice from the vantage point of the person who is on the receiving end. Her book was written for fellow librarians, but the advice she gives is useful for anyone seeking to persuade a legislator. Kinney lists a number of "do's" and "don'ts"; here are some of them:

WHEN LOBBYING

Do	*Don't*
Know your issue	Don't lie, withhold information
Be absolutely honest	Don't threaten, scold, demand
Be thorough, but concise	Don't get personal
Be appreciative	Don't be arrogant, or pushy or argumentative
Be positive	Don't break promises
Talk to all legislators, ignoring none	Don't unleash the grass roots unnecessarily
Respond quickly to requests	Don't burn bridges
Respect legislators who disagree	
Have a sense of humor	

Senator Kinney's hints should be useful as well for students who want more money from home, a change of a grade, or an excuse from a regularly scheduled exam. Students who lobby successfully in school and at home may have bright futures in state capitols.

Source: Drawn from Lisa F. Kinney, *Lobby for Your Library* (Chicago: American Library Association, 1992)

kill a bill. The governor can often veto entire bills or line items in a budget. State agencies can frequently drag their feet in putting new programs into effect or in implementing old ones. Governors, state senates, and senate committees can halt an administrative appointment.

Because the very structure of the system favors those who seek to stop something from happening, special interest groups are in an advantageous position in terms of their ability to thwart action. However, they are much less influential when they attempt to deal with a policy proposal from its inception to its implementation.

Failure and Success

In spite of special interest groups' image as powerful and influential entities, they are not always successful. Legislators respond to strong voter preferences regardless of what lobbyists may argue or contend. In addition, special interest groups may encounter a number of problems that can weaken their chances of success. For example, they may be frustrated by the opposition of other groups or face hostile public opinion. Politicians may vigorously oppose a group's desires. Members' differences of opinion may fragment a group internally and thus reduce its effectiveness.

Two case studies, one involving a special interest group in New Jersey and the other a group in Minnesota, illustrate the factors that lead to group failure or success.

New Jersey Farmers Fail

The New Jersey case involves the unsuccessful attempts by an organization of New Jersey farmers in the mid-1960s to stop the state's imposition of regulations requiring farmers to provide hot water for migrant workers.[14] Enforcement of the regulations, which were supported by the governor, was assigned to the Migrant Labor Board.

The growers argued that the costs of compliance would hurt them financially and that the rules were unfair because the rules would not affect growers in adjacent states. New Jersey farmers attended a public hearing held by the Migrant Labor Board to protest the regulations. The state secretary of agriculture subsequently sought a delay in the enforcement of the regulations, during which time the farmers successfully pushed a bill through the state legislature nullifying the hot-water rule. They were unsuccessful, however, in preventing the governor from vetoing that legislative ruling. After the governor's veto, the farmers appealed the rule in court but lost.

The farmers' group was well organized. It possessed money, able leadership, and a good image. It also knew how to attempt to influence the system. Even so, it failed in its effort to affect the system's decision. It could move the legislature, but not the governor.

Minnesota Business Interests Succeed

A more recent case in Minnesota produced a different outcome, one in which business interests triumphed after a temporary defeat. In the 1980s the Minnesota legislature passed legislation creating a state mini-superfund along with expanded liability for businesses whose hazardous waste discharges cause harm to people. Republican Governor Albert H. Quie vetoed the bill. Later, however, with a new governor, Democrat Rudy Perpich, the legislation was passed again and became law. It was characterized politically as protective of the public health and the environment.

The business community opposed the law, arguing that it put companies at excessive and unfair risk of lawsuit and costly damage payments, sometimes for problems that the defendant company may not have created. In their efforts to modify the legislation business lobbies sought to change the focus of the political debate from protecting public health and the environment to protecting the health of the Minnesota business climate. Business lobbies thus argued that companies might leave the state because of the increased number and cost of lawsuits. At one point Lloyd's of London declined to offer environmental impairment liability insurance to Minnesota firms.

Business won. Legislation modified the law and the business lobbies won a number of issues. Plaintiffs would now carry a heavier burden to prove that actions by the defendant company actually caused the alleged damage. The breadth of liability was narrowed and a victims compensation fund was created.

With the protection of the Republican governor's veto gone in 1983, business lobbies had to change their tactics, and they did so successfully. They were able to affect public opinion by altering the political context in which they were viewed—from one of irresponsible handlers of the public health and the environment to that of victims in need of legislative relief.

Strong Parties Weaken Special Interest Groups

There is some evidence that organized interests are more influential in one-party states than in states with two-party competition. Zeigler and van Dalen argue that "with regard to political variables, pressure groups are strongest when political parties and legislative cohesion are weakest."[15] When parties are weak and political struggles revolve around **factions** and personality conflicts, a vacuum of sorts is created. There are no strong, viable parties to recruit and support candidates, forge a well-defined package of policy proposals, or form the legislative majority needed to see the proposals safely through the political process. Instead, candidates are forced to look beyond the party for help, and this often leads them to form ties with and incur obligations to special interests. The absence of a cohesive legislative majority leaves what policy proposals there are to the mercy of the "veto" of the special interests. Politics becomes semianarchistic in nature, with each special interest seeking its own agenda.

The interesting question is who will be most influential and under what circumstances. Will strong-willed individual legislators who chair critical committees become one-person dictators on the legislation that passes through their committee? Will the legislative process be plagued with disorganization and ineffective leadership to the extent that affluent lobbies will be able to influence the votes of a majority of legislators? Will the majority party leadership be strong enough to control the power of committee chairs, hold the membership in line in the face of lobby pressures, and thereby push through party programs?

The important issue here is not whether influence is exerted in decision-making bodies but how that influence is distributed and used. Some commentators suggest that the interests of the public are best served by strong political parties in control of decision-making bodies because weak parties cause influence to flow to lobbies, legislative factions, and individuals. Political parties may not be perfectly reflective and representative of the general public, but they are typically more in tune with the public's preferences than are the more narrowly based interest groups and small legislative factions.

Special Interest Groups in a Democracy

The effects of special interest groups on the political system in the United States have long been a focus of political scholars and politicians alike. In 1788 James Madison wrote about "factions" in *The Federalist Papers*.[16] He considered property the source of all political conflict. When people banded together in attempts to influence the decisions of government in ways that would protect the property they had and allow them to acquire even more, Madison viewed this as dangerous. He argued that such groups could influence public decisions in ways that reflected their narrow, selfish preferences at the expense of the public interest. Neither Madison nor any other political writer since has ever come up with a satisfactory definition of the **public interest**. However, most agree on what the public interest in a democracy is not—it is not defined solely on the basis of the preferences of any single special interest group, no matter how large or powerful it may be.

While Madison articulated a problem that continues to concern many people today, he was unable to propose a viable remedy. One extreme and unrealistic suggestion is to make illegal the formation and operation of any special interest group. But to outlaw special interest groups would be tantamount to making it illegitimate for people to cooperate in the collective articulation of their desires to the government. Moreover, the freedoms of assembly, speech, press, and petition would be seriously compromised.

Another argument suggests that the potential ill effects of special interest groups are mitigated somewhat by the competition among the groups. Labor, management, the professions—these and other groups, it is argued, counterbalance one another's impact on the political system. However, not all groups are interested in all of the issues. Truckers may be interested in lowering the license tax on large trucks and teachers in policies dealing with educational issues, but not vice versa. As a result, only a few, if any, organized interests may exist to counterbalance the truckers on matters of truck license fees and the teachers on educational issues. Special interests may in this way dominate certain areas of public policy.

While James Madison worried about the potential ill effects of factions on public policy, others have chronicled and lamented some real ones. In a classic work entitled *The Semi-Sovereign People*, E. E. Schattschneider contends that pressure within the American system of politics is dominated mainly by business interests to the exclusion of the bulk of the population.[17] Similarly, Theodore Lowi argues in *The End of Liberalism* that in numerous policy areas relatively small coalitions of interested parties have come to dominate public choices on matters of vital concern to themselves. In addition, Lowi laments what he sees as the tendency of elected lawmakers to relinquish too much public authority and too many public resources to those small coalitions.[18]

On the positive side, special interest groups perform a supplementary, or functional, representation role in the political system. The representation schemes employed at all levels of American government define interests geographically. Senators, representatives, mayors, and county commissioners represent people according to where those people reside, not according to their political ideology, occupation, religion, or color. This means that lawmakers are called on to represent a host of diverse interests simultaneously. Any given district is apt to contain physicians, lawyers, merchants, laborers, teachers, and public employees, and it is highly unlikely that these people will agree on most or even many issues. The task of determining the public interest for a district thus falls to the representative. The preferences of a single special interest group within a representative's district are unlikely to be fully conveyed to the decision-making arenas themselves.

Special interest groups also act as gauges of the intensity of citizens on political issues. As a result of the democratic demand for political equality and the Supreme Court's interpretation of the Fourteenth Amendment relative to legislative apportionment, the vote of every American is equal to that of every other American—regardless of how intense some people may feel about a particular issue or candidate. For example, in a voting situation involving some issue and nine voters, five who are mildly in favor of the issue and four who are vigorously opposed to it, whose preferences should prevail? Given the democratic dictum of majority rule, of course, the desires of the five indifferent voters will prevail over those of the four intense voters. It would be difficult to have things any other way, for if people were allowed multiple votes on the basis of their intensity on issues, how would it be decided who gets two or more votes? Any deviation from the one person, one vote principle would create many operational and ideological problems. In this sense, then, **special interest group intensity** on issues helps to identify the issues about which the members of that group feel most strongly.

Summary

The political landscape of the American states has been changing in recent years and continues to do so. Among the many changes are an increase in the number and diversity of special interest groups, a rise in the number of lobbyists, and the growing sophistication of the tactics used by special interest groups. The expanded role of government generally, coupled with the devolution of many functions from the national government to the states, means that an increasing number of special interest groups have a stake in the decisions made by state and local governments. More special interest groups also mean more political pressure as well as more money being spent on state politics. The proliferation of such groups may have rendered the old-time powers of the rich less dominant, for while there is more money being spent, it is more widely distributed.[23]

Special interest groups and lobbyists are important players in the political game because they influence to varying degrees the content of public policies. At the same time, they do not control the making of public policy. Lobbyists tend to be most influential when they represent groups that decision makers hold in high esteem and perceive as in tune with the public good. However, elected decision makers defer to voter preferences when these outweigh the desires of an interest group.

Democracy in the states and localities, then, is not a contest that excludes the American voter. Rather, it is more like a game in which those who participate actively, organize themselves, and employ tactics of persuasion can have more influence on the shape of public policy than those who by choice or necessity are relatively inactive in politics.

In recent years there have been more and more groups and lobbyists active, and more lobbying. There has been more money in state and local politics. This is worrysome to many observers who fear that political influence is more and more concentrated in the hands of the organized and the rich. In attempts to counter this trend, states have adopted a variety of laws to regulate lobbying and campaign contributions.

Policy Perspective: What's Our Policy on Special Interests? . . . .

What should be our public policy stance with respect to special interest groups? Are they a threat to the public interest, or do they enhance representative government? Do they buy politicians with campaign money, or do they enrich representative government through the injection of additional information and citizen perspectives? Do their lobbyists simply peddle information, or are they a part of inside games in which influence is traded for favors? Should special interest groups be outlawed altogether, or would such a ban be, as James Madison feared, a cure worse than the disease itself?

These are tough questions and state legislatures struggle with them continuously. There is no doubt that special interest groups and their lobbyists help steer the direction of public policy; why else would unions, businesses, and professions organize and hire lobbyists? State government scholar Alan Rosenthal writes that "from 1985 to 1990, lobbyists in California and New Jersey increased by almost 50 percent."[19] The numbers have grown in similar fashion in other states.

This is a troublesome issue for both the public and lawmakers. One national poll found that nearly 70 percent of us believe that the influence of special interests is excessive. Another found that almost two-thirds of the respondents believe that lobbying poses either "somewhat" of a threat or a "very serious" threat to our system.[20]

Decades ago, the states had very little policy on the books addressing the matter of groups and lobbyists, and it showed. Stories abound of old-time influence peddlers who could make available to public officials gifts ranging from illicit booze and sex to meals and cash. Not too long ago lobbyists were allowed on the floors of some state legislatures and a few even chimed in on voice votes. Today lobbyists, perfectly honest ones, joke that their moms are afraid to tell family friends what their children do for a living.

But what to do? Among our most cherished constitutional rights are those that allow us to associate, speak, and petition government for redress of grievances. Isn't that the essence of special interest group formation, and lobbying? It is, and Madison recognized it as such.

Still, there has been a need to act, and the states have done so. Beginning in the 1970s, on the heels of the Watergate scandal, and in the throes of the state legislative reform movement, the states began to crank out policies designed to expose the activities of groups and lobbyists and to mute somewhat their influence. In many states, lawmakers were stampeded into passing new or tighter laws by scandal-driven waves of public opinion.

The policies of the states have addressed two major areas of special interest group activity. The first is the operation of lobbyists, and the second addresses the role of group money in campaigns. Let's look at each area.

Watching the Lobbyists

Every one of the fifty states now has laws on the statute books that define lobbying and lobbyists and in some fashion govern their behavior.[21] They all define attempts to influence legislators as acts of lobbying, and thirty states do the same for attempts to sway administrative officials. Half of the states define public employees who push their agency's interests as lobbyists, and ten states do the same for elected officials who lobby other elected officials. Individual citizens who may talk with their elected officials or who testify at hearings on their own behalf are not considered to be lobbyists. But once someone takes money to do so, or speaks for an organization of other citizens, he or she becomes a lobbyist by law and is then subject to other provisions of the lobbying statutes.

These other provisions generally identify activities that are not allowed, and require periodic reports of various information. Roughly half the states now make it illegal for lobbyists to contribute to a lawmaker's campaign war chest during a legislative session, and five states ban such gifts altogether. In sixteen states the law tells lawmakers that they may not solicit campaign contributions or other gifts. And thirty-seven states outlaw **contingency lobbying**. This is a practice of linking client payments to lobbyists on the condition that the lobbyist achieves some specified objective—such as killing a certain bill or causing an appropriation of some amount to be authorized. The logic here is that the connection of money to a goal tempts lobbyists to go over the legal and ethical edge when they try to influence the behavior of public officials. If one's meal hinges on success, it's tempting to cheat—or so goes the reasoning.

Nearly all states now require lobbyists to report their income and activities, although the amount of information required varies. Twenty-five states ask lobbyists to identify the bills or administrative decisions that are the targets of their activity. Twenty states tell lobbyists to report their total lobbying income and twenty, although not exactly the same ones, require that income be reported by source; that is, lobbyists with multiple clients must report separately the incomes received from each.

Finally, all but eight states have lobbyists report the spending they do for lobbying purposes, and in most of these the reports must be broken down by category of expenditure—food, entertainment, publicity, campaigns, and so forth.

As suggested earlier, most of the group and lobbying policy in the states is of fairly recent origin, and some has been driven by scandal and the resultant public demand for reform. As one study of legislative ethics observed, lawmakers are generally more interested in reforming education or welfare or some other policies than the laws that directly relate to their own activities.

A case in point is the state of Kentucky. Kentucky now sports some of the strictest laws, but they were developed in 1993 in the wake of a scandal having to do with legislation on horses, horse tracks, and betting. The new law requires extensive disclosure of lobbyist activities and finances, and restricts expenditures for wining and dining to $100 per year per legislator. The new law has nearly wiped out that practice. Other parts of Kentucky law prevent lobbyists from making campaign contributions, and keep former legislators from becoming lobbyists for two years after they leave office.

No two states have identical lobbying statutes, and most are less constrictive than Kentucky's. But unlike the situation just a few decades back, lobbying policies of some sort are now on the books in all fifty states.

Campaign Money

As with lobbying, all states have enacted laws governing campaign financing[22] and this includes the role of special interest groups in bankrolling candidates or seeking to affect the outcome of ballot issues. State policies require candidates and political committees to file with the state; usually, but not always, filed with the secretary of state. Often there is a spending threshold that triggers the need to file; in Kansas it is $100, and in Connecticut it is $1000. In New York it varies according to the level of government.

Beyond the filing requirements, limitations on the contributions may be made by both individuals and organizations including unions, corporations, political action committees, and the parties. The pattern is a curious one. Eighteen states ban corporate contributions altogether, while in seven others the corporate amount is unlimited. In the other half, there are limits, but they vary in amount. The constraints on labor unions are similar but by no means identical. In general, unions have more latitude.

The policies on PAC giving are widely varied. In some states they are identical to those for unions, in some they match the limits on corporations, and in still others they parallel neither, and vary from one type of election to another. The most general observation one can make is that a dozen states have no limits on PAC contributions whatsoever, while the others do, albeit at a variety of levels.

Finally, just under twenty states have sought to mute the impact of special interest money by instituting some form of public campaign financing. The particulars vary widely from one state to another with respect to the sources of the funds, the amounts available, and the races in which candidates, or in some instances the political parties, are eligible.

Factions: To Control or Not Control?

We're back to the dilemma cited by James Madison. His remedy for protecting the public interest from the mischief of factions was a complex and extended republic, one in which authority was partitioned to a number of institutions and persons. But clearly that hasn't gotten the job done fully.

So now the states have taken to enacting policies that, while they fall short of compromising the freedoms of association, speech, and petition, do require influence peddlers to do their work in public, and without resort to big bribes (cash) or little bribes (martini and club sandwich), and/or threats, either physical or political.

Now in the states not only are there policies for kids (education), the poor (welfare, Medicaid), travelers (roads), sportsmen (stadiums), and businesses (economic development), but there are policies for the policy players themselves—the groups, their lobbyists, and the public officials who are the lobbyist's targets.

KEY TERMS

lobbyist	legislative liaison	faction
special interest group	techniques of influence	public interest
single-issue interest group	political action committee (PAC)	special interest group intensity
employee lobbyist	political efficacy	contingency lobbying
contract lobbyist	veto point	
volunteer lobbyist		

ADDITIONAL READING

Hrebenar, Ronald J., and Ruth Scott. *Interest Group Politics in America*. 2d ed. Englewood Cliffs, N.J.: Prentice-Hall, 1990.

Hrebenar, Ronald J., and Clive S. Thomas, eds. *Interest Group Politics in the Southern States.* Tuscaloosa: University of Alabama Press, 1992.

Rosenthal, Alan. *The Third House: Lobbyists and Lobbying in the States*. Washington, D.C.: Congressional Quarterly Press, 1993.

Schattschneider, E. E. *The Semi-Sovereign People: A Realist's View of Democracy in America.* New York: Holt, Rinehart and Winston, 1960.

Thomas, Clive, ed. *Politics and Public Policy in the Contemporary American West.* Albuquerque: University of New Mexico Press, 1991.

Walters, Jonathan. "A Night on the Town Isn't What It Used to Be in Jefferson City." *Governing* (July 1989): 26.

Welch, Randy. "Lobbyists, Lobbyists, All Over the Lot." *State Legislatures* (Feb. 1989): 18.

NOTES

1. Quoted in Bill Schluter, "Contributions Don't Affect Votes? Don't You Believe It," *Governing* (Aug. 1990): 98.
2. E. E. Schattschneider, *The Semi-Sovereign People: A Realist's View of Democracy in America* (New York: Holt, Rinehart and Winston, 1960).
3. Among the best studies of lobbying and special interest groups in the states, see Alan Rosenthal, *The Third House: Lobbyists and Lobbying in the States* (Washington, D.C.: Congressional Quarterly Press, 1993). See also Ronald J. Hrebenar and Clive S. Thomas, eds., *Interest Group Politics in the Southern States* (Tuscaloosa: University of Alabama Press, 1992).
4. These observations are related in and suggested by the research of Professors Clive S. Thomas and Ronald J. Hrebenar.
5. Linda Wagar, "Balancing the Demands of Single-Issue Voters," *State Government News* (Nov. 1989): 34.
6. Randy Welch, "Lobbyists, Lobbyists, All Over the Lot," *State Legislatures* (Feb. 1989): 18; and Robert Pear, "Number of Ballot Initiatives Is the Greatest Since 1932," *New York Times*, 5 November 1990.
7. Tom Watson, "Dale Florio: A Lobbyist's Middleman Who Helps Business People Navigate State Capitol Halls," *Governing* (Feb. 1989): 32–38.
8. Welch, "Lobbyists," p. 19.
9. See Rosenthal, *Third House*, for more extensive treatment of this subject.
10. This discussion is drawn from a wide array of sources within the extensive literature on the group basis of politics, including V. O. Key, Jr., *Politics, Parties and Pressure Groups*, 5th ed. (New York: Thomas Y. Crowell, 1964); Schattschneider, *Semi-Sovereign People*; and Harmon Zeigler, *Interest Groups in American Society* (Englewood Cliffs, N.J.: Prentice-Hall, 1964).
11. Anne E. Kelley and Ella L. Thomas, "Florida: The Changing Patterns of Power," in *Interest Group Politics in the Southern States*, ed. Ronald J. Hrebenar and Clive S. Thomas (Tuscaloosa: University of Alabama Press, 1992), pp. 125–51. For more on campaign spending, see Sandra Singer, "The Arms Race of Campaign Financing," *State Legislatures* (July 1988): 24–28; and Rob Gurwitt, "California, Here We Come: The Professional Legislature and Its Discontents," *Governing* (Aug. 1991): 65–69.
12. Gabriel Almond and Sidney Verba, *The Civic Culture* (Princeton, N.J.: Princeton University Press, 1963).
13. See Paul R. Abramson, *Political Attitudes in America* (San Francisco: W. H. Freeman, 1983).
14. Richard A. Hogarty, *New Jersey Farmers and Migrant Housing Rules* (New York: Bobbs-Merrill, 1966), Interuniversity Case Program no. 94.
15. Harmon Zeigler and Hendrik van Dalen, "Interest Groups in the States," in *Politics in the American States*, 2d ed., ed. Herbert Jacob and Kenneth Vines (Boston: Little, Brown, 1971), p. 127.
16. Alexander Hamilton, James Madison, and John Jay, The Federalist Papers (1788; reprint New York: New American Library, 1961).
17. Schattschneider, *Semi-Sovereign People*.
18. Theodore J. Lowi, *The End of Liberalism*, 2d ed. (New York: Norton, 1979).
19. Rosenthal, *The Third House*, p. 4.
20. Rosenthal, *The Third House*, pp. 6–7.
21. *Book of the States*, 1996, pp. 357–58; 480–84.
22. *Book of the States*, 1996, pp. 167–208.
23. Rosenthal, *Third House*; and Hrebenar and Thomas, *Interest Group Politics*.

CHAPTER 9

• • •

Elections

• • •

Indiana's gubernatorial candidates debate in October 1996 at Old Lake County Courthouse in Crown Point, Indiana. Republican candidate Steve Goldsmith *(left)* and Democratic candidate Frank O'Bannon *(center)* listen to Libertarian candidate Steve Dillon during his closing statements. Frank O'Bannon won the election. *(AP/Wide World Photos)*

• • • **Election Laws**

Voter Registration
Constitutional and Federal Rules
Campaign Financing Rules

Focus 9.1: From Classrooms to Boardrooms

• • • **Electoral Participation**

Widespread Apathy
Young People Don't Vote
Women Voters
Ethnicity
Level of Education
Women and Minorities in Public Office
Legislatures Are Changing

Focus 9.2: Women in the Legislature

• • • **The Impact of Institutions on Electoral Participation**

Low Turnout in Local Elections
Levels of Turnout Affect Outcomes
Turnout Varies among the States

• • • **Modern Campaigns**

The Candidate-Centered Campaign
The Expensive Campaign
Incumbent Self-Promotion: An Endless Campaign
The Challenger's Dilemma
Sophisticated Campaign Strategies
Campaigns Reflect U.S. Institutions and Politics

• • • **Direct Democracy**

The Referendum
The Citizen Initiative
The Recall

• • • IS DIRECT DEMOCRACY GOOD GOVERNMENT?

• • • SUMMARY

• • • POLICY PERSPECTIVE: THE VOTING RIGHTS ACT AND THE STATES

In the United States elections are a common occurrence. The prime seasons for elections are late summer, November, and the spring. Partisan primary elections (where candidates are identified by party labels) are often held in early spring, though some states hold primaries in August and September. **Primary elections** are nominating elections in which Republican and Democratic voters decide who will represent them in the November general elections. In **general elections** voters elect governors, state legislators, members of Congress, the U.S. president, and many local officials. A large proportion of local governments hold elections in the springtime. Summer and fall primaries and most November general elections are **partisan elections**. Many local elections, particularly those below the level of county government, are **nonpartisan**, at least nominally, since candidates do not carry a party label and the parties are not formally involved in the nomination and campaign processes.

It is no mystery why Americans have so many elections; Americans have a lot of governments. Voters elect a president, members of the two houses of Congress, members of the state legislatures, governors, secretaries of state, attorneys general, governing boards of universities and school districts, mayors, city council members, boards of county commissioners, sheriffs, coroners, governing boards for sewer, water, recreation, flood, and hospital districts, and many, many more. Ironically, given the well-known cliché that "he couldn't get elected dogcatcher," very few jurisdictions in the United States elect dogcatchers, most of whom are appointed.

Representative democracy in America thus abounds. But how can American voters keep track of all the governments and elections and stay informed about the issues and candidates? The answer is that most do not.

Election Laws

State and local elections are governed by state law and subject to a few U.S. constitutional restrictions. State constitutional and statutory law determines which public offices are elective. It governs the procedures by which candidates are nominated, and it outlines citizen requirements for voting. Some local governments are allowed to impose additional requirements for voting and holding office, but even in these cases state law still constitutes the basic legal framework for the electoral process.

Historically, state laws imposed voting requirements with respect to age, residency, registration, and, in a few states, literacy. With the 1971 ratification of the Twenty-Sixth Amendment to the Constitution, the minimum voting age was standardized at eighteen years across the country. Immediately before the ratification of the Twenty-Sixth Amendment, two states allowed eighteen-year-olds to vote, one state allowed nineteen-year-olds to vote and one state allowed twenty-year-olds to vote; the remainder required that voters be at least twenty-one years old. In the past, residency requirements varied among the states, typically requiring an individual to reside from six months to one year in the state, from sixty to ninety days in the county, and from ten to sixty days in the district (or precinct) before becoming eligible to vote. Many states have changed these minimum residency requirements, however, recognizing that the high rate of mobility of the American public, combined with residency requirements, disenfranchises millions of would-be voters. Twenty states now require thirty days residency, twenty others have no residency requirement, and the remainder have requirements of various lengths.

Voter Registration

Most states require citizens to register to vote around thirty days before an election, though the number of days varies from none to fifty. Voters in all states except North Dakota must register. In just over 80 percent of the states, voter registration is permanent; that is, once people register to vote, they do not need to re-register for subsequent elections unless they move or fail to vote for a specified period of time. Those relocating to another precinct or state must register in their new place of residence. If they fail to do so, their names eventually will be purged from the voter registration list.

In nearly three-quarters of the states, voters must identify their partisan preference when they register. They may register as Republicans, Democrats, or Independents. Voters who register as Independents generally are not eligible to vote in party primary elections, whereas those who identify with one of the two major parties may vote only in that party's primary. In addition, there are situations in which voters must register separately for certain elections; for example, in some urban areas voters must register separately for city elections.

The states are also allowed to administer literacy tests to prospective voters, as long as such tests do not discriminate on a racial basis. Until 1965, literacy tests were often used in the South to deny the right to vote to African Americans. Today, however, no states use literacy tests. Until the 1960s, a poll tax payment was required by some states to register for state and local elections. However, the poll tax was outlawed in 1964 by the Twenty-Fourth Amendment to the Constitution for federal elections, and in 1966 by the U.S. Supreme Court in state and local elections.

The trend in the states has been to make voter registration easier. Fifteen states now provide for registration at state agencies often frequented by citizens, such as motor vehicle departments. In addition, roughly two dozen states now permit voter registration by mail. In 1986 Congress passed the Voting Accessibility for the Elderly and Handicapped Act, which requires the states to make the voting booth accessible to all eligible voters. In 1992 President George Bush vetoed a bill that would have provided for automatic voter registration whenever a person renewed a driver's license. Following the 1992 presidential elections, however, Congress passed a similar bill and President Bill Clinton signed it into law in 1993. The bill is known as the **motor-voter law** and allows people to register to vote simply by renewing their driver's license.

Constitutional and Federal Rules

Although state law governs the basic aspects of voter registration and of elections in general, several provisions of the U.S. Constitution and federal statutes also affect the conduct of elections in the United States. The Fourteenth Amendment stipulates that no state shall deny to any citizen the equal protection of the laws. It is on the basis of this provision that the Supreme Court has mandated the **one person, one vote** requirement in state and federal elections. It requires, when candidates run for election in districts (such as a state senate election), that the districts contain approximately the same number of people.

The Fifteenth Amendment makes illegal any discrimination on the basis of race, color, or previous condition of servitude. In 1944, in *Smith v. Allright*, the Supreme Court banned the southern "white" primary, under which southern political parties had declared themselves private clubs and barred African Americans from participating in primary elections. In the one-party South of that period, where the Democratic Party virtually was the only competitive party, the only meaningful electoral choice was made in the primary; thus, disenfranchisement from the primary was tantamount to complete and total disenfranchisement.

Similarly, the Seventeenth Amendment orders the direct popular election of senators, the Nineteenth Amendment guarantees the right to vote to women, and the Twenty-Sixth Amendment establishes the minimum voting age of eighteen years for federal elections. The 1965 Voting Rights Act, renewed several times, empowers the U.S. attorney general to take action under certain conditions to ensure fair and impartial voter registration procedures.

Campaign Financing Rules

In recent years the states have begun to exert some control over various aspects of campaign financing and reporting. Many states have enacted laws governing the amount of money that individuals and organizations may contribute to a single campaign. In addition, some states provide partial public funding of campaigns along with limits on how much may be spent. All states require some form of campaign finance reporting, though the rules are generally lax. (See Focus 9.1 "From Classrooms to Boardrooms.")

Reporting Finances

Campaign finance reporting requirements vary among the states. Wisconsin requires such reports from candidates or committees that spend more than $25. In Michigan, Minnesota, North Carolina, North Dakota, and Texas, those who exceed $100 must report. In California reports are required of candidates and officeholders whose salaries are or will be in excess of $100 per month.

Other states have similar dollar thresholds triggering the need to file financial reports.[1] These reports usually are filed with the secretary of state or the county clerk. In most states it is common for financial reports to be submitted after deadlines have passed, sometimes even after the elections are over, and for the sanctions for such tardiness to be mild.

Contributions

The states impose a variety of limitations on the ability of organizations to make financial contributions to candidate campaigns. Eighteen states prohibit corporations from making any contribution and fourteen others restrict the size of contributions. Again, there are wide variations among the states. Michigan disallows corporate contributions to candidate campaigns except for those that are issue-centered. Wisconsin prohibits them except for referenda matters. The states also regulate contributions from labor unions, regulated industries, and political parties. The limits on party contributions are few; those that apply to unions and regulated industries are similar to but slightly less restrictive than the ones for corporations.

Over half of the states limit the amount individuals may contribute to candidate campaigns, though these limits also vary widely among the states. Sometimes the ceilings are placed on statewide elections only; other times there are separate limitations on primary and general elections. The interstate variety is enormous.

The attempts to curb election finance abuses, both nationally and in the states, generated a response in the form of political action committees (PACs),

Focus 9.1
FROM CLASSROOMS TO BOARDROOMS

• • •

Who says you have to be old and jaded to be a politician? Two college kids proved otherwise in the 1996 elections. Twenty-two-year-old Maureen "Mo" Johnson and twenty-three-year-old David Korbelik won their elections following spirited campaigns.

Mo Johnson is a political science major at the University of Colorado in Boulder. Her school, along with CU campuses in Denver and Colorado Springs, and the Colorado University Health Sciences Center in Denver, is governed by a Board of Regents who are elected on a partisan ballot. She ran for a seat on that board and now you can call her Regent Johnson.

As regent, Ms. Johnson will join an interesting crowd. Board members are elected in a partisan, statewide race, and have been a controversial bunch. A few years back they rejected all candidates for the CU system presidency following an expensive search process, and in a secret meeting, they appointed a person who had not previously been a candidate.

Ms. Johnson ran as a Republican, although she says she is liberal on such issues as abortion and gay rights. She secured the party's nomination at the summer state convention, where she defeated three male opponents, one of whom was a veteran state representative. Mo gave a four-minute address to the delegates, who interrupted her with applause several times.

Ms. Johnson was at a disadvantage in terms of campaign finance. Her opponent had money for radio ads, but Mo says she had to save up quarters just to do her laundry. She did manage to raise $15,000 for her statewide campaign, and she got around in her old car, which already had logged 180,000 miles.

Mo won big. She received 58 percent of the vote and took a majority of the votes in fifty-two of the state's sixty-three counties. Although records are sketchy, the secretary of state believes that Mo is the youngest statewide office holder in Colorado's history. If so, she is the youngest just barely as Korbelik was elected the same day as County Commissioner in Kit Carson County.

Sources: Denver Post, "New Regent State's Youngest Official," 7 November 1996, and *Rocky Mountain News*, "Student Regent," 7 November 1996.

which have become a pervasive and important source of influence in modern politics. When the ability of organizations and individuals to contribute generously to campaigns is restricted by the states, those seeking to contribute pool their more limited sums and place them in the hands of PACs, which then act on their behalf. The irony is that the attempts to keep campaign financing honest and at reasonable levels have led to the creation of the PACs, which have served, instead, to make even more money available to candidates.

Expenditures

While some states seek to limit campaign spending as well as contributions, expenditure limitations are much less prevalent. In large measure this is because of the difficult legal issues associated with spending limits. The Supreme Court has ruled (*Buckley v. Valeo*, 1976) that in the absence of a public election financing system in which candidates voluntarily participate, spending limits constitute impermissible infringements on free speech. For candidates to effectively express themselves and communicate their political views to the voting public they must spend money. Thus, spending limits constitute speech limits.

Incumbent Advantages

Some argue that there is a political problem associated with spending limits—that they constitute an unfair advantage for incumbents. Incumbency, this reasoning goes, creates an advantage in any campaign, and to overcome that edge, challengers must spend heavily to advertise themselves to the public. Spending limits handcuff challengers. Not everyone agrees, of course. Others contend that since challengers receive far less in campaign contributions than incumbents, spending limitations would help challengers by limiting heavy spending by the already advantaged incumbents.

Variation among the States

Given the political and legal complications of expenditure limitations, it is not surprising that the states do less to limit campaign spending than they do to control campaign contributions. Many states have laws that specify who may authorize expenditures from a campaign fund and what campaign money may be spent for. Currently, only a few states limit the amounts that can be spent in certain elections, and roughly half of the states disallow any spending until an initial financial statement is filed with the state. It is not coincidental that the public officials writing this legislation are the same people who need the money to run for reelection. As a result, serious campaign financial reform has yet to emerge from the legislatures.

Approximately half of the states have some form of public campaign financing, but the plans vary widely among the states. Some make it possible for citizens to provide public financing through income tax credits or deductions, or by contributions by a check-off on the tax return form. A number of other states appropriate state funds directly. In some instances, taxpayers may specify the party to which their contributions will go. In others, state support is given to both political parties or is available only to candidates for governor. As is the case with all aspects of state election law, the interstate variations are great.

Electoral Participation

The American political system is based on a number of normative assumptions, including the belief that the people are sovereign. Authority may be exercised by elected representatives or appointed administrators, but authority rests ultimately with the people. Another assumption is that the sovereign citizens exercise their authority by voting.

But do they? The answer is both yes, some do, and no, many don't. In recent decades Americans have become increasingly less interested in voting. They also show a weakening attachment to the political parties, which are, after all, major components in the U.S. elective system.

Figure 9.1 tracks voter turnout in presidential elections from 1960 to 1996. The trend—with the exception of 1992, when the presence of a third party candidate (Ross Perot) sparked renewed interest—clearly has been downward.

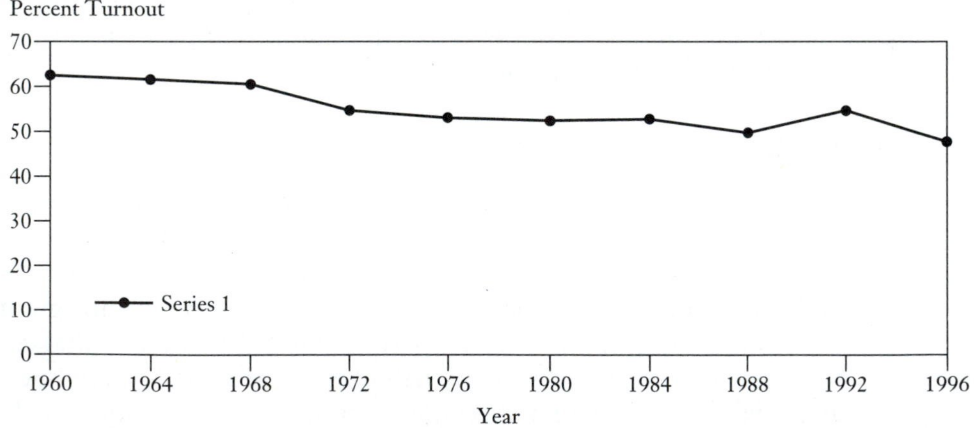

Figure 9.1 Presidential Election Participation by Voters, 1960–1996
Source: Statistical Abstract, various years.

The voter turnout in the 1996 presidential election was the lowest turnout since 1924. It is important to note that the data in the figure are for presidential contests, and that voter turnout is lower in almost all other types of elections. Occasionally, a hot local issue stimulates a massive turnout in a community. But voter participation in nonpresidential-year congressional elections, in elections for state offices, in local elections (especially those held in the spring), and in primary elections is often much lower than participation in presidential elections.

Widespread Apathy

The apparent lack of interest in self-governance is reflected also in a decline in citizen attachment to the parties. As Table 9.1 demonstrates, our identification with the two major parties has been slipping along with voter turnout. A recent study suggests that while professed party affiliation has declined, in reality many who describe themselves as independents in fact are very similar to Democrats and Republicans in voting habits, public opinion, and views of the two political parties. Genuine independents, it is argued, have never exceeded 11 percent of those who vote in a national election.[2]

Political participation, as measured by voting, varies considerably throughout the electorate. Table 9.2 shows the levels of voter turnout in national elections in two presidential election years—1976 and 1988. The table also shows how turnout varies with age, gender, ethnicity, education, and employment. As in Figure 9.1, the data indicate a decline in overall voter participation.

Young People Don't Vote

The youngest Americans participate the least. That may be understandable. Most eighteen-year-olds, as compared to those in their thirties and forties, for

TABLE 9.1 POLITICAL PARTY IDENTIFICATION, 1960–1994

Political Party	Percent Identifying			
	1970	*1980*	*1990*	*1994*
Strong Democrat	20	18	20	15
Weak Democrat	25	23	19	19
Strong Republican	16	9	10	16
Weak Republican	14	15	15	15

Source: U.S. Bureau of the Census, *Statistical Abstract of the United States, 1996* (Washington, D.C.: GPO, 1996), p. 285.

TABLE 9.2 VOTER TURNOUT BY AGE, GENDER, ETHNICITY, EDUCATION, AND EMPLOYMENT, 1988, 1992, AND 1994

	Voter Turnout (percent)		
Voter Category	*1988*	*1992*	*1994**
Age			
18–20 years	33.2	38.5	16.5
21–24 years	38.3	45.7	22.3
25–34 years	48.6	53.2	32.2
35–44 years	61.3	63.6	46.0
45–64 years	67.9	70.0	56.0
65 years and older	68.8	70.1	60.7
Gender			
Male	56.4	60.2	44.4
Female	58.3	62.3	44.9
Ethnicity			
White	59.1	63.6	46.9
African American	51.5	54.0	37.0
Hispanic	28.8	28.9	19.1
Education			
8 years or less	36.7	35.1	23.2
High School			
1–3 years	41.3	41.2	27.0
4 years	54.7	57.5	40.5
College			
1–3 years	64.5	68.7	49.1
4 or more years	77.6	81.0	63.1
Employment			
Employed	58.4	63.8	45.2
Unemployed	38.6	46.2	28.3

*1994 was a congressional election year, 1988 and 1992 were presidential election years.
Source: U.S. Bureau of the Census, *Statistical Abstract of the United States, 1996* (Washington, D.C.: GPO, 1996), p. 286.

example, are much less likely to be established, employed, knowledgable about, and interested in the workings of government. Rather, they may be transient, as is the case with many college students, and they may have yet to plant roots in a community and perceive personal stakes in political activities. By contrast, older voters often have developed habits of participation as a result of years of exposure to the workings and consequences of the system. In general, a mobile eighteen- or twenty-year-old with other preoccupations is less apt to vote than are his or her parents, who realize that they have a personal and economic stake in political outcomes.

Women Voters

Although at one time men voted more regularly than women, that is no longer the case. In the 1988, 1992, and 1996 elections, slightly more women voted than men. Coupled with the fact that women outnumber men, the female vote has become increasingly important. Some studies indicate that men and women tend to differ in their political views and preferences, placing women voters in a position to determine the outcomes of elections.[3]

It is not surprising that women's participation, in relation to voter participation generally, has increased with their expanded role in the workforce. Researchers have documented that the employed, and especially those in professional, prestigious, and high-paying jobs, vote more regularly than the unemployed (see Table 9.2). In recent decades the social and occupational roles of American women have changed, and today more women are part of the workforce. As women have assumed many of the roles formerly dominated by men, they too have become more politically active. In addition, national events such as the Clarence Thomas–Anita Hill hearings in 1991 on Thomas' nomination to the U. S. Supreme Court serve to encourage women to become more active politically.

Ethnicity

Voter turnout also varies by ethnicity. As Table 9.2 shows, whites vote more regularly than African Americans, though the gap is narrowing. Hispanics are less likely to vote than either whites or African Americans. As this very young population comes to political maturity, however, the sheer numbers of America's fastest-growing ethnic group are likely to translate into political power at the polls, and, as the chances of winning increase, so likely will the voter turnout. In the Rio Grande Valley of south Texas, where 80 percent of the population is Spanish-surnamed and where this vote often is seen as the key to a statewide race, it is not unusual for the voting turnout figures to run ahead of the statewide turnout percentages.

Level of Education

In addition, voter participation fluctuates by level of education (see Table 9.2). The more education one has, the more likely one is to vote. Clearly, education is associated with the other factors shown in the table. It takes time to go through school, and thus persons in their thirties are likely to have more schooling than an eighteen-year-old. A well-educated person is also less likely to be unemployed. Historically, men and whites have had more education than others. These factors can be cumulative and reinforcing. They can, and have, led to broader participation and a more extensive impact on the political system by well-educated, successfully employed middle-aged and older white men. This is changing, though not rapidly.

Women and Minorities in Public Office

The relative growth in voter participation by women and African Americans is reflected in Table 9.2. It is also manifest in increased success by women and African Americans in winning public office. Table 9.3 shows the increase in the number of African-American elected officials in a variety of positions at the national, state, and local levels. Although African Americans still do not hold public offices in the proportion in which they are represented in the general population, their presence is growing. More specifically, the recent political careers of such mayors as Thomas Bradley of Los Angeles, the late Harold Washington of Chicago, Coleman Young of Detroit, and David Dinkins of New York attest to the growing African-American political presence. There have been increases in the number of Hispanic officeholders as well, but the growth has been more modest.

Women have also been making significant strides in gaining elective offices, such as in state legislatures. Recent governors include Christine Todd Whitman

TABLE 9.3 NUMBER OF AFRICAN-AMERICAN ELECTED OFFICIALS, 1970, 1990, AND 1993

Position	Number of Officials 1970	1990	1993
U.S. state legislators and administrators	179	436	561
City and county officials	719	4,481	4,819
Local and state educational governing bodies	368	1,645	1,682

Source: U.S. Bureau of the Census, *Statistical Abstract of the United States, 1996* (Washington, D.C.: GPO, 1996), p. 284.

in New Jersey, Barbara Roberts in Oregon, Kay Orr in Nebraska, Joan Finney in Kansas, Ann Richards in Texas, Madeleine Kunin in Vermont, and Rose Mofford in Arizona. The 1992 election year was called the "year of the woman" by some observers because of women's role in the electoral arena. In 1992 California, the largest state in the nation, became the first to have two female U.S. senators. Similarly, in 1988 five states had women lieutenant governors, eleven had women secretaries of state, and nine had women state treasurers.

Legislatures Are Changing

Elections in the first half of the 1990s produced record numbers of women in state legislatures as well. In 1993 women constituted a record 20 percent of state legislators; twenty years ago that figure was only 5 percent. Over a third of the state legislators in Arizona, Colorado, New Hampshire, and Vermont are women.[4] (See Focus 9.2 "Women in the Legislature.")

There have been notable gains at the local level as well. Darcy, Welch, and Clark report that, from 1975 to 1982, the number of women in county offices

Focus 9.2
WOMEN IN THE LEGISLATURE

• • •

Elections in the early part of the 1990s produced several additional women state legislators, bringing the national total to 20 percent. The distribution is uneven, however. Over 30 percent of the legislative membership is female in Arizona, Colorado, Idaho, Maine, New Hampshire, Vermont, and Washington, whereas the proportion is only 10 percent in Alabama, Kentucky, Louisiana, and Oklahoma.

Does gender diversification make a policy difference? Some researchers suggest that women legislators are more liberal than their male counterparts on many issues; that they are less supportive of abortion restrictions and the death penalty; that they focus on health, child, and family issues more than men; and that their interpersonal and negotiation styles are less confrontational.

There are organizational consequences, too, as women are moving into leadership positions and providing the foundation for bipartisan coalitions. In 1993, for example, the Alaska house elected its first woman

Focus 9.2 *(continued)*

speaker; indeed, women took over the entire slate of leadership slots in that state. In the state of Washington, where almost 40 percent of legislators are female, women from the two parties organized the Ladies' Terrorist Society and Sewing Circle, indicating that gender cohesiveness may cross party lines.

Sources: Karl T. Kurtz, "The Election in Perspective," *State Legislatures* (Jan. 1993): 16–19; Rob Gurwitt, "Legislatures: The Faces of Change," *Governing* (Feb. 1993): 28–32; and Susan J. Carroll, Debra L. Dodson, and Ruth B. Mandrell, *The Impact of Women in Public Office: An Overview* (New Brunswick: Rutgers University, Center for the American Woman and Politics, 1991).

tripled, the number of women mayors grew from 566 to 1,770, and the count on town and city councils jumped from 5,365 to 12,963.[5] Mayors in twelve of the nation's hundred largest cities have recently been women, including Dallas, Houston, Pittsburgh, Chicago, San Diego, San Francisco, and Spokane. At one point in the late 1980s, five of the ten largest cities in Texas had women mayors. In cities larger than 30,000, over 11 percent had female mayors.[6] Figure 9.2 shows the increase in the number of women officeholders from 1977 to 1997.

It is argued that there would be even more women officeholders if not for a shortage of candidates. A variety of factors, including the presence of children at home and the inflexibility of regular working hours, may restrict the number of available women candidates.[7] If the recent past is any indication, however, the number of candidates is likely to increase.

There is some evidence that the election of minority and women officeholders affects public policy outcomes. Kenneth Mladenka reports that in the cities he studied, the election of minority council members, Hispanics especially, led to more minority municipal employment.[8] Others argue that women are more likely than men to vote Democratic and that this can determine the outcome of elections. In addition, women and men tend to differ in their views on a variety of issues. For example, women are said to be more supportive of programs assisting the economically disadvantaged and tend to emphasize racial equality, protection of the environment, and control of drugs, pornography, and gambling.[9]

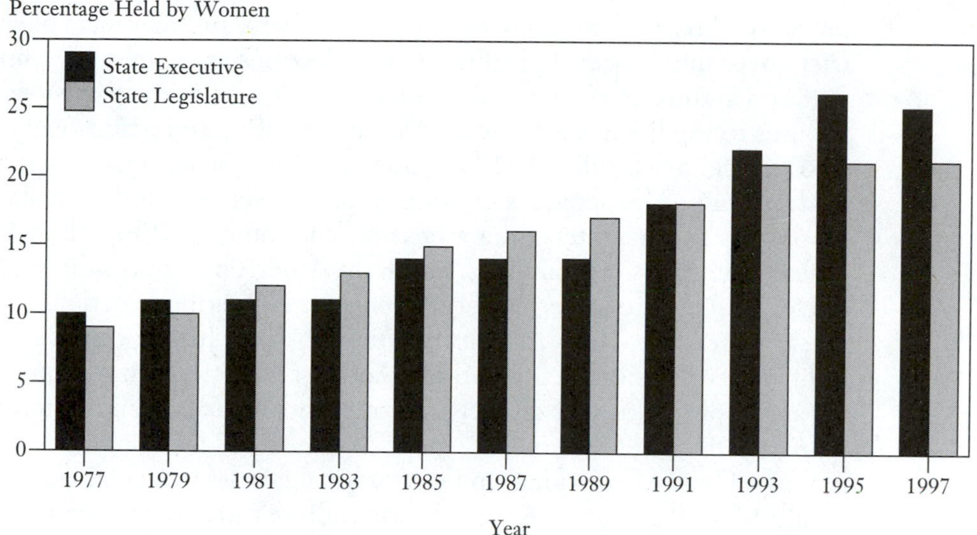

Figure 9.2 Increase in Number of Women Officeholders
Source: Rutgers University, Center for the American Woman and Politics, "Women in Elective Office, 1997."

Changes in patterns of political participation and the emerging electoral successes of women and minorities are far more than symbolic. They have translated into policy differences that are likely to become increasingly important.

The Impact of Institutions on Electoral Participation

In addition to the differences associated with age, gender, and ethnicity in electoral participation outlined in Table 9.2, voter participation varies as a result of institutional factors. These include level of government election, time of election, presence or absence of political party involvement, and items on the ballot. Consistently, the highest levels of voter turnout occur in presidential elections, which are held every four years in November. Turnout drops in the off-year November elections, when there are congressional contests and state and local races.

Low Turnout in Local Elections

For all the talk about how Washington doesn't understand the real problems, and that the government closest to the people works best, voter turnout is notoriously low in local elections. Often held in the spring, they include elections for school board members, city council members, and members of special district governing boards. In addition, local elections are generally nonpartisan—that is, candidates do not run as members of a political party—which contributes to the low voter turnout. The impact of these institutional conditions is to reduce the visibility of the elections and thus the interest and participation of the voters. The activities of political parties serve to focus media attention on politics and heighten voter awareness and interest. When these factors are absent, voter participation falls. Similarly, Americans are conditioned to think of electoral politics in terms of the even-year November elections. Springtime does not seem, to many, a "natural" time to vote. It is not unusual, then, for nonpartisan elections held in March, April, or May (featuring contests for seats on a school or hospital district governing board, for example) to attract less than 10 percent of the voters.

The blend of individual and institutional factors has a major impact on the results of local elections. As noted earlier, those most likely to vote are well educated, employed, middle aged or older, white, and hold prestigious and professional jobs. In local elections, when institutional factors such as time of election and absence of party combine with these differential voting patterns, the small sector of the population that actually votes tends to have a distinctive upper-class cast.

Levels of Turnout Affect Outcomes

Elections with extremely low voter turnouts can work to the advantage of particular special interest groups. A well-organized group, even though few in number, can often control the outcome.

Turnout Varies among the States

Electoral participation varies among the states. In general, voter turnout in the Midwest is higher and turnout in the South is lower than the national average. Five of the six states with the highest levels of voter turnout are in or adjacent to the Midwest, whereas four of the lowest five are southern states.

History and culture explain some of the state variations in voter turnout. Historically, the South has been so solidly Democratic that most meaningful electoral competition has been in the primaries, and not in the general elections. Thus, the incentive to vote in November has been lacking. The remnants of this heritage can still be seen in some southern states, where voters tend to vote Republican in the presidential and other statewide elections, but the Democrats are still relatively strong in the down-ballot races.

Some features of the moralistic culture of many midwestern states imply a civic responsibility to the community, and thus a moral obligation to participate in civic affairs such as elections. In any case, turnout varies among the states as well as within them, as evidenced by the impact of institutional factors.

Modern Campaigns

There are several pronounced characteristics of modern state electoral campaigns. They tend to be candidate-centered rather than party-centered campaigns and are increasingly costly, with political action committees playing an ever-larger role in their funding. In addition, modern campaigns tend to feature incumbents who campaign year-round, who almost always win because they often run unopposed, and whose campaigns are increasingly sophisticated and often managed by professional consultants.[10] In these ways, contemporary state campaigns are becoming more similar to those for national office.[11]

The Candidate-Centered Campaign

The decline in the electoral role of the political party in America, the diminished attachment that American voters have to the parties, and the increased importance of campaigning style together have led to the development of the **candidate-centered campaign**, in which the candidates, not the parties, run the electoral campaigns. The candidate works with professional campaign consultants and office staff to raise money, prepare strategy, assemble the campaign agenda, deal with the media, and do the polling and mass mailings. The parties may help with mailing lists and get-out-the-vote efforts, and may provide some technical assistance and a little money, but most activity is undertaken by the candidate and the candidate's advisers.

The Expensive Campaign

State races are increasingly costly. The growth in political ambition and careerism prompts incumbents to raise and spend more to extend their political careers. Serious challengers must then respond in kind with heavy spending. The expanded use of the visual media increases costs as well, especially in statewide races for governor, attorney general, and other executive branch posts. These costs are particularly acute in such large states as California, Texas, and New York, where there are several television markets.

As noted earlier in the chapter, gubernatorial contests routinely run into the millions of dollars. It is also common for competitive state legislative races, even in small states, to cost each candidate more than $50,000. In the 1988 elections in California, each winning state senate candidate reportedly spent an average of $277,000, and house winners averaged $190,000 each. Incumbents enter races with a major advantage; not only do they enjoy name familiarity with the voters, but they also receive a disproportionate amount of PAC campaign contributions.

Incumbent Self-Promotion: An Endless Campaign

In one sense many state-level campaigns are run year-round, just as they are in Congress. The modernization or "professionalization" of state legislatures, the growing importance of the office of governor, and the reduced limitations on the ability of governors to succeed themselves in office together have increased the attractiveness of state elective offices.

In many state legislatures the pay is better than it used to be, the staff help is more abundant, and the physical surroundings are much improved. More state legislators are making elective office a career, or at least a longer run enterprise, and more governors are seeking reelection.

Not surprisingly, state officeholders use the resources available to them while in office to promote themselves politically and to solidify their base for subsequent elections. Incumbents engage in extensive constituent casework; indeed, they seek it. Newsletters and questionnaires are mailed, each one conveniently pushing the incumbent's name, often a photograph as well, into voters' homes. Notes are mailed by the thousands congratulating constituents and their children on everything from receipt of a scholarship or job promotion to victory in the state wrestling tournament. Each note also gets the politician's name into someone's house. Local newspapers carry notices inviting citizens to have coffee and chat with the officeholder in local restaurants on Saturday mornings. Few people may show up, but the notice gains the desired publicity.

The increased desire by incumbents to continue in office is the stimulant for the modern so-called **endless campaign**; the expanded availability of staff, money, and other resources provides the means. These are not, of course, the kinds of things a competent representative should be addressing in the course of representing a constituency; nonetheless, they contribute mightily to an incumbent's advantage.

Similarly, incumbent governors can use their office for political self-promotion, albeit not with exactly the same tactics employed by legislators. As chief executives, governors are positioned to develop and maintain a high public profile.

Legislatures, the press, and the attentive public await the unveiling of the governor's policy initiatives. The governor can command statewide attention with a news conference or an announcement at a moment's notice. The governor's activities—public, social, and personal—make news. The ability to stay in the public eye works greatly to the political advantage of the incumbent state chief executive. Thus, it is not surprising that incumbent governors who seek reelection are successful nearly nine times out of ten. Though long in existence at the national level, a career-oriented political class is now emerging at the state level as well.

The Challenger's Dilemma

Given the growth in state-level political careerism, the decline of the political party, and the growth in PAC monies targeted primarily at incumbents, state contests have become increasingly less competitive. Incumbents almost always win, and many legislative seats go uncontested. Alan Rosenthal, a leading authority on state politics, notes that the success rate of incumbents in state legislative races is now well over 90 percent, and that most seats are now safe for one party or the other.[12] In addition, the number of competitive seats continues to decline.

Challengers thus face overwhelming odds. They generally lack name familiarity with the voters. To gain it, they must spend money, but most campaign donations go to incumbents. Challengers need people to help them, but it is generally the incumbent, not the challenger, who has paid staff. State-paid staffers are not supposed to work directly on campaigns, but the act of helping a constituent with a problem or of providing information to someone is, in itself, a boost to the officeholder.

Modern reforms have diminished the political party as a source of support to challengers as well. It is no wonder, then, that many state legislative seats go unchallenged. The minority party in these circumstances often has difficulty even finding a candidate willing to run against an entrenched incumbent.

Hence, the mix of careerism, modernized state legislatures, PAC campaign funding, and weakened political parties makes state contests increasingly less competitive. Some argue that incumbency has replaced political party affiliation as the major cue for voters. This does not mean, however, that incumbent officeholders are completely free of political risk. Some do lose, but these are the exceptions, not the rule.

Sophisticated Campaign Strategies

Modern state campaigns are more sophisticated than ever before. Candidates use polling and focus groups to identify supporters, opponents, and campaign positions. They track, sometimes on a daily basis, voters' feelings on selected issues and then adjust their campaign agendas accordingly. Literature is prepared for various segments of the voting public, with different messages targeted to groups characterized by gender, race, age, or interest in particular issues. Similarly, radio and television advertising is tailored to the voter responses and preferences gauged by polling.

The type, the timing, and the locality of an election may also affect the nature of the campaign strategy that candidates pursue. In a statewide race for governor or attorney general, for instance, candidates have to organize statewide and seek support from party regulars in all or most counties. They need a rather sizable campaign staff. Campaigning is expensive, for candidates have to advertise in newspapers with statewide distribution as well as in local papers. They need expensive spot advertisements on metropolitan radio stations. They have to purchase television time. In their appeals to the voter, candidates seek not only to create an identity for themselves and demonstrate that their platform differs from those of their opponents, they also seek to make clear the distinctions between their own political party and that of the opposition.

The situation differs somewhat in contests for state house and state senate seats. Here, the district may be located in a metropolitan, suburban, or rural area, and this influences choices of campaign strategy. In an urban or metropolitan area, candidates have to pursue strategies similar to those used by candidates for statewide office, such as purchasing the advertising services of the major newspapers, the expensive radio stations, and television. In rural areas, candidates find advertisements in major newspapers and on radio and television of limited use. Instead, they concentrate their efforts in the local, less expensive media. Since state legislative contests are partisan in nature (except in Nebraska), candidates work cooperatively with the local county party organizations. Although the candidates cannot depend on the party organizations for extensive help with funding or staffing, they can turn to the parties for relevant information, such as voter registration lists, the names of previous political donors, and the like.

The situation is different still in most local elections. Here, the political party usually is absent. Although a candidate's known affiliation with a party may bring in some votes on election day, the political parties do not play a major or formal role in local elections. In addition, campaign strategies are directly affected by the low voter turnout typical of such elections. Therefore, with the parties absent and voter participation low, the candidate for local office must be careful to target that small group of community influentials who do vote. Media blitzes targeting large areas are not an option—they cost too much and may cover areas the candidate does not need to reach. Some local media coverage is necessary to develop and maintain a presence in the election, and in this radio advertising often plays a key role. Door-to-door campaigning is important, as it is in all elections. Especially critical in local campaigns is careful targeting of the probable voters. In addition, contact with business associations, appearances at service club meetings, block work in communities with high voter participation, and a good public image—that of a community regular and a solid and moderate person—are all essential to a candidate's success in a local election.

Campaigns Reflect U.S. Institutions and Politics

The shape of U.S. institutions is reflected in American politics. The system is highly decentralized, with thousands of governments. Most of these jurisdictions conduct elections, but they differ in size, function, political character, and internal organization.

All fifty states feature partisan, statewide contests for governor, forty-nine states have partisan races for members of two-house legislatures (Nebraska is the one exception), and over half of the states have elections for judges (some of them are partisan and others are nonpartisan). In addition, the local contests in most states are nonpartisan. Special districts and school districts feature races for policy bodies only, for they hire their chief executive. Some city races may be hotly contested, whereas in some small towns public service is viewed not as a prize but as a public duty.

In terms of competitiveness, partisanship, voter turnout, and many other respects, therefore, extensive variety exists in the American electoral system. (Chapters 11 and 12 examine in greater detail local elections and community power and politics, respectively.)

Direct Democracy

Although the American political system is widely viewed as a democracy—one based on the direct participation of voters—in large measure it is really more of a representative democracy. Most policy choices are made by representatives, not directly by the citizens. Most ballots cast by voters are for their representatives, rather than direct expressions of voter preferences on specific issues. However, the voters do, in some instances, participate directly in policy choices. The processes that provide for their direct participation include the referendum and the citizen initiative. As discussed in Chapter 3, such processes are forms of **direct democracy**.

The Referendum

The **referendum** is a measure by which legislation is submitted to the people for their approval. Most referenda are "referred" to voters by their representatives. In some instances, however, a referendum may be initiated by citizens. By way of a petition, citizens may oppose a decision made by some board or legislature by forcing the matter to be referred to voters.

Most referenda are at the local level, in cities and school districts especially, though they occur at the state level as well. Examples include elections on whether to approve city issuance of bonds (borrowing) for building a new stadium, civic center, or park or for resurfacing streets. Communities have held elections to decide such matters as whether to allow eating and drinking establishments to serve mixed drinks, whether to fluoridate municipal water, and whether to preserve environmentally sensitive areas. Recently, there has been a spate of referenda concerning gay rights at both the state and local levels. School districts frequently go directly to the voters, seeking approval of borrowed funds to build additional schools or of increases in the property tax to support annual operating budgets.

Matters may be referred to the voters because a city council or school board wants a showing of public support for a decision that it could by law make on its own. Other times, state law, local ordinances, or local charter provisions require direct voter approval. Borrowing against anticipated tax revenues, for example, often requires direct voter approval. The laws in almost all states provide for the referendum process, but they vary in their applicability as well as to whether they are required by state statutes or local charters and ordinances.[13]

The Citizen Initiative

The **citizen initiative** is similar to the referendum in that it involves direct voter action. However, unlike most referenda, which begin with a referral by elected officials, the initiative begins with action by citizens. Although initiative procedures vary considerably, the basic steps of the process are similar.[14]

Citizens may organize interest groups when they want a law passed or repealed or a state constitution or city charter amended. They may draft their proposal, have it reviewed and approved for proper wording by a specified state body, and secure a certain number of valid signatures on a petition. The number of signatures required varies greatly among the states. If the required number of signatures is obtained by a deadline set in law, and the signatures are found to be valid, the measure is then placed on the ballot at the upcoming election.

The Recall

The citizen **recall** is the third side of the direct democracy triangle. The recall serves as a mechanism by which citizens can remove ("recall") elected officials from office prior to the end of the term of office. As with the initiative and referendum, the recall requires the obtaining of a stated number of signatures prior to implementing the recall process.

Is Direct Democracy Good Government?

As we discussed in the policy perspective at the end of Chapter 3, the growth in citizen lawmaking has become a matter of controversy in and of itself. Some argue that, because lawmakers can be insensitive and unresponsive, it is important for citizens to have access to a mechanism through which they can affect public policy directly. Indeed, the initiative, recall, and referendum were developed for precisely this reason. Besides, what could be more democratic than direct citizen control over public choices?

Critics contend, however, that the initiative process can lead to bad and poorly constructed law because citizen input is often uninformed. Virtually all legislation relates to other laws on the books and has complicated repercussions. For example, limitations on one tax are likely to have impacts on other taxes. Further, tax limits at the state level have a host of consequences for cities, counties, and schools, as well as for state programs themselves. The campaigns for and against the various initiatives and referenda now take on all the trappings of modern elections, with slick thirty-second soundbite commercials that may do less to inform viewers than to appeal to their emotions.

In addition, critics contend that big money interests often outspend opponents in supporting or opposing a measure, and thus the public is further deprived of a balanced view of the issue. Bottle companies and the insurance industry, for example, spend millions to quash initiatives that they believe will hurt them financially. Big money does not always determine the outcome, but it almost always distorts the picture.

Clearly, there is a trade-off to be made with direct democracy. Ultimately, citizens must retain the authority to structure their governments and choose their policies. But must the exercise of that authority be direct, and, if the answer is yes, must it have the potential to be applied to all policy questions? Does the extensive use of direct democracy invite voters to make mistakes? Does it keep government more in tune with the public? There are no correct answers to these questions. Thomas Cronin expresses the sentiments of some scholars when, in the introduction to his extensive study of direct democracy, he states: "Although my heart tends to side with populism, my head is skeptical about the workability and desirability of direct democracy devices."[15]

Summary

In no area of American politics is the diversity of the states as well represented as in the election systems. Election systems vary from state to state, within states, and from office to office. Elections vary in terms of partisanship, function, and turnout. Statewide races usually are partisan; local races usually are not. Turnout tends to be directly related to ballot position; the higher the office being filled, the higher the turnout. The use of direct democracy methods—the initiative, the referendum, and the recall—has added to the number and types of elections held each year.

Policy Perspective: The Voting Rights Act and the States

Historically, election and voting requirements are policy areas reserved to the states. That is why constitutional amendments have been required when establishing uniform protections for the franchise; the Fifteenth, Seventeenth, Nineteenth, and Twenty-Sixth Amendments were ratified for this reason.

In 1965, in one of the most far-reaching pieces of legislation in the nation's history, Congress passed the Voting Rights Act (VRA), designed initially to protect the rights of African Americans to register and vote. Although the VRA directly involved the national government in an area of policy traditionally reserved to the states, the legislation sustained a constitutional challenge in *South Carolina v. Katzenbach* (1966). The VRA has been extended several times and its scope expanded to cover language as well as racial and ethnic minorities.

Initially, the focus of the enforcement of the VRA was on voter registration procedures. However, beginning in the 1970s and accelerating during the next two decades, the VRA began to be used at congressional, state, county, and municipal levels to achieve the policy goal of increasing the number of candidates elected to office by minority populations. Most often, the remedy involved drawing election districts composed primarily of minority populations (usually at least 65 percent of the district would be minority); these districts replaced at-large elections where the white numerical majorities had been able to win virtually all the elections because of racially polarized voting (i.e., white voters voting for white candidates and minority voters voting for minority candidates). Usually the legal challenge would be initiated by one of several interest groups organized to represent racial and ethnic interests (e.g., the NAACP on behalf of African Americans and the Mexican American Legal Defense and Education Fund [MALDEF] on behalf of Latinos).

Districting as a remedy usually was quite successful, and throughout the South and Southwest, congressional delegations, state legislatures, city councils, and school boards begin to include minority representatives where none had been before.

Initially, these actions were approved by the federal courts; indeed, most often the districting occurred as a result of a successful federal court challenge brought by minority plaintiffs against a city council or school district. Beginning in the early 1990s, however, the U.S. Supreme Court signaled that it was going to take a second look at the use of the VRA to force local communities to district. In a series of decisions beginning with *Shaw v. Reno* (1993) and continuing through the mid-1990s, the Court indicated that districts drawn solely for the purpose of producing minority winners would not pass constitutional muster. These cases focused on the drawing of congressional districts, but there is no reason to believe the Court will accept state, county, and municipal districts drawn for the same purpose. Court challenges to such districts are almost certain to make their way through the judicial process.

Consequently, local jurisdictions have sought alternatives to districting as a way of enhancing minority representation. Perhaps the best-known alternative is the use of cumulative voting, a process where each voter is given the same number of votes as there are seats to be filled in a particular election. The voter may cast all of his or her votes for one candidate or divide them among several candidates. Thus, if there are five seats to be filled in an election, a voter may cast all five votes for one candidate or spread the votes among the other candidates in any combination. This allows a minority population to "plump" or aggregate their votes for one minority candidate. Recent studies have indicated that cumulative voting does enhance minority electoral success.[16]

Another alternative is the Single Transferable Vote, whereby the voter ranks candidates in order of preference. As soon as a candidate receives the requisite number of votes to be elected to, say, a city council, any additional votes cast for that candidate are routed to the voter's second preference, and so on until all the seats up for election have been filled.

Cumulative voting and the single transferable vote seem strange at first glance (and maybe even at second glance), but they are being discussed increasingly as measures by which to reach equity in our electoral process.

KEY TERMS

primary election
general election
partisan election
nonpartisan election
motor-voter law
one person, one vote
candidate-centered campaign
endless campaign
direct democracy
referendum
citizen initiative
recall

ADDITIONAL READING

Dionne, E. J., Jr. *Why Americans Hate Politics*. New York: Simon and Schuster, 1991.

McNitt, Andrew. "The Impact of State Legislation on Political Campaigns." *State Government* (Summer 1980): 135–39.

National Civic League. *A Model Election System*. New York: NCL, 1973.

Salmore, Barbara G., and Stephen A. Salmore. *Candidates, Parties, and Campaigns*. Washington, D.C.: Congressional Quarterly Press, 1989.

NOTES

1. *The Book of the States, 1990–91* (Lexington, Ky.: Council of State Governments, 1991), pp. 237–60.
2. Bruce Keith, et al., *The Myth of the Independent Voter* (Berkeley: University of California Press, 1992). pp. 198–99.
3. Center for the American Woman and Politics, "The Gender Gap" (factsheet) (New Brunswick: Eagleton Institute of Politics, Rutgers University, July 1987).
4. Center for the American Woman and Politics, "Women in Elective Office" (factsheet) (New Brunswick: Eagleton Institute of Politics, Rutgers University, July 1988); Karl T. Kurtz, "The Election in Perspective," *State Legislatures* (Jan. 1993): 16–19; and Rob Gurwitt, "Legislatures: The Faces of Change," *Governing* (Feb. 1993): 28–32.
5. R. Darcy, Susan Welch, and Janet Clark, *Women, Elections and Representation* (New York: Longman, 1987).
6. Center for the American Woman and Politics, "Elective Office."
7. Darcy, Welch, and Clark, *Women*; and Karen Beckwith, *American Women and Political Parties* (New York: Greenwood Press, 1986).
8. Kenneth Mladenka, "Blacks and Hispanics in Urban Politics," *American Political Science Review* (March 1989): 165–92.
9. Center for the American Woman and Politics, "Elective Office."
10. Barbara G. Salmore and Stephen A. Salmore, "The Transformation of State Electoral Politics," in *The State of the States*, ed. Carl E. Van Horn (Washington, D.C.: Congressional Quarterly Press, 1989), pp. 175–208; and Alan Rosenthal, "The Legislative Institution—in Transition and at Risk," in *The State of the States*, 2d ed., ed. Carl E. Van Horn (Washington, D.C.: Congressional Quarterly Press, 1993).
11. Bob Benenson, "Changing Money's Role Is No Easy Task," *Congressional Quarterly Weekly Report* (4 Nov. 1989): 2,987.
12. Rosenthal, "The Legislative Institution."
13. David D. Schmidt, *Citizen Lawmakers* (Philadelphia: Temple University Press, 1989).

14. Schmidt, *Citizen Lawmakers*; Thomas E. Cronin, *Direct Democracy* (Cambridge, Mass.: Harvard University Press, 1989); and *The Book of the States, 1990–91*, pp. 267–76.
15. Cronin, *Direct Democracy*, p. x.
16. See, for example, Richard Cole and Delbert Taebel, "Cumulative Voting in Local Elections: Lessons from the Alamagordo Experience," *Social Science Quarterly* 73 (1992): 194–201; and Richard Cole, Delbert Taebel, and Richard Engstrom, "Cumulative Voting in a Municipal Election," *Western Political Quarterly* 43 (1990): 191–99.

CHAPTER

10

. . .

The American Metropolis

. . .

One of the most famous urban redevelopment projects: the Renaissance Center in Detroit, Michigan. Does the Center improve the city or only emphasize the city's problems? *(John Maher/Stock, Boston)*

• • • **Population Shifts in the United States**

From Rural to Urban
From Urban to Suburban

• • • **Some Consequences of the Population Shifts**

Racial Segregation
Urban Struggles
Economic Segregation
Fragmented Government

• • • **Problems Associated with Fragmentation and Suburbanization**

Jurisdictional Inequities

Focus 10.1: Avoiding Annexation in Portage Township

Intergovernmental Conflict
Planning Difficulties
Financial Trouble for Core Cities
Other Problems

• • • **Benefits of Suburbanization**

• • • **Extreme Proposals for Reform**

Consolidation

Focus 10.2: Abolish the Suburbs?

The Metropolitan Federation

• • • **Modest Proposals for Reform**

Annexation
Intergovernmental Service Agreements
The Lakewood Plan
Metropolitan Councils of Government

• • • **The Politics of Metropolitan Reform**

Reform Sounds Rational
People Want a Choice
The Law Favors the Status Quo
Supporters versus Opponents

• • • **THE DOWNSIDE OF THE METROPOLITAN SCHEME**

Communities Want Local Control
A Clash of Values

• • • **FUTURE TRENDS**

Radical Reform Is Unlikely
Urban Villages
A Divided Nation?

• • • **SUMMARY**

• • • **POLICY PERSPECTIVE**

What exactly does it mean when a man who says he is from Dallas meets a woman who claims she lives in Los Angeles? Does the man really live in Dallas, or does he just say that to avoid having to explain where Garland, Irving, Grand Prairie, Arlington, or another Dallas suburb is located? And is the woman from Los Angeles, or is her home really in nearby Inglewood, Burbank, or Santa Monica? It probably doesn't make much difference to the two of them anyway, because they may not at the moment be worrying about zoning restrictions, property taxes, or an upcoming municipal election.

But to many people and in many circumstances it does matter. Dallas is not Garland and Los Angeles is not Burbank. These are separate governments with separate mayors, councils, zoning and taxing laws, and each with its own police, fire, sewer, and water services. Metropolitan America is literally strewn with governments. The Los Angeles, Chicago, New York, and Kansas City areas each sport literally hundreds of individual cities, not to mention scores of school districts and special districts and dozens of counties. This means that a lot of people have the chance to be mayor or to sit on a school board. It also means that the quality and quantity of public services vary from one place to another, and that planning for regionwide transportation, land use, and pollution abatement is hard to accomplish.

Population Shifts in the United States

From Rural to Urban

Both the absolute and proportionate increases in the **urbanization** of the U.S. population over the past two centuries have been astounding. The U.S. population grew from just over 3 million people in 1790 to over 255 million today. In the twentieth century alone it more than doubled. From 1980 to 1992, the U.S. population grew by more than 28 million, an increase of over 12 percent. In addition to its absolute growth, the urban population rose from just over 5 percent in 1790 to over 75 percent in 1990 (see Figure 10.1). The bulk of the populace is now crowded into urban areas, with extremely high concentrations found along the Atlantic and Pacific coasts, along the southern edge of Lake Michigan, and in a few other locations. In 1992, more than 13 percent of the population lived in the nine urban places of greater than 1,000,000 population. In 1994, over 18 million people resided in the New York metropolitan area, over 15 million in the Los Angeles area, 8.5 million in metropolitan Chicago, and almost 6 million in the Philadelphia metropolitan region.[1]

Critical factors underlying the dramatic growth in urbanization include technology and public policy. Modern technology greatly increased economies of scale on the farm, making it possible for fewer people to produce the needed food and fiber and driving the overhead and capital costs of farming upward. In 1840 the average farmer could produce enough food to feed 3.95 people; by 1972 the farmer could grow enough food for 52.4 persons. Similarly, the average farm covered 147 acres in 1920 but 478 acres in 1994. The larger farms generally meant more mechanization to work them, and so the demand for agricultural labor was greatly reduced. As a result, large numbers of people moved to the cities in search of work. Whereas in 1920 about 30 percent of the U.S. population lived on farms, only 1.6 percent resided there in 1990.[2]

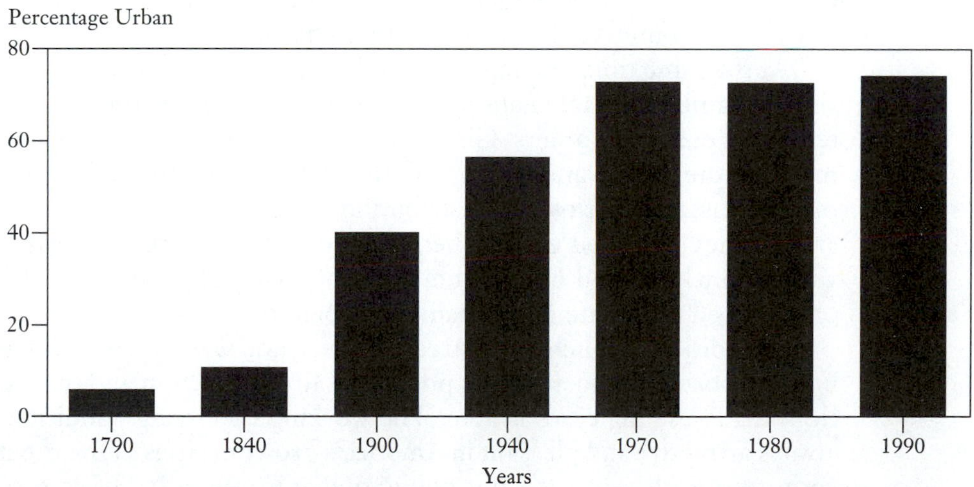

Figure 10.1 Urban Dwellers as a Percentage of the U.S. Population, 1790–1990
Source: Statistical Abstract of the U.S., various years.

Technology

Technology produced a **factory-based economy** that served to attract people to the cities. The advancing technology of the nineteenth and twentieth centuries gave rise to an economy based on specialized labor and mass production. Steel mills, automobile plants, shoe factories, and garment mills have sprung up in many urban areas. The mass production of the factory, in turn, gave rise to the physical concentration of people. The available transportation systems were such that workers had to live close to their jobs. The factory also encouraged the growth of urban centers.

Public Policy

Certain government policies encouraged the massive migration from farms to cities. For decades, the national and state governments had used public funds to subsidize agricultural research. A number of states supported large agricultural and engineering universities, whose impetus was the early federal land grants. Through the U.S. Department of Agriculture, the federal government supported a network of agricultural experiment stations, an economic research service that focused on agriculture, and a nationwide extension service that disseminated the knowledge of these research-related agencies. Today, these federally supported units are commonly housed within the land grant universities, such as Texas A&M University and the University of California at Davis.

The knowledge produced and disseminated by publicly financed research, in turn, greatly increased the productivity of American agriculture and triggered the trend toward larger, highly mechanized, and more expensive farms. It also contributed to the exodus from the farm.

At the same time, the rapid growth of big business was accelerated by a desire to maintain a viable national economy and the government's refusal to interfere in economic affairs. Giant corporations sprang up in textiles, oil, automobiles, the media, and dozens of other areas. These huge enterprises, based on the mass production and distribution of goods, located in the major urban areas. They provided employment for millions of displaced farm workers as well as newly arrived immigrants. Thus, public policy in regard to the economy helped to initiate and sustain the urban migration.

In addition, publicly built streets, sewers, and water systems, as well as publicly supported services such as police and fire protection and mass transportation, made the big cities livable. The working and living conditions were not always attractive and pleasant in America's growing cities of the nineteenth and early twentieth centuries, but public policy in regard to basic services made them viable.

From Urban to Suburban

No sooner had the nation experienced a massive migration to urban centers than a new migration began—this one from the cities to the suburbs. Whereas in the mid-1800s the United States was a rural nation and by the turn of the century it was well on its way to becoming an industrialized, urbanized nation-state, during the mid-1900s millions of American families were moving to the fringes of the large cities in a move toward **suburbanization**.

The magnitude of the move to suburbia was, and still is, staggering. The rapid growth of the cities began to slacken after World War II, giving way to the growth in suburban areas. Between 1950 and 1960, nine of the nation's ten largest cities, including Baltimore, Boston, and Chicago, lost population despite nationwide population growth. Of the ten largest cities, only Houston experienced population growth during this decade, largely as a result of extensive annexation of fringe areas.

The data in Figures 10.2 and 10.3 demonstrate the trend toward suburbia. While the national population grew by nearly 20 percent from 1950 to 1960, the suburbs (the portion of the metropolitan statistical area that is outside the central city limits) grew by more than 45 percent, and the central cities grew by just slightly over 10 percent. (A **metropolitan statistical area**, or **MSA**, includes a county with a central city whose population is at least 50,000 and the

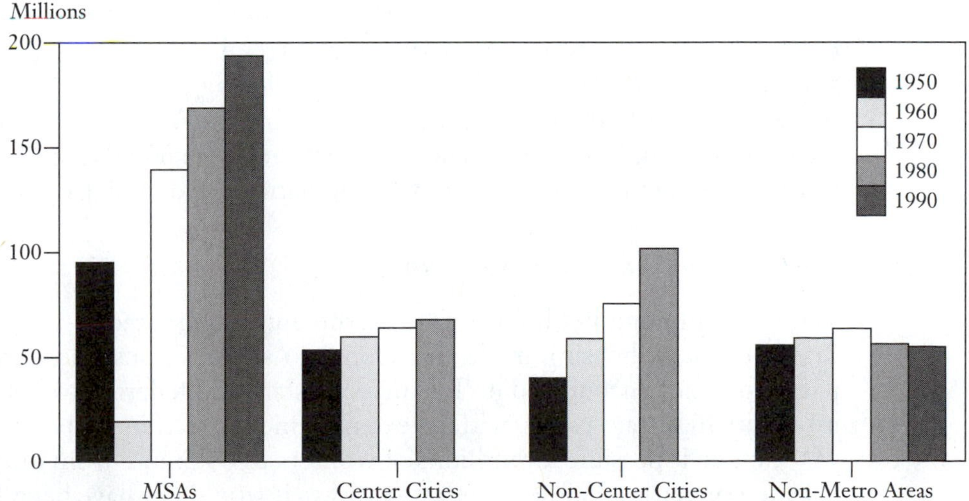

Figure 10.2 Population by Year
Source: U.S. Statistical Abstract, 1981, p. 16; 1992, p. 29.

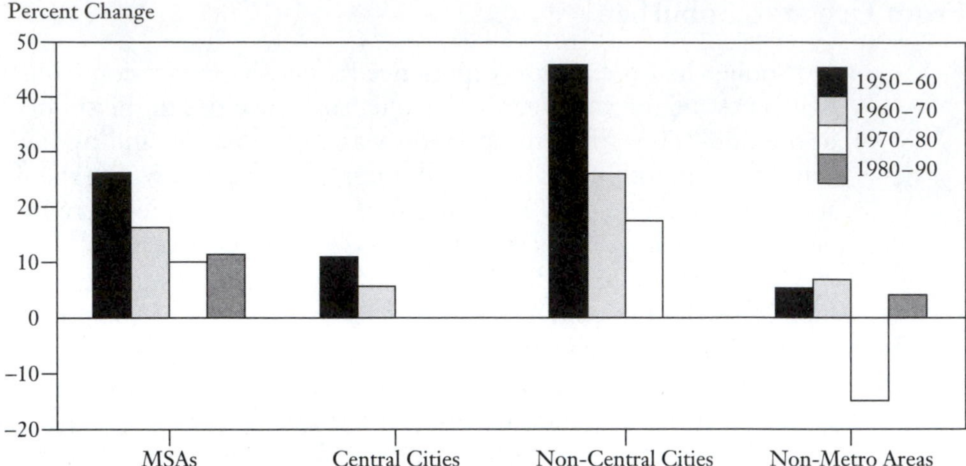

Figure 10.3 Percent Change in U.S. Population 1950–1990
Source: U.S. Statistical Abstract, 1981, p. 16; 1992, p. 29.

urbanized area of surrounding counties.) In the following decade, suburban growth slackened somewhat, though the growth ratios remained relatively stable. Looking at the thirty-year period of 1950 to 1980, the data in Figure 10.3 show that the population grew in central cities by about 14 million and in suburban areas by 60 million. In 1980 suburbanites outnumbered central city dwellers at 101.5 million and 67.9 million, respectively. More recent population estimates indicate a continuation of this trend; the suburban population is still growing and many central cities are still losing population. For example, in 1960, cities of 500,000 or more inhabitants had 24.7 percent of this country's population; in 1990 they had 19.6 percent of the population. By 1992, almost 80 percent (79.7 percent) of the population lived in metropolitan areas.

Technology Continues to Advance

While technological advances such as the automobile, radio, telephone, and mass-produced housing made the spread to suburbia possible, a number of public policies encouraged it. The massive state and federal investment in the interstate highway system, with its extensive network of metropolitan expressways, made it possible for millions of workers to commute from outlying suburbs to core cities. Without the expressways it would not have been feasible to travel twenty, thirty, or even fifty miles to work, as millions began to do.

Public Policy Continues to Broaden

Federal government support of the spread of consumer credit helped make it possible for millions of families to purchase radios and television sets for communication, automobiles for commuting, and, during the 1950s to early 1970s, single-unit suburban homes with small or no down payments. Through Veterans Administration and Federal Housing Administration insurance of home loans, millions of families were able to move into new suburban tract homes for just a few hundred dollars down. The banks were willing to make such loans largely because the federal government agreed to insure them.

The purchase of new suburban homes was made even more attractive to American families because the interest on the loans and the property taxes were deductible on federal income tax returns, as they are today. It was not unusual for middle-income families to have many thousands of dollars in tax deductions. In effect, the tax policies set in place subsidized middle-class homeowners and provided a boon to suburban developers.

Other Factors

Other factors also contributed to the rush to suburbia. While technology made it possible and government policies encouraged it, the more abundant space, the cleaner air, and the newness of suburbia, as well as the traditional American association of virtue with the small community, made it highly attractive. Many people began to associate the large city with high crime rates, dirty streets, air pollution, old housing, and undesirable types of people. In contrast, the suburb was perceived by many as having clean air, green grass, lower taxes, "nonpolitical" local government, good schools, and a more congenial living environment generally. Of course, sometimes these assessments were accurate and sometimes they were not.

Some Consequences of the Population Shifts

The consequences of the massive population shifts have been enormous. Urbanization has brought serious problems, including slum housing, a need for land use control, unemployment, sewer and water service difficulties, insufficient police and fire protection, smog, crime, and a host of others. The spread to the suburbs has created difficulties in land use, ethnic distribution, taxation, transportation, and environmental pollution.

Racial Segregation

The movement to the suburbs has contributed significantly to ethnic and economic segregation, since not everyone can afford to live in suburbia. Doing so usually involves home ownership, a down payment to purchase a home, numerous expenses associated with such housing, at least one automobile, and the ability to make steady payments on home and automobile loans. These are obstacles for a large portion of the middle-income class and virtually insurmountable problems for the lower-income class. Since a disproportionate number of ethnic minorities fall in the lower-income category, the result is continued segregation of minorities in the core cities and of middle- and upper-class whites in the suburbs.

There have been political consequences of the racial division in the nation's urban areas. As the minority populations grew between the 1960s and the 1980s, many cities came under their political control. As a result, African Americans gained a political base from which to influence the policies of the states and the national government. Demands for social programs designed to address urban issues such as poverty, education, and employment are expected to continue.

Urban Struggles

The nation's cities are increasingly in trouble. The disproportionately large numbers of city dwellers who fall into the lower categories in terms of income, education, and job status mean that, as the need for urban social services and the costs of city government increase, the capacity of the urban population to pay the bill is likely to decline relative to both costs and national wealth.

Given the heavy reliance of local government on the property tax, the cities are likely to continue to face a cost-revenue squeeze, further aggravated by recent cuts in federal funding and in some states, such as California, Colorado, and Massachusetts, by state tax and spending limits as well. Some argue that alterations in the tax base of local governments and continued state and federal assistance are needed to bail the cities out of their financial dilemma.

Economic Segregation

Suburbia also tends to segregate people of all races according to their economic status. Most tract housing developments provide homes in a given price range, with little variation. However, this sort of standardized mass development made the single-unit structure economically feasible for many in the 1950s and later.

The price of housing in any given suburban area tends to vary only slightly, though there are numerous exceptions. Such standardization, in turn, has led to the development of many communities that are homogeneous in terms of residents' income, occupation, age, and lifestyle. While this may or may not be good, its impact on ethnic and economic segregation is clear.

Fragmented Government

Suburbanization has had a tremendous impact on the pattern of government organization in metropolitan areas. In particular, the outward expansion has led to the development of new government units. In many metropolitan areas today, there are hundreds of cities, school districts, and special districts. For example, more than 1,000 units of government exist within the Chicago metropolitan area; the San Francisco–Oakland and St. Louis areas each have around 400; Denver, Los Angeles, Detroit, Kansas City, and Newark each have more than 300; and the Phoenix and Boston areas each have over 100. These examples represent the norm in most metropolitan areas.

A slight increase in the number of special districts and a dramatic decline in the number of school districts nationwide were observed between 1952 and 1992 (see Figure 10.4). The number of school districts declined due to the

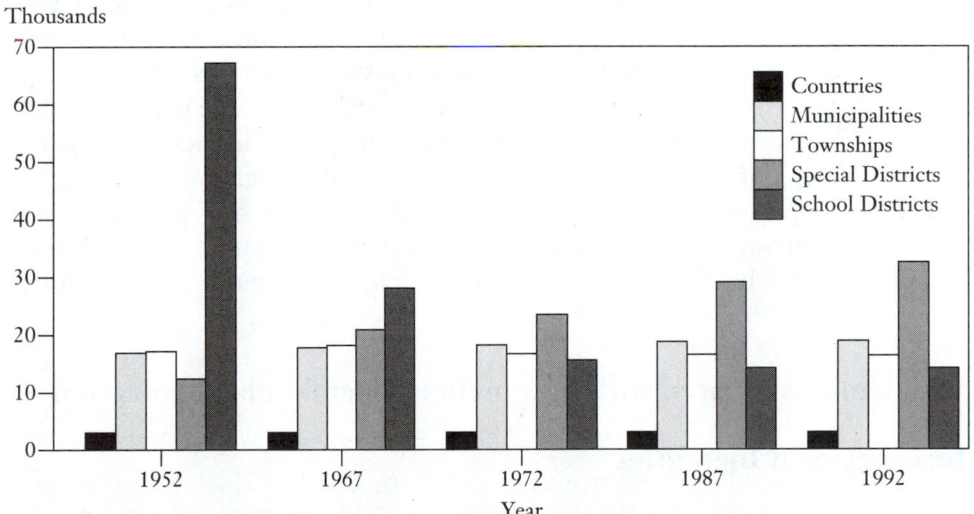

Figure 10.4 Local Governments in the United States
Source: U.S. Statistical Abstract, various years.

massive consolidations promoted by state governments, made possible by increased use of the school bus, road improvements, and more specialized and expensive instruction.

But why, as urban centers spread out into the hinterland, did new cities and special districts emerge? Why didn't the existing core cities extend their legal boundaries outward to include the developing suburbs? And why did the legal boundaries of local governments develop in ways that do not reflect social and economic realities? The answers to these questions are complex, involving the nature of state law, the behavior of central city governments, and the preferences of suburban residents. In terms of state law, for example, in most states it was easier for a new suburban area to secure a charter from the state and to **incorporate**—that is, become a new city—than it was for an existing central city to annex the new suburb (see Focus 10.1 "Avoiding Annexation in Portage Township"). As new housing developments sprang up in the suburbs, the existing core cities found it financially impossible to supply the new areas with water, sewer, police, and fire protection services. Therefore, to secure these necessary services, the residents of some suburban areas sought the status of a city, which would permit them to tax, borrow, and spend in order to provide needed services. Once a suburban area gained city status through incorporation, the core city found it virtually impossible to annex it. Most states' laws today require a majority vote at the polls in both the central city and the suburban area for **annexation** (in which a city expands by taking in more territory) or **consolidation** (in which two or more units of government are joined).

However, in many cases suburban developers or residents wanted neither annexation by an existing core city nor the formation of a new municipality—and so they created special districts instead. A **special district** is a single-function unit of local government, established under state law. Examples include fire protection districts, hospital districts, and water districts, among numerous others. Through a special district, residents of an area can create a government and empower it to tax, borrow, and spend in order to provide a service. There has been significant growth in the number of special districts in recent decades, which has further complicated the fragmented nature of government.

Problems Associated with Fragmentation and Suburbanization . . . .

Jurisdictional Inequities

The jurisdictional fragmentation created by suburbanization has led to a number of problems. For example, because the legal boundaries of metropolitan area governments do not reflect the location and distribution of various urban problems, it is increasingly difficult to consolidate solutions to such problem

Focus 10.1
AVOIDING ANNEXATION IN PORTAGE TOWNSHIP

• • •

In states that allow cities to annex unincorporated suburban areas without the consent of those affected, often suburban residents seek incorporation for the purpose of avoiding annexation.

In the early 1960s Portage Township, a suburban area located to the south of Kalamazoo, Michigan, took action to gain city status through incorporation and thereby avoid annexation by Kalamazoo. The Upjohn pharmaceutical firm, an extremely large enterprise and a major source of property tax revenues for Kalamazoo, had at that time decided to relocate from downtown Kalamazoo to an area in what was then part of Portage Township. Thus, the city of Kalamazoo acted to annex the suburb in order not to lose the tax revenues generated by Upjohn.

However, the residents of Portage objected and town officials initiated an incorporation campaign, because once Portage obtained city status, an independent majority vote at the polls in both Portage and Kalamazoo would be required for annexation. Portage successfully attained city status before Kalamazoo could annex the area. By winning at the polls, Portage maintained its independence from Kalamazoo and captured the valuable tax revenues from the relocated pharmaceutical firm.

areas as air and water pollution, mass transit, housing, and land use planning. These problems typically span entire metropolitan areas yet no single government has the jurisdiction or the resources to deal with them adequately.

In addition, considerable inequity exists among the jurisdictions in levels of taxation and quality of services. Some cities and school districts have within their legal boundaries manufacturing plants, shopping centers, or other sources of commercial tax revenue that increase the amount they can spend on public services. Other areas do not have a strong commercial tax base, so they must place a heavier tax burden on the homeowner or offer inferior public services.

Intergovernmental Conflict

Jurisdictional fragmentation often leads to intergovernmental squabbles over various issues, such as the annexation of prime-tax-producing property. It is not unusual for two or more cities or school districts to seek the annexation of a piece of land following the construction of a new plant or business. Although each government unit's interest in increasing its tax base is understandable, the wrangling that such battles precipitate can affect intergovernmental relations in other areas of potential cooperation.

In many cases jurisdictional conflicts extend to the state level. For example, suburban and rural coalitions may oppose blocs of urban representatives on issues related to transportation, taxation, natural resources, and other measures.

Planning Difficulties

It is difficult to plan effectively in jurisdictionally atomized areas. In most metropolitan areas, dozens of cities, school districts, county governments, water and sewer districts, and other units all make decisions that can affect transit, housing, or air quality, for example. Yet each government unit must respond to a slightly different constituency, each has a unique set of functions and problems, and each has its own difficulties in regard to tax resources, the demands placed on it, and state restrictions. Thus, the decision makers in each government unit tend to respond to their immediate and proximate pressures; they have neither the time nor the resources to focus on long-range, comprehensive problems.

Financial Trouble for Core Cities

Today's core cities are in great financial trouble. The massive movement to the suburbs has eroded the tax base of central cities. In general, the wealthy moved to the suburbs and those in the lower income brackets remained in urban centers. Most new commercial and industrial development also followed the path to suburbia.

While the costs to the central cities for police and fire protection, public assistance, and other public services have increased, the most valuable revenue-producing commercial properties have left. The result is severe financial crisis in most large American cities.

Other Problems

Other problems are associated with fragmented government as well. In some areas inefficiency results from the provision of similar services by multiple small governments. For example, police and fire protection services may be provided by a host of amateur departments.

Neil Pierce, an astute scholar of urban America, sums up the problems of fragmented government in this way:

> Americans are finding they have more and more governments, special authorities and agencies in their hair, but they are getting less and less governance that ties the problems together, sets priorities and comes up with coherent solutions on the level that counts—the region, our true, new city.[3]

Benefits of Suburbanization

There are many obvious benefits to the suburban phenomenon. It has provided comfortable housing, good schools, and a pleasant lifestyle for millions of American families. Small local governments often provide citizens with greater access to their public officials. Jobs for millions of workers are provided by the housing and automobile industries.

However, the proliferation of governments in the suburbs continues to be the object of widespread criticism. Not surprisingly, there have been numerous proposals for jurisdictional reform, some of them extreme and others more modest.

Extreme Proposals for Reform

Consolidation

Efforts at substantial reform, though psychologically appealing to some, have been unappealing to most and largely unsuccessful. These efforts have involved attempts to reduce the number of metropolitan area governments by consolidation of county government and several cities into a single government unit. However, like city limits, county boundaries seldom encompass entire metropolitan areas, and even consolidation fails to include an entire socioeconomic region within one jurisdiction. Still, counties typically cover sizable portions of metropolitan areas; some argue that city–county consolidation would thus reduce jurisdictional atomization. (See Focus 10.2 "Abolish the Suburbs?")

City–county consolidation has proven ineffective as a means of metropolitan reform in most cases. There were local governmental mergers in New York, New Orleans, Boston, and Philadelphia in the 1800s, but these were accomplished by state legislatures. In the twentieth century, successful mergers included Baton Rouge, Louisiana; Nashville, Tennessee; and Jacksonville, Florida. But the failures far outnumber the successes. Since 1950 consolidation attempts have been frustrated in Newport News and Richmond, Virginia; Knoxville, Memphis, and Chattanooga, Tennessee; Macon and Columbus, Georgia; Albuquerque, New Mexico; Durham, North Carolina; St. Louis,

Focus 10.2
ABOLISH THE SUBURBS?
• • •

Given the serious nature of the urban crisis, urbanist David Rusk, ex-mayor of Albuquerque, has proposed an extreme and potentially revolutionary solution—"abolish" the suburbs.

According to Rusk, the basic economic unit of the country is the metropolitan area, including both center city and suburbs. Allowing the suburbs to exist as separate economic units, he argues, denies the center cities the ability to grow and change—to become "elastic." Further, he sees this as the basic problem underlying today's declining center cities and growing suburbs. Rusk's strategy is aimed at bringing suburbs and the center city together as one economic unit, giving the latter some "elasticity." In addition, to overcome the political obstacles, he advises providing some sort of tax incentive to suburbanites. Rusk argues that his plan is a potential solution to the urban crisis.

Source: Reported in Mickey Kaus, "City Limits," *New Republic* (3 May 1993): 6.

Missouri; and Tampa, Florida. Even in Miami and Nashville defeat predated their later successes at city–county consolidation.[4]

A more recent, albeit partial, consolidation involved Indiana's Marion County and the city of Indianapolis; it is referred to as "unigov." But this alteration was put into place by the Indiana state legislature, with no local votes taken on the question. In the Miami area, the structure of Dade County was modernized through the use of a council–manager form of government, and the county's powers were expanded. The existing municipalities, however, remained intact.

The Metropolitan Federation

Another extreme approach to reform involves the formation of a metropolitan federation, though it too has been largely unsuccessful. The **metropolitan federation** involves the division of functions between government units. Although proposed for a number of U.S. cities, it has never secured adoption. Proposals for the creation of a metropolitan federation in the Boston area failed to gain state legislative approval in 1896 and 1931. Federation proposals were either discussed or formally proposed but never adopted for the areas in and around Oakland and San Francisco, California; Pittsburgh, Pennsylvania; Miami, Florida; and St. Louis, Missouri. The best-known example of an operating metropolitan federation is Toronto, Canada.

Most U.S. states today have laws that permit some form of local consolidation, cooperation, or modernization. These statutes are intended to allow the voters a choice of forming regional service authorities or modernizing county government, thereby better equipping local government to address modern urban-area problems and service needs. However, only in rare instances are such reforms actually instituted. Clearly, both the power of the existing arrangements and the broad public resistance to change are strong.

Modest Proposals for Reform

Unlike the generally unsuccessful efforts at consolidation and metropolitan federation reform, which aim to alter substantially the shape of government in metropolitan America, there have been some successful reforms of a more modest, though slowly developing, nature. These include municipal annexations, intergovernmental service agreements, such as the Lakewood Plan, and metropolitan councils of government.

Annexation

Although core city annexation of surrounding suburbs does not entirely eliminate fragmentation from metropolitan-area government, it can in some instances provide an alternative to the creation of even more cities or special districts. When a city annexes land, it redraws its boundaries to include the new area. But annexation is not often easy, legally or politically. As noted earlier in the chapter, many states require approval of annexation by a majority of the voters in both the annexing city and the area to be annexed. Other states give the option of initiating the annexation process to the people in the affected outlying area. However, because many U.S. cities are already surrounded by other cities, there are only limited opportunities for annexation.

A few states provide easier paths to annexation. In some states, it may be accomplished without any action by residents of the city or the affected outlying area. For example, in Virginia annexation is done by an annexation court, and in Texas some city councils are empowered to annex territory. In addition, some states' legislation prohibits new incorporation within a certain distance from an existing city, and other laws give existing cities some measure of control over planning and zoning just outside their boundaries (extraterritorial jurisdiction). In Arizona, no new cities may be formed within six miles of a city with over 5,000 people.

As observed earlier in this chapter, one criticism of the fragmented organization of government in metropolitan America is the lack of efficiency in the provision of municipal services. Some critics contend that it would be less expensive and more efficient for public services, such as police and fire protection and sewer and water service, to be provided by fewer, but larger, government units. However, others point out that bigger governments may not necessarily lead to lower unit costs. In addition, the optimal size for all government units may not be the same because an efficiently sized government for police protection may be far too small for an efficient water system.

Intergovernmental Service Agreements

The problem of government unit size and, in part, the political problems associated with the extreme reform proposals are mitigated by the more modest approach involving **intergovernmental service agreements**—contractual arrangements made between governments for the performance of public services. One government may sell its water or sewer services to another government. A city may purchase space at a county landfill or beds in a county jail. A city and a fire protection district may enter into a legal arrangement involving shared assistance. The approach permits governments to provide services to areas of various sizes. The area encompassed by a fire protection agreement, for example, may be either larger or smaller than an intergovernmental water supply area.

Furthermore, intergovernmental service agreements do not entail extensive alteration of the status quo. They can be formed without threatening government employees' jobs, without eliminating some mayors' and council members' governments, and without long, abrasive election campaigns. However, such service agreements can legally complicate intergovernmental arrangements and make government more difficult for the citizen to understand and follow. In addition, they can make one government overly dependent on another, a situation that public officials tend not to favor.

The Lakewood Plan

The most extensive network of intergovernmental contractual arrangements is the so-called **Lakewood plan**, used in southern California to provide a variety of public services effectively and efficiently to more than seventy participating cities. The scheme involves the provision by Los Angeles County of over forty different types of public services, including animal control, building inspection, fire protection, law enforcement, planning and zoning, street construction and maintenance, tax assessment and collection, and tree trimming. The participating cities can contract with the county for any package of services they desire.

Acquiring its name from the city of Lakewood, which in 1954 was the first city to enter into such an agreement with Los Angeles County, the Lakewood plan now involves contracts with most cities in the county for some or all of the available services. The participating cities benefit from their ability to maintain both their existence and a high level of service without massive capital investments in water, sewer, and other public services.

Although the Lakewood plan represents the most extensive example of intergovernmental service arrangements, such schemes are common throughout the nation. Some 63 percent of all U.S. cities have some type of service agreement with another unit of government, and well over 10 percent of those cities receive packages of services.

In sum, it is likely that extreme reform proposals aimed at dramatically restructuring government in metropolitan America will to continue to fail. The more moderate approach involving intergovernmental service agreements is a more politically feasible route to reform.

Metropolitan Councils of Government

Another modest reform proposal focuses on **metropolitan councils of government (COGs)**. These councils are not government units and, technically, do not rearrange the metropolitan government pattern. Further, they are not creatures of the state and they do not provide municipal-type functions (such as police and fire protection). Rather, COGs are composed of representatives from the local governments in an area and provide a forum for communication among governments and public officials. In addition, COG staffs study and report on areawide problems.

Before 1983, metropolitan councils of government were also involved in what was called the A-95 review process. Area governments reviewed and commented on applications for federal grants by local governments. The initial purpose of the A-95 process was to promote coordination, and to this end President Lyndon Johnson instructed the Office of Management and Budget (OMB) in 1965 to coordinate federal grant programs relating to metropolitan areas. OMB subsequently issued a series of circulars, including circular A-95, which required local government applicants for federal grants to have their proposals reviewed by areawide metropolitan-planning bodies in order to improve planning and program coordination among local governments. When A-95 was issued, many metropolitan areas had no such areawide planning bodies, so they moved quickly to create councils of government. Some observers in Washington, D.C., in the states, and in the localities viewed the emergence of COGs as a possible first step toward eventual full consolidation of services in metropolitan areas. But this has not happened. COGs remain researching, coordinating, and planning bodies. They are not units of government, nor are they empowered by the states to provide government functions or to impose taxes.

The Politics of Metropolitan Reform

Efforts to reform metropolitan areas by reducing the number of government units have met with very limited success. Why do reform efforts aimed at consolidation consistently fail? Why do most voters favor the existing fragmented metropolis? There are two basic answers to these questions. First, suburbanites strongly value their local autonomy and independence. Second, proponents of metropolitan reform typically have not achieved the level of political organization required to win elections.

Reform Sounds Rational

Proponents of metropolitan consolidation schemes have tried to sell their plans through all sorts of logical and rational arguments. Consolidation, they point out, increases efficiency and economy in government. Why have twenty police departments in a metropolitan area when one can do a better job? Why have ten water and sewer systems instead of one? Why elect fifteen mayors and city councils when one could do the job? Why, in other words, pay to have a host of governments all using public funds to pay salaries to hundreds of semiskilled public servants? Consolidation, they contend, could bring both tax savings and better-qualified firefighters, police, planners, and other public employees.

The promises of improved services, lower taxes, more professional public officials, and a greater capacity to wrestle with modern public problems through consolidation have not convinced the average voter that the existing government structure should be replaced by a dramatically different one. Thus metropolitan reform has been repeatedly defeated at the polls.

People Want a Choice

People want to be able to select from among a variety of lifestyles and service and tax levels. In the suburbs, they can purchase a home in a neighborhood with tax levels, service levels, school services, and housing costs that suit their needs or budget. They can have an impact on the quality of education, on planning and zoning, and on police and fire protection. They can enjoy relatively easy access to local public officials. They have worked to create and maintain these and other features of suburban life that they value highly.

While proponents of reform measure the costs and benefits against a model of efficiency and economy, opponents measure the costs and benefits against a model of autonomy and choice. Thus, many voters are unwilling to merge their communities with the larger metropolis.

The Law Favors the Status Quo

Metropolitan reform efforts also have not been successful because many consolidation plans require a majority vote at the polls in both the core city and the outlying jurisdictions. Winning a majority vote in a consolidation election, as in any other election, is largely a matter of effective political organization, a task that proponents have generally not done well. Typically, the reform movements are supported by academics, businesspeople, and planners impressed by the neatness and order that the new schemes promise. Their campaign tactics typically involve an appeal to the logic of the voter through mass-media advertising. Only rarely have the reform movements employed the existing party structure or attempted to create new ones that might better penetrate the grass roots.

Political parties in both the central cities and the suburbs, ethnic minorities in the core cities, and suburbanites all resist attempts at reorganization for fear of losing their political power relative to other groups. Suburban Republicans and central city Democrats may both fear a potential dilution of their power. Similarly, core city minorities and suburban whites may resist mergers for fear of losing control of their locality to the other group. The considerable uncertainty associated with dramatic reform creates widespread resistance.

Supporters versus Opponents

Social scientists have attempted to identify the factors associated with citizen support for or opposition to structural reform of metropolitan political arrangements. In general, some found that people who are dissatisfied with the present level of public services, who are not suspicious of the core city, and who have a relatively high level of formal education are apt to be more supportive of reform than those with the reverse characteristics.

In addition, some social scientists contend that reform is less likely to occur in older areas, presumably because residents have long enjoyed their independence. Furthermore, cities employing the city–manager system were found to engage in annexation more often than other cities. When state law makes it less difficult to alter the status quo, reform is more often successful. Moreover, the least drastic reform proposals are most likely to gain passage. Finally, a state's level of political party competition appears to have little or no effect on the reorganizational propensities of people at the local level.[5]

The Downside of the Metropolitan Scheme

Some observers do not support the creation of large metropolitanwide governments, arguing in favor of various other arrangements instead. Vincent Ostrom, Charles M. Tiebout, and Robert Warren suggest that there are several criteria by which one should measure the effectiveness of a metropolitan organizational scheme.[6] They argue that an all-encompassing central government may not always be the best choice. Their criteria include "packageability" or control (that is, whether the boundaries are broad enough to cover problem areas), efficiency, political representation (that is, appropriate political interests should not be denied a role in the decision making), and local autonomy or self-determination. They also point out that a very large jurisdiction—or one of any size for that matter—is not necessarily appropriate for meeting all these criteria. For example, a government package for the elimination of air pollution may differ in terms of size than those needed for health and public assistance services. Thus, metropolitan government, like the polycentric arrangement (discussed later in this section), can do some things but not all things well.

Robert Stein suggests that nearly half of the entire service mix provided by local governments is "planned, financed, produced, or delivered with the active participation of an entity or entities other than the municipal government."[7] Thus, there is currently a lot of variation in what cities do.

A 1970 publication from the Committee for Economic Development suggests that neither a very small nor a very large jurisdiction is most appropriate.[8] The proliferation of small units—the so-called **polycentric system**—is plagued by the obvious shortcoming of not being able to get a handle on issues that affect entire metropolitan areas (for example, air pollution and transit). But the larger units have two critical shortcomings of their own. First, in most cases, they simply are not publicly acceptable. Second, they may fail to provide representation for subcommunities within the metropolitan area (such as urban minorities seeking more control over the institutions that affect them). The committee proposes multilevel government with different functions performed at different levels.

Communities Want Local Control

In an interesting essay published in 1971, Francis Piven and Richard Cloward argue that metropolitan-area governments became consolidated to the detriment of urban African-American residents.[9] They contend that consolidation occurred as a result of the federal requirement that areawide planning and coordination precede receipt of federal grant monies. What could not be done at the polls, they argue, was done administratively as a result of federal intervention.

The Department of Housing and Urban Development, through such programs as the Model Cities and Metropolitan Development Act of 1967, forced the creation of metropolitan areawide planning and coordinating agencies. The federal government made it difficult or impossible for local governments to obtain federal grant funds. The result was that a new cadre of bureaucratic planners, in regional and federal agencies, became politically influential. According to Piven and Cloward, the implications were as follows:

> Black populations are now building to electoral majorities in the larger American cities, but the promise of urban political power will be frustrated, for the new administrative government will be responsive to a majority coalition of suburban and inner-city whites. As blacks rise to power in the city, the city will lose power to the metropolis.[10]

More recently, African-American citizens in a sizable sector of Boston proposed to secede from the city and take control of their own affairs by creating the separate city of Mandela. Among their concerns were the costs of converting neighborhood housing to upscale residences for well-to-do outsiders and the impact on housing availability. On November 2, 1993, in another bid for independence from a metropolitan government, the citizens of the borough of Staten Island voted overwhelmingly in favor of seceding from New York City.

A Clash of Values

Thus, some reformers want to consolidate and centralize metropolitan America, whereas others want to decentralize it further. On the one hand, extensive fragmentation of authority creates some loss of efficiency and renders systematic attack on such problems as transportation, housing, and air pollution difficult or impossible. On the other hand, authorities and power structures in large governments are often out of touch with and insensitive to the needs of neighborhoods. The only way to centralize and decentralize at the same time is through a system of federalism. But even federal systems present problems, such as deciding the authority of the central versus regional units and providing for the resolution of jurisdictional disputes.

Future Trends

Radical Reform Is Unlikely

What are the prospects for metropolitan restructuring in the future? As far as formal redrawing of city, county, and special district lines is concerned, the prospects are slim. The law as it exists today in many states requires an independent majority vote in each incorporated jurisdiction involved in an annexation or consolidation effort, and voters are not likely to change drastically their past voting behaviors. Given the increasing deterioration of U.S. cities and the ongoing migration of whites to the suburbs, the opposition to metropolitan reorganization may grow even stronger. Similarly, the existing cities are not likely to allow secession by unhappy neighborhoods.

In addition, state legislatures are not likely to modify state law in ways that would make reorganization easier to accomplish. The Supreme Court reapportionment decisions of the 1960s, coupled with over thrity years of suburbanization, have thrown enormous political strength in state legislatures to representatives in suburban areas. Suburban representatives have an obligation to represent their constituents' preferences, so they will remain disinclined to make reorganization easier through altering state law.

If any changes in the nature of metropolitan decision making are forthcoming in the future, they are likely to be in the form of coordination and cooperation among existing units of government. COGs may continue to promote communication and some coordination of grant applications. Continued growth in the use of intergovernmental service agreements can be expected, because they provide some increased efficiency without major or politically difficult changes to the status quo. Sweeping reform measures such as consolidation are highly unlikely, as the faltering attempt to consolidate San Antonio–Bexar County, Texas demonstrated in late 1996.

Urban Villages

Some observers claim that metropolitan America is experiencing yet another shift in settlement patterns, one that will only aggravate the problems created by the earlier shifts from urban to suburban areas. This movement involves the development of **urban villages**—growing "satellite" cities located on the fringes of the core cities.[11] Urban villages are larger, more complex, and more self-sufficient than traditional suburbs. They may begin with the development of a major regional shopping mall, which is then followed by other retail and service enterprises, office complexes, high-rises, and housing. New airports can spark the development of urban villages. New expressways that loop the core cities can stimulate the development of such satellite communities. Many grow very large and become homes to insurance or financial institutions. Citizens can work, eat, shop, and play without traveling to the older core city.

Urban villages have emerged throughout the nation—in southern California, on the East Coast, in the Atlanta area, and elsewhere. Denver may have one in the making. To the south of Denver is a large complex of hotels, office buildings, and service industries called the Denver Tech Center. It even sports its own skyline. To the north, Denver is undertaking the construction of a huge new international airport. A semi-independent public entity is constructing a toll road that will loop Denver to the east, connecting the developments of the south and the north. Although the core city of Denver will likely remain an important part of the economic and political system, in many ways the complexes to the north and the south will themselves become cities.

It is interesting to note that decades ago upper- and middle-class citizens often sought to live some distance from the sites of major economic activity. Those who could afford to do so moved away from factories, away from markets, away from downtown, to cleaner, newer, and more spacious suburban surroundings. The old housing left behind became occupied by the poor and ethnic minorities. In the newer urban villages, however, a different trend is emerging. Workplaces are now offices, small businesses, and clean and light industries. The structures are new and built in less dense, or more spacious patterns. Parking is available; landscaping is generous. Upscale housing is built in rather close proximity. And it is now the lower-class service personnel, rather than well-to-do businesspeople, who must commute some distance to work. Many executives who formerly drove to downtown from the suburbs now live close to work in the urban village, whereas lower-status workers now struggle to commute to work from the older and somewhat distant core city.

The emergence of these **satellite cities** (urban fringe areas that have developed into centers of significant economic and/or residential activity) has also altered expressway traffic patterns. Increasingly, as business and light industry locate outside the urban core, commuting is from one suburb or fringe city to another. No longer is all the traffic going in the same direction, either into or out of the city.

These developments have benefits and drawbacks. For some, the shift means the pleasure of living near one's place of work and in relatively new and clean surroundings. Yet the trend is also contributing to American urban blight. Most new jobs—some say up to 90 percent—are located in urban villages, as is most new housing and as are many recreational and cultural opportunities.

A Divided Nation?

While cities offer a wealth of diversity and opportunity, they are also beset by many problems. Our core cities have increasingly high concentrations of the poor, the unemployed, the marginally skilled and educated, and individuals and families lacking the means to secure and then travel to well-paying jobs. Large numbers of city dwellers are African Americans or Hispanics or single mothers. The fancy car, the three-piece suit, the nice house, and the well-paying job characterize many residents of urban villages, whereas poverty, crime, and gangs characterize life in many core cities. Increasingly, the same problems are being faced in the older suburbs by both whites and minorities.

The political dilemma of core city leaders multiplies as they face problems related to housing, social services, and law and order with an inadequate tax base. The urban village continues to divide Americans along such lines as color, opportunity, wealth, and location. If it is true, as some contend, that the redistribution of wealth and opportunity is essential to the long-term viability of American society, then the new urban village may be taking the nation in the wrong direction.

Summary

American metropolitan areas are still growing. Public policy and technological change have supported the growth of urban areas into metropolitan areas and continue to do so. Among the consequences of this expansion are jurisdictional problems and inequities, intergovernmental conflicts, planning difficulties, and in many cases a residual core city in severe fiscal distress. However, metropolitan growth offers opportunities as well. New "urban villages" and other kinds of fringe development offer metropolitan residents a variety of settings in which to live and work. There is little doubt that the immediate future of America is a sprawling metropolitan one.

Policy Perspective

Americans live in a metropolitan society but want local control. Americans also want efficiency in their local governments. In metropolitan America, this clash of values has turned into a clash of competing policy options. At the heart of the issue is a normative question—What is the best governmental structure in metropolitan areas today? Teaford argues that the legacy of the 1980s was a perpetuation of the governmental balance of post-suburban American.[12] This assessment seems to be correct. There is little evidence that residents of metropolitan areas want to abandon their "edge cities" to the sprawl of commercial development. Instead, the evidence seems to be quite overwhelming that the mix of governments in the metropolitan areas is fairly satisfying to most residents, if not to the urban "purists." Some years ago, Tiebout made the classic argument in which he characterized metropolitan governance as a competitive market for residents.[13] People can, in effect, vote with their feet.

Policy change in metropolitan areas is most likely to come incrementally—as is the case with much of American public policy making. The creation of area-specific as well as service specific governments is the form of metropolitan governance that has the greatest likelihood of adoption in most of America's metropolitan areas. Another is that more metropolitan services will be privatized or "contracted out." The days of the mammoth, large scale multipurpose governmental entity apparently have passed from the scene. Given this scenario, what are the most likely consequences for the metropolitan areas? One is that there probably will not be huge cost saving from these reform activities. The research of Robert Stein[14] suggests this. Another is that creation of a metropolitan identity is not likely. Television news might talk about the "Southland" when referring to southern California, or persons in the Midwest talk about "Chicagoland" but residents will continue to think of themselves as residents of Ponoma or DuPage. It seems that there is a requirement of some more deeply felt attachment to create a sense of identity. The lack of that sense of identity causes problems for the creation of a metropolitan-areawide multipurpose government.

So, for the foreseeable future, the policy mix of governments in metropolitan America will probably be much as it is today—uneven, a bit chaotic, but reasonably satisfying to most of the residents. This is not to say that there will not be proposals for metropolitan reform. In January 1997, a consolidation of San Antonio–Bexar County, Texas was actively discussed. However, it is unlikely that such large-scale reform will be the norm.

KEY TERMS

urbanization
factory-based economy
suburbanization
metropolitan statistical area (MSA)
incorporation
annexation
consolidation
special district

metropolitan federation
intergovernmental service agreements
Lakewood plan
metropolitan council of government (COG)
polycentric system
urban village
satellite city

ADDITIONAL READING

Bish, Robert L., and Vincent Ostrom. *Understanding Urban Government.* Washington, D.C.: American Enterprise Institute, 1979.

Kantor, Paul. *The Dependent City: The Changing Political Economy of Urban America.* Glenview, Ill.: Scott, Foresman, 1983.

Lyons, W. E., David Lowery, and Ruth Hoogland DeHoog. *The Politics of Dissatisfaction: Citizens, Services and Urban Institutions.* Armonk, N.Y.: M. E. Sharpe, 1992.

Peterson, Paul. *City Limits.* Chicago: University of Chicago Press, 1980.

Walker, David B. "Snow White and the 17 Dwarfs: From Metro Cooperation to Governance." *National Civic Review* (Jan.–Feb. 1987): 14–28.

Stein, Robert M. *Urban Alternatives: Public and Private Markets in the Provision of Local Services.* Pittsburgh: University of Pittsburgh Press, 1990.

Teaford, Jon C. *Post-Suburbia: Government and Politics in the Edge Cities.* Baltimore: Johns Hopkins University Press, 1997.

NOTES

1. U.S. Bureau of the Census, *Statistical Abstract of the United States, 1995* (Washington, D.C.: GPO, 1995); and *Agricultural Statistics* (Washington, D.C.: GPO, 1991).
2. Ibid.; and Drew A. Dolan, "Local Government Fragmentation: Does It Drive Up the Cost of Government?" *Urban Affairs Quarterly* (Sept. 1990): 28–45.
3. Neil Pierce, "Fragmentation Is the Bane of U.S. Cities," *Denver Post*, 10 Dec. 1989.
4. John C. Bollens and Henry J. Schmandt, *The Metropolis*, 2d ed. (New York: Harper & Row, 1970), chs. 11–12.
5. "Towns Have Written the Book on Sharing," *Governing* (June 1990): 18. See also Vincent L. Marando and Carl Whitley, "City-County Consolidation: An Overview of Voter Response," *Urban Affairs Quarterly* 8: 181–203; John C. Bollens et al., *Exploring the Metropolitan Community* (Berkeley: University of California Press, 1961).
6. Vincent Ostrom, Charles M. Tiebout, and Robert Warren, "The Organization of Government in Metropolitan Areas: A Theoretical Inquiry," *American Political Science Review* (Dec. 1961): 831–42.
7. Robert M. Stein, *Urban Alternatives: Public and Private Markets in the Provision of Local Services* (Pittsburgh: University of Pittsburgh Press, 1990), p. 54.
8. Committee for Economic Development, *Reshaping Government in Metropolitan Areas* (New York: CED, 1970).
9. Francis Fox Piven and Richard A. Cloward, "Black Control of Cities," in *Black Politics*, ed. E. S. Greenberg, N. Milner, and David J. Olson (New York: Holt, Rinehart and Winston, 1971), pp. 118–30.
10. Ibid., p. 119.
11. Christopher B. Leinberger and Charles Lockwood, "How Business Is Reshaping America," *The Atlantic* (Oct. 1986): 43–52.

12. Jon C. Teaford, *Post-Suburbia: Government and Politics in the Edge Cities* (Baltimore: Johns Hopkins University Press, 1997) p. 205.
13. Charles M. Tiebout, "A Pure Theory of Local Expenditures," *Journal of Political Economy* 65: 416–24.
14. Robert M. Stein, *Urban Alternatives: Public and Private Markets in the Provision of Local Services* (Pittsburgh: University of Pittsburgh Press, 1990).

CHAPTER 11

• • •

Local Governments

• • •

City Hall, Los Alamos, New Mexico. This modern city hall symbolizes the growth of cities in the so-called Sun Belt. It is at the military base outside Los Alamos that the first atomic bomb was constructed. *(Peter Menzel/Stock, Boston)*

• • • **CHARACTERISTICS OF CITY GOVERNMENT**

Creatures of the State
Controlled by the State
Home Rule
Incorporation
The Functions of City Government

• • • **THE ORGANIZATION OF CITY GOVERNMENT**

The Strong Mayor–Council System
The Weak Mayor–Council System

Focus 11.1: A CONSERVATIVE BIG CITY MAYOR?

The Commission Plan
The Council–Manager System

• • • **THE DISTRIBUTION OF STRUCTURAL FORMS OF CITY GOVERNMENT**

• • • **POLITICAL INFLUENCE AND CITY GOVERNMENT STRUCTURE**

Budget Control and Personnel Appointments
Control of Information and the Agenda
Strong versus Weak Mayors
Commissioners and City Managers

• • • **CITY GOVERNMENTS DIFFER IN MANY WAYS**

Structural Scheme Variations
Differences in Public Policy and Opinion
Variations in Political Behavior
Some Generalizations

• • • **COUNTIES, SCHOOLS, AND SPECIAL DISTRICTS**

County Government
School Districts

Focus 11.2: COUNTY REFORM

Focus 11.3: POLITICS IN THE NEW YORK CITY SCHOOLS

Focus 11.4: EDUCATION AND TAXES: THE MICHIGAN MODEL

Special Districts

• • • SUMMARY

• • • POLICY PERSPECTIVE: EDUCATIONAL REFORM
School Choice
Charter Schools

As noted in earlier chapters, the relationship of local governments to the states is quite unlike that which exists between the states and the national government. The state–national relationship is federal in nature; each level of government derives its authority from a source legally superior to both—the U.S. Constitution. Although the states and the national government perform a number of overlapping functions, the states and the national government exist and operate in parallel fashion.

A different relationship exists between local governments and the states. All units of local government, be they cities, counties, school districts, or special districts of some sort, are legally inferior to the state government. They are created by the state through legislative statutes or constitutional provision, they derive authority from the state, the state imposes duties and limitations on the local units, and the state may, if it so chooses, legally abolish local governments. In short, there is no such thing as an inherent right to local self-rule.

Characteristics of City Government

Cities are actually **municipal corporations**—they exist because they possess a charter from the state. Through statutes or constitutional provisions, states classify cities according to size. They may be classified as having one million or more residents, 100,000 to 500,000, or 2,500 to 100,000. In addition, the state may permit the creation of **towns**, that is, municipalities with fewer than 2,500 residents. When a city falls into one of these categories and operates with the charter authorized by the state for that size city, it is termed a **general law city**. These cities operate under the same charter, which, by a general act of the legislature, is authorized for any city that falls into that population classification.

Creatures of the State

For each class of city, the state constitution and statutes indicate, in considerable detail, the government structure, the electoral system, and the powers, duties, and limitations of the cities. Cities in the largest population categories may be required to employ a strong mayor form of government, have a city council of nine members, elect both the council and mayor for four-year terms, and employ a partisan ballot when electing council members from wards or districts. Cities in the next class size may be given an option of either a council–manager form of government or a weak mayor form of government. They may be required to use a seven-member council, to elect council members to two-year terms of office, and to employ at-large and nonpartisan elections. Cities in the smallest class size may be required to do the same.

State constitutions and statutes also prescribe local government powers, duties, and limits, usually in great detail. As mentioned earlier, the statutes may specify the form of government, the length of terms for council members and the mayor, and the time of year when elections can be held. In some cases, even the salaries of such local officials as the fire and police chiefs are specified. The statutes may tell the cities what type of taxes they may levy and at what level. For example, for cities in the smallest population class, the state may permit a property tax up to a certain millage level and a sales tax up to a certain percentage, but it may bar the imposition of an income tax. A millage rate is a tax rate expressed in terms of tax dollars assessed per $1,000 of the assessed value of real property. For example, homeowners might be assessed a tax of $1 for every $1,000 their property is worth.

Controlled by the State

State specifications of local government powers and duties can be extremely detailed. The statutory list of duties and functions for Colorado's cities and towns addresses numerous issues—water facilities, fences and walls, buildings and fire escapes, fire hazards, steam boilers, packing houses, breweries, stables, foundries, mills, ditches, houses of vice, fights and misconduct, riots and disturbances, vagrants and prostitutes, children's play (involving kites, balls, hoops, and other amusements), bail bonds, railroads, peddlers, games, sale of bread, weights and measures, secondhand stores, streets and sewers, utilities, parking facilities, and a host of other minor details. This sort of detail reduces the operational flexibility of local governments and forces the legislatures to focus often on altering state statutes that relate to local government.

Although the powers and duties of local governments are spelled out in great detail by the states, historically the courts have chosen to interpret them conservatively. Whereas the U.S. Supreme Court typically has interpreted the constitutional powers of the nation rather broadly, state courts have held that cities and other units of local government have only those powers that are clearly given to them in state constitutions and statutes. When some question about the intent of the law emerges and when the courts could conceivably interpret the power of local governments liberally, they have consistently chosen not to do so. This behavior not only keeps tight limits on the activities of local governments, but it is also a powerful and symbolic illustration of the legal inferiority of local governments vis-à-vis the states. The 1872 ruling by Supreme Court Judge John F. Dillon is often cited as illustrative of the legally inferior position of local governments:

> It is the general and undisputed proposition of law that a municipal corporation possesses, and can exercise, the following powers, and no others; First, those granted in express words; second, those necessary or fairly implied in, or incident to, the powers expressly granted; third, those essential to the declared objects and purposes of the corporation—not simply convenient, but indispensable.[1]

Dillon's rule (discussed more fully in Chapter 2) demonstrates that local governments have only those powers expressly granted to them.

Home Rule

States have attempted to loosen the legal shackles that constrain local governments by instituting constitutional or statutory home rule, especially for the largest cities. Simply stated, **home-rule provisions** are intended to allow local governments some freedom to choose the form of government and range of functions they will perform, without interference from the legislature.

However, generally state legislatures and state courts have been reluctant to grant much legal freedom to local governments, even to those with home-rule status. Although a majority of the largest cities in the United States operate with home-rule charters, the use of such charters is not widespread in medium- and small-sized cities.

Incorporation

Just as state law prescribes the powers, duties, and government form of cities, it also specifies the process by which communities can incorporate, obtain a state charter, and thus become a city.

The incorporation process typically goes like this: The residents of an area discover that their need for such services as sewers, water, and police protection cannot be met adequately by the county government. Given their powers, limitations, and government structure, counties usually cannot provide the services that a city can. Thus, in line with the dictates of state law, the residents must secure a given number of signatures on a petition asking for an election to decide whether a majority of those in the community wants to form a city. If the issue passes, a second election is held to elect members to a charter commission, which then draws up a **charter**—or basic law—for the city. The charter is subject to the confining requirements of state law. (In actual practice, the charter commission election may be held concurrently with the initial election.) Once a charter acceptable to the state is written, the residents vote on it. If it is adopted, as it almost always is, elections are then held to choose city officials.

The Functions of City Government

Cities are multifunctional government units established to provide a wide variety of essential services in areas of high population concentrations. The primary municipal functions are designed to ensure public safety and health. Police and fire departments provide for public safety, and water and sewer systems promote public health. Other primary municipal services include street and park maintenance and recreation. Some cities also operate hospitals and schools or administer some aspect of the social service system. Clearly, for the most part, cities provide those services without which people could not live in highly concentrated fashion.

The Organization of City Government

Cities must be organized with a view to providing citizens with municipal services. While there is almost infinite variety in the shape of city governments nationwide, four major forms exist—the strong mayor–council system, the weak mayor–council system, the commission plan, and the council–manager system.

The Strong Mayor–Council System

The **strong mayor–council system**, common in the largest cities, includes a popularly elected mayor and a unicameral city council. Elections are usually partisan, with each of the two major parties running candidates for mayor and council. Council members typically represent wards or districts. The mayor is a full-time politician. Like governors and the president, mayors are highly visible. They have a policy platform and program that they attempt to put into effect; they are the chief administrative officer in that they are situated at the top of the city bureaucracy and are able to hire and fire high-level administrators; they often have the power to veto council action; and they play a major role in preparing the city budget each year. Structurally, the strong mayor–council system resembles the model shown in Figure 11.1.

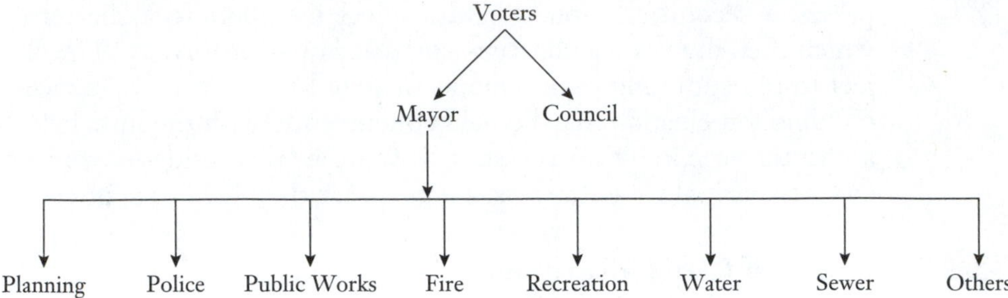

Figure 11.1 The Strong Mayor–Council System

The Weak Mayor–Council System

The **weak mayor–council system** is similar to the strong mayor scheme except that the powers of the mayor in areas of personnel, finance, and political leadership are considerably weaker. The weak mayor plan, typically found in small- and medium-sized cities, is often accompanied by nonpartisan elections. Weak mayors are seldom full-time politicians. Moreover, because the political parties are not as dominant in city politics, the weak mayor seldom receives the public attention that strong mayors enjoy. In addition, weak mayors may not possess a veto over council action; they play a minor role or no role in budget formation, they have little or no power to appoint administrative personnel; and they do not play a major role in the formation and introduction of a policy platform.

Although the weak mayor plan looks like the strong mayor plan shown in Figure 11.1, the powers of the weak mayor are considerably reduced. In addition to the structural features depicted in the figure, both strong and weak mayor cities may have one or more elective boards or commissions that oversee some city activity.

It is important to note that the weak and strong mayor forms are not pure models. Many cities contain some structural and operational features that strengthen the mayor and other features that weaken the position by forcing the mayor to share power with the council or some semi-independent boards and commissions. The extent of variety among America's cities in this respect is vast.

In mayor–council cities in the United States, the terms of the mayor and council members vary in length; 31 percent of mayors serve two-year terms, and 68 percent serve four-year terms. Council members serve two-year terms in 37 percent of these cities and four-year terms in 61 percent. The shorter council member terms are more common in the Northeast. About half of all mayors possess a veto over all council actions, while 91 percent may veto some types of council action but not others. In nearly 80 percent of all mayor–council cities, the council has between six and fifteen members.[2] (See Focus 11.1 "A Conservative Big City Mayor?")

Focus 11.1

A CONSERVATIVE BIG CITY MAYOR?

• • •

Traditionally, the largest American cities are resource centers for the Democratic party. As a consequence, most elected leaders of these cities are Democrats. Generally these Democratic mayors tend to focus on raising revenues to meet the demands of their constituencies.

Stephen Goldsmith, the recently elected mayor of Indianapolis is a Republican and convinced that a large American city can be governed from the political right. He says that the philosophy of liberal government has let the physical and social infrastructure of urban America descend into awful disrepair. When the young management specialist became mayor, the city, now twelfth largest in the country, had not had a Republican leader in seventy-five years. Goldsmith believes that the city is in a struggle with its neighbors for business as well as population. Thus, the city has to respond. Unlike some cities, he believes that his city cannot raise revenues by simply raising taxes. Thus, he has begun a program to privatize and downsize city government. More than seventy city services have been "privatized"—opened up to competition between city workers and private firms. He notes, "Sometimes private firms win, sometimes city workers win. But in every case, taxpayers get better service at lower cost thanks to 'competing out.'"

Additionally, he has fostered a plan of decentralization that returns substantial power to neighborhood groups—neighborhood empowerment or "municipal federalism." While it is yet too early to tell if neighborhood empowerment will move much beyond this early stage, Goldsmith clearly is convinced that big cities can solve many of their problems—at least in part by becoming smaller.

Sources: Rob Gurwitt, "Indianapolis and the Republican Future," *Governing* (February 1994): 24–28, and Stephen Goldsmith, "Commentary," *The McAllen Monitor*, 13 Oct. 1996, p. 5F.

The Commission Plan

The **commission plan** differs considerably from the strong and weak mayor–council forms. Under the commission plan there is no separation of powers, as the legislative and executive functions are merged. The voters elect a city commission (typically composed of five or seven members) that acts as the policy-forming body and whose members serve as the chief administrators for the city administration. In other words, each commissioner functions as the head of one of the city departments (for example, public works, police, or fire). Theoretically, the city commission, as a collective entity, supervises the various administrative departments. In actual practice, however, each commissioner oversees one department. The commission plan is depicted in Figure 11.2.

The commission plan differs from the mayor–council systems in several respects. First, there is no directly elected single chief executive, either weak or strong. Second, there is no check on commission action in the form of a veto. Third, there is a built-in incentive for **log-rolling**—the process of accumulating votes in order to build up a majority coalition. At budget time each commissioner goes along with the budget demands of the other commissioners in order to gain their loyalty in subsequent matters.

The commission plan is not widely employed by cities. It was supposedly invented in Galveston, Texas, in 1901 following a hurricane. In the wake of the disorganization that accompanied the disaster, a committee of "leading citizens" was formed to reinstitute domestic health and safety. Its remedial activities were apparently so exemplary that it was decided to continue under the plan, using it as the permanent form of government. Then, in 1907, the city of Des Moines, Iowa, refined the plan, which was subsequently adopted by other

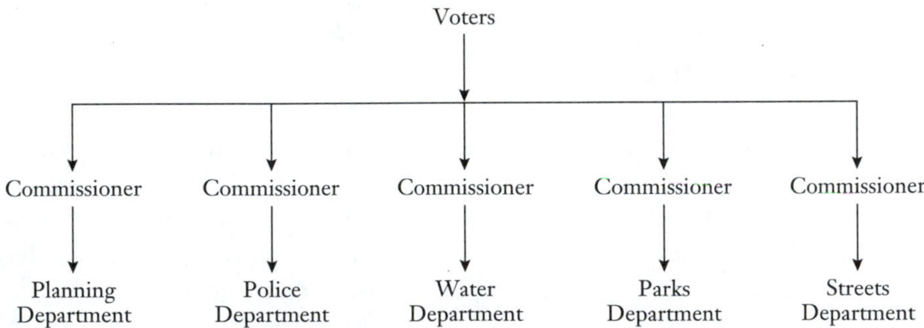

Figure 11.2 The Commission Plan

cities as well. But the commission plan has not gained the widespread acceptance accorded the other plans.

The Council–Manager System

Some cities employ the **council–manager system** of government (see Figure 11.3). Here, the **city council**—which is often composed of five, seven, or nine persons (ten or fewer in 97 percent of all council–manager cities) typically elected in at-large and nonpartisan elections—acts as the legislative or policy-forming body. The council appoints a professional manager to act as the chief administrative officer and, in effect, to run the city. The manager, who is hired and can be fired by the council, need not be a resident of the city. The office of mayor exists, but the position is filled in various ways. Generally, the mayor is simply "first among equals," and the title serves only a ceremonial function.

As the chief administrative officer, the **city manager** typically prepares the budget, makes recommendations to the council, appoints administrative personnel who are not under civil service, and, in general, runs the administrative affairs of the city without interference from the city council. In fact, some city charters and state statutes specifically prohibit council members from interfering with the city manager's operations. The council can fire the manager if it chooses to do so, but council members are not supposed to deal directly with

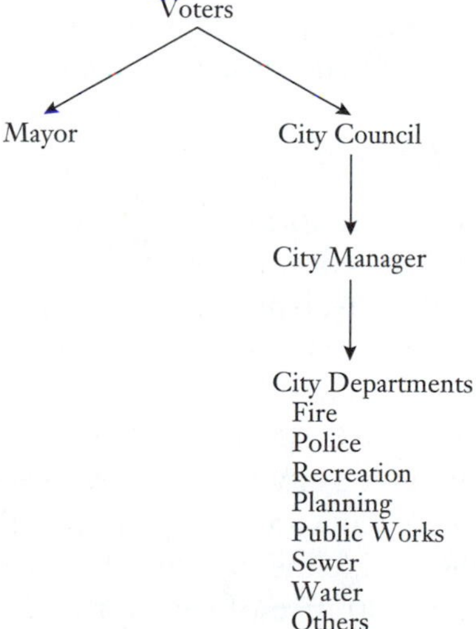

Figure 11.3 The Council–Manager System

administrative officers in such departments as police and fire. Rather, all communication with the lower ranks of administration is supposed to be through the city manager's office.

A Product of Early Twentieth-Century Reforms

The council–manager form of government is a product of an early-twentieth-century reform movement that emerged in the context of the larger national Progressive movement. Toward the end of the nineteenth century and into the early twentieth century, many city governments were dominated by corrupt politicians or political machines. These "machines" operated as the key to elaborate exchange systems, in which they bought the votes of masses of incoming immigrants in exchange for such favors as jobs, handouts to needy families, the conduct of funerals and wakes, and other commodities desperately needed by immigrants who had recently left their homelands. When necessary, the political machines supplemented the immigrant vote with outright manipulation of elections. Phony votes were cast, deceased people's names were kept on the rolls, and ballot boxes were stolen or "lost" when the situation demanded.

Muckraking writers such as Lincoln Steffens and business reformers such as Richard Childs (who later became the president of the National Municipal League) led the fight in the early part of the twentieth century to curb the activities of political machines. One of their primary aims was to remove politics and the politician from government and substitute instead efficient businesslike management. Part of their plan involved replacing the mayor–council system with the council–manager form of city government.

A Managerial Model

The council–manager form of government is patterned after the managerial model of the private corporation, as Figure 11.3 shows. The voters are viewed as the functional equivalent of corporate stockholders. While stockholders select a board of directors to oversee the activities of a corporation, voters elect a small city council to guide the affairs of government. In place of the company president, whom the board of directors hires to manage the corporation, the city council employs a city manager, who is supposed to be politically neutral, technically competent, and uniquely qualified to run the affairs of the city within the policy guidelines set forth by the city council. The city manager acts as the chief administrative officer of the city. Supposedly, the manager is politically neutral and only administers the policy handed down by the council. The city manager is empowered to hire and fire administrative subordinates, is generally instructed to prepare the city budget, and, supposedly, operates without daily interference by the council. Rather, the city council grants the city manager the freedom to conduct the job as he or she sees fit, but the council can fire the manager if they are unhappy with performance.

Underlying Assumptions

There are a number of interesting assumptions underlying the council–manager plan. For example, there is the assumption that alterations in both individual behavior and the operations of entire governments can be accomplished by tinkering with organizational structure. The elimination of the position of strong mayor, the substitution of a small city council for a large one, the use of at-large rather than ward elections, and the employment of a city manager as an equivalent to a corporate manager all try to eliminate graft and promote a businesslike and efficient economy. Students of administrative behavior suggest that while government structure is not unimportant, it alone does not govern behavior. Professional norms, ideology, training, working conditions, personal contacts, and opportunities are equally important in affecting both individual behavior and the general tone of government operations. One cannot eliminate greed, the potential for under-the-table payoffs, or communication based on personal acquaintances simply by juggling the lines on an organization chart.

Another assumption underlying the council–manager system is that the operations of government can and should be nonpolitical. The major target of early reformers was the political machine, controlled by a highly organized political network running from the ward supervisor to the manager. The words *politician* and *politics* became dirty words. Through use of a nonpolitical city manager, at-large rather than ward elections, and the elimination of partisan designations on the ballot, it was assumed that politics could be removed from the operation of government and that many of the evils of the political machine would disappear. But the notion that politics could be eliminated from government was based on the narrow assumption that politics involve only those activities undertaken by a partisan party. It was thought that politics would cease to exist if party labels were omitted from the ballot. In practice, politics involves much more than political parties. It also includes the competitive struggle among individuals and groups to affect the content and implementation of public policy. Politics is partisan combat, carried on according to a set of rules in which the competitors try to place their problems on the public agenda and secure public resources for the services and other benefits they desire; they try to secure, in short, benefits at public expense. Tax policy, the provision of police and fire protection services, zoning and educational decisions, and other public services are the outcomes of partisan political struggles.

Yet another assumption of the council–manager plan, one implicit in the early-twentieth-century reform movement, is that the values of economy and efficiency in government are supreme. Most would agree that economy and efficiency are desirable in government, but not at the expense of effective response to citizen desires. Some would argue that in a democratic system the primary task of government is to respond to the desires of the people, and that, while efficiency and economy in government are important, they are secondary to that primary function.

The political machines that were the object of reformers' attacks were interesting institutions. There is no question that they were corrupt and self-centered and that they made off with large amounts of illicitly obtained funds. At the same time, they performed a number of functions, which have since been taken over by government agencies, that provided much-needed aid and much desired upward mobility for many newly arrived immigrants. The old machines helped widows, orphans, unemployed, and those generally in distress. Some critics argue that, because the power of the political machine was partially dependent on the vote of the urban masses, it was much more responsive to their needs than modern bureaucracies, which are staffed with people protected by elaborate civil service provisions.

Although the reformers contributed significantly to the demise of the old machines, other factors helped as well. Changes in the national immigration laws reduced the number of new immigrants and eventually dried up the pool of new voters. At the same time, many second- and third-generation immigrant children were so successful—thanks in part to activities of the political machines—that they no longer had to sell their vote in order to receive assistance in getting jobs or other aid. Instead, they could afford to vote as they pleased.

Although the magnitude and character of machine politics have changed significantly since the turn of the century, Raymond Wolfinger argues that the urban machine is not gone from American politics.[3] Given the growing number of urban poor and the proliferation of urban-oriented public programs, the conditions favorable to thriving machine politics are present. In other words, according to Wolfinger, the poor provide the political machine with an electoral base, and new public programs generate opportunities for considerable patronage.

The Distribution of Structural Forms of City Government . . . .

The reform features developed in the early twentieth century—the council–manager system and at-large and nonpartisan elections—are unevenly distributed both geographically and in terms of city size. The mayor–council form of government is the older, more traditional form and is found most often in the East and Midwest. The council–manager plan and nonpartisan elections are especially prevalent in the Midwest, the West, and the South. The explanation for the trend in western states may be simple—western cities were just coming into existence when the early-twentieth-century reforms were in full swing. Western cities adopted the structural plans that were popular at the time, and most have maintained them ever since.

As Table 11.1 indicates, the council–manager system is most common in cities with populations over 25,000, whereas the mayor–council system is predominant in very large cities (those whose population exceeds 500,000) and very small cities. In recent years the council–manager system has gained popularity in every size category and in every region of the country.

Cities employing the council–manager model usually use other reform features, including at-large and nonpartisan elections. Eighty-eight percent of council–manager cities have nonpartisan elections, and 76 percent of those cities employ the at-large model for at least some council seats.[4]

Political Influence and City Government Structure

The structure of a city government helps to determine its internal distribution of political influence. The person or persons who control the formation of the budget, personnel appointments, the flow of information within the administration, and the council's agenda are in an extremely influential position. The governmental structure helps to determine this influence.

TABLE 11.1 FORM OF CITY GOVERNMENT BY CITY SIZE, 1992

	Number of Cities		
City Population	*Mayor–Council*	*Council–Manager*	*Commission*
Over 100,000	77	102	8
25,000–100,000	354	564	37
Less than 25,000	3,369	2,017	127
Total, all cities	3,800	2,683	172

Source: The Municipal Year Book (Washington, D.C.: International City Management Association, 1992), p. xiv.

Budget Control and Personnel Appointments

In an age when most government budgets are large and complicated, city councils, often composed of part-time politicians who devote a few hours a week to public affairs, seldom have the time or expertise necessary for a complete and careful budget review. As a result, the budget submitted to a council by an administration seldom undergoes extensive modification.

In a *de facto* sense, the administrative officials—whether the mayor, the mayor's staff, or the city manager—exercise extensive control over budgetary matters. Their budget control can extend into other forms of influence, since department and agency heads cannot afford to ignore the demands and preferences of those who control the operating budget. In a strictly legal sense, the legislative branches of all American governments control spending, and the problems and political pressures in a community help to structure program and budgetary priorities. But in practice, the people who work out the details of a budget and submit it for review to a city council control in large measure the internal distribution of government dollars.

In addition, the authority to hire and fire personnel contributes to the power of an administrator. The ability to hire employees permits administrators to fill positions with people who are sympathetic with their views and who are likely to accede to their preferences. The power to dismiss an employee is, of course, an effective tool to secure compliance with orders.

Control of Information and the Agenda

The ability to control the flow of information in an organization and the capacity to structure its agenda give an administrator an enormous amount of influence. Policy-making bodies such as city councils spend their time deliberating the items on their agenda, but matters do not get on the public agenda by accident or chance, just as problems do not define themselves. Among the infinite range of possible public issues, some are selected and placed on the public agenda for consideration and others are not.

Typically, some items that do reach the public agenda are those identified as problems by city administrators. Parks departments point to the need for more parks, firefighters point to the need for more staff and new equipment, and so on. Administrative departments and special interests push constantly to place their problems on the public agenda. With the abundance of potential issues and agenda items, the person who structures the public agenda is in a position to put some things on it and leave others off—thereby narrowing the range of options.

In addition, the person who sits atop the flow of information in a city administration is in a position to choose what the council will hear and what it will not hear.

Strong versus Weak Mayors

In strong mayor–council cities, the mayor has an independent constituent base, is empowered to hire and often to fire top administrative personnel (such as department heads), is empowered to veto council action, is the top administrator (with considerable legal administrative authority), and plays major roles in structuring the budget and the public agenda. It is the mayor's program and the problems that the mayor identifies that become the focus of city government.

In weak mayor–council cities, the situation is different, since political power is more widely diffused. The weak mayor typically does not have veto, budget, and appointive powers of the strong mayor. Instead, the council controls appointments and, in some cases, puts the budget together from the beginning. Likewise, because the weak mayor is not a highly visible figure with the power to structure the public agenda, agenda setting is more apt to be done by the council or individual department heads. In short, power is more broadly shared in the weak mayor–council system than in the strong mayor–council scheme.

Commissioners and City Managers

In commission plan cities influence is also rather diffused. Executive leadership and even coordination of activities may be lacking. Each commissioner may be powerful within his or her own department, but none has the legal authority and political visibility of the strong mayor.

In contrast, influence in council–manager cities is concentrated in the city manager, who is not directly elected. The budget is prepared by the city manager or the manager's staff. The council's agenda is set and top-level administrative appointments are made by the manager. As a full-time chief administrator who generally operates with a council composed of part-time politicians, the city manager has a monopoly on information and technical expertise. Council members' knowledge of the city's problems and alternative solutions tends to reflect that of the manager. This is not to suggest that city managers manipulate the flow of information from their administration to the council, but they do sit in the most critical position in the information process. Even though the early rhetoric regarding the role of city managers suggested that they were nonpolitical administrators, they actually play an extremely influential role in the policy-making process.

City Governments Differ in Many Ways . . . .

For years social scientists have tried to describe and explain the different characteristics and behavior of American cities. While they have been successful in identifying differences in the social, economic, and political realms, the exact causes of these variations are still unknown.

Structural Scheme Variations

Cities with different structural schemes tend to differ in other respects as well. According to a 1965 study conducted by Alford and Scoble, council–manager cities, in comparison with mayor–council cities, are likely to have higher growth and higher levels of citizen education, to be more homogeneous (socially, ethnically, and religiously), and to have more mobile populations.[5] In other words, they are more apt to fit the model of a middle-sized, growth- and business-oriented, middle-class community.

Similarly, in a summary of the research findings of a number of 1960s studies, Lewis Froman observes that council–manager cities are most likely to be medium size, growing, and white collar; to have high-value housing; to contain fewer foreign-born and nonwhite citizens; to have a higher-educated and wealthier population; and to display more occupant ownership of single-family housing units.[6] In addition, they are likely to spend more money per capita, to have lower municipal debt and higher property taxes, and to hold both at-large and nonpartisan elections. Wolfinger and Field contend that there is a geographic pattern to the distribution of government forms, and that cities with reformed structures are more likely to be found in the West than in any other region.[7]

Council–manager cities differ from council–mayor cities in the behavior of the electorate as well. Voter turnout tends to be lower in cities with the manager plan, in part because the plan is usually accompanied by nonpartisanship and at-large elections.[8]

Differences in Public Policy and Opinion

Just as the structural characteristics of cities tend to correlate with social, economic, and demographic factors, so too differences in the public policies of cities tend to vary with different government structures, as well as with social, economic, and demographic characteristics. In a 1967 study of two hundred randomly selected cities, Lineberry and Fowler examine the relationship between the use of reform features and policy output in cities.[9] Their conclusion is that structure has some impact on policy output, as measured by taxing and spending levels, as well as on the political style of a community. Reformed council–manager cities, they argue, tend to tax and spend less, with the exception that council–mayor cities with ward elections spend less when their elections are partisan.

However, in a 1980 study involving twenty-two cities tracked over eleven years, David Morgan and John Pelissero conclude that government structure does not affect fiscal behavior.[10] Robert Stein notes in a book published in 1990 that the provision of services by cities is related to the nature of those services, beginning with collective goods and moving to private goods.[11]

In addition, in a 1963 study of local referenda results, Edward Banfield and James Q. Wilson argue that some citizens, particularly people of Anglo-Saxon descent and Jews, are most likely to display a so-called "public-regarding" ethos, whereas other citizens, such as ethnic minorities, are more inclined to be "private regarding" in their outlook and electoral behavior.[12] That is, the private-regarding individuals tend to support only those public programs from which they will receive some direct benefit. Banfield and Wilson imply that cities containing a high proportion of public-regarding citizens are more likely than other cities to support the adoption of reformed government structures and new public programs designed to benefit the entire community. In a later study, published in 1971, Wilson and Banfield modify their earlier conclusions but do not abandon the ethos theory of political behavior.[13] In this ethos study, they contend that political ethos is more pronounced among individuals who exhibit so-called leadership qualities and that it likely played a role in cities' initial selection of government forms.

Variations in Political Behavior

A number of studies examine the behavior of city councils in relation to public policy and political processes. In a 1968 study, Bryan Downes suggests that city council members from high socioeconomic backgrounds are inclined to support high city expenditure levels.[14] However, Downes also notes that other factors, such as the wealth of a city and the nature of its political system, affect expenditure patterns as well.

A 1991 study by David Morgan and Sheilah Watson indicates that collaborative policy leadership is most likely to occur in large cities, with mayors as the dominant figures in most cases.[15] James Clingermayer and Richard Feiock, in their 1993 study, found that representatives from reformed political structures (at-large elections) tend to focus less on constituency casework and more on the "high politics" of policy formation.[16]

Some Generalizations

What can we conclude from the aforementioned studies? A few generalizations can be made with some confidence. First, government forms are not randomly distributed throughout the nation. Cities with certain economic, educational, ethnic, religious, age, and locational characteristics tend to adopt certain structures. Second, while these factors may be taken as indicators of structures, policies, and styles of political activity, they are not completely reliable. Third, political structures do have some impact on voter behavior and public policies, as indicated by the lower levels of voter turnout and expenditures in reformed cities. Finally, it appears that, in a sense, the antipolitical machine reformers have had their way. If differences in values and policy preferences within a community are muffled (as the preponderance of evidence suggests is the case in the reformed cities), if a wide range of issues are not placed on the public agenda and, therefore, not accommodated by official decision makers, then politics to a degree has been removed from government just as the reformers intended. However, democratic theory demands most of all that governments and public officials be responsive to the people and that community concerns be the primary business of the government.

Counties, Schools, and Special Districts

Most of the thousands of units of government in the United States are made up of counties, school districts, and other special districts. As with cities, they are all creatures of and legally subordinate to the states. They employ thousands of public servants, perform hundreds of functions, and spend billions of dollars.

County Government

To most Americans the **county** (the largest political subdivision of the state structure) is not among the most visible or salient units of government, but it is important nevertheless, and among the most changed of American governments.[17] Counties administer the voting system of the states, keep vital records, house the courts and maintain jails, collect local taxes, and run much of the social service system.

There are more than three thousand counties in the United States, and enormous variation exists among them. In Alaska, counties are called boroughs, and in Louisiana, parishes. Connecticut and Rhode Island have no functional county governments. Delaware has just three counties, whereas Texas has 254 counties. Eight states have fewer than twenty counties and seven other states have more than a hundred. The range of population in the counties is vast. Loving County, Texas, has 154 people; Los Angeles County is home to over 8 million residents. Most counties operate with an antiquated political structure that widely disperses authority; however, a few have adopted modern arrangements that centralize administration.

The existence of counties dates back over a thousand years in Britain. Initially arms of the royal government, through the years counties became the providers of education, aid to the poor, police protection, roads, courts, and more. In the American colonies and later the states, the county served as the arm of the state. Today, some counties perform only housekeeping functions, such as keeping records, maintaining jails, and holding elections. Other counties perform services much like those performed by the cities. As noted in Chapter 10, under the Lakewood plan, Los Angeles County provides many municipal-type services to cities.

Functions

Traditionally, counties typically perform several basic functions. They play a critical record-keeping role. Births, deaths, voter registrations, election returns, property ownership, land transactions, and other information are recorded and kept by the county. In addition, counties exercise a number of police powers. In areas outside of incorporated municipalities, they provide police protection through the sheriff's office. Liquor licenses and building permits may be controlled by the county. Some counties administer zoning and building codes, inspect food-dispensing establishments, and guard against disorderly behavior and houses of ill repute. Many counties have their own court systems and thereby help to administer the business of the state trial courts. The county sheriff often maintains the county jail.

Counties also play an important role in elections by registering voters, preparing ballots, supervising elections, and keeping some election records on behalf of, and as administrative subdivisions of, the state government. Finally, counties provide a range of services. They construct and maintain roads; they assess property and collect taxes for both themselves and other local government units within their boundaries; and they may maintain parks, libraries, airports, hospitals, stray animal kennels, sanitary landfills, and public assistance programs.

As the preceding description of county functions suggests, most activities undertaken by counties tend to be of a housekeeping nature in comparison to the broader range of activities performed by cities. Most county functions are the product of earlier decades when the activities of government were minimal. Those functions are spelled out in detail in state statutes; counties have relatively little freedom of policy choice.

Structure

The structure of county government bears a slight resemblance to the plural executive model employed in state government (see Chapter 5). County government is composed of what some call **row officers**—a directly elected sheriff, coroner, clerk, recorder of deeds, superintendent of schools, and board of supervisors. They are referred to as row officers because on an organizational chart they all line up in a row, and they all have independent constituent bases. In other words, the county lacks elective executive leadership.

The legislative branch of county government generally is composed of the county board of supervisors, often called county commissioners. The boards typically have three, five, or seven elected officials, though in some states (such as Michigan, Tennessee, and New York) the boards are much larger. Texas is fairly typical in that the voters of each county (by single-member district) vote for four county commissioners and, in a countywide election, for a presiding officer. The chief executive of Texas counties is called the county judge, though the position has only limited judicial functions. Unlike most city and school board elections, those for county officials are by partisan ballot. County board activities may include the formulation of the budget, the enactment of zoning and building codes, the parceling out of liquor licenses, and others. The legislative functions of the board are usually fairly restricted, because many of the duties of the county are spelled out in state law.

Other directly elected county officials include the sheriff, coroner, clerk, treasurer, registrar of deeds, and, in some states, the county superintendent of schools. Like the members of the county board of supervisors, these individuals run for office on partisan ballots and serve two- or four-year terms. The duties of the sheriff include law enforcement in those parts of the county not within municipal boundaries, the maintenance of jails, and the delivery of court summons. The coroner's job is to establish death and determine the cause. In some states coroners must have some medical training, but this is not a universal requirement. The duties of the county clerk (in those states where the office exists) include such clerical activities as issuing marriage and hunting and fishing licenses, registering voters, preparing ballots, and assisting the board of supervisors. County treasurers collect the tax revenues for the various local governments within the boundaries of their county and disperse them to each local government according to the legally established mill levies. The treasurer also keeps financial books and acts as custodian of the funds. The duties of the registrar of deeds involve just what the title implies—to keep an official record of property ownership, including the registration of deeds, property sales, mortgages, and estate titles.

Counties in over half of the states elect a superintendent of schools. However, this official performs only minimal duties; the actual job of running the schools falls to the school districts themselves, not to the county. In addition, the counties in some states elect an assessor, who makes estimates of property values for tax purposes; a highway superintendent; an auditor; and a surveyor.

There is some limited structural variety among the American counties. County executives (similar to mayors) are elected in 388 counties; another 786 counties operate with a chief administrative officer (similar to a city manager). Twenty-seven of the 3,042 counties have merged with other local governmental units, while nineteen states indicated in a 1992 survey that some structural change had occurred.[18]

Criticisms

County government has been the object of intense criticism in recent decades. The most common complaints are that the county is structurally incapable of generating effective political leadership and of attacking problems successfully; that it lacks the legal authority to provide the broad range of services that people now demand; and that it is plagued by other dysfunctions, such as a lack of a civil service system and of skilled personnel. With the multimember board of supervisors, plus the sheriff, the clerk, the assessor, the treasurer, and others all directly elected at the polls, and each possessing an independent constituent base, it is argued that the county is without an individual executive capable of identifying problems, leading a ticket, pushing a platform, and bearing the responsibility for the administration of county affairs.

Similarly, since state law largely deprives the county of anything other than housekeeping powers and duties, it has limited ability to tax, spend, and act to deal effectively with such modern issues as public assistance, police protection, housing, pollution, and water and sewer service. In addition, because most counties use the spoils system of employment rather than a civil service system, it is argued that they lack skilled personnel. Additionally, counties have faced increased state oversight as fiscal pressures mount for the states. Indeed, many states have shifted responsibility for activities. The 1996 welfare reform legislation promises to have even more consequences for county governments.

Reform Proposals

Not surprisingly, county government reforms have been proposed. Proponents of reform suggest that the row officers be replaced by a structural arrangement involving an elective or appointive chief executive, that a civil service system be adopted to replace the spoils system, that steps be taken to ensure that certain officials (such as the coroner, the treasurer, and the assessor) receive adequate training for their job, and that state laws be modified to broaden the powers of the county, especially in the areas of taxation and zoning.

Several counties, including Cook County in Illinois and Milwaukee County in Wisconsin, have adopted reforms instituting a chief executive. Dade County in Florida's Miami area and California's Los Angeles County have assumed broad municipal-type functions in order to serve millions of people as a city would. Although there have been other attempts to merge governments or update structures in order to allow counties to meet the growing demands of an urban and suburban society, county government in twentieth-century America still resembles that of the nineteenth century in many respects.

Many state governments have acted to make it possible for counties to modernize their structures. Thirty-seven states now allow some form of county home rule, but voters in the counties themselves have been very slow to make changes. In those states, about 4 percent have adopted home-rule charters.[19] (See Focus 11.2 "County Reform.")

Like America's modern cities, counties today face a variety of challenges. They remain creatures of the state and as such they are subject to the limitations imposed by the states. The states require counties to provide certain services but restrict the types and amounts of taxes that counties may levy and collect to pay for those services. The issue of unfunded or underfunded state mandates is highly controversial in many counties today.

School Districts

With a few exceptions, elementary and secondary education in the United States is administered by local **school districts**—single-function local governments that, like cities and counties, are creatures of and legally subordinate to the state government. As of 1992 there were 14,422 school districts in the United States, less than one-quarter the number that existed in 1920. The decrease in the number of school districts is the result of widespread district consolidation, made possible by improvements in roads and bus transportation, encouraged by rising costs and the savings associated with consolidation, and required by state legislation.

As single-function units of local government, school districts operate independently of other local units. The only exceptions are that the counties help school districts collect the property tax on which the latter largely depend and that the local schools are subject to oversight by state departments of education. Like cities and counties, school districts have their own legal boundaries, which may or may not parallel those of other local governments. In some communities in the eastern part of the United States, elementary and secondary education is provided by municipalities.

Focus 11.2
COUNTY REFORM

• • •

Recently two western states have adopted reforms that would allow significantly more local autonomy and variation among counties. Montana is the only state that requires that the voters revisit the question of the structure of local government every ten years. In 1994, Montana voters voted to review 112 jurisdictions. In only two cases were significant modifications made, and those involved city-county consolidation and adoption of a self-governing home rule charter. The two Montana counties that changed are the only two with self-governing powers in the state, as well as the only two consolidated counties and the only two with charters.

In 1994, Idaho voters approved HJR 17, which allows the establishment of optional forms of county government. Idaho counties would be able to select from a list of options approved by a commission and the state legislature. After a series of public meetings in 1995, the commission approved for recommendation two alternative forms of county government. According to the terms of the joint resolution, once a county has changed the structure of county government, it may not revisit that question for four years.

It is notable that these significant reforms come from some of the more conservative areas of the country, albeit areas with a solid tradition of faith in local government.

Source: Report of the Optional Forms of County Government Committee, 16 August 1995. Boise, Idaho.

Structure

In many ways the government structure of school districts resembles that of the council–manager plan in city government. In what are nominally nonpartisan elections, voters elect a multimember school board that, like the council in city government, acts as the policy-making body. The school board, in turn, hires a school superintendent, the school district's counterpart to the city manager. The superintendent, who acts as the chief administrative officer for the district, is supposed to have purely administrative-type duties and, theoretically, is nonpolitical. The superintendent is hired on the basis of administrative abilities and may be dismissed by the school board, which often involves a contract buy-out.

The rest of the school district government is structured hierarchically under the direction of the superintendent. Each school is headed by a principal, though in large school systems there may be an intermediate level of organization between the superintendent and the individual school principals. In addition, school districts, like other government units, may employ a staff organization including offices for budgeting, planning, and purchasing.

Are Schools Political?

An old, staunchly defended myth about American schools holds that they are nonpartisan and nonpolitical entities. For most Americans, education is an extremely important business, and this is reflected in the fact that more is spent on education than on any other single state or local function. Since education is so important, many believe that it is crucial that it is kept out of the hands of politicians and that local control be maintained. Thus, Americans hold strongly to the notion that schools should be controlled locally, that they should be kept nonpolitical, and that district elections should be nonpartisan.

However, in school district government as in anything else, politics involves much more than simply keeping party labels on or off the ballot (see Focus 11.3 "Politics in the New York City Schools"). Politics involves interpersonal and intergroup competition to control the content and implementation of public policy. It involves the authoritative resolution of conflict among individuals and groups with different values and images of the public good. Questions about the property tax rate, the establishment of expenditure priorities and item-by-item allocations in the school budget, the content of the curriculum, segregation and busing, as well as contests for seats on the school board are competitive and political in nature. The schools employ most state and local employees, spend most state and local tax dollars, and are a part of the political process.

Financial Problems

Schools in the United States are facing an increasingly serious financial crisis. The financial position of the schools and, indeed, of most local governments has been undercut by inflation, by the constant demand for more and better services, and by the decreased propensity of people to hold their wealth in the form of taxable real estate. Inflation and the demand for more and better services have driven the total cost of elementary and secondary schooling up from $103,100,000 in 1960 to $228,917,000 in 1992. However, the property tax—

Focus 11.3
POLITICS IN THE NEW YORK CITY SCHOOLS
• • •

One recent example of politics in the educational system is the experience of the former chancellor of the New York City school system. In 1993, Chancellor Joseph A. Fernandez was deemed responsible for an alteration in the curriculum of some New York City schools that included the incorporation of materials designed to foster tolerance for alternative lifestyles. The reading materials selected for young children shocked many traditional-minded parents and church leaders in the New York City area. Given the public response, it was soon apparent that the New York City school system had crossed a political boundary and, regardless of the appropriateness of the curriculum changes, Chancellor Fernandez, as leader of the system, had to go. He resigned early in 1993. Schools and school leaders are subject to political pressures.

the financial mainstay of the schools—has been increasingly hard pressed to supply the funds. Whereas previously many people may have held their wealth in the form of land and estates, fewer do so today. Instead, the wealthy accumulate stocks and bonds, with the result that the brunt of the property tax burden falls to the elderly, those on fixed incomes, and young, newly married couples with children—persons whose ownership of taxable real property (or payment of rent, which has the property owner's taxes built in) is high relative to their income.

The ability of the schools to escape their current cost–price squeeze is further hampered by rigid state laws limiting the taxing and spending powers of local governments. Some states impose an absolute millage ceiling on the property tax; that is, they limit the extent to which the schools can tax property. Others demand that a popular referendum be held to approve school district borrowing for building or operating purposes or to raise the tax levy beyond a certain level. Popular approval of property tax hikes is increasingly difficult to come by. Almost annually, a few school districts across the country are forced to close their doors for days or even weeks because they are financially destitute. In 1992, the Los Angeles schools were on the verge of bankruptcy. Given today's taxpayers' moods, as reflected in such actions as the passage of California's Proposition 13, and more recent reductions in federal support for schools and educational programs generally, these problems are sure to grow even more severe.

Inequities in Quality of Education

A problem related to school financing results in inequities among school districts. The schools rely heavily on the property tax, and some districts are richer than others. Within the borders of one district there may be industrial or commercial property, such as a shopping center, plus a considerable amount of high-cost housing. But an adjacent district may be poor; it may contain little or no industry and low-cost housing. The result is obvious: The tax bases vary, the incomes of the districts vary, and the quality of education varies. Indeed, the poor districts, in which high-cost remedial educational programs may be needed the most, tend to be least able to afford them.

The states have equalization programs designed to counteract the financial imbalances among school districts, whereby the states' share of the cost of elementary and secondary schooling is apportioned to benefit the poorer districts. Although equalization formulas help to eliminate some of the worst inequities, they do not solve the problem. There is growing concern that the very use of the property tax to support the schools results in the denial of equal opportunity to the nation's schoolchildren. There have been court cases in several states challenging the property tax as contributing to the "denial of equal protection of the law"—a Fourteenth Amendment guarantee. The Supreme Court, however, has ruled that an absence of dollar equality in district-to-district support of education does not constitute denial of equal protection of the law under the U.S. Constitution (*San Antonio Independent School District v. Rodriguez*, 1973). In some states, challenges under the state constitution have been upheld, and in others, states themselves have moved beyond the use of the property tax. (See Focus 11.4 "Education and Taxes: The Michigan Model.")

Creatures of the State

Although the relationship between the local school districts and their parent governments, the states, varies considerably, state offices or departments of education typically require periodic reports from the local districts, establish standards for teachers and certify them, and, in some states, select the textbooks and prescribe some of the course curricula for the local schools.

The state seldom involves itself in the daily operations of the local districts. However, it does maintain general surveillance and supervision.

Focus 11.4

EDUCATION AND TAXES: THE MICHIGAN MODEL

• • •

In the summer of 1993, the Michigan legislature passed and the governor signed Public Act 143, designed to eliminate the property tax as a source of operating funds for school districts. A major complaint was that the property tax, with differences in local bases—that is, some districts had a substantial amount of property to tax, while others did not, led to gross inequities in funding. The reform bill simply removed the property tax as a source of funding. No alternative source was provided. Later the legislature passed a reform bill that led Michigan voters to choose between raising either the state sales tax or the state income tax. The voters raised the sales tax. They also increased the tax on cigarettes from 25 cents to 75 cents. A number of other funding mechanisms were also provided. In essence, the legislature allowed a tax (18 mills) on nonhomestead property if districts want to get full funding. The legislature also provided a guarantee that each district had a minimum amount of money, with some overages. The basic amount was $5,000 per student. In the case of wealthy districts that historically spend above that amount, the reform measure allows them to tax property to keep spending at current levels. Districts that wanted to raise spending in their schools above current levels would be allowed to approve an additional three mill tax ($1 in tax per $1000 value).

Sources: George Weeks, "A Green Parachute for Michigan Education," *State Legislatures* (March 1994), pp. 24–27 and Robert Denny, "Michigan School Funding Law Worth a Hard Look," <http://www.jml.com/denny>.

Special Districts

Like all units of local government, **special districts** are also creatures of the state. State law provides for their existence, outlines the processes by which they may be formed, and specifies their powers, duties, and limitations. Typically, special districts are unifunctional in nature; that is, they perform a single function, such as the creation and maintenance of parks or sewer facilities. They generally have the authority to tax, spend, and borrow money. Some are governed by boards that are popularly elected. Like cities, counties, and school districts, special districts have legal boundaries that seldom parallel those of other governments.

The number of special districts has increased dramatically in recent decades, and by the 1990s the number exceeded 30,000. Almost two-thirds of these were in only eleven states, including over two thousand in both Illinois and California and more than one thousand in Pennsylvania, Kansas, and Texas.

Types

The variety of special districts is extensive. Nearly one-third of them deal with some aspect of natural resources, such as soil conservation, drainage, irrigation, or flood control. Another 17 percent provide fire protection, 10 percent provide urban water supply, and others deal with cemeteries, housing, highways, parks, hospitals, and other such facilities. Figure 11.4 shows the variety of special districts that exist within the state of Florida.

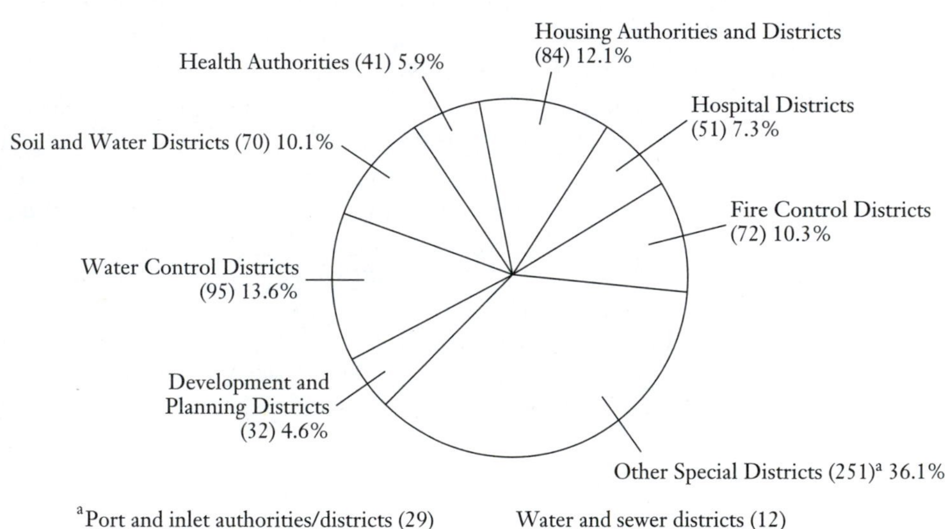

[a]Port and inlet authorities/districts (29)
Housing finance authorities (28)
Library districts (23)
Industrial development authorities (23)
Park and recreation districts (22)
Miscellaneous (20)
Utilities authorities/districts (18)
Mosquito control districts (13)
Aviation districts/authorities (13)
Water and sewer districts (12)
Regional planning councils (11)
Road and bridge districts (10)
Improvement districts (10)
Lighting districts (7)
Water management districts (5)
Transit authorities (3)
Community development districts (3)
Mobile home districts (1)

Figure 11.4 Number and Types of Special Districts in Florida (as a percentage of all special districts)
Source: Special District Accountability in Florida (Tallahassee: Florida ACIR, Nov. 1987).

The number of cities in the United States is growing very slowly, the number of counties remains stable, and the number of school districts continues to fall due to consolidation efforts; the number of special districts, however, continues to increase.

Functions

There are two primary reasons for the fairly recent and dramatic growth in the number of special districts. First, special districts can span an area and "package" a problem with which existing cities and counties cannot cope. For example, as new housing subdivisions spring up in areas adjacent to existing cities, they develop a need for both water and sewerage service. At first, these needs may be adequately provided for by water wells and septic tanks. As the density of the population increases, however, more modern water and sewerage facilities may become mandatory. The city to which the new developments are adjacent may be unable to extend its lines and provide the service. The city's facilities may already be operating at full capacity, and it may not have the resources with which to expand them. At the same time, the taxing and borrowing powers of the county within which the new developments exist may not be sufficient to permit the construction and maintenance of the needed facilities, or the county may be barred altogether by state law from providing such services. Therefore, in this situation, the formation of a new special district may be the only alternative. The boundaries of the district can be drawn to include only the area where the new services are needed, and the district can borrow the funds needed to build the facilities and impose a property tax sufficient to retire the bonds.

Situations similar to the hypothetical case just described are numerous given the rapid, widespread suburban growth in recent decades. Service needs have developed in the areas of sewerage, water, police, fire, parks, hospitals, and dozens of others. Thus, it is not surprising that the number of special districts has increased rapidly.

The other reason for the growth in the number of special districts is related to the fiscal limitations that state laws frequently impose on local governments. It is not unusual for a state to limit local governments about the kinds of taxes they may impose, the amount of taxes they may levy against property or retail sales, and the amount of debt they may incur. As a result, the formation of another government—a special district—may be an attractive way to get around the limitations. Since special districts can borrow, tax, and spend just like other local governments, they can act as a mechanism for borrowing the money and imposing the taxes that are beyond the legal limits of the existing cities and counties.

Problems

While special districts are obviously critical to the provision of needed public services, they create some problems as well. For example, their mere existence further complicates the problems associated with governmental fragmentation. Comprehensive community planning is difficult when sewerage and water, education, police and fire protection, recreation and land use planning are all handled by different units of government. It is no easy task to generate cooperation among counties, cities, school districts, and a host of special districts. In addition, special districts can add to already widespread citizen confusion about government in that they make its structure and operation more complex.

Special districts can also represent a bonanza for local attorneys and a burden for the already overburdened property taxpayer. Both statutory and case laws regarding local governments are extremely complicated, especially as they relate to finances. As a result, it is imperative that special districts keep an attorney on retainer. The lawyers may or may not earn their wages; nevertheless, the taxpayer pays the retainer tab in literally thousands of special districts.

Finally, in some cases, the growth in the use of special districts has created new financial burdens for citizens. In Colorado, the special district share of the local property tax doubled in the past two decades. In some instances, when special districts were created by developers, bonds were floated to provide improvements and pave the way for massive housing developments, generally just outside metropolitan areas. In Texas, the state legislature authorized the creation of municipal utility districts (MUDs) that allowed developers to buy up open land and, after issuing bonds backed by the MUD, to develop the land. When a city grew close enough to annex the developed land, the city also took over the MUD bonds. However, when a city could not annex the developed area in light of the recent downslide of the real estate market, the few existing taxpayers living in those areas were stuck with astronomical property taxes, and the holders of tens of millions of bonds were in danger of losing their investments.[20]

Summary . . . .

The more than 86,000 units of local government that exist in the United States display a rich diversity in institutional design and reflect a variety of historical American perspectives on the nature of politics. U.S. counties feature a highly decentralized form of government organization, and one that largely reflects nineteenth-century Jacksonian notions of democracy. With its long string of directly elected positions—including the commissioners, the sheriff, the coroner, the treasurer, the assessor, the clerk, and the auditor—the county scheme was designed to be highly democratic; that is, to maximize the ability of citizens both to be officeholders themselves and, as voters, to keep officeholders on a short leash.

In contrast, the council–manager form of city government emerged from the early-twentieth-century campaigns for economy and efficiency in government. Whereas the line of row officers in the county scheme decentralized authority, the council–manager system concentrated it in the hands of a small city council and its hired city manager. While today the Jacksonian concern for citizen participation in a democracy is still evident in the county arrangement, the reformed council–manager model employed in many cities reflects the private-sector business preoccupation with a streamlined and centralized government structure that is geared more toward efficiency than representation.

Interestingly, twentieth-century reform movements—whether targeted at state institutions, the fragmented metropolitan scene, or local governments—reflect the tension among different traditions and images of politics. Some observers favor a governing arrangement that is highly representative of the wide range of interests and perspectives in a community. Representation, in this view, overrides concerns about economy and efficiency. Other observers prefer a form of government that emphasizes clarity and simplicity, speed in decision making, and economy and efficiency; for them, these concerns outweigh broad representation, extensive deliberation, and compromise.

Most U.S. institutions reflect some dimension of the different traditions. Many council–manager cities, for example, overlay their otherwise centralized and politically neutral structure with a string of boards and commissions, created incrementally over time and designed to provide a variety of groups with special influence over certain policy areas.

All U.S. institutions are, at any given point in time, a reflection of their political history. That history, which has featured a variety of experiences and ideas, is evident in our local institutions. With ongoing change and growth, the American political landscape will continue to evolve.

Policy Perspective: Educational Reform . . . .

Public education in this country historically has been under local control. Iannaccone and Lutz identify several distinctive features of contemporary local school district governance that help to strengthen the independent nature of school districts. They argue that the fiscal independence of the local school district, the fact that school districts generally are not coterminous with other local governments, and the practice of holding separate elections combine to make the reformed system independent of other governments[21]. Zeigler,

Kehoe, and Reisman report that almost 73 percent of school districts have pure at-large election and that of the school districts in the forty-nine largest cities, more than 80 percent elect their board members by at-large systems.[22] In effect, school districts are virtually pure examples of "reformed" governments. The "unreforming" of electoral structures of schools has been a long and slow process. Largely in response to litigation, school districts slowly began to change their electoral structure throughout the 1980s and early 1990s.

In addition to electoral structure reforms aimed at increasing minority membership on school boards, there have been a host of other recent reforms aimed at solving other "ills" of the American educational system. Among the most popular of these reforms are those involving school choice[23] and the development of charter schools.

School Choice

An argument has risen that the American educational system is failing, that the American system no longer can produce effective quality education for its citizens. A variety of test score comparisons and other data are used to support this position. This presumed failure of the educational system assumes that the United States will become an inferior nation, losing the ability to compete in the world marketplace. Henig notes that the case for radical reform is rooted in several assumptions: unless strong and dramatic steps are taken, the United States is headed into stagnation and mediocrity; conventional remedies—more money, better teachers—are failures; that the very organizational nature of the American education system is a root cause of the failure.[24]

One of the suggested remedies is to essentially abolish the current system in favor of a system generally known as "school choice." In this system, parents and students would be issued vouchers with which they could "purchase" the education [and by implication, the quality of education] that they want. The market, free from burdensome regulation, could then provide quality education. Competition would ensure the quality. The best-known general argument for school choice is credited to that of Chubb and Moe.[25] In addition to the academic arguments, school choice also received strong political support from the Bush administration.[26] Choice allows the marketplace to emerge as the savior of education. Choice systems would thus empower those people purchasing the education.

However, there are some drawbacks to the rosy scenario painted by school choice advocates. Fundamentally, both empirical and normative arguments suggest that the choice movement has problems. One empirical test of the choice argument has found that private schools result in "creaming'—that is, taking the better [and wealthier] students and leaving the public schools to handle the rest.[27] While choice advocates argue that this will not necessarily be the case, the evidence suggests otherwise. Also, the "best" schools will have an enrollment capacity, so that not all students who want to attend those schools will be able to do so. Given the free market metaphor used by choice advocates, the result will likely be an increase in the cost of attending the "best" schools. Some students will be priced out of these schools. Given that some schools will start with a performance advantage, it seems likely that a two-tier system will result.

A basic normative argument also arises against the choice movement. Most choice advocates suggest the use of vouchers or some other type of public subsidy. Many people believe that the expenditure of public monies to support what might be termed elitist private schools is undesirable. Chubb and Moe are fearful that the public majority might not want to continue to support the choice movement, therefore they argue for enshrinement of the choice system in the state constitution where it would be difficult to change.[28]

Charter Schools

The Charter School movement[29] shares some of the anti-bureaucracy sentiment of the school choice movement. As with school choice, the charter movement is a product of the early 1990s. By the beginning of 1996, twenty states had adopted some sort of charter school law and many other states had considered such laws.[30] California, Arizona, Colorado, and Minnesota are among the states considered to have "strong" laws.[31] Although there is considerable variation among the states, charter schools generally are schools that are developed to serve a special need. Typically, parents, teachers, and local officials band together to create a school. They petition to receive a charter (most state laws set limits on the number of charter schools that may be developed) either from the state or from the local school board depending upon the state. The charters of most schools allow exemptions from many state regulations and education codes. In return for this freedom from regulation, the charter schools are required to set specific academic goals and to assess progress toward the attainment of those goals.[32] The apparent belief is that involved local officials can better understand and meet the educational needs within their community than can a one-size-fits-all state bureaucracy.

One of the hallmarks of charter schools in parental involvement. Mulholland reports that more than half of the reporting charter schools required parents to sign contracts guaranteeing their participation.

As might be expected, there has been some resistance to the charter school movement. A federal court suit in Pueblo, Colorado sought to enjoin the creation of charter schools when two local public schools were closed. The court ruled that the two issues were separate. If the charter movement expands, many local school districts might begin to see it as a threat to their source of funding and conflicts will likely ensue.

These end-of-the-century educational reforms are likely to continue to carry both symbolic and political weight into the next century. Education is perhaps the dominant local political issue and it consumes an enormous amount of local (and state) tax dollars. Consequently, it is always at the top of the local political agenda. The reforms are likely to continue to develop even if there is not much evidence of educational improvement.

KEY TERMS

municipal corporation
town
general law city
home-rule provision
charter
strong mayor–council system
weak mayor–council system
commission plan
log-rolling
council–manager system
city council
city manager
county
row officer
school district
special district

ADDITIONAL READING

Fleishman, Arnold, and Joe R. Feagin. "The Politics of Growth-Oriented Urban Alliances: Comparing Old Industrial and New Sunbelt Cities." *Urban Affairs Quarterly* 23 (1987): 207–32.

Judd, Dennis R. *The Politics of American Cities: Private Power and Public Policy*. Glenview, Ill.: Scott, Foresman, 1988.

Swanson, Todd. "Semisovereign Cities: The Politics of Urban Development." *Polity* 21 (1988): 83–110.

Yates, Douglas. *The Ungovernable City*. Cambridge, Mass.: MIT Press, 1977.

NOTES

1. Quoted in Clyde Snyder, *American State and Local Government*, 2d ed. (New York: Appleton, 1965), p. 353.
2. *Municipal Year Book* (Washington, D.C.: International City Management Association, 1979), pp. 98–101.
3. Raymond E. Wolfinger, "Why Political Machines Have Not Withered Away and Other Revisionist Thoughts," *Journal of Politics* (May 1972): 365–98.
4. *Municipal Year Book*, p. 101.
5. Robert R. Alford and Harry M. Scoble, "Political and Socioeconomic Characteristics of American Cities," in *Municipal Year Book* (Washington, D.C.: International City Management Association, 1965), pp. 82–97.
6. Lewis A. Froman, Jr., "An Analysis of Public Policies in Cities," *Journal of Politics* (Feb. 1967): 94–108.
7. Raymond Wolfinger and John Field, "Political Ethos and the Structure of City Government," *American Political Science Review* 60 (June 1966): 306–20.
8. Robert R. Alford and Eugene C. Lee, "Voting Turnout in American Cities," *American Political Science Review* (Sept. 1968): 796–813.

9. Robert L. Lineberry and Edmund P. Fowler, "Reformism and Public Policies in American Cities," *American Political Science Review* (Sept. 1967): 701–16.
10. David R. Morgan and John P. Pelissero, "Urban Policy: Does Political Structure Matter?" *American Political Science Review* (Dec. 1980): 999–1,005.
11. Robert M. Stein, *Urban Alternatives: Public and Private Markets in the Provision of Local Services* (Pittsburgh: University of Pittsburgh Press, 1990).
12. Edward C. Banfield and James Q. Wilson, *City Politics* (New York: Vantage, 1963).
13. James Q. Wilson and Edward C. Banfield, "Political Ethos Revisited," *American Political Science Review* (Dec. 1971): 1,048–62.
14. Bryan T. Downes, "Suburban Differentiation and Municipal Policy Choices: A Comparative Analysis of Suburban Political Systems," in *Community Structure and Decision-Making: Comparative Analyses*, ed. Terry N. Clark (San Francisco: Chandler, 1968), pp. 243–67.
15. David R. Morgan and Sheilah S. Watson, "Policy Leadership in Council–Manager Cities: Comparing Mayor and Manager," paper prepared for delivery at the annual meeting of the American Political Science Association, Washington, D.C., Aug. 29–Sept. 1, 1991.
16. James C. Clingermayer and Richard C. Feiock, "Constituencies, Campaign Support and Council Member Intervention in City Development Policy," *Social Science Quarterly* 74 (March 1993): 199–215.
17. For articles on U.S. counties, see the Advisory Commission on Intergovernmental Relations' *Intergovernmental Perspectives* 17 (Winter 1991): entire issue.
18. David R. Berman and Tanis J. Salant, "The Changing Role of Counties in the Intergovernmental System," *The American County*, Donald C. Menzel ed. (Tuscaloosa, Alabama: University of Alabama Press, 1996), pp. 19–33 and Blake B. Jeffrey, Tanis B. Salant, and Alan L. Boroshok, *County Government Structure* (Washington, D.C.: National Association of Counties, 1989), p. 120.
19. Jeffrey, Salant, and Boroshok, pp. 131, 146.
20. See, for example, Michael Mehle, "Crackdown on Special Districts Brewing," *Rocky Mountain News*, 6 March 1991.
21. Laurence Iannaccone and Frank W. Lutz, *Politics, Power and Policy: The Governing of Local School Districts* (Columbus, Ohio: Charles E. Merrill, 1970), pp. 10–12.
22. Harmon Zeigler, Ellen Kehoe, and Hane Reisman, *City Managers and School Superintendents: Responses to Community Conflict* (New York: Praeger), p. 11.
23. This policy perspective draws heavily from Kevin B. Smith and Kenneth J. Meier, *The Case Against School Choice: Politics, Markets and Fools* (Armonk, New York: M. E. Sharpe, 1995) and Jeffrey R. Henig, *Rethinking School Choice: Limits of the Market Metaphor* (Princeton, New Jersey: Princeton University Press, 1994).
24. Henig, p. 3.
25. John E. Chubb and Terry M. Moe, *Politics, Markets and America's Schools* (Washington, D.C.: Brookings Institution, 1989).
26. Henig, pp. 3–4.
27. See Kevin B. Smith, "Politics, Markets, and Bureaucracy: Reexamining School Choice," *Journal of Politics* 56: 475–91.
28. Smith, p. 477.
29. This section draws heavily from the work of Lori A. Mulholland. See Lori A. Mulholland, "Charter Schools: The Research" (March, 1996, <http://edreform.com/pubs/morrison.html>).
30. Mulholland, p. 2.
31. See Ted Kolderie, "A Guide to Charter Activity (August 1996)" <http://www.csus.edu/ier/charterwho.html>.
32. See Gary K. Hart and Sue Barr, "Remove the Limits on Innovative Schooling," *Los Angeles Times*, 17 January 1996, <http:// www.caus.edu/ier/article/html>.

CHAPTER 12

Community Power and Politics

The Chicago, Illinois, city council in session. *(Steve Leonard/Tony Stone Images, Inc.)*

• • • **Power in the Local Community**

• • • **Who Cares Who Governs?**

Scholars Care
The Public Cares, Sometimes

• • • **Do Power Elites Govern the Community?**

Middletown's Royalty
Atlanta's Elite
Other Perspectives

• • • **Is Community Power Pluralistic?**

Pluralism in New Haven
Pluralism in Florida
Other Perspectives

Focus 12.1: Students and Community Power

• • • **Do Experts Govern the Community?**

Full-Time Managers Monopolize Information
Complexity Enhances the Experts' Power

• • • **Do Local Election Systems Benefit the Elite?**

Partisan versus Nonpartisan Elections

Focus 12.2: Term Limits—No Problem at the Local Level

Variations in Voter Participation
At-Large Elections
The Effects of Electoral Reform

• • • **Do the Federal and State Governments Rule the Community?**

Federal and State Mandates

Focus 12.3: The Impact of a Federal Mandate on a Small Town

Who Should Pay for Mandated Programs?

• • • **Summary**

• • • **POLICY PERSPECTIVE: ECONOMIC DEVELOPMENT AND OUTSIDE CAPITAL**
The Urge for Economic Development
Does Development Improve the Economic Health of Communities?
Outsiders Limit the Community's Power to Affect Policy

We often refer to the person or group in control of our communities as "they." They raised our taxes. They failed to patch potholes. They fouled up the traffic light sequence on Main Street. They put too little money into lighting parks. They discriminated in city hiring policies. They run the town to suit their own self-interests.

Who are "they"? Clearly, they are people in positions to exert power and to influence the outcome of community politics. But are they the leaders who occupy positions in the governments described in Chapter 11—the mayors, council members, county commissioners, and school and special district board members?

Over the years social scientists have found these to be interesting and important questions. In representative democracies, citizens are supposed to control the outcomes of community politics through their representatives. But to what extent does this actually happen? What is the role of the citizen and how much influence do elected officials have in the public affairs of the community? In an official sense, these are the people who make and implement all authoritative decisions. Policy proposals do not become law until majorities of school board members or city council members pass them. Proposals that pass are of little impact until city managers, school superintendents, and other chief executive officers, along with the public employees who report to them, put money and effort into implementing the policies. Some of these people, then, have the power of the official vote. Others construct the public agenda and implement policy. They are all influential in important ways. And they all play power roles in governing.

This chapter examines these and other related issues, as well as the relevant perspectives generated by scholars in the field. Does it matter who governs, whether power elites rule, or whether power is pluralistic? Do local election systems bias the choice of local leaders? To what extent do state and federal governments and the financial capital of businesses and industry drive local choices?

Power in the Local Community

Many social scientists and others have long suspected that hidden powers lurk behind the scenes of community government—that so-called **power elites** selfishly manipulate community decisions to their own benefit rather than to the public good. However, as Norton Long points out, it is more popular to believe in the existence of power elites than it is to verify their existence:

> It is psychologically tempting to envision the local territorial system as a group with a governing "they." This is certainly an existential possibility and one to be investigated. However, frequently, it seems likely, systems are confused with groups, and our primitive need to explain thunder with a theology or a demonology results in the hypostatizing of an angelic or demonic hierarchy. The executive committee of the bourgeoisie and the power elite make the world more comfortable for modern social scientists as the Olympians did for the ancients.[1]

The view of the local community as run by an executive committee of the bourgeoisie is widespread, but it is not universally accepted. Other schools of thought and inquiry hold that community power is distributed in pluralistic, not monolithic, fashion; that it is so widely diffused that, in effect, nobody rules. More recently, some scholars have questioned whether community politics is controlled by anyone within the community itself; they ask whether community events are dictated by outside institutions and forces, and, if so, whether this diminishes the importance of community politics.

It is important to note the manner in which U.S. institutional arrangements affect patterns of community power. Nonpartisan elections held in the spring depress voter participation, which, in turn, can result in an elitist electorate. Some argue that at-large elections diminish the numbers of ethnic minorities on city councils and school boards, and that the use of part-time bodies to govern schools and cities enhances the influence of such hired experts as city managers and school superintendents. In addition, it is argued that the federal system with its unitary local–state ties conditions the way in which local decisions are preempted by other governments and external factors.

Who Cares Who Governs?

Scholars Care

Theoreticians concerned with democratic thought care who governs local communities. From time to time, almost everyone cares who governs in particular situations. However, most citizens are too busy with their jobs, their families, their homes, and their finances to worry much about the morality or virtue associated with elite or democratic political systems. Some people do worry about it. Some argue that elites should rule because, given their special qualifications, they are better equipped than others to make collective choices, or have a moral right or duty to do so, or both. Their membership in the correct political party, the correct church, and the correct race, together with their superior socioeconomic status or intelligence, endow elites, it is argued, with the right or ability to rule.

Advocates of democracy, however, argue that all elitist systems are illegitimate and that decision-making influence should be equally distributed throughout the community. Individuals are the best judges of their own best interests, and they do not need a self-selected elite to tell them what they want or need. People concerned with normative political theory, then, elitists and democrats alike, care who governs.

The Public Cares, Sometimes

From time to time the average citizen becomes aware of or concerned with the distribution of community influence. Government decisions are authoritative in nature; they are coercive; they help to determine who gets what, when, and how much. At the local level, government decisions affect the payment of traffic fines, the value and use of land, the distribution of the tax burden, the location of parks, the effectiveness of police and fire protection, and a host of other aspects of daily life that can affect millions of citizens, their families, and their pocketbooks.

City decision makers decide whether to spend public money to waive utility fees to attract and subsidize business development, or to use that money to improve parks. Decision makers can see to it that good streets and sewer hookups are available in low-income neighborhoods, or they can respond to citizen needs by the squeaky-wheel principle, thus letting most city investment go to middle- and upper-class areas. School officials also face choices. They can insist that the best teachers work in the schools where the children need the most help, or they can let those teachers transfer to upper-class neighborhood schools and hire inexperienced teachers for what are often the most difficult and least desired positions. School leaders can tailor curricula to the interests of the gifted and talented or focus resources on basic instruction in reading and writing for the entire student body. There are choices to be made that are not without significant consequences.

Do Power Elites Govern the Community?

Some studies conducted by scholars in community politics suggest that business- and economic-oriented power elites govern many local communities in the United States. The studies employ the **reputational** and **stratification approaches** to the question of how power is distributed in a community.

Basically, their method proceeds as follows. First, an effort is made to identify persons in the community who are likely to be knowledgeable about important community matters and who are apt to know of the most influential people. Once a list of community knowledgeables is completed, the informants are interviewed and asked to identify the powerful people in the community. A score is kept of the nominations to the influential list, and those receiving the most votes are then presumed to constitute the community's power elite.

The reputational and stratification approaches are, of course, more complicated than this brief description indicates, but basically they amount to a reliance on other people's perception of an individual's influence as a measure of community power. That is, some people are considered to be part of a power elite because other people think they are. Only rarely is the actual behavior of power elites intensely examined.

Middletown's Royalty

A well-known example of a community study involving the reputational and stratification approaches was conducted by Robert and Helen Lynd in 1929.[2] The study focused on Muncie, Indiana, or "Middletown" as the Lynds called it. Gathering their information from personal observation, interviews, and newspaper reports, the researchers concluded that virtually every aspect of community politics and economics in Muncie was controlled by a single family—referred to as the "X" family in the study or actually the glass-manufacturing Ball family.

According to the Lynds, the Ball family controlled the banks, the churches, the lawyers, the YMCA, the newspapers, the political parties, the chamber of commerce, the mayor, the community meeting halls, the breweries, the dog pounds, the hospitals, the local college—nearly everything, in other words. In the Lynds' words:

> Middletown has, therefore, at present what amounts to a reigning royal family. . . . the Middletown situation may be viewed as epitomizing the American business-class control system. . . . The ownership of banks, factories, colleges, breweries, dog pounds, hospitals, mayors and county chairmen, centered in this millionaire group, has produced an appalling economic pressure on citizens who find themselves in the house of bondage.[3]

Atlanta's Elite

Another well-known community study was conducted in 1963 by Floyd Hunter.[4] It focused on identifying the power elite in Atlanta, Georgia, a "regional city" as Hunter called it. He described his findings in terms of a **power pyramid**; that is, those at the top of the pyramid of power were often nominated as influential and, therefore, they constituted the community power elite. Hunter claimed that they controlled the important decisions in Atlanta, even though others actually carried out the plans and programs.

The following excerpts from Hunter's study convey his conclusions:

> The "men of independent decision" are a relatively small group. The "executors of policy" may run into the hundreds. . . .
>
> A group of men have been isolated who are among the most powerful in Regional City. . . .
>
> The pattern of business dominance of civic affairs in Regional City is a fact. . . .
>
> Most institutions and associations are subordinate, however, to the interests of the policymakers who operate in the economic sphere of community life in Regional City.[5]

Other Perspectives

While the investigations of the Lynds, Hunter, and others have led some scholars to conclude that ruling power elites exist in many communities and control decision making, other investigators harshly criticize the power elite school of thought. Among the most severe critics is Nelson Polsby, whose attacks are aimed at researchers' methods of studying the power elite as well as their interpretations of the data.[6] In *Community Power and Political Theory* (1963), Polsby outlines what he perceives to be the basic assertions of the elitist, or stratification, school. First, they contend that the upper class, which is composed of those in the top economic, occupational, and status brackets, rules the local community. Second, they argue that politicians and political decisions are actually subordinate to the economic elite; that is, that the economic big shots pull the decision strings. Third, it is assumed that the elite is a united and all-purpose group that rules in its own self-interest. Finally, community conflict is viewed as essentially class conflict in that lines are drawn on the basis of class status.

The critique of the elite model by both Polsby and Raymond Wolfinger is effective.[7] They note that the information obtained through interviews is based on vaguely worded questions, such as "Who is the most powerful person in town?" In this case, the word *powerful* can mean different things to different people. The reputational approach, according to Polsby and Wolfinger, may produce unreliable data for this reason.

The elitist method is also criticized for failing to distinguish between power in general and power in specific issue areas. In other words, the reputational approach does not distinguish between questions of who governs and who could govern, for in political and social life not every individual or group is interested in every community issue.

Finally, and perhaps most importantly, is the question of whether the existence of a power elite even conveys much about politics in a community. In some cases, the elite may be small, homogeneous, and united in its values. In other cases, the elite may be rendered impotent by conflict among its members. Therefore, in some communities the values of the upper class might coincide with those of most other members of the community, whereas in other communities upper-class values may conflict with those of the rest of the community. The mere reputational existence of an elite group does not guarantee its influence in community affairs.

Is Community Power Pluralistic?

Another major school of inquiry and theory holds that, in some communities, power is pluralistic rather than monolithic. In **pluralism**, power is not monopolized by a single elite but is distributed among many groups. In addition, the holders of power often vary with the issue involved. Influence may not be perfectly distributed throughout the community according to some ideal model of political equality, but neither is it monopolized by a small elite.

Pluralism in New Haven

The pluralistic theory of community power is generally associated with Robert A. Dahl and his 1961 study of New Haven, Connecticut.[8] Essentially eclectic in nature, the study relied on a variety of methods and data sources in order to discover who governed in New Haven. According to Dahl, the investigation included the following: (1) an examination of the socioeconomic characteristics of city public officeholders to determine if any major changes had occurred as a result of the type of persons in office; (2) the identification of a particular socioeconomic class and observation of the extent of its activity in local politics; (3) the examination of several issue areas to determine who was active and influential in each one; (4) a survey of a random sample of voters to determine what kinds of people were politically active and at what levels of political activity; and (5) an examination of changes in voting patterns among different strata of the population.

Employing a method quite unlike the reputational approach of power elite theorists, Dahl arrived at a very different set of findings. In particular, he found that decision making in New Haven displayed several characteristics. For example, only a few individuals were directly influential on policy matters in the various issue areas. Rather, voters exerted considerable influence on decision making—they selected the public officials and their preferences represented boundaries that those directly involved in decisions could not safely go beyond. In addition, influence tended to be specialized; that is, not everyone was interested in or active on every issue.

According to Dahl, the old families that made up the social elite in New Haven were once dominant in community affairs but their influence had given way to an **executive-centered coalition** formed around the mayor and the mayor's close associates. While political resources were not evenly distributed throughout the community, neither were they totally monopolized by a small elite. Every citizen possessed the vote, and the most influential tended to concentrate their influence in those specialized issue areas of greatest interest to them. In addition, it was found that some people used their political resources more skillfully than others. Political resources took many forms, including money, status, access to decision makers, skill, and time. There were also slack political resources in the community—that is, individuals and groups that had the ability to influence decisions but chose not to much of the time. Finally, Dahl found that the distribution of power changed with time and issue area.

Pluralism in Florida

A major study of a growing south Florida area—Broward County, the second most populous area in that state—was conducted by Ronald Vogel in 1992. Using the reputational method, which commonly leads to the conclusion that elites rule communities, Vogel found a pluralist decision-making system:

> Twenty-six of the leaders described a community that we would commonly label pluralist. . . . Nobody described Broward's decision-making structure as elite, though a few respondents indicated that Broward had an elite.[9]

Vogel noted that "leaders talked of the need to build a new coalition for every decision or issue."[10] His findings appear to fit nicely with an observation made by Nelson Polsby back in 1963:

> If a man's major life work is banking, the pluralist presumes he will spend his time at the bank, and not in manipulating community decisions. This presumption holds until the banker's activities and participation indicate otherwise.[11]

Other Perspectives

The pluralist perspective is not without its critics. Some of them argue that the pluralist's focus on a series of important issue areas is faulty in that it fails to provide a criterion for distinguishing between important and unimportant issues. Critics also consider the pluralist approach unwieldy because it demands that behavior be carefully scrutinized before making generalizations about who has power; ultimately, the behavior of each individual should be studied, an obviously impossible task.

In addition, the pluralists are criticized for refusing to acknowledge even that an imagined power elite has some impact on human behavior. It is argued that, when people believe a power elite not only exists but also has the power to negatively impact those who refuse to accede to its desires, then decisions may be based on placating the elite—whether the elite is real or not. In other words, potentially influential members of the community can affect decisions without even trying, since others' perceptions of their ability to affect decisions may influence actual outcomes. When decision makers assume that a community elite will oppose the imposition of a high income tax, for example, that perception may prevent the imposition of that tax—whether or not the elite would actually oppose it. (See Focus 12.1 "Students and Community Power.")

Peter Bachrach and Morton Baratz point out that the reputational and pluralist approaches each shed some light on the distribution of community influence.[12] The insights provided by the pluralistic investigation are obvious. Using an eclectic approach, the pluralist can identify in specific terms who was active in which issue areas and with what result. The reputational approach is most useful in providing something the pluralist approach cannot—a view of the prevailing political ethos. Although the reputational approach does not entail a careful and systematic inventory of community attitudes, it does give an indication of the types of people who are perceived as influential in a community, including their socioeconomic characteristics and value systems. This information, in turn, may provide clues to the kinds of issues and alternatives most and least likely to reach the public agenda in a given community. According to Bachrach and Baratz:

> . . . Power is exercised when A participates in the making of decisions that affect B. But power is also exercised when A devotes his energies to creating or reinforcing social and political values and institutional practices that limit the scope of the political process to public consideration of only those issues which are comparatively innocuous to A. . . . to the extent that a person or group—consciously or unconsciously—creates or reinforces barriers to the public airing of policy conflicts, that person or group has power.[13]

Focus 12.1
STUDENTS AND COMMUNITY POWER
• • •

An alert student might ask herself why she should care about the politics of community power—after all, somebody has to "run the place." Many of her fellow students might well agree with her. One student in a state and local government class was among that group. Unfortunately, he had to write a paper and chose the power structure in his university town. The student went into the project thinking that there might be something of interest, but he doubted it. After a few fruitless hours of preliminary research, the student decided to see if there were political elites who were running the town. One interesting fact that the student discovered was that the university president, the local district attorney, a few business people, and a wealthy attorney or two met every Saturday morning in a local coffee shop. This informal gathering had been conducted for several years. General university and community topics were routinely discussed and, although no recorded votes were taken, several consensus decisions were routinely made. One of these decisions concerned the possible building of a new facility that could serve as an athletic fieldhouse/convention center. There seemed to be substantial support among the community and university leaders for the proposed building. Most of the university community, including students, were not consulted. In fact, much of the financing of the proposed building would be done with student athletic fees.

The student concluded his research paper with the conclusion that community power did matter.

Do Experts Govern the Community?

Another research-based image of decision making in certain kinds of American communities places a considerable amount of community power in the hands of experts—those who operate the executive branches of government. This tendency is particularly pronounced in governments where the legislative or policy-making body is composed of part-time lay personnel. City councils, in council–manager cities especially, are composed of people who do other things for a living, who devote just part of their time to government business, and who are paid little or nothing for it. The same is true of school board members, boards that govern such state agencies as universities and colleges, and special districts. These boards may contain homemakers, bankers, drugstore operators, dentists, and small business owners, for example.

Full-Time Managers Monopolize Information

The effect of these governing arrangements is that, generally, the decision-making power flows to the full-time government employees. For example, when a school board meets, it deals with the agenda brought to it by the superintendent of the school system. The superintendent and his or her administration present recommendations supported by budgetary, legal, technical, and other types of evidence and arguments. Other members of the administration may be present to offer evidence or answer questions. A board member, a nonpaid part-timer, may ask probing questions, make other recommendations, or oppose the recommended course of action. That board member may have been pressured by some person or group or may have alternate information or recommendations from someone within the school system. But this is an unusual situation. Generally, school board members, at a disadvantage in terms of information and time, ask few questions, rarely oppose the superintendent's recommendations, and tend instead to praise the administration's work.

The power of permanent administrators and their bureaucracies should not be underestimated. They work at their jobs full time. They have access to all sorts of data. They are familiar with the problems and issues. They are viewed as the experts. It is no small task for council or board members to challenge successfully the stance of the managers, superintendents, and other chief executive officers. Few members of councils or boards have the time to do the kinds of research needed to challenge the administration. There may be problems, data, or perspectives within the organization that never come to the attention of the councils or boards because the organizational ethic is that council and board members seek data only through the chief executive officer. Furthermore, it may be risky for persons of lower rank within the organization to convey information or questions to council and board members directly. Thus, when university governing boards, city councils, or other such bodies meet, the chief executive officer of the organization and his or her administration generally have their way.

Complexity Enhances the Experts' Power

The role of the unelected expert is growing as intergovernmental relations become increasingly complicated and the number of local special districts and intergovernmental contracts continues to multiply. In matters of education, corrections, environmental protection, and virtually all other policy areas today, bureaucrats at all levels of government deal with their counterparts at other levels. And they are all specialists of some sort—engineers, lawyers, planners. Not only is their work complex, but so are their interactions with other governments. It is becoming ever more difficult for a citizen to follow and understand public affairs.

With the growth in special districts, there are more decision points and government players in the system; with the growth in intergovernmental contracting, local relations are increasingly complex. When the complexity of public affairs diminishes the role and influence of citizens and of council and governing body members, the full-time expert in control of the daily operation of government becomes the *de facto* political power.

Do Local Election Systems Benefit the Elite? ....

With tens of thousands of local governments in the United States, all holding periodic elections, Americans surely do not lack the opportunity to participate in self-governance. Most Americans live within the jurisdiction of many governments—a city, a county, a school district, and one or more special districts. Under these circumstances one would expect citizen involvement to be extensive and informed Americans to vote in great numbers. Unfortunately, this is not the case. Instead, most local elections are characterized by low voter turnout, with the percentage of registered voters often failing to reach even double digits. Turnout rates in the area of 20 percent are common; rates as low as 5 percent are not rare.

As is the case at the state level, numerous elections are held every year at the local level. Indeed, with over 19,000 cities, 3,000 counties, 15,000 school districts, and 30,000 special districts, there have to be a lot of elections. Some local officials are elected for two-year terms, others for four-year terms, and still others for even longer terms. Some local elections are held in the fall, concurrently with state and national elections; others are held in the spring. Some local elections are partisan, whereas others are nominally nonpartisan, revealing the effects of government reforms. (See Focus 12.2 "Term Limits—No Problem at the Local Level.")

Partisan versus Nonpartisan Elections

Elections for office in U.S. counties are partisan in nature; that is, the candidates run as Republicans, Democrats, Independents, Libertarians, or on some

Focus 12.2

Term Limits—No Problem at the Local Level

• • •

One major concern among the American public recently has been term limits. However, that concern does not appear to be significant at the local level. Currently, less than 10 percent of local jurisdictions impose term limits for council members.

It may be that the situation at the local level differs from the state and national level because of the large number of nonelected personnel and the reduced advantages of incumbency at the smaller, more visible level of government. Further, the existing high rates of turnover at the local level suggests that the "problem" cures itself.

The associate director of the Colorado Municipal League says that it is "a solution looking for a problem." Recently in Colorado, 20 of 171 local city elections were canceled due to lack of competition. Also, in Colorado about 320 special district elections are canceled every two years due to lack of competition. Along with this lack of competition is the fact that at the local level reelection rates for city council incumbents, while high, lag behind those of Congressmen.

Thus, while many people agitate for term limits at the state and national level, there does not seem to be the same level of cause for concern at the local level.

Sources: Victor S. DeSantis and Tari Renner, "Term Limits and Turnover Among Local Officials," *The Municipal Yearbook* (Washington, D. C.: ICMA, 1994), pp. 36–42 and Kit Miniclier, "Term Limits Meaningless at Local Level, Critics Say," *Denver Post*, 4 December 1994, p. 14A.

other party label. County government has been less affected by reforms than any other unit of government in the American system. Elections for school board members generally are nonpartisan.

The situation in American cities is mixed. Some cities conduct partisan elections and others nonpartisan ones. The nonpartisan election is an integral part of the municipal reforms developed during the early twentieth century. As a result, it typically is accompanied by at-large rather than ward elections and is often found in council–manager cities. As Table 12.1 indicates, elections in most American cities are conducted with nonpartisan ballots. In addition, cities

TABLE 12.1 CITY ELECTION AND GOVERNMENT SYSTEMS

Government System	Election Type	
	Partisan (percent)	*Nonpartisan (percent)*
Mayor–council system	39.0	61.0
Council–manager system	18.1	81.9
Commission plan	25.4	74.6
All cities	27.4	72.6

Source: Data from *Municipal Year Book* (Washington, D.C.: International City Management Association, 1988), p. 8.

with one of the two reform-era structures—the council–manager or the commission plan—are more likely than mayor–council cities to eliminate the role of the political party. Like the council–manager form of government, nonpartisan elections tend to be most prevalent in medium-sized cities and in cities in the southern and western United States.[14]

Nonpartisan elections were intended by reformers to reduce or destroy the influence of the political parties in local politics, and to a large extent they have done so. In areas where nonpartisan elections are employed, the parties no longer perform their traditional functions—recruiting candidates, raising funds, conducting campaigns for office, criticizing the policies and behavior of the incumbents' party, and providing voters with a means of identifying those responsible for failures and successes. Instead, candidates in nonpartisan campaigns work independently to raise funds and win office, or they rely on special interests for support. (The latter is common in factional politics in one-party-dominant areas.) In addition, the public is deprived of the use of the party label as a way to identify politicians in and out of office and their stances on issues. Traditionally, the political parties serve as useful sources of political information for voters. According to a study conducted in 1988, as voters gain knowledge of partisan information in nonpartisan contests, this provides voting cues and influences their vote.[15]

Most social scientists addressing political partisanship and elections contend that the absence of the party label in local elections works to the advantage of the higher-income, higher-status class in a community. When elections are nonpartisan, voter turnout declines, and it is more difficult for voters to keep track of the candidates or identify the candidates' policy positions. It is argued that less educated, poorer, and lower-status voters are disadvantaged by nonpartisan elections because they are less likely than other members of the community to be associated with the groups that function as alternate sources of information and voting cues (such as churches, service clubs, and the like). As a result, the upper-class, well-informed, group-joining members of the community may exert a disproportionately high impact on electoral outcomes.[16] In other words, as the level of voter turnout declines in a local election, the elitist character of the voting electorate increases.

In elections with very low turnout (which is generally true of nonpartisan local elections), the elitist cast that characterizes voters tends to be even more pronounced. When voter turnout is in the range of 10 percent to 15 percent, for example, the electorate may be heavily representative of community professionals and businesspeople; of people active in churches, service clubs, and other forms of political activity; of those with high incomes and levels of education; and of those residing in upper-class neighborhoods. As voter turnout declines, the electorate tends to become less representative of the community as a whole and more representative of the elitist minority. So, as a result, do those who are elected.

However, when cities change leaders do policies change? Some recent research indicates that electoral change, such as changing mayors, does have an impact on public policy in cities. Wolman, Strate, and Melchior found that changing mayors—especially when an incumbent was defeated—had a dramatic effect on public policy in that city.[17]

Variations in Voter Participation

Voter participation varies among localities. In a 1968 study of voter turnout in American cities, Robert Alford and Eugene Lee contend that the form of government employed by a city influences participation levels more than any other single factor.[18] Cities in the study that lacked the council–manager form of government (that is, were unreformed) and that held partisan elections had higher turnouts than cities with other systems. In addition, voter turnout tended to be higher when a race for mayor was held concurrently with other contests than when council races were alone on the ballot.

Alford and Lee also contend that voter turnout varies with the locality and age of a city. Older cities, those located in the eastern part of the country, and cities with a stable population demonstrated higher turnout than cities in the West and South, newer cities, and cities with high levels of in-migration.[19]

Many of these findings can be explained by voting behavior and the impact of government structure on it. People tend to know more about and be more interested in elections, candidates, and issues when institutions exist that operate to inform voters about the elections. In addition, informed and interested voters are more likely to vote. Not surprisingly, then, voter participation is low in reformed cities because nonpartisan elections do not involve the political parties, which in partisan elections act to inform and involve citizens in electoral politics. Voter turnout is higher in eastern cities, proportionately more of which remain unreformed. Finally, the higher levels of participation in stable cities may be explained by the higher levels of citizen knowledge about and identification with the community.

According to Eugene Lee, voter participation fluctuates with the time at which a local election is held, with the highest turnouts occurring when the election is held concurrently with state or national elections.[20] Although the original intent of independently held local elections was not to depress voter turnout, this has been the result. Because national and state elections tend to receive wide publicity, they often attract large numbers of voters to the polls. When a local election is held independently, the lack of publicity results in low voter turnout.

At-Large Elections

One main aspect of the municipal reform movement was the institution of the **at-large election**, in which voters in all parts of a city vote for city council candidates.[21] It was designed to remove what the reformers considered a major problem of the ward system—concentration by each council member on one area of the city to the disadvantage of the city as a whole. For many years, at-large elections were the dominant form of municipal election, especially in small- to medium-sized cities.

Recently, however, the at-large election system has come under both political and legal attack and, in some cases, the courts have required cities to modify the system to provide district representation. The criticism is based on national voting rights legislation, which disallows election system features that discriminate against ethnic minorities. At-large balloting can work to prevent African-American and Hispanic citizens from electing their representatives of choice.[22] As numerical minorities, the effect of their vote can be minimized. Without substantial white voter support, a city with a 35 percent Hispanic population could go indefinitely with absolutely no Hispanic council members. When the courts found that at-large systems prevent fair minority representation, they insisted on modifications in the form of partial or full districting systems.

The increase in changes in the system are shown in Table 12.2. As can be seen in the table, large numbers of American cities proposed representational structure changes in those years. And, the rate of successful adoption increased in 1991 over the 1986 rate. Clearly the mixed form has a higher rate of successful adoptions. The mixed system allows for minority representation but also retains some at-large seats, thus preserving at least some of the reform style.

Table 12.2 Changes in Election Systems, 1986 and 1991

Year	Change to Ward or District System	Change to Mixed System
1986		
Proposed	214	45
Adopted	68	36
1991		
Proposed	169	61
Adopted	86	36

Source: Tani Renner and Victor S. DeSantis, "Contemporary Patterns and Trends in Municipal Government Structures," *The Municipal Year Book* (Washington, D.C.: ICMA, 1993), pp. 57–69.

The Effects of Electoral Reform

Studies of contemporary urban institutional reform—primarily changing election structures from at-large to single-member districts—examine changes beginning in the early 1970s and continuing to the present day. These changes are often motivated by demands for equal representation by minority groups and facilitated by the federal government through the Voting Rights Act. In general, empirical research suggests that greater representational equity exists under single-member-district election systems.[23] Some scholars argue that city size, not election structure, is most related to representational equity; and that if election structure ever played a role, its impact has diminished over time.[24]

Most scholarly discussion of representational equity focuses on the election of minority candidates by minority voters. Such descriptive representation, while important, usually does not address the policy consequences for the minority community when representation is enhanced. Exceptions include studies linking district election structures with more equitable minority employment patterns in cities and less discriminatory education policy in schools.[25] Research indicating that institutional structure and representation affect policy challenges other research that indicates cities are limited in their ability to affect local policy or make a difference in the lives of their residents.[26]

The role of minorities in local politics is changing, particularly in large metropolitan areas. Beginning with the civil rights movement of the 1960s, ethnic minorities (African Americans especially) have been increasingly active as both candidates and voters. Civil rights legislation has broken down the barriers to participation that existed for decades. In addition, demographics are changing, since a growing number of cities are developing African-American or Hispanic majorities as whites move to the suburbs.

The impact of these changes is manifest in the impressive list of major cities that have or recently have had African-American mayors, including Denver; New York; Los Angeles; Chicago; Atlanta; Philadelphia; Cleveland; Washington, D.C.; and Gary, Indiana. Denver and San Antonio have had Hispanic mayors. The 1991 mayoral contest in Denver featured a white attorney, an African-American city auditor, and an African-American city attorney in a three-way contest to succeed Hispanic Mayor Frederick Pena. None of the three received a majority in the initial ballot, so the two top vote recipients challenged each other in a run-off. Both individuals in the run-off were African American. Minority membership on county and city councils and on state and local school boards is growing as well, as indicated in Table 12.3. These local minority officeholders make up more than 50 percent of the nation's minority officeholders.

It is clear that both African Americans and Hispanics have made impressive gains in recent years. Clearly there is a different route to empowerment chosen by the two minority groups. African-American presence on county and city councils outstrips service on state and local education boards by a ratio of almost three to one. The ratio for Hispanics is just over one (and in favor of service on education boards).

In summary, the institutional form that a community employs has an impact on the distribution of political power and on politics. The use of the at-

TABLE 12.3 MINORITY MEMBERSHIP ON COUNTY AND CITY COUNCILS AND ON STATE AND LOCAL EDUCATION BOARDS

	African-American			Hispanic		
Unit of Government	*1970*	*1988*	*1993*	*1984*	*1989*	*1994*
County and city councils	719	4,089	4,819	1,276	1,724	2,197
State and local education boards	368	1,542	1,682	1,173	1,341	2,412

Sources: U.S. Bureau of the Census, *Statistical Abstract of the United States, 1991* (Washington, D.C.: GPO, 1991), pp. 266–67 and *Statistical Abstract of the United States, 1996*, p. 284.

large election may disadvantage minorities and low-income candidates generally. The nonpartisan ballot takes away a voting stimulus and cue—the political parties—thus depressing turnout and the ability of voters to track decisions and hold representatives accountable. It may also increase the saliency of the candidates' race. Holding elections at times other than when state and national elections occur, which many reformed cities and school and special districts do, can depress voter turnout. Low turnout, in turn, may lead to an electorate that is within the upper class economically, occupationally, and socially. What American communities have by way of representation and leadership, then, may be determined to some extent by institutional arrangements.

Do the Federal and State Governments Rule the Community? ....

Several developments in recent years raise questions about the extent to which community politics is still guided from within the communities themselves. As noted in the discussion of federalism in Chapter 2 and on finances in Chapter 13, the federal government has imposed a variety of mandates on state and local governments in recent years, and the states have done the same to their local units. In addition, with the growth in the mobility of investment capital and the renewed willingness of states and localities to chase after business and industry, some observers now suggest that local politics is becoming less relevant because the major decisions that affect communities are being made by outsiders. They suggest that perhaps local politics has become a series of processes by which community leaders decide how to pander to outside forces such as federal money, state government mandates, and industry in an effort to survive economically. Mark Gottdiener describes the situation in this way:

> Local politics has long since passed over into the hands of professional managers, giant multinational corporations, local capital caught up in a predatory jungle of fierce small-business competition, provincial politicians making do on dwindling party resources, and, certainly not least, federal interventions promulgated by the long series of crises befalling the country since 1960. . . . Local politics is hemmed in presently by the power of corporations, programs at higher levels of government, and a failure to generate enough revenues without the need for finance capital's administration of public budgets.[27]

Local governments have always been the legal creatures of the states, and as such they are legitimately subject to state laws. Thus, state statutes that require counties to conduct elections and keep vital records, that control police officer and firefighter pension funds, or that set the number of school days for local districts are not new, are not especially burdensome to the local units, and certainly are not inappropriate. Similarly, the national government has long issued requirements along with grants to state and local governments, as in the specification of construction and accounting standards in the use of federal highway money.

Federal and State Mandates

The past couple of decades have witnessed an increase in the number of demands placed by one government on another, and in many instances the nature of the demands has changed. Congress has passed a veritable flood of laws that compel both states and localities to comply with their requirements or risk losses of federal funds (sometimes in program areas not directly related to the mandate), or civil penalties, or both. Mandates have been issued in such areas as clean air standards, wastewater pollution, storm drainage runoffs, Medicaid eligibility, accessibility for the disabled, on-the-job drug use, the speed limit, the drinking age, and so on. However, the mandates are almost never accompanied by the funds needed to pay for and implement the programs required. This has resulted in a redirection of state and locally derived tax monies and federal preemption of state and local priorities and policies. Will a city spend money for parks, open space, and better streets? Or will it first upgrade its sewage treatment facilities and redesign access to its buildings? If resources are inadequate to do it all, the city will do what Congress and federal agency rules dictate, which may or may not be what citizens, local influentials, or the elected council wants.

Similarly, the states have increasingly imposed requirements on their own local units, often without providing the funding that the local units need to comply with the mandates. Some mandates relate to governing procedures, others to programs, and others still to fiscal limitations. For example, from 1981 to 1989 the Florida legislature enacted 326 new mandates on local governments having to do with process, programs, and limits.[28] During the 1980s the state of Illinois placed $148 million in mandated costs on its local governments, but more than two-thirds of the total cost was not reimbursed by the state.[29]

State-imposed mandates affect all sorts of policy areas, including personnel, health, transportation, recreation, public assistance, and the environment. For example, states have required that certain school employees be fingerprinted, that drinking water be tested for lead, that landfills be closed, that school buses undergo certain safety examinations, and that the special educational needs of deprived or handicapped children be addressed adequately. Generally cities and counties are told how to regulate and handle underground storage tanks, asbestos, and hazardous materials. Counties are instructed in the handling of foster child care. Local units are told how to recycle materials. (See Focus 12.3 "The Impact of a Federal Mandate on a Small Town.")

Focus 12.3
THE IMPACT OF A FEDERAL MANDATE ON A SMALL TOWN

• • •

A small Colorado town with 1,200 residents operated a sewage system with an old set of collection lines but a fairly modern double-cell lagoon. The system was run by a single public works director, who also helped the town's two maintenance people with the streets, parks, and cemetery. The director did most of the book work on the sewer system, including filling out reports and forms for the state health department.

During irrigation season, the leaky sewage-collector pipes took in excess water and caused bacterial problems in the lagoons. At times the lagoons overflowed and, due to electric failures or vandalism, the pumping system failed, resulting in unplanned spills into an adjacent creek. The spills violated the rules of the state health department, which was doing the bidding of the Environmental Protection Agency by administering the clean water laws of Congress. The state health department sent letters to the town's officials ordering immediate remedies and threatening fines. The town looked to the public works director to handle it—in addition to his street work, lawn mowing, sewage testing, and work on reports for the state health department. Although the town struggled mightily to comply with the law, the town was poor, was not growing, and just did not have the money or staffing to comply fully with the dictates of Congress as passed down through two huge bureaucracies. The town still struggles.

As with federal mandates, those imposed by the states on local communities are reasonable and in the public interest. Few would argue with claims that drinking water should not contain lead, that school buses should be safety inspected, or that counties should address the special educational needs of handicapped children. Thus, the ends or goals of the mandates are generally not at issue.

Who Should Pay for Mandated Programs?

The cost of the mandated programs and which government will foot the bill are at issue. With the federal government running large annual budget deficits, it is difficult for Congress to fund new policy initiatives. But by using mandates

Congress can appear to be responsive to public concerns without spending much money; that is, Congress can respond to citizen and group demands by mandating programs and requiring states to pay for them. For example, recent legislation requires schools to adopt and enforce laws banning drug use in the workplace. Although the development and administration of this policy are costly, Congress can require schools to fund it but Congress can take the credit for the new antidrug initiatives.

The same situation characterizes many state mandates. State lawmakers respond to public calls for safer school buses and drinking water and the local decision makers pay the bill. A 1990 study of state mandates conducted by the Advisory Commission on Intergovernmental Relations describes the political issues involved:

> The major mandate issue for many local governments is whether they can meet the financial demands of state mandates within the financial limits imposed by the state. . . . essentially, a mandate substitutes [state] priorities for local ones.[30]

Thus the changing nature of intergovernmental relations has implications for community power and policies, as well as for the question of who governs. Without question some people and some groups are more influential in community affairs than are others. At the same time, some decisional latitude and the ability to set local priorities are slipping from the grasp of the communities themselves. According to Mark Gottdiener, "three decades of change have transformed the city from a formidable engine of growth to a federal and state client dependent on a form of municipal welfare."[31]

Summary

It is not at all easy to grapple with questions of community power and politics. The local political landscape is extremely diverse. Many of these governments are clustered together in large metropolitan areas where one can travel through a city, a county, and a school district without even noticing. Some of the units are enormous, such as New York City and Los Angeles, whereas others are tiny, such as Elsa, Texas.

Many cities and most counties operate with partisan political systems, whereas schools, special districts, and the majority of municipalities use nonpartisan systems. Some elect representatives from districts, others select them at-large, and a few use both methods. Some old cities have long-standing traditions of ethnicity-based partisan politics. Many new cities use a nonpartisan reformed system of government. The scale, age, histories, and economies of American communities are so varied that it is difficult to generalize much about their power and politics.

Further, the environments in which modern American communities operate are complicated by recent political and economic developments. The states and the national government are increasingly intrusive in local affairs, wrapping the communities in a web of dictates and requirements. The nationalization and internationalization of the economy, as well as the ebb and flow of economic circumstances, leave local communities with a shrinking ability to control their own fortunes.

Still, questions of power, of who governs, fascinate political scholars. Some contend that local communities are still run by elites, whereas others see a more diverse and pluralistic system emerging. None fail to recognize the growing power of fundamental experts—city managers, planners, computer and legal experts, and other professionals who occupy bureaucratic slots. Modern research increasingly focuses on the growing role of external forces in community politics, particularly the state and national governments and external and mobile capital. Finally, scholars are interested in the role of citizens in governing their own communities, and hence election systems and elections remain matters of interest in a representative democracy.

Policy Perspective: Economic Development and Outside Capital . . . .

Gottdiener highlights the interpretation of contemporary community power and politics held by many modern observers. He claims in his book *The Decline of Urban Politics* (1987) that the meaningful decisions impacting the local community are no longer made by popularly rooted representative bodies. Rather, much of the political life of the community is directed by external capital and business interests as well as by state and federal governments and bureaucratically rooted specialists.[32]

Similarly, the external preemption of local politics is addressed in a widely cited 1981 study conducted by Paul Peterson.[33] He argues that the primary political drive of the modern city is to survive economically. To survive, cities must grow. They must attract capital, which is mobile. The search for capital takes the form of local policies designed to enable a city to compete with other communities in attracting new business and residential development. In Peterson's words, "the primary interests of cities [are] the maintenance and enhancement of their economic productivity."[34]

The Urge for Economic Development

The cities' development strategy is to invest in infrastructure, local investment in roads, utilities, and industrial parks, along with taxing and zoning policies that are attractive to development interests with capital to invest. The underlying assumptions in such policies are that new growth will more than pay back the costs associated with its procurement; and that the city will have jobs and tax revenues adequate to meet its needs. In a 1985 study of Cleveland, Todd Swanstrom notes that "by lowering taxes on mobile wealth, cities will eventually increase tax revenues through an expanding tax base."[35]

According to Peterson, community policies devoted to development and growth come at a price—the neglect of social policies and programs that have a redistributional impact.[36] That is, money spent to attract more business and industry is money that is not spent on recreational programs, on health and hospitals, or on a variety of other services that would benefit those who do not profit from the aggressive economic growth policies. A variety of potentially redistributive local policies are thus preempted by policies designed to placate the interests of economic enterprises external to the community.

Several urban politics researchers challenge Peterson's model of urban policy making, arguing that cities have a considerable amount of policy discretion. In other words, they contend that politics does matter and cities can have sufficient resources and authority to make effective public policy.[37] The relevance of election structure and representation is clear; it is linked with the models of urban governance outlined by several scholars.[38]

Does Development Improve the Economic Health of Communities?

Some scholars of urban politics suggest that local communities may be wasting their time chasing business and industry. John Herbers reports that after the expenditure of billions of dollars in public funds over several decades, the extent of economic development remains unclear.[39] Disappointment, Herbers argues, has often overshadowed success.

Mark Schneider argues that the locational decisions of business and industry are based on a host of factors, of which local fiscal policies are just one, and that the latter therefore have but a marginal impact on location choices.[40] In addition, the economic health of a community is the product of a blend of many factors, including the health of the national economy, the regional economy, and national and state decisions. Community growth and development may help to keep taxes low and services high—to enhance the economic health of the community. But it is not at all clear, in the context of state, national, and even international politics and economics, that growth and development can be successfully manipulated with local policies. In Schneider's view, decisions by local politicians have relatively little impact on a community's economic fortunes; rather, the locals simply respond to demands originating from outside the community.

A prime example of local response to external demands is Denver's efforts in 1991 to assemble a public subsidy package large enough to lure a huge United Airlines maintenance facility to its new international airport. In an effort to beat out locations in Oklahoma and Virginia, Denver offered United over $200 million in an assortment of facilities and tax breaks. But that wasn't enough for the airline's management. They also wanted a package that would total $600 million over thirty years, include state tax credits of $2,000 per year per new employee, and pay the credits to United from the state treasury if the airline would suffer profitless years. The city, in concert with the governor, then pressured the state legislature to meet in special session to enact legislation to give United what it wanted. In this instance, the agendas of both the community and the state were driven by outside economic interests. (In the end, Denver's efforts proved futile; United Airlines received a better offer from Indianapolis and decided to locate its facility there.)

Outsiders Limit the Community's Power to Affect Policy

Clearly, much of the power to affect policies in the modern American community lies well beyond the city or town limits. Clarence Stone puts it this way:

> While local officials enjoy considerable formal authority, they must respond to external inducements and penalties beyond their influence. To a large extent, they must play by rules they have not made.[41]

Stone also notes the inherent constraints under which urban governing coalitions must operate:

> Because centrifugal forces are always strong, achieving cooperation is a major accomplishment and requires constant effort. . . . Cooperation across institutional lines is valuable but far from automatic; and cooperation is more likely to grow under some circumstances than others.[42]

Stone's analysis seems to be to the point. Communities have to deal daily with the impact of outside forces. A recent work by Pagano and Bowman suggests that city investment in and regulation of development projects is the most effective means that a city can use to control its growth and its future cityscape.[43] City leaders should pay heed to the words of Pagano and Bowman.

KEY TERMS

power elites
reputational approach
stratification approach
power pyramid
pluralism
executive-centered coalition
at-large election

ADDITIONAL READING

Dahl, Robert. *Who Governs?* New Haven: Yale University Press, 1961.

Hunter, Floyd. *Community Power Structure.* Chapel Hill: University of North Carolina Press, 1953.

Jones, Bryan D., and Lynn W. Bachelor. *The Sustaining Hand: Community Leadership and Corporate Power.* Lawrence: University Press of Kansas, 1986.

Stone, Clarence N. *Regime Politics: Governing Atlanta 1946–1988.* Lawrence: University Press of Kansas, 1989.

Vogel, Ronald K. *Urban Political Economy: Broward County, Florida.* Gainesville: University Press of Florida, 1992.

Pagano, Michael A. and Ann O'M. Bowman. *CityScapes and Capital.* Baltimore: Johns Hopkins University Press, 1995.

NOTES

1. Norton Long, "The Local Community as an Ecology of Games," *American Journal of Sociology* (Nov. 1958): 252.
2. Robert Lynd and Helen Lynd, *Middletown* (New York: Harcourt Brace, 1929), cited in Willis D. Hawley and Frederick W. Wirt, *The Search for Community Power* (Englewood Cliffs, N.J.: Prentice-Hall, 1968).
3. Ibid., pp. 43, 50.
4. Floyd Hunter, *Community Power Structure* (New York: Doubleday/Anchor Books, 1963).
5. Ibid., pp. 66, 74, 76, 81.
6. Nelson Polsby, *Community Power and Political Theory* (New Haven: Yale University Press, 1963).
7. Ibid.; and Raymond E. Wolfinger, "Reputation and Reality in the Study of Community Power," *American Sociological Review* (Oct. 1960): 636–44.
8. Robert A. Dahl, *Who Governs?* (New Haven: Yale University Press, 1961), p. 331.
9. Ronald K. Vogel, *Urban Political Economy: Broward County, Florida* (Gainesville: University Press of Florida, 1992), p. 40.
10. Ibid.
11. Polsby, *Community Power*, p. 117.
12. Peter Bachrach and Morton S. Baratz, "Two Faces of Power," *American Political Science Review* (Dec. 1962): 947–62.
13. Ibid.: 948, 949.
14. Raymond E. Wolfinger and John O. Field, "Political Ethos and the Structure of City Government," *American Political Science Review* (Dec. 1962): 948.
15. Peverill Squire and Eric R. A. N. Smith, "The Effects of Partisan Information on Voters in Nonpartisan Elections," *Journal of Politics* (Fall 1988): 169–79.
16. Willis D. Hawley, *Non-Partisan Elections and the Case for Party Politics* (New York: Wiley, 1973).
17. Harold Wolman, John Strate and Alan Melchior, "Does Changing Mayors Matter?" *Journal of Politics* (Feb. 1996): 201–223.
18. Robert R. Alford and Eugene C. Lee, "Voter Turnout in American Cities," *American Political Science Review* (Sept. 1968): 796–813.
19. Ibid., p. 804.
20. Eugene C. Lee, "City Elections: A Statistical Profile," in *Municipal Yearbook* (Washington, D.C.: ICMA, 1963), pp. 74–84.
21. Susan Welch and Timothy Bledsoe, *Urban Reform and Its Consequences* (Chicago: University of Chicago Press, 1988).

22. Chandler Davidson and George Korbel, "At-Large Elections and Minority-Group Representation: A Re-Examination of Historical and Contemporary Evidence," *Journal of Politics* (Nov. 1981): 982–1,005; Richard Engstrom and Michael D. McDonald, "The Effect of At-Large versus District Elections on Racial Representation in U.S. Municipalities," in *Electoral Laws and Their Political Consequences*, ed. Bernard Grofman and Arend Lijphart (New York: Agathon Press, 1986), pp. 203–25; and Peggy Heilig and Robert J. Mundt, "Do Districts Make a Difference?" *Urban Interest* (Spring 1981): 62–75.
23. Susan Welch, "The Impact of At-Large Elections on the Representation of Blacks and Hispanics," *Journal of Politics* 52 (Nov. 1990): 1,050–76.
24. Delbert Tabel, "Minority Representation on City Councils: The Impact of Structure on Hispanics and Blacks," *Social Science Quarterly* (March 1978): 142–52; Welch, "The Impact of At-Large Elections"; and C. E. Teasley III, "Minority Vote Dilution: The Impact of Election System and Past Discrimination on Minority Representations," *State and Local Government Review* (Fall 1987): 95–100.
25. Kenneth R. Mladenka, "Barriers to Hispanic Employment Success in 1,200 Cities," *Social Science Quarterly* (June 1989): 391–407; Kenneth R. Mladenka, "Blacks and Hispanics in Urban Politics," *American Political Science Review* (March 1989): 165–92; Kenneth J. Meier and Joseph Stewart, Jr., *The Politics of Hispanic Education: Un Paso Pa'Lante y Dos Pa'tras* (Albany: State University of New York Press, 1991); and Kenneth J. Meier, Joseph Stewart, Jr., and Robert E. England, *Race, Class and Education: The Politics of Second Generation Discrimination* (Madison: University of Wisconsin Press, 1989).
26. Paul Peterson, *City Limits* (Chicago: University of Chicago Press, 1981).
27. Mark Gottdiener, *The Decline of Urban Politics* (Newbury Park, Calif.: Sage Publications, 1987), pp. 14, 16.
28. Advisory Commission on Intergovernmental Relations, *Mandates: Cases in State-Local Relations* (Washington, D.C.: ACIR, 1990), p. 3.
29. *Governing* (May 1991): 14.
30. ACIR, *Mandates*, p. 4.
31. Gottdiener, *Urban Politics*, p. 6.
32. Ibid.
33. Peterson, *City Limits*.
34. Ibid.
35. Todd Swanstrom, *The Crisis of Growth Politics* (Philadelphia: Temple University Press, 1985).
36. Peterson, *City Limits*.
37. Clarence N. Stone and Heywood T. Sanders, eds., *The Politics of Urban Development* (Lawrence: University Press of Kansas, 1987); Vogel, *Urban Political Economy*; and Mark Schneider, *The Competitive City* (Pittsburgh: University of Pittsburgh Press, 1989).
38. Clarence N. Stone, *Regime Politics: Governing Atlanta, 1946–1988* (Lawrence: University Press of Kansas, 1989); and Rufus P. Browning, Dale R. Marshall, and David H. Tabb, *Protest Is Not Enough: The Struggle of Blacks and Hispanics for Equality in Urban Politics* (Berkeley: University of California Press, 1984).
39. John Herbers, "A Third Wave of Economic Development," *Governing* (June 1990): 43.
40. Schneider, *The Competitive City*.
41. Clarence N. Stone, "The Study of the Politics of Urban Development," in *The Politics of Urban Development*, ed. Clarence N. Stone and Heywood T. Sanders (Lawrence: University Press of Kansas, 1987), p. 3.
42. Stone, *Regime Politics*, p. 8.
43. Michael A. Pagano and Ann O'M. Bowman, *CityScapes and Capital* (Baltimore: Johns Hopkins University Press, 1995).

CHAPTER 13

State and Local Fiscal Policy

The soaring federal budget deficit has created fiscal worries for state and local governments, which today tend to receive less federal aid than they did a decade or two ago. Here, U.S. Congressman Maurice Hinchey explains the federal deficit at a town meeting in Kingston, New York.
(D. Ogust/The Image Works)

• • • **The Public Demand: More Services, No More Taxes**

• • • **Fiscal Policy: A Complex System of Institutions and Budgets**

State and Local Spending
Sources of Revenue
Tax Burdens
Tax-Collection Policies
Borrowing: A Major Source of Financing
Revenue and General Obligation Bonds

• • • **Trends in Fiscal Policy**

Reduced Federal Funding
Increased Spending
New Taxes
Other Trends
Tough Times Ahead

• • • **The Politics of Money**

The Federal Role
Tax Revolts
Privatization of Public Services
Comparing Regressive and Progressive Tax Systems

Focus 13.1: The Return of the Toll Road?

Expanding the Tax Base
Tax-Base Disparities

Focus 13.2: Would You Like Higher Tuition and Pay Toilets?

Chasing Industry: A Risky Business?
Earmarking Tax Revenues
Taxation and Public Opinion
Tax Reform

• • • **The Problems and Politics of Budget Making**

The Executive Budget Process
Influential Experts
Special Interest Group Influence
The Uncertainty of Budgeting

Incremental Annual Budget Changes
Failed Methods of Budgeting

• • • Summary

State and local finances are complicated because state and local governments are complicated. State governments spend billions on schools, social services, corrections, and so on. Local governments spend for schools, public safety, parks, and utility services. Major state revenue sources include sales and income taxes; local governments rely heavily on property and sales taxes. Of course, all of these taxes hit the poor harder than the wealthy, though the particular mix of services, taxes, and tax burdens varies extensively among the states and among the localities. Americans generally like to receive government services but are less enthusiastic about paying taxes. Recent years have witnessed many tax revolts and budget crises. The fiscal problems facing state and local officials today are increasingly difficult.

The American public is demanding more services from its governments, and politicians promise to provide them if they win elections. Softball players demand more baseball diamonds, lights, and umpires at city park. Golfers want better greens. The library is a fire hazard and may be closed unless sprinklers and more exits are installed. The police are angry at the offer of a 4 percent salary increase and the rejection of their staff expansion demands. So are the firefighters. The federal government, working through the state health department, has found in the city illegal discharge of treated sewage; the state will fine the city unless costly improvements are made. The city council just gave the city manager a 5 percent raise; the flood of mail and phone calls indicates that voters noticed, don't like it, and want the council to stop spending "recklessly." They demand a tax cut in place of escalating administrative salaries.

Parents complain bitterly at a school board meeting about the closing of an elementary school due to low enrollment. Some also object to an economy measure that rerouted school buses; others want expanded marching band activities. At the same time, teachers threaten a slowdown unless their 6 percent pay and benefits hike is approved. Yet one month earlier the voters had defeated a measure that would have increased the millage rate (or property tax level) to provide more money for the general operation of the schools. The school board and council members meet with a state senator who lives in the community. They tell the senator that their financial woes are, in part, the fault of the state legislature, because it is not allocating enough money to the schools and is imposing too many duties on the city, most of which are costly and unaccompanied by financial support. The state senator mentions an upcoming statewide vote on a tax-limitation measure, the soaring costs to the state of prisons and health care, and the lack of funds to repair even decaying state buildings and roads.

The Public Demand: More Services, No More Taxes

The American public has developed an enormous appetite for collectively provided goods and services over the past two centuries, and that appetite continues to grow. Americans have long expected government to protect them against external threat and to see to it that their mail is delivered. The national government, whose job it is to attend to these matters, has done so. But throughout much of U.S. history Americans have also assumed that internal public safety would be maintained; schools would be built, staffed, and heated, and children would be educated; roads and bridges would be built and maintained; drinkable water would come out of the faucet; elections would be conducted at the proper times; vital records would be kept in accurate and accessible fashion; and so on. These goods and services, however, do not come from the national government; rather, they are provided by the states and localities.

Today, though, the American public is asking state and local governments for even more. The demands include libraries in most communities; day-care facilities and public housing for moderate- and low-income citizens; parks with lighted softball diamonds and tennis courts; and skating, basketball, football, and baseball facilities. Feeding this colossal public appetite is expensive and, given the public's collective aversion to taxes, not easily accomplished. Governors, state legislatures, city councils, school boards, and county commissioners struggle mightily to bridge the gap between the public's collective wants and its reluctance to pay for them. State and local governments are successful in providing a wide range of essential services—water, roads, schools, and public safety, for example. However, public officials struggle with demands for more services without more taxes.

Fiscal Policy: A Complex System of Institutions and Budgets

A knowledge of the structural arrangement of the full American government system is essential to an understanding of state and local finances. The complex and varied character of that system is our focus in this chapter. The elaborate and structurally complicated nature of the American political system is evident in the fiscal systems and policies that are employed to provide services and pay for government. **Fiscal policy** refers to the state and local laws that govern the levying of taxes and the spending of money by state and local governments, respectively. Counties operate social service systems, conduct elections, keep vital records, and maintain jails, rural roads, and bridges. Cities provide streets, police and fire protection, utilities, and so on. States provide roads and operate colleges and universities, parks, and prisons. Much of what the various levels of government do is intergovernmental. For instance, while local school districts run the elementary and secondary schools, states provide much of the money and exercise some control. States collect fuel taxes and share the revenues with cities and counties. States and counties cooperatively operate social service systems.

Similarly, the fiscal system employed to raise money and pay bills is complicated and intergovernmental in that it tracks to a complex array of institutions. Citizens pay property taxes to cities or townships, counties, school districts, and special districts. They pay sales taxes to states, cities, and counties. They pay income taxes to states and sometimes to cities as well. Gasoline is taxed by the federal government and the states, and the revenues are shared with local governments. Many government services carry special user fees, such as fishing and hunting licenses. Charges are levied for driver's licenses, automobile license plates, and teacher certification.

All levels of government levy taxes, though the type and level of tax vary widely. Sales, income, property, and fuel taxes vary among states and among cities. So do levels of spending. And so do methods of budgeting.

State and Local Spending

As Table 13.1 shows, various kinds of services are made available to the American public by the nation's states, cities, townships, counties, schools, and special districts. Education—including elementary, secondary, and higher education—constitutes the largest portion of state and local budgets (or about 40 percent of total expenditures). Other services that require significant financial support include public assistance (20 percent), health and hospitals (11 percent), roads and highways (8 percent), and police protection (4 percent). About 7 percent is spent on interest on the general debt.

The particular services provided vary by the type of government. The leading expenditure categories for the states are education, public assistance, highways, and health and hospitals. Other state services include parks, corrections, police protection, regulation of activities (ranging from haircutting to mining), and paying for the courts and legislatures.[1] Cities, counties, schools, and special districts provide different types of services. Local schools provide education and special districts provide sewerage, water, and other services. The major service areas of American cities include police and fire protection, sewers and water supply, streets and roads, edu-

TABLE 13.1 STATE AND LOCAL EXPENDITURES, 1992

Function	Expenditures ($U.S. per capita)	Total Expenditures (percent)
Elementary and secondary education	$898	29
Higher education	331	11
Highways	261	8
Public assistance	605	20
Health and hospitals	345	11
Police protection	135	4
Fire protection	56	2
Natural resources	48	2
Sanitation and sewerage	127	4
Housing and community development	67	2
Parks and recreation	62	2
Interest on general debt	217	7

Source: U.S. Bureau of the Census, *Statistical Abstract of the United States, 1995* (Washington, D.C.: GPO, 1995), p. 300.

cation, airports, and parks and recreation programs. Some cities also provide natural gas and electrical services. Counties provide public assistance, education, hospitals, roads, and police, though their spending patterns vary dramatically nationwide.

Sources of Revenue

The revenue sources for all state and local governments are listed in Table 13.2. Although there is a bewildering assortment of user fees and charges, the **sales tax**—applied to the purchase of goods and, sometimes, services—is the single largest source of revenue, accounting for 17 percent of the total. At 15 percent the **property tax**, a tax levied on homes, businesses, and other real estate, is also a major revenue producer; it is used almost exclusively by local governments. Although the federal government is an important revenue source, its contribution is declining. Other sources of revenue for states and localities include insurance trust funds and the state **income tax**, which is levied on personal and business income.

Just as state and local units vary in the services they provide, they also differ in their sources of revenue. For the states, the sales tax is the leading source,

TABLE 13.2 STATE AND LOCAL REVENUES, 1992

Source	Revenue Amount ($U.S. per capita)	Total Revenues* (percent)
Federal government	$703	15.1
Property taxes	700	15.1
Sales tax and gross receipts	769	16.5
Individual income tax	452	9.7
Corporate income tax	93	2.0
Miscellaneous user fees and charges	932	20.1
Utility and liquor store fees	245	5.3
Insurance trust funds	588	12.7
Other	165	3.5

*Because of rounding, figures do not add up to 100 percent.
Source: U.S. Bureau of the Census, *Statistical Abstract of the United States, 1995* (Washington, D.C.: GPO, 1995), p. 304.

accounting for 22 percent of the total. The sales tax is followed by federal money derived from a host of different programs, amounting to 18 percent of the total. The individual income tax is also a major revenue source, accounting for approximately 10 percent of all state and local government revenue.[2]

However, cities derive 22 percent of their money from other governments, another 22 percent from an assortment of fees, 16 percent from utility charges and liquor sales, and 17 percent from the property tax.[3] America's 3,042 counties differ still. Nearly one-third of their funds comes from the state, 26 percent is generated by the property tax, and 24 percent comes from fees and charges.[4]

There is considerable variation in both spending and revenue systems across the country. In 1993, state general expenditures ranged from $2,892 per person in Missouri to $10,112 in Alaska. Even within regions of the United States the differences can be significant; Wyoming spent $5,126 in 1993 compared to nearby Idaho at $3,145.[5] These inter- and intra-regional differences reflect not only the resource availability of the states, but also their political cultures.

Moreover, not all states employ all of the traditional taxes. Alaska, Florida, Nevada, South Dakota, Texas, Washington, and Wyoming do not have an individual income tax. Nevada, Texas, Washington, and Wyoming all lack the corporate income tax. Alaska, Delaware, Montana, New Hampshire, and Oregon operate without a general sales tax.[6]

In states that employ all traditional taxes, the rates of taxation vary greatly. Some states use a graduated income tax similar to that of the federal government; others impose a flat percentage rate irrespective of income. For example, Alabama's individual income tax ranges from 2 percent to 5 percent and Colorado's is a flat 5 percent. Kansas has a 4.25 percent state sales tax, whereas Pennsylvania has set its sales tax at 6 percent.[7] Arizona, Michigan, and New Jersey are among the more than two dozen states that exempt food (except for prepared foods) from the sales tax. Mississippi, Virginia, and a few other states impose a tax on food items. In the tobacco-producing state of North Carolina the tax on cigarettes is just 2 cents per package; in Connecticut and New Jersey it is 40 cents. Hawaii taxes cigarettes at 40 percent of the wholesale price. State taxes on motor fuels vary as well, ranging from less than 10 cents to 20 cents per gallon.[8]

The amount of money the states and localities collect ranges widely. In 1993, Alaska took in $4,940 per capita, whereas Mississippi averaged just $1,534 for each person. The mean in 1993 was $2,294 (see Figure 13.1). Similar differences prevail among the states for specific taxes. In 1993, New Hampshire and its local governments collected $1,411 per capita in property taxes; in Wyoming the figure was $890, in New Mexico, $238, and in Alabama, $183. In the category of the personal income tax, New York and Massachusetts collected over $800 per person in 1993 and two states collected under $100. In 1993, the state of Washington, which has no income tax, was second among all states in 1993 in per-capita collections of the sales tax at $1,009. Hawaii, which ranks low with respect to the property tax, was first at $1,117 in sales tax col-

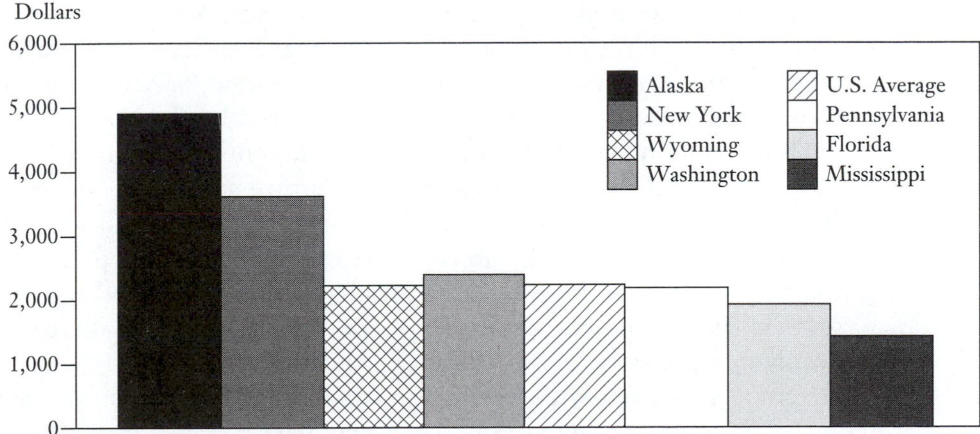

Figure 13.1 State and Local Per-Capita Tax Collections in Selected States, 1993
Source: "State and Local Source Book," *Governing*, 1997, p. 34.

lections.[9] Minnesota has a highly progressive income tax. Alaska leans hard on its extractive industries for tax revenue. New Mexico has a large "permanent fund" derived from taxes on extracted minerals and petroleum and interest on fund monies accounts for a substantial portion of general fund revenues. New Hampshire leads the nation in allowing the local units to do the taxing.[10]

Tax Burdens

The variation among the states in total tax collection is to some extent a reflection of their uneven wealth, but other factors also play a role. On average, state and local governments collected $110 in taxes per $1,000 of personal income in 1993. But that figure ranged from $216 in Alaska and $147 in New York to just $88 in Missouri and $94 in Alabama.[11] Clearly, the desire to provide goods and services collectively varies considerably among the American states.

The relationship between a state's wealth and its taxes can be illustrated by examining the case of New Mexico. New Mexico ranked twenty-fourth among the states in the total amount of state and local tax collections. It collected $2,132 per capita in 1993, or 7 percent less than the national average. Yet New Mexico ranked third among the states in its level of state and local taxes per $1,000 in personal income, the figure being 20 percent above the national average. New Mexico is not a wealthy state, but it has imposed upon itself a state and local tax burden that is higher than the national average in order to provide services for its citizens.[12] It also has its large permanent fund.

Tax-Collection Policies

There is another important way in which the fiscal policies of the states vary—the extent to which they impose and collect taxes or leave those tasks to the local governments. In some states almost all the money raised to pay for state and local government goods and services is collected by the state, with a substantial portion then allocated to the local governments. As Figure 13.2 shows, that proportion is as high as 82 percent in Delaware and as low as 34.8 percent in New Hampshire. The average for all states is 59.9 percent, though that figure has been increasing steadily in recent years. The growth is partly the result of the new federalism, wherein the states have assumed a growing share of program costs and the need, sometimes under court order, to increase and more evenly provide state support for local schools.

State variations with regard to tax-collection methods can have political and economic consequences. A state may have a conservative legislature but some politically liberal cities. If the state does the taxing, public programs are likely to be less well funded than if tax policies and levels were left to the lo-

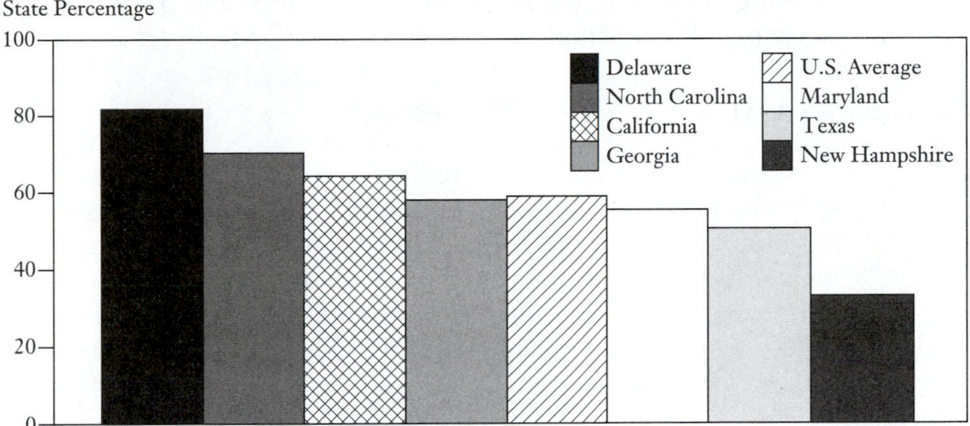

Figure 13.2 State Government Percentage of State and Local Tax Revenue, 1993, Selected States

Source: Adapted from Colorado Public Expenditures Council, *How Colorado Compares*, 1996 edition, p. 4.

calities. In addition, state-level politicians in states with centralized tax systems are in a better position to exert their will over local priorities and programs than are their counterparts in fiscally decentralized states. They can simply set conditions that go along with the distribution of funds. **Fiscal decentralization**—the tendency of some states to give local governments the taxing and spending responsibilities—can lead to wide disparities in the ability of local units to pay for public goods and services.

When local units are left to fend for themselves, those located in economically poor sections of a state may simply be unable to raise as much money as their more well-to-do counterparts, and the quality of such services as public education can suffer. Inequities are less likely to occur when the state collects the taxes and supports local schools and other local programs with direct annual state appropriations. However, in this case, the state is also in a better position to tell the localities how to run their affairs and the development of distribution formulae becomes a contentious issue in the legislature.

The pattern of taxation has changed significantly over the years. In the early part of the twentieth century, the property tax was the primary source of revenue for the states. Today, sales and individual income taxes generate most state revenue and the property tax is the major revenue source for local governments. In 1993, 33 percent of all state taxes came from the sales tax and 32 percent from the income tax.[13] At the local level, income and sales taxes are growing in use, as is the employment of user fees. The pattern of taxation tends to change slowly with time.

Borrowing: A Major Source of Financing

Forty-seven of the fifty states prohibit by way of their own constitutional or statutory provisions **deficit spending** for general operations—that is, spending more than they take in for the normal yearly operation of their governments. Indiana, Vermont, and Wyoming are the exceptions.[14] But that does not mean they refrain from borrowing money or that they are without debt. Indeed, borrowing is a major and very important source of money for state and local governments.

Revenue and General Obligation Bonds

When a state or local unit borrows money, it does so by issuing or selling **bonds**—legal instruments in which the government unit promises to repay the bondholder a certain amount of money at a specific time. In effect, a bond is a pledge to pay back what is borrowed, plus interest, at a certain date. Most bonds are issued by investment banks and brokerage houses, which handle the borrowing logistics for government units. Usually the government seeks to raise a large amount of money, and the brokerage house breaks down that amount into smaller denominations. These are then sold to lenders, generally huge financial institutions such as banks, insurance companies, and brokerage houses themselves. Some bonds may then be further broken down into smaller denominations and sold to individuals.

There are two general types of bonds that states and localities employ to borrow money—revenue bonds and general obligation bonds. A **revenue bond** is just what its name implies; it is a pledge to the lender to be paid off with the revenues from the facility or program built with the borrowed money. For example, a city might issue several million dollars in revenue bonds to obtain the money needed to build a convention center or a sports facility. Those frequenting the facility would then be charged a user fee, which would eventually provide the revenue to pay off the bonded debt.

A city faced with decaying streets may need to embark on an extensive repair program. It might cost millions of dollars that the city just does not have in its annual operating budgets. It might then seek to raise the funds for the road repair program by issuing "general obligation" bonds. A **general obligation bond** involves a pledge by the city to repay lenders with money derived from current revenues or from a small additional tax imposed only until the debt is satisfied. It is called a general obligation bond because the municipality pledges the "full faith and credit" of the taxpayers as security for the payback.

Careful Borrowing Prevents Deficit Spending

State and local governments, like private businesses, would find it difficult to operate without the ability to borrow money. Major capital investments, such as roads, buildings, and land acquisitions, are far too expensive to finance on a cash basis out of any single year's tax revenue. In addition, such investments usually have long-term benefits spanning several generations of citizens. So just as an industry borrows to finance plant expansion and pays off the debt with years of profits, so do cities, schools, utility districts, and states borrow money for capital projects.

State and local governments almost never allow deficit spending—that is, borrowing money to finance the ongoing expenditures of government (for example, employee salaries, as opposed to capital spending on roads, buildings, and the like). They are generally prohibited from doing so by state law, and borrowing for current operations is considered unwise and dangerous, for it just postpones financial trouble and promises to transform current difficulties into future disasters. Many of the past and recent financial difficulties in New York City are the result of deficit spending for ongoing operations.

The Impact of Federal Tax Laws

For years the ability of state and local governments to borrow money was enhanced by provisions in federal tax laws that permitted **tax-exempt bonds**; that is, the interest a lender earned from state and local bonds was exempt from federal taxation. This not only made the bonds easy to sell but also allowed the states and localities to borrow money at interest rates below the then-current level. It was worthwhile for persons in high tax brackets to earn, say, 7 percent rather than 10 percent on their money if in the process they could escape all income tax on the earned interest. In addition, the purchase of state and local bonds was usually a secure investment, especially if the full faith and credit of the taxpayers guaranteed the loans. Indeed, such general obligation bonds could be sold at interest rates below the going rate for the slightly riskier revenue bonds.

However, in 1986 Congress made sweeping changes in the federal tax code, some of which affected state and local borrowing.[15] For example, the tax rates in the top income brackets were lowered considerably, with the result that tax-exempt bonds became less attractive to those with high annual incomes. The tax-free nature of some earned income is less useful if one pays 28 or 33 percent in taxes on the last increment of income than if that last portion is taxed at 50 or even 70 percent. Surely state and local bonds will continue to be attractive to many investors, but clearly a little less so, and the interest rates that those governments will have to pay will be closer to the market for other forms of capital.

Another 1986 congressional change in the federal tax law has placed restrictions on the type of state and local borrowing for which the interest on bonds is tax-free. During the decade preceding the 1986 federal tax law changes, localities sought to promote growth and development by issuing what were called **industrial development bonds (IDBs)**. In doing so, however, the localities were simply lending their name to borrowing by private interests for investments ranging from new golf courses to fast-food outlets. Local officials assumed that such development would strengthen their communities economically. Business and industry leaders liked the IDBs because with the cloak of government backing, the interest paid to lenders was tax-free just as with other state and local bonds, and thus money could be borrowed at a rate a few percentage points below the going market rate. Some argued that the IDB arrangements were thinly disguised and fraudulent schemes to avoid taxes; others touted them as clever ways to help communities. Since 1986, federal tax laws restrict the kinds of bonds that qualify for tax-exempt status, and so IDBs are no longer tax-free.

Trends in Fiscal Policy

The fiscal policies and financial circumstances of the American states and localities have undergone significant changes over the past decade or so. The most dramatic change has been in the extent to which the federal government has reversed a trend that began some six decades ago and accelerated during the 1960s and 1970s—that of being the source of an ever-larger proportion of the revenue of state and local governments.

Reduced Federal Funding

In 1958 funds provided to the states and localities through various federal programs amounted to roughly 11 percent of state and local revenues. By 1980, just twenty-two years later, that figure had grown to nearly 26 percent, following an explosion of new federal support programs during the Great Society era of the 1960s. During the 1980s, however, in the context of the Reagan administration's desire to eliminate much of this fiscal dependency and the tremendous federal deficits, federal aid declined as a proportion of state and local budgets. By 1990 it had dropped to 19.4 percent, although by 1994 it had risen to 23 percent.[16]

Increased Spending

In spite of public pressure to hold down taxes, and in the face of tax revolts in California, Massachusetts, Michigan, and a host of other states, both state and local spending and tax rates have tended to increase since the late 1970s, in spite of some tax cuts in the mid 1980s. From 1979, state and local per-capita revenues grew faster than inflation and faster than the growth in federal spending. Indeed, from 1984 to 1988, per-capita revenue growth measured in real dollars grew by just 6 percent at the national level but by 17 percent in the states and localities. As at other times in the past when national spending policy has been conservative, the rate of state and local spending has grown.

New Taxes

In 1978, forty-five states employed a sales tax, and that number has not changed. The tax rates have changed, however, with roughly half of the states increasing the rate. Similarly, there were major increases in the rate of taxation of cigarettes and gasoline in most states, and marginal jumps in the rate of taxation of alcoholic beverages.[17] Forty-one states taxed individual income in 1978 and that number has not changed either, although New Hampshire and Tennessee tax income on interest and dividends only.[18] The changes that transpired during that period were in the form of modifications of rates for various income brackets and, in several states, a reduction of the rates at the higher end. This was done in efforts to hold wealth within the states by keeping high-income people from leaving. At the same time, many states joined the national government in seeking to give full tax relief to the very poorest citizens.

In times of **taxpayer revolt** (when grassroots movements to limit taxation and spending arise) and public resistance to taxes increases, it is easier politically for policy makers to seek additional revenues through the more subtle user fees or small increases in **sin taxes** (cigarette and alcohol taxes) than through more visible and politically costly hikes in income taxes or altogether new taxes. It is fair to say that in many, if not most, states the issue of taxation is less an economic issue than a political one.

Other Trends

Other trends in state and local fiscal policies during the past decade or so include an increased reliance on user fees and the institution of state-sponsored, money-making games of chance. More governments have chosen to tax the users of particular services directly, as with park fees, higher gasoline taxes, and increased college and university tuition rates.[19] And while just thirteen states employed lottery systems a decade ago, roughly thirty-six states do so today.[20]

The clear reason for the increased reliance on such fees and money-making schemes has been to patch together revenues and make ends meet in times of declining federal help and taxpayer resistance.

Tough Times Ahead

The 1990s have been a difficult time for the states. The economy has grown slowly, and so have state revenues. But costs keep rising, especially in the area of public health. In 1980 less than 10 percent of the states' budgets was spent on public health; that figure grew to 17 percent by 1992 and is expected to rise, especially in light of changes in the national welfare system. The underlying causes are a combination of generally rising health costs (fees for physician care, hospitals, and medicine) and expanded Medicaid coverage as mandated by Congress. Some states are hit harder than others, including California and states in the Northeast and mid-Atlantic area, because they are also suffering from a decline in the defense industry.

The Politics of Money

Fiscal policy and budget making are matters of high-stakes politics, for here it is decided in authoritative fashion who will receive what government has to offer and who will pay for it. Among the most enduring issues is whether taxes should be progressive or regressive; that is, how much should we tax the wealthy in comparison to the poor? In theory, a **progressive tax** means that taxes are tied to personal income; as income rises, so does the tax rate. As measured in dollars, a **regressive tax** falls equally on everyone regardless of personal income. But those who make less pay proportionately higher taxes than those in the upper-income brackets because they must spend proportionately more of what they earn on goods and services that are subject to taxes. Other fiscal issues to consider include the role of the federal government in state and local finances,[21] the propriety of taxing services as well as goods, and the morality of state-promoted and state-sponsored gambling.

The Federal Role

The role of the federal government in providing financial support for state and local activities grew from a minor one in the early twentieth century to a major role by the 1970s. At the start of the Great Depression in the early 1930s, federal programs then in existence collectively supplied about 3 percent of the total revenues for states and localities. By 1958 that number had climbed to about 11 percent as a result, largely, of the new programs enacted by Congress during the Depression to stimulate the economy and provide needed social services.

Federal Programs Grow from the 1950s through the 1970s

The late 1950s and the decades of the 1960s and 1970s witnessed a growth in federal support for education, prompted by the Soviet scientific advances made manifest in the launching of Sputnik, the world's first orbiting satellite; by President Lyndon Johnson's Great Society programs, which were enacted in the wake of President John F. Kennedy's death in 1963 and designed to reduce poverty and discrimination, advance education, and clean up cities; and by a national awakening to environmental and consumer protection concerns. Congress passed laws establishing new programs by the hundreds, and by 1978 this assortment of federal programs provided almost 30 percent of all state and local revenue.

By the end of the 1970s, and in many policy areas well before that, federal money was helping states and localities with education, highways, sewer and water systems, airports, an assortment of welfare programs, all sorts of research, law enforcement, mental health, and so on. But there were hitches—lots of them. As conditions for the receipt of federal money, state and local governments had to meet a bewildering array of federal objectives, ranging from elimination of architectural barriers to the handicapped to certain accounting and personnel practices. As the flow of federal money grew, so too did the paperwork associated with grant application, processing, and reporting. States and localities had difficulty just keeping track of all the federal programs that imposed requirements, or provided funds, or both.

The growth of the federal role in funding state and local programs was accompanied by ideological conflict as well. Some conservatives objected to federal spending for such programs as early education for handicapped children, food stamps for needy persons, and tuition aid, job training, and related support for college students. Others fought the trend for fear that the autonomy of the states and localities would be eroded.

Change in the 1980s and 1990s

By the 1980s the confusion and paperwork involved in intergovernmental relations were frustrating for almost everyone who had to deal with them. In addition, conservatives, joined by many moderates and liberals, began to worry about the vast federal preemption of state and local political autonomy. Ronald Reagan, a two-term governor of California, was among them; in his quest for the presidency he made it clear that if elected he would seek to diminish state and local dependency on federal money as well as federal strictures on state and local decision making.

Reagan was elected president in 1980 and reelected in 1984. By the end of his second term in office, federal money as a proportion of state and local revenue had declined to approximately 16 percent, from the 1978 high of 28 percent. Although there is disagreement about the causes of the decline, two major factors likely played a role. First, although the Reagan administration had only limited success in convincing Congress to eliminate or combine a host of programs that made funds available to the states and localities, it was able to pressure Congress into either reducing funding levels or holding increases to levels below the annual inflation rate. Second, and perhaps more importantly, beginning early in his first term, President Reagan and Congress teamed up to cut taxes and increase spending, resulting in enormous and precedent-setting federal deficits. The deficits, in turn, precluded the expansion, even the maintenance, of prior federal levels of state and local program support.

The 1980s were a time of heated political arguments. Mayors, governors, and many conservatives called for a reduction of the paperwork and federal dictates that accompanied the flow of federal money to state and local units. Many conservatives wanted the money pipeline to dry up because they opposed the liberal programs that the money funded. Mayors and governors generally wanted the money flow to continue but without the constraints. Everyone wanted less paperwork. Client groups that benefitted from federal funds in such areas as education and housing fought hard to keep the money coming.

The issues and arguments surrounding the changed level of federal support were a mixture of philosophy and practicality. Some claimed that the national government was obligated to provide money to care for all Americans. That is, while the states and localities actually operate education, health, and other programs, the federal government should provide adequate support. Others sidestepped the question of obligation, focusing instead on the sovereignty of the states. The founding fathers, some contended, did not intend for the central government to tell the states how to conduct their business. The issues for still others were much more practical; they did not want to lose the funds for the programs with which they were involved or from which they benefitted. The 1996 changes in the welfare system will produce still more modifications in the fiscal relations of the national, state, and local governments.

Entitlement Programs

In recent years much of the debate over the federal role has centered around the funding of **entitlement programs** such as Medicaid. An entitlement is a legally created benefit that is available to all citizens who meet the specified criteria. The Medicaid program provides medical care for the poor and is jointly funded by the national government and the states. The national government sets the standards and eligibility requirements for the program, however, and thus national decisions translate into fiscal responsibilities for the states. During every year since 1984, the national government has expanded eligibility for Medicaid; as a result, the costs are soaring and squeezing state budgets. From 1991 to 1992, state Medicaid costs rose 12 percent, or nearly three times as fast as overall state budgets.[22] State lawmakers are increasingly frustrated, arguing that federal decisions are controlling state budget choices and, as a result, education, corrections, transportation, and other state-run social programs are being shortchanged.

Many issues and arguments surround the federal role. Which government—federal or state—should take on the financial responsibility to provide health care for all Americans? Or should government be involved at all? Should the federal government be allowed to determine a state's speed limit on highways, a state's legal drinking age, a state's responsibility for indigent health care, or how a tiny rural town cleans its sewage before discharging it into a local stream? Should standards and services be leveled nationally by strings tied to federal money and mandates, or are policy questions best left to the local decision makers?

Federal mandates can be costly when local governments are left holding the bag for the funding. The small Colorado town of Windsor, population 5400, recently spent $3 million to upgrade its wastewater plant. This is $556 per resident. Paonia, Colorado, population 1531, doled out a sum equal to $200 per person on surface water treatment. Unfunded federal mandates such as these not only cause hardships for small communities, but they can skew the direction of policy as well.

Tax Revolts

Just as state and local officials were having to adjust to the slowed flow of federal money in the 1980s and later, activists in a number of states took action to cut or limit the ability of the states and localities to raise their own money. An early and spectacular move to limit taxation occurred in California in the form of Proposition 13, a citizen-initiated ballot item.

California's Proposition 13

In the late 1970s property values were soaring in California; property tax rates were growing, too. Homeowners faced rapidly escalating property taxes. Two businessmen, Howard Jarvis and Paul Garn, spearheaded an initiative effort to place on the ballot a measure to roll back and then limit property taxes. They captured the frustration of voters and, in 1978, Proposition 13 passed by a two-to-one margin.

The provisions of Proposition 13 limit property taxes in California to one percent of the market value, cap increases at two percent of the previous year's level, allow reassessment only when property changes hands, and require a two-thirds vote (both locally and in the state legislature) to levy any new taxes. The impact of the measure has been to cut property tax revenues for California's local governments by more than half.

Before Proposition 13, California had been running a sizable budget surplus and was, in the short run, able to provide some relief for the local governments. In the longer run, however, Proposition 13 has placed severe constraints on the budgets of California's local governments and cut deeply into public programs and services. It has led to staffing cutbacks, hiring and pay freezes, and reductions in recreational, library, and cultural programs, and even in public safety. Schools have been especially hard hit. The state is last in per-capita spending for highways. Over time, however, the state and local governments have made up much of the tax losses with hikes in user fees.[23]

Other States Respond to Tax Reformers

Several states followed California's lead with respect to tax reform. In Massachusetts, a measure referred to as Proposition Two and One-Half was designed to hold property taxes to a high of 2.5 percent of assessed valuation. In 1980 Massachusetts voters passed the measure; though taxes did indeed decline, so too did some public services. Other states soon followed with tax-limiting laws, including Arizona, Hawaii, Idaho, Louisiana, Michigan, Nevada, Oregon, Washington, and Colorado. The specter of such tax revolts has made policy makers in virtually all states more cautious about tax hikes.

Some Unexpected Consequences of Tax-Limiting Measures

There have been some interesting and ironic consequences to the tax-limiting actions (see Focus 13.1). In California, for example, roughly two-thirds of the tax relief went not to the millions of homeowners who had supported Proposition 13 but to owners of commercial and farm properties. In both California and Massachusetts, as well as in some other states, the limitations placed on local revenue-raising powers have led to more local reliance on state money, which, in turn, has contributed to a diminution of local autonomy. Conservatives, while they generally favor low taxes and small government, also tend to favor local control of policy.

The wrath of some taxpayers has been felt directly at the local level, too. In 1993 in Kalkaska, Michigan, school officials were forced to end the school year in March instead of June for 2,300 students because the district couldn't afford to remain open. Voters in the district had rejected on three separate occasions a property tax increase to keep the schools open.[24]

The Impact of the Tax Revolt Movement

The impact of the tax revolt movement has gone beyond the actual legal imposition of taxing and spending limits. It has also caused politicians to be extremely cautious in their handling of issues involving tax increases. In the wake of the experiences in California, Michigan, and elsewhere, candidates in both parties regularly run on promises to cut taxes or at least to resist any new ones. Rumblings of grassroots movements to place tax-limit measures on the ballot still command the attention of decision makers, causing them to assure the public of their dedication to fiscal conservatism. Indeed, the growth in user fees and sin taxes on such items as alcoholic beverages and cigarettes is in part stimulated by a desire to raise more money without broaching the question of increases in the property or income tax. Collected just pennies at a time, these taxes are relatively painless, and tobacco and alcohol are not widely viewed as essentials.

Politicians are wary of tax increases, and for good reason. Larry Sabato, in a book on state governors, notes that after 1960 the tax issue more than any other contributed to the electoral defeat of incumbent governors who lost bids for reelection.[25]

The tax revolt movement, the relative decline in federal financial support, and economic downturns have together made financial survival especially tough for some states and communities. The fall in oil prices hit hard in such states as Texas, Oklahoma, and Louisiana, and tourism-dependent states such as Colorado and Utah are fiscally vulnerable to snow-short winters.

Privatization of Public Services

In response to the financial squeeze felt by many states and communities, many have considered the **privatization** of public services; that is, shrinking government by turning over the provision of goods and services to the private sector. The idea, popular among conservatives especially, received a boost during Reagan's presidency in the 1980s.

In recent years proposals to privatize everything from public hospitals to the issuance of driver's licenses have been on the agendas of state and local governments. Indeed, Donna Dudek cites a survey of cities conducted by the International City Management Association in 1982 that reports that 41 percent of solid waste collection and 31 percent of residential garbage collection was being done privately. In addition, private contractors handled 26 percent of street maintenance, 78 percent of vehicle towing and storage, and 19 percent of building and grounds maintenance.[26]

Of course, much of what government has done routinely for decades has involved some reliance on private businesses. Governments purchase vehicles, equipment, and supplies from private vendors. Huge construction companies build government buildings and construct roads. At the national level, private corporations build virtually all the hardware for the defense establishment. However, the primary assumption underlying the current push for more privatization is that slow, lazy, and inefficient government can become more efficient through involvement with the lean, ambitious, and innovative private sector. In addition, many elected officials, conservatives especially, are ideologically committed to the notions of small government, free enterprise, and the private sector. Of course, many in the private sector support private provision of government goods and services because it promises to open markets and thus increase the private sector's profits. In combination, these factors fuel the ongoing political push toward requiring state and local governments to contract with private vendors for their goods and services.

Proponents' and Opponents' Views

Privatization is a controversial political issue that is likely to continue to receive attention. While opponents such as public employees want to keep their jobs, proponents in the private sector want profits (see Figure 13.3). Both sides use public-interest rhetoric to press their particular arguments.

Advocates of privatization contend that the private sector can provide services of equal or higher value for less money. They often cite a profit-making fire department in Scottsdale, Arizona, as an example. In addition, the management of some public hospitals in Florida has been turned over to the private sector, and in New Jersey, Sears, Roebuck and Company issues driver's licenses. There are many proposals to privatize prisons, and a few are indeed operated privately.

Public employees and their organizations counter with several arguments. One is that private vendors may be unreliable. Often they provide inferior services, experience cost overruns, or simply fail to complete the task for which they are contracted. Indeed, there are numerous instances of problems with private contractors, and public employee unions keep careful records of such failures. Some opponents of privatization point to such failures as the bankruptcy and government bailouts of Penn Central, Chrysler, and Lockheed and the ineptitude and fraud in the savings and loan industry as indications that there is no guarantee of efficiency, honesty, or success in the private sector. Others argue that the protection of civil liberties might be harder in privately run prisons.

In addition, privatization is criticized because its cost savings, when they occur, tend to come at workers' expense. The private vendors are often nonunion, pay substandard wages, and provide little job protection and few if any benefits. These conditions, opponents argue, produce marginal savings or

DON'T LET THE PRIVATEERS' FLAG FLY!

Privatizing public services is not a simple matter. Any radical change in the way things are done includes dangers — so there are important questions that you should ask before you allow any of your services to be privatized. For example:

Why charge the taxpayers to build a facility, then give it to a private company to make a profit from it?

Who'll do the job if private companies move on to more profitable customers when the economy is healthier?

What happens to services that don't return a profit?

Here's what happened when Los Angeles County signed a contract with a private firm to manage and maintain most county vehicles. Their need to show a profit resulted in cost overages, repair order errors, billing irregularities, unsatisfactory quality and a failure to establish an effective maintenance program. The Board of Supervisors voted unanimously to cancel the contract.

The ultimate question: What is really the best way to serve the public?

Capitalize on the experience that's already in place.

No one has more experience than CSEA members – in protecting our neighborhoods and our environment, maintaining our parks and roads, nurturing our children and our elderly, caring for our sick and mentally ill.

Keep that experience. Join CSEA in the drive to keep public services public. For a free copy of *"265,014 Reasons Why New York Shouldn't Be Plundered"*, call toll-free: **1-800-836-CSEA.**

Figure 13.3 The Civil Services Employees Association Opposes Privatization
Source: Copyright Civil Service Employees Association. Reprinted with permission of Civil Service Employees Association.

no savings at all by moving the costs elsewhere—either to the workers or the social service budgets when employees who lack benefits are unable to pay for health and other services.

Researchers' Findings

A path-breaking 1990 study by Robert Stein of Rice University suggests that privatization, while efficient, does not automatically provide cost savings to municipal governments:

> Research on contracting for goods and services has consistently found this mode of service arrangement to be more cost efficient than direct service provision and production. This, however, has not proven to be sufficient when it comes to reducing the spending levels of municipal governments and the taxes needed to support these levels.[27]

There are some real problems and dangers associated with privatization. Before a city, state, county, or school district moves to abandon public provision of a service, it must be sure that there are competent private vendors available. Unless there are several established and reputable vendors from which to choose, privatization can be risky. If there is only one vendor, problems can emerge down the road. The vendor may raise rates once the government has dismantled its own service provision system. Without private sector competition, the public may find itself gouged rather than saving money. The government also needs to monitor private providers carefully. Cost overruns, shoddy goods or services, or violations of contracts can occur, and vigilance is wise. It is important, too, to know how private vendors treat employees lest other costly problems result from deficient salary, safety, or benefit systems. (See Focus 13.1 "The Return of the Toll Road?")

Comparing Regressive and Progressive Tax Systems

Who pays a particular tax? Who picks up the tab for public goods and services? The answer to these questions varies from one tax to another.[28] As noted earlier, progressive taxes extract a disproportionately high portion of the income of those in high-income brackets, whereas regressive taxes hit the poor disproportionately relative to their income. The adoption of either tax policy has consequences. Indeed, tax-related politics is a high-stakes, often heated, affair.

The taxes employed by state and local governments are, by and large, regressive, as both the sales tax and the property tax hit the poor harder than the wealthy. The latter pay more in actual dollars, but the former pay much more as a proportion of their income. That is, the poor spend most of their income on essentials—food, clothing, transportation, shelter—so all or most of their money is hit by the sales tax or the property tax. Although the wealthy spend

Focus 13.1
THE RETURN OF THE TOLL ROAD?

• • •

You could be paying both to park and to get to school. As America's infrastructure ages and financially strapped states and localities face costly capital construction and repair bills, the notion of private investment is in the midst of a resurgence. In Puerto Rico, a $126 million private toll bridge is being constructed over the San Juan lagoon, which will shorten commuters' trip to the Isla Verde airport. In Orange County, California, plans are in place for using private enterprise to construct four express lanes down the median of crowded Highway 91.

Many other large-scale private ventures are planned or under way across the nation, and they have certain attractions. They relieve government of the need to come up with the cash to fund the capital construction and of the operating and maintenance costs that can dwarf construction costs and last for decades. Sometimes, too, private contractors can complete a job more quickly than the government. The 1991 federal Intermodal Surface Transportation Act, which allows the states to use some federal money to subsidize private projects, has stimulated private or public–private cooperative ventures.

But there are drawbacks to privatization of services as well. Sometimes private outfits have difficulty raising the enormous sums needed to get a project under way. Shifts in the economy and the cost of borrowing money can derail a project. And some politicians and voters alike philosophically oppose public subsidy of private for-profit ventures.

Nevertheless, the nation's aging infrastructure and the public's distress with the size and cost of government are likely to spawn a variety of private experiments similar to those in Puerto Rico and California's Orange County.

Source: Julie C. Olberding, "Paving the Way for Private Roads," State Government News (March 1993): 6–9.

more in dollars on transportation, shelter, and so on, what they spend represents a smaller portion of their income. Certain exemptions help to moderate the impact of regressive taxes. Just over half the states exempt food from the sales tax and all states exempt prescription drugs, for example.

The income tax may or may not be regressive, depending on its structure. A flat-rate income tax, coupled with exemptions that can be taken more readily by the wealthy than by the poor, tends to have a regressive impact. The types of exemptions include capital gains, which are profits from the sale of such items as real property and stocks, and business expenses. In contrast, a graduated income tax, which is based on one's earned income, is progressive. The income tax rate climbs as earned income increases, thus the wealthy pay taxes as a larger proportion of their income than do the poor. One study showed that in the aggregate, state and local tax systems are regressive and hard on the poor. Work by the Citizens for Tax Justice showed that in 1995 the poorest 20 percent of non-elderly married couples pay 12.5 percent of their income in state and local taxes while the richest one percent paid just 7.9 percent. For the middle 60 percent, the figure was 9.8 percent.

The states with the most regressive systems were Washington, Florida, South Dakota, Tennessee, Louisiana, Pennsylvania, Illinois, Arkansas, and Michigan. These states rely heavily upon the sales tax or have a flat income tax structure, or both. Michigan recently increased its sales tax to substitute for property taxes for the support of local schools. The impact of this "reform" was to make the state's tax system more regressive. The least regressive systems were in the states of Delaware, Montana, California, and Vermont.[29]

Significant differences of opinion exist about the best, or fairest, tax system. Proponents of the progressive tax system argue that taxes should be based on one's ability to pay. Those in favor of the regressive tax system adhere to a "benefits received" theory of taxation. That is, they argue that people should be taxed in proportion to the public goods and services they use, and regressive taxes come closer to taxing all people an equal dollar amount. The regressive tax position rests on a conception of government benefits as consisting of such tangibles as streets, sewers, parks, and the like. Thus, people should pay only for what they use and no more, the argument goes.

An alternative perspective that leans toward progressive taxation is based on a more expansive view of public goods and services. In this view publicly provided benefits include opportunities as well as tangibles. That is, it holds that certain people who parlay publicly provided educational and occupational opportunities into lucrative arrangements for themselves bear an extraordinary responsibility to reinvest in the system that they have used and from which they have benefitted.

Professionals in the field of medicine are an example. Physicians may be educated in public institutions—from kindergarten through high school to college and medical school—for which the public pays. The physicians may enjoy public scholarship support, intern in a public hospital, and practice at least some of the time in such a facility. Further, much of the costly equipment that physicians use in school and in private practice is provided by government. While physicians pay tuition to universities and medical schools, it represents only a small fraction of the total educational cost and of the value of their medical practice, which may generate a six-figure annual income.

It is argued, then, that physicians and others, such as professors, in a similar position owe to society what it paid for their educational and occupational opportunities—that they have an obligation to reinvest a substantial amount in the system in order to perpetuate the same opportunities for current and future generations that taxpayers did for them. This theory views the benefits received by wealthy physicians and others rather broadly, since it includes not just streets and parks but career opportunity as well. Therefore, it favors a progressive tax structure—one with a rate that increases with income—as a way to recapture some of the public investment.

Arguments over the systems of taxation are based on both philosophical concerns and self-interest. State and local tax systems are rife with special exemptions wrung politically from state legislators and local government decision makers. Such exemptions include waivers of sales taxes for Sunday supplement newsprint and various types of farm machinery; property tax breaks for church properties (some of which are also used as private day-care centers, counseling centers, and grocery cooperatives); and rebates or delays in the payment of taxes for the elderly. Special interests lean on state and local legislators to provide them with some special service and excuse them from the taxes that others must pay. The decision makers agree to some of their requests and reject others.

In the 1980s the changes in the structure of the federal tax system and the Reagan administration's cutbacks in the flow of federal money to the states and localities helped to create an even more regressive tax system. The 1986 changes in the federal law reduced the progressivity of the tax system, with the biggest tax breaks going to the wealthiest taxpayers. At the same time, state and local government replacement of some of the lost federal money with their own has contributed to a more regressive tax structure. With the devolution of programs in the 1990s, the overall tax system promises to become even more regressive.

There are some considerations, apart from the philosophical and self-serving arguments, that decision makers must consider. Some taxes are quite stable, providing governments with a steady and predictable flow of revenue, whereas other taxes can be more volatile. The property tax is stable. Should the economy of a community decline for a long period of time, property owners may default on their taxes and lose their homes, businesses, or land. But as this tends not to happen except in the most dire of circumstances, the property tax provides a reliable stream of revenue for local governments.

However, the sales tax can be volatile, and income taxes and mineral extraction taxes can be unsteady. When an economic downturn hits the nation or some region, people cut back on purchases and sales tax collections drop. In boom times they rise. If Utah or Colorado has a warm winter, the ski and tourist business will fall, sales tax revenues will drop, and the state will have difficulty balancing its budget. Similarly, if oil imports rise or national fuel demands fall, the oil extraction tax revenues of Texas, Oklahoma, and Louisiana will drop, unemployment will rise, and the region will face difficult times in terms of state and local budgets, and otherwise. Long secure in their reliance on oil and gas revenues, Texas, Oklahoma, and Louisiana had a particularly tough time adjusting to the economic changes of the 1970s and 1980s. Thus, when decision makers establish expenditure habits based on the good times, economic dips can wreak budgetary havoc on the downward side of an economic cycle.

Expanding the Tax Base

In the current era of tax resistance and unrelenting public pressure for government services, the states and localities are constantly seeking new sources of income as alternatives to tax increases. Their nickel-and-dime efforts include expanded use of user fees and sales of designer license plates. Though some other alternatives hold a promise of considerable revenue-raising potential, they are highly controversial. These include expansion of the sales tax base to include services, taxation of goods sold through mail-order houses located outside a state's boundaries, and the institution of state-sponsored gambling through lotteries.

Sales Taxes on Services

Mississippi inaugurated the first sales tax back in 1932. Over the years many other states adopted a tax on sales and today forty-five states impose some sort of sales tax. The breadth of the sales taxes varies, with some states taxing goods only and others taxing both goods and some range of services. The use of the sales tax at the local level is expanding, too.

As the U.S. economy has become increasingly service based (76 percent of all employment was in service-producing industries in 1987), the rationale for extending the sales tax to services has grown stronger. But the political opposition to taxing services is stiff. In 1987 Florida, in the context of reenacting laws subject to sunset provisions (which stipulate that programs be reviewed periodically to determine whether they should be continued), and beset with revenue problems, expanded its sales tax to cover a wide range of services, including business and consumer services and services made available from out-of-state vendors.[30] In doing so Florida became only the fifth state (after

Hawaii, Massachusetts, New Mexico, and South Dakota) to tax virtually all types of services. The action set off a firestorm of political protest in Florida; five months after its enactment, the state's tax on services was repealed and replaced with a one-cent sales-tax increase on goods. The mass media, concerned with the taxation of television, radio, magazine, and newspaper advertisements, used its considerable resources to try to turn a previously supportive public against the tax. The effort was successful, and the Florida legislature bowed to the public pressure.

As noted earlier in the chapter, state sales tax systems are riddled with special exemptions—ranging from exemptions on food to property tax relief for the elderly—all wrung from state legislatures by various interest groups at one time or another. Proposals to eliminate some exemptions and thereby broaden the tax base often surface when states face tight economic times.

Out-of-State Mail-Order Taxes

Struggling to increase their revenues, some states have attempted to tax goods purchased by citizens within their boundaries from mail-order houses located in other states.[31] In a 1967 decision the U.S. Supreme Court ruled that states could not compel out-of-state vendors to collect sales taxes on goods shipped into the state, though they could require the in-state purchaser to pay the tax if the state knew of the purchase (*National Bellas Hess v. Illinois Department of Revenue*). In 1992, however, the Court overturned in part the *National Bellas Hess* ruling. In *Quill Corporation v. North Dakota* (1992), the Court reaffirmed its 1967 ruling that such taxes placed an undue burden on interstate commerce but modified its position by noting that Congress could authorize states to levy such taxes.

The 1992 decision, of course, threatens the booming mail-order catalog business and is likely to result in a fierce battle between the mail-order corporations and the states and local governments over the direction Congress should take. The states and localities lose hundreds of millions of dollars annually as a result of their not being able to require the mail-order firms to collect state and local sales taxes. It is estimated that each year California loses $389 million, Tennessee $62 million, and the state of New York and New York City a combined $330 million. Thus far the lobbying efforts by the direct-marketing interests have forestalled such action by Congress.

Lotteries and Gambling Systems

Over the past decade or so, state-sponsored gambling has emerged as a significant source of revenue for the states. Stimulated by the states' own search for more revenue, and pushed by the gambling industry, games of chance spread until today every state except Hawaii and Utah are in the gambling business. All but 14 states have lotteries, 29 now have casinos on Indian reservations, and there are six with riverboat gambling.

The public is heavily involved with gambling, even if it is of mixed opinion on the desirability of government sponsorship. A recent study showed that 60 percent of the public has gambled at least three times in their lives. Most want lotteries to continue, but there is less support for casino-type gambling. Gambling is most prevalent in the West and least in the South. In Minnesota, nine of ten people say they've gambled, although over half believe that there is too much gambling.[32] Louisiana's former Governor Edwin Edwards is clearly not one such non-chance taking southerner, as in his 1993 tax returns he showed gambling profits of over $300,000.[33]

In the early years revenues from state-run lotteries grew rapidly. Indeed, by 1995 they were the second largest source in Oregon, behind only the income tax. But more recently, lottery revenues have flattened out, in part due to increased competition from reservation casinos and other state-run gambling operations such as video poker and dog and horse track wagering. In Oregon, for 1995, the revenues fell $87 million short of projections. Louisiana has seen a 30 percent decline in its instant lottery sales since 1992. Other states have experienced declines as well.[34]

State-sponsored lotteries are not without controversy, however. Some opponents argue that gambling in general is morally wrong and that states should not sponsor games of chance and thereby encourage citizens to participate. Opponents also argue that lotteries send a bad message to children—that the path to riches is through gambling rather than education and hard work. Still others object because of the alleged regressive impact of lotteries. With the states keeping roughly half of the proceeds, lotteries are simply another form of taxation. Citing studies that indicate lottery players come disproportionately from the middle- and lower-income strata of society, critics contend that the lotteries have a regressive impact.[35]

Opponents' objections, however, have not carried much weight politically, for voters and legislators in an increasing number of states have approved state-sponsored gambling systems as a means to raise revenue, and especially in lieu of the political costs of raising taxes. Educators, state and local officials, the elderly, and others repeatedly contribute to the reservoir of political support for the games, which bring in new money for their budgets and programs.

Researchers who have studied lotteries warn of certain dangers associated with their use.[36] The first is the tendency of decision makers to be optimistic and overestimate expected revenues. Another, related danger is the failure to account for second-year sales slumps, when the novelty of the game has worn off, which appear to affect all lotteries. There is also the danger that decision makers will view the lottery as a fiscal-problem cure-all, giving less attention to the broader and long-term fiscal needs of state and local governments. Finally, many critics argue that it is inappropriate for government to encourage behavior that is viewed as addictive and destructive. A professor at the University of Illinois who studies gambling made this observation:

> Governments used to be the protectors that provided police and fire [protection]. Now they're predators, advertising and preying on the public.[37]

User Fees

State and local governments have imposed an expanded array of **user fees**, direct charges to citizens for such services as entrance to public parks and golf courses. In the eleven-year period of 1976 to 1987, collections from local user fees tripled, from $30 billion to $98 billion. Whereas in 1976 user fees brought in 45 cents for every dollar in taxation, by 1987 the amount increased to 61 cents per dollar. As a percent of total local revenue, user fees rose from 17 percent in 1976 to 21 percent in 1987.[38]

Two primary incentives work to encourage governments to employ user fees. First, the fees represent a nontax method of raising revenues, which is important in the current wake of public hostility to new taxes. Second, for local governments user fees are a way to raise money, usually without having to seek permission of the state legislature. (See Focus 13.2 "Would You Like Higher Tuition and Pay Toilets?")

Tax-Base Disparities

Among the many consequences of the jurisdictionally fragmented government system of the United States is that some governments are rich and others are poor. The per-capita state government revenue in Alaska is almost three times that of Mississippi. The disparity is in large measure the result of the different levels of wealth in the two states. Similar variations exist among cities, counties, and school districts within the states.

Tax-base disparities lead to chronic political and legal controversy. Central cities generally face high costs for police and fire protection, social services, and maintenance of old utility systems while they watch their tax-producing property age and newer business, industrial, and residential development move beyond the city limits to the suburbs. Although core cities such as Boston, St. Louis, Detroit, and Denver are the economic, social, and cultural hubs of their respective regions, suburbanites and others benefit from their services and activities generally. Squeezed between high costs and weakened tax bases, core cities look for revenues from the state governments and often

Focus 13.2
WOULD YOU LIKE HIGHER TUITION AND PAY TOILETS?

• • •

Norm King is the president of the International City/County Management Association and a former city manager. He wants you to pay for the government services you use—as opposed to paying for the services used by others, or using services for which others pay.

Mr. King chastises politicians for accusing government of waste, inefficiency, mismanagement, and targeting them as the causes of high government costs and high taxes. Rather, the root of high costs and citizen discontent, he argues, is that we don't directly feel the dollar consequences for the services we use. In a bar, two beers usually costs twice as much as one. But the extent to which we use the public parks or pollute the air is generally not tied directly to any tax bill that comes in the mail.

Mr. King thinks that should change, and if it did, he claims, we'd behave differently. Here are examples of what he advocates, some of which already exist:

- Charges for the disposal of hazardous materials, such as old batteries
- Charges when police or fire personnel respond to false alarms
- Toll roads
- Higher airplane landing fees for peak periods
- Room-and-board charges for inmates

What else might Mr. King support? How about college tuition to cover the full cost; in state-supported schools it is now around a quarter of actual cost, with the rest covered by taxpaid state appropriations. Or how about pay toilets on college campuses and in public parks? Why not bottled water vending machines instead of drinking fountains? Maybe we should charge for elevator rides in public buildings, and sell tickets to watch the city council or school board in action.

Is Mr. King correct? What should be the underlying philosophy for paying for government? Should minimizing usage and efficiency be the driving values? Do fairness and ability to pay count?

These are tough policy questions.

Source: Drawn in part from Norman R. King, "Manage Demand, Not Supply," *Governing*, September, 1966.

resort to taxes designed to get at nonresidents and nonproperty-owners who work in the cities (for example, local sales and income taxes or commuter taxes). Citizens and lawmakers in the suburban and out-of-state areas, in turn, resist what they view as inappropriate subsidization of the core city.

Similarly, the financing of public schools is controversial. In all states except Hawaii the state government pays for some portion of the cost, with the local school districts or municipalities picking up the tab for the rest. The question arises, then, as to how to allocate state funds to the local districts. Some favor skewing the state's per-pupil allocation toward the poorer districts to compensate for the local district's difficulty in raising its share from a relatively poor population and poor tax base. Others object and support instead state allocation systems, which reward those districts that show a willingness to reach into their own pockets and pay generously for schooling. Many courts over the past two decades have disallowed state allocation systems that make some, but inadequate, effort at and progress in moderating extreme disparities among jurisdictions. Indeed, in 1993 nearly half of the states were in litigation concerning the constitutionality of school funding disparities.[39]

Chasing Industry: A Risky Business?

Another political issue that flows in large measure from the jurisdictionally fragmented system of U.S. government involves state and local attempts to develop jobs and promote economic health by attracting new business and industry into the state or town with public money. Some of the public money is used to hire people to recruit new businesses and to advertise the benefits of the state or community. But some of it is spent in the form of straight-out grants or tax breaks. For example, a community may waive a series of sewer, water, curb, and gutter installation fees for an incoming firm, or a state may make land available at cut-rate prices and grant exemptions from certain state taxes. Many of the debates over tax policy revolve around the question of what an increase or decrease in the property or corporate income tax might do to the attractiveness of the area for new businesses, or what it might do to drive existing ones out.

Attempting to attract business with policy tinkering can be a tricky business. Overly high taxes may keep development out. Excessively low ones may leave a government without the money needed to provide good utility, education, and transportation services and thus leave a community unattractive for the business and its employees. Failure to provide any incentives may mean losing a prospective business. Jumping too quickly can involve giving away public money to a business that might come anyway. Once decision makers begin to reach into the public treasury to help one private enterprise, others line up for their share. In addition, the subsidies can grow when jurisdictions seek to outdo each other in the use of collective resources to benefit private operations.

Still, governments engage in these activities all the time and with increasing frequency. Political leaders in most states consider economic development a prime responsibility; at election time they tout their past successes and promise more. There is little evidence, however, that the use of public money to try to stimulate economic development works, in the short run anyway. Yet many public decision makers argue that quick fixes for deeply rooted economic problems are possible, and their promises of economic development seem to work well at election time.

Earmarking Tax Revenues

The practice of **earmarking** certain tax revenues for specified purposes is popular. Gasoline taxes are typically earmarked—by either statutory or constitutional provision—for use on roads only. That is, the money may not be used for schools or health care or corrections. Special interest groups tend to favor earmarking because it provides a guaranteed source of money to support the programs they favor.

However, earmarking restricts a state's flexibility. When funds are earmarked for one purpose, the state cannot use those funds to respond to a crisis in another area. To some extent, every state earmarks some of its revenue—some for roads, some for schools, some for parks, and so forth. Rhode Island law earmarks just 5 percent of the revenue of that state, whereas in Alabama 89 percent of state revenue is designated for specific purposes. Most states fall somewhere in between these two extreme cases, however. California earmarks 12 percent, Illinois earmarks 21 percent, and Texas and Florida each earmark 25 percent of state revenue.[40]

Taxation and Public Opinion

Since the 1970s the American public's view of the value and efficiency of state and local governments has improved. In 1972 the federal government led both states and localities in positive citizen responses to the question "From which level of government do you think you get the most for your money?" However, when, in 1995, the American public was asked, "From which level of government, do we get the *least* for our money?", an amazing 46 percent named the national government. (See Figure 13.4.) Local governments were the best-rated level of government (only 19 percent named local governments as the ones from which we get the least for our money.) However, the local property tax was named as the most unfair tax barely beating out the national income tax (28 percent to 27 percent).

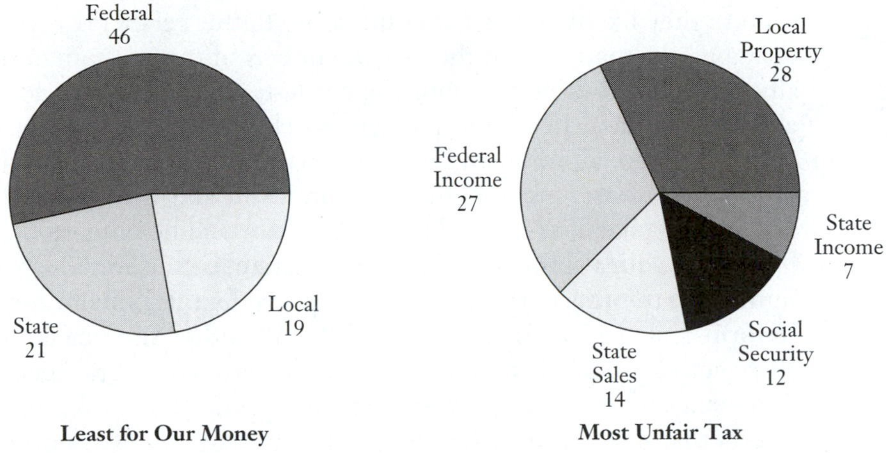

Figure 13.4 Public Attitudes Regarding Government and Taxes
Source: ACIR Intergovernmental Perspectives.

Several factors may have contributed to the improved image of state and local governments. Under the Carter and then the Reagan administrations, the states and localities had to assume more responsibility for funding their programs. They tightened their fiscal belts and squeezed more out of each tax dollar. At the same time, the flow of rules and regulations from Washington, D.C., increased, and with it irritation and impatience with the federal government spread. Although the public appetite for taxes has certainly not grown, an increased number of citizens are more comfortable than before with the performance of their state and local units.

Tax Reform

The views of many scholars and some legislators on tax policy are reflected in a report published in 1988 by the Lincoln Institute of Land Policy, the National Conference of State Legislatures (NCSL), and another published in 1994 jointly by NCSL and the National Governors Association.[41] The report defines a good tax policy as one that (1) generates revenues in a reliable and stable manner, (2) is broadly based and does not result in any single excessively high tax, (3) is efficient in collection and easily understood, (4) makes policy makers accountable for the tax, (5) minimizes interjurisdictional competition, and (6) is antiregressive. In similar fashion, the 1994 report stipulated that a tax system "should provide appropriate and timely revenues, distribute burdens equitably, promote economic efficiency and growth, be easily administered, and ensure accountability."

However, the tax policies of the states do not meet most of these criteria, nor are they likely to do so anytime soon. Rather, state tax revenues are often unstable, fluctuating with the ups and downs of the economy; they are generally regressive, hitting the poor the hardest; and exemptions for special interests are common. In addition, given our shift from a goods to a service economy, the nationalization and internationalization of business activities and the growth of interstate competition for industry and the jobs and taxes it produces, the current state–local tax system may well be outdated.

The political processes that characterize U.S. governments today make significant reforms in the direction proposed by the Lincoln Institute of Land Reform and the NCSL highly unlikely. Wealthy Americans, who are much more active politically than those in the lower income brackets, are not apt to support a shift in the tax burden in their direction. In addition, the special interests that have been so successful in extracting tax exemptions would resist attempts to eliminate their special status.

Tax policy, insofar as it changes at all, tends to change slowly and incrementally. Sweeping tax reform of any sort is difficult to sell politically because it would impact too many interests simultaneously, and their collective resistance to the reforms would likely be too weighty to overcome.

The Problems and Politics of Budget Making

In addition to having to decide whom to tax and for what and how much, governments must devise yearly budgets that outline how they plan to spend the money. This is not a simple or easy task, nor is it without controversy. Many parties are involved in the budget-making process—from bureaucrats fighting for more money for their programs and interest groups seeking more money for private benefits to the governor, mayor, or city manager who may be responsible for drafting budget proposals and the legislature, city council, or school board that ultimately controls the budget. The various participants in the budget process encounter a number of difficulties, many of which are related to the politics of taxation.

The Executive Budget Process

Until early in the twentieth century, government budgets were prepared by legislatures, often through the work of a legislative budget or finance committee. The various bureaus, agencies, and departments in the executive branch would submit budget requests to the budget committee, and it would aggregate all requests into one or more budget documents for approval by the legislature, council, or board. This system worked well in an era of small government. However, as the size of American governments grew, the **legislative budget** process became increasingly less functional.

Thus, beginning with the Budget and Accounting Act of 1921 at the federal level, and in state and local governments in the years and decades that followed, many American governments moved to the **executive budget** process. Under this system, department and agency budget requests are not sent to a legislative committee first; rather, the requests are first reviewed by the governor, mayor, city manager, school superintendent, or the special district manager, or their staff members, before going to the legislative body for enactment. The rationale for the executive budget is to permit chief executives, who are responsible for the administration of public policy, to review and coordinate the host of budget requests and bring them in line with their priorities. Advocates of this method say that, because chief executives must ultimately supervise the administrative apparatus, they should be empowered to assemble a budget that best enables them to get the job done.

However, the task of budget assembly involves much more than simple coordination; indeed it translates into political power. Legislatures, whether they are state legislatures, city councils, or school boards, control the purse strings of government and they have the authority to modify a chief executive's budget proposal. However, authority is not always the same as ability. Government budgets today are huge and complicated. Legislatures confront a host of controversial issues, and the budget bill is just one of them. As a result, most legislatures do not possess the time or knowledge of detail needed to examine thoroughly a massive and complex budget. Moreover, because legislatures are multimember bodies composed of individuals with different priorities, it is not always possible to assemble a majority vote to change items in a budget bill.

Considerable variation exists in the extent of budget involvement and budget power among state and local chief executives. In most states, the governor and the governor's staff are central to the budget-making process and, as a result, enjoy vast influence in this area. However, in some states, such as Colorado, the legislature still controls the budget-making process; here a joint house-senate budget committee and its staff are the centers of budgetary power. Similarly, in some cities, the council performs the basic work of budget construction, whereas in others, usually the larger cities, the mayor and the mayor's staff do the initial budget work. In council–manager cities, school districts and special districts, the hired chief administrative professionals—the city managers, school superintendents, and district managers—control the initial budget-making process.

Influential Experts

Much of the actual detail work on the budgets is done by full-time, salaried professional staff members. They analyze budget requests and make recommendations. As a result of their full-time status and expert knowledge, they may gain influence and power.

In council–manager cities, school districts, and special districts, this special expertise can be controlling. Council and board members are usually part-time politicians and often do not serve enough terms in office to gain comprehensive knowledge about the budgetary process. Thus, the administrative professionals with their expertise, experience, and continuity are true budget decision makers.

An example of the power of expert staff members comes from a story about Robert L. Mandeville, former chief of the budget bureau in Illinois, a state that has had annual budgets in excess of twenty billion dollars. The budget bureau served as an arm of the Illinois governor. Mandeville was experienced, tough, and respected. When Mandeville did not concur with the budget requests of an agency, the legislative appropriations staff would kill it. The governor went with Mandeville's recommendations and so did the legislative appropriations staff. Legally, the Illinois legislature controlled the purse strings, but Mandeville exerted considerable influence.[42]

Special Interest Group Influence

Often special interest groups are very influential participants in the budget-making process. For example, teacher's organizations have a stake in the budget because it impacts their salaries and professional working conditions. Truck and automobile interests have stakes in transportation funding, softball fans have an interest in parks and recreation funding, and so on.

Groups try to influence budget decisions in several ways. They provide much of the money for legislative campaigns and have access to lawmakers that they employ to enlist legislator help to preserve or enhance the appropriations that affect their interests. Groups also seek good relations with access to staff members, both in the executive budget office and in legislative committees. Good relations can translate into supportive staff recommendations as well as access to vital information. In addition, special interest groups try to create favorable public images for themselves on the assumption that goodwill will translate into support.

One tangible result of special interest group attempts to influence budgets is the earmarking of certain revenues. In all states and many communities, some tax revenues are set aside or earmarked by law for special purposes. Reserving a portion of a tax on gasoline for highways is an example. Special interest groups lobby hard to get their special projects funded with earmarked funds. However, as noted above, earmarking restricts the ability of a government to respond flexibly to changing circumstances.

The Uncertainty of Budgeting

Budget making annually is affected by inflationary pressures and the demands of numerous governmental and nongovernmental interested parties. Agencies always want more staff, more supplies, more equipment, more building, and more money. The public demands more and higher quality services, coupled often with a demand for lower taxes. In the Sun Belt states the size of the population grows each year with immigration from the Frost Belt. The increase in the population of the area means that the governments of those areas must serve more people. Often, revenue flows can be fickle, for they reflect the ups and downs of the economy. If spending is down, states that depend upon sales tax revenues are hurt more.

As noted earlier in the chapter, except for borrowing for capital construction purposes, state and local governments may not deficit spend. Instead, they must balance their budgets each year. A **balanced budget** involves months of work before the start of a fiscal year. Revenues must be estimated and balanced against the total expenditures expected to accrue in the fiscal year, which usually ends fifteen, eighteen, or more months later. Revenue forecasting is not an easy task. Many important sources of state and local revenues—the sales, income, and extraction taxes, especially—can be volatile, subject to the ups and downs of economic trends that are beyond government's control. For example, in Utah the legislature cannot predict snowfall on the state's ski slopes, but snowfall will affect revenues collected from sales-tax-paying tourists. Similarly, Louisiana can do little to control the politics of the Middle East, which affects oil imports and oil prices. Even revenue surpluses can create problems. The expenditure of windfall revenues can inflate the cost of government in subsequent years when the economy is less healthy.

The difficulty of revenue forecasting is reflected in the state budget itself, for most states include in it a reserve of 3 percent to 5 percent to accommodate any unexpected revenue fluctuations. Many states also look to more than one revenue forecast; they may examine the statistics generated in both the legislative and executive branches as well as some independently created estimates. Still, there are years when state and local governments misjudge revenues and are forced to reduce agency budgets midyear. This is a problem because small budget cuts on an annualized basis become large cuts when less than the full year remains to find the savings, and when clientele groups and the general public are not accustomed to midyear curtailment of services.

Furthermore, revenue forecasting can be politically manipulated. Governors, mayors, legislators, and others are often tempted to overestimate revenues rather than face the political heat of denying some requested increases in order to assemble a fiscally conservative and safe budget. Even though purposeful overestimating is a dangerous practice, elected officials sometimes risk it to postpone political controversy.

Incremental Annual Budget Changes

Budget changes from year to year tend to be incremental rather than large or dramatic for several reasons. First, growth in available resources tends to be small each year, so the money is rarely available for a huge increase. Second, political and legal realities preclude large downward adjustments. Buildings must be maintained, utility bills must be paid, hospitals must operate, water and sewage must flow, and police officers and firefighters must be on the job. Schools have to stay open throughout the school year and forest fires must be extinguished. Big cuts on an annual basis wreak havoc in these and other program areas, which neither decision makers nor citizens are apt to allow. As a result, states and localities add to their budgets, and occasionally subtract, incrementally, a little at a time.

Failed Methods of Budgeting

There have been times in U.S. political history when alternative administrative techniques of budgeting have been attempted in an effort to add rationality to government. In the 1970s, zero-base budgeting (ZBB), popularized by President Jimmy Carter, called for each expenditure item to be reconsidered and rejustified every year, thereby eliminating automatic increments. In the 1960s the planning-programming-budgeting system (PPBS) enjoyed some popularity; here budget categories were tied to programs rather than to administrative units or budget line items.

However, neither ZBB nor PPBS worked very well. The former encouraged the rehashing of old political issues and thereby led to time wasted justifying obviously needed expenditures. The latter generated confusion in general and hindered lawmakers' desire to examine specific budget lines. In essence, neither scheme could remove the human element or the politics inherent in government generally and in budget making in particular.

Summary

American government is a system of multiple, varied, and interrelated institutions made up of literally hundreds of parts, such as multiple branches, boards and commissions, and semi-independent agencies. As a result, state and local government finance is characterized by multiple, varied, and interrelated patterns of taxation and spending. Revenues come from income taxes, sales taxes, property taxes, user charges, fines and fees, sales and services, lotteries, and other governments. Revenue and expenditure patterns vary among cities, among counties, and among states.

The financial systems and patterns, like the institutions of government themselves, are interrelated. Although state and local units receive some federal funds, those funds come with mandates attached. The state government is the parent of the local units, and as such it sets the parameters for local finance systems. The local units administer many programs on behalf of the state, such as schools and social services, and they often do so in part with state money.

To many Americans the varied and interrelated nature of state and local finance is unclear. Citizens pay property taxes to a city or township, a county, a school district, and possibly many special districts. The county usually collects the property taxes and distributes the funds among the other governments. In April citizens pay income taxes to the national government and, in most states, to their state government. When they go shopping, citizens pay a sales tax, often to the state, a city, and possibly a county all at the same time. Anglers pay the state for a license; so do hunters and drivers. Recipients of social services are helped by people and programs paid for with local, state, and federal government funds. Students attend schools supported largely with local and state money and in part by federal dollars.

Politics also affect state and local finance. Special interest groups lobby for tax breaks and funding advantages. The public demands more services of better quality as well as tax relief. Tax reformers seek measures that limit the ability of governments to increase the taxpayers' burden. Indeed, few policy areas more clearly reflect U.S. government institutions and political power than do state and local finance.

KEY TERMS

fiscal policy
sales tax
property tax
income tax
fiscal decentralization
deficit spending
bond
revenue bond
general obligation bond
tax-exempt bond
industrial development bond (IDB)
taxpayer revolt
sin tax
progressive tax
regressive tax
entitlement program
privatization
user fee
earmarking
legislative budget
executive budget
balanced budget

ADDITIONAL READING

Anton, Thomas J. *The Politics of State Expenditures in Illinois*. Urbana: University of Illinois Press, 1966.

Gold, Steven D., ed. *The Unfinished Agenda for State Tax Reform*. Denver: National Conference of State Legislatures, 1988.

Wildavsky, Aaron. *The Politics of the Budgetary Process*. 4th ed. Boston: Little, Brown, 1983.

NOTES

1. U.S. Bureau of the Census, *Statistical Abstract of the United States, 1995* (Washington, D.C.: GPO, 1995), p. 300.
2. Ibid., p. 288.
3. Ibid., p. 298.
4. Ibid., p. 297.
5. Colorado Public Expenditures Council, *State and Local Taxes and Spending* (Denver: CPEC, 1996), p. 18.
6. *Book of the States, 1996–1997* (Lexington, Ky.: Council of State Governments), pp. 275–78.
7. Ibid., p. 60.
8. Ibid., p. 60.
9. Colorado Public Expenditures Council, *State and Local Taxes and Spending* (Denver: CPEC, 1996), pp. 9, 12, 13, and 16.
10. Ibid., p. 8.
11. Ibid., p. 9.
12. Ibid., p. 9.
13. Ibid., p. 29.
14. *The Book of the States, 1996–1997* (Lexington, Ky.: Council of State Governments), p. 230.
15. See Jeffrey H. Birnbaum and Alan S. Murray, *Showdown at Gucci Gulch* (New York: Vintage Books, 1987).
16. U.S. Bureau of the Census, *Statistical Abstract of the United States, 1995* (Washington, D.C.: GPO), p. 302.
17. *The Book of the States, 1978–1979, 1990–1991 and 1996–1997* (Lexington, Ky.: Council of State Governments), pp. 309, 316, and 260, respectively.
18. Ibid., *Book of the States, 1996–1997*, p. 263.
19. Penelope Lemov, "User Fees, Once the Answer to City Budget Prayers, May Have Reached Their Peak," *Governing* (March 1989): 24–30.
20. Elaine S. Knapp, "Lotteries No Gamble," *State Government News* (March 1988): 14–16; Marilyn Marks, "Florida Ends Tax Services, Raises Sales Tax," *Governing* (Jan. 1987): 57; and Elder Witt, "States Place Their Bets on a Game of Diminishing Returns," *Governing* (Nov. 1987): 52–55, 57.
21. For more on this topic, see Robert Gleason, "Federalism 1986–87: Signals of a New Era," *Intergovernmental Perspective* (Winter 1988): 9–14; John Shannon, "The Faces of Fiscal Federalism," *Intergovernmental Perspective* (Winter 1988): 15–17; John Shannon, "Federalism's Fiscal Fable," *State Government News* (Oct. 1988): 26–27; and John Shannon, "The Return to Fend-for-Yourself Federalism: The Reagan Mark," *Intergovernmental Perspective* (Summer–Fall 1987): 34–37.
22. Carol S. Weissert, "Medicaid in the 1990s: Trends, Innovations and the Future of the 'PAC-Man' of State Budgets," *Publius* (Summer 1992): 93–109; and Cornia Eck et al., "State

Budgets and Tax Actions, 1992," paper presented at the National Conference of State Legislatures, Denver, Colorado, July 1992.

23. John Herberts, "Read My Lips: The Tax Revolt Hasn't Had All That Much Impact," *Governing* (April 1990): 11.

24. "School System Goes Broke," *Denver Post*, 25 March 1993.

25. Larry Sabato, *Goodbye to Goodtime Charlie* (Lexington, Mass.: Lexington Books, 1978), p. 110.

26. Cited in Donna Dudek, "Going Private . . . Paying Less?" *State Legislatures* (March 1987): 26–29.

27. Robert Stein, *Urban Alternatives: Public and Private Markets in the Provision of Local Services* (Pittsburgh: University of Pittsburgh Press, 1990), pp. 187–88.

28. Steven D. Gold, "Wanted: A Good State Tax Policy," *State Legislatures* (April 1988): 24–27; and Steven D. Gold, "Taxing the Poor," *State Legislatures* (April 1987): 24–27.

29. Reported in *Fort Collins Coloradoan*, 27 June 1996.

30. Steven D. Gold, "Florida's Sales Tax on Services: Aberration or Innovation?" *State Legislatures* (Jan. 1988): 10–13.

31. See Michael H. McCabe, "States Eye Mail Order Sales Taxes," *State Government News* (March 1988): 22–23; and William T. Warren, "Closing the Bellas Hess Loophole," *State Legislatures* (Feb. 1989): 10–14.

32. Ellen Pearlman, "The Gambling Glut," *Governing* (May 1996): 49-56.

33. *Rocky Mountain News*, 16 April 1994.

34. Pearlman, *op. cit.*

35. See John Mikesell and Kurt Zorn, "State Lotteries for Public Revenue," *Public Budgeting and Finance* (Spring 1988): 38–47; and Daniel Suits, "Gambling Taxes: Regressivity and Revenue Potential," *National Tax Journal* 30 (1978): 19–35.

36. See Jeffrey L. Katz, "Lottery Fatigue," *Governing* (Sept. 1991): 62–66; and Steven D. Gold, "Lotteries: Still Small Change," *State Legislatures* (July 1989): 14–15.

37. Pearlman, *op. cit.*

38. Lemov, "User Fees."

39. See Charles Mahtesian, "The Quagmire of Education Finance," *Governing* (Sept. 1993): 43–46.

40. Martha K. Fabricius and Ronald K. Snell, "Earmarking State Taxes," paper presented at the National Conference of State Legislatures, Denver, Colorado, 1990.

41. Steven D. Gold, ed., *The Unfinished Agenda for State Tax Reform* (Denver: National Conference of State Legislatures, 1988); and Gold, "Wanted: A Good Tax Policy," in *Financing State Government in the 1990s* (NCSL and NGA, 1994).

42. John M. Downing, "The Financial Wizardry of a Fiscal Spin Doctor," *Governing* (Jan. 1989): 42–47.

CHAPTER

14

• • •

Commencement

• • •

The skyline of Albany, New York. The tall buildings are the Empire State Plaza, which includes the state capitol. The plaza symbolizes the complexity of governing a populous state. *(Joseph Schuyler/Stock, Boston)*

• • • **Pluralism**

• • • **Decentralization**

• • • **Power**

• • • **Is the System in Crisis?**

• • • **Future Trends**

We've chosen the term commencement as the title to this final chapter because it connotes both an end and a beginning. The word commencement is most often associated with graduation from a high school, college, or some other educational program or institution. For students, it may well mean "the end—we're out of here!" But for Webster, the dictionary folks, commencement is a beginning. So it is here; this is the end of the book, but it may well be the beginning of years of civic involvement for those who have read the book and completed the course.

Very few of us will ever serve in the U.S. Congress or occupy the White House making foreign policy or declaring war, but many of us will serve in decision-making roles in state and local governments. And as we discussed at length in the first chapter, we all rub elbows every day with state and local policies, programs, and personnel. We all live and work in states, counties, and school districts. Most of us live in cities. Most of us also reside within the jurisdictions of one or more special districts. Indeed, there are well over 80,000 such governments in the United States. That means, then, that literally millions of us serve as members of city councils, school boards, water and hospital district boards, and more. Tens of millions of Americans are employed by these units, as policemen, teachers, engineers, accountants—the list goes on and on. The odds are very high that the readers of this book will someday become elected state or local decision-makers, members of some advisory board or task force, or an employee of some state or local unit. Indeed, for many that may already be the case. Your civic life will be state and local.

But even if you never seek public office or serve on a board, commission, or task force, and if you work your entire life in the private sector, state and local governments will be ever present in your world. They'll pave your streets and provide your water. They will regulate your speed and your use of land.

They'll tax your purchases and perhaps your income as well. You'll need licenses to practice law, to teach, and to own and operate your boats, bikes, and cars. Even your dog will need the sanction of local government. Fun family times will likely be in city or state parks, and your troubles may lead you to state and local courts. Having read the book, you know all of this.

As we look forward to involvements with state and local governments, either as players in the decision-making arenas or simply as consuming and taxpaying citizens, what should we remember from the preceding chapters?

Pluralism

We live in a pluralistic world. We don't all share the same view of the public interest. We want different things from government. We tend to like services but not responsibilities or taxes. We tend to equate our preferences with the public good.

If you serve as a city, county, school, or special district administrator, get ready for both the highs and the lows. The highs will come when your fellow citizens show confidence in you by electing you to public office. There's nothing like winning an election. You'll also feel good when citizens thank you for decisions you've made in their favor, when school kids express gratitude for your presence in and talk to their class, and when an editorial in the local paper thanks you, at the end of your term, for your sacrifice and political service.

Then there will be the lows or, better put, the stomach aches and sleepless nights. Your issues will be complicated, contentious, difficult. Should the behavior of the police be scrutinized by a citizen review board? How much of the school's budget should be spent on individualized programs for special needs students? Can girls be on the wrestling team? What should you do with a landowner's request to build a convenience store adjacent to a nice residential area? If the zoning board or city council on which you are a member says yes, the neighbors will want to lynch you. If you say no, the landowner may sue the city.

The police department wants to use cameras to catch speeders—photo radar it's called. Angry speeders call it "big brother" government and remind us of Waco. The owner of the football team threatens to move the "Gladiators" to another town if we don't agree to let him have the profits from parking, advertising, and beer sales at the Sunday games. If we agree, taxpayers lose. If not, the team leaves. What to do?

This is just a short list, a very short list, of the kinds of issues that millions of well-meaning state and local decision makers must face. Partisans come on both sides of every issue. Often they are our friends and neighbors. Sometimes they are business and industry people whose choices can impact the economic health of our state or community.

Public service can be very rewarding. Without citizens who are willing to serve, we have no democracy. But different people have different notions of what constitutes the public interest and so serving in positions of public trust is not easy and it is not always comfortable.

For those of us who decline public service in elective or appointive capacities, there are highs and lows as well. It's nice to use a new city tennis court or ice rink. It feels good to receive a rezoning approval or a teaching license. Sliding out of a speeding ticket triggers a smile. But then there is the property tax bill, the fine for the wandering dog, and the school fee for participation in sports. The problem, of course, is that it's hard for our neighbors who sit on city councils and school boards to fund facilities and programs and provide essential public utility and safety services without revenue.

Decentralization

Our governmental system is highly decentralized and complicated. This can and does produce confusion and frustration for decision makers and their constituents alike. School board building location decisions impact traffic on city streets. State criminal sentencing policies may produce prisoner backlogs in county jails. Congressional choices drive special education costs in local schools. As a member of a city council or school board it can be frustrating indeed to find that your choices are constrained and major portions of your budget are driven by choices over which you have no control.

Decentralization and the associated complexity can be irksome for ordinary citizens too. Do you obtain your dog tag from the city or the county? Which senator, state or national, should you call to complain about jet aircraft noise? How many permits do you need, and from whom, to build and operate a sidewalk hot dog stand?

But our system is constructed as it is for reasons, and the reasons are not pernicious attempts to produce frustration and inefficiencies. Rather, they stem largely from desires to realize two values—protection and representation.

Decentralizing features such as federalism, separation of powers, and bicameralism are employed to help curtail potentially dangerous concentrations of political power. Some state boards and commissions were created for the same reason. Others, at both the state and local levels, were instituted to provide expansive citizen involvement in decisions ranging from land use to school curricula. And the plethora of cities, counties, and school districts exist to help keep decisions and decision makers accessible and close to the people.

So while we often struggle with fragmented and complicated government, we do so as payment for values that we want to preserve, namely political power that remains in check, and responsive and responsible government. It is good to remember this when impatience and frustration tempt us to damn our government and our politics.

Power

As seen in the chapters on legislatures, elections, interest groups, parties and community power especially, political clout is not evenly distributed. Businesses, unions, professions, even associations of local governments, are organized and are well funded, and they push their preferred agendas with considerable success.

But what of others? Students are seldom well organized or effective politically but it's a little hard to feel sorry for them since college graduates soon became a part of the organized elite who are politically strong. There are others, though. The unemployed, single parents, those without the mental or physical resources or skills and training to enter effectively the economic and political mainstream—what of them? They too are citizens and constituents.

It is the responsibility of persons in positions of public trust to search for an inclusive public interest, and not just one that responds to the demands of the already privileged, those who are strongest politically, or the noisiest citizens. Political power alone should not drive public choices. Too often it does, of course, but those millions of citizens who sit on state and local decisional councils must search for a larger, richer image of the public good. The rest of us should support their attempts to do so. Indeed we must demand that they do so.

Our state and local governments are not businesses. They are not designed to generate profits or pay dividends. They are not there to make some folks happy and comfortable at the expense of others.

Our state and local governments are us. They are all of us, collectively, and we've established them to produce collective benefits. Since they are us, we all have a right, indeed an obligation, to contribute to their effective operation, as well as to enjoy the results.

Is the System in Crisis?

Some observers, ranging from Ross Perot to columnist George Will, contend that today's system of state and local government is in the midst of a crisis as it attempts to deal with the growing costs of service demands, insufficient resources, eroding public confidence in government, and a declining sense of community. Increasing public demands for state and local services have had many consequences. The task of the schools, for instance, has been enlarged to include functions related to the decline of the family unit and other social conditions, so that schools now counsel and feed students as well as educate them. Illegal drugs, guns, gangs, AIDS, and homelessness are among the many other societal problems that local law-enforcement and social services agencies must address. As a result, the cost of operating the government system has risen considerably.

The states are forced by federal mandates to administer necessary but costly public services, and often without any significant financial support from the national government. Expanded Medicaid coverage and programs aimed at addressing the needs of the disabled, the special educational needs of handicapped children, the reduction of automobile emissions, the cleaning of wastewater, and the closing of landfills are a few examples of federally mandated programs that are carried out and funded by the states. As members of Congress enact these policies, however, the costs are increasingly being taken on by the states and localities because the enormous national deficit precludes any significantly expanded federal spending. To some extent, the states are doing the same to their local units. Cities, counties, townships, and school districts must abide by state-imposed service mandates, sometimes without any state money for implementation.

At the same time, the American public is demanding tax relief. Increases in the property, sales, and state income tax as well as in user fees (such as for college tuition, automobile license plates, hospital bills, and fishing licenses) are met with public opposition. State and local officials are thus in a difficult dilemma as they feel the need to raise more revenue to meet the dictates of Congress but have an obligation to represent the public's preferences regarding public demands for more services on the one hand, and with the antitax movement on the other.

The American public's disaffection with government and politics generally may be tied in part to the nation's declining sense of community. States and communities compete for new industry, often by promising tax giveaways or other benefits. Communities battle each other in their efforts to drive away the homeless and to keep public housing out. In communities with aging populations, there is often reluctance among voters to fund public schools. Proposals to move public money from public to private schools are common on modern state legislative agendas.

A reciprocal relationship may exist between the growing size and complexity of the U.S. political system and the public's declining confidence in government and decreasing sense of community. As all levels of government have grown in size and function, and as state and local activities have become increasingly directed from Washington, the American public has found it more difficult to sort out the vast complexities of the system and, therefore, has come to view its relationship with government as remote and distinct. For example, the consolidation of the 130,000 school districts that existed in the 1930s into the roughly 14,000 districts in operation today means that schools are much larger and more impersonal.

Future Trends

Observers who contend that the state/local system of government is facing a crisis in citizen confidence in and support for public institutions—one born, at least in part, of excessive institutional size, centralization, and distance—propose the rethinking of the evolutionary direction of the federal system. Perhaps smaller and closer governing is better than larger and distant, they argue. Rather than seeking efficiency through municipal consolidations, perhaps government should focus on fostering a sense of community by way of limitations on city size. Perhaps the largest school districts should be split up and community-based schools re-created. And perhaps it is time to resurrect the states' rights debate, not to retreat to a discriminatory society but to give back some decision-making power to the localities and to reduce the number of federal mandates.

If a heightened sense of community and a restoration of public confidence in government are tied to increased local control and citizen proximity to decision-making centers, then the nation's political future may rest with the localities and the states. It is these government units that provide what Americans need daily—water, streets, safety, schools, and the like. Moreover, unlike members of Congress, state and local officials are neighbors with whom community residents can enjoy direct, personal contact. In conclusion, it is interesting to note that the American revolutionaries, viewing their enemy as a large, distant, remote, and illegitimate government, fought to replace that distant authority with local units of government and local control.

Glossary

• • •

accountability The degree to which public agencies, public officials, and individuals are responsible for their actions.

Aid to Families with Dependent Children (AFDC) A major social services program that provides aid to needy families and is funded primarily with federal funds and administered by the states and their local governments.

Alternative Dispute Resolution (ADR) Methods, such as arbitration, for resolving civil disputes. The purpose is to reduce the case load of the courts.

amendment A modification made to an existing or proposed law or bill, such as a state constitution, a statute, or a proposal for a new law. See also *amendment process.*

amendment process The procedures used to amend state statutes or constitutions, such as legislative or citizen proposal of a change and ratification by voters at the polls. See also *amendment.*

annexation Expansion of the boundaries of a city to take in new territory.

apportionment Apportioning, or allocating the seats in a legislative assembly. As a result of U.S. Supreme court decisions, apportionments of state legislatures must be based primarily upon population.

appropriation A legislative act authorizing the expenditure of public money for some specified purpose.

Articles of Confederation The document that, prior to the adoption of the U.S. Constitution, established a loose union of the original thirteen states.

assessment The determination of the value of property for the purpose of taxation.

at-large election An election without districts; rather, the candidates are voted on by all electors within a jurisdiction and voters may vote for any of the candidates. Such elections are common in local government.

balanced budget A budget that authorizes only the expenditure of as much revenue as is expected to be collected. State constitutions or statutes require the states to balance their budget—to balance revenue and expenditure at year's end.

Badham v. Eu A 1988 U.S. Supreme Court case on partisan gerrymandering.

bargain justice The practice by prosecuting attorneys of striking plea-bargains with defendants.

bicameral legislature A two-house legislature, generally with a house and a senate. The U.S. Congress and forty-nine state legislatures are bicameral in nature. See also *unicameral legislature.*

bipartisan coalition An alliance of legislators, voters, and local officials from various political parties who join together to support or oppose an issue of special interest to them.

block grant Federal money granted to a state or local government with a certain amount of flexibility as to the purpose for which it can be used. Block grants developed when, during the Reagan presidency, a number of categorical grant programs were "blocked" together into more broadly defined categories.

bond The legal pledge of a government to repay what it borrows from a lender plus interest by a specified date. See also *general obligation bond* and *revenue bond.*

broker role The view of the representative in government as one who bargains, trades, and compromises with other lawmakers to accomplish what is necessary to serve a district's needs. See also *mirror role* and *oracle role*.

calendar committee A legislative agenda-setting or scheduling committee. See also *rules committee*.

candidate-centered campaign With the decline of the political party as a support base for candidates, and the increasing cost of campaigning, the task of organizing and funding political campaigns falls more and more to the candidate and his or her own organization.

categorical grant A federal grant-in-aid to a state or locality that must be used for a specific and narrowly defined purpose (in other words a specified "category" of activity).

caucus A meeting of party members—for example, all Republicans or all Democrats in a state legislative body. Caucuses meet to discuss issues, take policy positions, and elect their own leadership.

centralized (or unitary) system A political system in which all authority is concentrated, or centralized, in one place. In the states, for example, authority resides with the state and is not decentralized to local governments except as the state allows.

charter A basic foundational document that sets forth the powers, duties, limits, and organizational structure of city government.

citizen initiative A form of direct democracy by which a proposed law may be placed on the ballot through the gathering of citizen signatures on a petition. See also *direct democracy*.

citizen legislature model A legislature whose members serve part-time as representatives, and have other jobs. Unlike the U.S. Congress, they are not full-time professional legislators.

city council The "legislature" or policy body of a city, usually composed of from five to seven members.

city manager The chief executive or administrative official in a city that employs a council-manager system. The manager is hired by the city council, rather than elected by voters, and is accountable to the city council. See also *council–manager system*.

civil liberties Freedom to function as a citizen without undue restraint by government. Civil liberties include freedom of expression through speech and press, along with other freedoms such as those contained in the U.S. Constitution's Bill of Rights and the bills of rights in state constitutions.

clientele group An interest group or organized section of the public that interacts with government agencies in order to gain benefits from agency programs.

coercive federalism A national–state relationship typical of today's United States, in which the national government employs its spending, regulatory, and other powers to place restraints and mandates on states and localities, thereby reducing the range of state and local decision-making latitude.

commission plan A form of city government in which usually five persons are elected to function both as members of the policy-making body and as administrators of city departments.

committee on committees A legislative committee that either appoints legislators to standing committees or recommends appointments to party caucuses.

confederacy A loosely knit association of governmental units, such as existed among the states prior to the adoption of the U.S. Constitution.

conference committee A small group of representatives and senators that meets to resolve differences in a bill that has passed the two legislative houses in different versions.

consolidation A merger of government units.

constitution The fundamental document of a government that sets forth its basic structure, powers, duties, and limitations. The national government has the U.S. Constitution and each state has its own constitution. Many state constitutions are long and contain outdated provisions, although this is not always the case.

constitutional convention A convention held in the state or nation for the purpose of drafting a new state or national constitution or revising the current one.

constitutional politics The high stakes political activity associated with creating new constitutions or amending current ones.

contingency lobbying An arrangement in which a lobbyist is paid by the client only if he succeeds in doing the job the employer wants, such as getting a bill passed or defeated. Some states forbid contingency lobbying.

contract lobbyist A person who represents, or lobbies for, many clients on a paid contractual basis.

council–manager system A form of city government that emerged from the early-twentieth-century reform movement and features a hired full-time city manager who administers city affairs for the city council. See also *city manager*.

county A unit of local government that performs many administrative functions for the state, such as administering local tax systems, maintaining vital records, and administering elections. Counties typically have elected sheriffs, clerks and recorders, assessors, treasurers, and other officials.

cowboy coalition A group of rural farm-ranch legislators who vote as a bloc, sometimes across party lines.

crossover sanction A national law, or rule, or regulation contained in one program area and imposed on a state or locality that also "cross over" to apply in other program areas. For example, failure to comply with the dictates of a particular program might lead to penalties or loss of federal funds in another area.

cult of the robe The myth that judges shed all biases and prejudices when dispensing justice, and that judges are not political.

Davis v. Bandemer A 1984 U.S. Supreme Court cases on partisan gerrymandering.

decentralized system One in which most major political decisions are made by the regional units and the central government is weak. A confederation is an example of a decentralized system.

deficit spending Occurs when a government spends more than it takes in a fiscal year. States prohibit deficit spending and require balanced budgeting. See also *balanced budget*.

Dillon's rule The notion that local governments are empowered to perform only those functions clearly authorized by state law. Local governments do not possess "implied" powers.

direct democracy The creation or ratification of law directly by voters at the polls. The *citizen initiative*, the *referendum*, and the *recall* are methods of direct democracy.

direct primary The selection of candidates for government office by way of direct election by the voters of a political party.

due process The notion that established procedures must be used in administrative or judicial proceeding and that shortcuts and violations of rights must be avoided.

earmarking The specification that certain tax revenues are to be used only for a specific and identified purpose. Gasoline taxes, for example, generally are only used to maintain and build roads.

employee lobbyist Someone who lobbies for the organization for which he or she works as contrasted to those who lobby on a contract basis or as volunteers.

endless campaign A modern phenomenon in which career politicians never stop campaigning but begin working for reelection the day they are elected.

entitlement program A public program that guarantees benefits for anyone who meets legally specified criteria. Social Security and Medicaid are two examples. By meeting the criteria, one is "entitled" to the benefits.

exclusionary doctrine The prohibition of the use in a trial of evidence that was obtained by illegal means.

executive branch One of the three branches of American government. The executive branch is headed by governors and other state-elected officials and is responsible for executing or implementing legislative policy.

executive budget A state's budget proposal assembled by the governor and the governor's staff and submitted to the state legislature for approval.

executive-centered coalition First identified in New Haven, Connecticut, by the researcher Robert Dahl. This is a political coalition centered around the mayor.

expressed powers The authority of the national government, as expressed in the U.S. Constitution's Article I, Section VIII. The expressed powers are those explicitly enumerated and include, among others, the authority to regulate interstate commerce, coin money, and establish an army.

faction A term for *interest group* as used by James Madison in Federalist paper No. 10. See *interest group*.

federalism A governmental arrangement in which the central unit has authority to make some decisions whereas regional units are authorized to make others. The U.S. Constitution creates a federal system.

fiscal decentralization The tendency for some states to give local governments much of the responsibility for raising and collecting taxes and spending, rather than the state collecting the taxes and distributing the monies among its local units.

fiscal policy The political budgetary decisions that affect government taxation and spending policies.

formal powers The legal authority of the state governor, including the power to appoint people to certain positions, prepare budget proposals, and veto legislation. See also *gubernatorial roles* and *informal powers*.

full faith and credit The U.S. Constitution stipulates that each state must acknowledge the public acts, records, and judicial proceedings of the other states. This stipulation is meant to prevent legal chaos among the states.

general election A group of local, state, and national elections held in November in which voters elect candidates to office. See also *primary election*.

general law city A city that is established and operates under the provisions of a state statute that governs all cities of that size category. This is in contrast to a *home rule* city, which, under a different provision of a state's laws, is given the flexibility to design its own structure and processes and, sometimes, to define its own powers as well.

general obligation bond A form of government borrowing that involves a legal document and a government's pledge to repay a loan by a specified date with general revenues derived from taxes. General obligation bonds are used, for example, to repave city streets. See also *bond* and *revenue bond*.

gerrymander The configuration of legislative districts in ways that benefit one political party or group of voters and leave others at a disadvantage.

grand jury A body of citizens that convenes to review a prosecutor's evidence and to decide whether there are grounds for a trial. If there are, it issues an indictment.

grants-in-aid Funds made available to states and localities by the national government and under federal laws to support specified public programs, such as schools, highways, and utility systems.

Great Society The proliferation of national programs and funding to address domestic problems and improve the quality of life in the United States during the presidency of Lyndon Johnson. Great Society programs targeted areas such as poverty, urban blight, education, and unemployment.

gubernatorial power Governors' powers come from formal, legal grants of power embodied in state constitutions and statutes, as well as from informal influence gained through media exposure and prominence in the political party. See also gubernatorial roles.

gubernatorial roles The many activities and responsibilities of the state governor, including both formal responsibilities and informal activities. See also *formal powers* and *informal powers*.

gun control Laws regulating the purchase, possession, and use of firearms.

habeas corpus A court order directing that reasons be shown for detaining someone.

home-rule provision A provision in a state's constitution that authorizes cities (and sometimes counties) to design their own unique governmental structure and processes and, sometimes, powers as well.

implied powers Powers of the national government that have emerged from U.S. Supreme Court decisions. The Court, in a succession of cases, found the existence of certain powers was "implied" by other powers explicitly stated. The authority to regulate interstate commerce, for example, was found to imply that the national government could regulate a variety of activities of corporations engaged in interstate commerce.

income tax A tax based on the amount of earned income or salary. See also *progressive tax* and *regressive tax*.

incorporation The formation of a city government by residents of a particular area.

incorporation theory Constitutional doctrine applying U.S. Bill of Rights freedoms to states and localities.

incumbent The current, or sitting, holder of political office.

individualistic political culture One of three political cultures posited by Daniel Elazar, the individualistic political culture values self-advancement without governmental interference.

industrial development bond (IDB) Government-backed borrowing by a private party to establish or expand a business enterprise.

informal powers The extralegal political clout of a state governor; may include influence within the political party or the ability to affect public opinion. See also *gubernatorial roles* and *formal powers*.

informal rules Norms, or generally accepted legislative behavior patterns, that newcomers must learn.

inherent powers Powers of the national government that, the U.S. Supreme Court has said, are "inherent" in the nature of a central, or national, government—for example, the power to conduct a variety of activities in international relations.

initiative A form of direct democracy developed during the Progressive era. The initiative allows citizens to use the petition method to place proposals for new laws directly before the voters. See also *direct democracy*.

integrated executive A reformed model of state executive branch organization in which departments and agencies performing similar functions are consolidated or coordinated.

intergovernmental service agreement A legal cooperative deal made between two governments to provide collectively, or cooperatively, public services such as trash collection. See also *Lakewood plan*.

intermediate appellate court In the U.S. state judicial system, a court that sits below the state supreme court but above the major trial courts. These courts hear appeals from lower courts and reduce the case load burden on state supreme courts.

iron triangle A term used to describe the close and powerful political relationship that frequently exists among legislative committees, executive agencies, and special interest groups. These three form a triangle that is politically strong enough to win legislation and funding for programs that benefit the three parties.

joint committee A joint senate–house committee in a state legislature. Many states have a joint appropriations or budget committee, for example, on which members from both bodies sit together. Some states have many joint committees.

judicial activism and restraint The tendency of judges to allow themselves liberties in interpreting law or legal precedent, or to deny themselves such flexibility by exercising restraint.

judicial branch One of the three branches of American government. The judiciary, or the courts, are responsible for interpreting laws and for applying the law in specific criminal and civil cases.

judicial restraint See *judicial activism and restraint*.

judicial review An activity of a court in which the court is asked to review the constitutionality or legality of an action by a legislature or an executive official. Generally, the question before the court is whether legal authority exists for the action in question.

jurisdiction The purview that a court or some other government entity has with respect to policy or legal matters.

Lakewood plan An intergovernmental service agreement, initially developed in Lakewood, California, in which participating cities purchase an extensive range of services from another government instead of providing such services themselves. See also *intergovernmental service agreement*.

latent functions Secondary and sometimes unintended results. Political parties, for example, work to win elections, but in the process their activities have the "latent" function of informing the public about politics.

leadership powers The authority and responsibilities of leaders, such as those possessed by the house speaker and the senate president.

legal precedent Occurs when decisions made in prior court cases guide decisions in current cases.

legislative branch One of the three branches of American government. Legislatures are charged with representing citizens and forming policy. They also control the purse strings.

legislative budget The name for a budget-making process in which the legislature itself, and not the governor, prepares the state budget proposal, which is examined and ultimately adopted by the state legislature.

legislative committee One of the subgroups of state legislators to conduct hearings and examine bills before they are considered by the full state house or senate.

legislative liaison A lobbyist employed by governmental agencies or other governments. See also *lobbyist*.

legislative override A vote in the legislature to pass a bill over the veto of the governor.

legislative process The procedures by which bills become laws. They include both formal stages and informal bargaining, lobbying, and compromising.

legislative turnover The election of new members (nonincumbents) to a legislature.

legislative veto Action taken by a legislature to cancel a decision made by the executive branch.

levy The imposition of a tax.

limited government The notion that government may perform only those functions clearly authorized by law.

line-item veto The veto of a part (or line) of a bill, usually an appropriations bill, rather than the entire bill.

lobbyist A person who represents the interests of an individual, group, or organization before a decision-making body such as a legislative committee.

logjam A backlog of bills, common near the end of a legislative session.

log-rolling Gaining the support of legislators for bills that contain benefits for all involved.

lower court These courts constitute the lowest level of the state judiciary. They hear cases involving minor crimes and relatively low-stakes civil cases, and they do not have appellate jurisdiction. Often they are not courts of record (in which a full recording of the proceedings occurs).

malapportionment A representative districting system in which some districts have many more people than others. Outlawed by the Supreme Court in 1962, malapportionment allowed a numerical minority of voters to elect a legislative majority.

marble-cake federalism A term used to describe the state–national relationship in which the federal government makes funds available to states and localities to support state and local programs. The system can be said to resemble a layer cake, with the three sets of governments stacked atop one another and federal funds running vertically throughout the system.

McCulloch v. Maryland An 1819 U.S. Supreme Court case in which the implied powers were first established. See also *implied powers*.

Medicaid A major social services program jointly funded by the national and state governments that provides medical care for the poor.

Medicare A national government program created by amendments to the 1935 Social Security Act that provides medical care for elderly Americans and certain others adjudged to have disabilities.

merit pay A salary based on a supervisor's estimate of a worker's contribution rather than seniority.

merit plan A public employment system in which the initial hiring of an employee is based upon the "quality" or "merit" or his or her education, experience, and prior performance, and in which pay raises and promotions are similarly based on merit as determined by administrative superiors.

metropolitan council of government (COG) A cooperative organization of local governments in a metropolitan area, generally employed to do planning and conduct studies of areawide needs and problems.

metropolitan federation A reform proposal entailing a government arrangement in which a central government performs some functions for an entire area and local governments do the rest.

metropolitan statistical area (MSA) A metropolitan area as defined by the U.S. Bureau of Census.

mirror role A view of the representative as one whose actions reflect constituents' views rather than the representative's own judgments. See also *broker role* and *oracle role*.

Missouri plan A system of judge selection, sometimes called a *merit plan*, in which a panel of lawyers and laypeople nominate several candidates for openings on the bench and the governor appoints one of them. Generally, later the appointed judge has to run in a retention-only election.

moralistic political culture One of the three political subcultures posited by Daniel Elazar, the moralistic political culture is community-oriented and emphasizes the collective good. It has been embodied by settlers in the Great Lakes and upper Midwest regions.

motor-voter law Permits voter registration at driver's license bureaus and other state offices.

mud-slinging Political campaign tactics involving the levying of personal, questionable, "dirty" accusations against an opponent.

municipal annexation The expansion of the legal boundaries of a city in order to take in new territory.

municipal bond A legal pledge issued by cities to lenders to repay any borrowed monies.

municipal corporation The legal term used to describe a city.

municipality A city or municipal corporation.

national supremacy Article VI of the U.S. Constitution provides that the Constitution itself and laws and treaties made under its authority are the supreme law of the land. State constitutions are thus subordinate to the U.S. Constitution.

New Deal National government programs of the 1930s, associated with Franklin D. Roosevelt and designed to stimulate the economy, put people back to work, and rescue the United States from the economic depression.

new federalism A term used to describe a series of efforts by presidents Richard Nixon and Ronald Reagan, for example, to reassert the place of the states in the federal system; in other words, to decentralize the nation's system of government.

new judicial federalism A recent pattern of state supreme court decisions in which civil rights and liberties are asserted on the basis of state constitutional provisions.

NIMBY This acronym for "not in my backyard" refers to community reluctance to have prisons, group homes, drug rehabilitation centers, and other services found objectionable located nearby.

nonpartisan election An election in which the candidates do not run on political party labels. See also *partisan election*.

one person, one vote Equal protection of the law; in other words, all congressional districts must contain approximately the same number of individuals.

oracle role A view of the representative in government as one whose best judgment, rather than constituent's views, guides decisions. Sometimes called a "trustee" role. See also *broker role* and *mirror role*.

partisan election An election in which candidates run for office on political party labels. See also *nonpartisan election*.

party caucus A gathering of members of one political party in a legislative chamber, usually to select leaders, discuss party positions on bills, or plot legislative strategy.

patronage Occurs when the criterion for filling government jobs is political party loyalty.

petit jury A trial jury that determines guilt or innocence. A petit jury may consist of up to twelve members.

plea bargaining A form of bargain justice, employed by prosecutors in criminal cases, in which the defendant pleads guilty to a lesser offense. See also *bargain justice*.

plural executive An organizational scheme common within the executive branch of state government, in which voters directly elect many officials; authority is thereby decentralized and the governor's powers are lessened.

pluralism Exists where a society or polity is composed of multiple groups and centers of power. See also *power pyramid*.

pocket veto The refusal of a governor to sign a bill within a specified period of time. The term is also used to describe a similar practice of legislative committee chairs when they decline to schedule a bill for a hearing.

police powers Those powers exercised by local and state governments to protect and promote the public health, safety, and welfare.

policy coordinator One of the many roles of modern state governors is to seek to coordinate policies in such interrelated areas as economic development, transportation, and taxation.

political action committee (PAC) A group that collects funds from members and contributes the money to political candidates and their campaigns.

political efficacy One's ability to affect the political decisions of government.

political machine A term used to describe the tightly organized and disciplined political party organizations that operated in American cities in the early 1900s.

politics The resolution of conflicts over collective matters.

polycentric reform A locality, state, or nation in which political power is neither centralized nor evenly distributed, but instead is shared by a number of influential groups or parties.

poverty line A federally defined level of income below which a person or family is defined as eligible for various categories of public assistance.

power elites Those few individuals who may monopolize political power in a locality.

power pocket A point in the legislative process at which an individual or group with power (a house speaker, a committee chair, or a rules committee, for example) can determine the fate of a bill.

power pyramid A visual conception of political power as existing in a hierarchial, or nonpluralistic, form. See also *pluralism*.

powers denied In addition to allocating certain authority, or powers, to both the national government and the states, the U.S. Constitution specifically denies to both powers in certain areas—for example, in the establishment of *ex post facto* laws.

precinct A portion of a political jurisdiction geographically delineated for purposes of holding elections. People register to vote by precinct, they vote in their precinct, and political parties use precincts as their organizational base.

primary election An election held to select political party nominees for an upcoming general election. Normally, registered Democrats and Republicans can vote only in their own party's primary. In most states, independents cannot vote in primary elections.

privatization The practice of using private contractors or firms to perform functions traditionally provided by governments, such as trash collection and custodial care of public buildings.

progressive tax A levy that taxes larger incomes at a higher percentage than smaller ones, thereby affecting the wealthy more than the poor. Most taxes, however, are not progressive. See *regressive tax*.

Progressives Those who, in the late 1800s and early 1900s, pressed for political reforms to counter corruption in government. The reforms included the initiative, the recall, the referendum, as well as a variety of municipal government reforms.

property tax A levy, or tax, applied against the value of property, most commonly real estate.

Proposition 13 This tax limitation measure was passed in California in 1978 and is considered to have triggered similar "tax revolts" in other states.

pro tem The person chosen to preside over a legislative chamber in the absence of the presiding officer.

public entity A government or organizational creation of a government, such as a park or stadium authority.

public interest A term that is variously defined on the basis of individual values but that most agree is somewhat larger than the interests of one group or individual. Also referred to as the "public good."

public services Services provided to the public by government, rather than sold privately.

Reaganomics The conservative and decentralized approach to public programs and economic policy characteristic of the presidency of Ronald Reagan.

reapportionment The redrawing of legislative district boundaries, generally after a new census.

recall A Progressive-era invention that, in many states and localities, permits citizens to use petitions to force elections designed to remove a public official from office.

referendum A popular yes-or-no vote by the people on a measure or proposal placed on the ballot, usually by the legislature, for voter approval. A form of direct democracy. See also *direct democracy*.

reformed legislature A state legislature featuring upgraded legislative staffing, facilities, and pay, as well as lengthened and annual legislative sessions.

regressive tax A tax that affects the poor more than the wealthy. Most state and local taxes (for example, sales taxes) are regressive. See also *progressive tax*.

reputational approach A method of identifying the distribution of community power, and the members of the local elite, by asking knowledgeable community members who the "influentials" are. See also *stratification approach*.

reserved powers Powers reserved for the states by the Tenth Amendment of the U.S. Constitution. The original intention was to reserve to the states and to the people all governmental powers not given by the Constitution to the national government. Recent Supreme Court decisions seem to indicate that the reserved powers may not do much to protect state authority from national mandates.

revenue bond A government-issued pledge to repay a lender with funds generated by the activity or facility created with the borrowed money (for example, a stadium). See also *bond* and *general obligation bond*.

row-officers A term used to describe the organizational structure of county governments in which several officials are directly elected by voters, and on an organizational chart line up in a row, rather than hierarchically.

rule of law The assumption in our representative democracy that the activities of government and of public officials should be guided and constrained by what is in the written law, and not by the views and preferences of governmental personnel.

rules committee Exists in many state legislative chambers. Generally its task is to schedule bills for consideration by members. Also called *calendar committee*.

safe seat A legislative seat held by someone who is not likely to be defeated in an upcoming election.

sales tax Applied to the purchase of most nonfood items and some services, the sales tax is a major source of revenue for all states and some cities.

satellite city A concentration of new business and commercial activities and residential housing that develops on the fringe of an existing city.

school board The elected policy-making body in a local school district. See also *school district*.

school district The most common organizational government unit for public education in the United States.

selective incorporation U.S. Supreme Court decisions that have selectively read into the meaning of the Fourteenth Amendment (which applies to state and local governments) many freedoms found in the first nine amendments (which apply to the national government).

sentencing commission A group existing in most states that studies the patterns of criminal sentencing and makes recommendations for modification to the state legislature.

sentencing guidelines Provisions in state criminal codes that instruct judges on the range of punishments for those convicted of particular crimes.

service-based economy An economy, such as that of the United States in the late twentieth century, in which most businesses and jobs provide services, as opposed to an economy dominated by manufacturing.

sin tax A tax applied to the purchase of such products as beer, wine, liquor, and cigarettes.

single-issue interest group An interest group that presses its views on one or just a few issues. Both pro- and antiabortion groups are examples. At times these groups present difficulties for state legislators because they are reluctant to compromise on an issue, whereas compromise often is integral to legislative politics.

sovereignty The independence or autonomy of a government to make decisions affecting its fate.

speaker The presiding officer of a state house of representatives. Usually a very powerful position.

special court One of a variety of state courts that handle specific types of cases, such as juvenile courts (for those below the legal age of adulthood) and probate courts (which settle questions of wills and estates).

special district A unit of local government established to provide one service for a designated area such as water, sewerage, or recreation.

special interest group A group of people with similar interests who band together to pursue activities of benefit to themselves or their cause. See also *special interest group intensity* and *techniques of influence*.

special interest group intensity The degree of sentiment that a special interest group possesses on a particular matter.

spin doctor A term given to political spokespeople who try to put a particular, usually positive, twist or "spin" on a political statement or event.

state bill of rights Each state constitution contains a bill of rights. These are similar in many, but not all respects.

state constitution The most basic, or fundamental, legal document in a state. State constitutions establish the structure and procedures of the state government. They vary considerably in their length and detail. Some states have had several constitutions.

statute The laws passed by the legislature and signed by the governor. They provide the structural and procedural detail for state government, establish local governments, define criminal behavior, and so forth.

stratification approach A way of identifying a community's power elite by associating those at the top of the social and economic strata with the holders of political clout. See also *reputational approach*.

strong mayor–council system A form of city government in which the mayor possesses significant budgetary, personnel, and agenda-setting powers. See also *weak mayor–council system*.

subgovernments A term often used to refer to state and local governments.

suburbanization The population migration to areas that lie within metropolitan areas but outside the boundaries of core cities.

sunk costs The results of prior decisions and investments that restrict the latitude of current decision makers.

sunset provisions Parts of a law that establish a government program or agency and stipulate that the program or agency shall expire after a certain date (seven years after creation, for example) unless it is renewed by the legislature.

supreme court This is the top court, or the court of last resort, in a state's judicial system. Supreme courts deal mainly with appeals from lower courts but may also have original jurisdiction.

tax base The value of all property within the boundaries of a local government upon which taxes can be levied.

tax burden The financial impact of a tax, relative to other income.

tax-exempt bond A bond issued by an entity declared not to be liable for national income taxes. Traditionally, bonds issued by municipal governments were tax exempt.

taxpayer revolt Action in several states, starting in California in 1978 with Proposition 13, in which the electorate has voted to change the constitution or statutes to limit either taxes or the permissible level of spending, or both.

Taxpayer Bill of Rights (TABOR) A 1992 constitutional amendment in Colorado that restricts the ability of the state and local governments to tax and spend.

techniques of influence Methods employed by special interest groups, such as donating to candidate campaigns, seeking to influence public opinion, and lobbying in legislatures. See also *special interest groups*.

third party One of a number of small parties other than the Democratic and Republican parties. There are many third parties in American politics, but they seldom succeed in electing their candidates.

ticket-splitting Occurs when voters cast some votes for Democrats and others for Republicans rather than supporting a straight one-party ticket.

tort reform Changes in state laws that make it more difficult for persons to sue each other, or to claim excessive damages for alleged damages or "wrongs."

town A form of municipal corporation, similar to a city but generally very small.

township A form of local government found in some eastern and midwestern states.

traditionalistic political culture One of three political cultures posited by Daniel Elazar. In this culture, the status quo is the norm, while change is not, and those who head the social hierarchy also dominate government and politics. See also *moralistic political culture* and *individualistic political culture*.

trial court The major courts in state judicial systems. They sit above the lower courts and below the appellate courts. Major trial courts hear felony criminal cases, domestic cases involving matters such as divorce and paternity, and civil cases where money or property of substantial value is at stake. State statutes define the jurisdiction of these and all other courts.

two-party system A system such as the American political system which generally is characterized by the existence of two major political parties. However, two parties do not operate in all localities. See also *third party*.

U.S. Constitution See *constitution*.

unicameral legislature A one-house legislature. Nebraska is the only state with a unicameral legislature, although most cities, school districts, and special districts have one-chamber policy bodies.

unified court system A neatly configured and hierarchial state court system in which jurisdictions are clearly defined. This is in contrast to court systems that have developed in incremental fashion, and where neither boundaries nor jurisdictional lines of appeal are clear.

unitary system See *centralized system*.

urban village A residential and commercial development on the fringes of a core city, the hub of which is often a large shopping center, a new airport, or an office complex.

urbanization The movement of large numbers of people from rural areas to urban areas.

user fees A payment that citizens must make to use a public facility, such as a city swimming pool, a toll road, a park, or even a school.

veto The authority of the governor to nullify a bill passed by the legislature.

veto point A point in the legislative process where strategically placed legislators can kill bills (a rules committee, for example).

volunteer lobbyist Someone who lobbies legislative and other government decision makers on an unpaid basis.

vote broker A local political organization, other than the party, that can deliver a bloc of votes for those seeking support (for example, support for the party's nomination).

weak mayor-council system A form of local government in which the city council is dominant and the mayor generally lacks the power to control the budget, the public agenda, and major administrative appointments. See also *strong mayor-council system*.

whip A member of the legislative leadership team whose task it is to count votes and try to coax party members into voting the party line.

white flight The movement of large numbers of white citizens out of the core cities into the suburbs. See also *suburbanization*.

yellow-dog Democrat One so loyal to the Democratic party as to vote Democratic even if the candidate were a yellow dog.

Index

• • •

administrators
  power in communities, 387
  of schools, 363–64
Advisory Commission on Intergovernmental Relations, 398
African Americans
  electoral participation by, 295, 308–9
  as judges, 208, 212
  as jurors, 209
  as legislators, 132
  local elections and, 392, 394
  metropolitan area governments and, 333
  in public office, 132, 296, 394
  See also ethnic minorities; racial bias
agency-clientele ties, 170–71
agenda, city government and control of, 354–55
Aid to Families with Dependent Children (AFDC), 6, 52, 138
Alabama
  constitution of, 77
  taxes in, 411, 412, 436
Alaska
  executive branch of, 164, 166
  fiscal policy, 410, 411, 412
  judicial system in, 211
  women legislators in, 133, 297–98
Alford, Robert R., 356, 391
Almond, Gabriel, 271–72
alternative dispute resolution (ADR), 213, 217
amendments
  to state constitutions, 45, 77–78, 82, 89–92
  to U.S. Constitution, 42–43
  See also specific amendments
A-95 review process, 329–30
annexation of suburban areas, 322, 327–28
Anti-Terrorism and Effective Death Penalty Act (1996), 217
Anton, Thomas, 49
apathy toward electoral participation, 293
appointment power of governors, 159, 200, 202
appointments
  by city administrative officials, 354
  of judges, 197, 198–99, 200
apportionment (districting), 120–31
  gerrymandering and, 126–30
  minority electoral participation and, 308–9
  Supreme Court decisions on, 124–26, 129
Arizona
  apportionment in, 123
  citizen initiatives in, 91
  interest groups in, 257–58
  judge selection in, 197
  plural executive in, 162
  taxes in, 411
Arkansas
  constitution of, 82, 86–87
  taxes in, 428
Articles of Confederation, 33, 34, 36
Atlanta, Georgia, 381–82
at-large elections, 392
attorney general, 175–76

Bachrach, Peter, 385
Badham v. Eu (1988), 129
Baker, John, 134
Baker v. Carr (1962), 98, 100, 125
balanced budgets, 441
  state constitutions and, 88–89
Banfield, Edward, 357
Baratz, Morton, 385
bargain justice, 210–11
Barnes, Ramona, 133
Barron v. Baltimore (1833), 214
Bexar County, Texas, 334, 337
Beyle, Thad, 147, 150, 181–82
Bibby, John, 233
bicameral legislatures, 108–9
Bill of Rights, U.S., 74, 214, 215
bills. *See* legislative process; *specific legislation*
bills of rights, state, 74, 214
bipartisan coalition, 112
Bird, Rose, 201
Blair, Diane, 86
Bledsoe, Carl "Bev," 105
block grants, 45
  under Reagan, 52
boards, 19
  parole boards, 221–22
  school boards, 6, 363, 364, 372, 394
bonds, 414–16

borrowing by state and local governments, 414–16
Boston, Massachusetts, 333
Brady Bill, 58, 60
Breaux, David, 134
broker role of representatives, 131
Broward County, Florida, 384
Brown, Jerry, 163
Brown, John Y., 148
Brown, Willie, 113–14
Brown v. Board of Education (1954), 59
Brown v. Thompson (1983), 126
Buckley v. Valeo (1976), 291
budget deficits
  federal, 53, 420
  state, 414–16
budgeting and budgets, 438–42
  balanced, 88–89, 441
  city, 354
  executive budget process, 438–40
  experts and, 440
  failed methods of, 442
  governors' role in, 159–60
  incremental changes in budgets, 442
  uncertainty of, 441–42
  See also fiscal policy
bureaucracies, 20
  governors and, 164–71
  power in communities, 387
Bush, George (Bush administration), 53, 216, 288, 372
business interests, as interest group, 257

calendar committees, 106
California
  apportionment in, 123, 129–30
  Bill of Rights of, 74
  campaign financing rules in, 289
  citizen-initiated propositions in, 51, 90–91, 366, 421–22
  governors in, 149–50, 173–74, 181
  judicial system in, 201, 211, 215–16
  legislature of, 113–14, 116, 134, 135
  Proposition 13 in, 51, 366, 421–22
  taxes in, 428, 436
campaign financing, 16–17
  from interest groups, 280, 281–82
  political action committees (PACs) and, 267, 281, 289, 291
  rules on, 280, 281–82, 289, 291–92
campaigns. *See* electoral campaigns
candidate-centered campaigns, 238–39, 301
Cardozo, Benjamin, 215
Carter, Jimmy (Carter administration), 147, 437, 442
case law, civil liberties and, 215
categorical grants, 45
caucuses
  in precincts, 234
  in state legislatures, 110
central cities (core cities)
  financial difficulties of, 320, 324
  See also cities; city government; metropolitan areas
centralization, 31–32
Chandler, Happy, 148
charters, city, 345
charter schools, 373
chief administrator, governor as, 153
Childes, Lawton, 175
Childs, Richard, 350
Chubb, John E., 372, 373
cities
  incorporation of, 344–45
  See also communities; city government; metropolitan areas
citizen initiative. *See* initiative
citizen legislature model, 100
Citizens for Tax Justice, 428
citizenship
  government function summarized, 9
  political issues and, 16–17
city commission, 348–49
city council
  in council-manager system, 349–53, 355
  in strong mayor-council system, 345–46, 355
  variations in political behavior, 357
  in weak mayor-council system, 346–47, 355
  women and minorities on, 298, 394
  See also council-manager system of city government; mayor-council systems of city government
city government, 342–58
  differences among, 356–58
  elections, 389–90
  forms of, 345–53
    commission plan, 348–49, 355
    council-manager system, 349–53, 355, 356, 357
    distribution of, 352–53
    elections and, 389–90
    political influence and, 353–55
    strong mayor-council system, 345–46, 355
    weak mayor-council system, 346–47, 355
  functions of, 345
  home-rule provisions and, 344
  state constitutional and statutory provisions and, 342–45
  women and minorities in, 298
  See also city council
city managers, 349–53, 355
civil liberties
  case law and, 215
  state courts and, 203–4, 213–15
  See also Bill of Rights, U.S.; bills of rights, state

civil life
  government function summarized, 9
  political issues and, 16–17
civil service, 238
Clark, Janet, 297–98
Clements, Bill, 173
clientele groups, agency ties with, 170–71
Clingermayer, James, 357
Clinton, Bill (Clinton administration)
  citizen initiatives and, 91
  governorship of Arkansas and, 147
  motor-voter law and, 288
  state-federal government relations and, 30, 41, 53–54, 55
  welfare reform under, 137, 139
Cloward, Richard, 333
Cnudde, Charles F., 245
coercive federalism, 33–34, 35. *See also* federalism
cohesion of interest groups, 269
Colegrove v. Green (1946), 124–25
Colorado
  apportionment in, 123
  citizen initiatives in, 91–92
  city government in, 343
  governors in, 150–51, 182
  judge selection in, 212
  legislative tenure limits in, 91, 135
  lobbyists in, 260
  local elections in, 389
  mandates on local governments in, 396, 421
  special districts in, 370
  taxes in, 91–92, 411
  women legislators in, 133
Commerce Clause, 58
commissioners, city, 348–49, 355
commission plan (city commission), 348–49, 355, 390
commissions, 19
Committee for Economic Development, 332
committee on committees, 116
committees, legislative, 104–6, 112, 119
  assignments to, 115–17
communication, 48
communities
  economic development and, 400–401
  elections in, 299–300, 304–5, 388–94
    at-large, 392
    partisan vs. nonpartisan, 388–91
    reforms, 393–95
    voter participation, 388, 391–92, 395
  federal and state governments and, 395–98
  outside capital and, 399–401
  See also local governments; power, in communities
community-based corrections, 222
Conant, James, 169
confederacy
  defined, 31
  See also decentralization
conference committee, 104
conflict resolution, as function of political parties, 232–33
Congress, U.S., under Articles of Confederation, 34, 36
Connecticut, taxes in, 411
consolidation of metropolitan area governments, 322, 325–26
Constitution, U.S., 36–43
  amending process, 42–43
  as compromise, 42–43
  correctional systems and, 219–20
  national and state government powers, 37–43
    expressed powers, 38–39
    guarantees to states, 41–42
    implied powers, 39–40
    inherent powers, 40
    interstate and state-national relations, 40–41
  national supremacy clause, 41–42
  See also Bill of Rights, U.S.; *and specific amendments*
constitutional conventions, 82
constitutions, state
  amendments to, 45, 77–78, 82, 89–92
  city government and, 342–44
  contents of, 73–76
  criticisms of, 78, 80–81
  differences and similarities among, 68
  functions of, 68, 70–71, 88–89
  length and detail of, 76–77
  levels of law and, 71–73
  limits imposed by, 71
  political factors and, 83–87
  state-local government relations under, 43–44
  structure of state governments and, 71
Continental Congress, 32, 36
contingency lobbying, 280
contract lobbyists, 261
Cook County, Illinois, 362
cooperative federalism, 35, 48
Cornwell, Elmer, 85
corrections
  community-based, 222
  growing prison population, 222
  political issues and, 11–12, 219–20
  sentencing and, 221–22
  as state and local matter, 5, 220
corruption, legislatures and, 98
council-manager system of city government, 349–53, 355, 356, 357
  council-mayor systems compared to, 356–57
  elections and, 389, 390
councils of government, metropolitan (COGs), 329–30
counties, party organization in, 234–35
county government, 358–62
  criticisms of, 361
  ethnic minorities in, 394
  functions of, 9, 359

county government *(continued)*
- reforms proposed for, 361–62, 363
- structure of, 360–61
- women in, 297–98
- *See also* metropolitan area governments

courts, federal, 190–92, 217
courts, state, 188–95
- civil liberties and, 203–4, 213–15
- contemporary problems in, 206–13
  - attitudes and values, 207–8
  - bargain justice (plea bargaining), 210–11
  - judicial delay, 209–10, 221
  - lack of diversity, 212
  - searches for remedies to, 213
  - unequal resources, 212
- democracy and, 203–4
- expediting processing of cases in, 217–18
- gender and ethnic fairness in, 208, 209, 212, 218
- intermediate appellate courts, 192–93
- jurisdiction of, 190–92, 217
- legislative control of, 194
- lower courts, 193–94
- new judicial federalism and, 215–17
- as political entities, 188–89
- recent developments in, 215–18
- special courts, 194
- supreme courts, 192
- trial courts, 193

crime
- as state and local matter, 5, 220
- *See also* corrections

Cronin, Thomas, 307–8
crossover sanctions, 50–51
cult of the robe, 186
cumulative voting, 309

Dade County, Florida, 326, 362
Dahl, Robert A., 383–84
daily life, government in, 2–4, 447–48
Darcy, R., 297–98
Davis v. Bandemer (1984), 126, 129
Dawson, Richard E., 245
Dean, Howard B., 156
decentralization, 32–33
- consequences of, 30, 449–50
- defined, 31
- of executive branch, 178
- federalism and, 17–18
- fiscal, 413

deficit spending, 53, 414–16, 420
Delaware, taxes in, 410, 428
democracy
- courts and, 203–4
- direct, 77, 78, 89–92, 305–8
- interest groups and, 276–78

Democratic party, 240–43, 347
Denver, Colorado, 335, 401
Des Moines, Iowa, 348–49
Dillon, John F., 44, 344
Dillon's rule, 44, 344
direct communication, as interest group influence technique, 263–64
direct democracy, 305–8
- state constitutional amendment by, 77, 78, 89–92

direct primaries, 238
district attorneys, 210–11
districting. *See* apportionment
Downes, Bryan, 357
dual federalism, 35
Dudek, Donna, 423
due process, 204, 214–15
Durham, Christine, 216
Dye, Thomas R., 123, 245

early release programs, 222
earmarking tax revenues, 436, 440–41
economic development
- communities and, 400–401
- fiscal issues, 401, 435–36
- government function summarized, 8
- political issues and, 15

economic segregation, suburbanization and, 320–21
education
- inequities in quality of, 366
- political factors and, 12–13, 364, 365
- *See also* schools (school systems); teachers

educational level, electoral participation and, 295–96
educators, as interest group, 256
Edwards, Edwin, 432
Ehrenhalt, Alan, 100
Elazar, Daniel, 23
Eldersveld, Samuel, 247
election laws, 286–92
- campaign financing rules, 280, 281–82, 289, 291–92
- constitutional and federal rules, 288, 308–9
- residency requirements, 287
- voter registration, 287–88

elections, 16
- county governments and, 359
- general, 286
- government function summarized, 9
- gubernatorial, 149–52
- institutional design and, 60–61
- of judges, 197, 199–200, 202–3
- local, 299–300, 388–94
  - at-large, 392
  - campaign strategies, 304–5
  - ethnic minorities and, 392, 393–95
  - partisan vs. nonpartisan, 388–91
  - reforms, 393–95
  - voter participation, 299–300, 388, 391–92, 395
- nonpartisan, 286, 388–91
- partisan, 286, 388–91
- primary, 238, 286
- school district, 371–72
- *See also* election laws; electoral campaigns

electoral campaigns, 301–5
- candidate-centered, 238–39, 301

challengers in, 303
cost of, 301–2
endless (by incumbents), 303–4
sophisticated strategies in, 303–5
U.S. institutions and politics reflected in, 305
See also campaign financing
electoral participation, 292–99
apathy toward, 293
city government structure and, 356
educational level and, 295–96
ethnicity and, 295
institutional factors and, 299–301
interest groups, 300
in local elections, 299–300
variations among states, 300–301
legislatures and, 297–99
in local elections, 299–300, 388, 391–92, 395
by women, 295
by young people, 293–95
Eleventh Amendment, 58
Emmert, Craig, 203
employee lobbyists, 261
endless campaign, 303–4
Engler, John, 180
entertainment. See public fun
entitlement programs, 420–21
Environmental Protection Agency, 326
equality, political, 205–6
ethnic minorities
electoral participation by, 295, 308–9
electoral reform and, 393–95
judicial system and, 208, 209, 212, 218
local elections and, 392, 393–95
in public office, 296, 298, 394
as legislators, 131–32
on school boards, 372, 394
suburbanization and, 320
exclusionary doctrine, 214
executive branch, national, 38
executive branch, state. *See* governors; state executives
executive budget process, 438–40
executive-centered coalition, 384
experts
in budgeting process, 440
power in communities, 386–88
expressed powers, 38–39

Fair Labor Standards Act, 56
federal funding (federal aid), 418–21
of Great Society programs, 49–50, 416, 419
Reaganomics and, 51–54
reduced, 416
See also block grants; federal grants
federal grants, 45–48, 64. *See also* block grants
federalism, 33–43
coercive, 33–34, 35
as compromise between centralization and decentralization, 33
cooperative, 48
decentralization and, 17–18
defined, 17
expressed powers and, 38–39
functional theory of, 61–62
implied powers and, 39–40
inherent powers and, 40
legislative theory of, 61–62
marble-cake, 48–49
party organization and, 237
public policy making and, 62–64
types of, 35
U.S. Constitution and, 36–43
federalism (federal system), 31
Federalist Papers, The, 276
federal system, 31
Feinstein, Dianne, 150
Feiock, Richard, 357
Fernandez, Joseph A., 365
Field, John, 356
Fifteenth Amendment, 288, 308
Finney, Joan, 181
First Amendment, 214, 215
fiscal decentralization, 413
fiscal policy
city government structure and, 356, 357
definition of, 407–8
political aspects of, 418–38
entitlement programs, 420–21
federal role, 418–21
Reagan administration, 419–20
trends in, 416–18
See also budgeting and budgets; taxes
Florida
apportionment in, 129–30
citizen initiatives in, 91
judicial system in, 211
mandates on local goverments in, 396
pluralistic power in communities in, 384
special districts in, 368
taxes in, 91, 410, 428, 430–31, 436
food stamp program, 7, 138
formal powers of governor, defined, 156
Foss, Philip, 169
Fourteenth Amendment, 214–15, 216, 277, 366
Fowler, Edmund P., 356
fragmented government, in metropolitan areas, 20, 321–25
Francis, Wayne, 134
Froman, Lewis, 356
full faith and credit, 40, 41
functional theory of federalism, 61–62

Galveston, Texas, 348
gambling, 431–33
Garcia v. San Antonio Metropolitan Transit Authority (1985), 56
Garn, Paul, 421

gender bias, in judicial system, 208, 218
general law city, 342
general obligation bonds, 414–15
Georgia
  constitution of, 82, 91
  governors in, 173
  initiative on legislative terms, 91
  judge selection in, 204, 212
gerrymandering, 126–30
Gideon v. Wainwright (1963), 215
Gitlow v. New York (1925), 215
Glick, Henry, 203
Goldsmith, Stephen, 347
Gomillion v. Lightfoot (1961), 126
Goodman, Jay, 85
Gorman, Kenneth, 151
Gottdiener, Mark, 395, 398, 399
governors, 146–74, 179–82
  bureaucracies and, 164–71
  competition for job of, 149–52
  elections for, 149–52
  greater visibility of, 148–49
  image of, 149–52
  increased responsibility of, 147
  powers of, 156–73
    appointment power, 159, 200, 202
    budget power, 159–60
    formal executive authority as source of, 157
    formal vs. informal, 156–57
    integrated executive model, 163–64
    limits on, 161–71
    lobbying as source of, 161
    plural executive and, 161–63
    political party as source of, 157–58
    separation of powers, 177–78
    state constitutions and, 88
    strength and leadership of governors, 173–74
    tenure as source of, 160
    veto power, 88, 106, 158–59
    visibility as source, 157
  roles of, 152–56
    chief administrator, 153
    party leader, 153–54
    policy coordinator, 156
    policy leader, 154–56, 179–82
    state symbol, 154
  terms of office, 160
  veto power of, 88, 106, 158–59
grand jury, 209
grants-in-aid, 45–48, 64
grass roots activism, as interest group influence technique, 265
Great Britain, 272
Great Depression, 137
Great Society, 49–50, 416, 419
Grodzins, Morton, 48
Gross, Donald, 104
Grunseth, Jon, 150
guarantees to states under U.S. Constitution, 42
gubernatorial power. *See* governors, powers of
gun control, 58, 60
Gun-Free School Zones Act, 58
Gurwitt, Rob, 114

habeas corpus relief, 217
Hamm, Keith, 117
Hawaii
  judicial system in, 195
  taxes in, 411–12, 431
Hayden, Mike, 149
health care. *See* Medicaid
Herbers, John, 400
Hispanic Americans
  electoral participation by, 295, 309
  as judges, 212
  as legislators, 132
  local elections and, 392, 394
Hobby, Bill, 173
Hofferbert, Richard I., 245
home-rule provisions, 344
houses of representatives, state. *See* legislatures
Howard, A. E. Dick, 85
Hunter, Floyd, 381–82

Idaho
  constitution of, 82
  county government in, 363
  fiscal policy, 410
Illinois
  budgetary process in, 440
  constitution of, 76, 82
  mandates on local governments in, 396
  taxes in, 428, 436
image. *See* public image
image building, as interest group influence technique, 264–65
implied powers, 39–40
income tax
  federal, 49
    Reaganomics and, 54
  state, 409, 410–11, 413–14, 417, 430
  regressive vs. progressive, 428
incorporation
  of cities, 344–45
  of suburban areas, 322
incumbents
  advantages of, 291
  electoral campaigns of, 303–4
Indiana
  judicial system in, 211
  legislature of, 96
Indianapolis, Indiana, 326, 347
individualistic subculture, 23
industrial development bonds (IDBs), 416
informal powers of governor, defined, 157
information, administrators' ability to control, 354–55, 387
inherent powers, 40
initiative, 86, 306, 307
  state constitutional amendment by, 77, 78, 89–92
Innaccone, Laurence, 371
institutional design, consequences of, 59–62
integrated executive model, 163–64
interest groups. *See* special interest groups
intergovernmental conflict, jurisdictional fragmentation and, 323–24

intergovernmental relations, 45–59
  correctional systems and, 220–21
  grants-in-aid and, 45–48, 64
  marble-cake federalism, 48–49
  public policy making and, 62–64
  in 1980s, 51–54
  in 1990s, 55–59
  in 1960s and 1970s, 49–51
  See also specific topics
intergovernmental service agreements, 328
intermediate appellate courts, 192–93
Intermodal Surface Transportation Act (1991), 427
Iowa, judicial system in, 195
iron triangles, 49

Jacob, Herbert, 123, 202
Jarvis, Howard, 421
Jefferson, Thomas, 97
Jewell, Malcolm, 106, 114, 134
jobs
  government function summarized, 8
  political issues and, 15
Johnson, Gary, 181
Johnson, Lyndon B. (Johnson administration), 49–50, 329, 419
Johnson, Maureen "Mo," 290
joint committees, 115
Jones, Charles O., 236
judges
  attitudes and values of, 207–8
  gender differences among, 208
  as human beings, 187–88
  new judicial federalism and, 216
  selection of, 196–203
    by appointment, 197, 198–99, 200
    by elections, 197, 199–200, 202–3
    Missouri plan, 196–97, 200–201
    political nature of methods of, 202–3
    variations among states, 197–98
    Voting Rights Act and, 204
  sentencing policies and, 221–22
  See also courts, state
judicial activism, 188
judicial branch, national, 38–39. *See also* courts, federal
judicial branch, state. *See* courts, state; judges; judicial systems, state
judicial delay, 209–10, 221
judicial restraint, 188
judicial review, 72, 186–87
judicial systems, state, 187–223
  most justice administered by, 187
  reform of, 195–96
  structure of, 189–95
  See also corrections; courts, state; judges
juries, 208–9
jurisdictional fragmentation, in metropolitan areas, 20, 322–25
jurisdiction of federal vs. state courts, 190–92, 217
jurors, prejudices of, 208–9

Kalamazoo, Michigan, 323
Kalkaska, Michigan, 422
Kansas
  governor's influence on policy in, 181
  taxes in, 411
Katz, Vera, 133
Kean, Thomas, 150–51
Kehoe, Ellen, 372
Kennedy, John, 50
Kentucky
  governors in, 173
  laws on lobbying in, 281
Key, V. O., 243
King, Norm, 434
King, Rodney, 190–91
Kinney, Lisa, 273
Korbelik, David, 290

Lakewood plan, 328–29
land use control
  government function summarized, 7–8
  political issues and, 14–15
Landy, Marc, 148
law, levels of, 71–73
Lee, Eugene, 391, 392
legal precedent, 205–6
legislative branch
  under U.S. Constitution, 38
  See also legislators; legislatures
legislative budget process, 439
legislative committees. *See* committees, legislative
legislative liaisons, 161, 262
legislative process, 102–8
  committee system and, 104–6
  recent improvements in, 107
legislative support, 119–20
legislative theory of federalism, 61–62
legislative turnover, 99, 115
legislative veto, 106
legislators
  alcohol consumption by, 99
  demographics of, 131–33
  ethnic minorities, 131–32
  roles of, 130–31
  support staff of, 119–20
  tenure and turnover of, 91, 99, 109, 115, 133–35
  women, 131–33, 297–98, 299
legislatures, 96–136
  committees (*see* committees, legislative)
  as dominant institution, 97
  electoral participation and, 297–99
  functions of, 101–2
  historical background of, 97–98
  informal rules and strategies in, 107–8
  judicial branch and, 194, 202
  organization of, 108–15
    division of labor, 109
    leadership positions, 110–11
    party caucuses, 110

legislatures *(continued)*
powers of leadership, 111–12, 117–19
trends in leadership, 112, 114–15
political corruption and, 98
political parties and, 230
in public policy formation, 137–40
reform of, 98–101
representation and, 120–31
apportionment, 120–30
roles of representatives, 130–31
staff and financial support, 119–20
See also legislative process
levels of law, 71–73
lieutenant governor, 174–75
Lincoln Institute of Land Policy, 437–38
Linde, Hans A., 72
Lineberry, Robert L., 356
line-item veto, 106
literacy tests for voter registration, 287
lobbyists, 254, 259–62
contract, 261
"do's and dont's" for, 273
employee, 261
governors as, 161
as industry, 263
institutional design and, 59
legislative campaign funding from, 114, 115, 280
public policy on, 279–81
in state politics, 272–76
volunteer, 262
See also special interest groups
local communities. *See* communities
local elections. *See* elections, local
local governments
as interest groups, 256
state constitutions and, 75
See also city government; county government; metropolitan area governments; state-local government relations
Loftus, Tom, 117–18, 268
logjams in legislatures, 100
log-rolling, commission plan and, 348
Long, Norton, 379
Lopez v. U.S. (1995), 58
Los Angeles, California schools, 365
Los Angeles County, California
county government in, 359, 362
metropolitan area government in, 328–29
lotteries, 431–33
Louisiana
constitution of, 76, 77, 82
judicial system in, 211
revenue sources of, 428, 430, 432
Lowi, Theodore, 277
Lutz, Frank W., 371
Lynd, Helen, 381
Lynd, Robert, 381

Mackay, Buddy, 175
Madison, James, 276, 277, 279, 282
mail-order houses, sales taxes on purchases from, 431
majorities, forming, as function of political parties, 232
malapportionment, 121–25
managerial model, council-manager form of government patterned after, 350–51
managers. *See* administrators; city managers
mandates, unfunded, 55–56, 396–98, 421, 451
Mandeville, Robert L., 440
Mapp v. Ohio (1961), 215
marble-cake federalism, 48–49
Marion County, Indiana, 326
Marshall, John, 39–40, 47
Martinez, Bob, 149
Maryland, judge selection in, 197
Massachusetts, taxes in, 411, 422, 431
mayor-coucil systems of city government
council-manager system compared to, 356–57
elections and, 390
strong mayor system, 346–47, 355
weak mayor system, 346–47, 355
mayors. *See* city government; mayor-council systems of city government
McCrone, Donald J., 245
McCulloch v. Maryland (1819), 39–40, 47
McVeigh, Timothy, trial of, 187
media, governors and, 150–52
Medicaid, 6–7, 52, 138, 140, 421, 451
Meier, Kenneth, 168
Melchior, Alan, 391
merit (Missouri) plan, 196–97, 200–201
metropolitan area governments
disadvantages of, 332–34
fragmentation of, 20, 321–25
public policy and, 336–37
reform of, 325–34
"abolition" of suburbs, 326
annexation, 322, 327–28
consolidation, 322, 325–26
disadvantages of, 332–34
future trends in, 334
intergovernmental service agreements, 328
Lakewood plan, 328–29
metropolitan councils of government (COGs), 329–30
metropolitan federation, 326–27
political factors and, 330–32
See also city government
metropolitan areas, 314–37
future trends in, 334–36
See also central cities (core cites); metropolitan area governments; population shifts; urban areas
metropolitan councils of government (COGs), 329–30

metropolitan federation, 326–27
metropolitan statistical area (MSA), 317–18
Mexico, 272
Miami, Florida, 326
Michels, Robert, 247
Michigan
  campaign financing rules in, 289
  judicial system in, 211
  plural executive in, 162
  school funding in, 367
  taxes in, 411, 428
Middletown, 381
Miller, James N., 81
Milwaukee County, Wisconsin, 362
Minnesota
  campaign financing rules in, 289
  gambling in, 432
  1990 gubernatorial campaign in, 150
  interest groups in, 275
  taxes in, 412
mirror role of representatives, 130
Mississippi, taxes in, 411, 430
Missouri
  governor's power in, 182
  judicial system in, 211
  taxes in, 412
Missouri plan, 196–97, 200–201
Missouri v. Holland (1920), 42
Mladenka, Kenneth, 298
Model Cities and Metropolitan Development Act of 1967, 333
Moe, Terry M., 372, 373
Montana
  constitution of, 82
  county government in, 363
  taxes in, 410, 428
moralistic political subculture, 23
Morgan, David, 357
Motor-Voter law, 58, 288
Muchmore, Lynn, 147
Mulholland, Lori A., 373
Muncie, Indiana, 381
municipal corporations, 342
municipal utility districts (MUDs), 370

Nagel, Stuart, 207–8
National Bellas Hess v. Illinois Department of Revenue (1967), 431
National Conference of State Legislatures (NCSL), 437–38
national government. See courts, federal; federal funding; federalism
National Governors Association (NGA), 148, 172–73, 180, 437
National League of Cities v. Usery (1976), 56
National Municipal League, 82
National Rifle Association (NRA), 117–18
national supremacy clause, 41–42
Nebraska, legislature of, 108–9
Nevada
  legislative process in, 103
  taxes in, 410
New Hampshire, taxes in, 410, 411, 412, 417
New Haven, Connecticut, 383–84
New Jersey
  citizen initiatives in, 91
  governors in, 150–51, 181
  interest groups in, 274
  judicial system in, 211
  taxes in, 91, 411
new judicial federalism, 68, 215–17
New Mexico
  citizen initiatives in, 91
  governor's influence on policy in, 181
  judge selection in, 197
  taxes in, 91, 411, 412, 431
New York (state)
  constitution of, 82
  judicial system in, 192, 195, 211
  taxes in, 411, 412
New York City
  schools, 365
  secession of Staten Island from, 333
  St. Patrick's Day parade in, 206
Nineteenth Amendment, 288, 308
nonpartisan elections, 286, 388–91
North Carolina
  campaign financing rules in, 289
  constitution of, 82, 88
  governor's powers in, 159
  taxes in, 411
North Dakota
  campaign financing rules in, 289
  constitution of, 82
Office of Management and Budget (OMB), 329
Ohio
  interest groups in, 257–58
  judge selection in, 197
  legislative tenure and turnover in, 134
Oklahoma
  constitution of, 77, 91
  executive branch in, 164, 165
  legislative tenure limits in, 91, 135
  taxes in, 430
Oklahoma City bombing case, 187
Omnibus Budget Reconciliation Act (1981), 52
one person, one vote requirement, 125, 288
oracle role of representatives, 130–31
Orange County, California, 427
Oregon
  Bill of Rights of, 74
  citizen initiatives in, 91
  constitution of, 82
  revenue sources of, 410, 432
organization of governments, 28–62. *See also* centralization; decentralization; federalism; and specific levels of government
Orr, Kay, 149
Ostrom, Vincent, 332

Palko v. Connecticut (1937), 215
Paonia, Colorado, 421
parliamentary system, 249
parole boards, 221–22
parties. *See* political parties
partisan elections, 286, 388–91
party caucuses, in state legislatures, 110
Pelissero, John, 357
penal system. *See* corrections
Pennsylvania
  constitution of, 81
  taxes in, 411, 428
Perot, Ross, 292, 450
Perpich, Rudy, 150, 275
personal income, per-capita, 22
personnel exchanges, as interest group influence technique, 266
Perverill, Squire, 134
Peterson, Paul, 61–62, 399
petit jury, 209
Pierce, Neal, 324–25
Piven, Francis, 333
planning, jurisdictional fragmentation and, 324
planning-programming-budgeting system (PPBS), 442
plea bargaining, 210–11
plural executive, 161–63
pluralism, 448–49
  community power and, 383–85
pocket veto, 158
police powers, 220
policy coordinator, governor as, 156
policy leader, governor as, 154–56, 179–82
political action committees (PACs), 101, 267
  campaign financing and, 267, 281, 289, 291
political campaigns. *See* electoral campaigns
political corruption, legislatures and, 98
political cultures, 271–72
political efficacy, interest groups and sense of, 271–72
political equality, 205–6
political involvement (political activism), 229. *See also* electoral participation
political machines, 237–38
  council-manager system of government and, 350, 351, 352
political parties, 227–50
  caucuses in state legislatures, 110
  competition among, 239–46
    advantages of, 244
    divided party control, 240–43
    downside of factional politics, 243–44
    third parties, 245–46
  as controlled by a few party leaders, 247
  criticisms of, 246–48
  as directionless, 247
  functions of, 228–33
    educating the public, 228–29
    forming majorities, 232
    fusing fragmented system, 230–31
    increasing political involvement, 229
    organizing the lawmaking process, 230
    policy formation, 249
    recruiting candidates, 229–30
    resolving conflict, 232–33
  governors as leaders of, 153–54
  identification with, 293
  interest groups and, 275–76
  organization of, 234–39
    at county level, 234–35
    in one-party states, 235
    at precinct level, 234
    at state level, 235
    as structurally untidy, 236–38
    variations among states, 235–36
    weakening of, 238–39
  in policy formation, 249
  responsible party system model, 248–50
  resurgence of, 239
  as too much alike, 247–48
politics (political factors), 9–10
  city government structure and, 350, 351, 352, 353–55
  metropolitan area government reform and, 330–32
  schools and, 364, 365
  specific government functions and, 10–17
    citizenship and civil life, 16–17
    crime and corrections, 11–12, 219–20
    education, 12–13, 364, 365
    jobs and economic development, 15
    land use control, 14–15
    public entertainment and recreation, 15–16
    public health and safety, 10
    public utilities, 10–11
    social services, 13–14
  state constitutions and, 83–87
  See also fiscal policy, political aspects of; specific topics
poll tax, 287–88
Polsby, Nelson, 116–17, 382, 384
polycentric system, 332
Poor Laws (England), 137
population shifts, 314–22
  consequences of, 319–27
  from rural to urban, 314–16
  from urban to suburban, 317–22
Portage Township, Michigan, 323
power, in communities, 378–88
  critique of elite model of, 382–83
  of experts, 386–88
  pluralism, 383–85
  power elites, 378–83, 386
  studies by scholars, 380–82
  who cares about, 379–80, 386
power, political, 450. *See also* power, in communities
power elites, 378–83, 386
power pockets, 105
power pyramid, 382
powers denied, 40
precincts, 234

primary elections, 286
direct, 238
Printz v. U.S. (1995), 58, 60
prisons, 220, 221–22. *See also* corrections
privatization of public services, 423–26
professionals, as interest group, 256
progressives (Progressive Movement)
council-manager system of government and, 350
direct democracy and, 89–90
progressive taxes, 418, 426–30
property tax, 409, 410, 429
Proposition 13 in California and, 51, 366, 421–22
as regressive, 426
school funding and, 364–66, 367
Proposition 13 (California), 51, 366, 421–22
Proposition Two and One-Half, 422
public agenda, city government and control of, 354–55
public assistance. *See* social services; welfare
public education. *See* education; schools
public fun
government function summarized, 8
political issues and, 15–16
public health and safety
government function summarized, 4–5
political issues and, 10
public image
of governors, 149–52
of interest groups, 264–65, 270–71
public interest, interest groups and, 276
public opinion
city government and, 356–57
interest groups and, 264–65
taxation and, 436–37
public policy
citizen initiatives and, 89–92
city government and, 356–57
federalism and, 62–64
governors and, 179–82
on interest groups and lobbyists, 279–82
legislatures and, 137–40
metropolitan area governments and, 336–37
political parties and, 249
population shifts and, 316, 319
See also specific topics
public services, privatization of, 423–26
public utilities
government function summarized, 5
political issues and, 10–11
Pueblo, Colorado, schools in, 373
Pulsipher, Allan, 124

Quie, Albert H., 275
Quill Corporation v. North Dakota (1992), 431
racial bias
in judicial system, 218
voting rights and, 287, 288
racial segregation, suburbanization and, 320
Racicot, Marc, 157
Ransome, Coleman, 147
Reagan, Ronald (Reagan administration), 51–54, 147
crime and corrections policy, 221
fiscal policy of, 416, 419–20, 429, 437
judicial appointments, 216
Reaganomics, 51–54
reapportionment, 121
recall, 86, 307
recreation. *See* public fun
referendum, 86, 306
reform (reformers)
bureaucratic, 167–69
of county government, 361–62, 363
of judicial systems, 195–96
of legislatures, 98–101
of local elections, 393–95
of schools, 371–74
state constitutions and, 84–85
of taxes, 437–38
of welfare, 7, 138–40, 361
See also metropolitan area governments, reform of
regressive taxes, 418, 426–30
Reinertson, Karen, 260
Reisman, Hane, 372
representation, 120–31
electoral reform and, 393
interest groups and, 277
See also apportionment; malapportionment; reapportionment
representatives
roles of, 130–31
See also legislators; legislatures; representation
Republican party, 240–42, 347
reputational approach, 380–81, 384, 385
reserved powers, 40
residency requirements for voting, 287
revenue bonds, 414
revenue sources, 409–12. *See also* taxes
Reynolds v. Sims (1964), 125
Rhode Island
earmarking of taxes in, 436
judge selection in, 197
Richards, Ann, 150, 161
Robinson, James A., 245
role reversals, as interest group influence technique, 266–67
Romer, Roy, 151–52
Romer v. Evans (1996), 91, 92
Roosevelt, Franklin, 137
Rosenthal, Alan, 112, 279, 303
row officers, 360
rule of law, 205
rules committees, 106
Rusk, David, 326

Sabato, Larry, 423
St. Patrick's Day parade, 206

sales tax, 409, 410, 411–12, 413–14, 417, 430
  as regressive, 426
  on services, 430–31
San Antonio, Texas, 334, 337
San Antonio Independent School District v. Rodriguez (1973), 366
satellite cities, 335–36
Schattschneider, E. E., 255, 277
Schlafly, Phyllis, 247
Schluter, Bill, 254–55
Schneider, Mark, 400
school administrators, 363–64
school boards, 6, 363, 364, 372, 394
school choice proposals, 372–73
school districts, 321–22, 362–67
schools (school systems)
  changing roles of, 450–51
  charter schools, 373
  financing of, 6, 13, 364–66, 367, 435
  governance of
    school administrator, 363–64
    school boards, 6, 363, 364
    state role, 6, 367
  political factors and, 12–13, 364, 365
  reform approaches, 371–74
  school choice proposals, 372–73
  See also education; teachers
Scoble, Harry M., 356
secretary of state, 176–77
segregation, racial, suburbanization and, 320
selective incorporation, 214–15
Seminole Tribe of Florida v. Florida, 58
senates, state. *See* legislatures
sentences, 221–22
sentencing guidelines, 221
separation of powers, 18
  governors and, 177–78
Seventeenth Amendment, 288, 308
Sharkansky, Ira, 245
Shaw v. Reno (1993), 309
Simpson, O. J., trial of, 187, 209, 218
single-issue interest groups, 258–59
Single Transferable Vote, 309
sin taxes, 417
Sixteenth Amendment, 49
Smith v. Allright (1944), 288
Social Security Act (1935), 6, 137, 138
social services
  funding shift from federal to state, 55, 138
  government function summarized, 6–7
  political aspects of, 13–14
  programs of, 138
    Aid to Families with Dependent Children (AFDC), 6, 52, 138
    Food Stamp program, 7, 138
    Medicaid, 6–7, 52, 138, 140, 421, 451
    Supplemental Security Income (SSI), 7, 138
  rising costs and, 138
  See also welfare
South Carolina v. Baker (1988), 56
South Carolina v. Katzenbach (1966), 308
South Dakota, 56
  citizen initiatives in, 91
  taxes in, 410, 428, 431
South Dakota v. Dole (1987), 56
special districts, 321, 322, 367–70, 387–88
special interest group intensity, 278
special interest groups, 254–59
  budgeting and, 440–41
  business interests as, 257
  campaign financing and, 114, 115, 280, 281–82, 289, 291
  case studies of failure and success of, 275–76
  democracy and, 276–78
  educators as, 256
  factors in effectiveness of, 267–72
    cohesion, 269
    image, 270–71
    leadership, 269–70
    money, 268
    political efficacy, 271–72
    size, 267–68
  influence techniques used by, 262–67
    common interests, 265–66
    direct communication, 263–64
    grass roots activism, 265
    image building, 264–65
    PAC money, 267
    personnel exchanges, 266
    role reversals, 266–67
  institutional design and, 59
  legislative leaders' power and, 117–18
  local governments as, 256
  party strength and, 275–76
  professionals as, 256
  public policy on, 279–82
  reasons for formation of, 259
  similarities and differences among states, 257–58
  single-issue, 258–59
  state constitutions and, 84
  strategies of, 272–74
  volunteer groups as, 257
  voter turnout and, 300
  See also lobbyists
spending, government, 408–9
  deficit, 53, 414–16, 420
  increase in, 417
  See also fiscal policy
spin doctors, 229
state aid to local governments, 55
state and local governments
  continuity and change in, 23–24
  crisis in, 450–52
  differences among, 22–24
  functions summarized, 4–9
    citizenship and civil life, 9
    crime and corrections, 5
    education, 6
    jobs and economic development, 8
    land use control, 7–8

public entertainment and recreation, 8
public health and safety, 4–5
public utilities, 5
social services, 6–7
future trends, 452
shared characteristics of, 21–22
state constitutions. *See* constitutions, state
state courts. *See* courts, state
state executives, 146–82
women as, 296–97, 299
See also governors
state governments
framework under state constitutions, 74–75
local communities and, 395–98
school districts and, 367
See also specific topics
state houses of representatives. *See* legislatures
state legislatures. *See* legislatures
state-local government relations
Dillon's rule and, 44
legal relations, 43–44
state senates. *See* legislatures
state symbol, governor as, 154
state treasurer, 177
statutes, under U.S. Constitution, 72
Steffens, Lincoln, 350
Stein, Robert, 332, 337, 357, 426
Stolberg, Irving, 112
Stone, Clarence, 329
Strate, John, 391
stratification approach, 380–81
strong mayor-council system of city government, 345–46, 355
subcultures, political, 23
subgovernments, 49
suburban areas
annexation of, 322, 327–28
incorporation of, 322
suburbanization, 317–22
benefits of, 325
problems associated with, 322–25
suburbs, "abolition" of, 326
sunk costs, 171
Supplemental Security Income (SSI), 7, 138
Supreme Court, U.S. *See specific decisions*
supreme courts, state, 192
Swanson, Wayne, 85
Swanstrom, Todd, 400
Symington, Fife, 149

taxes
attracting new business and industry and, 401, 435–36
city government structure and, 356, 357
collection policies and methods, 412–14
demands for more services without more, 407
earmarking revenues, 436, 440–41
expanding the tax base, 430–33
federal tax laws, 415–16
moves to limit, 421–23
new types of, 417
per-capita, 22
progressive vs. regressive, 418, 426–30
public opinion and, 436–37
reform of, 437–38
regressive vs. progressive, 418, 426–30
school funding and, 364–66, 367
sin, 417
as sources of revenue, 409–12
tax base disparities among states, 433, 435
variation among states, 409–14
See also fiscal policy; income tax; property tax; sales tax
tax-exempt bonds, 415–16
taxpayer revolts, 51, 417, 421–23
teachers, as interest group, 256
Teaford, Jon C., 337
techniques of influence, 262–67
technology, population shifts and, 316, 318
Teeter, Robert, 150
Tennessee, taxes in, 417, 428
Tenth Amendment, 40, 60
terms of office
of governors, 160
of legislators, 91, 109, 115
at local level, 389
Texas
apportionment in, 129–30
campaign financing rules in, 289
citizen initiatives in, 91
constitution of, 76–77, 82
electoral participation in, 295
governors in, 149, 150, 173
judicial system in, 204, 210, 215–16, 216
municipal utility districts (MUDs) in, 370
taxes in, 91, 410, 430, 436
women in public office in, 298
third parties, 245–46
Thompson, Tommy G., 88, 148, 159, 180, 181
ticket-splitting, 239–40
Tiebout, Charles M., 332, 337
Tomlinson, Danny, 263
tort reform, 216
totalitarian states, 205
towns, 342
traditionalistic political subculture, 23
transportation, 48
treasurer, state, 177
trial courts, 193
Twenty-Fourth Amendment, 288
Twenty-Sixth Amendment, 287, 288, 308
two-party system, 245

unfunded mandates, 55–56, 396–98, 421, 451
unicameral legislature, 108–9
unified court system, 195–96
unitary system, 31–32
United Nations, 33
United States v. Curtis-Wright Export Corporation (1936), 40
Unruh, Jesse, 114

urban areas
population shift from rural areas to, 314–16
See also cities; metropolitan areas
urbanization, 314–16
urban villages, 334–36
user fees, 433, 434
Utah, citizen initiatives in, 91
utilities, public. *See* public utilities

values of judges and juries, 207–9
Van Dalen, Hendrick, 275
Van de Kamp, John, 149–50
Verba, Sidney, 271–72
Vermont
apportionment in, 123
balanced budget requirement in, 88
gubernatorial policy leadership in, 155–56
taxes in, 428
veto points, 272
veto power of governors, 88, 106, 158–59
Violence Against Women Act (VAWA), 58
Virginia
constitution of, 82
legislature of, 97, 116
taxes in, 411
Vogel, Ronald, 384
volunteer groups, as interest groups, 257
volunteer lobbyists, 262
vote brokers, 235
voter registration, 287–88
county governments and, 359
voter turnout. *See* electoral participation
voting. *See* elections; electoral participation
Voting Accessibility for the Elderly and the Handicapped Act (1986), 288
voting laws. *See* election laws
Voting Rights Act (VRA) (1965), 204, 212, 288, 308–9

Wagar, Linda, 259
Wahlke, John C., 107–8
Walker, Bob, 156
Warren, Earl, 125
Warren, Robert, 332
Washington (state)
citizen initiatives in, 91
taxes in, 91, 410, 411, 428
women legislators in, 298
Watson, Sheilah, 357
weak mayor-council system of city government, 346–47, 355
wealth, judicial system and inequities in, 212
Weatherby, James, 124
Welch, Susan, 297–98
welfare
county government and, 361
definition of, 13–14
funding shift from federal to state, 55
government function summarized, 6–7
history of, 137–38
political aspects of, 13–14
public policy on, 137–40
reform of, 7, 138–40, 361
See also social services
Wesberry v. Sanders (1964), 125
West, Paul, 150
West Virginia, constitution of, 81
Whitman, Christy, 181
Will, George, 450
Williams, Clayton, 149, 150
Wilson, James Q., 357
Wilson, Pete, 181
Windsor, Colorado, 421
Wisconsin
campaign financing rules in, 289
governor's power and authority in, 88, 159, 180
interest groups in, 117–18
speaker of the house in, 117–18
Witt, Elder, 72
Wolfinger, Raymond E., 352, 356, 382
Wolman, Harold, 391
women
electoral participation by, 295
judicial system and, 208, 212
as legislators, 131–33, 297–98, 299
in local government, 297–98, 298
in state executive offices, 296–97, 299
Wyoming
apportionment in, 126
constitution of, 85–86
fiscal policy, 410, 411
judicial system in, 192

yellow-dog Democrat, 244
young people, electoral participation by, 293–95

Zeigler, Harmon, 275, 371–72
zero-base budgeting (ZBB), 442